Dictionary of Judaism
in the Biblical Period

Dictionary of Judaism in the Biblical Period

450 B.C.E. to 600 C.E.

VOLUME 2

Jacob Neusner, *Editor in Chief*

William Scott Green, *Editor*

MACMILLAN LIBRARY REFERENCE USA
Simon & Schuster Macmillan
NEW YORK

Simon & Schuster and Prentice Hall International
LONDON   MEXICO CITY   NEW DELHI   SINGAPORE   SYDNEY   TORONTO

Simon & Schuster Macmillan
866 Third Avenue, New York, NY 10022

PRINTED IN THE UNITED STATES OF AMERICA

printing number

1   2   3   4   5   6   7   8   9   10

LIBRARY OF CONGRESS CATALOGING-IN-PUBLICATION DATA

Dictionary of Judaism in the biblical period : 450 B.C.E. to 600 C.E.
      Jacob Neusner, editor in chief : William Scott Green, editor.
        p.   cm.
      ISBN 0-02-897292-9
      1. Judaism—History—Post-exilic period, 586 B.C.–210 A.D.—
Dictionaries.   2. Judaism—History—Talmudic period, 10-425—
Dictionaries.   3. Rabbinical literature—Dictionaries.
I. Neusner, Jacob, 1932-   .   II. Green, William Scott.
      BM50.D525   1996   95-31543
      296'. 09'01—dc20   CIP

This paper meets the requirements of ANSI/NISO Z39.48-1992
(Permanence of Paper).

J

Jacob son of Isaac and Rebekah; Esau's younger twin. God is often called the God of Abraham, Isaac, and Jacob in the Bible and in Jewish and Christian tradition. Esau sold his birthright to Jacob for a bowl of stew. Rebekah and Jacob tricked Isaac into giving the firstborn's blessing to Jacob, who became the bearer of the promises (Genesis 25:29–34; cf. Jub. 19:15–31, 26, which justifies the deception). Jacob's name probably derives from the verb "to supplant" (Heb.: *kb*). Paul takes this to mean that election depends on grace, not descent (Rom. 9:10–13).

Jacob had twelve sons and one daughter. The twelve sons were the eponymous ancestors of the Israelite tribes, so all Israel is the "House of Jacob," or simply "Jacob." Returning from Mesopotamia, Jacob wrestled one night with a mysterious "man" (Gen. 32:24–30; cf. 35:9–15). The man changed Jacob's name to Israel, originally meaning "may God strive." From that time on, Jacob's descendants were also called children of Israel or Israel.

Stories about the patriarchs are used to explain later relationships. Jacob's brother, Esau, moved to Seir (Gen. 33:16), and his descendants became the Edomites (later, Idumeans). This posits a kinship between Israel and the Edomites and asserts Israel's superiority. Jubilees 37–38 tells of antipathy between Jacob and Esau, reflecting rivalry between Jews and Idumeans in the author's own day. Theodotus, in *On the Jews,* rewrites from Genesis 34 to describe Jewish-Samaritan relations.

In Genesis 49 Jacob blesses his sons before dying. This testamentary setting is a prototype for the many testaments of ancient heroes written throughout the period of early Judaism. (The Testament of Jacob is a Christian work, not to be dated before the second century.) Jacob's prediction that the scepter would not pass from Judah (Gen. 49:10) was taken messianically in Jewish and Christian tradition. Balaam's prophecy of the star of Jacob and the scepter of Israel (Num. 24:17) was used in the Dead Sea Scrolls to refer to two messiahs (CD 7:18–21; 1QM 11:6–7; 4QTest. 9–13).

In Philo and in Jubilees, Jacob and the other patriarchs become models of Torah-abiding behavior. The Wisdom of Solomon 10:10 attributes Jacob's escape from Esau to Jacob's righteousness, and the Damascus Rule calls Jacob a friend of God and member of the covenant forever. In Joseph and Asenath 22, Jacob is described in angelic and even divine terms, and agrees to be a father to Asenath, a convert to Judaism.

Within the rabbinic literature, Jacob's life is viewed as symbolic of later Jewish history. Especially insofar as he was called Israel (Gen. 32:28), Jacob represents the nation as a whole, while his chief antagonists, Esau and Laban, are equated with Rome. In this reading, the conflict between the Israelite nation and Rome was predestined, represented in the struggle that took place in Rebekah's womb even before Jacob and Esau's birth (Gen. 25:22; Gen. Rabbah 63:6). The rabbis further represented this conflict in their claim that, although Jacob and Esau both were given equal opportunities to learn Torah and follow the ways of God, only Jacob did so, with Esau becoming instead an idolater (Gen. Rabbah 63:10). The irreconcilable opposition between Jew and non-Jew was depicted, finally, in the contrast between the handsome Jacob, representing the spiritual beauty of Judaism, and the ruddy and ugly Esau, characterizing what the rabbis saw as the warmongering and contemptible world of paganism (Gen. Rabbah 63:8).

Much attention is given to explaining the apparently devious methods by which Jacob acquired the birthright and blessing of the firstborn. The rabbis explain that Jacob did not act out of selfishness but wished only to acquire from the spiritually unworthy Esau the right to offer family sacrifices, at that time given by the firstborn (Gen. Rabbah 63:13). Comparably, Jacob did not intend to deceive his father by telling him, "I am Esau, your firstborn" (Gen. 27:19). The sentence is properly understood as laconic and actually included the following, bracketed words: "I am [the one who will receive the Ten Commandments, which begin with the word 'I'], [but] Esau [is indeed] your firstborn" (Gen. Rabbah 65:14).

While generally treated as a model of piety, Jacob is not above criticism. The dreadful result of Jacob's preferential treatment of Joseph proves the importance of a parent's treating all of his children equally (B. Shabbat 10b). Jacob is criticized further for failing to intercede with God to prevent the Israelites' enslavement in Egypt (B. Shabbat 89b). Overall, however, Jacob is seen as a model of proper behavior, for which he was appropriately rewarded. Along with Abraham and Isaac, he was one of only three people to whom God gave a foretaste of the life of the world to come and over whom the evil inclination had no control. He was one of six people over whom the angel of death had no power (B. Baba Batra 17a). According to one source, like the immortal Jewish people, Jacob never died at all (B. Taanit 5b).

Jacob b. Iddi Palestinian amora at the end of the third century C.E.; a student of Yohanan. He and Isaac b. Nahman were community leaders in Tiberias (Y. Peah 8:9, 98b). Later, he lived in Tyre, to which Zera sent rabbis traveling between Palestine and Babylonia, so that they could learn Jacob's views on various issues (B. Erubin 80a; B. Baba Metzia 43b; B. Hullin 98a).

Jacobites followers of a form of Monophysite Christianity, named for Jacob Baradaeus, bishop of Edessa. In 559 C.E., Baradaeus visited Khusro I to gain tolerance of the Jacobite Christians. The Jaco-

bite sect eventually became the national church of Syria. Baradaeus was martyred in 578 for converting a member of the royal family.

Jambres *see* JANNES AND JAMBRES

James, brother of Jesus brother of Jesus of Nazareth; also called James the Just. Various New Testament passages refer to James and other brothers and sisters of Jesus (Mark 6:3; Matt. 13:55–56; Acts 1:14). Christian tradition has regarded these brothers and sisters as either children born to Joseph and Mary after Jesus, as stepbrothers and stepsisters, or as cousins (the last two positions preserve the traditional belief in the virginity of Mary). Paul refers to Cephas (Peter) and "James the brother of the Lord" as leaders ("pillars") of the Jerusalem community of Jews who followed Jesus (Gal. 1:19; 2:9, 12). James is also listed with those to whom the risen Jesus appeared (1 Cor. 15:7). Acts of the Apostles refers to James without introduction as a leader in the Jerusalem community (12:17, 15:13, 21:18). According to Josephus, Ananus (son of Ananus), who was high priest when Festus died (62 C.E.), took advantage of the interregnum to execute James and others for transgressing the law.

James, Epistle of an early Christian writing by James; a book of the New Testament. This brief writing known as the Epistle, or Letter, of James has been the subject of controversy since ancient times. Which person named James wrote it? Is it really a letter? Why does it disagree so sharply with the point of view expressed by Paul in his letters?

Of all the people named James (Gr.: Iakobos) in the New Testament, the one most likely meant is James, the brother of Jesus, who after Jesus' death became leader of the church in Jerusalem (Mark 6:3; Gal. 1:19; Acts 15:13). The author of the Epistle of James rejects Paul's teaching (Rom. 3:21) that one can gain acceptance from God on the basis of faith without obedience to the law of Moses (James 2:14–17). But the epistle is written in highly philosophical language (reflecting Stoic and Cynic teachings) that seems unlikely for a pious Jew from a small town in Galilee (Nazareth). The style of the work resembles an essay in the form of a letter claiming to have been written by the Greek philosopher Socrates, but it presents ideas common around the beginning of the second century C.E. Unlike the letters of Paul, where specific issues are addressed that have arisen in the community to which he is writing, this work deals only with general principles of moral behavior.

Neither does the Epistle of James deal with the broader issues that James debated with Paul:

whether Gentile Christian males should be circumcised and whether Gentiles should observe the Jewish dietary laws (Gal. 1–2). When James discusses temptation, it is not testing done by the devil or trials that the faithful must endure before the end of the present age, as in Paul and the Gospels. Instead, temptation is an inner struggle, whose desired outcome is the triumph of morality and the life of conformity to the ethical principles embodied in the laws. Even the images the author uses for guiding the moral life—horse and bit, ship and rudder, fire out of control, water produced by springs, trees bearing fruit (3:3–12)—are just those found in the Cynic-Stoic writings of this period. Two popular themes of contemporary philosophy that are mentioned in James are (1) the transmigration of souls from one body to another—the "wheel of life" or cycle of nature (3:6)—and (2) the predictability of the movement of heavenly bodies as an inference from solstices and eclipses through which they move (1:17). Heavenly wisdom is to manifest itself in purity and peace, and mercy and impartiality within the community of faith (3:13–4:12). The return of Christ in triumph is still expected (5:7), and members should seek to restore to the faith those who have wandered from the truth (5:19–20). The writing is clearly an attempt to formulate faith and practice in ways that build on earlier traditions but are in conversation with the intellectual developments of the Roman world at the start of the second century C.E.

Jamnia *see* YABNEH

Jannaeus *see* ALEXANDER JANNAEUS

Jannes and Jambres the names given to two magicians identified as the opponents of Moses and Aaron in Pharaoh's court (cf. Exod. 7–8). The first extant references to these named characters are in the Damascus Document (CD 5:18–19) and 2 Timothy 3:8–9, where they are identified as false teachers. The names recur in a variety of later Jewish, Christian, and pagan texts.

A book about Jannes and Jambres is mentioned by Origen in the third century. Fragments of the book are extant in one Latin manuscript and two Greek papyri of the third and fourth centuries. The narrative, such as it can be reconstructed, is shot through with references to magic, necromancy, and cosmic portents. Jannes is struck dead for his sins, but his shade returns to warn his brother of the punishments suffered in the netherworld.

Japhia Synagogue synagogue site 3 kilometers southwest of Nazareth at the south edge of Lower Galilee. Japhia, also known as Yaffa or Yafia, is usually identified with the Yafia of Joshua 19:12.

Josephus knew of the town in the first century C.E., mentioning it as the largest village in Galilee, strongly fortified, and containing a large population (*Vita* 230). Japhia also played a role in the First Revolt. Josephus records that the Romans took 2,150 captives there, while they killed the rest of the inhabitants (*War* 3.7.31: 289). No literary references to the town appear after the First Revolt, but there were surely Jewish inhabitants here in the third and fourth centuries who built the synagogue. The building is partially covered by modern structures, so that only its width of about 15 meters could be found. Interior space was divided by two rows of columns into a nave and aisle. The columns had been set upon square column bases about 74 centimeters square and 41 centimeters high. A lintel stone from the synagogue, recorded in 1921, depicts two eagles with spread wings on either side of a wreath. A second stone depicts two rosettes on either side of a seven-branched menorah. The synagogue was finished with an ornate mosaic that appears to have included a zodiac. The frame around the zodiac was once elaborately furnished with depictions of animals; the surviving images in the frame include an eagle with outstretched wings, the head of a medusa, and a tiger. Two of the twelve circles intended for signs of the zodiac are extant. One shows a bull, while the other depicts a horned animal, perhaps a wild ox. Since the wild ox is not normally part of a zodiac, the excavator hypothesized that this was actually a calendar or other pattern with animals as symbols for the twelve tribes of Israel. The building is oriented east to west, which is a surprise.

Jason Jewish high priest (175–172 B.C.E.). Jason (Heb.: Joshua) is said by 2 Maccabees 4:7–10 to have replaced his brother Onias III by promising the Seleucid king Antiochus IV Epiphanes large sums of money. Jason is portrayed in 2 Maccabees 4 as fostering a program aimed at Hellenizing the Jewish people of Jerusalem. He in turn was outbid for the high priesthood by Menelaus in 172 B.C.E. After a futile attempt to regain power in 168 B.C.E., Jason died in exile and disgrace (2 Macc. 5:1–10).

Jason of Cyrene Jewish historian in the Hellenistic period. The author of 2 Maccabees states at 2:19–23 that he has abridged a five-volume history by Jason with a content that roughly corresponds to 2 Maccabees. Other than this reference, we know nothing about Jason, but there is no reason not to take the claim in 2 Maccabees at face value.

Jeconiah *see* JEHOIACHIN

Jehohanan son of Eliashib; a person in whose chamber Ezra rested (Ezra 10:6). His identity is greatly disputed. He may be the high priest who was the grandson of Eliashab (Neh. 12:22–23) and was mentioned in an Elephantine papyrus (408 B.C.E.). Since the names are common among priests and nonpriests, he may also have been a hypothetical earlier high priest or a nonpriest. The identification of Jehohanan depends partly on the dispute over the date of Ezra's mission to Jerusalem.

Jehoiachin king of Judah; also known as Jeconiah. The son of Jehoiakim, he became king in 597 B.C.E. and was taken captive to Babylon three months later. 2 Baruch 1:1 suggests that he (rather than Zedekiah) was king when Jerusalem fell in 587 B.C.E.

Jehovah transliteration of the divine name, based on a misunderstanding of the Hebrew Tetragrammaton YHWH. Jews did not pronounce the name of God; they referred to God as *adonai* (lord). Translators took the vowels of *adonai* and added them to the consonants JHVH, hence JeHoVaH. *See also* GOD, NAMES OF; I AM.

Jerahmeel (Heb., may God have mercy) most likely the correct name of the angel who appears in various Jewish sources under the names Remiel, Jeremiel, Eremiel, and Ramiel (1 Enoch 20:8 [Greek Codex Panopolitanus]; 4 Ezra 4:36; Apoc. Zeph. 6:11–17; 2 Bar. 55:3). He is often connected with traditions relating to the resurrection of the dead (cf. also Rev. 6:9–11 with 2 Esdras 4:33–37), whence very possibly the transformation of his name to a form of the Hebrew *rum* (to lift up).

Jeremiah 1. son of Hilkiah; prophet in Jerusalem from 627 to 587 B.C.E. Of priestly lineage, Jeremiah was from the village of Anathoth, to which David's high priest Abiathar was expelled by Solomon. The biblical Book of Jeremiah contains many of his oracles, as well as narrative material bearing on his life. His opposition to religious and social abuses earned him the enmity of many in Jerusalem, including other prophets. His famous Temple sermon (Jer. 7 and 26) warns against complacency that God will protect Jerusalem despite covenant violations. He also counseled submission to Babylonian rule. After Jerusalem's destruction in 587 B.C.E., he was taken forcibly to Egypt, where he died. The Epistle of Jeremiah is not by the prophet, but it builds on the anti-idolatry theme of Jeremiah 10 and uses the epistolary form of Jeremiah 29. The Book of Lamentations has often been attributed to him, incorrectly.

Most later traditions about Jeremiah concern Jerusalem and the Temple. The legend arose that before the destruction of the Temple, Jeremiah hid the ark and the vessels, and that they would be found again in the last days (2 Macc. 2:4–8; Eupolemus [frg. 4]; Lives of the Prophets 2:11–19; 4 Bar. 3:6–11; cf. 2 Bar. 6:7–9). 4 Baruch is also called Paraleipomena Jeremiou, Jeremiah being its main character. According to 2 Baruch 2:1 and 4 Baruch 1:1–2, Baruch and Jeremiah had to leave Jerusalem before it could be destroyed, because their righteousness and prayers protected it. In 2 Maccabees 15:12–16, Judas Maccabeus has a vision in which he sees the high priest Onias praying for the Jews. Beside him is Jeremiah, who is described as one who "loves the family of Israel and prays much for the people and the holy city—Jeremiah, the prophet of God" (2 Macc. 15:14). Jeremiah then gives Judas a golden sword with which to strike down his enemies.

Lives of the Prophets 2 preserves a tradition in which Jeremiah drove the asps and crocodiles out of Egypt, and another that claims that Alexander the Great scattered the remains of Jeremiah around Alexandria to protect it. The work claims that the Egyptians held Jeremiah in great esteem. In some sources, he is said to have died by stoning (Lives 2; 4 Bar. 9). In Matthew 16:14, Jesus is said by some to be Jeremiah raised from the dead.

2. Palestinian amora of the fourth century C.E.; born in Babylonia, later lived in Caesaria as a student of Abbahu and others; after a period of exclusion from the academy, and after the death of his principal teacher, Zera I, he became a recognized authority and head of the school at Tiberias. He spoke with disdain of Babylonian authorities (e.g., B. Pesaḥim 34b).

Jeremiah, Letter of treatise against idolatry ascribed to Jeremiah. The work takes its inspiration from biblical polemics against idol worship, notably Jeremiah 10:2–15, as well as from the prophet's letter to the Babylonian exiles (Jer. 29). The superscription of the work claims that it is a copy of another letter by Jeremiah (v. 1), but apart from the introduction in verses 2–7 and the use of second person address in the book's refrains, it has none of the typical features of a letter. The Letter of Jeremiah is known from the Greek Bible, where it is placed either between Lamentations and Ezekiel or, more often, as the last chapter of 1 Baruch. The earliest testimony to the work is a fragment of the Greek text found at Qumran. The date of composition is uncertain; the text could have been composed at any time between the fourth century B.C.E. (cf. v. 3 and its reference to an exile of seven generations) and 100 B.C.E., when the author of 2 Maccabees made reference to it (2:2).

This text is satirical and mocking in its tone, like

other works polemicizing against idolatry, such as Bel and the Dragon and the Apocalypse of Abraham 1–8, and irony is a major rhetorical device. The author's strategy is to lay out a series of repetitive evidences and arguments that idols are not the gods that Gentiles suppose them to be. Each of its ten sections is punctuated by a refrain that underscores this point (vv. 16, 23, 29, 40, 44, 52, 56, 65, 69, 73). The point is further emphasized through the repeated use of the negative. Idols are *not* gods because of all the things they do not and cannot do (vv. 8, 19, 34, 35). Specifically, they do not and cannot do all the things that gods do: they do not control the universe, they are not sovereign over kings, and they cannot act as the beneficent deliverers of humankind. Indeed, they cannot do even the things that humans do: speak, see, and breathe (vv. 8, 19, 25). With scathing irony, the author describes the topsy-turvy situation in gentile religion. These would-be divine helpers of humanity are the helpless objects of human actions, and in fact they are themselves fabricated by human beings. Made of wood and overlaid with gold and silver, they are symbols of their own falseness—of their not being what they are claimed to be (vv. 44, 50). In the end, they are lifeless, disintegrating (vv. 12, 20, 72), and useless. Hence the refrain: they are not gods; therefore, do not fear them.

Jeremiah, Paraleipomena of (from Gr., the things omitted from Jeremiah) a narrative about the Babylonian destruction of Jerusalem, Jeremiah's exile to Babylon, his return, and his martyr's death. The text is preserved in a long and a short form, in a large number of Greek manuscripts and in several daughter versions. Although its conclusion indicates that it is Christian in its present form, the work is probably a Jewish composition from the early second century C.E.

Chapters 1–4 are a legendary account of the destruction of Jerusalem that closely parallels 2 Baruch 1–10, but with Jeremiah rather than Baruch playing the primary role as interlocutor with God. Before Jeremiah is taken to Babylon (contrast Jer. 43:5–44:30), he sends Abimelech to the vineyard of Agrippa outside Jerusalem with a basket of figs. When Abimelech awakes from a sixty-six-year sleep, he finds the figs ripened and not spoiled. This is interpreted as a symbol of the resurrection and a sign that the exiles are to return to their homeland. Baruch sends a letter to Jeremiah via eagle informing him of these events (chaps. 5–7). Jeremiah leads the returnees back to Judah; those who had married Babylonians are turned away from Jerusalem and they found the city of Samaria

(chap. 8). In the Jerusalem Temple, Jeremiah has an ecstatic trance in which he sees God and the Son of God and learns of the founding of the church. When his soul returns to his body and he recounts the vision, the people stone him for blasphemy.

The Paraleipomena of Jeremiah has numerous parallels with other Jeremiah and Baruch literature: the opening narrative; the figure of Abimelech; Baruch's letter sent by eagle (2 Bar. 78–87, esp. 87:1); the story's movement from destruction and exile to return (1 Baruch). A Jeremianic legend about the burial of the Temple vessels in 3:7–20 is alluded to in 2 Maccabees 2:1–8 (cf. Lives of the Prophets 2:11–19), which indicates that the core of the narrative stems from the second century B.C.E., where it may have been related to Antiochus Epiphanes' seizure of the Temple vessels (1 Macc. 1:21–24). The length of Abimelech's long nap suggests that the Paraleipomena was written approximately sixty-six years after the destruction of Jerusalem, around 136 C.E., perhaps in connection with events surrounding the Second Jewish Revolt (132–135). The legend of Jeremiah's death by stoning is alluded to in the Life of Jeremiah (Lives of the Prophets 2:1) and probably also in Hebrews 11:37, immediately before an apparent allusion to a similar legend about Isaiah's death (see Isaiah, Martyrdom of).

Jeremiah, Targum to   *see* TARGUM TO THE PROPHETS

Jeremiah b. Abba   rabbi of the late third and early fourth century C.E. Born in Babylonia, he lived in Israel where he served as the head of the academy at Tiberias. He is especially known for his pronouncements regarding prayer. In the Jerusalem Talmud, he is sometimes referred to without the patronymic or, alternatively, as Jeremiah b. Va.

Jeremiah b. Va   *see* JEREMIAH B. ABBA

Jeremiel   *see* JERAHMEEL

Jericho   oasis city in the Judean Desert that succeeded the biblical city of the same name, though in the Hasmonean period it was built on either side of the Wadi Qelt, about one mile south of biblical Jericho. In the Hellenistic and Roman periods it became an economic center for balsam and dates. Alexander Jannaeus (103–76 B.C.E.) built a palace at Jericho. The principal edifice of this palace was a square building (about 50 by 50 meters) with square towers on each corner, built largely of mud brick. The central building was surrounded by a moat on the north, west, and east. In the interior of the building were rooms with beautifully painted stucco. West of the central building were two small swimming pools measuring about 8 by 8 meters.

Less than a generation later, the palace was enlarged on the northeast with a peristyle garden, two much larger swimming pools, and a pavilion. By the time of Queen Alexandra Shlomzion (76–67 B.C.E.), the palace experienced a second enlargement. On the south were added twin central courtyard palaces, each about 25 by 25 meters in size. Three more swimming pools were built. Within the new complex were found rooms decorated with frescoes, a bathhouse, and ritual baths. The Hasmonean palace was destroyed by the earthquake of 31 B.C.E.

Herod the Great built a single large structure at Jericho, south of the Hasmonean palace, as his first winter palace. Later, as his second winter palace, he rebuilt and enlarged the complex, adding a personal villa, a bath house, palatial rooms around peristyle courtyards, and service areas. About 15 B.C.E., Herod built a third palace at Jericho, and the three structures then functioned together as his winter palace. The third palace occupied both sides of the Wadi Qelt and covered about seven-and- one-half acres. There was a large triclinium with columns on three sides, a sunken garden, a long colonnade, many rooms decorated with frescoes, and a Roman style bathhouse. The exterior of the structure was built with decorative, Roman-style masonry in square stones and concrete called *opus reticulatum* and *opus quadratum*.

A synagogue is known at Jericho from the late Byzantine period, as are other buildings and occupations. Extensive cemeteries are known at Jericho from the Hellenistic through the Byzantine periods, including coffin burials of Jewish families during the early Roman period.

Jericho Synagogue synagogue found just north of Tell es-Sultan (ancient Jericho) about 10 kilometers north of the Dead Sea. From paleographic analysis of the inscriptions, the synagogue was probably used during the eighth century C.E. This date is also supported by the fact that several eighth-century Arab coins were found at the site. Other small finds, however, consisting of three glass vessels and a fragmentary bronze lamp have led to the suggestion of a founding date of either the late sixth or early seventh century. Since the date of the synagogue is uncertain, it is also unclear whether there is any relationship between the use of this synagogue and Byzantine Jericho, located about 2 kilometers south of Tell es-Sultan.

The floor plan of the synagogue was a rectangular, basilica shape. Its walls were 13 meters by 10 meters. Four pairs of square pillars laid in two rows serve to divide the building. There is a nave in the middle, and two aisles on the sides. The apse at the front of the synagogue faces southwest, directly toward Jerusalem. Two stone steps in front of the apse connect it to the central nave. There is only one entrance, located in the middle of the northeast wall.

The floor is paved with a geometric mosaic in three panels, all of which avoid human and animal figures, as was common during this period. In the middle panel of the mosaic, a menorah is placed in a circular frame. A lulab and shofar adorn each side of the menorah, and a brief Hebrew inscription is found directly below the menorah. It reads, "Peace upon Israel."

There is also an Aramaic inscription of six lines in the mosaic pavement near the entrance to the synagogue, which is particularly important because it explicitly connects contributions toward the construction of the mosaic to an eschatological reward. The entire inscription reads, "Be remembered for good the memory of the entire holy community, the old and the young, whom the Lord of the Universe aided and were strengthened and made the mosaic. He who knows their names and those of their children and of their families, may He inscribe them in the Book of Life [together] with all the pious, friends to all Israel. Amen."

The inscription explicitly connects "be remembered for good" with an eschatological meaning. The petition to God to have the donors' names inscribed in the "Book of Life" shows that it was believed that the donation had a direct connection with receiving life in the end-time. It is also important to note that the phrase "Book of Life" is written in Hebrew, not Aramaic like the rest of the inscription. This is probably because the phrase was used in the prayers for the New Year and the Day of Atonement, which also carry eschatological connotations.

Jerome (342–420 C.E.) Latin church father. He was born Eusebius Hieronymus at Strido, Dalmatia. After studying in Rome, where he was baptized as Jerome, he spent his early life in Gaul. In about 370 he renounced his career as a civil servant and joined a group of ascetics in Aquileia. From 375 to 378 he lived as a hermit in the desert of Chalcis in Syria, where he met an apostate Jew who taught him Hebrew. He was ordained in Paulinus's "little church" and traveled to Constantinople to argue for the recognition of the "little church" before the council of 381. There he met Gregory of Nazianzus and heard his exegeses of the Bible. From 382 to 385 he served as secretary to Pope Damascus I in Rome. Upon the pope's death in 384, he traveled with his female friend Paula to Bethlehem. There he continued his Hebrew studies with several Jewish teachers, one of whom, Bar Ḥanina from Tiberias, visited him at night because he was afraid of the Jews attacking him for teaching the Christians.

Jerome became extremely proficient in pronouncing Hebrew, and his transliteration of Hebrew is an important source for our knowledge of Hebrew pronunciation during his time. His intimate knowledge of Hebrew served him well in his Latin translation of the Bible. This translation along with his Latin translation of the Greek New Testament, known as the Vulgate, was accepted as the official version of the Bible by the Catholic Church at the Council of Trent in the sixteenth century. The translation was done in several stages. At times he relied on Origen's texts, at others he relied on the Greek texts of Aquila and Symmancus. He also rendered many of the books of the Apocrypha into Latin. Among conservative Christians his translation was condemned; they accused him of following the Jews and ignoring the Christian interpretive traditions. Jerome also wrote many biblical commentaries in which he was influenced by Origen and Gregory of Nazianzus, as well as by some of his Jewish teachers. In fact, his commentaries seem to contain some examples of Jewish midrashim that have been otherwise lost.

Despite his contact with Jews and his studies with them, Jerome had a negative attitude toward Jewish observances and Jewish law. Jerome condemns Judaizing Christians, and in a series of letters between Jerome and Augustine we find the former criticizing the early Christians who accepted Jewish practices. In his commentary on Galatians 2:1, Jerome wrote that Peter and Paul had fabricated their dispute concerning the importance of Christians following Jewish observance in order to convince their followers in Jerusalem that Jewish ritual was meaningless and unnecessary. While Augustine wrote that Peter and Paul continued their Jewish observance, Jerome argued that they could not have done this. Jews who become Christians must stop their Jewish observances, "what they have initiated in the synagogues of Satan."

Jerusalem In the first centuries of the common era the city was the focus of two wars for Jewish independence. The war of 66 to 70 C.E. resulted in the destruction of the Second Temple and of the city. The Bar Kosiba Revolt of 132 to 135 C.E. was instigated in part by Hadrian's establishment of a Roman colony, Aelia Capitolina, on Jerusalem's ruins. The failure of the Bar Kosiba Revolt led to a prohibition against Jews entering the city at all, upon penalty of death. Beginning with Emperor Constantine, the city was under almost unbroken Christian control from 324 C.E. until the Arab conquest of 638.

Jerusalem's theological significance stemmed from the presence there of the Temple and the Ark of Covenant, which meant that the city was the center of Israelite religion and cult. Prophetic writings and the Book of Psalms depict Jerusalem's Mount Zion as God's permanent home, located at the center of the world. These writings hold that, at the end of days, all nations will come to Jerusalem to recognize God's rule (Isa. 2:2–4). As a result of the Israelite people's sins, the city might have been destroyed. But the nation should find consolation in the certainty that Jerusalem will be rebuilt and enjoy greatness (Jer. 30:18–19; Isa. 40:1–2; 52:1–10; Zech. 8:3–8).

Like scripture, rabbinic writings and later Judaism understand the destroyed Jerusalem to symbolize the nation's fortunes. Through longing for the city's restoration, Jews express hope for the fulfillment of God's messianic promise. Rabbinic texts hold that the city's western wall, Gate of the Priests, and Huldah Gate will never be destroyed and believe that, despite the destruction of the Temple, God's presence still dwells at the western wall. Seeing Jerusalem as central to the redemption of all humanity, the rabbis depict all people as mourning the city's destruction and rejoicing at its future restoration. At the end of days, Jerusalem will become a home to all nations (Abot deR. Natan 35), marking a time of universal peace and brotherhood under the rule of the one God.

Jerusalem, archaeology of excavation and survey of the holy city. Archaeological remains indicate that the returnees to Jerusalem in 538 B.C.E. occupied the ridge of the city of David. Later rebuilding has all but obliterated the Persian period city, but it is clear that it was quite small compared to Solomon's city. Nehemiah's wall (Neh. 3:1–32) has been identified with a short segment on the summit of the eastern slope of the city of David. The water gate, mentioned in Nehemiah 12:37, has been found in the wall above the Gihon spring at the foot of the east slopes of the city of David. In the remains of the city more than seventy seals were found with names like Ahazai and Hanania. Many Yehud (Judah) seal impressions were found, reflecting the name of the area around Jerusalem in this period. Persian period occupation did not extend to the modern Jewish quarter of the Old City. The "broad wall" of Nehemiah 3:8 and 12:38

is mentioned as a marker of the extent of Nehemiah's work. This wall has been identified in the Jewish quarter of the Old City and is apparently a surviving Israelite wall that Nehemiah did not elect to repair. The First Temple was restored in its place north of the city of David.

In the fourth and third centuries B.C.E. the city slowly began to expand west of the Temple Mount into quarters remaining from the previous Iron Age occupation. Ancient literary sources such as the Letter of Aristeas mention extensive building activities. The main public work in this period was the building of the Baris Fortress northwest of the Temple Mount. Since this was later torn down for the construction of the Antonia Fortress on the same site, no remains of the Baris have been identified archaeologically. Also built in this period were the aqueduct to Jerusalem from Bethlehem, which has been identified, and the two sheep's pools found north of the Temple Mount.

In the Hasmonean period (167–37 B.C.E.) expansion to the western hill continued. The construction of the city wall was the major building project of the Hasmoneans and expanded the thirty-acre Persian city to about 160 acres. Extensive construction on this wall commenced in mid-second century B.C.E. The wall was built in stages, with the erection of the western wall as the first stage. This wall was built at the far west of the western hill, about 900 meters west of the western wall of the Temple Mount, and its foundations and towers have been identified at several places. A steep scarp protected the eastern and southern sides of this new Upper City until the building of the wall from west to east to the intersection of the Hinnom and the Kidron valleys, just south of the city of David. Ancient literature mentions Hasmonean building projects such as the Hasmonean palace, the council building, and the gymnasium and its attached courtyard, but so far none of these have been located archaeologically.

During the Hasmonean period a bridge was built across the Tyropeon Valley linking the Temple Mount with the Upper City on the western hill. This bridge was discovered in excavations during the last half of the nineteenth century. Also, Hasmonean towers were built against the walls around the city of David. The Acra fortress was built by the Seleucid ruler Antiochus IV in 168 B.C.E. and was located somewhere south of the Temple Mount. Several large cisterns, walls, and other remains of this period have been advanced as remnants of this fortress, but its precise location is unknown.

Small finds from houses of this period include pottery vessels of many types, including imported wares. Rhodian jar handles stamped with Greek inscriptions attest to the wine and the name of the Greek priest in Rhodes under whose aegis the wine was exported. Some jar handles are known with seals of a pentagram and the word Jerusalem stamped between the points of the pentagram. Many coins of the Hasmonean rulers were found, including a hoard of coins of Mattathias Antigonus, the last Hasmonean king.

During the Herodian period, Jerusalem underwent growth and prosperity, as revealed in the archaeological finds. The Temple Mount was expanded to 35 acres within its retaining walls and was the largest building project in the city. Herod also built a palace to the west, the outside towers of which have been found. Just north of his palace he built a fortress with three towers, one of which, the Hippicus tower, can be viewed today at the Jaffa gate and the appended "David's tower." Herod strengthened the city walls. Excavations have unearthed extensive remains of houses of this period, including the "burnt house," a mansion, perhaps of a priestly family, and others. The houses were rectilinear in plan, with rooms around central courtyards. Basement areas included work spaces, storage, and pools interpreted as mikveh, or ritual baths.

Archaeology attests to the violent end of Jerusalem in 70 C.E. Roman arrowheads, round stone ballistae, the equivalent of modern artillery, and a thick ashy layer were found everywhere within the walls of Jerusalem. Equally clear is the evidence of the quartering of the Tenth Legion Fretensis (Ironsides) within the area of the Armenian quarters and Jewish quarters in the modern Old City. Roof tiles stamped with variations on "Leg. X.F." have been found in abundance, as well as clay pipes, bricks, pottery, coins, and other evidences of Roman occupation. This camp seems to have covered about 380 by 250 meters. Equally sudden was the urban renewal under the emperor Hadrian in 135 C.E., when Jerusalem was re-founded as Aelia Capitolina. Coins of Hadrian minted in Aelia Capitolina show a temple to the Capitoline triad of Jupiter, Juno, and Minerva, but the remains of such a temple on the Temple Mount have not yet been traced. Archaeological investigation has revealed the main, northern gate and its inner plaza, the Tyropeon Valley street with its columns, and other streets in the new northeast quarter, Beth Zatha, and its small forum. A large forum occupied the area of the modern Muristan shopping area, and the foundations of a temple to

Aphrodite have been found beneath the Church of the Holy Sepulcher on the north side of the forum. A Roman arch was erected in the northeast of the city, a portion of which today is known as the Ecce Homo Arch. Nearby a temple to the god of healing, Asklepios, was built over the double sheep's pool. Latin inscriptions have been found here and there, and no evidence of Jewish remains anywhere are known.

In the Byzantine era there was a burst of building activity in Jerusalem, especially with the adoption of Christianity as the emperor Constantine's religion in 324 C.E. A series of churches were built in Jerusalem. A detailed map of Jerusalem of the sixth century survives in the floor of a church at Madeba in Transjordan. It shows the city walls and six gates, the Church of the Holy Sepulcher, the colonnaded streets, and other details. In the middle of the fourth century the emperor Julian (r. 361–363 C.E.), called "the Apostate" in Christian sources, returned to the old Roman religion and decreed freedom of worship for all his subjects. He also granted the Jews permission to rebuild the Temple, but no archaeological vestiges of that short-lived attempt survive. The carving of Isaiah 66:14 on the western retaining wall of the Temple Mount is usually associated with this event. Since it is in Hebrew it shows that Jews indeed were to be found in Jerusalem. On the other hand, another possibility dates it from the fifth century, when the empress Eudocia allowed Jews to visit Jerusalem. From the Byzantine period is the massive Cardo or colonnaded street, recently opened to the public. The Church of the Holy Sepulcher was also built in the fourth century, but embellished by successive Christian emperors.

Jerusalem log *see* LOG

Jerushalmi, Targum *see* TARGUM TO THE PROPHETS

Jesse father of David, from Bethlehem of Judah; grandson of Ruth, Boaz's Moabite wife (Ruth 4:13–17). Jesse's importance resides in his being the father of King David, who is often called "son of Jesse." In 1 Samuel 16, Jesse does Samuel's bidding by summoning David from among the sheep, and Jesse later sends David to Saul with gifts. Isaiah 11:1–10 describes an idyllic future when a "root from the stump of Jesse" (a reference to a Davidic king) will rule. In the Book of Biblical Antiquities 59:4, David blames his parents for not calling him when Samuel came to anoint him. Jesus, son of David, is also son of Jesse (Matt. 1:5–6; Luke 3:32; Rom. 5:12; Acts 13:22–23).

Jesus, son of Gamaliel high priest (63–64 C.E.), appointed by Agrippa II. According to rabbinic literature, he was married to Martha, daughter of Boethus. His supporters engaged in street battles with those of his predecessor, Jesus, son of Damnaeus. He was among the chief priests who counseled against the war with Rome and opposed the Zealots. He and Ananus, son of Ananus, were killed by the Idumeans when the latter slaughtered the nobility of Jerusalem in the winter of 67–68 C.E. His father's name is also rendered as Gamla or Gamlas.

Jesus of Nazareth a Jewish popular reformer or leader who was active in Galilee, especially along the northwestern shore of the Sea of Galilee around Capernaum; in the New Testament, the Messiah and the Son of God. The name Jesus is from the Hebrew Jeshua, an abbreviated form of Joshua. According to Matthew, chapter 2, and Luke 1:5, Jesus was born during the reign of Herod the Great (d. 4 B.C.E.) in Bethlehem, though Luke places his birth also during the governorship of Quirinius in Syria and during a census (6 C.E.). John treats him as a native of Nazareth in central Lower Galilee (1:46, 7:42); all agree that he grew up there. He was executed in Jerusalem sometime during Pontius Pilate's governorship (26–36 C.E.), probably because he was perceived as a potential troublemaker. (The Gospels tend to stress the responsibility of the national Jewish authorities as part of an anti-Jewish polemic.) His exact roles and teaching are very difficult to reconstruct since the Gospel accounts are second- or third-generation theological narratives, reflecting both early traditions and later interpretations of Jesus. Most scholars hold that he taught a renewal of Judaism or fulfillment of God's promises to Israel, using the symbol of the Kingdom of God, understood as an eschatological and/or present reality. He was also a popular healer and miracle worker, who reached out to marginal members of society. His followers experienced him as risen from the dead and quickly acknowledged him as the Messiah. This title in Greek, Christ, very soon functioned as a second name.

jewelry objects (often precious or semiprecious) that were used for personal ornamental decoration. From the earliest of prehistoric times, people have adorned themselves with jewelry. The various types of jewelry found within a culture can reveal beliefs about the afterlife, religious superstitions, customs, and tenants, but the jewelry may also simply be used for personal beauty. Of the archaeological discoveries of jewelry in the Holy Land, various forms are known from the Chalcolithic periods down through the Second Temple and Byzantine periods.

The earlier finds of jewelry from Israel are characteristic of the ancient Near East. The earliest gold object in Israel comes from an Early Bronze Age II tomb near the Sea of Galilee. Similar objects are known from Gazer, Byblos, and Troy. Israelite objects from the Late Bronze Age have appeared at such sites as Beth Shemesh and Achzib. Much of this jewelry is reminiscent of Egyptian religious motifs and contains images of Isis, Hathor, and other religious symbols. Other finds from the Late Bronze and various stages of the Iron Age also exhibit Canaanite as well as Egyptian motifs.

Beginning in the Persian period, much of the jewelry from Israel begins to resemble the types known from Hellenistic cultures. In the Hellenistic and Roman worlds, the centers for jewelry production were Alexandria and Antioch-on-the-Orontes. An abundance of the jewelry from Israel during the Second Temple period resembles this Hellenistic jewelry, and many scholars feel that much of the jewelry even originated from these production centers.

Two important finds from the City of David excavations in Jerusalem provide explicit evidence that at least some of the jewelry with these Hellenistic motifs was produced in Israel itself. The City of David excavations uncovered two molds that were used for manufacturing jewelry. The first mold was designed to produce five different types of jewelry: two different forms of earrings, a rectangular pendant, a bud pendant, and a ball pendant. All of these forms have parallels in the late Hellenistic and early Roman periods, and several actual pieces of jewelry resembling these molds have been found in Israel. The second mold dates from the late Byzantine period and is fragmentary, so the type of jewelry is uncertain. It seems to have been used to make either a pendant or an earring.

Common motifs from the Persian period through the Roman period include various Greek and Roman gods, Eros figures, snakes, goats, and dolphins. During the Roman period, medallions with the head of an emperor became common. In Nahal Raqafot in Jerusalem, several pieces of jewelry that were discovered at this site illustrate this Hellenistic influence. These pieces are not displayed in the Israel Museum and include an earring with a rosette connected to a horizontal bar with animal figures. Three pearls are attached. Another piece is a brooch in a gold frame with inlaid semiprecious stones enclosing an onyx cameo. The cameo contains a representation of the bust of Minerva that holds a shield with the image of a gorgoneion. Finally, there was a gold ring that contained a blue onyx decorated with the figure of an elephant, a common motif of Roman jewelry.

During the Byzantine period, the Hellenistic and Roman motifs tend to be replaced with Christian symbols. At Acre, several burials were discovered that are particularly helpful in understanding jewelry with Christian motifs.

A tradition from the Hebrew Bible (cf. Exod. 28:17–20, 39:10–13 and Ezek. 28:13) and from the historian Josephus relates that the high priest in both the First and Second Temple period wore a breast plate decorated with twelve gems. The exact identity of the gems is still somewhat debated, because there are variances among the Hebrew accounts and the Greek translations. The best climate is that this breastplate contained the following gems: sardius, topaz, carbuncle, emerald, sapphire, diamond, jacinth, agate, amethyst, beryl, onyx, and jasper.

Jewish Literary Aramaic *see* ARAMAIC, JEWISH LITERARY

Jewish Palestinian Aramaic *see* ARAMAIC, JEWISH PALESTINIAN

Jewish War, The a historical work by Josephus in seven books that is often referred to by its Latin title, *Bellum Judaicum*. The work, whose title is abbreviated as *War* or *B.J.*, begins about the time of the Maccabean revolt and moves through Hasmonean and Herodian rule; the bulk of its content, however, is devoted to the beginnings and course of the Revolt against Rome in 66 to 70 C.E.

Jews *see* ISRAEL, PEOPLE OF

Joazer, son of Boethus high priest appointed by Herod the Great in 4 B.C.E. and removed by Archelaus after Herod's death. He had become high priest again by 6 C.E., when Quirinius conducted a census. He convinced the people to accede to the census but lost influence to his popular opponents. In 6 C.E. Quirinius replaced him with Ananus, son of Seth.

Job, daughters of Hemera, Kasia, and Amaltheia's Horn—Job's three daughters—appear in the Testament of Job 46–50 (dependent on Job 42:14, where the daughters are named Jemimah, Keziah, and Keren-Happuch). Responding to his daughters' concern about being passed over by his testament in favor of their seven brothers, Job promises the daughters a better legacy: three miraculous, multicolored bands (phylacteries) that will enable them both to earn a living and to live in heaven (47:2). For Job, the phylacteries have provided healing; for the daughters, they function both as amulets and as catalysts for ecstatic speech. Chapter 51 claims that the daughters' hymns and accompanying explanations are preserved in books by their uncle, Nereus. *See also* JOB, TESTAMENT OF.

Job, targums to There are two targums to Job: one found in Qumran Cave 11 (11QtgJob), the other from the rabbinic period. The Qumran targum is in fragments, with its only consecutive section being from Job 37:10–42:11. This highly literal targum has been dated from the first century C.E. The rabbinic targum to Job is complete and may date from the fifth century. There seems to be no relationship between the two texts; they differ not only in word choice but also in dialect. The later targum is more expansive, often giving several different renditions of the same passage—both literal and aggadic. Its language contains elements of both Jewish Palestinian Aramaic as well as Eastern Aramaic. In addition to these targums, there are reports of early rabbis condemning a targum to Job.

Job, Testament of an account of Job's life, told in the form of his testamentary instructions to his children. It is preserved in three Greek manuscripts from the twelfth to sixteenth centuries, a Slavonic version, and a manuscript of a Coptic version dating from the fifth century. It was composed in Egypt, very likely in the first century C.E., in Jewish circles that some scholars have related to the Therapeutai. Its original language was Greek.

Central to the book is the contrast between heavenly realities and this world, which is the area of Satan's activities. Job's primary characteristic is his insight into these realities and his ability to perceive and combat Satan's deceptions.

The narrative opens by explaining the origin of Job's knowledge and the reason for Satan's attack on him (Test. Job 1–5; cf. Job 1–2). God reveals to Job that the local idol temple is really Satan's dwelling, and Job burns the temple (cf. Jub. 12:1–14, of Abraham).

In a set of duels with Satan, in which he loses his possessions, his children, and the respect of his wife, Job emerges as a spiritual athlete, sustained in his contest by the virtues of patience, endurance, and perseverance (1:6–27:7). The second major narrative section describes Job's debate with his friends; he is depicted as king of Egypt and they as monarchs from other countries (chaps. 28–43). Identified as a mouthpiece of Satan, Elihu contrasts Job's former glory with his present degradation. When Job appeals to his possession of a throne in heaven, Baldad and Sophar diagnose him as mentally deranged. Job proves his point by mediating a vision in which his wife and the kings see the enthroned Deity flanked by the children crowned with heavenly glory.

The retrospective narrative returns to the testamentary situation (chaps. 46–51), and Job distributes his restored wealth to the seven sons of his second family. Then, in what is perhaps the most remarkable feature of the book, he bestows on his daughters a set of sashes, which allow them to tune into heavenly realities and to sing with the tongues of angels. This event reverses the book's general tendency to depict women as lacking in insight. The story concludes with Job's death and burial and the ascent of his soul to the heaven to which he had constantly appealed (chaps. 52–53).

Connections between the Testament of Job and Jewish and Christian literature are manifold and complex. The book's cosmic dualism recalls the world view of apocalyptic literature and, perhaps more relevant, Wisdom of Solomon 1–6. Job's portrayal as a spiritual athlete parallels tales of the martyrs and employs motifs typical of some Greek philosophical literature. The celebrated "patience of Job" (James 5:11) derives from this tradition rather than the biblical story. Similarities to some of the Abrahamic literature indicates how traditions and motifs can be transferred from figure to figure. In some of its details, the Testament parallels the Greek rather than the Hebrew version of the Book of Job. The book, with its references to female inspiration, was valued by members of the Christian Montanist movement in the second and third centuries.

Jobab the second king of Edom, according to Genesis 36:33. In the Testament of Job 1–3, Job, who is king in Egypt (28:7), is identified with Jobab the son of Esau; a similar identification appears in the Septuagint of Job 42:17.

Jodfat *see* YODFAT

Joel, Targum to *see* TARGUM TO THE PROPHETS

Johanan *see under* YOḤANAN

John, Jews in the Gospel of The most sectarian and polemical of the Gospels, the Gospel of John criticizes and attacks various Jewish groups, Samaritans, Gentiles, and other followers of Jesus with whom it disagrees. The Gospel has undergone several stages of composition and thus reflects a series of battles against diverse opponents. The Johannine community had its origin as a group of Jews in Judea who followed the teachings of Jesus. References to being expelled from the synagogue (9:22, 12:42, 16:2) testify to a later schism between the Johannine group and Jewish communal authorities. The term Jews occurs frequently in the Gospel. Sometimes it refers neutrally to the Jewish people or Judeans, but mostly it is used as a code for the Jewish opponents of Jesus, mainly the authorities, such as the chief priests and Pharisees. The Pharisees are depicted as communal authorities with judicial responsibilities (9:13), a much more substantial role than they have in the other Gospels. The Jewish people as a whole are not explicitly attacked. The author distinguishes true Israelites (1:47), who are open to Jesus, from the authorities, who are depicted as plotting against him. He also alludes disapprovingly to Jews who believed in Jesus but feared to say so openly (12:42–43). Nevertheless, the complex rhetoric and symbolism of the Gospel are used to distance the Johannine community from its original home in the Jewish community. The choice of the term Jews for the community's opponents has the same effect and tends to stigmatize all Jews, rather than the authorities to whom the references are made. Thus the Gospel of John has been a source of later Christian polemics against Jews.

John Chrysostom (c. 347–407 C.E.) famous preacher in Antioch who became bishop of Constantinople in 398. He was baptized in 368, ordained priest in 386, and earned the name "golden-mouthed" for his popular series of sermons on New Testament books and other subjects. His sermons and other works quickly became widely read in the Eastern Church. He also preached eight notoriously anti-Jewish sermons, which actually were addressed to and against Christians who were participating in Jewish festival celebrations. His polemics reveal that many Christians were drawn to Jewish practices, teaching, and synagogues. The invective in these sermons sought to denigrate the powerful, well-established, and attractive Jewish community in favor of the more recent, insurgent Christian community. Chrysostom, like many early Christian teachers, interpreted the Bible, especially the prophets, in a way that supported Christianity and delegitimated Judaism after Jesus. Later, as bishop of Constantinople, Chrysostom became involved in imperial and ecclesiastical political disputes, was removed from office, and died in exile.

John Hyrcanus high priest and prince (r. 135/134–104 B.C.E.). He succeeded his father, Simon Maccabee, after Ptolemy, Simon's son-in-law, assassinated Simon and two of Hyrcanus's brothers. Hyrcanus then secured Jerusalem and besieged Ptolemy, who eventually fled. During John's first year, Antiochus VII Sidentes, the Seleucid ruler of Syria, invaded Judea in an attempt to reassert his rule. After Hyrcanus was besieged in Jerusalem for the better part of a year, he secured the Syrian's departure by surrendering his arms,

having the walls of Jerusalem torn down, paying a large tribute, handing over hostages, giving up some coastal cities, and subordinating himself again to the Seleucid monarchy. Hyrcanus accompanied Antiochus on his Parthian campaign in 129 B.C.E. When Antiochus was killed in battle, Hyrcanus used the internal disorder of the Seleucid kingdom as an occasion to cease paying tribute and to conquer territory adjacent to Judea, including Idumea, Medeba, and part of Samaria, where he destroyed the sanctuary on Mount Gerizim and Shechem. Late in his rule he also besieged and destroyed the town of Samaria. He was the first Hasmonean king to employ mercenaries.

Hyrcanus's title was high priest and his coins indicate that he ruled in conjunction with the "congregation of the Jews," probably meaning a council in Jerusalem. Josephus says that Hyrcanus's internal policy was influenced first by the Pharisees and then, after a dispute, by the Sadducees. The story by the Jewish historian Josephus and in the Talmud (B. Kidd. 66a) is clearly legendary and its historical worth is hard to assess. The dispute seems to have concerned Hyrcanus's legitimacy as a priest and thus as ruler. It may also have been motivated by factional politics among Hyrcanus's courtiers that led to the ascendency of the Sadducees and fall of the Pharisees from favor. The Talmud attributes the break to King Yannai, that is, Alexander Jannaeus, whom it viewed as cruel and wicked. The Mishnah (Maaser Sheni 5:15) attributes several rulings to Johanan the High Priest, that is, John Hyrcanus, and rabbinic commentary interprets these somewhat unclear rulings favorably. Under Hyrcanus, the Jewish kingdom achieved independence and stability and increased its size significantly.

John of Gischala first-century-C.E. Zealot, born in Gischala, a city in central lower Galilee; leader of the Zealot group in Jerusalem during the war with Rome. He was a popular leader who opposed the more cautious approach to war taken by Josephus, who was given command by the Jerusalem authorities. He unsuccessfully tried first to assassinate Josephus and then to have him removed. In late 67 C.E., when Galilee had been subdued and Titus was besieging Gischala, John escaped to Jerusalem, where he became the leader of the militants called Zealots. In the civil war that ensued in 68 and 69, John's party was one of three that killed the Jerusalem leadership, burned supplies, and turned on one another. He was captured by Titus in the conquest of Jerusalem, displayed in Vespasian and Titus's triumph, and sentenced to life imprisonment.

John the Baptist a lower-order priest (Luke 1) who preached a prophetic message of doom and repentance in the Judean wilderness (Mark 1; Luke 3; Matt. 3). The Gospels picture him as a forerunner of Jesus (Mark 1:7–8; John 1:29–35). He was imprisoned and executed by Herod Antipas at Machaerus because he was the leader of a large popular movement (Josephus, *Ant.* 18.116–119; Mark 6:17–29). His disciples continued his movement into the mid-first century C.E. (Acts 18:25, 19:3–4).

Jokneam *see* YOKNEAM

Jonah **1.** prophet who is the main character of the Book of Jonah; perhaps the Jonah of 2 Kings 14:25, who prophesied about the expanded borders for Israel that Jereboam II attained. In the Book of Jonah, God commands the prophet to preach against the gentile city of Nineveh. Jonah attempts to flee by sea, but a storm arises, and he tells the sailors to cast him overboard to evade God's anger. After they comply, he is swallowed by a fish. In the fish's belly, he prays to God, whereupon the fish spits him out onto dry land. God again demands that he prophesy against Nineveh. When he does so, the Ninevites repent and thus avoid punishment. This angers Jonah.

Later Jewish tradition identifies Jonah with the widow's son raised from the dead by Elijah in 1 Kings 17:17–24 (Lives of the Prophets 10:4–6; some rabbinic sources). In Luke 11:29–32, the sign of Jonah that Jesus says his opponents will receive seems to refer to Jonah's preaching, taken as a parallel to that of Jesus. At the judgment, the repentant Ninevites will condemn Jesus' generation, which did not listen to him. In the parallel passage in Matthew 12:39–41, the element of preaching remains, but the real sign becomes Jonah's rescue after three days in the fish's belly, taken as analogous to Jesus' stay in the tomb.

2. leading Palestinian amora of the fourth century C.E.; head of the academy at Tiberias; student of Zera I, Ila, and, in particular, Jeremiah. He was known for the efficacy of his prayers and for miracles that resulted from his pious behavior.

Jonah, Targum to *see* TARGUM TO THE PROPHETS

Jonah of Botzra Palestinian amora of the mid-fourth century C.E.

Jonathan Tannaitic authority active in the mid-second century C.E.; of the school of Ishmael. The name is not mentioned in the Mishnah, but does occur in the Mekhilta and Sifrei and may be equated with the infrequently mentioned Jonathan b. Joseph. In the talmudic literature, the name Jonathan without a patronymic refers to Jonathan b. Eleazar.

Jonathan, son of Mattathias second-century B.C.E. Maccabean leader. He carried on the Jewish revolutionary Maccabean movement begun by his father and his brother Judas. The fifth son of the priest Mattathias of Modein, and surnamed Apphus, Jonathan was the leader of the Maccabean movement from 160 to 142 B.C.E. He relied on diplomatic and military initiatives to increase and stabilize its influence. The exploits of Jonathan are described chiefly in 1 Maccabees 9:23–13:30. When the Seleucid pretender Alexander Balas offered him the Jewish high priesthood (vacant from 159 to 152 B.C.E.), Jonathan "put on the sacred vestments" (1 Macc. 10:21). Jonathan was captured by Trypho in 143 B.C.E. and later put to death in Bascama. He (or his brother Simon) may have been the "wicked priest" criticized in some Qumran scrolls.

Jonathan, Targum *see* TARGUM TO THE PROPHETS

Jonathan b. Amram student of Judah the Patriarch, active in the late second and early third centuries C.E., during the transition between Tannaitic and Amoraic authority. The few laws attributed to him concern levitical cleanness. Jonathan b. Amram was known for his extreme modesty and unwillingness to profit from his knowledge of Torah (B. Baba Batra 8a).

Jonathan b. Baayan commander of the area around En Gedi, a major port for supplies shipped across the Dead Sea, during the Bar Kosiba Revolt. He was a recipient of many of the Bar Kosiba letters, written between 132 and 135 C.E. One refers to the confiscation of produce of a wealthy landowner in En Gedi who refused to cooperate with the revolt and who seems to have been guilty of profiteering. Another letter was written in Greek because there were no scribes available who could write Hebrew or Aramaic. A third letter charges Jonathan and his co-commander with "sitting eating and drinking and caring nothing for their brothers."

Jonathan b. Eleazar Amoraic authority. He was born in Babylonia, but from an early age lived in the Land of Israel. In the talmudic literature and Midrash, he is referred to simply as Jonathan, without the patronymic. Active at the beginning of the Amoraic period, in the early third century C.E., he was in the circle of Ḥanina at Sepphoris, where he was referred to as "prince of the city." Known primarily for his exegetical teachings, he was a student of Simeon b. Yose b. Lakoniah and a teacher of Samuel b. Naḥman.

Jonathan b. Uzziel According to the Babylonian Talmud (B. Meg. 3a), Jonathan b. Uzziel was the greatest of Hillel's disciples, while Yoḥanan b. Zakkai was the least. Jonathan is credited with writing the Targum to the Prophets, an attribution that is apocryphal.

Jonathan of Beth Guvrin Palestinian amora of the third century C.E., cited exclusively in midrashic contexts

Joppa ancient port city located just south of present-day Tel Aviv, 56 kilometers from Jerusalem; also known as Jaffa or Yapho. The city is situated on a rock about 35 meters above the water. Its natural harbor was formed by a breakfront made up of a collection of rocks about 12 meters offshore, parallel to the coastline. Joppa served as a major port from the Middle Bronze Age down through the Persian and Hellenistic periods.

The name Joppa comes from the Semitic word for "beauty" or "beautiful." It is mentioned in both the Hebrew Bible and in many extrabiblical texts because it served as a major port and travel center throughout antiquity. Joshua 19:46 identifies Joppa as the northern boundary of the tribe of Dan. It is also mentioned in 2 Chronicles 2:16 and Ezra 3:7 as the place where cedars, sent via sea from Tyre and Sidon, were gathered before being sent to Jerusalem for use in constructing the First Temple and in its repair under Ezra. In the New Testament, Joppa is mentioned in conjunction with the missionary work of Peter (Acts 9:36ff.). Extrabiblical texts identify Joppa as an early fifteenth-century Egyptian victory stela of Thutmose III. It is again mentioned in two fourteenth-century-B.C.E. letters from Egyptian Amarna and in the conquest list of Sennacherib, an Assyrian emperor, from 701 B.C.E.

In the Hellenistic period, Joppa became a Greek colony and a major center of ancient Greek and Roman influence in Palestine. From this time on, the name Joppa is frequent in historical documents of the Greeks and Romans. These citations make the identification of modern Jaffa with ancient Joppa certain. Recent excavations from the 1950s and 1960s have unearthed remains of Joppa dating back to the Middle Bronze Age. Also discovered was a fortress from the Persian and Hellenistic periods. This fortress was used by the Greeks and by the Hasmoneans when Joppa was the central port for Judah.

During the Hasmonean period, Joppa was taken from the Seleucid Greeks and was used by the Judeans as a central port. The city soon became independent, and the Hellenistic citizens were known to have had anti-Jewish sentiments. There is even a tragic account of two hundred Jewish citizens being drowned by spiteful inhabitants in 164 B.C.E. Even though the Jewish monarch, Herod the Great, captured the city in 37 B.C.E., he established Caesarea (a harbor further north on the Mediterranean coast) as the central port of Judah. It seems probable that this action was taken in response to Joppa's resistance to him and to other Jewish leaders preceding him.

Jose *see under* YOSE

Joseph 1. eleventh son of Jacob (Gen. 30:22–24). The cycle of stories about Joseph in Genesis 37, 39–50 are shaped in general by a genre employed in the ancient Near East to recount tales about persecuted and vindicated courtiers (cf. Daniel 3 and 6, Esther, the story of Ahikar, and the Book of Tobit, as well as the Book of Susanna). Joseph's brothers conspire against him because his dreams foretell his future domination over them. He is condemned to death, rescued, installed as vizier of Egypt, and vindicated when his brothers bow down before him. His encounter with Potiphar's wife (Gen. 39) adds to the motif of his mantic wisdom and the emphasis on his righteous conduct, specifically his chastity. This, however, is balanced by the notice of his marriage to the daughter of an aristocrat (41:45).

The Testament of Joseph recounts a pair of stories that emphasize qualities of Joseph that are to be emulated (chaps. 3–9, 10:5–16:5). The first focuses on his chastity or moderation (Gr.: *sōphrosynē*) and draws on motifs from the classical Greek story of Phaedra. Joseph's character as a spiritual athlete contending for virtue is a typical feature of Hellenistic moral philosophy and Jewish martyr traditions (e.g., 4 Maccabees and the Testament of Job). The second narrative highlights Joseph's love for his brothers. These moralizing narratives are preceded by a poetic summary of Joseph's life that features the humiliation/exaltation pattern of the court-story genre.

In a different vein, the romantic tale of Joseph and Asenath explains how an Israelite patriarch could have married the daughter of an Egyptian priest: she abandoned her idols and converted to the true God. The story contrasts a pair of disparate motifs that are already implicit in the biblical accounts. Joseph is depicted as "a son of God," with certain angellike characteristics, and his chastity is emphasized. At the same time, true to its genre as a romance, the story highlights certain erotic features, and it may even reflect some elements from the Greek story of Eros and Psyche. Details from the stories in the Testament of Joseph and Joseph and Asenath are found in a wide variety of rabbinic texts.

339

In the New Testament, Joseph is especially important in Stephen's speech (Acts 7), which, following the genre of the Genesis story, cites him as an example of the kind of persecuted and vindicated righteous one (7:9–10) that is epitomized in the crucified and exalted Jesus (7:52–56).

2. Jewish convert to Christianity in the fourth century C.E. Epiphanius records his story. Joseph claimed that he was an important member of the patriarch's court in Tiberias and guardian of the child Judah IV. However, when he learned that Jesus' name had magical powers and could be used for healing, he became a Christian, making his conversion public while on a mission in Cilicia on behalf of the patriarch. Constantine honored him with the title *comes* (companion of the emperor). With the emperor's support he returned to Galilee and built churches in Tiberias, Sepphoris, Capernaum, and Nazareth.

Joseph, Prayer of   a pseudepigraphical Jewish (or possibly Christian) writing probably dating from the first century C.E. The work was most likely composed in Aramaic or Greek in either Palestine or Egypt. Although, according to one canon list, the Prayer originally had 1,100 lines, it survives today only in three short fragments quoted by Origen. The fragmentary nature of the work makes it difficult to formulate definite statements about its content or literary form.

The longest fragment, Fragment A, is quoted in Origen's *Commentary on John.* Fragment B is quoted in the Philocalia and also by Eusebius and Procopius of Gaza; Fragment C appears only in the Philocalia.

The surviving text of the Prayer presents some highly unusual material. In Fragment A, the patriarch Jacob identifies himself as "an angel of God and a ruling spirit" and "the firstborn of every living thing" (A 1, 3). Jacob then recounts a story, based on Genesis 32:24–32, about his wrestling match with the angel Uriel. Uriel acknowledges Jacob's angelic status; Uriel fights with Jacob out of envy over their relative positions; and Jacob identifies Uriel's status as being significantly below his own. Fragment B contains only one sentence, while in Fragment C, Origen reflects upon Fragments A and B.

Since Joseph is never mentioned in the extant text, its title, Prayer of Joseph, presents something of a mystery. Most commentators assume that Joseph is the recipient of Jacob's discourse in Fragments A and B and that the setting for the discourse was Jacob's blessing of Joseph's sons in Genesis 48. It seems probable that the lost portions of the work do contain "prayers" of Joseph.

Some scholars have argued that the text's focus on angelology and its identification of Jacob's angelic status reflect an interest in the mystical ascent to God's throne that is characteristic of Merkabah mysticism.

Joseph, son of Tobiah   tax collector in the reign of Ptolemy III Euergetes (246–221 B.C.E.). In the legendary tale found in Josephus (*Ant.* 12.4.2–11) Joseph was nominated by the people to act as their representative to Ptolemy when the high priest Onias II refused to pay taxes. Joseph placated the king and won his favor, gaining the contract to collect taxes in Coele Syria, Phoenicia, Judea, and Samaria. Joseph is said to have built up the Jewish nation and to have dealt harshly with the Hellenistic cities of Ashkelon and Scythopolis, who refused to comply.

Joseph and Asenath   a Jewish romantic tale that recounts the circumstances of Joseph's marriage to the daughter of an Egyptian priest (Gen. 41:45). The story is preserved in several text forms of long, short, and intermediate length, in sixteen Greek manuscripts of the tenth century and later, and in eight versions translated from the Greek. It appears to be a Jewish (rather than Christian) composition, written in an unknown provenance in Egypt during the first century B.C.E. or the first century C.E.

The story divides into three major parts (chaps. 1–18, 19–21, 22–29). In part 1 Asenath rejects her parents' decision that she should marry Joseph, but agrees to do so when his glorious appearance convinces her that he is "a son of God." Joseph, for his part, refuses her because her worship of idols and eating of food sacrificed to them have made her unclean. Devastated by this rejection, she repents of her idolatry and is visited by the chief of the heavenly host (Michael, though he is unnamed), who provides her with "the bread of life, the cup of immortality, and the ointment of incorruptibility," thus making her eligible to be Joseph's bride. Part 2 repeats in short form the sequence in part 1. Again Joseph visits Asenath's house, where he perceives the new life in her and accepts her as his bride. In part 3, Simeon and Levi foil a plot by Pharaoh's son to kidnap Asenath and murder Joseph.

Thus the story of Joseph and Asenath explains the patriarch's marriage to a gentile woman by positing her conversion to Judaism. In the account of her repentance and the appearance of the heavenly man, not only is she granted immortality and eternal life, she is commissioned to be "a walled mother-city of all who take refuge with the name of the Lord God, the king of ages" (16:16). Thus the story serves as a religious myth that explains the origins of proselytism. That this point is made in a marriage story may indicate that it is intended to deal specifically with the issue of Jew/Gentile marriages. In combining Egyptian mythological motifs with a strong emphasis on the uniqueness of Israel's God in a narrative told from the point of view of the proselyte, the author may have been creating the story that would be especially appealing to new or potential converts to Judaism. Although Joseph and Asenath is a polished literary composition, it incorporates traditional material. This is evident in some parallels with later Jewish stories about Asenath, in which she is said to have been the daughter of Dinah and Shechem (e.g., Pirkei R. Eliezer 38; Midr. Aggadah, Buber ed., I.97). According to these traditions, Joseph could marry Asenath because she was, in fact, the daughter of an Israelite woman. Remnants of the tradition may be seen in the description of Asenath (1:4–5), in the actions of Pharaoh's son, who is a counterpart of Shechem (chaps. 1, 23), and in the major role played by Simeon and Levi, Asenath's protectors (chaps. 22–29).

Joseph and Asenath speaks with much of the technical idiom of Jewish religious literature, notably in its critique of idolatry and its description of conversion as a movement from death to life. At the same time, the story is clothed in the trappings of contemporary Greek romantic literature and has occasional erotic nuances. Its extensive preservation in Christian circles suggests a perceived typology between Joseph "the son of God" and Jesus, between Joseph and Asenath's marriage and the marriage of Christ and the church (cf. Eph. 5:21–33), and between the rituals in chapters 15–16 and the Eucharist.

Joseph b. Ḥama Babylonian amora, active at Maḥoza and Pumbedita in the third century C.E.; the father of Raba; a student of Sheshet and Ḥuna. B. Baba Batra 29b and B. Baba Kamma 97a speak of his and his family's ownership of slaves, a practice contested by Raba.

Joseph b. Ḥiyya Babylonian amora; succeeded Rabbah as head of the academy at Pumbedita; died 333 C.E., after two years in that position. A student of Judah b. Ezekiel, he frequently is cited in both Talmuds. B. Ḥagigah 13a reports his knowledge of chariot mysticism. B. Horayot 13b states that because of his comprehensive learning, Joseph was called Sinai. Several medieval commentators attribute to him authorship of Targum Jonathan to the Prophets and the Targums to the Writings.

Joseph b. Judah   *see* YOSE B. AKABIAH

Joseph of Husal   *see* YOSE B. AKABIAH

Joseph the Babylonian   *see* YOSE B. AKABIAH

Josephus   Jewish historian who recorded the fall of the Second Temple. Born in Jerusalem to an aristocratic priestly family around 37 C.E., Josephus lived through the tumultuous years leading to the Revolt against Rome (66–70 C.E.). Just before the revolt he was sent to Rome on an embassy to secure the release of some priests imprisoned by the Roman authorities. In the early stages of the revolt he was appointed by the leadership in Jerusalem to a position of responsibility in Galilee. There he organized the resistance to Rome while trying to placate the diverse local factions. He was captured by the army of the Roman general Vespasian after the siege of Jotapata (Yodfat) in 68. After his capture he predicted that Vespasian would become emperor of Rome. When the prediction came true, Josephus was released and employed by Titus, Vespasian's son and successor, as head of the Roman forces during the siege of Jerusalem. From his vantage point in the Roman camp, Josephus witnessed the destruction of the city and the Temple in 70.

After the revolt Vespasian and Titus brought Josephus to Rome where he spent the rest of his days in literary activity, supported initially by the Flavian emperors, and then by a wealthy freedman, Epaphroditus. His first work, an account of the war written in Aramaic, probably as a warning to Jews not to rekindle any violent resistance to Rome, has not survived. He then composed an account in Greek, *The Jewish War,* which he published in large part by 79 C.E. This seven-volume work first gives a brief overview of the history of the Jews in the Hellenistic period and then describes in detail the campaigns of Vespasian and Titus, the factional strife that raged in Jerusalem before and during the Roman siege, and the destruction of Jerusalem and the aftermath, including the fall of Masada. Josephus blames the destruction of Jerusalem and its Temple on the revolutionary leaders while exonerating the Romans as instruments of the divine will.

In 93–94 C.E. Josephus published a longer and more comprehensive work, *Antiquities of the Jews,* in twenty books. Modeled on antiquarian historiography like that of Dionysius of Halicarnassus, the *Antiquities* surveyed the history of the Jewish people from Adam to the period just prior to the Revolt against Rome. The first ten books paraphrase the Bible and embellish scriptural narrative with devices of dramatic historiography: pathos, psychological analysis, set speeches, and moralizing touches. Book 11 recounts postexilic history, relying on 1 and 2 Esdras and Esther. Book 12 paraphrases the Letter of Aristeas and 1 Maccabees. Josephus also provides documentary evidence for Jewish rights in Greek cities (12:119–28; 138–53), information on the Samaritans (12:257–64), and a legend about the influential Tobiad family of the third and second centuries B.C.E. (12:154–256). Books 13 and 14 continue the history of the Hasmoneans, using 1 Maccabees and Hellenistic historical sources. Books 15 and 16 give a critical account of Herod's reign. Book 17 continues the account of the Herodian family. Book 18 deals with various episodes of first-century Jewish history, both in the Land of Israel and in the diaspora, and includes a report on Jesus, the so-called Testimonium Flavianum (18:63–64). Book 19 describes the accession of the emperor Claudius, in which Herod Agrippa I played a prominent role. Book 20 brings the account to the beginning of the Revolt against Rome.

As an appendix to the *Antiquities,* Josephus composed an autobiography, *Vita.* The work gives a brief description of his youth, when he sampled the religious options available within Judaism before deciding to conduct his affairs as a Pharisee. The bulk of the work gives another account of the participation by Josephus in the early stages of the revolt, when he served as "general" in Galilee. His reminiscences were apparently prompted by an unflattering report given by a rival historian, Justus of Tiberias. Josephus defends his actions and tries to portray his activity as that of a moderate.

The final work in the Josephan corpus is *Against Apion,* an apologetic tract written to refute a series of slanders against the Jews composed by an Egyptian opponent at the end of the Hellenistic period. The Jews were not, as Apion and others had portrayed them, antisocial misanthropes who descended from lepers expelled from Egypt and who conducted a bizarre cult worshiping the head of an ass in the Temple. The Jews were instead a people of revered antiquity, the Hyksos of Egyptian history. The excellent Jewish constitution and laws provide for a model human society.

The value of Josephus as a historian has been variously assessed. He is clearly tendentious, although his biases are generally obvious, and he is frequently inattentive to details. Nonetheless, he remains an invaluable source for the history of the period. He preserves valuable documentary sources, including a collection of laws and decrees relating to Jews (*Ant.* 14). For many events, such as the details of Herod's reign or the events in Adi-

abene in the first century, he is our only source. His labor as an apologist preserves a valuable record of the cultural conflicts of the Hellenistic and early Roman periods.

Joshua   successor to Moses (Deut. 31:23, 34:9). He led Israel into the promised land and apportioned it among the tribes, according to the Book of Joshua. His name means "Yahweh is salvation." A later form of the name is rendered into Greek as Jesus. Joshua's service to Moses included cultic and military duties (Exod. 17:9–13, 33:11). Of the twelve spies sent into Canaan, only he and Caleb brought back an encouraging report (Num. 13–14).

Sirach describes Joshua as a mighty warrior (and thus a savior of Israel, true to his name), a prophet, and faithful to God (46:1–10). Eupolemus (frg. 2) and Josephus (*Ant.* 4.7.2, sec. 165; 4.8.46, sec. 311) also see Joshua as a prophet. In 1 Macc. 2:55, he is remembered for his obedience to God's commands. In 4 Ezra 7:107, he intercedes for Israel (alluding to Joshua 7). Joshua's story in the Book of Biblical Antiquities occupies chapters 20–24 and emphasizes his division of the land as fulfillment of divine promises, his testamentary exhortation to remain faithful to the covenant (based on Josh. 23–24), and his opposition to the Transjordanian altar (Josh. 22). The Testament of Moses stresses Joshua's role as Moses' successor, and says that the revelations given to Moses were entrusted to Joshua. In Acts 7:45 he is remembered for bringing the Tent of Testimony into the promised land (see Heb. 4:8).

Joshua, Samaritan Book of   one of the Samaritan Chronicles, also known as Chronicle 4. It roughly parallels the book of Joshua in the Hebrew Bible in its first half, but the rest of the book continues to the time of Ba‎ba Rabba. Although an important work to the Samaritans, it is not a part of their canon.

Joshua, Targum to   *see* TARGUM TO THE PROPHETS

Joshua b. Galgula   commander of the area around Hebron during the Bar Kosiba Revolt (132–135 C.E.). In one of the Bar Kosiba letters, Joshua and his staff are threatened with imprisonment if they mistreat any of the Galileans residing in the area, probably a reference to refugees who had moved southwards as Rome conquered the north. Another letter, written toward the end of the revolt, indicates that the military situation was changing drastically. It refers to the approaching pagans and the fact that travel between the neighboring villages and the military headquarters at Hebron was impossible.

Joshua b. Gamla   (d. 69 or 70 C.E.) high priest in the last years of the Second Temple. According to several talmudic passages, he was married to one of the richest women in Jerusalem, Martha, daughter of Boethus (see B. Yoma 18a). He may be identical to Joshua b. Gamaliel, identified by Josephus (*Ant.* 20:213) as a high priest appointed by Agrippa II. According to B. Baba Batra 21a, Joshua b. Gamla established a system of public education that covered all of the Land of Israel.

Joshua b. Hananiah   rabbi in the Land of Israel from c. 70 C.E. to before the Bar Kokhba rebellion of 132–135. In Mishnah Abot 2:8 he is listed as a disciple of Yohanan b. Zakkai, the alleged founder of rabbinic Judaism. His teaching that a person's intention in an act should be central in determining liability appears to have been important in the development of the early rabbinic position on intention.

Joshua b. Iddi   Babylonian amora of the late fifth century C.E.; a contemporary of Ashi. B. Shabat 93a reports that he fasted to prevent an unfavorable dream and, accordingly, declined to participate in a meal at Ashi's house.

Joshua b. Korha   Tannaitic authority of the middle of the second century C.E., recalled for being bald, which accounts for his patronymic, Korha, which means bald-headed. Joshua opposed all cooperation with the Romans and called his student, Eleazar v. Simeon, who served as a police officer, "vinegar, son of wine." He is known primarily from exegetical comments. Rashi holds that he was the son of Akiba, who reportedly was bald (*korha*). The Tosefot reject this claim, which finds no support in the talmudic sources.

Joshua b. Levi   Palestinian amora of the first half of the third century C.E. A native of Lydda, he studied with Eleazar haKappar, Bar Kappara, and Judah b. Pedaiah. Joshua made trips to Caesarea and Rome to discuss Roman relations with the Jewish community (Y. Berakhot 5:1, 9a; Y. Terumot 8:10, 46b; Gen. Rabbah 78:5). He was known for his legal and, especially, exegetical abilities.

Joshua b. Nehemiah   Palestinian amora active in the fourth century C.E. Except for one reference in the Palestinian Talmud, he is cited exclusively in the midrashic literature. His name frequently is attached to parables.

Joshua b. Perahyah   along with Nittai of Arbel, one of the pairs listed at M. Abot 1:6. He was a scholar active in the second half of the second century B.C.E. At M. Hagigah 2:2, he holds that one does not lay hands on a festival sacrifice. M. Abot 1:7 reports his statement: "Keep away from a bad neighbor; and do not get involved with a wicked man; and do not give up hope of retribution."

B. Sotah 47a states that Joshua was a teacher of Jesus who, although finding Jesus guilty of a sin, was responsible for his failure to repent. Parallel stories involving other rabbis (see, e.g., Y. Hagigah 2:2, 77d) suggest that this report about Joshua b. Perahyah is a late elaboration of a stock story.

Josiah   Tannaitic authority of the second century C.E.; an eminent student of Ishmael. While his name is absent from the Mishnah, he is frequently cited in the Mekhilta, in dispute with Jonathan. Sifrei Numbers 123 refers to his presence in Nisibis, at the academy of Judah b. Batyra.

Josippon   a Hebrew version of the 66–70 C.E. Jewish war with Rome. The name Josippon (Yosippon) is a Hebrew form of the name Josephus. The book probably originated about the tenth century C.E., though some would date it earlier. The contents seem to be taken primarily from a Latin version of Josephus's *The Jewish War* passed down under the name of Hegesippus; however, it also contains some additional material from Latin versions of the Apocrypha and even some books from Josephus's *Antiquities of the Jews*. In addition, there is other aggadic material from various sources, such as a version of the legend that Alexander visited Jerusalem and bowed to the high priest.

Jotapata   *see* YODFAT

Jovian   Roman emperor (r. 363–364 C.E.). He took part in Julian's Persian campaign and was elevated to emperor by the army upon Julian's death. He made an unpopular peace with the Persians, returning to them the territory in the east that Diocletian had won, along with the cities of Nisibis and Singara. He was a devout Christian and restored to the Church the privileges that Julian had abrogated. At the same time, he denounced those who were intolerant toward the pagans. He reigned only a few months and died before he and his troops could return to Constantinople.

joy   a quality of the eschatological life. Although nouns and verbs denoting joy and rejoicing have many contexts and connotations, there is a long tradition for associating them with the end-time, especially in contrast to the sorrow and grief that have attended life in this world. A variety of words denoting joy run like a thread through the chapters of Second and Third Isaiah (Isa. 40–66), as they proclaim the return from exile, the hope of a new Jerusalem, and the promise of a new heaven and a new earth. At the end of the Epistle of Enoch (1 Enoch 92–105), having vividly depicted the oppression of the righteous by the sinners, the author explicitly contrasts former troubles and future joy (102:4–103:4, 104:12–105:2).

The notion of eschatological joy permeates the New Testament at many points. The birth of Jesus will be a joy to all the people and is cause for praise from the heavenly chorus (Luke 2:10–14). Paul's letter to the Philippians, its prison setting notwithstanding, is marked by repeated references to the apostle's joy. Matthew's parable about the great judgment describes the heavenly kingdom as "the joy of your Lord" (Matt. 25:21, 23).

Jubilees, Book of a narrative work, written in Hebrew in about 150 B.C.E., that retells the biblical stories from Genesis 1 through Exodus 20 as they were understood by the author. The book is now divided into fifty chapters and is a little longer than the Book of Genesis. The writer was probably a priest who lived in the Land of Israel. He seems to have been concerned that his contemporaries did not have a proper understanding of the first parts of the Bible and their crucial implications. To give greater authority to his words, he presented his book as a divine revelation communcated by an angel to Moses on Mount Sinai. The fourteen or fifteen fragmentary copies of the book that were found among the Dead Sea Scrolls demonstrate that Hebrew was its original language and provide the only evidence now existing for the original Hebrew text. However, it seems not to have been highly regarded by most Jews at a later time; hence it was not copied and went out of use. Before its disappearance it was translated into Greek and possibly into Syriac. No complete manuscript of either translation has survived, only citations from them in other works. The Greek translation served as the base for subsequent renderings of the text into Latin and Ethiopic—the latter is the only complete version of Jubilees that is available. Among Ethiopian Christians, the book seems to have enjoyed biblical status. European missionaries in Ethiopia brought copies of the book, which was believed to have been lost, to the attention of Western scholars in the nineteenth century. As a result, modern study of the book began only in the 1840s.

As he relates the biblical stories, the writer envelops them in a chronology that employs time units of seven and forty-nine years (= a jubilee)—a feature that explains the name of the book. The entry into Canaan will happen, according to his chronology, at the end of the fiftieth jubilee of years, that is, in the year 2450 since the Creation. He also relates that the angels revealed to Enoch the correct length of the solar year (364 days exactly—evenly divisible into fifty-two weeks). The moon was to play no role in measuring time.

Besides his interest in dating events, the author is concerned to show that the ancient biblical heroes engaged in practices that in the Bible arose only later. For example, Noah celebrated the Festival of Weeks, and Abraham inaugurated the Festivals of Unleavened Bread and the Festival of Booths. He seems intent on convincing readers that distinctive Jewish practices have ancient and authoritative roots and thus must not be rejected under cosmopolitan pressures in the Hellenistic age. The book shares a number of features with the Enoch literature (for example, the 364-day solar calendar) and, like that literature, must have been valued by the authors of the Dead Sea Scrolls. Its later influence, outside of Ethiopia, seems not to have been large, although a number of Christian writers refer to it or cite passages from it.

Jubilee year the fiftieth year, following seven Sabbatical cycles. During this year, agricultural labor is prohibited (as during the Sabbatical year), hereditary property (other than that which is in walled cities) is returned to its original owners, and Hebrew slaves who have not completed their six-year terms or who have refused to leave their masters are emancipated (Lev. 25:11–40). The Hebrew term for the Jubilee year, Yobel, refers to the ram's horn, blown to announce the Jubilee's start (Lev. 25:9). Sifra beHar Sinai 7:1 spells out the rabbinic notion that the Jubilee year preserves God's original allotment of property to the tribes and helps bring an end to slavery. Recognizing, too, that during the Jubilee, the land brings forth food without human intervention, the rabbis saw the fiftieth year as a return to the original, perfected state in which God created the world and intended it to exist.

Judaea capta Latin inscription meaning "Judea captive," found on a coin of Agrippa II, which also has a bust of Titus and a picture of Judea as a woman in chains. The coin seems to have been produced in 90 C.E. on the twentieth anniversary of the conquest of Judea by Titus.

Judah fourth son of Jacob and Leah; eponymous ancestor of the tribe of Judah. In Genesis 38, he has intercourse with his daughter-in-law Tamar, mistaking her for a prostitute. Judah's place in later tradition is as the progenitor of the royal tribe, since David was from the tribe of Judah. In Jacob's blessing, Judah's dominance as ancestor of the ruling tribe and his military prowess are prominent (Gen. 49:8–12).

Throughout the Testaments of the Twelve Patriarchs, the dominance of the tribe of Levi as the priestly tribe and of the tribe of Judah as the royal tribe is emphasized, though Judah is subordinate to Levi. The Testament of Judah 2–9 highlights Judah's military exploits (see Jub. 34, 38; LAB 10:3). Judah's lying with Tamar is seen as the result of drunkenness (Test. Jud. 12:3). Judah warns against drunkenness, fornication, and love of money (Test. Jud. 13–19). Jubilees legitimates Judah's and Levi's leadership positions through a blessing by Isaac (31:11–17) and says that Judah repented of his sin with Tamar and was forgiven (41:23–24).

The New Testament claims that Jesus was descended from Judah, since he was the Davidic Messiah (Matt. 1:2–3, 2:6; Luke 3:33; Heb. 7:14). Revelation 5:5 calls Jesus the "Lion of Judah," a phrase originating in Jacob's blessing (Gen. 49:9).

Judah, Persian province of After the collapse of the Neo-Babylonian empire in 539 B.C.E., Judah (Yehud) automatically passed under Persian control as a small province in the vast Fifth Satrapy, which included Babylon and the Trans-Euphrates region (Babili-Ebirnari). This administrative arrangement remained in place until Xerxes I (r. 486–465) made Babylon a separate satrapy after crushing a revolt there in the early years of the reign. The province seems to have had its own identity independent of Samaria from the beginning (see references to governors preceding Nehemiah in Ezra 5:14; Neh. 5:15; Hag. 1:1; Mal. 1:18), but was put on a firm footing only with the administration of Nehemiah during the reign of Artaxerxes I (465–425 B.C.E.).

Judah, Rab *see* JUDAH B. EZEKIEL

Judah II (d. 270 C.E.) Tannaitic authority and patriarch; the grandson of Judah I and son of Gamaliel III, whom he followed as patriarch; active in Tiberias in the mid-third century C.E. Referred to as Judah, as Judah Nesiah, or, sometimes, like his grandfather, as Rabbi. Accordingly, it often is difficult to determine to which Judah reference is made.

Judah III son of Gamaliel IV; patriarch from 290 C.E. to his death in 320 C.E.; a student of Yoḥanan. Judah III was in the circle of Ḥiyya, Ammi, and Assi, whom he sent to provide scribes and teachers for towns throughout the Land of Israel (Y. Ḥagigah 1:7, 76c). Y. Terumot 8:10, 46B–C, reports of a meeting between Judah III and Diocletian when the latter stayed in Tiberias while waging war against the Persians.

Judah IV son of Gamaliel V; patriarch in the late fourth century C.E. Apparently he was unpopular with contemporary rabbinic authorities, who refused to attend his sister's funeral (Y. Berakhot 3:1, 6a). Little is known about him.

Judah b. Baba Tannaitic authority of the second century C.E., known for his piety and modesty (T. Sotah 13:4). After Akiba was executed by the Romans, Judah ordained several of his students, a capital offense. Surprised by Roman troops, he told the students to flee while he remained and was martyred (B. Sanhedrin 14a).

Judah b. Batyra 1. Tannaitic authority active at the close of the Second Temple period. B. Pesaḥim 3b indicates that prior to the destruction, he moved to Nisibis, in Babylonia.

2. later Tannaitic authority of the same name, whose existence is posited on the basis of interactions between Judah b. Batyra, Akiba, and other authorities in the mid-second century C.E. This Judah apparently was born in Rome, educated in the Land of Israel, and, like the earlier Judah, ultimately went to Nisibis.

Judah b. Ezekiel Babylonian amora active in the third century C.E.; normally referred to simply as Judah, without the patronymic; the most prominent student of Rab. After Rab's death, he studied with Samuel, who called him Shinena (sharp-witted, or large-toothed). Judah founded the academy at Pumbedita, where he died in 299. He was known for his intensity and vigor in study.

Judah b. Ḥiyya Amoraic authority of the late second and early third centuries C.E.; born in Babylonia; moved with his twin brother and father to the Land of Israel, where he studied with Judah the Patriarch. His father-in-law, Yannai, referred to him as Sinai, indicating the breadth and depth of his scholarship.

Judah b. Ilai Tannaitic authority of the mid-second century C.E.; referred to simply as Judah, without the patronymic, in the talmudic literature. A native of Usha, Judah may have been a student of Tarfon in Lydda (see M. Nedarim 6:6). He cites principles of Akiba (e.g., T. Ohalot 4:2), whom scholars therefore consider also to have been his teacher. According to B. Sanhedrin 14a, he was one of the five students ordained by Judah b. Baba during the Hadrianic persecution that followed the Bar Kokhba Revolt. Judah played a leading role in establishing the rabbinical academy in Usha, and he also opened the Sanhedrin in Yabneh (B. Berakhot 63b). His importance was recognized by later talmudic authorities, who refer to the rabbis of Judah's period collectively as "the generation of Judah b. Ilai" (B. Sanhedrin 20a). The talmudic literature contains many of his laws and other statements, some given on his own authority and others in the name of past rabbis, including Eliezer b. Hyrcanus, who had been his father's teacher,

Akiba, Meir, and the Houses of Hillel and Shammai. In legal contexts, Judah is chiefly in dispute with Simeon b. Yoḥai. In exegetical settings, his principle disputant is Neḥemiah. Judah was a teacher of Judah the Patriarch (B. Shebuot 13a) and of Ishmael b. Yose (B. Sukkot 18a).

Judah b. Lakish (late 2d c. C.E.) Tannaitic authority; a contemporary of Judah the Patriarch. He frequently transmits statements of Simeon b. Gamaliel II in controversies with Yose b. Judah.

Judah b. Naḥmani Palestinian amora of the third century C.E.; the meturgeman of Simeon b. Lakish, charged with conveying the master's quietly spoken lectures to the students assembled at the academy at Tiberias. He was in his own right a learned and respected teacher (see, e.g., Y. Sukkah 5:1, 55a; B. Sanhedrin 7b).

Judah b. Pazzi *see* JUDAH B. SIMEON B. PAZZI

Judah b. Pedaiah Palestinian amora of the early third century C.E.; referred to in the Babylonian Talmud as Bar Pada, in the Jerusalem Talmud as Bar Pedaiah, and in midrashic compilations by his full name. He was a student of Judah the Patriarch or, alternatively, of Ḥiyya and of his uncle, Bar Kappara.

Judah b. Shalom Palestinian amora of the late fourth century C.E.; referred to in the Jerusalem Talmud as Yudan

Judah b. Simeon b. Pazzi Palestinian amora active at the beginning of the fourth century C.E.; also referred to as Judah b. Simon and Judah b. Pazzi. He frequently cites legal and exegetical statements in the names of his father, Joshua b. Levi, Yoḥanan, and Simeon b. Lakish. He often employs parables.

Judah b. Simon *see* JUDAH B. SIMEON B. PAZZI

Judah b. Tabbai along with Simeon b. Shetaḥ, one of the pairs referred to by M. Abot 1:2–15; active in the first century B.C.E. Attributed to him is the maxim: "Do not make yourself like an advocate before judges [while you yourself are judging a case]. And when the litigants stand before you, regard them as guilty. And when they leave you, regard them as acquitted, when they have accepted your judgment" (M. Abot 1:8).

Judah b. Tema Tannaitic authority; possibly a contemporary of Judah the Patriarch. At M. Abot 5:20, he is reported as saying: "Be strong as a leopard, fast as an eagle, fleet as a gazelle, and brave as a lion, to carry out the will of your Father who is in heaven."

Judah the Prince head of Palestinian Jewish community who promulgated the Mishnah in 200 C.E.

Judaism Judaism, the religion deriving from God's revelation to Moses at Sinai, is a monotheistic religion, as are Islam and Christianity, which affirm that same revelation. Distinguished from polytheistic and other nonmonotheistic religions, all three maintain that God is one and unique, transcendent, and not subject to the rules of nature but wholly other. Judaism differs from Christianity in recognizing as God's revelation the Hebrew scriptures, but not the New Testament. It differs from Islam in holding Moses to be unique among prophets and in recognizing no prophecy beyond the scriptural record. Differentiating Judaism from Christianity and Islam is easier than defining Judaism because the word "Judaism" applies to a variety of closely related religions, past and present. These share a number of traits. For example, all of them revere the Torah (literally, revelation; often mistranslated, the law) revealed by God to Moses at Sinai—even if they do so to different degrees. But they also differ among themselves in important ways. Thus to define Judaism as a unitary and uniform religion, unfolding in a single continuous history from beginning to present, is simply not possible.

Dealing with the diversity of Judaisms within Judaism proves somewhat easier if we speak not of a "religion" but of a "religious system." A religious system comprises three components: (1) It presents a worldview explaining who the people it encounters are, where they come from, and what they must do. In general, what a Judaism defines as "the Torah" will contain that worldview. (2) It prescribes a way of life, which expresses in concrete deeds the religious system's worldview. It thereby links the life of the individual to the community. For each Judaism, its way of life comprises what it sets forth as the things someone must do. (3) It designates a particular social group, which is the group to whom the worldview and way of life refer. For a Judaic system, obviously, that group is "Israel" or, more specifically, the group it considers to constitute Israel—beginning with itself. A Judaic system, or a Judaism, thus comprises a worldview, a way of life, and a group of Jews who hold the one and live by the other. A striking and also distinctive symbol expresses the whole all together and at once; such a generative symbol may be "Torah," God's revelation to Moses at Sinai, or it may be "Israel," God's holy people. Each Judaic system alleges that it represents the true and authentic Judaism, or Torah, or will of God for Israel, and that its devotees are Israel. And each Judaism ordinarily situates itself in a single historical line—hence, a linear history—from the entirety of the past. Commonly, a Judaism sees itself as a natural outgrowth, the increment of time and change. These traits of historical or even supernatural origin characterize nearly all Judaisms.

How, then, do we distinguish one Judaism from another? We can do so when we identify the principal symbol to which a given system appeals—when we uncover its urgent question and define the answer it considers "natural." All Judaisms, wherever formed and whatever type of question they have deemed urgent, must face up to the same persistent social facts that all Jews for all time have confronted. All Judaisms identify in common the Pentateuch, or the Five Books of Moses (the Torah). The Torah explains "where it all began" and forms a critical component of the holy writings of every Judaism ever known. The key question is, what problem does the Pentateuchal authorship—the people who put it all together as we now have it—find urgent? And can we translate that problem into terms that are socially relevant wherever Jews have lived, from then to now? If we can, then we can account for any Judaism and every Judaism.

Judaism finds its origins in two sequential happenings, which together form a single event—the Babylonian exile and the subsequent return to Jerusalem. In 586 B.C.E., the Temple of Jerusalem was destroyed. In addition, the political classes of the Jewish state and the persons of economic worth, the craftsmen and artisans—anybody who counted—were taken away to the homeland of the conquering empire. Around three generations later, toward the end of the sixth century B.C.E., the Babylonian Empire fell to the Persian one. The Persian emperor Cyrus, as a matter of public policy, sought to win the loyalty of his diverse empire by restoring to their points of origin populations removed from their homelands by the Babylonians. Consequently, the Jews of Babylonia were given the right to return to the Land of Israel. At this time, only very small numbers of them took the opportunity. These Jews made a start at rebuilding the Temple. And some time later, in the middle of the fifth century B.C.E. (c. 450 B.C.E.), a successor of Cyrus allowed a Jewish high court official, Nehemiah, together with a top bureaucrat and civil servant, Ezra, to go back to Jerusalem and, with the support of the state, to rebuild the Temple and establish a Jewish government in the surrounding region. These two events come together as "exile and return," and are framed in terms as mythic and transcendent in their context. The historical events of 586 B.C.E. and 450 B.C.E. are transformed in the Pentateuch's picture of the history and destiny of Israel into that generative myth of exile and return that characterizes every Judaism, then to now.

In order to grasp the Pentateuch's main point, the vital concern that its compilers dealt with, we have first to understand how it took shape. The Five Books of Moses (Genesis, Exodus, Leviticus, Numbers, and Deuteronomy) speak of the creation of the world and God's identification of the children of Abraham, Isaac, and Jacob (who also was called Israel) as God's people. The people of Israel are portrayed as taking shape in Canaan, which was promised to Abraham and his seed and would be called the Land of Israel. The people are portrayed as then going down to Egypt, being freed of the bondage of Egypt by Moses, who led the people to Sinai, and being given the Torah by God. The Torah is described as comprising rules that were to govern Israel's holy community and Israelites' service to God in the cult and in the temple that would be built in time to come. It also contained the message that when Israel kept the covenant, the contract made with God by the patriarchs and given substance at Sinai, then God would favor Israel, but when Israel did not comply, then God would punish it. The Pentateuch as we now have it is the work of an authorship of a particular period. Thus the message of the Pentateuch, encompassing diverse prior viewpoints and messages to be sure, is one that addresses the social world of the ultimate authorship, which has put everything together to say that one thing.

Each Judaism responded to events within the pattern laid out by scripture in the original encounter with the "single event" comprising the destruction of the Temple in 586 B.C.E. and the return to Jerusalem in the beginning of the fifth century B.C.E. That event was, to begin with, interpreted as a paradigm of death and resurrection. The destruction of the Temple and the subsequent exile symbolized death, while the return from exile, with the rebuilding of Jerusalem and reinstitution of the Temple cult, constituted resurrection. It answered the question, who is Israel? by defining the rules that govern what it means to be Israel. These rules involve the formation of Israel and its covenant with God, time and again insisting on the holiness of Israel and its separateness from other peoples. They also involve the conditional possession of the land as the mark of the covenant. The people of Israel have the land not as a given but as a gift. So long as the people honor the covenant, the land will be theirs and they will prosper in it. If the people violate the Torah, the conditions of the covenant, they will lose the land. The key scriptures are Leviticus, chapter 26, and Deuteronomy, chapter 32. But if one reviews the narrative of Genesis, with its account of how the people took shape and how they got the land, one sees that the relationship of Israel to the land is the theme throughout. Everything else depends upon it. When you get to the land, you build the temple. The condition of the people dictates their right to the land, and in losing the land, the people are warned to keep the Torah and the conditions that it sets forth. What that means, of course, is that in recovering the land, Israel enjoys a redemption that is conditional, as noted above, not a given but a gift.

The Torah stresses the distinctive rules that govern Israel and the unique character of Israel among the nations. Translating those stressed points into secular and neutral language reveals a chronic concern for defining Israel—for discovering (to slip into contemporary political language) the answer to the question, who is a Jew? In one way or another, Israel, that is, the Jewish people, wherever they lived, sought means of declaring themselves a group distinct from its neighbors. One reason that the concern with difference persists is that the Jews, wherever located, are simply a very small group surrounded by others that are larger, more powerful, and more important. If a small group under diverse circumstances wishes to sustain itself, it does so by underlining the points of difference between itself and everyone else. It will furthermore place a high value on these points of difference, going against the more common impulse of a minority to denigrate points of difference and so identify with the majority. Throughout the Torah's narrative—in Genesis, where the patriarchs go "home" to Babylonia to obtain their wives; in Leviticus, with its exclusion of the Canaanites, whom "the land vomited out" because of their wickedness; in Deuteronomy, with its command to wipe out some groups and to proscribe marriage with others—the stress is the same: form high walls between Israel and its nearest neighbors. The stress on exclusion of the neighbors from the group, and of the group from the neighbors, in fact runs contrary to the situation of ancient Israel, which, with its unmarked frontiers of culture, participated in the constant giving and receiving among diverse groups characteristic of ancient times. The persistent stress on differentiation, yielding a preoccupation with self-definition, also contradicts the facts. In the time of the formation of the Pentateuch, Israel was deeply affected by the shifts and changes in social, cultural, and political life and institutions. When, a century and a half after the formation of the Pentateuch under Ezra

and Nehemiah, the Hellenized Macedonians under Alexander the Great conquered the entire Middle East (c. 320 B.C.E.) and incorporated the Land of Israel into the international Hellenistic culture, the problem of self-definition came up again. And when the war of independence fought by the Jews under the leadership of the Maccabees (c. 160 B.C.E.) produced an independent state for a brief period, that state found itself under the government of a court that accommodated itself to the international style of politics and culture. What, then, was different? What made Israel separate and secure on its land and in its national identity? In that protracted moment of confusion and change, the heritage of the Five Books of Moses came to closure. And the same situation persisted that had marked the age in which the Pentateuch had delivered its message, answering with self-evident responses the urgent question of the nation's existence. Exile and return define the history of all Judaic systems or Judaisms.

Judaism in the first century B.C.E. and first century C.E. The common core of traits that characterized all the Judaic systems in the biblical period, with special reference to the first century B.C.E. and first century C.E., are defined by James D. G. Dunn (*The Partings of the Ways,* p. 18) as follows: "We can still speak of a common and unifying core for Second Temple Judaism, a fourfold foundation on which all these more diverse forms of Judaism built, a common heritage which they all interpreted in their own ways. We cannot say that the four common elements were Judaism, since each group or 'sect' differed in emphasis and understanding and in the way it brought the common core to expression. Even when Ioudaismos ('Judaism') is used in texts of the time, it may well have included something at least of a sectarian understanding of the term. Nevertheless, the fact remains that the word could be used; there was something recognizable as 'Judaism,' something common to these various diverse expressions of Second Temple Judaism(s)." Dunn's four pillars are (1) monotheism; (2) election: the conviction that Israel was chosen by God, "that the one God had bound himself to Israel and Israel to himself by a special contract or covenant"; (3) Torah: the centrality of the Torah in Israel's self-consciousness of being God's chosen people; and (4) Temple: the role of the Temple at the center of Israel's national and religious life at that time. Corollaries of the basic axiom of covenantal nomism are Israel's distinctiveness as the people specifically chosen by the one God to be his people and the sense of privilege in being the nation specially chosen by the one God and favored by gift of covenant and law. This was expressed in concrete terms in circumcision, the Sabbath, and the dietary laws. Dunn concludes: "These then can be fairly described as the four pillars on which the Judaism(s) of Jesus' time was built: the axiomatic convictions around which the more diverse interpretations and practices of the different groups within Judaism revolved." In these four points, we identify what we must call the lowest common denominator that characterizes all Judaic systems equally. What each Judaic system had in common with all the others proves systemically inert, hardly active, let alone definitive, in setting forth what to any given Judaism proved its critical point: its self-evidently valid answer to the question it identified as urgent and immediate.

The formation of the Judaism of the dual Torah. Defined by the Mishnah, the two Talmuds, and the Midrash compilations, the paramount Judaism known today, the one that focuses upon "the Torah" as its generative symbol and adopts the Talmud of Babylonia, in addition to scripture, as its authoritative document, took shape between the first and seventh centuries. The process of that Judaism's formation is detailed in the sequence of books that served to make its principal statements in succession. Stated in documentary terms, the formative history of the Judaism that appeals to the myth of the dual Torah, oral and written, revealed by God to Moses at Sinai, tells a story in three sentences, so to speak. First, the Judaic system emerged in the Mishnah (promulgated c. 200 C.E.) and its associated Midrash compilations (compiled c. 200–300 C.E.) as a philosophical structure comprising a politics, philosophy, and economics. These categories were defined as philosophers in general understood them: a theory of legitimate violence, an account of knowledge gained through the methods of natural history, and a theory of the rational disposition (and increase) of scarce resources. Second, this philosophical system was turned by the Talmud of the Land of Israel and related Midrash compilations (compiled c. 400–500 C.E.) into a religious system. The system was effected through the formation of counterpart categories: an antipolitics of weakness, an antieconomics of the rational utilization of an infinitely renewable resource, a philosophy of truth revealed rather than rules discovered. Third and finally, the religious system was restated by the Talmud of Babylonia and its companions of Midrash collection (compiled c. 500–600 C.E.). In those writings, the system was given theological re-presentation through the recovery of philosophical method for the formulation of religious conceptions. In the Hegelian tradition, one might say, the formation of Judaism took place through the second Talmud's final synthesis of the Mishnah's initial thesis and the first Talmud's consequent antithesis.

Theology is the science of the reasoned knowledge of God, in the case of a Judaism made possible by God's self-manifestation in the Torah. Seen in its whole re-presentation in the Talmud of Babylonia, the theology of Judaism sets forth two modes of knowledge of God. The first is to know God through God's self-revelation in the Torah. This requires that we know what the Torah is, or what torah is (in a generic sense, which can pertain to either message or media or modes of thought). Then knowing how to define and understand the Torah affords access to God's self-revelation. The second is to know through that same self-revelation what God wants of Israel and how God responds to Israel and humanity at large. That specific, propositional knowledge comes through reasoned reading of the Torah, oral and written, the Mishnah and scripture, represented by the Talmuds and Midrash compilations, respectively.

The schematic classifications of the successive, related Judaic systems as philosophical, religious, and theological, therefore derive from the character of the successive documents, the Mishnah, Yerushalmi, and Babli. What makes all the difference in the second Talmud's re-presentation of the Judaic religious system, therefore, is the character of that Talmud itself. Through analysis of the hermeneutics that conveys the intellectual program of that medium, a religion rich in miscellaneous but generally congruent norms of behavior and endowed with a vast store of varied and episodic but occasionally contradictory ideas was turned into a proportioned and harmonious theology, religious in character and theological in re-presentation. Earlier Midrash compilations undertook the task of showing the relationship between the two media of the Torah, the oral and the written, by insisting that the Mishnah rested on scripture. The goal was to show linearity and, of course, harmony. They furthermore began the definition of the Torah—in our terms, the reading of scripture—by systematizing and generalizing the episodic cases of scripture. The goal was to demonstrate the comprehensiveness of the Torah: its cases were meant to yield governing rules. The later Midrash compilations continued that reading of scripture by formulating syllogistic propositions out of the occasional data of scripture. The religious writings that formed the second stage in the unfolding of Judaism—the Talmud of the Land of Israel, Sifra and the two Sifrés somewhat earlier, Genesis Rabbah and Leviticus Rabbah somewhat later—finally were succeeded and replaced by the Talmud of Babylonia and related Midrash compilations, particularly Song of Songs Rabbah, Lamentations Rabbah, and Ruth Rabbah. These were documents that restated in rigorous, theological ways the same religious convictions, thus providing that Judaism, or Judaic system, with its theological statement. This point bears repeating: in these writings, the religious system was restated in a rigorous and philosophical way. The associated Midrash compilations succeeded in making a single, encompassing statement out of the data of the several books of scripture they presented. The re-presentation of the religious system in the disciplined thought of theology took the form of setting forth rules of reading the Torah—oral and written—and through those rules exposing the character of the intellectual activity of thinking as God does, that is, thinking about the world in the way God thinks.

The theology of Judaism—reasoned knowledge of God and God's will, afforded by God's self-manifestation in the Torah—affords access in particular to the mind of God, revealed in God's words and wording of the Torah. Through the Torah, oral and written, the sages work back to the intellect of God, who gave the Torah. Thus, through learning in the Torah in accord with the lessons of the Talmuds and associated Midrash compilations, humanity knows what God personally has made manifest about mind, that intellect in particular in which "in our image, after our likeness" we, too, are made. That defines the theology of the Judaism of the dual Torah and, in particular, forms the upshot of the Talmud's re-presentation of that theology. Then the formation of Judaism, correctly described, may be stated in a single sentence: The Mishnah, then the first Talmud, and finally the second Talmud, together with their respective sets of associated Midrash compilations, yield the history of a three-stage formation. The first tells how the document that set forth the first Judaic system formed a philosophy, utilizing philosophical categories and philosophical modes of thought (philosophy, politics, economics, Aristotelian methods of hierarchical classification for categories). The second explains how the categorical formation was recast into religious classifications, from philosophy to Torah, from a politics of legitimate power to an antipolitics of weakness, from an economics of scarce resources to an antipolitics of the abundant

resource of Torah-learning. The third then spells out how the received categorical system and structure was restated in its main points in such a way as to hold together the philosophical method and the religious message through a hermeneutical medium.

Judaism in Greek and Latin sources Early Greek reactions to Judaism were favorable. Aristotle's disciple Theophrastus (372–288 B.C.E.) noted Jewish sacrificial customs and commended the Jews' philosophical lifestyle (in Porphyry, *On Abstinence from Meat* 2.26). A similar assessment of Jews as philosophers appears in a fragment of another Aristotelian, Clearchus of Soli, around 300 B.C.E. (in Josephus, *Against Apion* 1.176–83). At about the same time the ethnographer Hecataeus of Abdera gave a moderately favorable account of Jewish origins. His work, preserved by the first-century historian Diodorus of Sicily (*Bibliotheca historica* 40.3), told of the Jews' expulsion from Egypt as undesirable aliens and of their migration to Judaea under Moses, who founded many cities, including Jerusalem! Hecataeus also spoke favorably of the Jews' imageless cult, sacrificial system, and legal traditions. Another positive account attributed to him survives in Josephus's *Against Apion* 1.183–204. It extols the Jews' steadfast adherence to their laws as well as the extent and character of their settlement. The fragment's authenticity is doubtful, and it may derive from a Jewish apologist writing after the Maccabean revolt.

National historians took note of Jews in various ways. Berossus of Babylon (early 3d c. B.C.E.) merely mentioned them as one of the peoples subjected by Nebuchadnezzar (in Josephus, *Against Apion* 1.130–41). Manetho, an Egyptian priest contemporary with Berossus, offered a polemical Egyptian reading of Exodus traditions (in Josephus, *Against Apion* 1.73–105 and 228–52). In his account, the original Jews were Egyptian lepers, condemned to banishment from Egypt. They revolted under the leadership of a priest from Heliopolis, named Osarseph, later called Moses. They designed misanthropic laws and customs in opposition to Egyptian ways. Elements of this tale are common in later anti-Jewish sources (e.g., the advice of the counselors of Antiochus IV Epiphanes in Diodorus, *Bibl. hist.* 35.1.2).

Hellenistic authors interested in exotic peoples added new and sometimes hostile touches. Mnaseas of Patara, around 200 B.C.E., claimed that Jews worshiped the golden head of an ass (in Josephus, *Against Apion* 1.215–16; 2.112–14), a slander repeated frequently (e.g., Apion in Josephus, *Against Apion* 2.80). A possibly related report in Diodorus's *Bibliotheca historica* 35.1.3 holds that Antiochus IV Epiphanes entered the inner sanctuary of the Temple and found a statue of a bearded man on an ass.

Not all Hellenistic authors were as negative. The Alexandrian historian Agathachides of Cnidus (second century B.C.E.) noted the Jewish observance of the Sabbath and attributed to it the capture of Jerusalem by Ptolemy I, king of Egypt (in Josephus, *Against Apion* 1.205–11). He deemed the Jewish practice foolish, but not reprehensible.

More virulent treatments appear in later Hellenistic authors. Apollonius Molon (early first century B.C.E.), an orator active on Rhodes, instructed many leading Romans in the last generation of the Republic. His monograph on the Jews, according to Josephus (*Against Apion* 2.79–80, 145, 148), attacked their vile worship (the ass's head), atheism, and misanthropy. Lysimachus (2d or 1st c. B.C.E.) added to Manetho's account of Jewish origins a tendentious etymology of Jerusalem as a derivative of "temple plundering," an activity attributed to the misanthropic Jews (in Josephus, *Against Apion* 1.304–11). Apion (early 1st c. C.E.), an Egyptian scholar and orator, represented the Alexandrian Greeks before the emperor Gaius. He repeated the Egyptian version of Jewish origins (in Josephus, *Against Apion* 2.1–25), argued that Jews did not enjoy citizens' rights in Alexandria (*Against Apion* 2.32–42), and castigated Jewish piety. To the tales of the worship of an ass Apion added a blood libel, recording the discovery by Antiochus IV Epiphanes of a non-Jewish prisoner in the Temple being fattened for sacrifice (*Against Apion* 2.91–96). Josephus (*Against Apion* 2.79) suggests that the Stoic philosopher Posidonius of Apamea (135–51 B.C.E.) was a source for such slanders, but direct evidence for Posidonius's views is scanty and his probable fragments, including those in Diodorus of Sicily (*Bibl. hist.* 35.1.1–5), are relatively positive to Jews.

A different anti-Jewish bias appears in the fragments of Pompeius Trogus (late 1st c. B.C.E. to early 1st c. C.E.), a historian from Damascus. An epitome of his *Historiae Philippicae* by the third- or fourth-century-C.E. author Justin repeats Egyptian views of the Jews as originally lepers but locates the ancestral home of Moses in Damascus. It also suggests that the Jews had always been ruled by priest-kings (Justin, *Hist. Phil.* 36, *Epitome* 1.9–3.9).

Not all attention to Jews in the late Hellenistic period was hostile. Alexander Polyhistor compiled a reference work for Romans after Pompey's conquest of the East in 63 B.C.E. His treatise, preserving fragments of many Greco-Jewish authors of the previous centuries, survives in Christian sources such as Clement of Alexandria and Eusebius. Diodorus of Sicily preserved various notices on Jewish history in the Hellenistic period, including the favorable view of Hecataeus (*Bibl. hist.* 40.3). The geographer Strabo (64 B.C.E.–20 C.E.) knows much about Palestine and has an extensive and favorable account of Jewish origins (*Geography* 16.2.34–46). Varro (116–27 B.C.E.), the learned Roman antiquarian, in a fragment from his *Antiquities Human and Divine,* praises the imageless worship of the early Romans and compares it favorably with the Jewish cult (in Augustine, *City of God* 4.31). Pseudo-Longinus in *On the Sublime* (early 1st c. C.E.) extols the literary quality of the opening of Genesis. Nicolaus of Damascus (64 B.C.E. to early 1st c. C.E.), a scholar and client of King Herod, treated Jewish history at various points in his 144-book universal *History.* Though it has not survived, the work provided material for Josephus's treatment of postbiblical Jewish history, particularly for Herod's reign.

Among the Romans, less favorable opinions were common. In 59 B.C.E. Cicero (106–43 B.C.E.) defended the governor of Asia, Flaccus, against charges of embezzlement, particularly of the gold sent to the Temple by Jews of his province. In the defense Cicero indicated his dislike of Jewish practices (*Pro Flacco* 28.66–69). Roman poets and satirists were also negative. Horace (65–8 B.C.E.), the major Augustan lyric poet, evinces the traditional Roman disdain toward a foreign cult (*Sermones* 1.4, 5, 9). Martial (late 1st c. C.E.) portrays Jews as lewd and lascivious (*Epigrammata* 7.30; 7.82). His younger contemporary, Juvenal, caricatures Jewish beggars, fortune tellers, and proselytes (*Satires* 6.542–47; 14.96–106).

Learned Romans generally regarded Jewish practices as superstitious. Seneca (late 1st c. B.C.E.–65 C.E.), the Stoic philosopher and adviser to Nero, castigates Sabbath observance and food laws (*Moral Epistles* 95.47; *On Superstition,* in Augustine, *City of God* 6.11). Quintillian (*Institutio oratorica* 3.7.21) simply refers to Jewish superstitions. The most hostile Roman account appears in the historian Tacitus (56–120 C.E.). In a lengthy excursus on the Jewish revolt (*Histories* 5.1–13), he repeats many of the charges against the Jews developed in the Hellenistic period.

Plutarch (c. 45–c. 125 C.E.) treats Jews, like other eastern peoples, as an exotic curiosity. He and his friends marvel at the abstention from pork (*Table Talk* 8.5) and debate whether the Jewish God was identical to Dionysus (*Table Talk* 8.6). He views Sabbath observance as simple superstition (*On Superstition* 3, 8). Some religious philosophers esteemed Jewish traditions more highly. Numenius (late 2d c. C.E.), whose system incorporated Pythagorean and Platonic elements, says that Plato was simply Moses speaking Greek (in Clement of Alexandria, *Miscellanies* 1.22.150.4).

Historians of the imperial period provide some information on Jews. Dio Cassius (160–230 C.E.) supplements Josephus and other sources for earlier Jewish history and offers the primary information on the Jewish revolts under Trajan and Hadrian (*Historia Romana* 68.32.1–3, 5; 69.12.1–14.3, 15.1).

Critics of Christianity use Jews and Judaism in their polemic. The philosopher Celsus (late 2d c. C.E.) found in Judaism the roots of the Christianity he despised. His *True Account,* preserved through its refutation by the third-century Christian theologian Origen, ridicules Jewish teachings on creation (*Against Celsus* 1.19) and claims that Moses and his followers were of the lowest classes, easily duped into monotheism (*Against Celsus* 1.23). While he disliked Jews, Celsus faulted Christians for abandoning a national tradition, and he put his own criticisms of Christianity in the mouth of a Jew. Polemic continues with Porphyry (232 to late 3d c. C.E.), a Neoplatonist disciple of the Roman philosopher Plotinus and the most astute ancient critic of Christianity. Even more positive about the Jews than Celsus, he prefers their worship of God to that of Christians (*On Philosophy from Oracles,* in Augustine, *City of God* 19.23). Yet Porphyry could be critical. A careful student of scripture, he argued for the dating of the book of Daniel in the second century (*Against the Christians,* in Jerome, *Commentary on Daniel,* Prologue). The emperor Julian (331–363 C.E.) culminates this polemical tradition. A defender of traditional Greco-Roman religion, he criticizes Jewish beliefs, including the account of origins in Genesis (*Against the Galilaeans* 89–94), and disdains the Jews' meager contributions to civilization (*Against the Galilaeans* 178). Yet he also praises Jewish sacrificial practice, since it conformed to his religious ideals (*Against the Galilaeans* 238). Julian even intended to support the rebuilding of the Temple (*Letter 204: To the Community of the Jews*).

Greco-Roman writers on Judaism are thus seldom neutral observers. Some are more favorable than others, but all felt the challenge of the Jews' vital but distinctive culture.

Judaizers term that implies acting like a Jew or practicing Judaism. It occurs in Greek texts (*ioudaisein*) and came to have two connotations. One was found in Jewish contexts and referred to those Jews who were faithful to their religion. The earliest usage seems to be in 1 Maccabees, where the "faithful" Jews at the time of the Maccabean revolt are called Judaizers, in contrast to the Hellenizers. A second usage is found in early Christian writings, where the word is used as a derogatory term for those who maintained—or were accused of maintaining—certain Jewish practices.

Judas, son of Ezekias Galilean messianic leader active after Herod the Great's death in 4 B.C.E. He was the son of Ezekias, the brigand chief whom Herod had killed in 47 B.C.E. He captured the royal arsenal at Sepphoris, armed his followers, and attacked other aspirants to power. He plundered the wealthy to accumulate wealth. In response, Varus, the Roman governor in Syria, suppressed a number of rebellions and destroyed Sepphoris.

Judas Maccabeus the third son of the priest Mattathias of Modein. He took over the leadership of the Jewish uprising begun by his father in 166/165 B.C.E. His surname, Maccabeus, is usually understood as deriving from the word for "hammer" (*makkaba*). His military and political exploits are described in 1 Maccabees 3–9 and 2 Maccabees 8–15, respectively. After early military successes against the generals of the Seleucid king Antiochus IV Epiphanes, Judas presided over the cleansing and rededication of the Jerusalem Temple (the first Hanukkah) in late 164 B.C.E. Then he launched military expeditions to other areas (see 1 Macc. 5; 2 Macc. 10–12), but failed to capture the enemy citadel in Jerusalem (the Akra) and suffered defeat at Beth Zechariah, a location between Jerusalem and Beth Zur (1 Macc. 6:32–47). Judas seems to have been reduced to guerrilla warfare, though his victory over Nicanor (1 Macc. 7; 2 Macc. 14) in 161 B.C.E. restored his fortunes to some degree. In an attempt to gain an ally against the Seleucids and other hostile neighbors, Judas sent an embassy to Rome and entered into a formal relationship with the Romans (1 Macc. 8:17–32). He was killed in battle with Bacchides at Elasa in 160 B.C.E. Judas kept alive the revolt against the Seleucids between 166 and 160 B.C.E., restored the traditional order of worship to the Jerusalem Temple, and became a symbol of religious and national resistance.

Judas the Essene person who predicted the murder of Antigonus by his brother, Aristobulus I. Judas, like other Essenes, was adept at prophecy and interpretation of dreams, according to Josephus.

Judas the Galilean also identified as Judas the Gaulanite from Gamala by the historian Josephus. If Gaulanitis is considered as part of Galilee in a wider sense, then Judas came from Gamala and received the nickname "the Galilean" when he was active as a teacher in Judea. Some claim that Ezekias, the brigand chief in Galilee (40s B.C.E.), was his father, but the Judas son of Ezekias who raided the armory in Sepphoris in 6 C.E. is not connected to Judas the Galilean. Josephus says that Judas and Zadok, a Pharisee, taught a philosophy that advocated resistance to Roman rule and taxation, promoted recognition of God alone as ruler, and recommended dependence on divine intervention. Josephus blames this teaching for all the unrest and resistance that led to the Revolt against Rome in 66. While Josephus does not clearly say that Judas personally led a revolt in 6 C.E. after the imposition of direct Roman rule and a census, Acts of the Apostles (5:37) does. Josephus at least connects Judas with popular tendencies toward revolt. Two of Judas's sons, James and Simon, were executed by the procurator Julius Tiberius Alexander (46–48) and another, Menahem, led the Sicarii in their capture of Masada in 66. Menahem was eventually killed by Eleazar ben Ananias's party in Jerusalem during the civil conflicts from 67 to 69.

Judas the Gaulanite *see* JUDAS THE GALILEAN

Judea, archaeology of archaeology and survey of the region extending south from Jerusalem and defined on the west by the coastal plain, on the east by the Judean wilderness, and on the south by the line of hills from Beer Sheba to Arad. In the Persian period, Judea was sparsely populated from Hebron to the south, perhaps with half the population as that from earlier periods. On the other hand, in the area from Jerusalem to about 30 kilometers south at Beth Zur, which marked the border with Idumea, the population density seems to have remained the same as before. Many sites of the Persian period appear to betray the purpose of the Persian province as mainly an immense granary, perhaps in service to the Persian army. A Persian period villa at Lachish may be a regional governor's palace. Also in this period, the Hebrew letters *yhd* or *yhdh* appear on coins, seals, and seal impressions. This is evidently the name of the province, Yehud or Yehudah. There are also fortified hilltop forts from the Persian period, again reflecting the military nature of the province. Nehemiah was active in Jerusalem at the beginning of this period. He is credited with building the "broad wall" (Neh. 3:8 and 12:38), which has been found in excavations in the modern Jewish Quarter in Jerusalem. On the other hand, Persian period occupation in Jerusalem was confined to the ancient city of David on the Hill of Ophel.

Things changed in the Hellenistic period, when the population returned to its former size. The main cities of Judea in the Hellenistic period were the biblical cities of Jerusalem, Hebron, Ziph (about 40 km south of Jerusalem), and Adoraim, known as Dura (about 11 km west and a little north of Ziph). The towns and villages of Judea steadily increased in size and number into the Roman period. Under King Alexander Jannaeus (104–76 B.C.E.), the total area of Judea returned to the same extent it had been under David, though Ashkelon remained a free city. Judea was in a world trade network in this period, which is characterized, for example, by the find of many imported amphorae from Rhodes from the fourth to the second centuries B.C.E. The diverse population of Judea is underscored by the find of several ostraca, or pottery sherds written with ink, at Khirbet el-Kom near Hebron. These were written in Greek or Aramaic (or both) and record the activities of Kos-Yada, a moneylender with an Idumean name. Hellenistic Jerusalem was remodeled in grand, Hellenistic fashion, particularly in the tomb monuments around the city. Antiochus IV built a new fortress in Jerusalem called the Akra. Excavators believe they have found this fortress just south of the Temple Mount. The Hasmonean city walls were impressive for their thickness and workmanship. The Upper City, the hill west of the Temple Mount, was resettled. Many Hasmonean baths, pools, and cisterns have been found but few houses, which were destroyed in renovations in the next period.

In the Roman period, the number of settlements and their sizes remained roughly stable, though with some setbacks after the first Jewish Revolt (66–70 C.E.) and the Bar Kokhba Revolt (132–135 C.E.). Jerusalem was the national capital, but Caesarea on the coast, founded by Herod the Great, became the economic and political capital of the province. It is Herod the Great's activities as a builder that are most easily detectable in the archaeological record. He built his palace in Jerusalem with an appended set of three towers, into which he could withdraw when threatened militarily. His most famous work was the rebuilding of the Temple, which necessitated the building of a second aqueduct from Bethlehem to Jerusalem. He also built the city walls anew. He built a huge palace in the wilderness near Bethlehem with a support village and named it after himself, the

Herodium. He also built up the sacred enclosure at Mamre near Hebron, and in Hebron itself, he built the structure over the Cave of the Patriarchs that is still used as a place of prayer to this day. He also built a palace on a natural butte at Masada on the western shore of the Dead Sea. He built splendid palaces at Jericho, remodeling and adding to the Hasmonean palaces there. It was after Herod's reign that Qumran on the northwest shores of the Dead Sea reached its heyday.

In the aftermath of the Jewish Revolt of 66 to 70 C.E., the Roman presence in Judea was materially strengthened. Herod's son Archaelaus had built little or nothing in Judea, even though he held the title of ethnarch of Judea (4 B.C.E.–6 C.E.). The Roman governors managed the status quo until the revolt, but under the Flavians the province did well. Major Roman constructions such as baths, theaters, amphitheaters, or aqueducts appeared at Beth Guvrin, Antipatris, Jerusalem, and elsewhere. Joppa on the coast was named a Flavian city. Hadrian built Roman roads in Judea between 120 and 130 C.E. Hadrian also refounded Jerusalem as a Roman city after the Bar Kokhba Revolt and named it for his tribe, Aelia Capitolina. Yet excavations within Jerusalem suggest that it was a much smaller city than before, with most of its occupation concentrated in the north. Archaeological traces of his works are found everywhere in Jerusalem. For example, today's Damascus Gate is apparently built over the earlier Roman gate, complete with an olive press in one gate chamber, and the inner finely paved plaza has been unearthed. The Arabic name for the gate, the Gate of the Column, preserves a memory of a Roman column erected in this plaza. Under Septimius Severus the status of Judea advanced again, for he designated Lydda (Diospolis) and Beth Guvrin (Eleutheropolis) as Roman cities.

During the Byzantine period, the number and size of settlements increased dramatically, a measure of the economic advances of the period. A veritable flurry of building activity, both by Jews and by Christians, distinguishes this period. Many synagogues have been excavated in Judea of this period, particularly in Daroma, or the southern area around Hebron, where Jewish occupation continued for several centuries after the Bar Kokhba Revolt. Byzantine Jerusalem was grand indeed, especially with the royal patronage of the emperor Constantine. The Cardo Maximus or main colonnaded street of Jerusalem has been found, as well as the shops on either side. Byzantine mansions were built at the south end of the Temple Mount, virtually in its shadow, though no new constructions appeared on the site of the Second Temple. There was a brief interlude under Emperor Julian (r. 136–363 C.E.) when the Jews were granted permission to rebuild the Temple. This rebuilding was never carried out, but some think that a Hebrew quotation from Isaiah 66:14 scratched on a stone on the west side of the Temple Mount dates to this effort: "And when you see this, your heart shall rejoice, and their bones shall flourish like an herb."

Judean Aramaic   *see* ARAMAIC, JEWISH LITERARY

Judean Desert   the arid region west of the Dead Sea extending to the middle of the Judean ridge. The bulk of modern research antedating the discovery of the Dead Sea Scrolls has focused on the Judean Desert Caves that contained various finds including the scrolls themselves. Yet, this region contained settlements apart from these caves that continued to play an important role in Jewish life from the Persian period through the early Arab period. In particular, the settlements at En Boqeq, Jericho, En Gedi, and Masada provide clues for understanding the role of the Judean Desert region in Jewish history.

The settlement at En Boqeq is the only one of those mentioned above where a synagogue has yet to be discovered. The site, however, played a significant role in Jewish history during the Herodian period and during the Jewish Bar Kokhba Revolt. The site is an oasis about 13 kilometers south of Masada. During the Herodian and Bar Kokhba periods, it served as an irrigation source for the southern Judean Desert area, a fortress, a trading post, and a center for the manufacture of pharmaceuticals and cosmetics.

The importance of Jericho in terms of understanding Jewish religion in antiquity is immediately apparent from the synagogue and the Jewish cemetery. Other finds show the important political role this city played in both the Hasmonean and Herodian kingdoms. Jericho is at the northern tip of the Judean Desert area, so it was natural that this site served as a strategic center for the Judean monarchs until the destruction of Jerusalem in 70 C.E. There are winter palaces at the mouth of the Wadi Qelt for both the Hasmonean and Herodian monarchs. Obviously, the warmer weather of the Judean Desert was preferable to the wet and cold of Jerusalem, so these kings established residential and political centers in the Jericho region for use during the winter months. It is unclear exactly when these palaces and economic centers ceased to be used, but it seems that by the destruction of the Temple in 70 C.E., they had ceased to play an important role.

The settlement at En Gedi was also an important Judean center for trade. Located near the water source of today's Nahal Arugot, the site served as a trading post and economic center from the end of the Iron Age until the late Roman and Byzantine periods. A citadel is notable among the Herodian period finds, indicating the importance of this site in the Judean trade and defense systems. The citadel was destroyed by fire, probably during the beginning of the First Jewish Revolt against Rome.

Masada is located toward the southern end of the Dead Sea on its west side and is one of the most famous sites of the area because of its role as the symbolic last stand against the imperial Roman army. The site was established by Herod as a resort, but is most famous for its use by Zealots as a final holdout against the Romans. All of its inhabitants committed suicide in 74 C.E. rather than be defeated by the Romans.

Judean Desert Caves   a set of caves located along the western and northwestern edge of the Dead Sea in the Judean Desert. The caves were used as places of refuge from the fourth millennium B.C.E. until at least the end of the first millennium of the modern period. The arid climate of the Judean Desert has preserved many organic items normally lost at other sites. Most of these items are the manuscripts of ancient religious and sectarian documents, also known as the Dead Sea Scrolls.

One of the principle sets of caves are known as the Nahal Zeelim Caves. Nahal Zeelim is one of the largest canyons in the Judean Desert and flows into the Dead Sea about 3 miles north of Masada. During the Bar Kokhba period, there were several Roman forts near the En Anava. The Romans built these forts to control the desert region and the refuges found there. Two caves in particular were important during this period. Cave 31, also known as the Cave of Arrows, contained various finds from the Bar Kokhba period including coins, sherds, and food. The most interesting find was a large store of arrowheads belonging to the Bar Kokhba rebels. Some of the arrowheads were still attached to the their shafts.

Another important cave from Nahal Zeelim is Cave 34, also known as the Cave of the Scrolls. Fragments of papyri and two coins from the third century C.E. were found in this cave. Among the documents are fragments of the *tefillin* prayer from Exodus 13:1–16 that contain the exact variation from the Hebrew Masoretic found in the Septuagint (the Greek translation of the Hebrew Bible). In addition to various other documents containing undecipherable Aramaic and Greek writing, there is a fragment of papyrus with Greek writing containing numerous Jewish names. It is believed that this is a partial list of the Bar Kokhba fighters.

Another famous cave in the region is known as the Cave of Treasure. It is found among the Nahal Mishmar Caves, located just north of Nahal Zeelim. The Cave of Treasure is located about 50 meters from the top of the cliff and about 250 meters from the bottom of the cliff. Because it was very secluded, it preserved an amazing store of treasures from the Chalcolithic period. There are also some important finds from the Bar Kokhba period, including various types of pottery and glass, measuring cups, lamps, and cooking pots. The written documents include fragments of papyri and ostraca with Aramaic and Greek inscriptions and one fragment with Jewish names similar to those found at Nahal Zeelim. Associated with these names is the Greek word for "brother." This fact has led some scholars to conclude that the Greek word "brother" was a title among the Bar Kokhba fighters, similar to the modern use of "comrade."

The Nahal Hever Caves are another set of important caves in this region. Nahal Hever flows into the Dead Sea about 4 miles south of En Gedi and is distinguished as one of the deepest canyons in the region. In this valley there are remains of several Roman camps. Like the others, they were used to keep an eye on rebels who might be hiding in the caves. One of the caves, the Cave of Horror, which contains various ceramic and written remains and more than forty human skeletons, provides an explicit example of what the Romans did when they found a rebel hideout. After locating a cave hideout, the Romans would guard the entrance of the cave (which in this case was about 50 meters below the top of the cliff) to seal off any means of escape. The rebels then simply starved to death. The remains in this particular cave suggest that this siege lasted more than a year. The finds of this cave also provide concrete support for legends of Jews who preferred death to capture by the Romans.

Another famous cave with many written remains, known as the Cave of Letters, is found in the En Gedi region near Nahal Arugot. It too has extensive remains from the Bar Kokhba period, but despite the name, these remains are not limited to written documents. Numerous metal and ceramic objects were also discovered that provide insight into how the Bar Kokhba warriors lived. The written documents from this cave are especially rich in variety. There are several biblical scrolls from Numbers and the Psalms dating to the first century C.E. There is also a set of documents known as the Archive of Babata, the daughter of Simeon. These papers were written in Nabatean, Aramaic, and Greek. They detail the various legal transactions of the family of Babata. There are also several Nabatean documents from the late first century C.E. Finally, there is a set of documents, known as the Bar Kokhba letters, that detail instructions concerning supplies and army shipments.

Other important caves in the region include the Nahal David caves, the Wadi Murabbaat Caves, and numerous other caves just to the northwest of the Dead Sea. The Wadi Murabbaat Caves are especially noteworthy for the numerous inscriptions from the Second Temple period found there. One inscription even dates back to the First Temple period. This cave is also famous for scrolls that contain substantial portions of the prophetic books of Amos, Obadiah, Jonah, and Micah.

Though most of these caves are in remote places that are difficult to reach, the area has been extensively surveyed and excavated due to the intense interest in the Dead Sea Scrolls. The exploration of these remote caves has revealed much data about the Bar Kokhba rebellion and Jewish resistance to the Romans that would have otherwise gone unnoticed.

Judges, Targum to *see* TARGUM TO THE PROPHETS

judgment, divine the act by which God sets matters right. Fundamental to God's role as judge is the biblical notion of covenant: the righteous deeds or disobedient conduct of God's people inevitably receive their due reward or punishment. In the view of most biblical writers, but especially the Deuteronomist, this covenantal recompense occurs during the course of one's life. The blessings include a long life, health, fertility, and freedom from oppression, while the curses involve a premature death, sickness, sterility, invasion and exile by foreigners, and oppression or persecution by one's fellow Israelites. When the nation and individual Israelites experienced what they perceived as injustice, they sought adjudication, appealing for vindication of themselves and punishment for their enemies. Similarly, when sinners repented of the sins that had brought punishment, they prayed for the return of the blessings promised to those who were faithful to the covenant. In short, Israelites understood the whole range of their experience, for better or for worse, within the framework of a covenantally related justice that was administered by the divine judge.

Texts from the exile onward focus increasingly on the disparity between human experience and divine justice. The speeches at the heart of the Book of Job are a major example of this, as is the last Servant poem in Second Isaiah (52:13–53:12) and some of the postexilic psalms. The rise of eschatology reflects a tendency to seek God's justice in a future, major act, a final judgment to be followed by a new age of blessing for the righteous. Increasingly the centerpiece for such a construct was the notion of postmortem judgment: vindication for persons unjustly put to death and, sometimes, punishment for those who escaped the punishment they deserved in this life. Thus, notions of resurrection, immortality, and eternal life, at least at the beginning, do not reflect a concern simply to extend one's earthly existence to the beyond, but express the belief that the divine judge will set right things that are seriously wrong and unjust. In time, belief in a resurrection of some of the righteous and some of the wicked was broadened into a concept of a universal resurrection and judgment. Integral to this complex of ideas is a proliferation of transcendent agents of divine justice—archangels called by name, the son of man, Melchizedek, and the like. Moreover, the heavenly realm, or an invisible dimension of the earthly, becomes the place where justice is administered through clashes of angelic armies, heavenly assizes, and hidden places of reward and punishment.

These developments notwithstanding, Jews in the Graeco-Roman period could also perceive divine justice in the events of history, and the Deuteronomic historical scheme was employed to make this point. Weal and woe were indicators of good or evil conduct or disposition. Health and prosperity demonstrated that one was a God-fearing person, and victory in battle vindicated the rightness of one's cause. Conversely, the opposite experience served as proof of wrongdoing. This viewpoint was constitutive of claims that the nation was suffering because the majority were not heeding a particular revealed interpretation of the Torah and was central to appeals for repentance.

These alternative approaches to an understanding of God's judgment could create an impasse between persons of differing persuasion. One might see death as evidence that one's opponent had been punished by God, while belief in postmortem vindication proved to others the validity of the opponent's claim to be righteous and the agent of God. The story of the persecuted righteous one in the Wisdom of Solomon 2–5 is a classical example of this kind of dispute.

Not surprisingly, this story and its parallels are constitutive in early Christian explanations of the death of Jesus. For many, the crucifixion was adequate proof that Jesus was not God's eschatological agent. However, an appeal to revelatory appearances of the risen one reversed these proofs: the crucifixion was evidence that Jesus epitomized the figure of God's suffering spokesman, and the resurrection completed the paradigm by vindicating the suffering righteous one. Acceptance or rejection of Jesus turned on one's acceptance or rejection of the paradigm and the claim that Jesus was raised from the dead.

Rabbinic Judaism further developed the concept that people are responsible for their lot in life, with evil actions bringing about punishment from God and proper behavior being rewarded. B. Berakhot 5a accordingly states: "If a person sees that sufferings afflict him, let him examine his deeds." The failure of this approach to explain either the unearned punishment of the pious or the prosperity of the wicked is accounted for in the rabbis' conception of immortality and afterlife. In the rabbinic view, final punishment or reward in a coming world explain apparent inequities in present life. The wicked are rewarded in this world for any slight good they might do. In the coming world, they will be severely punished. The righteous, by contrast, suffer in the present world for slight infractions they commit. They can, however, look forward in the coming world to a perfect and complete reward. In describing divine judgment, the rabbis hold that, while carefully and accurately evaluating each person's actions, God, who abounds in mercy, ultimately leans towards a judgment of mercy (B. Rosh Hashanah 17a). Central in this notion of God as judge is the concept of repentance, which the rabbis understood to be powerful enough to obliterate even the most sinful person's final judgment (B. Rosh Hashanah 17b). *See also* AFTERLIFE; ESCHATOLOGY.

Judith, Book of Likely composed in the second century B.C.E. in the light of Maccabean successes, this Hellenistic apocryphon celebrates the defeat of Nebuchadnezzar's general Holofernes by the cunning Judith (Jewess). The first eight chapters describe the progress of the Assyrian army, the Ammonite Achior's complimentary detailing of Jewish history, the siege of Bethulia, and the response of the community elders. The final eight chapters introduce Judith through an extensive genealogy and describe the means by which she rescues her people.

Judith—a wealthy, beautiful widow—engages in ascetic worship while her maid manages her estate. Taking action upon hearing that Uzziah, the town leader, has counseled surrender if divine aid does not swiftly intervene, Judith summons the elders—thereby demonstrating her own power—and berates them for lack of faith: The Deity is not to be tested; indeed, God may be testing them. Judith prays for the power to deceive "by the hand of a female," and events suggest her prayer has been heard. Beguiling the besotted general Holofernes with her beauty and a series of double entendres, she finally beheads him with his own sword. Returning the head to Bethulia, which occasions Achior's conversion, Judith leads the thyrses-bearing Bethulian women, followed by the men, to Jerusalem. There, she dedicates the spoils of her victory to the Temple. Then Judith retires to her home, refuses offers of remarriage, and, before dying at age 105, frees her maid and makes arrangements to distribute her property.

The text recapitulates several motifs from the Hebrew scriptures: Judith is a new judge who rescues her people and is a new Jael who, like her predecessor (Judg. 4–5), uses seduction and misdirection against a foreign general. She redeems the female-identified Bethulia just as her ancestor Simeon recovered Dinah from Shechem (Gen. 34). Like Esther, she takes initiative and works without the manifest help of the Deity; like Daniel, she insists on retaining Jewish dietary practices in the foreign camp, and she defeats the representative of a king who demands to be worshiped as a god (Dan. 3).

The book's earliest manuscripts are in Greek; no fragment has been found at Qumran. Debate continues over the text's original language, provenance, and relationship to historical events.

Julian Roman emperor (r. 361–363 C.E.), known as Julian the Apostate. Born at Constantinople in 332, Flavius Claudius Julianus was the younger son of Constantine I's half-brother, Julius Constantius, and Basilina. When Constantine died without a clear successor in 337, the army killed most of Constantine's relatives to secure succession for his three sons, but the youthful Julian and his brother Gallus were spared and were reared together in Nicomedia and Cappadocia. Meanwhile, Constantine's three sons, Constantine II, Constans, and Constantius II, fell on hard times. Constantine II was defeated and killed by Constans in 340, but the latter in turn was defeated and assassinated by one of his own generals, Magnentius, in 350. In 353, Constantius II, who until then had been preoccupied with the east, defeated Magnentius and united the empire. Constantius II then gave Gallus the title Caesar and sent him to protect the east, where the latter's failure to do so resulted in his murder in 354. Constantius II then turned to his cousin Julian. In 355 he gave Julian the title of Caesar, gave him his sister Helena in marriage, and sent him to Gaul. Julian had considerable military success against the Franks and Alamanni, but in 360 when Constantius II demanded some of Julian's best troops for a Persian campaign, the soldiers rebelled and proclaimed Julian emperor. Constantius II mobilized for civil war but died in 361 before hostilities had begun. In 363, Julian turned from his efforts to reinvigorate paganism to his plan to recreate Alexander the Great's eastern conquests by invading Persia. With an Armenian alliance, he routed the Persians at Ctesiphon, but was later wounded during a skirmish and died soon after. The army then declared its commander, Jovian, emperor.

Despite his considerable military successes, Julian is known for his revival of paganism, for which he was called "the Apostate." Although he was baptized and brought up a Christian, his years of seclusion included an education in Greek literature, particularly philosophy. Julian did not so much suppress Christianity as try to prevent the union of the Roman state with Christianity. To this end, he proclaimed religious toleration, recalled Christians exiled by the Arian Constantius I, and admitted Christianity into the religious pantheon. Julian believed that Graeco-Roman religions were more firmly tied to the traditions of the empire than Christianity; for that reason he took away Christian privileges in education, denied Christians public funds for charity, made Christians restore pagan lands and temples, and gave preference to pagans when filling offices. He was even prepared to rebuild the Temple in Jerusalem, less as a favor to the Jews than because they too opposed the Christians. Julian's particular brand of Neoplatonism was formed by Libanius and Maximus, and with their assistance, he attempted to create a pagan alternative to the Christian Church, with himself as pontifex maximus and with the sun-god as the popular focal point of the new faith. However, his Hellenism, colored by magic and superstition, was hardly less novel than the Christian practices he deplored and no easier to understand.

His prolific writings include *Orations, Satires, Letters,* and other works. Among the extant pieces are a panegyric to Constantius II, satirical depictions of the caesars, and a denunciation of the people of Antioch, who had mocked his philosopher's beard. Some of these are less important than his lost works on the Gallic campaign or his attacks on the Christian Church. Julian's was the last concentrated attempt to stem the rising tide of Christianity, but the current was too strong for such a tentative effort.

Julianus, Marcus Antonius procurator of Palestine. Minucius Felix cites the works of Josephus and Julianus as the source of his view that the Jews caused their own misfortunes under Vespasian. Josephus refers to Julianus as a procurator of Judea during the war with Vespasian and most think this is the same person to whom Felix refers.

Julius Caesar (100–44 B.C.E.) Roman general and dictator. A Roman aristocrat of the Julian gens (clan), Gaius Julius Caesar accumulated great power in the 50s B.C.E. in league with Pompey and Crassus. From 58 to 49 B.C.E., he prosecuted a successful war in Gaul (present-day France). In 49 B.C.E., he overran Italy; in subsequent years, he had himself made dictator, finally for life. He was assassinated in 44 B.C.E. by a group of nobles that included Brutus and Cassius. His rule led to the end of the Roman republic and the rise of the principate, or empire, under his successor, Octavian (Augustus).

Julius Quadratus Bassus *see* BASSUS, GAIUS JULIUS QUADRATUS

Julius Severus *see* SEVERUS, GAIUS JULIUS

justification the act of making or declaring a person in right relationship with God; it is a translation of the Hebrew root *tzdk* and the Greek stem *dikaio-,* stems which are also rendered as "righteousness." The term reflects the language of the law court (cf. Deut. 25:1). In the Tanakh (Old Testament), it designates fulfillment of the obligations of the covenant on the part of Israel and of God. For example, Genesis 15:6 describes Abraham's response to God's promises: "And he believed in God, and it was reckoned to him as righteousness." Daniel 12:3 promises eschatological reward to the wise who "make many righteous" (the *hiphil* [causative form] of the verb *tzadak,* NRSV "lead many to righteousness"; cf. Isa. 53:11). The same verb is used to describe God's vindication (salvation) of his servant in Isaiah 50:8.

In the Dead Sea Scrolls, which exhibit both a scrupulous concern for obedience to God's law and a keen awareness of human sin, a person cannot be justified apart from the grace of God: "If I stagger because of the sin of the flesh, my judgment (Heb.: *mishpat*) shall be by the righteousness (*tzdk*) of God which endures forever" (1QS 11:12).

In the New Testament, the idea that justification cannot be earned by human merit is a particular emphasis of Paul: "All have sinned and fallen short of the glory of God and are justified (made righteous) as a free gift by his grace through the redemption which takes place in Jesus, the Messiah" (Rom. 3:23–24). Paul interprets the death and resurrection of Jesus as the fulfillment of Jewish hopes that God would "demonstrate his righteousness," namely, that he would act decisively to restore his creation to himself. He argues that justification of the individual sinner, which is part of this general restoration of creation to God, is a divine gift, which one receives by having faith that God has acted in Christ. The example of Abraham (Gen. 15:6) shows that God justifies a person on the basis of faith, not "works of the law" (Rom. 4, cf. 3:28). James 2:14–26 gives a different interpretation of the Abraham story: "A person is justified by works and not from faith alone" (2:24). Paul's teaching on justification did not have wide influence in the early church but was reemphasized and reinterpreted by Augustine and Luther (cf. the principle of *sola fide,* justification by "faith alone," which summarizes Luther's disagreement with the medieval church). Protestant teaching on justification focuses mainly on the salvation of the individual, not on the broader sense of justification as part of God's eschatological demonstration of his righteousness. *See also* DEEDS, WORKS; RIGHTEOUSNESS.

Justin I Byzantine emperor (r. 518–527 C.E.). An Illyrian, he was commander of the imperial bodyguard before becoming emperor. During his last years, when Justinian I was the true power, an edict was published that expanded the definition of a Christian heretic to "anyone who is not orthodox," thus including the Jews. The Jews could not serve as city advocates or as members of the city councils. They could be lower-grade officials, for these posts involved many duties but little honor. They were also excluded from the more important military positions and were prevented from teaching in public institutions.

Justin II Byzantine emperor (r. 565–578 C.E.). He seized the throne from his uncle Justinian I with the aid of Tiberius, commander of the guard. After Justin became insane, Tiberius and the Empress Sophia ruled the empire. In 578 C.E., he sent Theophilus to suppress the Jewish-Samaritan revolt in Palestine. During his reign, some Jews were forcibly converted to Christianity. In 572, he refused to continue paying tribute under the treaty executed by Justinian and the Persians in 562, thereby provoking Khusro I to invade Armenia and Cappadocia. The Persians were forced to withdraw in 575.

Justinian (482–565 C.E.) Roman emperor (r. 527–565). He was born in a village near Naissus in present-day Serbia, taking the name Justinianus when he was adopted by his uncle Justin. Justinian became emperor in 527 upon Justin's death. He resolved to restore the glory of the Roman Empire by retaking the lost western provinces, ridding the governmental administration of its corruption, and rationalizing and codifying the Roman legal system. He improved the provincial administration by abolishing the sale of offices and increasing the status and salaries of the provincial governors. He reformed the provincial judicial system and revamped the municipal and military accounting procedures. He also believed that he could win God's support for his revived Roman Empire by adhering to orthodox Christianity, suppressing the heresies of Arianism and Monophysitism, and oppressing the ancient Roman cults. To this end, Justinian governed the Church, considering its hierarchy his employees. Although Justinian's interests lay in the West, he was forced to engage in a protracted war against the Persians in the East. Although he achieved an "Eternal Peace" with Persia in 532, he was forced to fight them again from 540 to 562.

In 528 he appointed a commission to codify all imperial legislation from the time of Hadrian, and the first *Codex Justinianus* was issued in 529. He further published the *Novellae* of his own laws. A *Digest* of the original code was published in 533, with a second edition of the *Codex* appearing in 534. These legal codes served to strengthen the state's and the emperor's power. In general, Justinian's laws dealt harshly with the Jews. In an early edict, the Jews were included among Christian heretics. Jews could not be appointed to civil or military posts, and they could not teach in public universities. He did allow Jews to hold offices as low-level officials, because these involved duties without bestowing honor. He increased the monetary penalty for a Jew found holding a Christian slave, and he ordered all Jews to release all their Christian slaves or any slave wishing to be baptized. Jews were declared unfit to offer testimony in court against Christians. Jews were forbidden from holding title in any way on land upon which a church had been erected. Justinian's *Codex* omitted the law that declared Judaism a legal religion, while at the same time stating that the Church's canons would have the force of law. The execution of laws against the Jews were entrusted to the bishops as well as to the provincial governors. The bishops could appeal directly to the emperor if they perceived that the civil authorities were lax in administering the laws affecting the Jews. Furthermore, the Jews could not observe Passover on its proper date if that date came before Easter. Justinian ordered that Greek versions of the Hebrew Bible be allowed in synagogues in an attempt to bring the Jews closer to Christianity. He also ordered the Jews to excommunicate anyone who doubted resurrection, the last judgment, or the existence of angels.

Justin Martyr (c. 100–c. 165 C.E.) Christian apologist. Justin composed, among other writings, the earliest extant apology against Judaism, entitled *Dialogue with Trypho, a Jew,* c. 160. Although claiming to record an actual debate between Justin and Trypho at Ephesus just after the Bar Kosiba Revolt (132–135), the dialogue cannot be seen as a transcription. Specialists debate whether Justin even addressed it to the Jews. It is more likely that he was responding to arguments that gentile polemicists had drawn from Jewish sources, and that he was attempting to stabilize wavering converts. By his day, Roman churches would not have had many members of Jewish background.

A native of Flavia Neapolis, Justin manifested a considerable knowledge of Jewish thought and customs, such as rabbinic rules of interpretation. He relied heavily, however, on proof-texting from the Greek Old Testament (citing brief passages to prove his point) and typology to answer the chief Jewish objections to Christianity and to establish Christian claims. Trypho, a layperson (not to be identified with Rabbi Tarphon of the Mishnah since he knew no Hebrew), voiced three standard sets of objections: (1) Christian failure to observe the ritual law, especially circumcision, (2) the doctrine of a crucified Messiah and the claim that Jesus was the Messiah, and (3) belief in Jesus' resurrection and divinity. In response to the first, Justin sought to establish from the Old Testament a pre-Abrahamic covenant that did not require adherence to the ritual law, citing prophetic passages criticizing Jewish observance of the Mosaic covenant and laws. Whereas the apostle Paul had viewed Abraham as the father of both Jews and Gentiles, Justin followed the Gospel of John in making Christian believers the true children of Abraham, thus taking a further step toward the disenfranchisement of the Jews. To establish Christian beliefs about Jesus as the fulfillment of Jewish messianic hopes, he argued strongly for two advents—one involving a suffering Messiah (according to the servant poems of Isaiah) and the other involving a triumphant Son of Man (according to Daniel and Ezekiel). To undergird Christian convictions about Jesus' Resurrection and divinity, Justin marshaled texts and types that he thought proved that the divinity of "Logos," the preexistence of Christ, the virgin birth, and the Resurrection, in general and of Christ. He added to these points a clincher from history: the dispersion of the Jews, the destruction of the Temple in Jerusalem, and the success of Christianity proved that God had shifted the divine favor from Judaism to Christianity. Christians, he argued, are the true Israel because they are spiritual, and the Jews have forfeited their status because of hardheartedness.

Justus of Tiberias Jewish historian of the first century C.E. He came from a prominent family in Tiberias, where he had a good education in Greek. During the early part of the Revolt against Rome (66–70 C.E.), Justus and his father were part of the Galilean resistance against the Romans; however, at some point he evidently fled and joined with King Agrippa II. Justus was presumably pardoned for his rebellion, as he became secretary to Agrippa after the war with Rome. Apparently in the early 90s he wrote an account of the revolt and possibly also a separate work on the Israelite kings. Unfortunately, details of his life and work are known mainly from Josephus, who was his rival. Evidently, Justus's account of the revolt differed from that of Josephus and even made certain accusations against the latter. Josephus responded with his *Vita*, in which he not only gave his version of events in Galilee, but also attacked Justus and his family. Although they are ignored in Josephus's *The Jewish War,* the parallel account in the *Vita* puts much of the blame for the war on Justus's family.

Juvenal (c. 60–130 C.E.) Roman satirist. His main literary works are his sixteen satires. In these are a number of references to Jews, some of them derogatory. He mentions the statue of the "Arabarch" (Alabarch), apparently a statue of Tiberius Julius Alexander. Jews are frequently represented as beggars who will tell fortunes for a small fee. They are caricatured as all having a wisp of hay in a basket, perhaps a means of keeping food warm during the Sabbath. The progress of adopting Judaism is described as a generational affair in which the father keeps the Sabbath and abstains from pork, while the son proceeds further and undergoes circumcision. Juvenal refers to Agrippa II and his sister Berenice, with whom he was rumored to have had an incestuous affair, commenting that even as royalty they went barefoot on the Sabbath, while in their country pigs were allowed to live to old age.

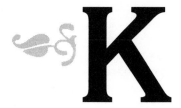

K

kab a dry measure, four times the volume of a log; *see also* LOG

kabbalah (Heb., reception) the major technical term for Jewish mysticism. Hebrew, in fact, has no special word for "mysticism," but this does not mean that there is no mysticism in Judaism. On the contrary, many forms and phases of mysticism have developed in Judaism from ancient times to the present day. In most cases that mysticism developed in the form of doctrines and theological positions that eventually crystallized into enduring traditions. Only in rare cases do we find, as in Christianity and Islam, individuals who became mystical saints in their own right.

Jewish mysticism began in postbiblical times. Mysticism requires a stance of spiritual distancing from its alleged scriptural sources. Jewish mysticism crystallized in interpretative attempts at revitalizing the spirit of scripture, but there are mystical traits in scripture itself. Jewish mysticism did not singularly develop in interpretative frameworks. Historically and phenomenologically speaking, Jewish mysticism can also be viewed in terms that link it with inner Jewish developments, even in such cases where the presence of mythical and magical materials is likely to suggest non-Jewish forms of influence.

Jewish mysticism is present wherever people attempt to experience God in an immediate way. This can happen during a prophetic experience on earth, in the course of visions in which certain persons see themselves going up to heaven (mainly in apocalypticism and *merkabah* mysticism), and in an intensive way of studying the Jewish scriptures, which are believed to embody the word of God. Quantitatively speaking, Jewish mysticism unfolds in interpretative modes. In this respect the Book of the Zohar occupies a central position. In fact, kabbalah is that kind of mysticism that reads scripture as a coded form of expression in which almost every word allegedly belongs to or represents one of the ten sephirot.

These sephirot (not necessarily spherical in nature and form) represent special configurations of the divine essence. Their official names are only labels that designate their contents, the words of scripture. The narrative unfolded in scripture is the exposure of the inner dynamics that prevail in the sephirot. That dynamics, when properly working or activated, is supposed to transmit the essence of the divine powers to the mundane world.

At stake for the kabbalists was the question: "How can one experience God outside of the country of Israel?" Although some rabbinic authorities are often quoted as postulating the presence of God everywhere, including for that matter in the various places of exiled Israel, the question was often raised as to how God could be experienced outside his cultic center. In the days after the destruction of the Second Temple (70 C.E.), rabbis often spoke of the preference that should be given to the spiritual, as opposed to cultic, ways of experiencing and worshiping God. The kabbalists believed that God is virtually incorporated in the words of the Torah. In this sense, his actual presence could be conceived and experienced wherever there was an active Torah center.

The Kabbalists believed they were in possession of the special secrets that made the realization of God in the words of scripture a lively and authentic experience. Accordingly, they developed a special technique of discovering and actually realizing the divine essence in the written words of scripture. This is a particularly interesting process, since not everything told in scripture necessarily bears the characteristics of a divinely inspired event. In short, the Kabbalists discover God in scripture, and the narrative of scripture is the unfolding of various ways of God in the sephirot. For instance, the historical events told about the patriarchs and the wanderings of the people of Israel in the desert are dry and apparently uninspired materials. As the Kabbalists conceived of them, they carried a divine stamp like everything else in scripture. In fact, all mundane events are reflections of celestial realities. In this respect, the ephemeral history of mankind is an evanescent appearance or projection of the eternal divine realities. In essence this is a Platonic concept, but it is variously represented in the religious thinking of the Jews long before the kabbalah gave it its particular phrasing.

History unfolds in patterns that are typical of the various configurations that the sephirot may take on. The sephirot emanated from God and in an interesting dialectical process were made to reflect both God and the mundane realities. The absolute unity of the world in which nothing, neither celestial nor earthly, is left out of the picture is thus achieved. Evil is also part of that picture. In fact, the Kabbalists think of evil in strong mythical terms. The existence of evil is not a philosophical or theological problem but a mythical reality. As such it encounters human beings on every step in their lives. Since the people of Israel lived in exile, they found the doctrine of evil postulated in kabbalistic writings a most powerful way of accounting for their historical misery. The nations were just one of the historical configurations of what others were used to viewing as metaphysical evil. The Kabbalists treated those nations in mythical terms.

In this respect, the doctrine of redemption developed by the Kabbalists aims at counterbalancing various components. On the one hand, redemption has to be effected in divine realms. Since the unifying dynamics of the sephirot were believed to be affected, actually damaged, by what came to be known as the original sin of Adam and Eve, redemption was interpreted to mean an act of restoring the perfect equilibrium in the divine world. What needed counterbalancing were the conflicting horizontal factors (grace vs. severe judgment) and the vertically conceived masculine and feminine elements in the sephirot. When that is achieved, mainly through the acts of the people of Israel who expectedly perform the laws of God in their kabbalistic orientation, final redemption will come. The divine and the human realms will be repaired, so to speak, at one and the same time.

Kabritha location referred to at T. Shebiit 4:11 as demarcating a border area of the Land of Israel. The reference is probably to Kabri, northwest of Nahariyyah, but it may be to Qabrath-al-kabri, several kilometers north of Acre.

kaddish (Heb., doxology) prayer in praise of God recited at the end of principal sections of Jewish service. The rabbi recites, "May his great name be magnified and sanctified in this world that He has created by his will, and may his kingdom come, in your lives and in the lives of all Israel," to which the congregation responds, "May his great name be praised eternally." The prayer is characterized by eschatological emphasis and hope for the speedy advent of the messiah. It is also recited by mourners.

Kafri town in Babylonia; location of the court of the exilarch Ukba I (B. Kiddushin 44b); birthplace of Rab and home of Hisda. The court at Kafri apparently was deemed by Samuel to be of a higher status than Samuel's own (B. Sanhedrin 55a; B. Kiddushin 44b).

Kahana **1.** Babylonian amora often associated with Assi; active in the period prior to Rab's return to Babylonia from the Land of Israel in the early third century C.E.; later, a member of Rab's academy. This Kahana ultimately emigrated to Palestine.

2. a student of Rab in the mid-third century C.E., who fled Babylonia after putting to death a Jew who threatened to denounce a fellow Jew to the Persian government (B. Baba Kamma 117a)

3. a student of Huna at the end of the third century C.E.

4. a student of Rabbah b. Nahmani at Pumbedita in the early fourth century C.E. He lived for some time in the Land of Israel, where he worked on the intercalation of the calendar.

5. a student of Raba; teacher of Ashi

6. at the end of the fourth and beginning of the fifth centuries C.E., the successor to Rafram b. Pappa as head of the academy at Pumbedita

Kaige a recension, or revision, of the Septuagint. The standard Hebrew text around the turn of the era differed in some cases from that on which the Septuagint was based, so the revision was intended to represent the current Hebrew text. The name comes from the Greek particle *kaige,* which was used to render the Hebrew *gam* (even, also).

Kallah   **1.** the gathering of Talmudic rabbis held in the Babylonian academies during the months of Adar and Elul. These annual assemblies provided an opportunity for study of scripture, a detailed discussion of legal issues, and perhaps an analysis of a particular mishnaic tractate, chosen as the topic of the convocation (see B. Taanit 10b). Talmudic sources speak of crowding at the Kallah, and apparently a large attendance enhanced an academy's status (see B. Berakhot 5b). Medieval sources describe a sophisticated ranking of each academy's authorities and a fixed procedure for discussing the assigned material and examining scholars on their knowledge. According to these sources, at the end of the month, the head of the academy produced a written statement of decisions on the legal topics covered. Describing the period of the geonim, it is unclear to what extent this picture reflects the situation in the Amoraic period itself.

In Hebrew, *kallah* literally means "bride." The reason for the association of this term with these rabbinical assemblies is unknown. There appears to have been no parallel institution in the Land of Israel.

2. a minor tractate on the *kallah* (bride), published at the end of the fourth division in editions of the Babylonian Talmud. The first known, shorter version of Kallah consists of a single chapter and originally was published in the Talmud and in Maḥzor Vitry. The longer version, referred to as Kallah Rabbati (the great Kallah), contains ten chapters. It was published in 1864 and, later, in the Romm edition of the Talmud. The only possible Talmudic reference to the tractate Kallah is at B. Taanit 10b and parallels, which speak of a Kallah tractate. The reference more likely is to the section of the Mishnah chosen for study during the annual rabbinical Kallah and is unrelated to tractate Kallah.

The shorter Kallah discusses betrothal, marriage, chastity, and moral purity. Its materials derive from Tannaitic citations in the Babylonian Talmud, and it is believed to have been compiled in the eighth century C.E. by Yehudai Gaon. Kallah Rabbati follows the format of the Talmud, including Tannaitic citations and discussion. Opinions concerning its origin range from the claim that it derived from Maḥoza in the third century C.E. to the more likely

position that its author was a student of Yehudai Gaon. Its first two chapters are a commentary on the shorter version of Kallah. The rest, except for chapter 8, develops the themes of Derek Eretz Rabbah and Zutta. Chapter 8 is related to "the Baraita of R. Meir," at the end of Pirkei Abot.

Kallah Rabbati   *see* KALLAH

kal vaḥomer   (Heb., from the light to the heavy) a logical argument *a fortiori,* or from a minor to a major premise; one of the thirteen rabbinic rules of inference attributed to Ishmael b. Elisha

karet   (Heb.) extirpation; dying before one's time, which is defined as prior to age sixty

karmelit   (Heb.) in Rabbinic literature, sides of the public way, classified as neither wholly public domain nor entirely private domain

Kartir   a founder of Sassanid Zoroastrianism in the Sassanid Empire in the third century C.E., at the time of Shapur I. After Shapur's death, he dominated the Mazdean church, becoming, under the Bahrams, a major political and religious figure. Under Shapur I, Kartir was called simply Herpat, Greek for "magus." Under successive kings, his powers and titles multiplied, to the point that he later was referred to as "Kartir, the soul-savior of Bahram and Ahuramazda's Mobad."

As chaplain to the king-of-kings, under Bahram I and Bahram II, Kartir undertook a program of elimination of foreign minorities: Jews, Christians, Brahmans, Masoreans, Manichaeans, and others. With his fellow magi, he gained sufficient power to arrange the execution by Bahram I of the Manichaean Mani, who had converted members of the royal family, including Shapur's brothers, and to destroy Christian churches. While the matter is subject to dispute, talmudic sources do not suggest a serious persecution of Jews at this time. B. Gittin 16b–17a refers to a magus's removal of a lamp from a study hall, apparently on a Zoroastrian festival; B. Taanit 8b alludes to a prohibition against fasting. The evidence for other measures, such as the destruction of Jewish scrolls or the removal of Jews from government positions, is tentative and, apart from extant statements of Kartir describing his persecution of Jews, would not be understood to refer to a serious persecution.

Little is known of Kartir's own religion. He encouraged traditional Zoroastrian practices—the cults of fire, water, and cattle, and incestuous marriage—and sought to establish a national cult that excluded aliens. By contrast, little is known regarding his formulation of religious doctrine. Some historians deem his period to be characterized by an eclectic official religion.

Kartir is the author of an inscription describing the ascent of Zoroastrianism, detailing Kartir's own establishing of new fire-temples in Sassanid and non-Sassanid lands, and claiming that, in the interests of Zoroastrianism, he persecuted Jews, Christians, and other religious groups in the empire.

Kashisha   *see* ABAYYE KASHISHA

kashrut   *see* DIETARY LAWS; FOOD TABOOS

Kavad I   king of Sassanid Babylonia (488–531 C.E.) during a period of weakened economy and government, the result of unsuccessful wars, revolts of vassal states, and a century of the nobility's interference in the line of succession. In the first period of his reign, Kavad embraced Mazdak, a religious figure who rejected marriage and ownership of property, holding instead that God required an equal division and sharing of everything. Mazdakites accordingly held that adultery, incest, and theft were necessary to reestablish the true laws of nature. In resistance to the disruptive power of this religious movement, the Mobads succeeded in deposing Kavad. In 498 he was forced to flee to Hephthalite territory, where he remained until 501.

Kavad's return to power was supported by the Hephthalite Khagan and was marked by a growing rejection of Mazdakite views. Ultimately, when Mazdakite leaders objected to the nomination of Kavad's son Khusro to the throne, Kavad sought to destroy the movement; in 528 C.E. he sponsored a massacre of Mazdakites and the burning of their books. A side effect of this was significantly to weaken the feudal nobility and to weld the country into a centralized state.

In 502 C.E., when Rome declined to continue to pay for the defense of the Caspian, Kavad, supported by Hephthalites and Arabs, invaded Roman Armenia. The battle ended in 505 C.E., with Rome's payment of one thousand pounds of gold. Over the following twenty years, however, tensions with Rome grew. Rome attempted to win the loyalty of Sassanid dependencies, and some tribes did convert to Christianity. After 528 C.E., this led to increasing hostilities, including a Sassanid defeat in an attack on a new Roman fortress near Nisibis and a continuing military engagement in Antioch. Kavad died in September of 531 C.E., in the beginning stages of this campaign.

The Jews in this period apparently favored and fought for the Sassanid cause. The Chronicle of Joshua the Stylite states that Jews in Constantina unsuccessfully conspired to surrender the city to Kavad by informing the Sassanids of how to enter the city. The result was a Greek massacre of the city's Jews. A second passage found in the Chronicle of Zachariah of Mitylene and elsewhere reports that, out of respect for a Jewish feast, Kavad asked his Roman opponent to postpone a battle. Apparently, despite previous Jewish opposition to the policies of Kavad the Mazdakite, during the second period of his rule, Jews supported Kavad and served in his army.

Kavad II   Sassanid emperor (r. 628–629) who ascended the throne after his father, Khusro II, was murdered. He made peace with Heraclius and returned Egypt, Palestine, Syria, Asia Minor, and Western Mesopotamia to Rome. The holy relics seized from Jerusalem decades earlier were returned. Rome granted safe passage to the retreating Persians and abandoned Eastern Mesopotamia. Kavad II executed all of the Sassanid princes he could, allowing only his sisters to live. He granted religious freedom to Christians. The Apocalypse of Zerubbabel pictures him as the antimessiah, who had assassinated his father and made peace with the Romans.

kavvanah   *see* KEBA

Kazinta   the present-day Qabrath Zawinta, 1 kilometer north of Kabritha, referred to at T. Shebiit 4:11 as demarcating a border area of the Land of Israel

keba   (Heb., fixity) the opposite of *kavvanah* (Heb., intentionality). Ideal rabbinic worship is composed of a fixed liturgical structure and the spontaneous and spiritual intention with which a worshiper invests its recitation at any given time.

Kedushah   sanctification of God, added to the third blessing in the Amidah: "Holy, holy, holy is the Lord of hosts; the whole earth is full of his glory"

Kefar Aziz   during the Tannaitic period, the location of a rabbinic academy, where Ishmael was active; located south of Hebron, near Idumea (M. Kilaim 6:4; M. Ketubot 5:8)

Kefar Baram   village of Upper Galilee located approximately seven miles northwest of Safed and near the village of Gush Halab. Although ancient sources mention it only in passing, it is noteworthy because of the remains of two monumental synagogues found there, both of which probably date to the third century C.E. Two doorways of the smaller synagogue were visible in the sixteenth century, but by the nineteenth only one remained. By 1905, H. Kohl and C. Watzinger found no remains of this building and excavated only the large synagogue. The Israel Department of Landscaping and Preservation of Historical Sites completed work on the synagogue in the 1960s.

The large synagogue (15.2 by 20 m) was found

inside the village. The entire first story of the southern facade is nearly completely preserved. It has the three entrances typical of Galilean synagogues: one large central entrance flanked by two smaller ones. The now-mutilated figures of two winged victories bearing a wreath decorate the lintel of the center entrance. Above the lintel is a convex frieze depicting a vine growing from an amphora. Above the frieze is a cornice beneath an arched window. Consoles in the form of double spirals once framed the lintel.

The side entrances bear their own friezes: a rope pattern in the east and a laurel leaf pattern in the west. Each lintel supports a rectangular window decorated with vine branches. The sill of the western window has a Hebrew inscription: "Built by Elazar son of Yudan." The eastern corner of a high cornice is still preserved. Although the synagogue probably had a second story, no remains were found.

Unique to this ancient synagogue is the porch—5.35 meters deep—in front of the facade. Six columns stood at the front and two at the sides. One column and the pedestal of a corner column are preserved on the east side. The columns stood upon attic bases and were topped by capitals molded with ovolo, cavetto, and abacus. The two corner columns were heart-shaped. An arched pediment led to the porch between the two central columns.

In the interior, fourteen columns on low walls surrounded three sides of the 6.2 meter-wide nave (two rows of five on the east and west sides and one row of four in the north). As on the porch, the two corner columns were heart-shaped. Low benches lined the east and west walls. The east bench was interrupted by an entrance in that wall. A lion's head and a fragment of a frieze carved with a meander pattern were found in the rubble.

Photographs and an unpublished plan drawn by C. Wilson describe the smaller synagogue, which was outside the city. The jams of the main entrance were decorated with molding and, like the larger synagogue, the lintel was decorated with the blurred image of winged victories holding a wreath. Beneath was a Hebrew inscription: "May there be peace in this place and in all the places of Israel. Jose the Levite, the son of Levi, made this lintel. May blessing come upon his deeds. Shalom."

Kefar Bilu Synagogue (Khirbet al-Asasfimra) ancient synagogue located about 1 kilometer south of the modern town of Rehovot in Israel. In antiquity, the synagogue was located on the ancient road between Jamnia and Lydda (Diospolis). From a paleographic dating of an inscription, the synagogue seems to have been used during the Byzantine period. This paleographic dating is uncertain, however, and the synagogue may have been used as late as the early Arab period.

A fragmentary Samaritan inscription on a marble tablet with eleven extant lines was found in the synagogue. The inscription contains the opening words from the Samaritan Decalogue (Ten Commandments) as well as the first two words from Genesis.

Kefar Hananiya small ancient Jewish village on the slope of a hill at the eastern end of the Beth Kerem Valley on the border between Upper and Lower Galilee. The name is mentioned in the Mishnah and Talmud as a border point between two districts of Galilee and as a center for clay vessel production.

At the upper part of the village, the foundations of a public building, which was probably a synagogue and was partly hewn to the natural rock, were observed. The remains of rock-cut stylobates are visible, some holes in the walls indicate marble plating, and remains of a door are in the west. There are some architectural elements scattered at the site that could be associated with the building, but the suggestion to identify another synagogue at the site where these elements were found should be rejected.

As limited excavations took place at the lower part of the site, the remains of a large potter's kiln dating to the third century C.E. were uncovered. Piles of broken shards and wasters were found, one of which covered the unused kiln and showed that manufacturing in another kiln went on into the fourth and fifth centuries C.E. Neutron activation analysis was used to check the ingredients of the clay in comparison with soil samples from the small valley of Hananiya; the results indicate that the potters of Kefar Hananiya used the local clay to produce their well-known pottery and traded it all over Galilee.

The excavations were limited to a small area at the industrial zone, dating the existence of the village from the first century B.C.E., or earlier to the second, and up to the medieval period. Although shards from late Hellenistic and early Roman periods were found, it seems that in this period the most important site was the neighboring one of Beer Sheba (Galilee), while at Kefar Hananiya only an industrial zone existed. Only at the end of the first century C.E. or the beginning of the second, during the decline of Beer Sheba of Galilee, did the site become more important and well known.

Kefar Kanna Synagogue synagogue site situated in a modern village of this name approximately 6 kilometers northeast of Nazareth. The synagogue seems to have been used during the second and third centuries C.E., as evidenced by the dating of an inscription. The site is probably most famous for the traditional identification with New Testament Cana, the location of Jesus' first miracle of turning water into wine (John 2:1–11). It is generally agreed today that Khirbet Qana, which is located in the Beth ha-Kerem valley farther to the north, is preferred as the site identified as "Cana of Galilee" in John 4:46.

The remains of a synagogue are evidenced by a mosaic pavement with a fragmentary Aramaic inscription found underneath a modern Franciscan church. The inscription can even be viewed by modern visitors to the church. It is evident that the inscription originally contained two columns of text of four lines each, separated by a dividing line. Today only the right column is complete. It reads: "Honored by the memory of Yosi, son of Tanhum, son of Bitah, and his sons who made this mosaic. May it be a blessing for them. Amen."

Kefar Ludim a location near Lydda, on the border of Palestine, treated as though it were outside of the Land of Israel. Accordingly, one who brings a writ of divorce from there to Lydda must declare that the writ was written and signed in his presence (M. Gittin 1:1). This is the same rule that applies to all writs brought from foreign territory.

Kefar Nahum *see* CAPERNAUM

Kefar Othani village defining the border of Galilee and Judah (M. Gittin 7:7); the home of Shemayah, a student of Yoḥanan b. Zakkai. M. Gittin 1:5 refers to Gamaliel's presence there, as well as to Samaritans in the area.

Kefar Signah an undisclosed location referred to at M. Kelim 5:4, M. Menaḥot 8:6, M. Eduyyot 7:8, and T. Terumot 3:18. On the basis of the reference at M. Menaḥot 8:6, it appears that Kefar Signah may have been in Lower Galilee, not far from Sepphoris.

Kefar Yatmah at M. Orlah 2:5, the home of the Tannaitic authority Dostai. The location is otherwise unidentified.

kehillah (Heb.) Jewish community

kelal ufrat (Heb.) a principle of reading scripture that holds that a general principle given in one verse followed by a particularization of the same governing principle in another verse is limited to the items particularized in the second verse. A particular rule may be generalized in the same manner. *See also* MIDRASH.

Kelim Mishnah tractate devoted to loci of uncleanness, in particular, the susceptibility to uncleanness of various pots and pans, made of diverse materials. The tractate discusses earthenware utensils (chaps. 2–10); metal utensils (chaps. 11–14); other materials, such as wood and leather (chaps. 15–18); susceptibility of utensils to diverse types of uncleanness, the end of susceptibility, and connection (chaps. 19–24); the components of an object as inside or outside (chap. 25); and leather objects, woven materials, fabrics, and glass utensils (chaps. 26–30).

kenas *see* FINE

Kenath a location on the east bank of the Jordan, southeast of Trachona, referred to at T. Shebiit 4:11 as a border area of the Land of Israel. Kenath is mentioned at Numbers 32:42, 1 Chronicles 2:23, and elsewhere in the Bible.

Kenaz **1.** grandson of Esau (Gen. 36:11)
 2. father of the first judge, Othniel (Josh. 15:17)
 3. grandson of Caleb (1 Chron. 4:15)
 4. in the Book of Biblical Antiquities 25–28, the first judge and an ideal leader of Israel. Kenaz embodies submission to God's will, enjoys military success, and receives a vision spanning Creation and the eschaton.

Kenesset Israel assembly of Israel; Jewish people as a whole

kere, ketib a series of notations in the margins of the biblical texts that indicate a tradition of reading the biblical text differently from what is written. These notes often derive from the Masorah. "What is read" (*kere*) appears in the margins and replaces "what is written" (*ketib*) in the text itself. These replace difficult consonantal readings in the Masoretic text, many of which stem from scribal errors. The corrections frequently comprise a grammatical change, a euphemism, or occasionally even an added word or two.

Keriat Shema recital of Shema; *see also* HEAR O ISRAEL

Keritot Mishnah tractate on sins that are punishable by extirpation (death before age 60) if the deed is deliberate, by a sin-offering if it is inadvertent, and by a suspensive guilt offering in the case of doubt. The tractate discusses occasions on which one is obligated to present a sin-offering (chaps. 1–2), a single sin-offering and multiple sins (chaps. 2–3); and a suspensive guilt offering (chaps. 4–6).

keriyah (Heb., cutting) the act of ripping one's clothes upon hearing the news of a death. In modern times, it often entails just cutting a black ribbon, which is affixed to one's lapel during the mourning period.

ketib *see* KERE AND KETIB

Kettina Babylonian scholar, active at Sura in the late third century C.E.; a student of Rab, mentioned frequently in the Babylonian Talmud

ketubah *see* MARRIAGE CONTRACT

Ketubim (Heb., writings) biblical books of Psalms, Proverbs, the Five Scrolls, Job, and so on. The term should not be confused with "written Torah" (Heb.: *Torah shebikhtab*), which refers to the entirety of the Hebrew scriptures (the Old Testament).

Ketubot Mishnah tractate on marriage settlements, dealing with the formation of a marriage, with attention to the material rights of the parties to the marital union. The tractate first addresses the formation of a marriage, discussing the wife (chaps. 1–2); the virgin and her marriage contract, and conflicting claims in that regard (chaps. 1–2); the material rights of the husband and the father (chaps. 3–5); the fine paid to the father (Deut. 21:22) for rape or seduction (chap. 3); the rights of the father (chap. 4) and the husband (chaps. 4–5). It then sets forth the reciprocal responsibilities and rights of the husband and wife for the duration of the marriage (chaps. 5–9), discussing the wife's duties to the husband, the husband's duties to the wife, and the dowry (chap. 7) and specifying the property rights of the wife (chap. 8). Finally, it discusses the cessation of a marriage and collection of the marriage settlement covered by the contract (chaps. 9–13), describing imposition of an oath, multiple claims on an estate and the wife's claim, support of a widow, rights to and collection of a marriage contract, and special cases. A collection of case reports is appended.

keYotze bo beMakom aher (Heb.) a principle of scriptural exegesis that holds that a difficulty in understanding a given verse may be solved by appeal to the comparison with another verse that exhibits points of similarity; *see also* MIDRASH

kezayit *see* OLIVE'S BULK

Khazars a Turkic group that functioned as an independent nation in Eastern Europe between the seventh and tenth centuries C.E. Their origins are unknown, as is the date that they reached the Volga-Caucasus region. Some have speculated that they may have belonged to the empire of the Huns. They probably belonged to the West Turkish Empire from 552 C.E. Kavad I was the first Persian emperor seriously to respond to the Khazars' raids by fortifying several border towns. After his treaty with Rome in 562, Khusro I was free to turn toward the Khazars, as well as toward the Hephthalites and the Ethiopians, on his northwestern and western borders, overrunning their territory.

He thus extended Persian influence to the Persian Gulf and the Red Sea. The situation changed under Hormizd IV. With the victory of Heraclius before Nisibis, the Khazars and the Arabs invaded Persia. After 650, the Khazars took over the Bulgars' region from the Danube to the Black Sea. There were Khazar officials in Bosporus and Phanagoria by 700 C.E. From this time onward, the Khazars became associated with the Crimea, the Volga, and the Caucasus. After the exile of Justinian II in 695, the Khazars played an important part in Byzantine politics. The Khazars were ruled by two rulers, the king and a chief (*khaqan*); however, it is uncertain when this double rulership was instituted. Sometime in the eighth century, the Khazars converted to Judaism. While they were known as Jews by their neighbors, they had little contact with the central Jewish organizations in Iraq; consequently they are infrequently mentioned by Jewish sources. Even after their conversion, there is evidence that they practiced a number of pre-Jewish and pre-Islamic customs. Their empire was crippled by a Russian attack in 961.

Khirbet Amudim *see* HORVAT AMUDIM

Khirbet Marus ancient Meroth, a village founded in Upper Galilee during the second century B.C.E. and destroyed at the end of the twelfth century C.E. It is mentioned twice by Josephus: once as marking the northern border of Upper Galilee, and once as one of the towns fortified in 66 C.E. during the Great Revolt.

Excavations uncovered remnants of a defense system, including parts of a wall, moat, and refuge tunnels, perhaps from the period of the Second Temple. The town's economic base was cattle and crops of olives, grapes, grains, and vegetables. Archaeologists estimate the population to have been between one thousand to twelve hundred.

The synagogue of Khirbet Marus was built in the late fourth or early fifth century C.E. The worship space of the building was divided by two rows of six columns each. The south-facing facade was pierced by three doors. Low benches lined both the eastern and western walls and the east and west ends of the northern wall. The floor was at first plastered, but later was renewed as a mosaic. One section of the mosaic floor depicts a young warrior surrounded by weapons, possibly a rendition of David with booty from his defeat of Goliath. The mosaic also bears an Aramaic name, Yudan bar Shimon Mani. The walls were finished with red and yellow painted plaster.

The synagogue underwent two major renovations. In the sixth century C.E., the mosaic was covered with a stone pavement and raised platforms, or *bimah*s, were added: two in the south, one in the east for a wooden Torah shrine, and one in the west as a platform for the Torah reading, serving as a lectern. Five stones for an arch above the central entrance were carved with signs of a zodiac. The second renovation in the seventh century was more drastic. The south facade was sealed and three doors were placed in the north, allowing those entering the building to face toward Jerusalem (as at Qatsrin, Beth Alpha, Naaran, and Jericho). The northernmost column of each row was removed. A staircase to an upper gallery and a vaulted storeroom to the west both date to this phase. Also, the courtyard was converted into a children's classroom in the northeast and a school in the southwest, both with low benches lining their walls. The lintel of the school is carved with two eagles flanking a garland with a Hebrew inscription: "Blessed shall you be when you come in, and blessed shall you be when you go out" (Deut. 28:6). The mosaic floor also depicts a lamb and a wolf on either side of an amphora and a Hebrew inscription: "The wolf and the lamb shall feed together" (Isa. 65:25). Another part of the floor shows two shofars, a structure (perhaps a Torah shrine), pomegranates, leaves, and grapes.

Under the eastern threshold in the northern facade a bronze amulet was found in which twenty-six lines of Hebrew and Aramaic ask God to give control of the village to Yose, son of Zenobia, perhaps a local leader. The synagogue treasury of 485 coins dating from the first century B.C.E. to the twelfth century C.E. was found in an alcove carved into the bedrock beneath the storeroom floor.

Khirbet Shura small ancient Jewish village on a low hill at Rosh Pina Plateau at the southern edge of the Hulla Valley. Decorated architectural elements were found at the site in the twentieth century; an Aramaic inscription, found in 1942, later disappeared. In 1980, a stone capital decorated with four menorahs on all sides was found at the site. Following this important find, a brief excavation, which uncovered the remains of an ancient Jewish synagogue, took place at the site in 1983.

The medium sized building has a north-south axis and measures 17 by 14.5 meters. It is built of large basalt ashlars and the floor is paved with cut basalt pavers. The remains of two rows of pillars were found; along the walls were found the remains of seating benches. There are a few well-cut and well-decorated arch stones, one of which is carved with the star of David and a rosette. The roofing system reclines on an arcade. The main entrance to the building was to the south, like many other Galilean sites. The architectural elements, such as pillars, pillar bases, attached half-pillars, decorated moldings, and fragments of windows, show the elegance of the building.

The design of the building is similar to that of Chorazin and also to some synagogues in Golan and Galilee. It was difficult to date the building because of later intrusions, but the coins that were found on the floor were dated to the fifth and sixth centuries C.E.

Khirbet Susiya Synagogue ancient synagogue site about eight kilometers south of Hebron in an area called Daroma (south) in ancient sources. Current research identifies the ancient name of the town as Carmel. The synagogue is located at the intersection of two main streets of the town or village. The synagogue building is called a broad-house because it is entered on its long or broad side. The long axis of the synagogue is oriented east to west, and it is entered from the colonnaded courtyard that stood at its east end. In the mosaic floor of the porch, at the southeast of the courtyard, is a long Hebrew inscription that honors Isai the priest who donated the mosaic and the plastering on the walls: "which he donated at a feast of Rabbi Yohanan the priest, the venerable scribe, his son. . . ." Other fragmentary Hebrew and Aramaic inscriptions in the narthex honor Yoshua Yudan, the Comforter Yoshua, Yudan bar Simeon the Levite, "all the people of the town . . ." and "the holy congregation." From the courtyard five steps led up to the narthex of the synagogue, which is a kind of porch before the facade. The prayer hall was then entered from the narthex through one of three doors in the facade, the central one being much larger than the other two. The interior of the prayer hall was decorated with beautiful mosaic pavements, and the north wall was built quite thick to hold three niches, the central one for the Torah. The two on either side may have displayed marble menorahs, as fragments of one such menorah were found. The fragments were inscribed in Hebrew: "Be remembered for good Lazar and Isai sons of Simeon ben Lazar." A tier of multiple benches were built on the south, west, and the west half of the north walls.

The worshipers used two raised platforms (*bimah*s) against the north wall. The central *bimah* was quite elaborate and may have been faced with marble. Its east side featured three round steps, and at its center were steps up to the central niche and the Torah shrine. To the east of the central *bimah* stood a secondary *bimah* from which scripture was read. No benches were built beside the *bimah*s.

The mosaic consists of three panels. The eastern panel shows birds in a geometric pattern based on two interlocking octagons. The central panel was originally a zodiac, though later in the history of the building it was replaced with geometric designs. The western panel was badly damaged, but apparently depicted Daniel in the lion's den. Simple geometric mosaics filled in the spaces east and west of the *bimah*s, but the mosaic directly in front of the secondary *bimah* depicts a Torah shrine with gabled roof and a shell at its center. On either side of the ark are two menorahs with lulabs, etrogs, and incense shovels. On either side of this depiction stand two rams looking toward the center. No curtain is rendered in the mosaic. A Hebrew inscription opposite the middle entrance into the prayer hall contains a fragmentary date from the creation of the world: ". . . the second of the week . . . four thousand . . . when the world was created."

The excavators believe that the synagogue was first built in the late third or early fourth century C.E. and continued to be used until the ninth century C.E. with at least three major renovations. It ceased to be a synagogue by 814 C.E., according to an Arabic inscription in ink on plaster indicating its transformation into a mosque.

Khirbet Tieba Synagogue a probable ancient synagogue site near the Jordan River and about 10 kilometers north of the Sea of Galilee. Only a few carved stones have been found at this site, whose alternate Hebrew name is Horvat Tuba. Two carved basalt lintels have been found. One is actually a pediment stone with a niche carved in it, as if for a Torah shrine. The second is decorated with plants flanked by eagles. These two stones have been deemed unambiguous enough to posit that the building, if it is found, will have an elaborate exterior like the synagogues at Chorazin in the Galilee and En Nashut in the Golan Heights. The moldings may be dated to the third or fourth century C.E.

Khusro I son of Kavad I through his marriage to a daughter of the Hephthalite royal household; Sassanid ruler (r. 531–579 C.E.) following the reign of his father. His reign was marked by political, social, and economic success, including the return of property seized during Mazdakite times, care for the women and children of the nobility seized by the Mazdakites, rebuilding of villages, repair of public utilities, and fiscal reform. While enjoying a long period of peace following years of disorder, Khusro secured his authority through the fortification of strategic passes, by reviving the practice of transplanting subject peoples for state purposes, and by executing all male sons and grandsons of Kavad. Additionally, he persecuted and martyred the remaining followers of Mazdak.

Of mixed Iranian and Hephthalite blood, Khusro victoriously concluded the bitter struggle with the Hephthalites that had engaged his father. In order to be able to turn his attention to this problem, he reached a peace agreement with Rome and, through an alliance sealed with a royal marriage, joined forces with the Turks. In 566 C.E. Sassanid and Turkish armies surrounded and devastated the Hephthalite forces. Khusro took control of Tokharistan, Kabul, and part of Transoxiana.

Following the previous chaotic reigns and periods of persecution of Christians and Jews, Khusro I was known for his liberal attitude toward minorities. His measures against heresy appear not to have been directed against Jews or Christians. The latter were employed in his administration and, following the Samaritan uprising in the land of Israel in 529 C.E., Jews and Samaritans sent an embassy to Khusro asking him not to make peace with Rome and assuring him of their continued support. Although this embassy had no impact on his actions, it indicates Jewish attitude toward Khusro.

Khusro died in 579 C.E., during a campaign in which Rome had taken the offensive and reached almost as far as Ctesiphon. Khusro's son and successor, Hormizd IV, is referred to as "son of the Turk," a reflection on his father's marriage to a member of the Turkish royal family.

Khusro II Sassanid emperor (r. 590–628 C.E.) following the removal of his father, Hormizd, from office. While palace rebels accepted him, Khusro initially struggled for control with Bahram VI, who defeated the loyalists and forced Khusro to flee to Circesium. There, in exchange for Khusro's ceding of all of Sassanid Armenia and Eastern Mesopotamia, Rome joined forces with him. In the spring of 591, the combined Sassanid, Roman, and Mesopotamian armies accepted the surrender of Ctesiphon, which Bahram had taken. Bahram fled to the Turks, and Khusro regained the throne, with the Byzantine frontier now extended to Lake Wan.

In this conflict, Jews had sided with Bahram. Khusro, for his part, had favored Christians and enjoyed the support of the Jews' Roman enemy. Bahram, by contrast, had overthrown Hormizd IV, known for closing Jewish schools and other acts of persecution. The Jews' choice was unfortunate. In the aftermath of Khusro's victory, many Jews who had supported Bahram were massacred. Additionally, for the remainder of Sassanid times, no Jewish government recognized by the state seems to have functioned in Sassanid Babylonia.

Following the murder of the Roman emperor Maurice and coronation of his murderer Phocas, Khusro initiated a campaign against his former allies. The result was that from 603 to 618 he built an empire extending from the Tigris to the Nile and controlled the entire Middle East. His campaign in Palestine in 614 and 615 had garnered substantial Jewish support, with Jews joining in the struggle against the hated Rome.

Khusro's conquests, however, were far from permanent. His armies brought destruction and anarchy, but no new governmental structure. The result was an additional ten-year struggle, in which Heraclius, a prefect of Egypt who had replaced the deposed Phocas, regained Rome's lost territory. On February 28, 628, Khusro was murdered by rebellious nobles and troops, securing Heraclius's military victory. Christians remember Khusro II favorably, as he offered prayers to the saints and martyrs, married a Christian, and supported construction of churches and monasteries in Ctesiphon.

kibbutz galuyot *see* GATHERING TOGETHER OF THE EXILES

kiddush (Heb.) sanctification recited over bread or wine on the eve of a Sabbath or festival

Kiddush haShem (Heb.) sanctification of the name of God. It applies to the conduct of Jews among non-Jews that brings esteem on Jews or Judaism; in medieval times, it denoted martyrdom.

kiddushin (Heb., consecration of betrothal) in rabbinic Judaism, the act that designates a woman as the future wife of a specific man, accomplished when an adult woman or the father of a minor accepts a token of betrothal worth a minimum sum of money. From that point, the woman is "consecrated" to that man and may not enter into betrothal, far less marriage, with any other; if she does, the offspring are *mamzerim. See also* MAMZER.

Kiddushin Mishnah tractate on betrothals. The tractate gives a general account of rules of acquisition of persons and property (chap. 1) and discusses procedures of betrothal (chap. 2); stipulations in a betrothal and doubts (chap. 3); and castes (priest, Levite, Israelite, and other) and who may marry whom (chaps. 3–4).

kidnapping abduction of a human being by force or fraud. Two passages in the Pentateuch describe abduction of a human being as a capital offense. One seems to prohibit the kidnapping of anyone, while the other refers only to Israelites; the former seems to prohibit kidnapping for any motive, while the latter specifies enslavement or sale as the kidnapper's motive. The Pentateuch also recounts Joseph's abduction by his brothers, who sold him into slavery. According to talmudic law, three separate acts—detention, enslavement, and sale—are required before kidnapping constitutes a capital offense. A separate warning had to be administered to the kidnapper before the commission of each of the three acts. The Talmud records no instances of prosecution of a kidnapper. According to a rabbinic interpretation, the Eighth Commandment, "Thou shalt not steal," refers to kidnapping.

Kidron, Brook of a valley separating Jerusalem from the Mount of Olives, on Jerusalem's eastern side, demarcating the border of the biblical city; referred to first at 2 Samuel 15:23. The Brook of Kidron is mentioned elsewhere in the Bible and with some frequency in the rabbinic literature.

Kilayim Mishnah tractate on the prohibition against hybridization. The tractate discusses plants (chaps. 1–7); animals (chap. 8); and mixed fibers, wool, and linen (chap. 9). Special attention is given to the following topics: growing different kinds of plants together; plants that are or are not regarded as diverse kinds with one another; grafting; sowing different kinds of crops in the same space or adjacent spaces; and vines and other crops.

king (Heb.: *melekh;* Gr.: *basileus*) ruler of a city or nation; the title is applied to actual kings (David, Manasseh, Herod, Agrippa I and II), future redeemers, and the Deity (Ps. 47:6–8, 95:3; see also Exod. 15:18). The Davidic monarchy effectively ended at the exile, although the Davidide Zerubbabel ruled briefly following the edict of Cyrus. With the Hasmonean and then Herodian dynasties, kingship returned to Israel. Speculations on royal redeemers occupy Sibylline Oracles 3 (a Ptolemaic king) and Apocalypse of Elijah 2. On the eschatological judgment of earthly kings, see 1 Enoch 46, 53–54, and 62; 3 Enoch 45; and 2 Baruch 40. Testament of Solomon 8:10 mentions demons who depose kings. The Letter of Aristeas comments in detail on the duties of kings (187–294; see also Ahikar). The Testament of Job elevates the three "friends" to kings. *See also* ANOINTED; DAVID; DAVID, SON OF; KING OF ISRAEL; KING OF THE JEWS.

kingdom of God an idea clearly present in the Hebrew Bible, although the phrase "kingdom of God" does not appear regularly. Developing probably from ancient Near Eastern mythical portrayal of the divine warrior as the king who orders the universe, YHWH was acclaimed as king over the cosmos in the enthronement psalms and eventually as king over all history in Isaiah 40–55. Implications of the Mosaic covenantal conception of YHWH as the true king of Israel and the portrayal of YHWH as defeating human kings in delivering Israel (e.g., Exod. 15) were drawn for God's rule over the nations and for possibilities of future deliverance of the people by God as king. The convergence of these two ideas of God as king and the kingdom he would bring to his people can perhaps be discerned in Daniel (mid-second century B.C.E.), where the world empires are ultimately to be overthrown by God, who bestows the sovereignty or his kingdom upon people symbolized by "the one like a son of man" (Dan. 7; cf. Dan. 2:44).

God's kingdom appears to be more or less imminent in various apocalyptic literature, such as the sections of 1 Enoch (25:3; 84:2) and the Testament of Moses (10:1). In both the Psalms of Solomon 17 (mid-first century B.C.E.) and the Dead Sea Scrolls (first century B.C.E.; e.g., 1QSb 5:20–21; 1QM 12:7–15), the kingdom of God has implications of liberation of the people (Judah/Israel) from oppressive foreign rule and the restoration of the people in their land. Both of the latter texts also connect the coming of God's kingdom with God's anointed agent(s): Psalms of Solomon 17:21–43 with "the anointed, the son of David" and the Dead Sea Scrolls (4QPB 1:4; cf. 4QFlor 10–13) with what appear to be two anointed figures, an anointed one of Aaron and an anointed one of Israel. The idea that God is the sole king of the people of Judah/Israel can be clearly discerned behind the passionate concern not to yield to the rule of Caesar. This is manifested in the movement Josephus labels "the Fourth Philosophy," which refused payment of the tribute to Rome in 6 C.E. (*Ant.* 28.4–5, 23).

"The kingdom of God" is the dominant theme of the proclamation of Jesus of Nazareth in the synoptic Gospels, connected both with suggestions of the renewal of Israel and with the identification of Jesus himself as the anointed one, in varying degrees. In Jewish kaddish prayer, which may be early, although preserved only in later rabbinic literature, the hope is expressed that God "may establish his kingdom in your lifetime and in all the house of Israel." The idea of God's kingdom in Jewish literature of the diaspora, such as the Wisdom of Solomon (6:17–20; 10:9–10) or the writings of Philo of Alexandria (*Abr.* 261; *Spec. Leg.* 4.164), has been heavily influenced by Hellenistic philosophy such that "kingdom" is individualized and spiritualized in virtual identification with the wisdom and immortality of soul attained by the wise. The rabbis (Y. Kidd. 59b; B. Ber. 2:2) also depoliticized the ideas somewhat, although the covenantal notion is retained, as in the phrase "take the yoke of the kingdom of heaven upon oneself." *See also* ESCHATOLOGY; KINGDOM OF HEAVEN.

kingdom of heaven the concept of the universal sovereignty of God, expressed by Exodus 15:18— "The Lord will reign for ever and ever"—and understood by rabbinic texts either to reflect God's reign over the Jews alone or to suggest the need for all people to accept the yoke of God's authority. The former meaning is implicit in M. Berakhot 2:2, which refers to the Jew's recitation of the Shema ("Hear O Israel, the Lord our God, the Lord is one") as an acceptance of the yoke of the kingdom of heaven. It is found as well in texts that associate the kingdom of heaven with Israelite political autonomy and argue that this kingdom will be re-created only when the Jews regain their political sovereignty. Elsewhere, however, the kingdom of heaven appears as a universal concept, referring to a period in which all idolatry ceases and God is recognized throughout the world as the only deity (Mekhilta deRabbi Ishmael, Amalek, chap. 2). The rabbinic concept of the kingdom of heaven in some ways parallels the early Christian notion of a kingdom of God. The terminology, however, is distinctive. The phrase kingdom of God is not used in rabbinic texts, while, in the Gospel of Matthew, the use of the phrase kingdom of heaven is probably an artificial attempt to duplicate rabbinic parlance. *See also* KINGDOM OF GOD.

king of Israel the monarchical leader of the Israelite people, enthroned in the capital city of Jerusalem. The talmudic literature understands the restoration of the Israelite monarchy to pertain to the Davidic dynasty in the messianic age. At the same time, rabbis deemed legitimate a non-Davidic king as long as he was an Israelite appointed by a prophet. Accordingly, they accepted as valid the Hasmonean kings, who were of pure Jewish descent. Such non-Davidic kings demanded the greatest respect and legitimately could confiscate property of rebellious subjects, impose taxes, force labor on men and women (although a wage had to be paid), conscript subjects into the army, and declare a required war (e.g., one in which Israel defended itself) without prior sanction by the Sanhedrin. *See also* ANOINTED; DAVID; DAVID, SON OF; KING OF THE JEWS.

king of the Jews title used to support a charge of sedition against Jesus of Nazareth when he was brought to trial before Pilate (Matt. 27:4; Mark 15:2, 9; Luke 23:3; John 18:23, 39). This title was written on the notice attached to the cross, which gave the cause of execution (Matt. 27:37; Mark 15:26; Luke 23:38; John 19:19). The title "king," unused since the Babylonian conquest of Jerusalem, had been assumed by Aristobulus I (r. 104–103 B.C.E.) and Alexander Jannaeus (r. 103–76 B.C.E.). Earlier, Simon, son of Mattathias, had been recognized as leader, governor, and ethnarch but not king (1 Macc. 14:35–47). Herod the Great (r. 40–4 B.C.E.) had been appointed king by the Romans. However, all these rulers had been opposed by some of the people, and the Romans only reluctantly appointed kings in some circumstances. The "Fourth Philosophy" described by Josephus adhered to the pre-Davidic biblical view that only God is king. The Dead Sea Scrolls speak of a prince or an anointed of Israel, without using the word "king." *See also* ANOINTED; KING OF ISRAEL.

Kings, Targum to *see* TARGUM TO THE PROPHETS

kings and mighty common designation in the Parables of Enoch (1 En. 37–71) for the enemies of the author's community. These otherwise unnamed rulers "possess the land" that belongs to "the righteous and chosen" and are doomed to judgment when the latter's heavenly champion (variously called son of man, chosen one, anointed one, and righteous one) appears on God's glorious throne. Although unnamed, the kings and the mighty are described as archetypical enemies of God (cf. Isa. 14 with 1 Enoch 46:4–8, and Ps. 2:10 with 1 Enoch 48:8–10). The reference to their idols (1 Enoch 46:7) suggests that they are gentile rulers, probably Romans of the 1st century B.C.E. The term recurs in Revelation 6:15.

Kinneret *see* GALILEE, SEA OF

Kinnim Mishnah tractate made up of conundrums on how bird offerings of various classifications are confused, and the way in which the confusions are to be resolved

kinyan *see* ACQUISITION OF PROPERTY

kippurim *see* ATONEMENT

Kislev third month of the Jewish calendar, corresponding to November/December

Kittim Hebrew designation for Cypriots (Gen. 10:4), a subgroup of the Greeks (Yavan). This term is used in Daniel 11:30 and the Dead Sea Scrolls (Pesher Habakkuk 2:12 and often) for the Romans.

knowledge technical terminology employed in a religious system that centers on revelation as a means to divine blessing or salvation. Relevant Semitic and Greek vocabulary includes the following: "to know, make known" (Heb. and Aram.

root: *yd'*; Gr.: *[epi]ginōskō, gnōsis*); "to disclose, show" (Aram.: *khavvei*; Gr.: *deiknymi*); "to reveal" (Heb. root *glh*; Aram. root *gl'*; Gr.: *apokalyptō*); "to give knowledge/wisdom" (Heb. and Aram.: *ḥokmah/mada natan/yehab*; Gr.: *sophian didōmi*).

The specific content, transmission, and function of saving knowledge varies in different (groups of) texts. In a wisdom text such as Ecclesiasticus, the sage expounds the wisdom resident in the Torah (chap. 24), which facilitates the obedience that grants life, and he searches out the mysteries of the prophets and the riddles of other sages (39:1–8). The authors of apocalypses also worked out of the wisdom and prophetic traditions; however, they claimed special knowledge about the secrets of the cosmos and the hidden future obtained from dreams and their interpretation, journeys through the cosmos, and trips to the divine throne room. The transmission of these revelations, written in the name of ancient worthies, such as Enoch and Daniel, exhorted the faithful to stand fast in persecution or affliction and to await vindication in the imminent judgment. The writings found at Qumran are difficult to place in the intellectual trajectories of wisdom and apocalyptic literature. Nonetheless, such texts as the Community Rule 10–11 place great emphasis on the esoteric knowledge of the religious group and its leaders and on the need to conceal this knowledge from outsiders (cf. 1QS 5:15–20). This knowledge included a revealed interpretation of the Torah (1QS 5:7–11) and revealed insight into the fulfillment of prophecy (1QpHab 7:1–5). Other texts like the Damascus Document 6:2–11 and Jubilees 23:26 highlight the importance of "searching" out the right interpretation of the Torah, which would make possible salvation from present disasters that have befallen the nation.

Although New Testament texts focus on Jesus' death and resurrection as events of divine salvation, the Gospel of John depicts Jesus as the divinely sent revealer, and the sayings source behind Matthew and Luke (so-called Q) portrayed Jesus as a teacher of life-giving wisdom (Matt. 11:25–30; cf. Ecclus. 51:23–30).

Gnostic religion bears many similarities to Jewish apocalypticism and was influenced by it. It claims esoteric, revealed knowledge that has the power to deliver the human soul from the evil world in which it is enmeshed. While the content of that knowledge differs significantly from apocalyptic revelation, its function is the same.

Although present evidence and the state of the discipline do not allow us to explain all the details of their relationships, Jewish wisdom texts and apocalypses, some of the Qumran scrolls, certain New Testament texts, and many of the Gnostic writings all attest variations of a religious system that enshrines revealed knowledge as the power that gives life to the faithful and delivers them in times and circumstances of evil and danger. *See also* SALVATION.

Kodashim the fifth division of the Mishnah, devoted to Holy Things, Temple offerings on ordinary days, and the maintenance of the Temple building and the priesthood

Kohelet, Targum to (Targum to Ecclesiastes) Written after the composition of the Babylonian Talmud in the fifth century C.E. and probably before the ninth century, the Targum to Kohelet contains linguistic elements of the eastern and western forms of Aramaic. This targum programmatically recasts Kohelet's cynical world view—his pessimistic brand of wisdom—into an endorsement and explication of the rabbinic Torah-based Judaism. Borrowing heavily from rabbinic documents such as Leviticus Rabbah and the Babylonian Talmud as well as Kohelet Rabbah, the Targum to Kohelet transforms the wisdom sage into the Torah sage.

kohen *see* PRIEST

Koine (Gr., common) term used to describe the type of Greek that became the lingua franca (common language) of the Hellenistic world. Koine or Hellenistic Greek represented a development from classical Greek, though many writers in Koine did attempt to imitate the classical writers. Both the Septuagint and the New Testament were written in a type of Koine (though the books of the New Testament tend to be written in the less literary form of the language).

Kokhav ha-Yarden (Arab.: Kaukab el-Hawa) site of a crusader fortress (Belvoir) and possible site of ancient Agrippina, a toparchy (head city) during the days of Herod the Great, though current scholarship identifies the site as ancient Kokhav or Kokhba. The site lies about 22 kilometers south of Tiberias and is also noted for the remains of an ancient synagogue at a site near a spring about 700 meters southeast of Belvoir. The remains of the synagogue occupy a low terrace near a spring and consist of basalt columns and a platform oriented north to south. On the other hand, several stones have been found in secondary use in the crusader fortress, some bearing grapeleaves and a double meander in fine relief. The most striking find is a basalt lintel with a relief of a seven-branched menorah in the center with an incense shovel to the left. To the right and left stand representations of Torah shrines with four columns each and a shell with an arch above the columns. To the right, in a recessed rectangular area (a tabula ansata), are the last four lines of what was originally a six-line Aramaic inscription: "[Be remembered for good X and Y] who have donated this lintel from their own and from public funds. Amen. Amen. Selah."

Kol Nidrei (Heb., all vows) prayer opening the Yom Kippur Eve service, declaring that all vows made rashly during the year and not carried out are null and void

kōmarches (Gr., ruler of a village, from *kōmos* [village] and *archon* [ruler, or official]) in the Graeco-Roman world, the village headman or mayor. This may have been the office held by Jeddous when he threw out the debt collectors from Zenon, as mentioned in one of the Zenon papyri.

konam euphemistic way of saying *korban,* the language of an oath; *see also* KORBAN

Korah **1.** son or grandson of Esau (Gen. 36:5, 16)
2. son of Hebron (1 Chron. 2:43)
3. Levite leader who instigates a revolt against Moses in the desert (Num. 16). Korah, Dathan, and Abiram protest the consolidation of priestly privileges by Moses and Aaron. Fire comes forth from the Lord and destroys the rebels, and the earth swallows up everyone and everything belonging to them. Josephus sees Korah as a rich Levite motivated by jealousy (*Ant.* 4.2.1–3.4, secs. 11–58). The Book of Biblical Antiquities (LAB 16:1) and rabbinic literature interpret Numbers 16 in terms of the law of tassels (a law to put fringes on the corners of garments) immediately preceding it (Num. 15:37–41). They see Korah as rebelling against Torah itself. In the Book of Biblical Antiquities, Korah is a foil to righteous Israelites who would die rather than disobey God's will; Korah dies rather than obey. In rabbinic literature, Korah illustrates wrongful controversy over Torah in contrast to legitimate scholarly debate. The Book of Biblical Antiquities (LAB 16:3) and some rabbis deny that Korah will participate in the Resurrection. This Korah is the eponymous ancestor of a group of Levitical singers (2 Chron. 20:19), gatekeepers (1 Chron. 9:19), and bakers (1 Chron. 9:31). The Book of Biblical Antiquities explains that Korah's sons opposed his rebellion, and rabbinic sources say that three of Korah's sons repented in time to escape disaster.

korban (Heb., as an offering) the language of an oath, which assigns to the object subject to the oath the status of a Temple offering, hence rendering the object forbidden for secular use

kosher (Heb., fit, proper) suitable for use according to Jewish law; *see also* DIETARY LAWS

koshering preparation of meat by removing blood, usually by salting the meat or roasting it over an open flame to drain out the blood

kotebet *see* DATE'S BULK

Kotel Maarabi *see* WESTERN WALL

koy a kind of deer or antelope exhibiting some characteristics of a domesticated beast and some of an undomesticated beast. Accordingly, the koy is in an anomalous legal status, discussed in detail at M. Bikkurim 2:8–11. As in the case of an undomesticated animal, the koy's blood must be covered when it is slaughtered (Lev. 17:13), it may not be slaughtered on a festival, and its fat conveys carrion uncleanness (Lev. 7:24). As in the case of a domesticated animal, by contrast, its fat is forbidden for consumption (Lev. 7:25), and it may not be bought with second-tithe funds and consumed in Jerusalem (M. Maaser Sheni 1:3). The koy differs from both domesticated and wild animals since under the laws of diverse kinds it may not be yoked with either, and, for purposes of inheritance,

it is deemed neither a domesticated nor an undomesticated animal. Like all other animals, however, the koy requires ritual slaughter before it may be eaten and conveys uncleanness on account of the laws of the carrion and of a limb cut off from a living animal (Lev. 11:8).

Kutim rabbinic name for Samaritans, treated under the law as Jews in cases in which their practice accords with rabbinic norms. Samaritans may be part of the group of three males who publicly recite the grace after meals (M. Berakhot 7:1), and they are understood to observe rabbinic rules for ritual slaughter (B. Hullin 4a) and menstrual impurity (B. Niddah 56b), among other laws. At the same time, because of divergences in marriage practices, Israelites were forbidden to marry Samaritans. *See also* SAMARITANS.

kyrios (Gr., lord) a generic term, though it is also used to refer to God in Jewish literature in Greek. It is the common translation for the Tetragrammaton in the Septuagint, with *theos* the normal translation of the Hebrew *elohim*. Some exegetes see significance in this difference.

L

L.A.   *see* LEGUM ALLEGORIARUM

Laberius Maximus, Lucius   procurator of Judea, 71 C.E. He served with Sextus Lucilius Bassus, who was the governor. The Acts of the Arval priesthood and a diploma of 83 refer to him. He was the prefect of Egypt in 83, and the prefect of the *annona* in 80.

Lag baOmer   The thirty-third day of the period called Omer (the time of the barley harvest), running from Passover to Shabuot. The Omer became associated with mourning, on account of a talmudic tale about a plague that devastated rabbis in Roman times, but Lag baOmer was reserved for festivity, on the grounds that the plague ended then. *See also* SEFIRAH.

Lake Tiberias   *see* GALILEE, SEA OF

lamb   animal that figures literally in the story of the Passover (Exod. 12) and figuratively in the Tanakh (Old Testament) and New Testament. In the story of the Exodus from Egypt, in preparation for the tenth and final plague on the Egyptians, God instructs the Israelites to slay a lamb and splash its blood on the doorposts of their homes. When the Lord slays the firstborn of the Egyptians, he will "pass over" all the houses marked by this sign. The narrative of the event in Exodus 12 served as the foundation story for the yearly festival of the Passover, at which each family was to slay and consume a lamb, in commemoration of the deliverance from Egypt.

The figurative use of the lamb in Isaiah 53:7 was to have considerable influence on Christian theology: here the enigmatic "servant of God" is compared to "a lamb led to the slaughter," whose suffering provides vicarious expiation for the sins of the exiled Israelites. In the "Animal Apocalypse" (1 Enoch 85–90; 2d c. B.C.E.), which uses animals to symbolize figures in the history of Israel, "lambs" (90:6–9) stand for the pious ones of the Maccabean times.

Several texts in the New Testament portray the crucified Jesus as the lamb who was slain. The words of John the Baptist in John 1:29 have had particular influence on the formation of christology and liturgy: "Behold the lamb of God who takes away the sins of the world" (cf. 1 Pet. 1:18–19, 1 Cor. 5:7). The title "Lamb of God" is used repeatedly in the Revelation to John. Jesus appears in the heavenly court of God as the "lamb who was slain," who is paradoxically also the victorious "lion of Judah" (Rev. 5). Jesus' death, interpreted as a sacrifice and as victory over the powers of evil, qualifies him to open the seven seals of the scroll and unleash the events of the end-time. These events will be completed when the Lamb, who is "Lord of lords and King of kings," will finish his victory over Satan and his earthly representatives (Rev. 17:14). The church looks forward to the "marriage supper of the Lamb" (19:9) as a celebration of this victory and part of the consummation of all things in the Kingdom of God.

Lamech   son of Methuselah and father of Noah (Gen. 5:25–31). The story of Noah's birth in 1 Enoch 106–107 plays on Lamech's name (Heb./ Aram.: Lamekh), stating that until his time "righteousness was brought low" (Aram.: *muk*; 106:1 in the Chester Beatty papyrus). The Qumran Genesis Apocryphon, which contains a version of this story, was first called the "Lamech Scroll" and was identified as "the Apocryphal Book of Lamech" because the patriarch's name occurred on one of its fragments.

Lamentations, Targum to   There are two related versions of the Targum to Lamentations, both composed sometime between the mid-fourth and early seventh centuries. Whatever the origins of this targum, its current text is heavily influenced by the Aramaic of Targum Onkelos. Lamentations was read on the Ninth of A<u>b</u>, and the targum reflects the concerns of that mournful day. Over its first four chapters, the targum attributes specific sins and misdeeds to the Israelites, which brought on different calamities as punishment. Chapter 4 concludes with a look to the messianic future in which Israel will be saved from its oppressed circumstances. *See also* A<u>B</u>, NINTH OF.

Lamentations Rabbah   (also: Lamentations Rabbati; Heb.: Ekhah Rabbati) compilation (c. 6th c. C.E.) of exegeses on the Book of Lamentations, focused on the themes of (1) Israel and God, with special reference to the covenant, the Torah, and the land; (2) Israel and the nations, with interest in Israel's history, past, present, and future, and how that cycle is to be known; (3) Israel on its own terms, with focus upon Israel's distinctive leadership; and (4) the Book of Lamentations in particular. The Rabbah repeats one point: the stipulative covenant still and always governs the relationship between Israel and God. Therefore everything that happens to Israel makes sense and bears meaning; and Israel is not helpless before its fate, but controls its own destiny. Israel's relationship with God is treated with special reference to the covenant, the Torah, and the land. By reason of the sins of the Israelites, they have gone into exile, with the destruction of the Temple. The founders of the family, Abraham, Isaac, and Jacob, also went into exile. Now they cannot be accused of deficiency in religious duties, attention to the teachings of the Torah and of prophecy, carrying out the requirements of righteousness (philanthropy) and good deeds, and the like. The people are at fault for their own condition. The dominant theme of Lamentations Rabbah is Israel's relationship with God. This is the one and whole message; everything else proves secondary and derivative of the fundamental proposition that the destruction proves the enduring validity of the covenant, its rules, and its promise of redemption.

Torah study defines the condition of Israel as follows: "If you have seen [the inhabitants of] towns uprooted from their places in the land of Israel, know that it is because they did not pay the salary of scribes and teachers" (II.i). As long as Judah and Benjamin were at home, God could take comfort for the loss of the ten tribes; once they went into exile, God began to mourn (II:ii). Israel survived Pharaoh and Sennacherib, but not God's punishment (III:i). After the disaster in Jeremiah's time, Israel emerged from Eden, but could come back (IV:i). God did not play favorites among the tribes; when any of them sinned, he punished them through exile (VI:i). Israel was punished because of the ravaging of words of Torah and prophecy, righteous men, religious duties, and good deeds (VII:i). The Land of Israel, the Torah, and the Temple were ravaged, to the shame of Israel (Jer. 9:19–21) (VIII:i). The Israelites practiced idolatry even more than did the pagans; God was neglected by the people and was left solitary, so God responded to the people's actions (X:i). If Israel had achieved the merit (using the theological language at hand), then it would have enjoyed everything, but since it did not have the merit, it enjoyed nothing (XI:i). The Israelites did not trust God, so they suffered disaster (XIII:i). The Israelites scorned God and brought dishonor upon God among the nations (XV:i). While God was generous with the Israelites in the wilderness, under severe conditions, he was harsh with them in civilization, under pleasant conditions, because they sinned and angered him (XVI:i). With merit, one drinks good water in Jerusalem; without, bad water in the exile of Babylonia; with merit, one sings songs and psalms in Jerusalem; without, dirges and lamentations in Babylonia. At stake is the people's merit, not God's grace (XIX:i). The contrast is drawn between redemption and disaster, the giving of the Torah and the destruction of the Temple (XX:i). When the Israelites went into exile among the nations of the world, not one of them could produce a word of Torah from his mouth; God punished Israel for its sins (XXI:i). Idolatry was the cause (XXII:i). The destruction of the Temple was possible only because God had already abandoned it (XXIV:ii). When the Temple was destroyed, God was answerable to the patriarchs for what He had done (XXIV:ii). The Presence of God departed from the Temple by stages (XXV:i).

laments   cries to God in times of need and suffering. Throughout the Hebrew Bible people address God in times of need, both personal and communal. The story of the deliverance from Egypt serves as a paradigm: the act of groaning, of crying out to God, is an essential element in the process of deliverance (Exod. 2:23–25). Over one-third of the psalms in the biblical Psalter fall into the category of lament.

In the postexilic period, we find a distinctive category of prayers that contain lamentation over the destruction of the city and the temple ("We have no ruler or prophet or leader, no burnt offering or sacrifice"), confession of sins, acknowledgment of God's justice in punishing ("for you are just in all you have done"), and plea for deliverance (Ezra 9; Neh. 9; Dan. 9:4–19; Bar. 1:15–3:8; Prayer of Azariah 1:3–22). These prayers, though now reused in other contexts, may have originated in liturgical lamentations at the time of exile. Other laments over the destruction of the city and the temple appear in 1 Maccabees in conjunction with the crisis at the time of Antiochus IV Epiphanes (e.g., 2:7–13; 3:45, 50–53). In 2 Baruch (10:5–19, 21:1–26, 35:1–4) and 4 Ezra (the first four visions, chaps. 3–10), lament over the destruction of Jerusalem and the human condition raises questions of theodicy, as the seer enters into extended dialogue with God about the reason for suffering.

Laments of the individual in times of personal need are illustrated by the parallel prayers of Tobit and Sarah (Tob. 3:2–6, 11–15). Other types of lament include the addition that the Book of Biblical Antiquities 40:5–7 makes to the text of Judges 11:38, which fills in the actual text of the lament sung by Seila, the daughter of Jephthah, before she is killed by her father. In the Testament of Job 40:9–14, the lamentation at the death of Sitis, the wife of Job, is described, but the actual text of the lament for her is said to be preserved only in another book.

lamp, hanging   minor motif in Jewish art, particularly synagogue art, in which a glass lamp is shown to be suspended from the Torah shrine, usually in the center of the pediment. For example, in the mosaic floor of the synagogue at Beth Alpha found near Beth Shean, a lamp is shown suspended from a chain attached to the top center of the pediment. A red dot in the center of the open mouth of the lamp may represent the flame. In the synagogue at nearby Beth Shean, the Torah shrine in the mosaic floor features a lamp suspended in the same central place as in the outer Torah shrine. In the Naaran Synagogue, near Jericho, the two menorahs depicted in the mosaic pavement show a glass lamp with a footed base suspended from either side of each menorah. The actual stone pediment of a Torah shrine recovered at Naburaya (Nabra-

tein) in Upper Galilee has a hole cut into the top of the projecting molding around the shell in the center of the pediment, presumably for a hanging lamp. A hanging lamp is an actual item of synagogue furniture in terms of lighting, as many fragments of hanging glass lamps have been recovered inside the ruins of Byzantine period synagogues. On the other hand, an example of a lamp that hung from the Torah shrine has yet to be recovered or recognized.

Land of Israel   *see* ISRAEL, LAND OF

languages in Palestine   Between the return of Babylonian refugees to Palestine in the sixth century B.C.E. and the invasion of Islam in the seventh century C.E., four languages were used in Palestine: Hebrew, Aramaic, Greek, and Latin. Although the linguistic situation was quite complex over these thirteen centuries, a few general observations can be made. Hebrew formed the native language of the Israelites before the exile and was used after the return as well. The returnees apparently brought with them Aramaic, which was the main language of the eastern empires. Over the centuries, Aramaic gradually became the most commonly used language in Palestine; by the first century it had pushed Hebrew largely into the role of a religious language. Greek was introduced into Palestine with the conquest by Alexander the Great in the late fourth century B.C.E., and it became the administrative language of the whole eastern Mediterranean region. It was later used by the Roman and the Byzantine empires in their administration of Palestine. Among the residents of Palestine, Greek became the language of the upper class—which dealt with the colonial administration—and the language of international trade. Those who participated little in those activities were more likely to use Aramaic. Latin was used almost exclusively among the Roman occupation and security forces. There is no evidence that it became widespread among Palestinian Jewry. *See also under* ARAMAIC; GREEK LANGUAGE; HEBREW LANGUAGE; KOINE; LATIN.

Laodicea, Council of   fourth-century-C.E. church council. The exact dates are uncertain. Canons forbid Christians from receiving gifts from Jews on their feast days, from holding feasts jointly with Jews, from fasting together with Jews, from taking oil from synagogues, from accepting Jewish unleavened bread, or from lighting candles on Jewish feasts. Other canons order the Gospels read in churches on Saturday, require Christians to work on Saturday, and forbid Christian priests from entering or praying in a synagogue.

laographia a type of poll tax in Egypt, introduced by Augustus at the beginning of Roman rule, from which citizens of the Greek cities and Roman citizens were exempt; everyone else paid. (Noncitizen inhabitants of the Greek cities paid at a reduced rate.) The Jews were humiliated by this new requirement. Much more important than the financial loss was the loss of status, since they were now classified with the native Egyptians at the bottom of society. This probably led to the Jewish agitation for citizenship in Alexandria.

laos (Gr., people) The term could be used generically, like the English word "laity," but it was used particularly to designate the people of the countryside who were not slaves but were often dependent laborers. These people often had a status much like that of serfs, being tied to the land.

lashon haRa (Heb., evil speech) slander or defamation, prohibited by rabbinic law even in a case in which the statement is true. According to rabbis, scripture provides numerous examples in which slander led to severe punishment, for example, Miriam's becoming leprous after slandering Moses (Num. 12:1–15) and the death of the spies who brought back a negative report about the promised land (Num. 14:36–37). Rabbis also interpreted debacles in Israelite history as resulting from *lashon haRa*, for example, the claim that David's kingdom became divided because he took account of slander (B. Shabbat 56a–b). The rabbis imagined stinging divine punishments for slanderers and their community, and held that *lashon haRa* hurts three people: the one who is slandered, the slanderer, and the listener (B. Arakhin 15b).

Late Aramaic *see* ARAMAIC, LATE

Late Jewish Literary Aramaic *see* ARAMAIC, LATE JEWISH LITERARY

latifundia (Lat., wide estates) estates engaged in high-profit agricultural production using extensive tracts of land farmed by large numbers of slaves. Although such estates were known in the Hellenistic world, production there was more often carried out by peasants tied to the land. In the Roman republic, the large number of slaves derived from conquest encouraged the use of *latifundia*. Even when they declined in Italy, they are attested there and elsewhere in the Roman Empire.

Latin an Indo-European language that was first spoken around Rome and was then spread throughout Europe and northern Africa by the Roman Empire. Latin is important for biblical Judaism because (1) early versions of the Bible survive in Latin, (2) several early Jewish pseudepigrapha have important versions in Latin, and (3)

numerous ancient Latin inscriptions provide evidence for Jews and Judaism.

Latin Bible *see* VETUS LATINA; VULGATE

Latter Prophets books containing anthologies of the sayings of different prophets. These are the books of Isaiah, Jeremiah, Ezekiel, and the twelve Minor Prophets. While these books contain some narrative material, they largely consist of prophetic statements in poetic form. They are called the Latter Prophets because they come after the Former Prophets in the arrangement of the Hebrew Bible. Together the two collections make up the division of the Hebrew Bible called the Prophets.

law, Graeco-Roman The law of the Graeco-Roman world that relates to the Jews has two main aspects: (1) the absorption of Graeco-Roman legal concepts or terms into Jewish law, and (2) the legal position of the Jews and the Jewish religion in Graeco-Roman law.

We know that from an early time, Jewish legal practice was already influenced by surrounding cultures. For example, the papyri of Elephantine contain many legal documents that show the influence of Egyptian and Aramaic law on Jewish law. Similarly, the many legal papyri of the first and second centuries C.E. from the Judean desert (Murabbaat, Nahal Heber) in Hebrew, Aramaic, and Greek show common or comparable phraseology, despite their language differences. In rabbinic literature many of the legal terms are borrowings from Greek (and occasionally Latin). In some cases, this borrowing involves Greek vocabulary. For example, the well-known Hebrew *prosbul* is from the Greek *pros boulē* (to the council). In other cases, however, the rabbinic term seems to be a loan translation; that is, the Greek has been translated literally into Hebrew or Aramaic. In both cases, the influence of Graeco-Roman law is clear, despite the cultural gap. It seems almost symbolic of this influence that even the Greek word for law (*nomos*) is found in the phrase "according to the law" in a Jewish marriage certificate of the first century C.E.

The treatment of Jews in Graeco-Roman law was a complex and often vexed question. It must be said that, for the most part, room was made to accommodate Jewish customs, laws, and even sensibilities. The Jews themselves sometimes found their position restrictive, but the Greeks and Romans seemed to have felt that they gave greater privileges to the Jews than they did to other ethnic groups. It would, in fact, be difficult to find another ethnic group scattered throughout the Mediterranean world that had equivalent rights to those generally accorded to the Jews. There are many examples of the Jews' superior privileges and, indeed, there is only one example in which the practice of Judaism was officially prohibited—the brief period of the "Abomination of Desolation" under Antiochus IV.

When Antiochus III took the Syro-Palestinian area away from Ptolemaic control about 200 B.C.E., he confirmed the right of the Jews to live by their traditional laws. For the Roman period, Josephus lists a long series of decrees that granted or confirmed Jewish rights or privileges. Although the authenticity of these decrees has been doubted, most of them conform with general practice in the Hellenistic period. Thus, even if the individual decrees cannot be confirmed, the broad picture gleaned from them seems to reflect the general situation of the time; that is, Jews were able to assemble and to eat together—rights necessary for their festival observances. When the *collegia,* or clubs, were prevented from meeting, Jewish religious assemblies were exempted. Jews were also able to obtain exemptions from conducting legal or other business on the Sabbath or during festivals. On the other hand, certain rights or privileges that Jews held in theory could not always be exercised without hindrance in practice. For example, on one occasion Herod the Great had to intervene with a member of Augustus's family when the Jews of Ionia complained of the local government's restrictions on their religious rights.

One of the privileges important to Jewish communities in the diaspora was the right to collect the yearly offering of a half-shekel (two drachmas) from every male Jew and transport it to Jerusalem. Civil authorities in the Graeco-Roman world were not always happy that so much precious metal was being taken out of their area of jurisdiction, and they sometimes interfered with the money's transfer. Josephus lists a decree, allegedly from Augustus, that affirms this right.

Military service was a problem for Jews because of such religious requirements as diet, Sabbath and festivals, and the like. We have evidence that Jews served in the Hellenistic and Roman armies, though the details of how their religious requirements were handled are not usually given. However, we have statements in Josephus to the effect that Jews were exempted (at least in some cases) from military service in the Roman period because of their need for kosher food and their inability to march or fight on the Sabbath.

The general Roman tolerance toward Jewish religious practice was not unusual. Religions were usually tolerated in the Graeco-Roman world as long as they posed no threat to the state. Concomitant with this tolerance was the expectation that adherents of local and ethnic religions also respected the rights of others. In a few instances where Jews attacked pagan cults, for example, Roman retaliation was swift and decisive. A particular example occurred under Caligula: when a pagan altar in a non-Jewish area was torn down by Jews, a plan was made to put a statue of the emperor into the Jerusalem Temple.

Strictly speaking, Jews were not exempt from the emperor cult. But since the cult's primary purpose was to express allegiance rather than to worship, it was possible to substitute an oath of allegiance for the cult. Thus, it was common for synagogues to have plaques dedicated to the emperor, and special sacrifices for the emperor and his family were offered each day at the Temple in Jerusalem. Indeed, it was the cessation of these sacrifices in 66 C.E. that marked the first event in the war with Rome.

When the Roman Empire became Christianized under Constantine, Jewish relations with it became even more complicated. There was considerable hostility toward the Jews by Christians. Certain Jewish rights, especially those that seemed to infringe on Christianity, were restricted: Jews were not permitted to own Christian slaves or to circumcise any of their slaves. Officially, however, Jewish worship was allowed.

law and prophets   term used in the Second Temple period to designate the Jewish scriptures. "Law" denotes the Torah, or Pentateuch, the first five books of the present Jewish canon, while "prophets" refers to both the group known as the Former Prophets—Joshua, Judges, 1–2 Samuel, and 1–2 Kings—and the group called the Latter Prophets—comprising the three Major and twelve Minor Prophets. Of the three literary groupings that constitute the present Jewish canon, the "law" and "prophets" were the first two to become fixed and regarded as authoritative; the "writings" gained a standardized form only later.

The first datable use of the term "law and prophets" occurs in the translator's preface to Ben Sira, from around 132 B.C.E. Each of the three references to the term here is followed by another, more amorphous designation such as "and the other books." 2 Maccabees, written at about the same time, uses "law and prophets" alone (15:9), as does 4 Maccabees (18:10; first century C.E.). The term appears with greatest frequency in early Christian writings, occurring nine times in the New Testament, which also attests the phrases "Moses and the prophets" (three times) and "the law of Moses and the prophets and the psalms" (Luke 24:44). For the latter expression, see also Philo's *De Vita Contemplativa* 25.

lawlessness (Gr.: *anomia*) actions that violate the Torah. In the Septuagint the term translates a whole range of Hebrew words denoting wickedness, transgression, and wrongdoing. The Greek negating prefix *alpha* before the root *nom-* (law) may give the word an explicit connotation of Torah violation not necessarily present in the Hebrew. In 1 Enoch 92–105 and the Psalms of Solomon, it is sometimes used in synonymous parallelism with "injustice" (Gr.: *adikia*), and in 1 Enoch it may translate the Aramaic noun *ḥamsa* (violence). It can be combined with verbs meaning "to do" to create an idiom for doing evil or committing sin (cf. 1 Enoch 99:15; Ps. Sol. 15:8; Matt. 7:23, 13:41). The latter two passages have been cited as proof that Matthew was polemicizing against antinomians in the early church, but more likely he is using an idiom meaning "evildoers." *See also* INJUSTICE.

Lazarus shortened form of El[e]azar (Heb., God has helped). The name of several Jews whose deaths are recorded in Jewish and Christian texts: a principal scribe martyred under Antiochus IV (2 Macc. 6:18–31); the fourth son of Mattathias the Hasmonean, who dies in battle (1 Macc. 6:43–46); a beggar whose death and ascent to paradise are the subject of a parable of Jesus (Luke 16:19–31); the brother of Mary and Martha of Bethany whom Jesus raises (John 11). The latter two are joined by the common theme of resurrection from the dead (cf. Luke 16:27–31), and the Hebrew name may be implied in their deliverance from death.

lease, rabbinic law of In the rental of land, rabbinic sources recognize as legitimate both fixed payments in produce and share-rental for a percentage of the crop. Houses and shops were rented for cash. A rental was considered a sale for a limited term, either specified or implied. Local rules governed the details of leases.

leaven (Heb.: *ḥametz*) grain that is leavened, which is forbidden for use on Passover

leaves major motif in Jewish art, especially grape leaves, ivy leaves, acanthus leaves, oak leaves, and olive leaves. The wreath or crown in a circlet is depicted realistically, that is, woven of olive leaves or ivy. Repeated leaf symbols appear on many flat surfaces in tomb art, on ossuaries and sarcophagi, in synagogue art, and on lamps and coins. Rosettes are formed of petals or leaves. Olive and ivy leaves appear on ossuaries of the first and second centuries C.E. Ivy leaves are known from sarcophagi and are painted on walls of tombs, particularly in Jewish funerary art from the catacombs of ancient Rome. These representations are usually heart-shaped. Leaves appear rarely on lamps of Palestine, except for the grape leaf or grapevine. Some kind of repeated leaf design appears in the mosaic floor of the synagogue at Jericho. Of course coins that depict the leaf of the grapevine are to be associated with Herod Antipas, the First Jewish Revolt, and also the Bar Kokhba Revolt. A simple, upright acanthus leaf is occasionally present in funerary art. The acanthus leaf forms the curls of the Corinthian capital, though this is not distinctive Jewish art. Other such leaves are a normal and ordinary part of popular decoration, but share this function with the rest of the Graeco-Roman world.

Leg. *see* DE LEGATIONE AD GAIUM

legalism overattention to details of the law. The term has flourished in Christian theological literature as a pithy description of postbiblical Judaism that has been colored by anti–Roman Catholic tendencies of Protestant New Testament exegetes. Evidence for legalism is found in New Testament texts like Matthew 23 and is supported by a reading of the Mishnah and Talmud that ignores their "archival" character as compilations of rabbinic opinions. The Apocrypha and Pseudepigrapha contain long stretches of text where appeals to righteous conduct are implicit or explicit in narratives and wisdom genres without reference to the details of the Torah's ordinances and the circumstances of their fulfillment.

Leg. All. *see* LEGUM ALLEGORIARUM

legate Roman provincial governor of the senatorial rank. Larger provinces, such as Syria, were ruled by a former consul and others by a former praetor. *See also* GOVERNOR.

Legum Allegoriarum the treatise *Allegorical Interpretation*, by Philo of Alexandria; its title is abbreviated as *L.A.* or *Leg. All.* The work consists of three books, each giving an allegorical explanation of a section of Genesis (2:1–3:19). Book 1 covers Genesis 2:1–17; Book 2 analyzes Genesis 2:18–3:1; and Book 3 explains Genesis 3:8–19.

Leo emperor of the Eastern Roman Empire (r. 457–474 C.E.). In 474 he recognized the occupation of the Island of Jotaba by Amorcessus, a Persian, and Amorcessus's expulsion of the Byzantine customs collectors, his levying of tolls on the ships passing along the Gulf of Elat, and his policy of leaving the community of Jewish merchants on the island unmolested.

Leontius convert to Judaism. According to Jacob, Leontius was a deacon and an ascetic in Acre, Palestine. After the Jews captured Acre in 614 C.E., they arrested and tortured Leontius, and he converted. Eventually, he met an old man sitting by the synagogue. During their conversation, Jacob reports, the sage quoted Matthew 10:33. Becoming distraught because he had denied Jesus, Leontius climbed the city walls and threw himself to his death in the sea. Jacob notes that the Jews were very upset because they had lost one of their own.

Leontopolis, Temple at Jewish temple built in the Heliopolitan nome of Egypt at what is now Tell el-Yehudiyeh. Josephus attributes this temple to Onias III (*War* 7.420–25) and to Onias IV (*Ant.* 13.62–73); the latter is probably correct. This temple, built c. 160 B.C.E., apparently served only the Jewish military garrison at Leontopolis, Egyptian Jewry in general remaining loyal to the Jerusalem Temple. The Leontopolis temple was destroyed by the Romans about 73 C.E.

leprosy (Heb.: *tzaraat*) the skin ailment described in Leviticus, chapters 13–14. Since the condition is described as affecting fabrics and wood and stone in the walls of houses as much as the skin of human beings, it is certainly not Hansen's disease (also referred to as leprosy).

lēstēs (Gr., robber, bandit) The term could designate an actual robber; however, it is often used in Josephus and elsewhere in reference to "social bandits" (those forced into brigandage by oppressive taxation and land seizure) and revolutionaries. Thus, one person's "bandit" might be another's "freedom fighter." *See also* BANDIT.

Levi Jacob's third son by Leah (Gen. 29:34). In the biblical narrative, Moses and Aaron were descendants of Levi, and through Aaron the dignity of the Israelite priesthood was accorded to the tribe of Levi, the Levites. As ancestor of the priesthood, Levi is assigned a special role in later Jewish literature. He is described as a visionary to whom the rituals of priesthood are revealed (Aramaic Test. Levi, 4QTLevi) and to whom one should listen because he knows the laws of God (Test. Reuben 6:7–8); he is depicted as a prophet who knows the unspeakable mysteries of God (Joseph and Asenath 22:11–13) and who hands on the book of mysteries given to Noah by angels (Sefer haRazim 12). Most known in the Bible for his and Simeon's attack and extermination of the men of Shechem for the rape of their sister Dinah (Gen. 34), Levi is frequently justified for his action, which is seen not as an act of vengeance, but as an act of punishment willed by God (Jdt. 9:2; Jub. 30:6–7; Test.

Levi 5:1–5, 6:8–11; Theodotus, frg. 6). The unrighteousness of the Shechemites is stressed since they had attacked Sarah and Rebecca earlier and had persecuted Abraham (Test. Levi 6:8–10; Theodotus, frg. 7). Only 4 Maccabees 2:19 blames Simeon and Levi for acting out of a rage not controlled by reason. On the other hand, Levi's action at Shechem becomes the reason why he is chosen for the priesthood, as he will uphold the law against intermarriage (Jub. 30:18–20). Elsewhere he is portrayed as a great warrior (Test. Judah 5; Joseph and Asenath 23:14–15, 27:6) and as self-controlled: Joseph and Asenath portrays him as restraining Simeon's anger (23:7–9) and as interceding for the life of Pharaoh's son and those of Jacob's sons by concubines (29–29). A messiah will come forth from Levi as from Judah (Test. Simeon 7), parallel to the messiahs of Aaron and of Israel found in the Qumran literature.

Levi, Testament of one of the Testaments of the Twelve Patriarchs. Its narrative section emphasizes Levi's divine call to the priesthood (chaps. 1–9). Chapters 14–18 are a historical summary that highlights the sins of the Jerusalem priesthood, which will be overcome with the appearance of an eschatological priest, described in part in language traditionally applied to the Davidic king (18:2–7; cf. Isa. 11:2–9).

In its present form, the Testament is an explicitly Christian component of a Christian collection. Chapter 10 refers to Jesus' crucifixion, and 18:6–12 reads like a description of Jesus' baptism and temptation (cf. Mark 1:9–11).

Different from the Testaments of the Twelve Patriarchs as a collection, there is clear evidence that the Testament of Levi has drawn heavily on Jewish traditions. The Cairo Geniza contained a medieval Aramaic manuscript of a Levi Testament. The Qumran caves have yielded fragments of several Aramaic manuscripts of a Levi apocryphon, one of which contains a passage that was interpolated, in Greek translation, into a manuscript of the Testaments of the Twelve Patriarchs at Testament of Levi 1:3. The account of Levi's ascent to heaven at Abel-Main (near Mount Hermon) draws on the tradition about Enoch's ascent in 1 Enoch 12–16. Aspects of the narratives about Levi's call and instruction for the priesthood are paralleled in Jubilees 30–32. The emphasis on an eschatological priest has important parallels at Qumran. All of this points to a Jewish prototype for the Testament, quite possibly from the third century B.C.E. This text may have underscored and justified the divine institution of the priesthood, perhaps a Levitic priesthood, and formed a member of a triad of testaments ascribed to Levi, Qahat, and Amram. Quite possibly it criticized aspects of the Jerusalem priesthood and featured the hope of an eschatological priest. Its composition can be placed in circles of pious Jews ancestral to the Qumran community. *See also* AMRAM, TESTAMENT OF; QAHAT, TESTAMENT OF; TWELVE PATRIARCHS, TESTAMENTS OF THE.

Leviathan mythological sea serpent, often associated with the land monster Behemoth. In Canaanite mythology, Leviathan (Lothan) is a twisting serpent with seven heads. Psalms 74:14 describes God's crushing of Leviathan's heads, an allusion to ancient Near Eastern creation myths centered on conquest of the chaos monsters (cf. Ps. 89:9–10, 104:26; Job 3:8, 7:12, 26:12–13; Jub. 2:11). In Job 41, a description of Leviathan's might counters Job's bold questioning of God, Leviathan's creator. In 2 Baruch 29:4 and 4 Ezra 6:49–51, Leviathan and Behemoth are created on the fifth day with the rest of the sea creatures, and they will be eaten at an eschatological banquet. 1 Enoch 60:7–10 claims that Leviathan is female and Behemoth is male. Revelation uses imagery associated with Leviathan and Behemoth to depict cosmic evil forces supporting the Roman Empire. The dragon representing Satan has seven heads (Rev. 12:3), as does the beast from the sea representing the Roman Empire (Rev. 13:1; cf. 17:3).

Levi b. Sisi Palestinian authority active in the late second and early third centuries C.E., at the nexus of the Tannaitic and Amoraic periods; a student of Judah the Patriarch. In the Babylonian Talmud, he generally is cited without the patronymic; in both Talmuds, his name appears without the title of "rabbi." This distinguishes him from the amora Levi II.

levir the surviving brother of a childless, deceased man. The levir is required either to marry his sister-in-law, that is, enter into levirate marriage, or to undertake the rite of removing the shoe (Heb.: *ḥalitzah*). *See also* RITE OF REMOVING THE SHOE.

Levitas of Yabneh Tannaitic authority, apparently of the early second century C.E. He is cited in the Mishnah only at M. Abot 4:4, where he states: "Be exceedingly humble, for the hope of humanity is the worm."

Levites caste of Temple acolytes and singers; *see also* LEVI

Leviticus, Targum to *see* ONKELOS, TARGUM, PALESTINIAN TARGUMS

Leviticus Rabbah compilation of comments on episodic verses of the Book of Leviticus, formed into thirty-seven propositional composites. In contrast to Genesis Rabbah, a verse-by-verse commentary, the paramount and dominant exegetical construction in Leviticus Rabbah is the base-verse/intersecting verse exegesis. A verse of Leviticus is cited (the base-verse), and then a verse from one of the other books, such as Job, Proverbs, Kohelet, or Psalms, is cited. The latter, not the former, is subjected to detailed and systematic exegesis. But the exegetical exercise ends up by leading the intersecting verse back to the base-verse and reading the latter in terms of the former.

The principal propositions are as follows. God loves Israel, so He gave it the Torah, which defines its life and also governs its welfare. Israel is alone in its category, so that which is a virtue to Israel is a vice to the nations, and that which is life-giving to Israel is poison to the Gentiles. True, Israel sins, but God forgives that sin, having punished the nation on account of it. Such a process has yet to come to an end, but it will culminate in Israel's complete regeneration. Meanwhile, Israel's assurance of God's love lies in the numerous expressions of special concern for even the humblest and most ordinary aspects of the national life: the food the nation eats and the sexual practices by which it procreates. These life-sustaining, life-transmitting activities draw God's special interest, as a mark of his general love for Israel. Israel then is supposed to achieve its life in conformity with the marks of God's love. These indications also signify the character of Israel's difficulty, namely, subordination to the nations in general, and to the fourth kingdom, Rome, in particular. Both food laws and skin diseases stand for the nations. There is yet another category of sin, also collective and generative of collective punishment, and that is social. The moral character of Israel's life, the treatment of people by one another, and the practice of gossip and small-scale thuggery draw down divine penalties.

The nation's fate therefore corresponds to its moral condition. The moral condition, however, emerges not only from the current generation. Israel's richest hope lies in the merit of the ancestors, and thus in the scriptural record of the merits attained by the founders of the nation, those who originally brought it into being and gave it life. The world to come upon the nation is so portrayed as to restate these same propositions. Merit overcomes sin, and performing religious duties or supererogatory acts of kindness will win merit for the nation that does them. Israel will be saved at the end of time, and the age, or world, to follow will be exactly the opposite of this one.

Lex Talionis (Lat., the law of retaliation) a principle of retribution graphically stated in Deuteronomy 19:21: "It shall be life for life, eye for eye, tooth for tooth, hand for hand, foot for foot." The principle reappears in apocalyptic literature in the woes in 1 Enoch 92–105, which envision God as the one who enacts punishment whose form is appropriate to the nature of the sin (94:6, 7, 8; 96:6). Thus, one is requited according to one's deeds (95:5). This latter shorthand appears in Psalms of Solomon 2:16, 34 and such New Testament judgment contexts as Romans 2:6, 2 Corinthians 5:10, and Revelation 20:13. A more positive form of the notion of appropriate recompense occurs in Matthew 5:7: "Blessed are the merciful, for they will obtain mercy" (cf. Luke 6:36). The Lex Talionis is explicitly rejected in Matthew 5:38–42, where Jesus counsels nonretaliation. The context may suggest that such action increases the culpability of the sinner, who will face God's wrath at the final judgment (5:43–45, cf. Rom. 12:19–21 and 1QS 10:17–20). Christian apocalypses from the Byzantine and medieval periods recount tours of hell, where sinners suffer in ways appropriate to their sins. *See also* JUDGMENT, DIVINE.

Libanius (314–393 C.E.) Greek rhetorician, born in Antioch. His surviving speeches, letters, autobiography, and numerous other works evidence many of the ideals of the non-Christian Greek urban upper class of late antiquity. His wealthy father sent him to study in Athens for four years. He taught rhetoric in Constantinople and Nicomedia. In 354, he returned to Antioch to take the official chair of rhetoric. It is likely that John Chrysostom, Theodore of Mopsuestia, Basil, and Gregory of Nazianzus were among his pupils. A friend of the emperor Julian, Libanius is a major source of information about the Palestinian patriarchate at the end of the fourth century. His letters from 388 to 393 reflect the cordial relationships between Jews and non-Jews after Julian's death. They indicate that the patriarch was educated in Greek culture and that his sons studied at Berytus under Libanius and one of his pupils. They claim that the patriarch was the leader of the Jews in the whole empire and that he appointed the archons of the Jewish communities. He writes that the decisions of the Jewish courts were accepted only if approved by the patriarch.

libation an offering of liquid poured out as a sacrifice. Libations served in the Israelite cult as an additional "pleasing odor" (Num. 15:7) alongside the offering burned on the altar. They were included with the daily offering (Exod. 29:40–41), with the Sabbath offering (Num. 28:9), with the offering for the New Moon (Num. 28:14), at other points in the festival calendar, and in some specified rites, for example, those of the Nazirite (Num. 6:17). In the rabbinic literature, libations made to pagan gods receive special attention, since rabbis assumed that, given any opportunity, a Gentile would pour out an offering of wine and thereby render the rest of the jug or vat forbidden for Israelite consumption.

Libertines Acts 6:9 mentions a synagogue of the Libertines (Gr.: *synagogos tōn libertinōn*). The meaning is most likely "synagogue of the freedmen"; that is, it was (allegedly) made up of a group of Jews freed from slavery. Whether such a synagogue existed before 70 C.E. is debatable.

Lies, Man of an opponent of the Teacher of Righteousness (the inspired leader of the group of Jewish sectaries who lived at Qumran). The Man of Lies (also known as Spouter of Lies, Liar, or Scoffer) appears in the Damascus Document and the Habakkuk Commentary, where he appears along with the Teacher as a leader in an already existing group in the early second century B.C.E. His quarrel with the Teacher concerned halakhic matters of purity, justice, and ritual (including the proper calendar). The Man of Lies led a breakaway congregation from the Teacher; in the Dead Sea Scrolls, this congregation was called the Seekers after Smooth Things, usually identified with the Pharisees. The Man of Lies' quarrel with the Teacher may have precipitated the Teacher's move to Qumran.

life, eternal (Heb.: *ḥay olam*; Gr.: *zōē aiōnios*) life of fabulous length or without end, appropriate to the new age (*olam, aiōn*). The first occurrences of this term in Jewish literature refer to the immortal, spiritual state of the heavenly watchers (1 Enoch 15:4, 6), who do not need progeny to perpetuate themselves. Although the expression is not used, 1 Enoch 5:6–9, 10:17, and 25:4–6, drawing on the imagery of Isaiah 65:17–25, promise that the righteous in the new age will live fabulously long lives on a renewed earth, as the patriarchs did in primordial times. Daniel 12:2 also alludes to Isaiah 65, and it is not clear that the "eternal life" promised to the resurrected righteous is an endless rather than a very long life. The heavenly exaltation of the wise teachers in Daniel 12:3, however, may posit a kind of astral immortality for these leaders of Israel. As "eternal life" is combined with terms like immortality and incorruption (4 Maccabees, Joseph and Asenath), and heaven rather than earth is seen as the locus of blessing, an everlasting overcoming of death appears to be indicated. Especially note-worthy in the New Testament is John's use of the term. In a world characterized by sin and dominated by the devil, those who believe in Jesus have already passed from death and possess the eternal life that is appropriate to the existence that awaits them in heaven (John 3:16, 5:24, 11:25–26, 14:1–3). The idea parallels texts like Joseph and Asenath and the Qumran Hymns. *See also* IMMORTALITY, INCORRUPTION.

life after death   *see* AFTERLIFE; LIFE, ETERNAL

light and darkness   This pair of opposites and each of its two elements occur frequently in biblical Jewish thought, where they have both literal and figurative meanings. In their figurative sense, the pair normally depicts a valuative dualism, in which "light" represents positive entities, and "darkness" represents those entities' negative opposites.

The Hebrew Bible furnishes many paradigms for light and darkness that become normative in later Judaism. In the Bible, light is generally a symbol of knowledge, life, hope, goodness, joy, and the presence of God. God is the bestower of light, and its qualities and benefits express God's constant presence in and concern for the world. The first explicit creation of God (Gen. 1:3), light established a contraposition to the primordial darkness. Darkness, on the other hand, represents evil, sin, foolishness, desolation, gloom, ignorance, the underworld, and, generally, God's absence.

Intertestamental Jewish literature maintains these biblical images of light and darkness and introduces three new elements into their use that begin to reflect some of the broader transformations in ideology, cosmology, and eschatology that characterize Second Temple Judaism. First, there is an increasing evocation of a dualism that is not only temporal and valuative but also spatial and ontological. For example, 1 Enoch states that some human spirits are "born of light" while others are "born in darkness" (108:11). According to 2 Baruch 17–18, Adam spread darkness on the earth, whereas Moses and the law gave light. This dualistic characterization is especially evident in the sectarian literature from Qumran, where the "two spirits" of truth and falsehood govern the "children of light" and "children of darkness," respectively (see especially 1QS 3–4).

Second, each of the elements in the dualism becomes more absolute. In Wisdom of Solomon 7:26, wisdom is a "reflection of eternal light." 1 Enoch 58:3 locates the elect "in the light of eternal life." In Tobit 14:10, Nadab goes into "eternal dark-ness." Philo, especially, tends to idealize the quality of light, emphasizing the contrast between perfect, divine light and everyday, earthly light.

Third, images of light and darkness are used increasingly in eschatological contexts. One theme is that the coming of the eschaton will result in darkness in the natural world (e.g., Test. Mos. 10:5). Another is that, after the eschatological judgment, the elect will enter a realm of light, while the damned will go into darkness (e.g., 1 Enoch 108:12–14). A third motif is that the final eschatological situation will be one of eternal light (e.g., 4 Ezra 7:42).

Images of light and darkness are also common in early Christian literature, especially in their juxtaposition as a contrastive rhetorical device, indicating either two states of being in the world or two cosmological realms (e.g., Matt. 6:22–23; 2 Cor. 6:14). In the Gospel of John, Jesus is the paradigmatic light, God's force of illumination in the world (e.g., 1:4–9). Other important motifs are the characterization of Christians as "children of light" (e.g., 1 Thess. 5:5) and the notion that the present world order is dominated by darkness (e.g., Eph. 6:12). *See also* DUALISM.

Lilith   female demon who, according to legend, endangers women in childbirth and kills newborn children. The sole reference to Lilith in scripture includes her among the wild animals and harmful spirits that will inhabit the ruins of the land on "the Lord's day of retribution."

lion   **1.** a major literary motif in Jewish and Christian writings. Lions were common in Palestine in antiquity. The Bible and early Jewish and Christian literature refer frequently to lions, both in literal and metaphorical senses. In the Bible, the image of the lion is generally that of a strong, bold, and cruel predator. The lion is sometimes characterized as the most powerful of the animals (Prov. 30:30), thus having royal qualities. In the ideal future age as described in the Book of Isaiah, lions will be either absent (35:9) or tame (65:25).

Metaphorically, in a positive sense, kings (1 Macc. 3:4; Apoc. Elijah 2:7) and even God (Job 10:16; Hos. 13:7) are compared to lions. Leonine characteristics are also ascribed to the Messiah (Rev. 5:5; 4 Ezra 11:36–12:35; cf. Gen. 49:9). The awesome, semidivine qualities of the lion are evident in symbolic treatments in Ezekiel 1:10, 10:14, and Revelation 4:7.

In a negative metaphorical sense, the apocalyptic beasts in Daniel 7:4, Revelation 9:8, and 13:2 have lionlike features. Joseph and Asenath 12:9 and 1 Peter 5:8 describe the devil as a lion.

2. a major motif in Jewish visual art for many centuries. Lions figure in the decoration of the Second Temple, according to written tradition. A late story tells that eighty-two virgins sewed the veils of the Temple twice a year, and upon these veils they embroidered lions and eagles (M. Shekalim 7.5; T. Shekalim 51b). In any case, lions figure strongly in synagogue art, where they occur both in relief and modeled in the round. Most commonly in synagogue art, a pair of lions appears flanking the Torah shrine and the menorah. This is so in the Beth Alpha mosaic floor and at Maon in its floor. The actual pediment of a Torah shrine found at Nabratein featured two lions in high relief on top, and they were not simply symmetrical. In gold glass depictions of Torah shrines from the Jewish catacombs of Rome, lions appear on either side of the shrine. On the other hand, the lion may be paired with another animal to flank an item of interest. For example, at Beth Alpha a lion and a bull flank the dedicatory inscription. Two lions flank the inscription at Hammat-Gader. Also, notably on sarcophagi, lions or lionesses flank objects of interest, for example, a bull's head and a vase at Beth Shearim. Lions modeled in the round are known from Chorazin, Baram, and Capernaum, all in the Galilee, and at Baram two were found. The lions or lionesses are typically depicted in body profile, either gazing straight ahead at the object of interest or with heads turned looking at the observer. It is notable that the lion never appears on Jewish coins, on ossuaries, or in early funerary art. The motif seems to be part of late Roman and Byzantine Jewish art.

listes *see* LĒSTĒS

literalists a group of Bible interpreters mentioned by Philo of Alexandria. They evidently interpreted according to the letter of the text, as opposed to using allegory, as many did; however, their "literal" interpretation is often not literal in the modern sense, but extends the plain meaning of the text.

literary genres, in Second Temple literature Contemporary biblical studies have emphasized the importance of literary form as a means of interpreting a text and gaining some insight into its function in the society for which it was created. The various literary forms and genres in which Jewish religious texts of the Graeco-Roman period were cast reflect the rich complexity of the culture that generated them. Especially in their differences from their biblical prototypes, they attest new religious and intellectual developments in the Second Temple period.

Narratives may be divided into two types. Some stories are loosely tied to biblical times, places, and characters (Tobit, Judith, Daniel 1–6, Bel and the Dragon, and Susanna). Others are aggadic elaborations of biblical texts, which reflect a developing tendency to interpret sacred tradition in light of contemporary events and concerns. Taken together, these narratives embody the belief that God's activity touches individual human lives and that one's fellow Israelites provide examples to be emulated or eschewed. Although *biblical* narratives celebrate the virtues of Israel's heroes and heroines and criticize their flaws, the narrative emphasis in later texts on example that is explicit reflects parallel trends in gentile literature of the period.

The genre of *testament* epitomizes the tendency to emphasize virtues and vices, and its postbiblical exemplars differ from their biblical prototypes (Gen. 49 and Deut. 33) in the emphasis on ethical instruction, which is sometimes presented through a combination of narrative, exhortation, and eschatological prophecy. The attribution of testaments to venerable figures of the past adds weight to the authority of their exhortation.

Works of *history* like 1 and 2 Maccabees and Josephus's *Antiquities of the Jews* and *The Jewish War* supply important information that provides a context for other literary material stemming from the Graeco-Roman period, although the data must be sifted in order to filter out an individual author's bias. 1 Maccabees is a piece of political propaganda that legitimizes the Hasmonean priesthood by claiming that Mattathias and his sons were God's chosen deliverers of Israel and by telling the story in the idiom of biblical history. Taking a totally different tack, the author of 2 Maccabees minimizes the Hasmoneans' accomplishments and uses the Deuteronomic historical scheme to explain Israel's sufferings, recounting the story in the idiom of contemporary Hellenistic historiography. Both texts emphasize God's ongoing activity, as judge and redeemer, in the events of Israel's recent past.

Wisdom instruction abounds in the literature of this period. Its most obvious example is Ecclesiasticus, or the Wisdom of Joshua ben Sira (Sirach). Analogous to the canonical Book of Proverbs, this text attests the ongoing creation and collection of proverbs. However, the book differs from its canonical prototype in at least two major respects. It explicitly identifies heavenly Wisdom and the Torah (chap. 24), and it demonstrates an interest in the events of Israel's history (chaps. 44–49; see also the prayer in chap. 36). Proverbial wisdom appears in other literary genres as well: the narrative Book of Tobit (4:5–21); the ethical sections of the Testaments of the Twelve Patriarchs; the exhortations in the apocalyptic collection of 1 Enoch (chaps. 91, 94). The Wisdom of Solomon and 4 Maccabees, on the other hand, expound wisdom in the form of a *philosophy* that is beholden to contemporary eclectic Greek traditions.

The most innovative literary genre in the Jewish literature of the Graeco-Roman period is the *apocalypse*. This class of texts synthesizes features of the wisdom and prophetic traditions, presenting them as revelations mediated by heavenly beings through human agents identified as heroes from Israel's past (e.g., Abraham, Moses, Baruch, Ezra, Daniel, and Zephaniah), or more radically, the primordial patriarch Enoch. Perhaps the major concern of the pseudonymous apocalypticists is the assurance of God's justice and power in a world that the faithful experience as devoid of divine justice and power. Myths about the origins of evil and its eschatological defeat, visions of the future and revealed summaries of Israel's history down to the present time, and revelations of the structures of the universe all serve to comfort and encourage readers during times of persecution, oppression, and other political, social, and religious upheaval.

Eschatological awareness, rooted in the prophetic tradition, is expressed in the *pesharim,* commentaries on biblical books composed by the community at Qumran. Written at a time when the prophetic writings had achieved canonical status, these texts explicate, verse by verse, how the ancient oracles are being fulfilled in the contemporary events of the community.

Psalms, hymns, and *prayers* were composed as expressions of Jewish piety in the Graeco-Roman period. Prayers of confession could serve as acts of repentance intended to return God's blessing to a nation thought to be suffering the curses of the covenant (Daniel 9, Prayer of Azariah, 1 Baruch 1–3). Hymns of praise might also express such contrition as they envisioned the restoration of Zion's glory (Tobit 13). The Psalms of Solomon are heavily didactic and emphasize the righteousness of God's judgment. The Qumran hymns recount the suffering of the righteous leaders of the community and praise God for the blessings that accrue to community's members, who have been rescued from damnation and brought into the realm of divine blessing.

These general observations notwithstanding, it is often difficult to classify Jewish literature by genre, because many texts are of mixed genres. The Book of Tobit is an extended narrative presented as a kind of testament. The Testament of Moses is an extended piece of biblical paraphrase with an apocalyptic oracle. Jubilees retells the events in Genesis 1–Exodus 12 with halakic interpolations and presents the narrative as an angelic revelation. The Book of Daniel and the Apocalypse of Abraham combine narrative and revelation mediated by angels. 1 Enoch contains an introductory oracle, mythic narrative, a prophetic call story, cosmic journeys interpreted by angels, prayers, dream visions, historical summaries, and proverbial sentences, as well as woes, exhortations, and predictions of the future that parallel prophetic texts. Torah can be taught through biblical paraphrase, proverbial instruction, accounts of journeys to the heavens, halakic expansions of biblical laws, and manuals of community rules.

A study of literary form is instructive in many ways for an understanding of the multiple facets of Jewish life in the Graeco-Roman period, but such analysis of form and genre must avoid oversimplifications, be sensitive to the unique contours of individual texts, and avoid rash conclusions about the settings and functions of the texts. *See also* AGGADAH; APOCALYPSES; PROPHECY, FULFILLMENT OF; TESTAMENT; WISDOM LITERATURE.

literature, rabbinic writings produced by sages who bore the title of honor "rabbi," meaning "my lord" or "sir," in the first seven centuries C.E. These writings include the Mishnah, a philosophical law code, promulgated c. 200 C.E., which was the first document of the oral Torah; the Tosefta, completed c. 250 C.E., a set of supplements to the Mishnah; the tractate Abot (The Fathers; The Founders), a collection of wise sayings; and two Talmuds, which amplified and explained the rules of the Mishnah: the Talmud of the Land of Israel (Heb.: Talmud Yerushalmi), completed c. 400 C.E., and the Talmud of Babylonia (Heb.: Talmud Babli), completed c. 600 C.E. In addition to the rabbinic documents that commented on the Mishnah, compilations of exegeses of scripture, the written Torah, were made. These were in three main groups. The first was made up of verse-by-verse comments on scripture, specifically, Mekhilta Attributed to R. Ishmael, which deals with the book of Exodus; Sifra, which concerns Leviticus; Sifrei to Numbers; and Sifrei to Deuteronomy, all compiled c. 250–350 C.E. The second group, compiled c. 400–500 C.E., involved the presentation, through citations of verses of scripture, of propositions and principles proved by the facts of scripture; this group includes Genesis Rabbah, Leviticus Rabbah and Pesikta deRab Kahana, which is organized around the special Sabbaths of the year. The third group, compiled c. 500–600 C.E., systematically set forth broad principles of theology through reading from a single perspective the verses of scripture; it comprises Song of Songs Rabbah, Ruth Rabbah, Lamentations Rabbati, and Esther Rabbah I, which covers Esther 1–2.

liturgy the public, fixed activity of worship. The term is sometimes limited specifically to words (hymns, prayers, readings) that form part of such worship, but it is often used much more broadly to include all elements of action, dress, movement, and setting. Liturgy is distinguished from individual private and spontaneous acts of devotion and prayer.

In Judaism prior to 70 B.C.E., the central liturgical activity was the offering of sacrifices at the Temple in Jerusalem. Sacrifices were offered by the priests and Levites twice a day (morning and afternoon), with additional sacrifices offered for feasts and other needs (purification and atonement) as set forth in the laws of Moses. In addition to the actual slaughter of animals and pouring of blood, liturgy involved the singing of psalms by the temple singers, the burning of incense, the blowing of trumpets, the priestly blessing, and the prostration of the people.

However, our knowledge of precisely how the Temple liturgy was carried out is very limited. The most detailed description is in the Mishnah (especially Tamid), but this was compiled circa 200 C.E. and presents a somewhat idealized and stylized picture. Of actual descriptions written before the destruction of the Temple, the most extensive is Sirach 50, which describes the actions and dress of the high priest Simon "the Just" (c. 200 B.C.E.); this poetic passage still conveys a sense of the awe and splendor of the Temple liturgy.

Scholarly opinion at present is divided about how much of a formal statutory liturgy of prayers and blessings had developed in institutions such as the synagogue prior to 70 C.E. While some scholars are hesitant to assume that there were any formal structures and texts (apart perhaps from gatherings for the reading of the Torah) while the Temple was still standing, others would date the beginning of set patterns of prayers and blessings as far back as the third century B.C.E. Some actual texts may have survived in the Dead Sea Scrolls, where we find collections of prayers and blessings for each day of the month, each day of the week, and for feasts; the language and theology of these texts suggest that they were not composed by a sectarian group but reflect more widespread developments within Judaism. Thus, they may give us a glimpse into a very early stage of what eventually became the standard synagogue liturgy.

In the Dead Sea Scrolls, a few examples of texts for specific liturgies of this community are preserved. For example, in the Community Rule we find a description of the ceremony for entering the covenant, with the actual texts of the words to be said as the confession of sin, the blessings of the priests on "those of the lot of God," and the curses of the Levites on "those of the lot of Belial"; the participants share in the liturgical action with the response of "Amen, amen." Other liturgies are described for the days of the final eschatological battle (War Scroll).

Livias *see* BETH HARAM

loans *see* BORROWING

Lod ancient city in Judea known in Greek first as Lydda, later as Diospolis; mentioned in Ezra 2:23, though it is probably far older than that. In 145 B.C.E., it was placed under Hasmonean hegemony when Demetrius I gave it to Jonathan the Hasmonean. In the first half of the first century, the apostle Peter visited Lydda to call on believers there (Acts 9:32). By 68 C.E. Vespasian's proconsul in Syria, Cestius Gallus, burned Lydda in the First Jewish Revolt. Vespasian resettled Lod with Jews loyal to Rome. By the second century C.E., it was a capital of its toparchy and was given its name Diospolis (city of Zeus) by the emperor Septimius Severus. Severus went as far as to give it the honor of being designated a colony under the full name of Colonia Lucia Septimia Severia Diospolis. Diospolis minted its own coins from about 200 C.E. to about 218 C.E. Pagan themes appear on these coins: the city goddess Tyche (Fortuna), Zeus, and Demeter. Many sages are associated with this city after the destruction of the Second Temple (M. Shebiit 9:2; Y. Megillah 70a). By the fourth century C.E., George, patron saint of England, was martyred at Lod (Lydda), and his shrine was venerated there. Many tombs are known to exist in the modern town, but archaeological excavation is precluded by the density of settlement.

log (Heb., no English equivalent) dry and liquid measure. One *log* = 2 *toman* = 4 quarter-*logs* (Heb.: *rebiit*) = 6 *betzah*. A wilderness *log* (Heb.: *log midbarit*) is equivalent to 503.5 cubic centimeters (30.7 cu. in.); a Jerusalem *log* is equivalent to 699.4 cubic centimeters (39.6 cu. in.); a Sepphorean *log* is equivalent to 777.4 cubic centimeters (47.4 cu. in.).

Logos literally, the Word; notion of knowable divine first principle derived from ancient Greek philosophy that became a key theological concept in Hellenistic Judaism (especially in the thought of Philo of Alexandria), from which it was adopted by early Christianity. The Greek word *logos,* usually translated as "word," comes from the root *leg-,* meaning (1) to gather or count and (2) to speak. From the former, the noun comes to mean ratio, proportion, order; from the latter, a wider spectrum of meaning results, including (from concrete to abstract): word, saying, account, oracle, speech, conversation, dialogue, definition, argument, theory, reason, or rationality. The term is very common in Greek philosophy, signifying the cosmic order (Heraclitus), the divine principle that causes and maintains that order (the Stoics), or more generally the principle of reason or rationality in man (Plato, Aristotle).

In Jewish tradition, the term first appears in the Septuagint, where it most often translates *dabar* in the Hebrew Bible. This results in a more dynamic element not present in the ordinary Greek usage, for example, when "the word of the Lord comes" to one of his prophets. Significantly, *logos* was used to indicate God's act of creation and his maintenance of cosmic order (e.g., at Ps. 33:6 [LXX 32:6]: "By the *logos* of the Lord the heavens were established," where *logos* clearly refers to the "and God said" of Gen. 1). In Hellenistic Judaism, the cosmological and theological use of *logos* is further developed, especially through the identification of the Logos with the figure of Sophia from the Wisdom literature (e.g., at Wisd. of Sol. 9:1–2). The term thus becomes to some degree personified (hence "Logos," with a capital letter).

The concept is most prominent, however, in the writings of Philo of Alexandria, who further exploits its Greek philosophical connotations. The Logos is a theological principle: it can be described as that aspect of God that stands in relation to his creation. It is also a cosmological principle: God uses his Logos as instrument in the act of creation or as the location for its ideal blueprint or model. Finally, it is also an anthropological principle: humankind is created "according to the image" (Gen. 1:26), which is the Logos. Through their reason (*logos*), humans are related to the Logos, and thus can attain to the knowledge and vision of God (though not of his essence). Philo's conception of the Logos is not easy to interpret. Sometimes it seems primarily aspectual, virtually a metaphor for God's power and presence in the world. Sometimes it is presented as a hypostasis (self-subsistent entity), separate from God Himself. There are even a few texts (later favored by Christian readers) in which Philo calls the Logos "God's first-begotten Son" or "Man of God." In other texts, angels are described as *logoi* (plural). These divergencies are probably to be explained through the diversity of traditions in earlier Jewish tradition upon which Philo is drawing.

Because the term *logos* is tied to the use of the Greek language, its presence in Judaism is curtailed by the reduction in preserved Jewish writings in Greek after the first century C.E. An important continuation occurs in early Christian thought. In the Prologue to the Gospel of John (1:1–18), the Logos is identified with Jesus Christ as the incarnated Son of God. Such a degree of personification goes beyond anything found in Hellenistic Judaism (although Philo regards the high priest as representing the Logos). This line of theological reflection is continued in the Christian Apologists (especially Justin Martyr) and Alexandrian theologians (Clement, Origen, Arius, Athanasius).

logos protrepticus (Gr., exhortatory discourse) Probably originating with the Sophists, this type of discourse formed a well-known genre of Greek literature, whose function was both to teach and to persuade. In Jewish literature, the Wisdom of Solomon seems to fit this form.

Longinus, Gnaeus Pompeius legate of Judea, 86 C.E. Many scholars identify him with Gnaeus Aemilius Pinarius Cicatricula Pompeius Longinus, who was governor of Moesia Superior in 93 C.E. and of Pannonia in 98 C.E. This is the only information we have about his career.

Longinus, Pseudo- author of an anonymous work with the title *On the Sublime.* Although the writing has been identified with the Neoplatonist Longinus, this attribution is generally rejected; the work is thought to be by a writer of the first century C.E. He is of interest because he shows knowledge of the actual biblical text, one of the few non-Jews to do so (it is generally agreed that he was Greek and not Jewish). He speaks well of Moses and gives a composite quotation made up of Genesis 1:3, 9–10, in the Septuagint version. Whether he got the quotation from the Septuagint or indirectly from Jews is unknown.

Loos name of a Macedonian month; appears in a number of Jewish sources, such as the writings of Josephus. Unfortunately, there was not a uniform usage; sometimes it corresponded to the Hebrew month of Tammuz (June/July) and sometimes to the month of Ab (July/August).

lord a designation that can be applied to any male who exercises primary authority over an individual, a household or any other social or political unity, and that is used in an ultimate sense as a title for the biblical God who is regarded as "Lord of all the earth" (Josh. 3:11; Ps. 97:5; Mic. 4:13; Zech. 4:14, 6:5; cf. Deut. 10:14), or more comprehensively as "Lord of heaven and earth" (Gen. 24:3; Deut. 4:39; Matt. 11:25; Luke 10:21; Acts 17:24). God is Lord of heaven and earth because he both created them and owns them (Exod. 9:29; 1 Chron. 9:29). Similar titles were attributed to other ancient deities; the Babylonian god Enlil, for example, was also called "Lord of the earth." The English word "lord," however, is used to translate three Hebrew terms in the Old Testament: *adon, adonai,* and YHWH (Yahweh). *Adon* means lord, master when applied to persons in authority (Gen. 45:8–9; Deut. 10:17; Judg. 19:26–27; 1 Sam. 29:8), and is occasionally used for God (Exod. 23:17, 34:23; Josh 3:11, 13). *Adonai,* on the other hand, is a plural form based on *adon,* but is used exclusively for God and is often used as a parallel to YHWH (Gen. 15:2, 8; Josh. 7:7; Isa. 25:8) or as a substitute for it (Isa. 13:17; Amos 7:7–8, 9:1; Ezek. 18:25). The most important divine title in the Hebrew Bible is YHWH (referred to as the Tetragrammaton because it consists of four consonants), regularly translated Lord, but transliterated as either Jehovah or more accurately as Yahweh. Yahweh is the personal name for the God of Israel and is never used of any other human or divine being. Sometime during the Second Temple period (i.e., after 516 C.E.), the practice arose during the public reading of the Torah of avoiding the audible pronunciation of YHWH because of its great sanctity (see Lev. 24:16), by substituting *adonai* (Lord) or *elohim* (God). Sometime during the Middle Ages the correct pronunciation of the name was lost. The sanctity of YHWH is reflected in the fact that it is frequently referred to as the Name or the Holy Name (Gen. 4:26; Exod. 6:3; Isa. 12:4; Jer. 10:16; Ezek. 20:39, 36:20; Mal. 1:11). This practice persists in Judaism to the present day. Attempts to explain the etymology of YHWH go back to Exodus 3:14. It is likely that YHWH is a causative formation from the verb *hyh,* to be, which may have originated as a shortened form, or hypocoristicon, of the phrase "YHWH El" (El [God] creates). In early Hebrew poetry YHWH is frequently depicted as a divine warrior.

In the New Testament, the term "Lord" is used as a translation of the Greek words *kyrios* and *despotês. Despotês* (lord, master) is used for people in authority (2 Tim. 2:21; 1 Pet. 2:18), for Christ (2 Pet. 2:1; Jude 4), and God (frequently in the Septuagint; Luke 2:29; Acts 4:24; Rev. 6:10). The most important word translated as "Lord" in the New Testament is *kyrios,* which occurs over seven hundred times. It is used as a term of respect meaning sir (Matt. 8:6, 21; John 4:11), as well as for people in authority (Matt. 20:8; Luke 13:8), for God (Matt. 5:33; Luke 1:6; Acts 7:33; James 1:7), and most frequently for Christ (1 Cor. 12:3, 16:22; Rom. 10:9; Phil. 2:11; Rev. 11:18), often in the compound forms of Lord Jesus or Lord Jesus Christ (Jude 17; 2 Pet. 1:8). When citing or alluding to Old Testament passages originally referring to YHWH or Adonai, early Christians regularly used the term *kyrios,* by which they mean Jesus (Mark 1:3; Acts 2:34; Rom. 10:13; Heb. 1:10), though it is sometimes unclear whether Jesus or God is meant (Acts 9:312; 1 Cor. 4:19; 2 Cor. 8:21; 1 Thess. 4:6). Surviving Jewish manuscripts of the Septuagint indicate that Jews themselves did not translate YHWH with *kyrios,* but either transliterated the Tetragrammaton or left it untranslated. *See also* GOD, NAMES OF.

Lot Haran's son; Abraham's nephew. He migrated to Canaan with Abraham. Their herdsmen quarreled over land, and they parted company; Lot later settled in Sodom (Gen. 13). When Lot was captured by Mesopotamian kings, Abraham rescued him (Gen. 14). Lot showed hospitality to two angels who visited him, and then tried to protect them from the Sodomites. When God destroyed Sodom, Lot was rescued. Lot's daughters got him drunk and committed incest with him (Gen. 19). They gave birth to Moab, ancestor of the Moabites, and Ben-Ammi, ancestor of the Ammonites. Jubilees 16:8–9 blames the incest on father and daughters both, and says that God will remove Lot's seed from the earth.

Later tradition is divided in its attitude to Lot. Rabbinic material often judges him negatively, and sees anything positive about him as due to his association with Abraham. In the Genesis Apocryphon, Abraham weeps when he hears that Lot has been captured (see Test. Abr. 5:13, 6:5). Jubilees 16:7 claims that Lot was saved because God remembered Abraham. In 2 Peter 2:7–9, Lot is righteous and is tormented by the Sodomites' iniquity. He is an example of how God saves the righteous. The story of Lot is also used to show the sureness of God's punishment, apart from any judgment on Lot himself (Sir. 16:8; Luke 17:28–32).

love translates several Hebrew words, including *ahabah* and *hesed* (the latter of which is also translated "grace"). The Tanakh (or Old Testament) speaks of "love" in erotic relationships (see especially the Song of Songs), and family life (Ruth 4:15). The words for love have a further sense not carried by the English word but common in the ancient Near East, namely loyalty in political relationships (e.g., treaties). When it describes the relationship between God and Israel, "love" reflects both the political and the familial usages. The classic summary of biblical faith in Deut 6:4–5, the Shema, includes the commandment, "You shall love the Lord your God with all your soul, and with all your heart, and with all your might." Here "love" designates Israel's loyal fulfillment of her obligations to God, as set forth in the Sinai covenant. "Love" refers more to action than to emotion, and the language of political treaties forms the background. Images from the realm of familial love are especially prominent in Hosea. The prophet describes God's love for his covenant people as that of a husband for his wife (3:1) and a father for his child: "When Israel was a child I loved him, and out of Egypt I called my son" (11:1). God's election of Israel and his deliverance of his people from its enemies are viewed as special signs of his love. Hosea uses his own love for his adulterous wife Gomer to exemplify God's love for his people, which endures despite Israel's constant seeking after other "lovers" (meaning worshiping other gods; 2:7). While many texts describe the gracious, forgiving nature of God's love (Exod. 34:6–7), it is not unconditional (Exod. 20:5–6), nor is it to be taken for granted. God's freedom is maintained.

In the Dead Sea Scrolls the language of love and hate is used to contrast the sectarians, the Essenes, with those outside. Humanity is divided into two camps, those who follow the spirit of darkness and those who follow the spirit of light: God "loves everlastingly" the spirit of light but "hates forever" the "ways" of the spirit of darkness (1QS 3:26–4:1). Members of the community are commanded to love what God chooses and to hate what God rejects (1QS 1:3, 1QH 14:12).

Love figures prominently in the New Testament; some form of the Greek term *agapē* occurs in every book (the verb *phileo* also is used). Of Jesus' teachings on love, two have been especially influential: his command to love one's enemies (Matt. 5:44) and his summary of the law (Matt. 22:37–40) by citing the commandments to love God (Deut. 6:5) and "to love your neighbor as yourself" (Lev. 19:18). A similar summary, a negative paraphrase of Leviticus 19:18, was made by Jesus' near contemporary Rabbi Hillel (died c. 10 C.E.): "Whatever is hateful to you, do it not unto your fellow. This is the essence of the Torah, the rest being just its corollary" (B. Shab. 31a; cf. Jub. 36:4–7, which

combines Lev. 19:18 with the command to fear God in Deut. 6:13). Paul declares that love is the "fulfillment of the law" (Rom. 13:8–10) and gives an extended tribute to *agapē* in 1 Corinthians 13:1–13. Love is a central theme in the Gospel of John and 1 John. The Gospel interprets the death of Jesus as a demonstration of the superabundant, self-sacrificing nature of God's love for humanity: "For God so loved the world that he gave his only son" (John 3:16, cf. 13:1, 1 John 4:9–10, Rom. 5:8). Jesus gives a "new commandment": to "love one another" (John 13:34), that is, one's fellow Christians, a command that figures prominently in the exhortation of 1 John. (Note the narrower focus in comparison with the commands to love one's neighbor or enemy). In 1 John, love is closely linked with knowledge of God (4:7), and the author even defines God as love (4:16).

luah *see* CALENDAR

Lucian satirical writer of the second century C.E. from Samosata (born c. 120 C.E.). He indicated that his own background was Syrian rather than Greek. He wrote mainly satirical works, with devastating mockery of those he regarded as religious impostors, but his works provide valuable information on contemporary Syrian culture and religion. He also made some references to Jews, though these are all brief and relate to magic. He refers to Jews who peddle magical spells and notes that a particular impostor would say some Hebrew or Phoenician words to fool the customers. He also mentions a "Syrian from Palestine" who exorcized evil spirits.

Lucianic recension a revision of the Septuagint, originally made around the turn of the era. Its purpose was apparently to bring the Septuagint text closer to the current Hebrew text. The earlier anonymous revision was revised around 300 C.E. by the church father Lucian of Antioch.

Lucuas leader of Jewish revolt in Cyrene in 115–117 C.E. Eusebius states that in 115 the Jews in Alexandria, Egypt, and Cyrenaica revolted against the Greeks. The Greeks fled to Alexandria where they were able to defeat the Jews. At this point the Jews of Egypt and Cyrenaica joined forces and plundered the rest of Egypt. In 116 the situation developed into a war with Rome, and at this point Eusebius describes Lucuas as "a king." Whether or not this is meant to imply that the uprising had taken on a messianic tone is unclear.

Luke, Jews in the Gospel of The Gospel of Luke and the Acts of the Apostles constitute a two-volume narrative that argues that God sought to bring the Gentiles to belief in God through Jesus Christ within a renewed Israel. The author is a Gentile who does not know Palestinian geography but is acquainted with diaspora Judaism. He constantly quotes and alludes to the Bible and consciously parallels the experiences of Jesus and his early followers to biblical figures and events. He understands Jesus' call to repentance to be addressed to both Jews and Gentiles. In Acts of the Apostles, Peter and Paul both appeal first to their fellow Jews and then to Gentiles. They experience both success and failure with each group.

Luke and Acts stress the connections of Christians with Jews. Various leaders, such as Gamaliel and Pharisees, are presented as sympathetic with Jesus' followers. Some Pharisees believe in Jesus (Acts 15:5) and Paul is depicted as engaging in learned discussion with Jewish leaders at the very end of Acts. On the other hand, harsh polemics are directed against Jews who reject Jesus' reform program and against the rich and powerful who exclude the poor, repentant sinners, and Gentiles from a renewed and enlarged Israel through which all are called to be saved. The author blames the Jerusalem authorities and people for Jesus' execution (e.g., 3:13–15) and frequently calls on them to repent. Thus Acts especially has contributed to later anti-Judaism and anti-Semitism among Christians.

lulab palm branch bound with myrtle and willow, associated with the Feast of Sukkot (Tabernacles), and well represented as a major motif in Jewish art. The lulab almost always appears with the etrog, shofar, and incense shovel in Jewish art of the Roman and Byzantine periods, and especially with the menorah in synagogue art. The lulab also appears alone on coins, glass, lamps, and small artifacts. Double lulabs appear on half-shekels of the First Jewish War of Year 4, or 69 C.E. On the reverse of one of these types there is an etrog. The lulab is covered in these depictions, though on yet another type, the lulab is free of its cover and one can see that it is a bound bundle. The lulab does not appear again until the coins of the Bar Kokhba Revolt of 132–135 C.E. Now the character of the lulab changes, for it appears that the exterior wrapping of limbs is trimmed at the top. On some coins the bundles of limbs are tied in such a way as to resemble an amphora. The lulab in synagogue art, namely in mosaic floors, is never so elaborately presented. In fact, it is usually a simple palm branch, though in some depictions it is tied so tightly to defy interpretation, except that it appears with shofar, etrog, incense shovel, and menorah. On a plate (about 49.5 centimeters in diameter) from Naaneh near Ramleh, the Torah shrine ap-

pears with lulabs. Further examples appear on tomb walls and sarcophagi at the Jewish catacombs of Beth Shearim. Where the Torah shrine appears, the lulab and the other cult objects also appear.

lunar calendar *see* CALENDAR

Lupus, Marcus Rutilius Egyptian prefect. In 115 C.E., the Jews of Alexandria, Egypt, and Cyrenaica rose up against the Greeks. Lupus's edict of 115 indicates that the revolt was widespread by October. Although the Greeks in Alexandria killed and imprisoned many Jews, the Cyrenaican and Egyptian Jews ravaged and plundered the rest of Egypt. The edict reports on the successful Greek reprisals against the Jews in Alexandria, but warns the Greeks to stop using their slaves and others to organize arson and murder in the city, saying that the Jews should be left to the recently arrived Roman army.

Lupus, Tiberius Julius prefect of Egypt (72–73 C.E.). In 72 some of the Sicarii (a Jewish revolutionary group) who had fled Palestine arrived in Alexandria to continue their anti-Roman activity. The Jewish community turned over to the Roman authority some six hundred Sicarii. Though he tortured them, Lupus was unable to force them to acknowledge the emperor's rule, so he executed them.

LXX *see* SEPTUAGINT

Lycinus, Publius Aelius Sempronius procurator of Palestine (198–209 C.E.). He previously had been procurator in Gaul, Dacia Porolissensis, and Egypt. He seems to have been appointed by Septimius Severus and to have continued as procurator under Caracalla. We do not have any information about his posts after leaving Palestine.

Lydda *see* LOD

Lysias Seleucid general who led expeditions against Judas Maccabeus, unsuccessfully in 165 B.C.E. and successfully in 162 B.C.E. In 162 B.C.E. he and Antiochus V lifted their siege of Jerusalem because of an attack on Antioch by the general Philip. They garrisoned Beth Zur, pulled down the fortifications in Jerusalem, and gave Jews the privilege of living according to their own laws.

Lysimachus **1.** Alexandrian writer, possibly identifiable with Lysimachus the Mythographer (fl. c. 200 B.C.E.), who wrote a book on Egypt called the *Aegyptiaca*. According to the quotations in Josephus, his work contained some gross slanders against the Jews. In Lysimachus's account the Jews were descended from impious and diseased individuals who took refuge in the Egyptian temples. These were expelled from Egypt by King Bocchoris at the direction of the oracle of Ammon, though there is some confusion since the leprous and diseased individuals were also said to have been executed. Not knowing what to do in the wilderness, the Jews lit torches and called a fast. (Although the Sabbath is not explicitly mentioned, Lysimachus may be giving here a version of its origin.) The expelled people were led north by Moses, who set himself up as leader and counseled them to show no one good will but to offer misleading advice. When they came to an inhabited land, they plundered it, showing no mercy to the native peoples, and overthrew the altars and temples. Lysimachus's account differs considerably from that of Manetho, suggesting a different tradition. Whether Apion borrowed from him is uncertain.

2. one of three influential brothers in Jerusalem in the mid-second century B.C.E. The most important brother was Menelaus, who took over the priesthood from Jason about 172 B.C.E. Lysimachus was eventually attacked and killed by the people for selling Temple vessels.

maamad one of twenty-four delegations corresponding to the priestly watches in charge of the Temple cult in Jerusalem. There were twenty-four priestly watches in charge of the Temple, and for each watch there was a delegation in Jerusalem, made up of priests, Levites, and Israelites. When the time came for a watch to go to Jerusalem, its priests and Levites accompanied it to Jerusalem, and its Israelites gathered together in their towns and studied the story of the works of creation (i.e., Gen. 1:1–2:3) day by day.

Maarib the evening prayer service. Maarib may be recited from the time when three stars become visible in the sky through midnight. In a case of special need, it may be recited as late as the beginning of the morning (M. Berakhot 1:1). In the synagogue, the Maarib service usually follows the afternoon (Minhah) prayers. This avoids the need to reconvene the prayer quorum later in the evening.

Maarib begins with a statement of God's mercy (*vehu rahum*) and the usual call to public prayer (*borkhu*). The Shema service follows. The first of the two blessings before the Shema praises God for bringing on the evening (*maarib arabim*). The second refers to God's eternal love for the Israelite nation. The Shema itself follows, comprised as always of recitation of Deuteronomy 6:4–10 and 11:13–22 and Numbers 15:37–41. The benedictions following the Shema proclaim the truth of the historical claims of Judaism (*emet veemunah*) and, finally, request God's protection, both during the night and through life in general (*hashkibenu*). The Eighteen

Benedictions (Amidah) follow. In contrast to the rule for the morning and afternoon prayers, even when Maarib is recited by a prayer quorum, these benedictions are not repeated by the leader.

The title Maarib derives from the first of the blessings before the evening Shema. In the talmudic literature, this service is called Tefillat Arabit (evening prayer). Since there had been no evening offering in the Temple, talmudic authorities deemed the recitation of the Eighteen Benedictions in the evening to be voluntary. In place of these benedictions, they followed the evening Shema with a recitation of eighteen biblical verses mentioning God. Only after the talmudic period did the recitation of the Eighteen Benedictions in the evening become common custom. Maimonides notes that their recitation in fact is voluntary, but holds that through common practice, the recitation has taken on the status of an obligation.

maaser *see* TITHE

Maaserot (Heb., tithes) Mishnah tractate on tithes; the seventh tractate in the Mishnaic Division of Agriculture (Zeraim), concerned with defining the classes of produce that are subject to the separation of agricultural tithes and with determining (1) when, in the course of the crop's growth and ripening, tithes may be separated, and (2) when, in the subsequent harvesting and preparation of the produce, heave-offering and tithes must be paid. The tractate often is thought of as concerning in particular first tithe, which is separated by Israelite householders and given to Levites (Num.

18:20–24). But its issues are much broader, dealing in general with how produce becomes subject to agricultural offerings and discussing the appropriate times for the separation of first tithe, second tithe, and heave-offering.

The tractate's first chapter defines what produce is subject to tithes, details when produce may be tithed during its growth, and indicates when produce must be tithed after the harvest. Its theory is that food must be tithed once it is acquired by an individual for use in a normal meal. On the basis of this theory, chapters 2 and 3 discuss exceptional circumstances under which one may make a meal of untithed produce (e.g., by doing so casually or without preparing the food in the normal way). The conclusions of chapter 3 and chapter 4 concern opposite situations, in which, either by finally acquiring the produce (e.g., by bringing it into the home) or by starting to process the food, one renders it liable for tithes and completely unavailable for untithed consumption. Chapter 5 concludes the tractate with ambiguous cases, in which the processes that normally render food subject to tithing are not completed (e.g., if harvested produce is replanted) or in which other ambiguities occur (e.g., the sale or purchase of inedible produce).

Maaserot has its foundation in the notion, foreign to scripture, that produce is not invariably subject to the separation of agricultural offerings. Its point is that the claim of priests, Levites, and the poor, who were designated by God for a share of what grows upon the Land of Israel, is effective only upon food that Israelites purposely cultivate and then take for their own use in the meals that provide their sustenance. In Maaserot's view, the claim upon food of those designated by God is not automatic. It is triggered by Israelites' own exploitation of the land. This exploitation of what belongs to God brings with it the obligation to set aside the agricultural dues that recognize God's role in providing the land and allowing the food to grow in the first place.

maaser sheni (Heb.) second tithe, separated in the first, second, fourth, and fifth years of the Sabbatical cycle and brought to Jerusalem for consumption there

Maaser Sheni Mishnah tractate on the second tithe. The tractate discusses eating second tithe in Jerusalem and the prohibited uses of produce designated as second tithe (chaps. 1–2); transferring the status of second tithe to coins, to be brought in its stead to Jerusalem and used for the purchase of food to be eaten there (chaps. 2–4); and some special problems (chap. 5).

mabo *see* ALLEY

Maccabean Revolt Jewish military and political uprising from 167 to 164 B.C.E., in which Judas, surnamed Maccabeus (probably from the Hebrew word for "hammer"), played a prominent role. In the early second century B.C.E., the province of Judea was administered by the high priest Onias III under the oversight of a Seleucid governor (2 Macc. 3:1–5). By the late second century B.C.E., Judea was ruled by John Hyrcanus I, the son of Simon and nephew of Judas, who combined in his own person the roles of religious (high priest), military (commander), and political (ethnarch) leader. Through the Maccabean Revolt, the Jews went from being clients first of the Ptolemies and then of the Seleucids to being an independent political entity, tied by treaty with the Romans and the Spartans. They also extended their control over large parts of the Land of Israel and revitalized the national identity that had been submerged since the exile in the early sixth century B.C.E.

The major literary sources for the Maccabean revolt are the Book of Daniel, 1 Maccabees, and 2 Maccabees. Taken together, these works make it possible to trace the course of events through the whole period from 175 to 130 B.C.E. But these works accompany their historical facts with theological interpretations, thus complicating their use by modern historians. Daniel appears to have been put in final form before the revolt proper made much headway (about 166–165 B.C.E.). By its stories (contests and conflicts) and its visions, Daniel indicates how one Jewish group looked on the chief opponent, King Antiochus IV Epiphanes, and hoped that his arrogance would soon be broken by the coming of God's kingdom and vindication of Israel. 2 Maccabees provides valuable (if sometimes legendary) information about the struggles over the Jewish high priesthood and the relations between Judea and the Seleucids that led up to the revolt. It emphasizes God's care for the Jerusalem Temple and use of Judas Maccabeus as a divine instrument. 1 Maccabees carries the story from its beginning under Mattathias and Judas through Jonathan and Simon down to the accession of John Hyrcanus in 134 B.C.E. It so focuses on the exploits of the "Maccabee" family that it is sometimes described as dynastic propaganda.

The Maccabean Revolt had its roots in the division of Alexander the Great's empire around 300 B.C.E. Throughout the third century B.C.E., Judea was controlled and administered to a large extent by the Ptolemies of Egypt. But in 200 B.C.E. Jerusalem and Judea came under the political control of the Seleucids of Syria, represented by Antiochus III (r. 223–187 B.C.E.). Throughout the second century B.C.E., the Seleucid kingship moved back and forth among the descendants (or would-be descendants) of Antiochus III. The dynastic struggles among the Seleucids form the background for the major events in the Maccabean Revolt.

After the death of Seleucus III Philopator (r. 187–176 B.C.E.), Antiochus IV Epiphanes gained the Seleucid throne in 175 B.C.E. Soon thereafter, the Jewish high priest Onias III was replaced by his brother Jason, who outbid Onias for the office at the Seleucid court (2 Macc. 4:7–8). Jason in turn established Hellenistic institutions at Jerusalem and sought to make it into a Hellenistic city. In 172 B.C.E. Jason was outbid for the high priestly office by Menelaus, a person with no legitimate genealogical claim. By 167 B.C.E. Antiochus IV, with the cooperation of Menelaus, plundered the temple, founded a military garrison near the temple (the Akra), abolished the Torah as the Jewish law, and established a new order of worship at the Temple (probably the cult of Baal Shamem [lord of heaven]).

The involvement and motives of Antiochus IV remain matters of controversy. He surely had some supporters among the Jews (see 1 Macc. 1:10–15). Was he merely responding to their invitation? Or did he use such people for his own purposes? And what were those purposes? The ancient Jewish sources portray Antiochus as the implacable enemy of the Jewish people and their religion. But this portrayal does not fit with non-Jewish sources that attribute to Antiochus a lively interest in and tolerance for various religions and philosophies. Some modern scholars contend that Antiochus stumbled into a religious or socioeconomic civil war among several Jewish factions. Others argue that he wanted to develop the eastern equivalent of the nascent Roman Empire. Still others maintain that Antiochus's chief motive was economic; he needed money from any source to pay his army and thus keep himself in power.

The author of 1 Maccabees placed the beginning of the revolt in 166/165 B.C.E. at Modein, under the priest Mattathias and his five sons. The author of 2 Maccabees 8 (see also 5:27) attributed the leadership to Judas and said nothing about the Modein incident and little about the brothers of Judas. Some interpreters find in Daniel 11:34 a dismissive comment ("a little help") on the first stages of the uprising. Not all Israel supported Judas. There were Jewish supporters of the high priests Jason

and Menelaus, as well as Hasideans, strict Sabbath observers, and the "Daniel" circle of apocalyptists.

Judas and his followers had some early military successes against the Seleucid armies, probably due to their familiarity with the land and its people. Meanwhile, Antiochus turned his energies to a major military campaign in the eastern parts of his empire and issued a conditional amnesty in early 164 B.C.E. However, Judas continued his attacks. His success in capturing the Jerusalem Temple and restoring the traditional worship there in late 164 B.C.E. (the first Hanukkah) gave substance to his movement and the symbolic significance of representing Israel (see 1 Macc. 4:36–59; 2 Macc. 10:1–8). About the same time, Antiochus IV died of a mysterious disease in Tabae in ancient Persia.

Though the restoration of the Jerusalem Temple may have been the immediate goal of the Maccabean Revolt, the movement continued in large part because of Seleucid efforts under Antiochus V Eupator (r. 163–162 B.C.E.) and Demetrius I Soter (r. 162–150 B.C.E.) to keep Judea under Seleucid military and political control. Though Judas managed to defeat the Syrian general Nicanor in 161 B.C.E., he fell in battle in 160 B.C.E. at Elasa (1 Macc. 9:1–22). But before his death, Judas had sent an embassy to Rome to seek to establish a treaty uniting Judea and Rome against the Seleucids.

With Judas's death and the emergence of Alcimus as a claimant to the high priesthood, the Maccabean Revolt seemed finished around 159 B.C.E. But the sudden stroke and death of Alcimus left the high priesthood vacant between 159 and 152 B.C.E. Toward the end of that period, there was another Seleucid dynastic struggle, between Demetrius I (r. 162–150 B.C.E.) and Alexander Balas (r. 150–145 B.C.E.). Both needed allies, and Jonathan, who carried on the Maccabean movement after Judas's death, was one of the few substantive leaders left in Israel. Thus Jonathan became the object of a bidding war between the Seleucids and came away with the Jewish high priesthood, bestowed on him by Alexander Balas in 152 B.C.E. (see 1 Macc. 10:21). Though the Maccabees were a priestly family (see 1 Macc. 2:1), the priesthood should by right have remained among the descendants of Onias III. Nonetheless, in 1 Maccabees, Jonathan's accession is described without apology. In the next dynastic struggle between Alexander Balas and Demetrius II and the subsequent intervention of the Egyptian Ptolemy VI, Jonathan diplomatically played one side against the other and further solidified his power. Though Jonathan first took the side of Antiochus VI and his chief minister Trypho, he was taken prisoner by them and executed in 142 B.C.E.

Leadership of the Maccabean movement passed to Simon, the brother of Judas and Jonathan, in 142 B.C.E. Following Jonathan's example of diplomacy and military daring, Simon, between 142 and 134 B.C.E., further consolidated the dynasty's rule and made the territory of Judea into an independent territory. He reestablished the diplomatic initiatives with Rome and Sparta and was proclaimed by Jews in their documents and contracts from 142 B.C.E. onward as "the great high priest and commander and leader of the Jews" (1 Macc. 13:42, 14:41–43). He also began to mint his own coinage (1 Macc. 15:6).

One clear sign that the Maccabean Revolt had succeeded was the capture of the Seleucid citadel (the Akra) in Jerusalem by Simon in 141 B.C.E. This garrison had been founded in 168 B.C.E. by Antiochus IV (see 1 Macc. 1:36). It had remained in Seleucid hands all through the days of Judas and Jonathan. Only when Simon dissolved this garrison (see 1 Macc. 13:50) was Maccabean control of Jerusalem complete and the revolution successful.

Revolutions often carry within them the seeds of their own undoing. The concentration of power in the Maccabean dynasty was probably necessary if the revolt was to succeed. The result was that by Simon's time, all the religious, political, and military power was in the hands of one person and one family. And that family soon fell into the sort of dynastic struggles that plagued the Seleucids and Ptolemies. The assassination of Simon by his son-in-law in 134 B.C.E. set off a cycle that lasted through the Herods.

Another seed of destruction was the alliance with Rome. The Romans were eager to make treaties in the second century B.C.E., though slow to follow through on them unless it suited their own interests. Judas, Jonathan, and Simon could point to Rome as a powerful protector against the Seleucids and the Ptolemies. Rome, for its part, had in Judea a client state and a foothold in the Middle East. These two destructive forces came together in 63 B.C.E., when the Roman general Pompey intervened in a Maccabean family dispute about the legitimate successor to Queen Salome Alexandra. The Herod family eventually married into the Maccabean line and usurped the powers won so courageously, patiently, and shrewdly by the Maccabees.

The Maccabean Revolt is significant for many historical, literary, and theological reasons. At its start, Jews in Israel were clients of the Seleucid Empire; at its end they had achieved political independence, were living under their own native rulers, and had powerful allies. Whereas in the period from 167 to 164 B.C.E. Jews were in danger of cultural and religious extinction, by the time of Simon they had a form of religious life that was both traditional (focused on the Torah and the Temple) and adapted to the realities of the Graeco-Roman world.

The events connected with the Maccabean Revolt seem to have inspired literary creativity, expressed in various forms: the apocalypse (Daniel, an early version of the Testament of Moses), history (1–2 Maccabees), the religious novel (Judith), and the biblical commentary (the Habakkuk Pesher). Indeed, the Qumran sect seems to have taken shape among Jewish religious dissidents who opposed the Maccabean movement for usurping the high priesthood. Their chief enemy, "the Wicked Priest," may have been Jonathan or Simon.

The chief figures of the Maccabean Revolt—Mattathias, Judas, Jonathan, and Simon—have functioned among both Jews and Christians as models for rebels against unjust governments, guerrilla warriors, and practical men of action skilled in the art of diplomacy. The martyrs described in 2 Maccabees—especially the mother and her seven sons (chap. 7)—have inspired both Jews and Christians to hold firm to their principles in the face of torture and death and to go to their death convinced that in the resurrection they will be vindicated and their tormentors will be brought to divine justice.

Maccabee popular name for Judas, son of Mattathias, who led the successful military uprising against Antiochus Epiphanes from 167 to 164 B.C.E. The name is probably from the Hebrew *makebet* (1 Kings 6:7), meaning "hammer," or *makban* meaning a "hammer-shaped" head (M. Bekhorot 7:1). Thus the epithet could refer to his appearance or his prowess in battle. Judas's family and followers became known as "the Maccabees." *See also* JUDAS MACCABEUS; MACCABEAN REVOLT.

1 Maccabees a narration of the events beginning with the accession to power by Antiochus IV Epiphanes to the Seleucid throne in 175 B.C.E. and ending with the death of Simon, one of the leaders of the revolt against the Seleucids, in 134 B.C.E. The book is written in a straightforward narrative style, combined with some poetic passages (e.g., 1:36–40, 3:3–9, 14:4–15). Its style is reminiscent of the Bible's historical books; for example, Mattathias's action against apostate Jews (1 Macc. 2:23–27) is modeled on that of Phinehas in Numbers 25:6–13; the Hasmonean leaders of the revolt are described as the judges had been depicted in ancient Israel, and their enemies are characterized in terms drawn from Deuteronomy 13:12–15. The author uses biblical imagery to portray the Hasmoneans as upholders of the ancestral faith. Although the book is now extant only in Greek, most scholars hold that it was composed in Hebrew, and this use of the ancestral language is another way in which the Hasmoneans are portrayed as preservers of tradition. The question of when the author of 1 Maccabees wrote the book is still being debated, although the book's friendly attitude toward the Romans (1 Macc. 8) would seem to exclude it from having a date after the invasion of Jerusalem under Pompey the Great (63 B.C.E.), and its concluding reference to a chronicle of the acts of John Hyrcanus I (1 Macc. 16:23–24) would suggest that his reign was over, or nearly so, when the book was written. The author probably finished his work late in the reign of John Hyrcanus I (135/134–104) or early in the reign of Alexander Jannaeus (103–76 B.C.E.).

The book's initial prologue (1:1–10) provides a setting for the narrative in the time after Alexander the Great, who is depicted as an arrogant ruler demanding tribute. Alexander's early death hints at what will happen to Alexander's arrogant successor, Antiochus IV. Then comes a description of the apostasy of base Jews (1:11–15) and the punishment that follows as Antiochus IV invades the land. A clear dichotomy is set up between loyal Jews who wish to maintain their ancestral traditions and others who wish to homogenize all nations in obedience to Antiochus IV, who has said that he wishes to abolish all particular national customs (1 Macc. 1:41–43). Laws concerning Temple sacrificial rites, kosher laws, and the law of circumcision are singled out for abrogation (1 Macc. 1:44–61). The rest of the book's narrative deals with the successful revolt of Mattathias and his five sons. First the exploits of Mattathias are narrated (2:1–70), followed by those of his successor Judas (3:1–9:27), Jonathan (9:28–12:53), and Simon (13:1–16:24). While Judas is heroic, one can see how the revolt would have been unsuccessful if the whole weight of the Seleucid forces had been concentrated against it. However, Jonathan was skillfully able to exploit the bickering between rival claimants to the Seleucid throne after the death of Antiochus IV. When finally captured, Jonathan is said to have had at least 40,000 men under his command (1 Macc. 12:41). He had rebuilt the walls of Jerusalem (1 Macc. 12:35–38) and he held the position of high priest (1 Macc. 10:21). The success of

Jonathan's policy is seen in the reign of Simon, which is described in almost messianic terms (1 Macc. 14:4–15). Despite all this praise, Simon dies an ignominious death, assassinated while drunk (1 Macc. 16:16).

The author of 1 Maccabees, steeped in his tradition, is an enthusiastic supporter of the war of liberation. He clearly supports the Hasmoneans: they were the family chosen to save Israel (1 Macc. 5:62).

2 Maccabees as now found, a composite work in which two letters are prefixed to an epitome of a five-volume history by an otherwise unknown, Jason of Cyrene. The first letter (1:19) is a festal letter addressed by the Jews of Judea to the Jews in Egypt in 124 B.C.E. After offering a long prayer for the well-being of the addressees, the senders refer to a previous letter of the year 143 and then invite the Egyptian Jews to celebrate the Day of Tabernacles in the month of Kislev. The second letter (1:10–2:18) bears no date, but claims to have Judas Maccabeus as one of its senders and, if authentic, would have been written in 164 B.C.E. The contents of this letter are intriguing. First comes an account of Antiochus IV's death that differs from the one found in 2 Maccabees 9, for in the letter's account, Antiochus IV dies as he attempts to rob the temple of Nanara at Elymeus. 2 Macc. 1:18 begins a series of narratives grouped around the theme of fire. The first narrative (1:19–36) stresses the continuity between the First Temple and the Second, as Nehemiah is said to recover in liquid form the sacred fire of the First Temple, which had been hidden. The second narrative (2:1–8) specifies that it was the prophet Jeremiah who ordered the fire to be hidden. However, the sacred vessels of the First Temple are to remain hidden until God gathers his people, when the cloud of the glory of the Lord will be seen as in the time of Moses and Solomon. All these stories are said to be recorded in the official records of Nehemiah, and alongside his activity is placed Judas Maccabeus's collection of the books of Judaism. Placing all these traditions together enhances the traditional character of the new festival in Kislev, conceived as a festival of fire, which was to be the Festival of Hanukkah.

The epitome begins in verse 2:19. At times—the quick succession of events in 13:23–26 and 14:25 and the mention of characters without any introduction, for example—one can see that the narrative is condensed. Most of the narrative, however, is written in the stylistic conventions of Hellenistic historiographers: the author has a particular penchant for emotional descriptions, epiphanies of divine helpers, and digressions from the narrative when the author speaks in the first person (5:17–20 and 6:12–17). The narrative itself spans the period from the reign of Seleucid IV (187–175) to the defeat of Nicanor, the Seleucid governor, in 161 B.C.E. It stops before the death of Judas Maccabeus and gives more attention to the events leading up to the Maccabean Revolt than does 1 Maccabees. The narrative is structured into three acts, which are all concerned with a threat to the Temple and its miraculous deliverance. The story in 3:1–40, the first act, is patterned after many stories in which a deity defends his or her temple from attack. Each of the other two acts (4:1–10:9, 10:10–15:37) ends with a decree, told in almost formulaic language, that a festival is to be celebrated every year to commemorate the victory wrought by God. The first festival is the Feast of Purification, that is, Hanukkah; the second is the Feast of Nicanor on the day before Mordecai's Day (Purim). Thus the author's concern is primarily with the Temple rather than with the Hasmonean family, for although Judas Maccabeus is certainly depicted as a hero, not all of his family is. That emphasis also helps explain why the author ends the book with the statement that, after Nicanor's defeat, the city has been in the possession of the Jews (15.37), whereas, in fact, just a year later, Judas has been killed and his army routed. The epitomist worries about threats to the Temple and its worship, not about political control. When and where the epitome was written is much debated.

3 Maccabees   a narrative of the miraculous deliverance of the Jews in Egypt set in the time of Ptolemy IV Philopator, king of Egypt (r. 221–204 B.C.E.). Written in a Greek of rich and varied vocabulary and abounding in rhetorical embellishments, the work also reveals (6:6) the author's awareness of the Greek additions to the Book of Daniel; the work also contains verbatim parallels to the Greek additions to the Book of Esther, and the punishment inflicted on Ptolemy (2:21–24) resembles that given to Heliodorus in 2 Maccabees 3:22–31. These correspondences as well as its author's focus on Egyptian themes suggest that 3 Maccabees should be dated from the early part of the first century B.C.E. and that it was possibly written in Alexandria.

The narrative opens abruptly, as though something is missing, in the midst of another narrative about the battle between the Seleucids and the Ptolemies at Raphia in 217 B.C.E. Ptolemy IV Philopator is saved by a Jew—Dositheus—from an assassination plot. When the king wins the day at Raphia, he sets out to visit his territories, including

Jerusalem. He arrogantly wants to enter the Holy of Holies but is rebuffed and divinely punished. Ptolemy vows revenge and returns to Egypt to enslave the Jews unless they participate in the cult of Dionysos, for which they would receive Alexandrian citizenship. In the second half of the book (chaps. 3–7), the narrative describes the refusal of most of the Jews to worship Dionysos and their persecution and divine deliverance. The story is similar to one told by Josephus (*Ag. Apion* 2:53–56) but set by him in the time of Ptolemy VIII Euergetes (r. 145–117 B.C.E.). Although 3 Maccabees emphasizes the differences between Jews and Gentiles and gives examples of accusations made against the Jews of their exclusivism and misanthropy, the book's author insists the Jews are good citizens. The narrative ends with the Jews executing apostates (7:14) and celebrating a festival of deliverance.

4 Maccabees   a philosophic discourse reflecting on the stories of the martyrs in 2 Maccabees 6–7. The author sets out to show that devout reason can master the passions. He writes with the skill of a trained rhetorician and also evidences knowledge of an eclectic blend of Platonic and Stoic philosophy. He lists the four cardinal virtues of prudence, temperance, justice, and courage (1:3–4). But the author is also a loyal Jew, faithful to his ancestral traditions, and he argues that the reason that can master the passions is the reason guided by the law: "To the intellect [God] gave the law, and if a man lives his life by the law, he shall reign over a kingdom that is temperate and just and good and brave" [2:23].

This emphasis on the law is evident in the discussion between Eleazar and King Antiochus. Eleazar, now called a distinguished philosopher (5:4, 35), holds against the Stoics that reason does not eradicate the passions but rather controls them (5:43). Antiochus cannot understand Eleazar's reluctance to eat swine's flesh and calls Eleazar's a preposterous philosophy, full of nonsensical calculations (5:11). In contrast, Eleazar sees true philosophy as reason guided by the law, since God is both creator of the world and the giver of the law (5:25). The author thus sets out to show how religious reason governed by the law controlled the passions that would have led the martyrs to violate the law. He first illustrates his thesis with a number of examples from biblical history (1:30b–3:18) and then quickly summarizes the events narrated in 2 Maccabees 3–5, being even more critical than the author of 2 Maccabees was toward Jason, the high priest.

The author describes, sometimes in graphic detail, the martyrdoms of Eleazar (5–7), the seven brothers (8–14:10), and the mother (14:11–17:6). All of these martyrs demonstrate the author's main thesis, particularly the mother, who shows how devout reason can triumph over even the deepest emotion of mother love. She is described as truly a daughter of Abraham, who was willing to sacrifice his son Isaac (Gen. 21). Her keen sense of wishing to avoid defilement is shown by her throwing herself into the fire so that no one would touch her body (17:1). The author intensifies the notion that the martyrs' deaths brought about God's mercy (18:4–5), using particularly the notions of purification and expiation for sin (6:28–29, 17:19–22).

4 Maccabees was most probably written in 19–54 C.E., since the book describes Apollonius as governor of Syria, Phoenicia, and Cilicia (4:2), and Roman sources suggest that Syria-Cilicia constituted one province only during this time. It has been proposed that the author composed the book in Antioch, but any large Greek city would have been as plausible a location for its writing.

Macedonians inhabitants of Macedonia, an area north of Thessaly and west of Chachidice and Thrace. They were of mixed tribes, which gradually became Hellenized. Macedonia was the frontier between Greeks and other tribes. Macedonian power reached its zenith in the fourth century B.C.E., when Philip of Macedon conquered Greece and then his son, Alexander the Great, conquered all of the Middle East.

Macrinus, Marcus Opellius (c. 164–218 C.E.) Roman emperor (r. 217–218 C.E.). Born in Africa, he was the first Roman emperor who was not a senator. A Praetorian prefect under Caracalla, he arranged for the emperor's assassination. In the spring of 217 he invaded Mesopotamia but was defeated by Ardavan V at Nisibis. The emperor sued for peace, bringing an end to Caracalla's Parthian war. Macrinus gave expensive gifts to the Parthian nobles and reported to the Senate that the peace was really a victory for Rome. He angered the army by cutting their pay and leaving the European legions in Syria. In 218 Bassianus was named emperor. Macrinus was defeated near Antioch and put to death.

Madeba town south of Heshbon, east of the Dead Sea, assigned along with the plain on which it is situated to the tribe of Reuben (Josh. 13:9, 16). During the Maccabean period, it was home to the band of robbers that murdered John, the brother of Simon and Jonathan Maccabee (1 Macc. 9:35–42). Later, it was captured by John Hyrcanus and Alexander Jannaeus (Josephus, *Ant.* 8:1ff.).

Magdala town on the western shore of the Sea of Galilee about 5 kilometers north of Tiberias. Its name in Aramaic was Magdala (tower), but in Greek sources it is called Taricheae (salted or pickled fish). The latter reveals its principal industry. Magdala is the traditional city of origin of Mary Magdalene in the New Testament (Matt. 27:56). The emperor Nero gave the city to the Jewish king Herod Agrippa II (*Ant.* 20.159). It played a role in the First Revolt against Rome. Josephus claims to have made it a military base for his resistance to Rome and to have fortified the city (*Ant.* 5.96f; *Vita* 156). The Romans successfully besieged the city and amassed the Jewish captives in its stadium. After the death of Herod Agrippa, the city reverted to the province of Judea.

This may be the same town as Migdal Nunayah (tower of fishermen) in ancient Jewish sources. Archaeological excavation has unearthed the Roman city with a major paved street running north and south and at least one cross street. At the southeast corner of the intersection stands the low ruins of what the excavators believe to be a first-century-C.E. synagogue or prayer hall. This building has a set of benches across the north, narrow side. Worshipers would evidently enter a doorway on that side and walk down to the interior space. Small columns supported the roof, and heart-shaped or double columns stood at the corners of the columnation. Only about twenty-five people could stand comfortably in the space within the columns. After the First Revolt the synagogue was converted into a fish pond. In the fifth century C.E., a Byzantine monastery was built here, but evidently was destroyed by the Arab conquest of 640 C.E.

magen david *see* STAR, SIX-POINTED, REPRESENTATION OF

Maghariya (Heb., men of caves) Jewish sect, described by Joseph al-Kirkisani as founded in the first century B.C.E. He reports that its members kept their books in caves, prohibited games, and possessed unusual commentaries on the Hebrew scriptures. The group believed that God is too transcendent to mingle with matter; therefore, its members rejected the notion that God was directly responsible for the Creation. They believed instead that the world was created by an intermediary angel, invented by God and, after the Creation, continuing to represent God in the world. On the basis of the group's name, date, theory of Creation, and the fact that al-Kirkisani does not include the Essenes on his list of sects, some scholars have equated the Maghariya with the Essenes.

magi Iranian religious leaders. Originally a tribe consecrated to the service of their deity, they became a hereditary priestly caste who controlled the state religion in whatever form it might assume. They probably expanded Zarathustra's teachings and incorporated the worship of Mithra, the god of light, and Anathita, the goddess of water and the moon, into Zoroastrianism. Agathias wrote that only those things of which the magus approves are considered lawful by the Persians. The magi performed priestly rites at the fire temples, legalized marriages, dominated law and culture, presided over legal disputes, taught basic reading, writing, and mathematical skills to the population, and provided ethical guidance to the Persians. The magi were governed by their own laws and customs. Ardashir I reorganized the magi's vast bureaucracy. The magus (the singular form of magi) was under the authority of the *herpat,* the chief of fire, and the *mobad,* the chief magus. The *herpatan herpat,* chief justice, and the *mobadan mobad,* high priest, were at the top of the hierarchical structure. With this reform, the magi became virtual state officials. Ardashir wished to convert all the people in his empire to the Mazdean religion, and the magi vigorously opposed other religions and allegedly imprisoned those who opposed the true faith, executing those who refused to confess the errors of their wrong beliefs. Under Shapur the situation changed radically, for he prohibited the persecution of minority cults and specifically encouraged Mani (the founder of Manichaeism) to create a syncretistic doctrine that would incorporate elements from Christianity, Buddhism, and Zoroastrianism. Kartir reversed Shapur's policy, executed Mani, and established fire temples in non-Iranian lands. However, Kartir's policies seem to be the exception. Rab argued that any Jew who learns even a single matter from the magi deserves death, because their teachings are blasphemy. Samuel argued that the magi were mere sorcerers.

magic a technique by which individuals who possess secret information can accomplish what they desire through the proper use of certain natural objects or the reciting of certain secret formulas. These techniques force the gods or natural powers to act for either the good of the one who initiated the action or the harm of that person's enemy or opponent. Ancient historians, such as the fifth-century-B.C.E. Greek writer Herodotus, traced the origins of magic to Persia, where one of the six native tribes was called the *magoi,* or magi, which developed and refined these methods of control over the natural order and over the behavior of others.

However, evidence for magicians or sorcerers goes back to the law of Moses, as reported in Exodus 22, Leviticus 19–20, and Deuteronomy 18, and includes direct mention of Egyptian magicians (Exod. 9:11). Although the dates of these magical traditions cannot be determined with certainty, they seem to reflect the situation faced by Israel after it began settling in the land of Canaan in the twelfth century B.C.E. By the fifth/fourth century B.C.E., magic had infiltrated Greece and was also a significant factor in Israel.

The most complete evidence of magical practices dates from the first-century-B.C.E. Egyptian manuscripts known to scholars as the Greek Magical Papyri. Written on writing material made from reeds (papyrus), they give details of the techniques and aims of magicians. In his extensive *Natural History* (30.6), the first-century-C.E. Greek author Pliny is ambivalent about magic but admits that it does work in a range of circumstances. Two examples he gives are the uses of human saliva as a safeguard against snakes and of female menstrual fluid to drive away hailstorms and whirlwinds (28).

In the Torah, there are direct warnings (Deut. 18:9–11) against consulting or having dealings with augurs (who could foresee the future), sorcerers (who had secret powers), charmers (who could cause harm or provide protection for clients), mediums (who communicated with the spirits of the dead), wizards (who performed extraordinary deeds), and necromancers (who predicted the future by consulting the dead). The people of Israel are not to rely on such magicians but should depend solely on God for their preservation in the present and the future. God's people are neither to practice augury or witchcraft nor to consult those who do (Lev. 19:26–31). Those who claim the ability to exploit these magical powers perform all sorts of stunts in the foolish hope that these will increase their magical powers: trimming their beard or the hair around their temples in a special way; making gashes on their bodies or having themselves tatooed. Those who practice magic or rely on those who do will find that God has "set his face against them" (Lev. 20:6). Men or women who become wizards or mediums are to be stoned to death (Lev. 20:27), and female sorcerers are not to be permitted to live (Exod. 22:17–18).

As explicit as the law is, when Israel's first king, Saul, is confronted by the armies of the Philistines (1 Sam. 28), he consults a female medium (or witch) and has her call up from the dead Samuel, who had guided the life of Israel and arranged for Saul's installation as king. Instead of advising Saul on how to withstand the Philistines' attack, Samuel tells Saul that the king and his army will be defeated.

The warning against consulting the spirits of the dead or false prophets is found in the prophetic books. Isaiah 8:19 reminds Israel that God is the only one whom it should consult, instead of "the mediums and the wizards who chirp and mutter." God himself will give his people "signs and portents," so that if they have God-given insight, they and their leaders will know what God expects of them and has in store for them. Ezekiel's condemnation (Ezek. 22:25–29) of the wicked city of Jerusalem and its misguided and disobedient leaders, both princes and priests, mentions their having consulted false prophets who mimic magicians by smearing themselves with whitewash and communicating false visions and predictions. The prophet Malachi, after describing the messenger who will come to prepare the way of the Lord and to purify God's people (Mal. 3:1–4), says that when God appears in order to judge his people, the first group that will be exposed and denounced are the "sorcerers." In 1 Enoch 7–8, the fallen angels who take human wives teach them "magical medicine, incantations, astrology" and the reading of the stars.

Sepher-ha-Razim (The Book of Mysteries) claims to be a collection of secret material that an angel gave to Noah as he was boarding the ark. Its contents assume the signs of the zodiac and the astrological secrets thought to control human destiny. A plausible date for this book's origin is the late third or early fourth century C.E. The pervasive influence of Graeco-Roman culture throughout the work is obvious. Prayers included in this material are offered not only to YHWH but to Helios (the Greek god of the sun), Hermes (the Greek messenger of the gods), and Aphrodite (the Greek goddess of love). The names of scores of angels are given who, at specified times of the year and in each of the seven firmaments or levels of the universe, may be called upon for help in relieving needs or in solving problems. The cure of a headache or the overcoming of a spirit causing blindness is as follows: take the fat that covers the brain of a black ox . . . write on it the names of these angels [in the second firmament] and place it in a silver tubular case, then bind the tube with seven colors and place it next to where the pain is. To be sure of effective results, one must abstain from meat, from wine, from contact with the dead or menstruating women, and from every unclean thing (2.180–185). This document clearly embodies a mix of factors: belief in the divine order of creation, the obligation to obey the law of Moses, and the conviction that hostile powers at work in the universe can be brought under control by the proper techniques. All of these are regarded as wholly compatible with trust in YHWH as creator and sustainer of the world.

Rabbinic Judaism condemned magic as one of the "ways of the Amorites" (M. Shabbat 6:10) and sanctioned its practitioners to death by stoning (M. Sanhedrin 7:7). One who so much as whispered over a wound the words of Exodus 15:26 ("I will put none of the diseases upon you that I have put on the Egyptians, for I am the Lord who heals you") was held to lose his place in the world to come (M. Sanhedrin 10:1). To quell magical practices, Simeon b. Shetah is said to have hung eighty witches on a single day (M. Sanhedrin 6:4).

Despite these severe admonitions against magic, the rabbinic literature depicts without condemnation both rabbis and common people who performed magical acts. A number of these instances are reported in B. Sanhedrin 67b–68a, which distinguishes an actual magical act, punishable by stoning, from an illusion, which is forbidden but exempt from punishment. The Talmud reports that every Friday afternoon rabbis Hanina and Oshaya would study the laws of creation and make for themselves a third-grown calf, which they would eat. Ashi knew of a person who could produce ribbons of silk from his nostrils. Yannai is said to have been given a drink that, when spilled out, turned into scorpions. He repaid the innkeeper with a potion that turned her into an ass, which he mounted and road in the market place until her girlfriend nullified the charm. Hiyya speaks of an Arab who chopped up a camel and, by ringing a bell, caused it to come together again. Eliezer states that he taught Akiba how to cause an entire field of cucumbers to grow and then to be harvested simply by saying a few words. These reports of magic performed by rabbis, common Jews, and non-Jews suggest that despite the biblical and rabbinic prohibitions, the use of magic within the general culture of the talmudic period had a significant impact upon Jewish society, which largely accepted such practices and deemed them appropriate methods of protecting people from harm or of accomplishing legitimate purposes.

magic bowl pottery bowl on which was written a magical formula used to drive away evil spirits or to invoke the help of a deity in preserving and protecting individuals or a family. During the talmudic period, roughly 300–600 C.E., such bowls were in common use in Babylonia by Christians, Mazdeans, Mandeans, and Jews. Bowls in use in Jewish homes often were prepared by Jews who were not involved with or representative of the rabbinical academies. At the same time, certain rabbinical figures were deemed potent in driving away particular demons and hence appear with frequency on these bowls. This indicates the extent to which the Talmudic image of the rabbi as a wonder-working holy man entered the popular culture of the day.

The formulas used on magic bowls and the deities invoked are common across religious traditions. The bowls apparently were prepared by professionals, for instance, by Jews for both Jewish and non-Jewish use. A particular practitioner would be hired to produce a bowl not because of his denomination but because of his reputation for success. Accordingly, while certain references signify the religious origin of a bowl (e.g., mention of the rabbi Joshua b. Perahia suggests a Jewish origin, while reference to Jesus the Messiah indicates a Christian context), for the most part identification depends upon the script in which the incantation was prepared: Aramaic letters are Jewish, Syriac script indicates a Christian source, and Mandean lettering suggests a Mandean origin.

The majority of extant magic bowls were found during excavations in Nippur in 1888 and 1889. They were found upside down in the ruins of houses, with one or more bowls found in almost every house as well as in cemeteries (where they apparently served to lay ghosts to rest). The bowls were used by individuals and families seeking protection for houses and property, for example, cattle, often with a particular concern for domestic sexual life and unborn babies. Lilis and Lilith, who personify sexual abnormality, prey upon women and children, and produce offspring with human beings, are common targets of the bowls.

The chief element of the bowls is an incantation composed of repeating phrases, words, or syllables believed to have the power to bind favorable powers or demons to some designated action. Angels, on Jewish bowls, and deities, on pagan ones, frequently are adduced, and there appears to have been an attempt to use as many names as possible. The spell's main power, however, derived from terminology declaring that the demon had been rendered unable to exercise its control, for instance, that it had been "bound, sealed, countersealed, exorcised, hobbled, and silenced." The separation of a Lilith from her victim often is expressed in terms of a writ of divorce.

The incantations generally begin with an invoca-

tion, followed by the name of the client or clients, the categories of demons to be purged, the names of the angels or deities in which the spells are pronounced, and a conclusion. Jewish texts frequently refer to the angels Michael, Gabriel, and Raphael. The name YHWH also occurs, often broken down into individual, repeated letters or syllables.

Magnesia, Battle of After rejecting a treaty with the Romans that would have meant giving up any claim to Thrace, Antiochus III invaded Greece in 192 B.C.E. He was driven off and pursued by Roman legions and allies. He was defeated by the Roman forces at Magnesia, in western Asia Minor between Pergamum and Ephesus, in 190 B.C.E. and was forced to accept harsh terms at Apamea in 188 B.C.E. *See also* APAMEA, PEACE OF.

magnify God *see* GLORIFY, MAGNIFY, SANCTIFY GOD

Magog *see* GOG AND MAGOG

Mah Nishtannah (Heb., how is this night different from all others?) opening words of four questions asked by the youngest person present at the Passover Seder

maḥor (pl., *maḥorim*) liturgical handbook that contains scripture readings for festivals. Some of these handbooks—Maḥor Vitry and the Worms Maḥor, for instance—contain pentateuchal readings for the seventh day of Passover (Exod. 13:17–15:26, the Song at the Sea) and the first day of Shabot (Exod. 19–20, the Giving of the Ten Commandments). These two *maḥorim* also include a targum that is similar to the Fragmentary Targum of Paris. The expansive material paralleling the Paris Targum derives from the Palestinian Targums to the Pentateuch, while the nonexpansive verses in the *maḥorim* derive from Targum Onkelos.

Maḥoz town in the coastal area in Samaria, referred to at M. Arakhin 3:2 as "the sand-plains of Maḥoz," contrasted with the lush gardens of Sebaste

Maḥoza town on the outskirts of Be-Ardashir and Ctesiphon, on the Nahar Malka, a canal that connects the Euphrates with the Tigris River. Situated on a caravan trading route, the Jews of Maḥoza reportedly were successful merchants (B. Baba Batra 29b; B. Gittin 6a). After the destruction of Nehardea (259 C.E.), Maḥoza became a center of rabbinic study. Upon Abayye's death (338 C.E.), the academy at Pumbedita and its scholars relocated to Maḥoza, where they worked under the leadership of Raba from 338 through 352 C.E. The city was populated by many Jews (B. Yoma 11a) and proselytes (B. Kiddushin 73a). With Julian's invasion in 363 C.E., Maḥoza was destroyed; the town was rebuilt after the Roman withdrawal. By the middle of the fifth century C.E., the growth of Nestorian Christianity had diminished its Jewish character and significance.

maiestas (Lat., a type of treason, especially against the Roman emperor) An accusation of *maiestas* was a useful way of getting rid of an enemy. There were a number of such trials under Tiberias, Caligula, Claudius, Nero, and Domitian, though in many cases the emperor himself did not encourage such denunciations.

Makhshirin Mishnah tractate devoted to elucidation of conditions set forth in Leviticus 11:34, 37 for susceptibility to uncleanness of produce. Produce is susceptible to uncleanness when harvested and then deliberately watered. The tractate discusses the issue of intentionality in watering the produce (chap. 1); water that is capable of imparting susceptibility mixed with water that is not (chap. 2); absorption of water (chap. 3); water that serves one purpose and status as to a secondary purpose (chaps. 3–5); the rule that liquids not used intentionally do not impart susceptibility (chap. 5); and liquids that can impart susceptibility to uncleanness (chap. 6).

Makkot Mishnah tractate devoted to those punishable by flogging for perjury (chap. 1), the penalty of exile and those who are subject to it (chap. 2), and others penalized by flogging and how the penalty of flogging is administered (chap. 3). Both Talmuds devote important and lengthy expositions to this tractate.

Makom (Heb., place) with the definite article, a designation for God, signifying omnipresence. Genesis Rabbah 68 explains the usage as follows: "Why is the name of the Holy One, blessed be He, changed and represented as 'the Place'? Because He is the place in which his world exists." *See also* GOD, NAMES OF.

Malachi, Targum to *see* TARGUM TO THE PROPHETS

malakh haMavet *see* ANGEL OF DEATH

Malalas, John (491–578 C.E.) Greek rhetorician and historian. The name Malalas means "rhetor" in Syriac. He wrote a universal chronicle covering the creation of the world to 565 C.E. Antioch is the focus of all but the end of book 18, which focuses on Constantinople. He is the only historian who speaks of an anti-Jewish riot in Antioch in 486. He states that after the war of 67–73, a theater was built in the suburbs of Daphne out of the proceeds of the booty from Judea. He is a source for the Samaritan revolt in Palestine in 529.

Malkhuyot *see* SOVEREIGNTY VERSES

mammon (Aram.: *mamona*) wealth or profit. The Greek transliteration of the word occurs four times in the Gospels, always with a negative connotation. Matthew 6:24 and Luke 16:13 (through different contexts) personify mammon as a god whose worship excludes worship of the true God. The story of the unjust steward appeals to the rich to give away their "unrighteous mammon" (i.e., ill-gotten riches) in order to gain heaven (Luke 16:1–11). In 1 Enoch 63:10, the kings and the mighty complain that their ill-gotten riches cannot save them from damnation. The word carries the same connotations in some rabbinic texts (Tg. Gen. 13:13; B. Ber. 61b). *See also* WEALTH.

mamzer (Heb.) in rabbinic law, the offspring of individuals unable to contract a legal marriage, in particular because it would be incestuous (Lev. 18). A *mamzer* is forbidden to marry an Israelite of unimpaired status. He or she may only marry another *mamzer* or a proselyte. The child of parents who are genealogically free to marry is never deemed a *mamzer*. Despite common usage, the term therefore cannot be translated as "bastard." The latter term, which has no rabbinic parallel, appears, for example, at Enoch 10:9, where it refers to the giants born of the heavenly watchers and mortal women. *See also* ADULTERY.

Mana *see* MANI I B. TANḤUM; MANI II B. YONA

Manasseh king of Judah (c. 687–642 B.C.E.). Manasseh is notorious in the biblical histories for instituting idolatrous cults (2 Kings 21:1–9; 2 Chron. 33:1–9) and inciting God's decree to destroy Jerusalem (1 Kings 21:10–15). Manasseh's sins and his responsibility for the events of 587 B.C.E. are recalled in 1 Enoch 89:53–58, 2 Baruch 64:1–6, and Apocalypse of Abraham 25:2 (cf. 2 Kings 21:6), and the chronologies in 1 Enoch 85–90 and Daniel 9 are keyed to the date of Manasseh's sin. The Martyrdom of Isaiah elaborates on 2 Kings 21:16 (he shed much innocent blood), while the apocryphal Prayer of Manasseh alleges to be the king's confession of sin described in 2 Chronicles 33:10–13.

Manasseh, Prayer of a penitential prayer ascribed to the seventh-century king of Judah. According to 2 Chronicles 33:10–17, the Assyrians took the apostate king into captivity in Babylon, where he prayed to God, who restored him to the throne. Different from the formal liturgical prayers in Daniel 9 and 1 Baruch 1–3, the Prayer of Manasseh does not employ the stereotyped language of Deuteronomy and Jeremiah, but makes numerous allusions to 2 Chronicles 33:1–13. Its viewpoint is personal rather than national, with an emphasis on the sincerity and internal sources of Manasseh's repentance. God's creative power is juxtaposed with God's covenant mercy, and different from texts that contrast the fate of the righteous and the sinners, the prayer has parallel addresses to "Lord, the God of the righteous forebears" (v. 1) and to "Lord, the God of those who repent" (v. 13). Manasseh concludes (v. 15) by acknowledging that "the host of heaven," before whom he had prostrated (2 Chron. 33:3), praise the God to whom he now "bends the knee" of his heart (v. 11). The prayer is of uncertain origin and date. It is included in two early Christian handbooks, the third-century Didascalia (2:22), and the fourth-century Apostolic Constitutions (2:22), where it is incorporated in an expanded, legendary version of 2 Chronicles 33. It is Ode 13 in the collection appended to the Book of Psalms in manuscripts of the Greek Bible. *See also* MANASSEH.

Mandaeans literally, knowers (*mandayi*); a baptist sect of southern Mesopotamia (present-day southern Iraq and southwestern Iran), the product of Jewish, Zoroastrian, and Gnostic influences on the indigenous religious traditions of the region. Mandaeans possess a complex literary tradition (written in a unique Eastern Aramaic dialect and script), dating in part back to the third century C.E., as well as a distinct married priestly class called the *nasuraiyi* (guardians).

The Mandaeans believe in a world of light and a world of darkness, eternally distinct and mutually hostile, ruled by abstract beings called the Great Alien Life and the Lord of Darkness, respectively. Our world (Tibil) occupies an intermediate zone, and was imperfectly crafted by the demiurge Ptahil, who was himself the mixed offspring of the worlds of light and darkness. The human spirit (from the world of light) abandons the body (from the world of darkness) at death, and eventually obtains unity with its soul-double (*nishimta*), which dwells in an interim paradise called Mshunia Kushta. The Mandaeans call upon many divine beings, never reduced to an ordered system, who operate on behalf of the Great Alien Life and the world of light. These include (1) Hibil Ziwa (Abel the Splendor), the savior spirit, whose descent into and reascent from the underworld forms the paradigm for Mandaean rites of purification and ascent; (2) Shitil Taba (Seth the Good), the archetype of human goodness and purity; (3) Anosh Uthra (Enosh the Angel), the patron of *nasirutha* (sacred knowledge), healer and guide to believers, and their rescuer in times of persecution; and (4) Manda dHaiya (Knowledge of Life), the "father" of Mandaeans and embodiment of their identity and aspirations (which are opposed at every step by the female evil spirit Ruha).

Mandaean rituals take place in compounds consisting of a specially constructed hut (*bit manda*) beside a baptismal pool (*yardna*), which is connected by a canal to a nearby river (stagnant water is considered impure). The all-important rites of baptism are arranged in an ascending order of complexity and power, culminating in the *masbuta,* which involves immersions, anointings, and further purifying acts, punctuated at points by the distinctive Mandaean handshake (*kushta*). The Mandaeans also frequently hold a special meal on behalf of the dead, called a *masiqta* (ascent). Commonly performed on the first, third, seventh, and forty-fifth days after a death, the *masiqta* is believed to feed the spirit and help it perfect its spiritual body. The full forty-five days marks the period during which the spirit of the deceased Mandaean traverses the purgatories (*matarata*) on its way to Mshunia Kushta. During the five days of the Parwanaiya festival, held every spring, the boundaries between earth and Mshunia Kushta dissolve, creating a period when the dead may ascend more easily and those who may have been deprived of proper funerary rites may be freed from the purgatories by retroactive rites on earth. Then follows Dihba Rba (New Year), a vigil that marks the reconstruction of the universe, and includes the rebaptism of all Mandaeans into their sacred community of "alien life."

Manetho Egyptian priest of the early third century B.C.E. at Heliopolis. He wrote the *Aegyptiaca,* a work on Egyptian history, which is still important for Egyptology, especially in listing the various dynasties and providing a framework for chronology. Only fragments of his work are preserved, in Josephus and Julius Africanus. According to Josephus, he made a number of slanderous statements about the Jews, though some scholars think this was not part of his original work but only of a later interpolator. His description of the Hyksos made them the founders of Judea, or at least caused Josephus to make this identification since they are said to be called Shepherds. In another passage, however, Manetho is said to ascribe the origins of the Jews to lepers, as Lysimachus did. Among the lepers were some learned priests who also had the disease, one of these being Moses. Under Moses, these afflicted individuals banded together and made a pact with the Shepherds (Hyksos). They also enacted laws to require the exact opposite of the laws of Egypt and agreed to refuse to have anything to do with outsiders. They successfully made war on the Egyptians for a time.

Mani (216–277 C.E.) the "doctor from Babylon" and "apostle of light" who founded the Manichaean religion. Known in Western literature as Manes or Manichaeus, and in Chinese as Mo-ni, he was born in Mesopotamia (present-day Iraq) to Parthian (Iranian) parents, and was raised in an Aramaic-speaking Elchasaite Christian community. He left the community at age twenty-four in response to a revelation from God, in which he met his divine alter ego, his "light-twin," who instructed him to start a new mission to the world. Mani traveled to India and then to the Persian court, where he gained the interest, though not the conversion, of the emperor Shapur I (r. 240–272).

Mani believed himself to be the last in a series of prophets that included Zarathustra, the Buddha, and Jesus. He sought to provide the definitive interpretation and synthesis of these earlier revelations, and to correct what he perceived as their corruption. In contrast to his prophetic forebears, Mani wrote his teachings down (in five principal Aramaic treatises, as well as letters, psalms, a Persian catechism, and a picture book for the instruction of illiterates) and formed a missionary organization to disseminate his ideas. Mani sent his disciples into the Roman Empire, India, and Central Asia, while he worked mostly in Mesopotamia and Persia. Manichaeism grew quickly, and became a serious rival to Christianity, Zoroastrianism, and Buddhism, eventually spreading from the lands of present-day Spain in the West to China in the East and thriving for nearly a thousand years.

Mani taught that the world was a battleground of two alien entities (characterized as good and evil, light and darkness, life and death), and that everything in the world was a catastrophic mixture of these two opposing forces. Everything contains a divine spark of life, Mani said, which seeks liberation from pain and death, and it is the duty of humans to cooperate with God's plan to accomplish this liberation. Mani felt that ordinary human life is filled with violence toward living things, and that the only road to purity was to stop interacting with the world in a manipulative and harmful way. Consequently, he insisted on a rigorous code of behavior that was ascetic, pacifist, and celibate (called the "three seals" of mouth, hand, and heart). Believers must first conquer the enemy within themselves and convert their own bodies into the instruments of God's saving will, through which the life force can reascend to the world of light.

The success of Mani's mission posed a threat to the Zoroastrian religious authorities in Persia, and the latter finally convinced Shapur to banish the prophet. Mani returned to Persia upon Shapur's death, but was eventually imprisoned on the orders of the emperor Bahram (r. 273–277). After twenty-six days in chains, Mani "took off the warlike dress of the body" and ascended to the moon, an event commemorated by his followers at the annual Bema festival. After centuries of relentless persecution, the religion of Mani finally succumbed, but not before leaving deep and lasting influences on its rival religious traditions.

Mani I b. Tanḥum Palestinian amora, known also as Mana; contemporary of Yoḥanan (3d c. C.E.). He sometimes is confused with the fourth-century-C.E. authority Mani or Mana b. Yona.

Mani II b. Yona Palestinian amora of the midfourth century C.E., active primarily at Sepphoris; cited frequently in the Jerusalem Talmud simply as Mana, without the patronymic

Manichaeans followers of Mani, a Mesopotamian prophet of the third century C.E. Also called Dualists (Arab.: Thanawiya) and Interpreters (Pers.: Zanadiqa), the Manichaeans referred to themselves as the Living Family and the Righteous, and took the name Religion of Light (Chin.: Ming-jiao) in China. They considered themselves God's army in a war against evil; but they insisted that this conflict was a spiritual one and rejected violence. The true Manichaean, in fact, was required to stop committing violence toward all living things and to lead an ascetic, celibate, and pacifist life of strict discipline and constant mindfulness. Those who could not live up to such a difficult code of behavior were to do everything in their power to support those who could. Through reincarnation, these less able followers could hope for another chance in their next life, when they, too, would count on the support of others.

The Manichaean community for this reason consisted of two classes: the disciplined "elect" or "righteous," and the supportive "hearers," who led a less rigorous existence. The propertyless elect were required to travel constantly, spreading the teachings of Mani throughout the world. Consequently, they were totally dependent on the hearers for food, clothing, and shelter. The hearers were required to pray four times each day and to fast once a week. The elect prayed seven times each day and fasted until evening, when they partook of a sacred meal as part of their religious duty to free the life force in food by means of their pure bodies. The human body was itself considered a battleground of hostile forces, and Manichaeans sought to overpower their own sinful behavior and inclination to evil. This struggle between virtues and vices was personified in a complex pantheon of spiritual beings, who were the respective emanations of the God of Truth (also called the Father of Greatness) and his eternal enemy, the anti-god and "father of lies." The Manichaeans developed an extensive hymnic tradition, in which they sang of their devotion to God and praised his light, power, and wisdom, the latter personified in his prophets, Zarathustra, the Buddha, Jesus, and Mani.

All Manichaeans theoretically obeyed the authority of Mani's successors in Mesopotamia (a kind of Manichaean "papacy"), but in actuality formed regional communities, which adapted deliberately to each cultural environment. Manichaeans in the West emphasized the religion's Christian elements, while in Central and East Asia Buddhist features gained prominence. This strategy of adaptation had been instigated by Mani himself, and it not only furthered missionary outreach, but also allowed Manichaean communities to go "underground" during frequent persecutions. In spite of nearly universal persecution, Manichaean communities extended from the region of present-day Spain to China by the eighth century C.E. Finally driven from the West by the triumph of Catholicism and then from its Near East homeland by the initially tolerant Muslims, Manichaeism persisted among the Uighur Turks (into the eleventh century) and in China, where the Manichaeans faded from history by the seventeenth century. *See also* MANI.

manna   also called "bread from heaven," a white, flaky substance, which according to accounts in Exodus 16:1–36 and Numbers 11:4–9 (cf. Ps. 78:24, 105:40) was provided by God for the Hebrews after the Exodus from Egypt. In Exodus 16:15 the etymology of the term is traced to the people's question, "What is it?" (Heb.: *man hu*). The provision of manna, in response to the people's grumbling about their lack of food in the wilderness, is presented as a demonstration of the glory and power of the Lord God. Details of the narrative highlight its miraculous character. According to Numbers 11:4–9, the people grew tired of the manna and resumed their grumbling, asking for the richer food they had eaten in Egypt.

In 2 Baruch, an apocalypse of the second century C.E., manna figures in the description of the abundance of food promised at the end-time, when the messiah will be revealed: "At that time the treasury of manna will come down from on high" (29:8). In the New Testament, "the hidden manna" is promised as an eschatological reward

for Christians who prove faithful (Rev. 2:17), and John 6 associates Jesus' miraculous feeding of the five thousand with the manna miracle. When the people compare Jesus to Moses, Jesus paraphrases Exodus 16:4: "It was not Moses who gave you bread from heaven, but it is my Father who gives you the true bread from heaven" (John 6:32). He goes on to identify himself with the manna, the food of eternal life, which is superior to the manna provided through Moses: "I am the bread of life. Your ancestors ate the manna in the wilderness, and they died. . . . I am the living bread that came down from heaven. Whoever eats of this bread will live forever, and the bread that I will give for the life of the world is my flesh" (6:49–51).

man pleaser   (Gr.: *anthrōpareskos*) one whose overt actions are calculated to gain the approval of others. Psalms of Solomon 4 employs the term in a scorching criticism of people who pretentiously sit in the "council of the pious," but whose life is a deceitful fraud, replete with secret affairs, crooked contracts, and illegal schemes. The text is significant for the study of first-century Judaism, because it demonstrates that pious Jews, and not just the Evangelists, were aware of the dangers of hypocrisy. Interpretations of the New Testament use of the term (Gal. 1:10; Eph. 6:6; Col. 3:22) often overlook the nuance of hypocrisy.

Manual of Discipline   *see* COMMUNITY RULE

Manue   ancestor of a second-century-C.E. Jewish family that moved to Armenia during Trajan's reign. Moses Xorenazi reports that a family called Amaduni came to Armenia from the eastern part of the country of the Arik during Trajan's invasion of Armenia and that the family was descended from a certain Manue. Manue appears to be the Armenian form of Monobases or Monobazes. It is possible that this family was related to Monobazes, the king of Adiabene. Monobazes' son, Izates, converted to Judaism in the first century C.E. Therefore, Xorenazi's story may be a further chapter in the history of the Jewish royal family of Adiabenia.

Maon Synagogue   ancient Jewish village and synagogue site about 20 kilometers southwest of Gaza, known today as Khirbet al-Main. In the Roman period it was part of the string of forts, known as the *limes Palaestinae,* that protected settled towns from marauders and bandits. The prayer hall found at this site measures about 19 by 15 meters and is built as a basilica with columns dividing the nave from the two aisles. There is an external apse built at the focus of worship at the northeast end of the building, which points toward Jerusalem. It is likely that three entrances opened into the worship space from outside at the end opposite the apse. The floor of the nave is paved with a remarkable mosaic, which is about one-third destroyed. The mosaic has a vine trellis forming fifty medallions (inhabited by animals and birds) to the left and right of the center column. This center column is composed mainly of baskets of fruit, but at the end, just before the center of worship, is a menorah flanked by two lions. Around the menorah, an etrog, a lulab, and a shofar are depicted. From the entrance one sees a peacock, an eagle with out-stretched wings, a leopard, two partridges, a flamingo, an ibex, a buffalo, two doves, a crane, a fat-tailed sheep, a hare, a guinea fowl, pheasants, a two-antlered stag, elephants, a central hen with egg on a water vessel, a duck, a bird in a cage, a hunting dog, and a gray goose. There is also a damaged Aramaic inscription beyond the menorah and the border of the mosaic: "Remembered be for good the whole congregation who have contributed this mosaic and furthermore Daisin and Thoma and Juda who have donated the sum of two [gold] denarii." The building was probably erected in the fourth century C.E. and was used through the sixth century C.E., which is the date assigned to the inscription. The latest coin found in the fill within the synagogue was 585 C.E. A water channel and a ritual bath (*mikveh*) stand to the east of the synagogue.

maot ḥittim   (Heb., money for wheat) funds collected to ensure a supply of flour so that the poor would have unleavened bread for use on Passover. Maot ḥittim is referred to at Y. Baba Batra 1:6 (12b), which states that residency in a town for one year obliged one to contribute or entitled one to receive "flour for Passover." In medieval Europe, the community's rabbi and elders made up a list of those who would give or receive maot ḥittim.

Maoz Hayim Synagogue   ancient synagogue site at the modern town of that name about 4 kilometers east of Beth Shean. The plan of the building during its whole history was that of a simple basilica with two rows of columns dividing interior space into a nave and two aisles. In its first phase, from the third century C.E., the building was almost square, or 12.5 by 14 meters. Two rows of columns divided interior space into a wide nave and two narrower aisles on either side. On the south side of the building a large raised platform or *bimah* extended into the worship space. This low *bimah* served for the Torah shrine. The excavator believes that the entrances were from the east, since in the later structure entry was from that direction. The interior floor of the first synagogue was a mosaic that con-

tained a representation of a seven-branched menorah and a shofar in the southern section. The rest appears to have been composed of geometric designs, namely, meanders, though a bird was also depicted. This building was not destroyed violently, but was evidently simply superseded in the fifth century C.E. by the later synagogue.

The renovated synagogue was extended northward 4 meters to make a building 12.5 by 18 meters. In this building an apse was constructed on the south side that extended 3 meters to the exterior. The apse now served as the *bimah,* and its floor was higher than the interior floor of the worship space. The floor was the reused mosaic floor of the earliest phase of the building. The apse was partitioned by a marble screen. Interior to the apse stood the Torah shrine, probably of wood, as no stone fragments were found. Entry into the building was from an exterior courtyard forming an L-shaped exterior space without columns. That part of the L in front of the facade functioned as a narthex or front porch. This outside area was paved with stone slabs. Entrance from the narthex into the synagogue was through a central door in the north facade.

Near the end of its use as a synagogue, perhaps in the sixth century C.E., a new mosaic floor was laid about 30 centimeters above the earlier floor. It appears to have been simple geometric patterns without birds or a menorah. Benches were added along the walls. The earlier stone columns were replaced with inferior columns, perhaps of wood. A *bimah* was built beside the apse and extended into the nave. A *geniza,* a place for storing unusable or damaged scrolls, was dug into the east side of the apse. A marble screen was in use to separate the apse and *bimah* from the nave. Two double doors opened inward to the courtyard to the east. Some kind of attached structures or rooms existed in this period, or from the second phase of the synagogue, on the southwest, but it is as yet impossible to determine what they were. The synagogue was destroyed and its settlement abandoned in the seventh century C.E., probably as a result of the Arab conquest.

Mar   in the Talmuds, a term of respect, often used to designate a scholar; literally, "master." In some cases, Mar is used as a title preceding the name (e.g., Mar Samuel and Mar Ukba). The term also is used when the Talmud quotes an anonymous Amoraic statement, which frequently is introduced: "A master said. . . ."

maranatha   an Aramaic sentence transliterated into Greek and found in 1 Corinthians 16:22 and

Didache 10:6. It is derived from *mar* (lord) and *ata* (come). Depending on how the sentence is divided, it can mean either "Our Lord has come" (*maran atha*), or "Our Lord, come" (*marana tha*). One of the concluding phrases of the Book of Revelation is "Amen. Come, Lord Jesus!" which probably derives from *maranatha* and so supports the sentence's second meaning. The contexts in which *maranatha* appears in both its transliterated and translated forms suggest that it has a liturgical origin.

Mar b. Ashi talmudic designation for Tabiomi, son of Ashi, a Babylonian amora active in the fifth century C.E.; head of the academy at Sura from 455 C.E. until his death in 468. The unusual circumstances surrounding his assumption of that post are narrated at B. Baba Batra 12b.

Mar b. Rabina Babylonian amora of the early fourth century C.E., known for his ascetic practice of engaging in fasts throughout the year, except on Pentecost, Purim, and the eve of the Day of Atonement (B. Pesahim 68b). In a similar spirit, when he believed that his colleagues were becoming inappropriately merry at the wedding of his son, he broke an expensive cup to sadden them (B. Berakhot 30b–31a).

Marcellus, Gaius Quinctius Certus Publicius governor of Syria. Leader of the only Syrian legion, III Gallica, known to have fought in the Bar Kokhba Revolt. He probably moved his troops into Palestine in 132 or 133 C.E. He apparently was the most competent general close to the fighting. Eusebius also mentions this reinforcement of the Roman forces.

Marcion (d. c. 160 C.E.) a wealthy shipowner who in 140 C.E. went to Rome, where he developed his own understanding of Christianity; he was expelled from the Christian community in 144. Many Christian writings of the late second century seek to refute Marcion and thus testify to the success of his teaching in attracting followers to his communities, which were very similar to Christian communities. Partly under the influence of Gnosticism, he taught that the God of the Old Testament was an evil and deceptive God of creation (demiurge) who was involved with the material world and a God of law who laid impossible and contradictory burdens on Israel. Marcion understood the God of the New Testament to be a spiritual God of love who sent Jesus Christ to reveal the spiritual world and overthrow the God of creation. He held that Jesus was a spiritual being who only appeared to be a human. He accepted as authoritative only certain books of the New Testament that were not "Jewish," namely, some of the Pauline Epistles, because they contrasted law and spirit, and an edited version of the Gospel of Luke.

Marcionites followers of the early Christian teacher Marcion. The Marcionites, with their teacher, were expelled from the Roman church in the middle of the second century and established numerous communities in the following decades. They were similar in ritual to Christian communities, but taught Marcion's interpretation of the Bible and New Testament, which involved a radical rejection of anything Jewish. Marcion's communities also taught a sharp division between spirit and matter and were absorbed into the dualistic Manichean communities in the late third century. *See also* MARCION.

Marcius Turbo *see* TURBO, QUINTUS MARCIUS

Marcus Aurelius Roman emperor (r. 161–180 C.E.). He was born in 121 and named Marcus Annius Verus. Hadrian became enamored of the boy and made him a Salian priest at age eight, betrothed him in 136 to the daughter of Lucius Aelius whom Hadrian had adopted as his successor, and hired only the best teachers to supervise his extensive education in rhetoric, grammar, philosophy, and law. Upon becoming emperor, Marcus Aurelius petitioned the Senate to grant Aelius's son, Lucius Verus, joint authority with him. After settling the revolts in Britain and Chattan, in 162 he sent Verus to respond to the Parthians' seizure of Armenia and their victory over two Roman legions. Although Verus was slow to arrive, Statius Priscus regained Armenia in 163–164, and Avidius Cassius succeeded in making Mesopotamia a Roman protectorate in 165–166. His attempts to finally place central and southeastern Europe north of the Danube under permanent Roman control were abandoned when Cassius revolted in 175. In 175 and 176, after Cassius's murder, the emperor visited Egypt and Syria to firmly establish his control. Ammianus Marcellinus writes that the emperor was "frequently exasperated by the Jews, who were malodorous and riotous," and he compared them unfavorably to his barbarian enemies in the north. Exactly what this means is unclear, but it does not appear that there was an open revolt or concerted opposition to the emperor. Marcus Aurelius is often claimed to have been the Antoninus with whom the rabbinic sources claim Judah the Patriarch was in conversation. In 177 he elevated his son Commodus to coemperor and set off on a campaign against the German tribes. Marcus's life was guided by Stoic philosophy, and he is one of the few Roman emperors whose writings have gained more fame than his practical accomplishments as ruler.

Marḥeshvan *see* ḤESHVAN

Mariamme **1.** second wife of Herod the Great and grandaughter of both Hyrcanus, the last Hasmonean high priest, and his brother, Aristobulus. She married Herod in 37 B.C.E., just before he became effective ruler of Palestine. She bore Alexander and Aristobulus, executed by Herod in 7 B.C.E., and two daughters. She was politically active in the struggles for power in the Herodian court. Herod became convinced of her infidelity and executed her in 29 B.C.E., an act for which he later suffered remorse.

2. Herod the Great's third wife, whom he married in 24 B.C.E. She was the daughter of Simon, an Alexandrian priest, whom Herod appointed as high priest so that he could marry her. She was the mother of Herod, son of Herod, who for a while was second in line for the throne. She was part of the group that supported Antipater as heir of Herod, for which Herod divorced her and disinherited her son.

Mariamne *see* MARIAMME

Mark, Jews in the Gospel of The majority of the people appearing in the Gospel of Mark, including Jesus, are Jews and are treated without prejudice. The Jewish crowds in Galilee who hear and follow Jesus are presented as curious, interested, and sometimes enthusiastic. Even when the Jerusalem crowd calls for Jesus' execution, they are pictured as having been misled by the Jerusalem leadership. Many stories and dialogues concern polemical exchanges between Jesus and Jewish opponents. In all cases the adversarial groups are differentiated so that Jews as a whole are not attacked. The Pharisees confront Jesus over interpretation of Sabbath, purity, and other laws. The scribes conflict with him over teaching authority. The Jerusalem authorities (chief priests, elders, and scribes) treat Jesus as a threat to political stability and seek his execution. The stories are stylized and of limited value for determining the historical relationship of Jesus to the Jewish community. The author of Mark also polemicizes against the Temple and proclaims divine judgment against it. It is likely that the author or at least his audience was mainly gentile. He explains the meaning of Jewish terms and customs and he feels free to teach that dietary and purity regulations no longer apply (7:19). In general, the author stresses the authority of Jesus and diminishes the importance of the Temple and its leadership.

Markah a fourth-century Samaritan hymnist and author of the *Memar Markah* (a theological work also known as the *Tibat Markah*) who lived in Nablus in the Palestinian hill country north of Jerusalem. According to tradition, an angel of the Lord named him Moses at birth, but his parents called him Markah, a name that has the same numerical value as Moses when the number equivalents of each Hebrew letter are totaled. He was the father of Noneh, who also became a writer of hymns. Markah was the most highly venerated of all non-biblical personages by the Samaritans, and later tradition described him as a priest, perhaps symbolizing orthodox acceptance (and co-opting) of his eclectic and possibly Dosithean views. For example, he is the earliest Samaritan to explicitly describe an afterlife, perhaps expressing a Dosithean tenet.

Markah's poetic style, though different from that of his near contemporary Amram Darah, also became a standard form of liturgical poetry. Like Amram, Markah did not use rhyme in his poetry. His poems were longer than those of Amram and did employ acrostics, usually alphabetical, in which subsequent verses began with the next letter of the alphabet. On one occasion he worked his own name into the first letters of a poem. In further contrast to Amram, he used a standard number of lines in a verse, usually four or seven. He had a rich vocabulary and good rhetorical skills that are evident both in his poetry and in his great theological commentary, the *Memar Markah*.

Part of his genius was his ability to both comprehend and blend ideas from various contemporary philosophies. There are traces of Gnosticism, Neo-Platonism, Stoicism, and the concepts of Philo in his work. John MacDonald, who has made the Memar Markah available in both Aramaic and English (*Memar Markah* [1963]), believes that Markah assimilated Christian concepts, attributing to Moses qualities that the Gospel of John and the Book of Hebrews used in reference to Jesus. Markah anticipated kabbalistic preoccupations with his mystic meditations on the letters of the alphabet. Although he did not believe that individuals need the intercession of Moses, he did believe that Moses met an intercessory "glory of God" on Mount Sinai rather than God Himself, thus resisting an anthropomorphic portrayal of God. He subtly associated Moses and God by referring to God as "The Standing One" and Moses as the one "Standing by God."

Mark Antony (c. 83–31 B.C.E.) Roman general and ally of Julius Caesar in his struggle for power in Rome. After Caesar's death, he was one of three rulers, with Octavian (later Augustus Caesar) and Lepidus. After the defeat of Brutus and Cassius at the Battle of Philippi (42 B.C.E.), Antony ruled the eastern half of the Roman Empire, where he formed a liaison with Cleopatra, the queen of Egypt. Octavian conspired against him and defeated him at the Battle of Actium in 31 B.C.E. Pursued to Egypt, Antony commited suicide.

maror (Heb.) bitter herbs, consumed at the Passover Seder in remembrance of the bitter life of slaves

marriage (Heb.: *nissuin*) the legal union of a man and a woman, consummated by sexual intercourse and providing the basic structure of the family. Traditionally, it follows the betrothal and is supported by the terms of the marriage contract (*ketubah*). Fidelity is required; polygamy is permitted; endogamy is advised; levirate marriage is occasionally practiced; celibacy is uncommon but accepted; progeny are desirable; priests are restricted from marrying particular women (Lev. 21:7–8; *Spec. Leg.* 1; *Ant.* 3.12.2); and the ideal marriage remains a dominant metaphor for the relationship between the husband/God and Israel or the Church. Concern with marriage appears in sacred and secular contexts and encompasses law, wisdom literature, narrative, and poetry.

The Book of Tobit emphasizes marriage: Sarah marries Tobias only after he exorcises the demon who has killed her first seven husbands; marital strains and their resolution between Tobit and Sarah, as well as the irenic relationship between Raguel and Edna, are depicted; endogamy is preached; and Tobit instructs Tobias on how to be a proper husband. Joseph and Asenath depicts love at first sight and provides information on betrothals and weddings (esp. Jos. Asen. 21). Ben Sira bewails the inability of husbands and fathers to insure the chastity of wives and daughters. More for eschatological than social reasons, Paul too recognizes difficulties the responsibilities of marriage can cause (cf. 1 Cor. 7). Warning against sexual sins, Pseudo-Phocylides nevertheless strongly encourages marriage and children (175–217).

According to Josephus (*War* 2.8.2; *Ant.* 18.1.5), Philo (*Hyp.* 11.14.17), and Pliny (*Nat. Hist.* 5.73), Essene (men) reject marriage; Josephus and Philo provide a reason: the Essenes view women as naturally unfaithful. Yet Josephus also mentions married Essenes (*War* 2.8.12). The Dead Sea Scrolls and archaeological evidence provide conflicting data. While the Damascus Document (CD 7:6–7), the Rule of the Congregation (1QSa 1:4), the War Scroll (1QM 7:4–5, with women and children removed from the camp during holy war), and the Temple Scroll (11QTemple, following biblical material) mention married members and marital laws, the Qumran cemetery has yielded almost only male remains.

Jesus' marital status is not discussed in early Christian texts. Marital imagery, however, is common (the wedding at Cana in John 2; bridegroom language; the "marriage supper of the Lamb" in Rev. 19:9). The Pastoral and Catholic Epistles commend women's subordination and patriarchal marriage (1 Tim. 2; 1 Pet. 3); some of these texts may be in reaction to Christian women's attraction to celibacy (see The Acts of Paul and Thecla).

In rabbinic Judaism, marriage refers to the consummation of a marriage and completion of the marriage bond. Rabbinic literature regards the natural state of humanity as marriage, and women in particular are assumed to be subject to the family bond, first as daughters and then as wives. The principal interest for the law of Judaism is the point at which a woman becomes or ceases to be holy to a particular man, that is, when she enters or leaves the marital union. These transfers of women are the dangerous and disorderly points in the relationship of woman to man, and therefore are dangerous to society as well.

Five of the seven Mishnah tractates concerning women are devoted to the formation and dissolution of the marital bond. Three of these five tractates, Kiddushin, Ketubot, and Gittin, treat that which is done by man here on earth, that is, formation of a marital bond through betrothal and the marriage contract and dissolution of a marital bond through divorce and its consequences. One of them, Sotah, is devoted to that which is done by woman here on earth. The fifth, Yebamot, deals with the corresponding heavenly intervention into the formation and end of a marriage: the effect of death upon the marital bond and the dissolution, through death, of that bond. The other two tractates, Nedarim and Nazir, draw into one the two realms of reality, heaven and earth, as they work out the effects of vows taken by women and subject to the confirmation or abrogation of the father or husband. These vows make a deep impact upon the marital life of the woman who has taken them.

In all, the system set forth in these seven tractates, which comprise the third division of the Mishnah, Nashim, delineates the natural and supernatural character of the woman's role in the social economy framed by man: the beginning, end, and middle of that relationship. The tractate Yebamot concerns the rule that the levirate connection is null in a case of consanguinity. The tractate also deals with marriage into the priesthood and the right to eat heave-offering, severing the marital bond, marital ties subject to doubt, the right of refusal, infirm marital bonds, the deaf-mute, the minor male, severing the marital bond through death of the husband, the woman's testimony, and identifying a corpse. The tractate Ketubot covers the material rights of the parties to the marital union (the wife, the father, and the husband). It discusses conflicting claims, fines paid to the father in the case of rape or seduction, the father's material rights, the husband's material rights, rules for the duration of the marriage, the wife's duties to the husband, the husband's marital rights and duties, the dowry, property rights of the wife while she is married, settlement of the marriage contract in the event of the husband's death, multiple claims on an estate, and the support of the widow. The tractate Nedarim deals with the language of vows, including euphemisms and language of no effect or of limited effect; the binding effects of vows not to derive benefit in general, vows not to eat some specific kind of food in particular, and vows not to use certain objects; the temporal application of vows; and the absolution of vows. The discussion of absolution covers grounds for absolution, annulling the vows of a daughter and of a wife, the husband's power to annul the wife's vows, and vows of a woman who is not subject to their abrogation. Invoking the ordeal of the bitter water, the tractate Sotah sets forth the narrative of the ordeal and the rules of the ordeal. It discusses exemptions and applicability, testimony, rites conducted in Hebrew, the anointed-for-battle and draft exemptions, the rite of the heifer, and the neglected corpse. Dealing with writs of divorce, the tractate Gittin discusses delivering a writ of divorce; preparing a writ of divorce; two irrelevant matters (confirming the prevailing supposition and fifteen rulings enacted for the good order of society); the law of agency in writs of divorce; receiving the writ; appointing an agent to prepare and deliver a writ of divorce; stipulations in writs of divorce; invalidity and impairment arising from improper delivery, improper preparation, improper stipulations, and improper witnesses; and grounds for divorce. Taking up the process of betrothal, the tractate Kiddushin defines the rules of acquisition of a woman in betrothal. It discusses procedures of betrothal, agency, the token of betrothal, stipulations, impaired betrothals, doubts in matters of betrothal, appropriate candidates for betrothal, castes and outcastes, the status of the offspring of impaired marriages, and marriage among castes. It also includes miscellanies and homilies. We see in this detailed account of the division's repertoire of themes that we have an encompassing account of the formation, duration, and dissolution of marriages. The topic is worked out in a fairly systematic and orderly way. *See also* BETROTHAL; BRIDEGROOM; DIVORCE; ENDOGAMY; MARRIAGE CONTRACT; MARRIAGES, PROHIBITED; WOMEN, POSITION OF.

marriage contract (Heb.: *ketubah*) contract describing a marriage settlement, stipulating obligations to the wife in the event of the husband's death or a divorce. The text is as follows: "This *ketubah* witnesses before God and man that on the . . . day of the week, the . . . of the month . . . , in the year [the year reckoned from creation], the holy covenant of marriage was entered between bridegroom and his bride, at. . . . Duly conscious of the solemn obligation of marriage the bridegroom made the following declaration to his bride: 'Be consecrated to me as my wife according to the laws and traditions of Moses and Israel. I will love, honor and cherish you; I will protect and support you; and I will faithfully care for your needs, as prescribed by Jewish law and tradition.' And the bride made the following declaration to the groom: 'In accepting the wedding ring I pledge you all my love and devotion and I take upon myself the fulfillment of all the duties incumbent upon a Jewish wife.'"

marriages, prohibited marriages that may not be consecrated in the first place or that are deemed null and void (despite having been consecrated) because the involved parties are relatives or have a personal status that precludes marriage. Rabbinic law deems null and void *ab initio* marriages proscribed by scripture because the parties are within a prohibited degree of kinship (see Lev. 18:6–30). In this category are marriages between siblings (whole or half), marriages between an aunt and nephew, marriage to a brother's wife or to a wife's sister while the wife is alive (even after divorce), marriage to the wife of an uncle, marriage to a son- or daughter-in-law, and marriage to someone already married. Offspring of any of these unions are *mamzerim* and entirely forbidden from marriage.

Certain other marriages are forbidden by rabbinic law, but if celebrated are deemed valid. Included in this category are marriages involving a person born of an incestuous or adulterous marriage (*mamzer*) or a castrated man; marriages between a man and a woman whom he had divorced and who had subsequently been remarried and then divorced or widowed; marriages between a priest and a divorcee or proselyte; marriages between an adulterous woman and her lover; a man's marriage to a second woman while he still is married to his first wife; marriages to a woman divorced or widowed less than three months; and marriages to a pregnant or nursing woman. These unions are deemed valid, and are treated under the law as normal marriages, with no stigma attaching to any children of the union. At the same time, the fact that the marriage was forbidden *ab initio* is grounds for either party to demand and obtain a divorce.

The Mishnah tractate Yebamot lists additional forbidden unions. The point in these instances is to prevent a man from benefiting from licentious behavior or from giving testimony or acting as a judge in a case in which he has a personal interest. For instance, a man suspected of having intercourse with a slave woman who subsequently was set free or with a gentile woman who subsequently converted to Judaism may not marry her. Comparably, one who seduces a married woman, whose original marriage then is dissolved by a court, may not marry the woman. If he does so anyway, a court can impose a divorce. Finally, individuals involved in a woman's divorce proceedings are forbidden from marrying that woman. This applies to a man who delivers a writ of divorce from overseas, who is responsible for attesting to the validity of the document (M. Yebamot 2:8), and to a judge before whom a widow refused to perform the rite of halitzah (M. Yebamot 2:10).

Mar Samuel *see* SAMUEL

Martial Roman epigrammist of the late first century C.E. He makes several references to Jews in his *Epigrams;* in some cases, it is only to have a joke at their expense, but this is not unusual since he does this with most of his subjects. For instance, he uses the "breath of Sabbatarian women" as one example of a bad smell. This may suggest that Jews were thought to fast on the Sabbath. Another epigram mentions Jews who were taught to beg, a stock image of the Jews. He also mentions a circumcised actor and a circumcised poet, indicating Jews could be in these professions.

Martialis, Quintus Rammius prefect of Egypt (117–119 C.E.). The Acta Pauli et Antonini, the longest chapter of the Acts of the Alexandrian Martyrs, discusses an episode in Alexandria in which the Greeks used their slaves as agents in the illegal release and beating of some prisoners. Sixty Greeks had been found guilty of instigating the violence, but the matter dragged on until Martialis issued an edict on the subject. The papyrus also deals with Martialis's reconstructions after the

revolt. Antoninus was one of the leaders of a Greek delegation to the emperor Hadrian to complain about the Jews in Alexandria. The Jews had recently been involved in a revolt and were not citizens of Alexandria, yet Martialis allowed them to reside in a place near the city from where they could easily attack the Alexandrians. It is clear to Antoninus that none of the delegation's letters reached the emperor. The implication of Antoninus's remarks is that Martialis had prevented the Greeks' communications from reaching Rome.

martyr (Gr.: *martys,* witness) one whose death or suffering for his or her convictions is construed as a witness to those convictions. Jewish and early Christian literature is replete with stories in which the protagonist comments on the meaning of her or his impending death. Most often they are cast in the genre of tales about the persecution and vindication of a wise courtier. Modifying older stories such as Genesis 37–50 (Joseph), the Story of Ahikar, and the Mordecai story in the Book of Esther, Daniel 3 and 6 characterize their heroes as righteous men prepared to die for the Torah. The three youths express their trust in God's ability to deliver them (3:16–18) and, retrospectively, Daniel ties his rescue to his faithfulness (6:22). In 2 Maccabees 7, much of the narrative about the deaths of the seven brothers and their mother consists of speeches in which the protagonists express their conviction that God (1) is punishing Israel for its sins; (2) will punish Antiochus; (3) will vindicate their innocent deaths for the Torah through resurrection. The story is preceded by an account of the death of Eleazar, who exhorts the young to imitate his willing death for the Torah (6:18–28). In the Story of Susanna, the heroine's testimony is embodied in a prayer that asserts her innocence. The Martyrdom of Isaiah depicts the dying prophet speaking from a Spirit-inspired trance (chap. 5). The story of the mother and her seven sons had long history in Jewish tradition and is attested in 4 Maccabees, Lamentations Rabbah 1:50 and B. Gittin 57b (where it is set in the time of Hadrian), and the history of Joseph ben Gorion (Josippon).

New Testament stories about Jesus' suffering and death imitate the Jewish narratives (Matt. 26–27; Mark 14–15; Luke 22–23; John 13–19). Jesus' testimony about the meaning of his death appears mainly in his comments to his disciples. However, in Matthew 26:64, Mark 14:62, and Luke 22:70, he confesses his identity when interrogated by the high priest, and in John 18:33–19:11 he converses with Pilate. References to his silence reflect Isaiah 53:7 and Second Isaiah's portrait of the Servant of

YHWH, which influenced Jewish texts about persecution and vindication. Among the accounts of Jesus' death, Luke's is noteworthy for the unique words of witness ascribed to Jesus (23:34, 43, 46), this being consonant with Luke's emphasis on the exemplary character of Jesus' death. Thus, in Acts 6–7, Luke employs the passion narrative genre to narrate Stephen's trial and death. However, this association between Jesus' death and that of his followers is explicit already in Mark 8:34 and is implicit in Mark 13:9, which mentions one's "testimony" (Gr.: *martyrion*) before kings and governors.

The explicit notion of innocent death as a witness appears in Jewish texts first in 1 Enoch 8:4, 9:10, and 22:7, where the blood of the righteous (Abel in 22:7) brings accusation and appeals for retribution. The earliest Christian uses of *martys* to refer to a martyr are in Acts 22:20 (of Stephen) and Revelation 2:13, although it may be implied in Hebrews 12:1 (cf. 11:4; 12:24 of Abel). The noun and related words meaning "martyrdom" and "to witness" come into wide Christian usage after 150 C.E. They appear frequently in the Martyrdom of Polycarp (mid-2d c.) and in the writings of Irenaeus and Clement of Alexandria. The story of Justin's trial depicts him testifying to his faith and describes him and others as "(holy) martyrs." Stories about the deaths of Christian martyrs come into wide currency from the late second century onward.

Martyrs, Ten the rabbis executed by Hadrian for their support of Bar Kokhba (134 C.E.): Simeon, Ishmael, Akiba, Hananiah b. Teradyon, Huspit, Yeshebab, Eliezer b. Shammua, Hananiah b. Hakhinai, Judah b. Baba, and Ishmael b. Elisha. Descriptions of their torture and death are taken from a gaonic midrash and are part of the liturgy for the Day of Atonement and for the Ninth of Ab. The latter's moving liturgy (probably 12th c. C.E.) mentions eight of the martyrs and includes the following expressions of grief: "The cedars of Lebanon, noble persons of the Torah, shield bearers of the Mishnah and Talmud, mighty heroes who toiled in it in purity—their blood was spilled and their heroism ended. Here are the ten holy martyrs of the realm, and for them I weep and my eyes pour forth tears. . . . They brought R. Akiba, whose powers of logic could uproot mountains and grind them together. And they combed his flesh with an iron comb to break him. His soul departed as he recited, '. . . is one.' And a heavenly voice said, 'Happy are you R. Akiba. Your body is purer than every kind of purity.'"

Mar Ukba I an early Babylonian exilarch (c. 210–240 C.E.); presided over the court at Kafri. Divergent stories report either that he honored the piety and learning of rabbis, who deferred to him in political matters, or that he was ignorant, imprisoned Rab, and did not properly observe the law.

Mar Ukba II grandson of Mar Ukba I; Babylonian exilarch (313–337 C.E.); father of Abba Mari. On his mother's side, he was a grandson of Rab. He is particularly known for having the rabbinic authority Geniba executed, apparently for teaching that rabbis (not exilarchs) should rule the Jewish nation. He is also referred to as Mar Ukban de Tzutzita, Akabiah, and Rabban Ukba.

marzeah (Heb.) technical term used to designate a form of religious association. The word is known from the Hebrew Bible, as well as from cognate Semitic languages, such as Ugaritic. The *marzeah* seems to have been mainly a funerary institution, with the purpose both of burying the dead and of commemorating the deceased with a periodic banquet. Thus, the *marzeah* also became known for its consumption of large quantities of drink. This and possible associations with pagan worship led to its condemnation in the Hebrew Bible. Overall, the *marzeah* seems to have functioned much as the *collegia* did in the Graeco-Roman world.

Mar Zutra **1.** Babylonian amora active in the late third and early fourth centuries C.E.; a friend of Ashi. He succeeded Kahana as exilarch in 401 C.E. and ruled until 409.

2. son of Huna. He served as exilarch from 512 until 520 C.E., when he rebelled against the Persian government and was imprisoned and executed.

Masabala b. Simon one of the commanders of the area around En Gedi during the Bar Kosiba Revolt. En Gedi was one of the administrative centers of the revolt, and it was the chief port for supplies shipped across the Dead Sea. One of the Bar Kosiba letters is addressed to Masabala b. Simon and his co-commander, Jonathan b. Baayan, and chastises them for "sitting eating and drinking and caring nothing for their brothers." He was probably also involved with confiscating the property of a certain wealthy landowner in En Gedi who refused to cooperate with the revolt.

Masada fortress from the Hasmonean and Herodian periods located on the west bank of the southern part of the Dead Sea about 14.5 kilometers from En Gedi. The fortress is located on the top of a plateau with cliffs on all sides and it towers 600 meters above the Dead Sea. The name "Masada" is extremely close to the Hebrew and Aramaic words for "fortress," and the name of this particular fortress occurs in numerous Greek and Latin inscriptions.

The earliest history of Masada is somewhat mysterious. Scattered sherds from the Chalcolithic and Iron II periods suggest that the site experienced some settlement, if only sparse and sporadic, since the fourth millennium B.C.E. There are no signs, however, of architectural remains from these periods. The next archaeological sign of settlement at Masada comes from the Hasmonean period with the discovery of some coins from the reign of Alexander Jannaeus (first half of the first century C.E.). The name Jannaeus on these coins is seemingly consistent with an account by the Jewish historian Josephus, which relates a speech by Eleazer during the final defense of Masada. In this speech, Eleazer refers to a tradition of the founding and naming of the fortress by a high priest named Jonathan, causing some scholars to identify this Jonathan with the coins of Alexander Jannaeus (*War*, VII:285). Nevertheless, another passage in Josephus (*War*, IV:399) clarifies that the establishment of Masada was carried out by the "ancient kings," suggesting the Hasmonean kings. With this passage in mind, the Jonathan mentioned by Josephus is most easily identified as the Hasmonean Jonathan Maccabeus who became high priest in 153 or 152 B.C.E. (cf. 1 Macc. 10:15–21).

The mystery lingers concerning the establishment of the fortress at Masada because the extensive excavations carried out on the summit of the site have yet to yield any certain architectural remains from the Hasmonean period. Two buildings show some signs of Hasmonean occupation, but the final report of the Masada excavation disputes a firm identification. On the other hand, the written sources indicate that some sort of fortress must have been established during the Hasmonean reign, both because of the above references from Josephus and because at least a small fortress was present when Herod the Great's brother Joseph and his eight hundred men guarded Masada from siege by the Parthian army in 40 B.C.E. Herod returned from Rome the following year and rescued his brother in 39 B.C.E. Realizing the military advantages of the site and the need for a place of refuge in case he was deposed, Herod overhauled the site from 37 to 31 B.C.E., extensively improving the fortifications, buildings, and cisterns. Since all, or almost all, of the early architecture from Masada dates from the Herodian period, one must assume that the entire site was either rebuilt or established by Herod during a six-year period.

After the Herodian complex was completed in about 31 B.C.E., it contained a sophisticated water collection and distribution system, extensive fortifications, storehouses, and palaces. The desert climate of course necessitated the elaborate water system and storehouses, which are quite impressive even by today's standards. Dams were constructed that trapped the flash floods that came through the Masada Valley during the rainy season. This water was then transferred via plastered aqueducts to extensive cisterns, which were cut into the rock cliffs. The total capacity of all the cisterns was close to 40,000 cubic meters. Smaller cisterns found adjacent to the various buildings provided further ways of collecting the periodic rainfall. In addition, food storehouses were constructed for public storage and for the various palaces.

The fortifications were equally impressive. The entire distance of the circumference (about 1,400 m) was enclosed by a casemate wall. There were numerous towers spaced at uneven distances along the wall, and there were five gates (though only four were in use during any one period). Of course, the most effective fortification was the natural location of Masada on the top of a plateau surrounded by steep cliffs on all sides.

As the fortress was also constructed with the Herodian family in mind, there were several groups of palaces at Masada: (1) the three-tiered northern palace-villa, which contained living quarters on the upper tier and entertainment facilities on the lower two tiers; (2) the western palace, which contained the administrative center as well as almost 4,000 square miles of residential space for royal guests; (3) an administrative wing and residence for palace officials adjacent to the western palace; and (4) three smaller palaces, which were found close by, just southeast of the western palace, which were probably used as residences for the royal family.

Other interesting finds from Masada include numerous coins and epigraphic materials. The written texts are particularly interesting because they include multiple ostraca (pottery sherds with ink writing) that illustrate how the rationing of food and water took place during times of siege.

A synagogue was also discovered at Masada that is particularly important for an understanding of Judaism because it is one of the few examples of a synagogue that was used before the destruction of the Second Temple. This synagogue at Masada and another Second Temple synagogue from Herodium both contain a vestibule and a hallway. In addition, both buildings were almost identical in their dimensions: the Masada building was 12 by 15 meters, while the building from Herodian was 10.5 by 15 meters. Like later synagogues, worshipers faced Jerusalem, but in both the Masada and Herodium synagogues, the worshipers faced Jerusalem immediately upon entering the building, instead of turning to face the Holy City at the Torah shrine. These two synagogues provide important data that point to a link between Second Temple synagogues and later synagogues constructed after the destruction of the Temple in 70 C.E. This link is particularly helpful in understanding written references in sources like the New Testament to synagogues that were contemporary to the Second Temple.

The defeat of Masada by the Roman army in 74 C.E. is probably the most famous story associated with the fortress. Four years after the fall of the Second Temple, the Romans crushed the last Jewish resistance that had taken refuge at Masada. Instead of allowing the Romans to kill and imprison them, the survivors committed suicide on the eve of what would have been certain defeat. After this conquest, a small Roman force was stationed at the site to keep it secure. A church was later built during the Byzantine period in the fifth and sixth centuries C.E.

mashgiah (Heb.) supervisor of rituals, particularly ritual slaughter. A *mashgiah* must be expert in law, pious, and God-fearing. An ignorant man, motivated by financial gain, cannot supervise religious rites.

maskil (Heb., master) one of the titles for a lay officer in the Qumran Community. The term *maskil* appears in three clearly sectarian texts, the Community Rule, the Damascus Document, and the War Scroll. In fact, the Community Rule contains an entire section of statutes for the *maskil* (1QS 9:26–10:8), in which he is admonished to be the living embodiment of the sect's rules. His duties include teaching and instruction (cf. 1QS 3:13, the introduction to the Treatise on the Two Spirits), the administration of justice, the admission of new members, and playing a pastoral role among the members of the Community. The section ends with the Hymn of the Master (1QS 10:9–11:22), which describes the characteristics prescribed in the preceding statutes.

There are two mentions of the *maskil* in the Damascus Document (CD 12:21, 13:22), both in formulaic closings to groups of statutes: "and these are the precepts in which the Master shall walk in his commerce with all the living. . . ." The *maskil*'s role is much more shadowy in the Damascus Doc-

ument than in the Community Rule; it has been argued that the *maskil* should be identified with the *mebaker,* or guardian, also found in the Damascus Document (and less prominently in 1QS), since in some cases their duties overlap, but the fact that two different titles are used militates against this identification. Finally, the heading of the War Scroll reads "To the m[askil]." Therefore, it is clear that the *maskil* holds a prominent position in the hierarchy of the Qumran Community. *See also* COMMUNITY RULE.

Masorah a collection of notes and signs aimed to ensure that the text of the Hebrew Bible would be pronounced correctly when read aloud and transcribed accurately when copied. Jewish scholars from different regions developed different Masoretic systems: Palestinian, Babylonian, and Tiberian. By the sixteenth century, the Tiberian Masorah came to be accepted as the most authoritative. To ensure correct pronunciation, scribes inserted vowels and accents into the otherwise consonantal Hebrew text. To ensure accurate copying, two different types of Masorah were developed. Masorah Parva consists of short notes—usually made up of abbreviations—written in the margins of the manuscript that identify unusual spellings, the number of times a word appears, and so on. It also indicates *kere* and *ketib.* The Masorah Magna (Great Masorah) consists of notes written in the margins and at the ends of books with lists of particular forms, where certain words appear as well as unique forms. Since their inception, the Masoretic notations have enabled the accurate copying of the Hebrew Bible, providing the biblical text with a stable manuscript tradition from the early Middle Ages. This is called the Masoretic Text. *See also* KERE, KETIB; MASORETIC TEXT.

Masorah to Targum Onkelos Like the Masoretic text of the Hebrew Bible, the text of Targum Onkelos was considered so authoritative by the medieval rabbis that they constructed a Masorah for it. For the Masoretic text, the Masorah's list of notes was designed to help ensure that the text was copied correctly. The notes in Targum Onkelos's Masorah served the additional purpose of preserving alternate readings.

Masoretes Jewish scholars who developed a system of notes and signs to ensure the accurate transmission and pronunciation of the text of the Hebrew Bible. They did most of their work between 500 and 950 C.E. Their systems have been recorded in texts called the Masorot (plural of Masorah). The most famous of the Masoretes were Ben Naphtali and Ben Asher.

Masoretic Text the standard text of the Hebrew Bible developed by the Tiberian Masoretes. This text provides a fixed model for the three main elements of the biblical text: the consonantal text, the vowel signs, and the accents. Of the three, the consonantal text is the oldest, deriving from the first millennium B.C.E. Both the accents and the vowel signs were developed in the second half of the first millenium C.E. *See also* MASORAH.

massoret (Heb.) handing down; that which is handed down; tradition; *see also* TORAH

mastema (from Heb., hostility) a characteristic of the chief evil spirit, or, in some sources, his name. In Jubilees, the term is predominantly associated with the chief of the evil spirits who came from the dead progeny of the watchers. The texts and individual manuscripts vary as to whether it is a proper name (the Prince Mastema) or an attribute (the prince of hostility). He obstructs God's purposes, leads people to sin, brings sickness, and acts as accuser (perhaps reflecting the related Heb. root *stn*). In the Qumran War Scroll, *mastema* is an attribute of the chief evil spirit, Belial (1QM 13:4, 11; 14:9; cf. Jub. 1:20; 17:16).

Mata Maḥasia town in southern Babylonia, near Sura, where the Euphrates River splits into two; first mentioned in the Talmud at the time of Ashi, who moved the academy of Sura to Mata Maḥasia. Ashi calls the people who live there "stouthearted," for "they witness the glory of the Torah twice a year [when the sages assemble], and yet a single proselyte has never come forth from among them" (B. Berakhot 17b). By contrast, Mesharshaya esteems the town's scholars over those of Pumbedita (B. Horayot 12a). In gaonic writings, Sura and Mata Maḥasia often are treated as the same town. This is an error.

Matenah Babylonian amora, of the late third century C.E.; a student of Samuel and, later, Raḇ. For a time he was at Nehardea, to which he returned after thirteen years (B. Kiddushin 70b). He is frequently cited in the Babylonian Talmud in exegetical as well as legal contexts.

Mattai of Arbel along with Joshua b. Peraḥiah, one of the five pairs referred to in M. Aḇot. His name alternately is recorded as Nittai. M. Aḇot 1:6 reports that he said: "Keep away from a bad neighbor, and don't get involved with a wicked man, and don't give up hope of retribution."

Mattan Torah *see* REVELATION

Mattathias a member of the priestly family of Joarib (1 Chron. 9:10, 24:7) who began the Maccabean revolt in 166/165 B.C.E., according to 1 Maccabees 2. (He is not mentioned in 2 Maccabees.)

He refused to obey the Seleucid king's order to offer sacrifice to foreign gods and put to death a Jewish collaborator and a royal official at his ancestral town, Modein (near Lydda). The movement he began was carried on by his five sons: John, Simon, Judas, Eleazar, and Jonathan. He died in 165 B.C.E. and was buried in Modein. His "testament" appears in 1 Maccabees 2:49–68.

Matthew, Jews in the Gospel of The Gospel of Matthew, written in the later first century, has long been recognized as the most "Jewish" of the Gospels. It is also notorious for its polemics against Jesus' Jewish opponents. The Gospel contains extensive teachings of Jesus, including sustained legal discussions that are more sophisticated than those in the other Gospels. The author encourages observance of the law according to the interpretations of Jesus and defines righteousness as observance of the law (not as faith in Jesus Christ as is found in Paul's letters). The crowds of Galilean Jews who hear Jesus in the narrative are either well disposed toward him or neutral. They symbolize the Jews in the late first century whom the author hopes to convince of Jesus' teachings. Despite the Christian use of Matthew for anti-Semitic attacks, the harsh polemics in the gospel do not attack Jews as a group but the leaders of the Jews (scribes, Pharisees, Sadducees, chief priest, elders) and those people who have been misled into hostility toward Jesus. The threat to give the kingdom of God to a nation/group bearing fruit (21:43) is directed at the chief priests and Pharisees (21:45) and expresses the author's hope to displace the Jewish teachers of his day. The Jerusalem crowd that calls Jesus' blood down on themselves and their children (27:25) is not the whole Jewish people but a part of Israel that has been misled by the chief priests and elders and has met disaster in the destruction of Jerusalem. Matthew nowhere claims that followers of Jesus are a new or true Israel, but rather seeks to convince Israel of the truth of his claims. In doing so, he attacks in a sustained way the rival program of the Pharisees who symbolized the early rabbinic movement (chap. 23). He uses the word "Jews" only once concerning those Jews who have believed the rumor that Jesus' body was stolen by his disciples after his burial (28:15).

Matthias, son of Boethus the high priest who led Simon bar Giora and his forces into Jerusalem in 69 C.E. in order to oppose John of Gischala and the Zealots. At the height of the siege, in 70 C.E., Matthias was executed, along with three of his sons and other leaders, by Simon in order to prevent them from negotiating a surrender to the Romans.

matzah (Heb.) unleavened bread, used during Passover

Mauricius (in full, Mauricius Flavius Tiberius) Byzantine emperor (r. 582–602 C.E.). In 580 the Romans planned an invasion of Babylonia, but Hormizd IV learned of the attack and forced Mauricius to retreat. From 584 to 586 the Romans continually invaded Iranian territory, and they succeeded in capturing various locations for a short period. By 588 anarchy raged in Persia, and fearing that the instability would invite others to invade Byzantium, Mauricius threw his support to Hormizd's son, Khusro. Mauricius was a devout Christian and we learn that Domitianus, the bishop of Melitene and a brother of the emperor, forced the Jews in his diocese to undergo baptism and accept Christianity.

Maximinus I Thrax Roman emperor (r. 235–238 C.E.); born a Thracian peasant. He was proclaimed emperor after a revolt overthrew Alexander Severus. He waged war throughout Germany and was in Germany when a revolt in Africa led to the proclamation of Gordian I and his son as emperors. Maximinus invaded Italy but was murdered by his own troops. Although he persecuted the Christians, he left the Jews alone. His low-born origins were marked by contempt in the rabbinic sources: "When the Gentiles want to have a king, they take him from anywhere and set him over themselves."

Maximus, Lucius Laberius *see* LABERIUS MAXIMUS, LUCIUS

Maximus, Marcus Junius governor of Palestine (198–209 C.E. or 211–212 C.E.). His dates are uncertain, and he is placed during the reign of either Septimius Severus or Caracalla. A dedication to him in Jerusalem identifies him as provincial governor and legate of the sole legion in the province.

Mazaca *see* CAESARIA IN CAPPADOCIA

mazal (Heb.) planet; often, planetary influence

mazal to<u>b</u> *see* ASTROLOGY

Mazdaism (properly, Mazdayasna) the worship of Ahura Mazda (the Wise Lord), the supreme God revealed by the Iranian prophet Zarathustra. Ahura Mazda is said to administer the universe primarily through seven divine assistants, the Amesha Spentas (Immortal Benefactors). But set against Ahura Mazda's divine hierarchy and his good creation is an antigod, Angra Mainyu (Aggressive Spirit), whose army of evil forces seeks to corrupt and destroy the world. Ahura Mazda first created spiritual existence (*menog*), and then perfected it by material existence (*getig*), which serves as a demarcated area in which the assault of evil can be trapped and destroyed. The material world, there-

fore, is a battlefield of good and evil. Humans are the soldiers of Ahura Mazda; every good deed they perform increases the power of good, while every moral failure weakens the good and assists the cause of evil. Three days after death, at the Chinvat Bridge (the bridge to the afterlife), the human soul must answer to Ahura Mazda for its conduct in life. If the soul led a life of good, it passes over the bridge to paradise; if it followed evil ways, it is knocked off the bridge into hell. The false description of Mazdaism as "fire worship" comes from the religion's reverence for fire as a symbol of purity and of the successful emergence of good from mixture with evil. Sacred fires perpetually burn in the religion's temples, and are kept free from contact with polluting substances. Careful funeral procedures and elaborate purification practices are employed to keep both the natural world and the human body free from contamination by death and the other polluting creations of Angra Mainyu. Adherence to Mazdaism involves a life of moral righteousness and generosity, as well as daily prayers, offerings, and meals of commemoration and communion celebrated on behalf of God, his divine associates, and ancestral spirits.

Mazdak son of Bamdad; Zoroastrian reformer contemporary with Kawad I of Persia (r. 488–531 C.E.), whose support he gained for a time. Mazdak interpreted traditional Zoroastrian principles of hospitality and generosity into a radical social program of egalitarianism and nonviolence, while deemphasizing ritual practices. He advocated the abolishment of monogamous marriage and private property, which he thought to be the bases of Persian feudal society and its inherent injustices. Mazdak lost Kawad's support when his utopian program disrupted Persian society (and after Mazdak tried to manipulate the royal succession), and he was assassinated, along with many of his followers, in 528 C.E.

Mazdakites followers of the Zoroastrian reformer Mazdak (fl. late 5th and early 6th c. C.E.), whose teaching they called Dristden (the religion of justice). They believed that the social ills of envy, hatred, wrath, want, and avarice could be resolved by freely sharing the world's bounteous resources—including women—with everyone on the basis of individual need. They condemned excess in consumption and violence toward living things, and they promoted the leveling of social rank into a utopian community of equal believers.

The Mazdakites adhered to the dualistic metaphysics fundamental to Zoroastrianism, involving the eternal coexistence of two opposite principles of good and evil, personified by the god Ahura Mazda and the antigod Angra Mainyu, who battle for control of the world. But they were also influenced by materialist and fatalist notions and taught that a person's good or bad character is the accidental outcome of a random mixture of good and bad elements; a person of bad character is inherently ungenerous to others and has to be controlled by the good in society. They played down traditional Zoroastrian ritual practices in favor of social justice and self-discipline, the latter involving self-examination in terms of twelve aspects of daily behavior, seven modes of human agency (modeled on seven administrative positions of the Persian government), and the cultivation of discernment, intelligence, memory, and joy.

The Mazdakites rejected traditional Zoroastrian marriage practices (such as *sturih,* or levirate marriage), undermining the patrimony so central to Persian feudal society by the practice of freely sharing wives with fellow believers and by advocating the tracing of descent through the mother. But they were unsuccessful in their effort to revolutionize traditional Zoroastrian lifestyles. After the assassination of Mazdak and many other leaders in 528 C.E., the Mazdakites survived as an underground sect and later adopted the public identity of Muslims, while secretly retaining their teachings and practices.

meal-offering offering of grain, a handful of which is burned on the altar and the residue eaten by the priests, in the Jerusalem Temple

meals Since ancient times, breaking bread or eating a meal together has been an accepted way of establishing or reaffirming a relationship with a divine or human partner. In the Hebrew Bible, eating a meal together is an expression of hospitality and friendship, as when Abraham entertains (divine) visitors by the Oaks of Mamre (Gen. 18:1–5). A meal is also a way of ratifying a covenant: in Exodus 24:1–2 and 9–11, Moses and the seventy elders eat a meal with God on Mount Sinai in order to ratify the covenant between God and Israel. Finally, it was believed that in the eschatological age the messianic banquet would celebrate the victory of God over his enemies (cf. Isa. 24:6).

In the Second Temple period, common meals continued to be a way of emphasizing relationship. The Pharisees, forming themselves into *haburot,* or fellowships, took their meals together, observing ritual purity regulations that set them apart from other Jews. Among the Essenes, according to Josephus and the Qumran texts, the common meal took on great importance as a way of emphasizing

their separation from the rest of Judaism. Therefore, every communal meal was blessed by a priest (1QS 6:4–5), and an initiate could only participate in these meals after a two-year probationary period (1QS 6:21–23). The Essenes also looked forward to a messianic banquet, to be presided over by the Priestly and the Davidic Messiahs (1QS^a 2:17–21a).

The early Christians also attached a great importance to common meals. Thus in the Gospels, Jesus is often portrayed as eating with his followers, and, in the resurrection narrative of Luke, the risen Jesus is recognized by his disciples only after he has broken bread with them (Luke 24:28–35, 41–43). In the Book of Acts, the earliest portrayal available of the first Christian community, members are portrayed as taking meals together (Acts 2:42, 46). Finally, in 1 Corinthians 11:23–26, we have the earliest record of the Christian celebration of the Eucharist, where followers of Christ came together to break bread and drink wine together ritually to commemorate the passion of Jesus. This celebration was often followed by a less formal meal. This celebration of the Eucharist, the "common meal" of the church, continues to be the centerpiece of the liturgy in Christianity today.

Rabbis engaged in common meals characterized by detailed ritual practices and formulaic behaviors (T. Berakhot 4:8ff). Seating was according to stature, and the individual's conduct at each stage in the meal was controlled by concern for cultic cleanness. Specific foods were consumed in a formalized manner. Such meals heightened the rabbinic sense of differentiation from the rest of society and concretized a system of recognition for the honor due those with the greatest accomplishments in the study of Torah, who were seated in positions of respect and served first. Such meals thus legitimated and naturalized the social and intellectual hierarchy the rabbis developed through the study of Torah. The best known example of such a meal is the Passover Seder, a ritualized symposium incorporating many of the behaviors required at rabbinic meals.

Measha 1. early Tannaitic authority, referred to at M. Peah 2:6

2. Palestinian authority; grandson of Joshua b. Levi. Y. Betzah 1:6, 60c, reports that he had himself carried to the synagogue on Saturday in order to preach.

3. Palestinian amora of the fourth century C.E.; a colleague of Samuel b. Isaac and Zera; referred to in both Talmuds

mebaker (Heb., guardian, or overseer) official title for a lay leader of the sect, usually identified with the Essenes, that produced the Damascus Document and the Community Rule. The office of *mebaker* is given prominence in the Damascus Document, where an entire section (CD 13–14) is headed "the Rule for the *mebaker* of the camp," presumably the individual settlements of the Essenes in the towns and villages of Judah. The *mebaker* is to be a man between thirty and fifty years of age, well versed in the teachings of the sect, whose duties include instruction, the administration of justice, the admission of new members, taking a pastoral role among the members of the camp, and overseeing the financial contacts between the sectarians and outsiders.

In the Community Rule the *mebaker*'s role is less well-defined. He is called the Guardian of the Many—in control of the meetings of the Community's members (1QS 6:11b–12a)—and also the Guardian of the Property of the Many—in charge of the pooled property of the sect's members (1QS 6:18–21a). It is not clear whether these offices are the same or separate. It has been argued that the office of *mebaker* is the same of that of *maskil,* also found in the Damascus Document and the Community Rule, because of their similarity of function, but then the two separate titles are left unexplained. It seems certain that the *mebaker* played the leading role in the Essene camps to which the Damascus Document is addressed, and a less prominent one in the Qumran Community of the Community Rule.

Media country south and west of the Caspian Sea, in the vicinity of present-day Azerbaijan, associated with Noah's grandson Madai (Gen. 10:2). Having risen to power in the seventh century B.C.E., the Median Empire was absorbed into the Achaemenid Empire under Cyrus II. Throughout Achaemenid history, the Medes remained an important component of the empire. The princes and kings of Media are referred to in the Book of Esther as a distinct component of the Persian Empire.

medicine, talmudic References to this subject, interspersed throughout the Talmud and rabbinic literature, show that the rabbis had a significant level of medical knowledge. The physician was recognized as a source of authority in questions regarding healing and injuries. The Talmud makes mention of specialists akin to modern internists, psychiatrists (San. 75a), dentists (Kid. 24b), surgeons, and obstetricians (Arakh. 7b). Rabbis are said to have dissected birds or animals to gain knowledge of anatomy (Hul. 57b) or to have experimented on themselves (Ned. 50b) to learn about disease. Talmudic tradition asserts that the body is made of 248 limbs and 365 sinews, more than the number commonly accepted by early medicine. They sought out a corresponding number of commandments in the Torah, indicating their more immediate interest. Rabbinic sources show familiarity with the blood, the structure of the heart and other features of the circulatory system (Hul. 45b), and note many aspects of the nervous (Hul. 45a), the digestive (Hul. 43b), and the respiratory systems as well. Details that the Talmud represents in the genital and urinary systems and in its understanding of embryology (Nid. 30b) are consistent with the medical knowledge of the day.

In some instances, the sources recognize that a disease or dysfunction is caused by a physical agent, by unsanitary conditions, or by improper consumption of alcohol or foods (Hul. 59a). Many times, however, the agents of rabbinic pathology are demons or other mystical and spiritual causes. Incantations and amulets were effective against these forces (Ber. 53a). Folk medicine plays an important role in talmudic therapeutics. An amulet containing a scroll with names of God inscribed on it, for example, might cure rabies from the bite of a mad dog (Yoma 84a). Of course, circumcision was a universally practiced surgical procedure, and other surgeries are described, including the discussion of a caesarian section. A variety of mental disorders are acknowledged in the sources, which recognize some as congenital and some as transient. Study of the Torah helps to prevent senility (Shab. 152a).

medinah (Heb., city, or province; Aram.: *medintah*) a basic administrative unit under the Persian Empire, being a subunit of the large satrapies and a more manageable and coherent entity. The Persian Empire divisions seem generally to have been continued under the Greeks.

Megillah Mishnah tractate containing the laws for the reading of the Scroll of Esther on Purim (chaps. 1–2), the laws of synagogue property and liturgy, and lections of scripture read in the synagogue (chaps. 3–4)

Megillat Taanit (Heb., scroll of fasting) a listing of thirty-six days on which happy events or victories occurred during Second Temple times and on which the rabbis forbade fasting. Megillat Taanit is written in Aramaic and appears to derive originally from the second century C.E. Its current form is much later, and through later accretions, the document has evolved into two distinct versions.

Among the dates on which fasting is prohibited (listed in chronological order according to the original occurrence of the event being commemorated) are the fourteenth of Iyar, the second Passover; the fourteenth of Adar, Purim; the twenty-third of Iyar, when, during the Maccabean revolt, Jerusalem was captured (1 Macc. 13:49–53); the fourteenth of Sivan, when the citadel Zur was seized (1 Macc. 11:65–66; 14:33); the fifteenth and sixteenth of Sivan, when the sons of John Hyrcanus captured Beth Shean and the Jezreel Valley (Josephus, *Ant.* 13:280; id., *War* 1:66, 14:33); the twenty-third of Ḥeshvan, when the Maccabees removed a certain structure from the desecrated Temple; the twenty-fifth of Ḥeshvan, when John Hyrcanus conquered Samaria (Josephus, *War* 1:64, *Ant.* 13:275–81); the twenty-first of Kislev, when John Hyrcanus destroyed the Samarian Temple on Mount Gerizim (Josephus, *Ant.* 13:255); the twenty-fifth of Kislev, which is Hanukkah; the twenty-eighth of Shevat, when Antiochus was driven from Jerusalem; the thirteenth of Adar, marking the defeat of the Syrian commander Nicanor (1 Macc. 7; 2 Macc. 15); the third of Kislev, when the images of the emperor were removed from the Temple court; the twenty-second of Shevat, marking the rescinding of Gaius Caligula's order to erect a statue of him in the Temple (Josephus, *War* 2:195–203); the twenty-fifth of Sivan, marking the suspension of tax payments to the emperor, probably in 66 C.E. (Josephus, *War* 2:235–401); and the seventeenth of Elul, when the Romans left Jerusalem.

Megillot, Five   *see* FIVE SCROLLS

meilah   (Heb., trespass) the improper use of sacred property

Meilah   the eighth tractate of the division Kodoshim in the Mishnah, Tosefta, and Talmud Babli. Its six chapters specify the cases and extent of liability for violations against sacred property.

Meir   Tannaitic authority of the second century C.E. and leader in the period following the Bar Kokhba Revolt; a student of Ishmael and later of Akiba; the husband of Beruriah. Meir resided primarily in Tiberias but died in Asia. He is one of the most frequently cited rabbis in the Mishnah.

Midrashic statements hold that Meir was descended from proselytes and that his given name was Nehorai (B. Erubin 13b). He reportedly was one of the five scholars ordained by Judah b. Baba during the persecutions following the Bar Kokhba Revolt. Discussions of his ordination by Akiba also are extant. After the persecution, he was a major figure in the newly convened academy at Usha, where he served as *ḥakham,* a position of leadership over the Sanhedrin.

Meir's centrality in the formulation of the Mishnah is indicated by the talmudic statement that anonymous mishnaic rules represent Meir's view, based upon Akiba's teaching. While this statement is not literally true (the Mishnah reports numerous anonymous rules that disagree with statements of Meir), it indicates Meir's overall importance as well as the respect in which later authorities held him.

Talmudic stories report a number of tragedies in Meir's life. His wife, Beruriah, was the daughter of the martyr Ḥananiah b. Teradion. After the Bar Kokhba Revolt, her sister was enslaved in a brothel, from which Meir rescued her. Beruriah was known for her erudition and intelligence, but reportedly was seduced by one of Meir's students.

Meiron   ancient town and synagogue site in Upper Galilee on the eastern foothills of Mount Meiron (Jebel Jarmaq) about 5 kilometers northwest of modern Tsfat (Safed). Meiron or Meron is mentioned by Josephus (*Life* 188) as one of the localities he fortified in the First Revolt against Rome. He also mentions the town as a border town of Upper Galilee (*War* III.40). Later rabbinic sources regard the town as the place of ministry of Rabbi Shimon bar Yohai (T. Dem 4,13).

The lower city of Meiron was organized in blocks, at least two of which have been partially excavated. Living and working rooms (carpentry, etc.) were arranged around open courtyards. Many cisterns were cut into bedrock beneath the houses. At least one ritual bath or immersion pool (*mikveh*) was excavated beneath one of the houses. In one room of the structure that the excavators called the Patrician House, a large assemblage of storage jars with foodstuffs were found: peas or beans, walnuts, wheat, and barley. These pantry items were evidently deliberately burned, as one of the storage jars was inscribed in Hebrew "fire." Another jar was inscribed in Greek with the name of the owner: "belonging to Julianos." The excavators believe that the burning represents a pious act of the individual or family, who burned or otherwise rendered unusable items dedicated as consecrated to the Lord. Most of the remains date from 250 to 363 C.E., the peak of village life, though the village was probably founded about 200 B.C.E. On the other hand, village life at Meiron continued to about the fourteenth century, when it began to wane.

The synagogue stood at the very top of the steep promontory upon which ancient Meiron rests. The building is a long basilica, about 13.5 by 27 meters, oriented south, with a finely built facade with three portals, two of which are still standing. A porch with stairs in front and six columns stood before the facade. Entry into the worship space was through the three portals. Two long rows of columns divided the interior space into a nave and two side aisles, with a third aisle across the back. The floor of the building was probably paved with slabs of stone, and a stone-cut bench stood on the west side. In fact, most of the west wall of the building was cut from the bedrock of the hill. Evidently a small Torah shrine stood between the central portal and the west portal against the south wall. The synagogue was built during the third century and was evidently destroyed by the earthquake of 363 C.E.

Mekhilta of Rabbi Ishmael Midrash compilation devoted to the Book of Exodus, divided into nine freestanding tractates, compiled sometime after 600 C.E. Mekhilta, the first scriptural encyclopedia of Judaism, joins together expositions of topics and disquisitions on propositions, generally precipitated by the themes of scriptural narrative or the dictates of biblical law, and collects and arranges in accord with scripture's order and program the exegeses—paraphrases or brief explanations—of clauses of biblical verses. A sustained address to approximately half of the Book of Exodus, Mekhilta of Rabbi Ishmael presents three kinds of materials: (1) a set of ad hoc, episodic exegeses of some passages of scripture; (2) a group of propositional and argumentative essays in exegetical form, in which theological principles are set forth and demonstrated; and (3) a set of topical articles, some of them sustained and many of them well crafted, about important subjects of the Judaism of the dual Torah. Lacking all interest in cogent and sustained argumentation and demonstration of propositions set forth for argument, the authorship of the document scarcely aspires to make a statement of its own.

Mekhilta of Rabbi Simeon b. Yohai a lost, presumably Tannaitic midrash compilation to Exodus reconstructed by D. Hoffman in 1905 from fragments interspersed in the medieval Midrash haGadol.

Melchiresha (from Heb., king of wickedness) a name for the chief of the evil spirits, probably formed in parallel to Melchizedek (king of righteousness), his heavenly opponent. The name occurs only at Qumran (4QAmram^b 3:3; 4Q280 2:2), although Malchira (king of evil) is a name for the demon Sammael in Martyrdom of Isaiah 1:8.

Melchizedek (from Heb., king of righteousness) "the king of Salem" and "the priest of the Most High God," who meets Abraham after the war with the kings, blesses him, and receives tithes from him (Gen. 14:18–20). The only other reference to

him in the Hebrew Bible is Psalm 110, a royal psalm similar to Psalm 2, in which the king, enthroned at God's right hand, is called "a priest forever after the order of Melchizedek."

The abruptness with which Melchizedek appears and disappears in the Genesis narrative and the mystery surrounding him provided fertile ground for Jewish and Christian speculation. In the Melchizedek text (11QMelch, a fragmentary Qumran text), he is a high angel, the opponent of Belial and champion of the righteous. He executes judgment on Belial and his spirits and proclaims freedom and atonement for the righteous. Although the text is too fragmented for certain interpretation, the occurrence of cultic language suggests that Melchizedek has priestly functions as well as those of warrior and judge. In another fragmentary Qumran text (4QAmram), the wicked angel's name, Melchiresha, suggests that one of his opponent's three names (lost in a lacuna) is Melchizedek. Thus, Melchizedek is ascribed roles elsewhere attributed to Michael (and to an extent the son of man in 1 Enoch). An identification between Michael, the heavenly high priest, and Melchizedek is explicit in two medieval texts (Yalkhut hadash f. 15, col. 3.19; Midrash haNeelam Lech. 25). Two other texts identify Melchizedek with Shem (B. Ned. 32b; Tg. Neof. Gen. 14:18).

Early Christian speculation about Melchizedek is concentrated in the Epistle to the Hebrews, where Jesus, the preexistent Son of God, now exalted at God's right hand, is said to be a priest forever after the order of Melchizedek (chap. 7). The comparison suggests that this author was aware of Jewish ideas about an angelic Melchizedek. A fragmentary text in Nag Hammadi Codex IX indicates ongoing related speculation about Melchizedek in third-century Christian Gnostic circles.

Chapters 71 and 72 of 2 Enoch preserve a narrative about Melchizedek's miraculous conception and birth by Sopanim, Noah's sister-in-law, and his assumption to heaven before the flood. Because of its many similarities to Matthew 1, scholars dispute whether the story is of Jewish or Christian origin. However, a tradition in B. Sukk. 52b identifies Melchizedek, along with Elijah, as one of the four smiths in Zechariah 1:20 (2:3 in Heb.) This may reflect knowledge of a tradition about Melchizedek's assumption to heaven.

Melito of Sardis Christian bishop of Sardis in the second century C.E. (d. c. 190 C.E.). He was a Quartodeciman, that is, a Christian who kept the (Christian) Passover, or Easter, on the fourteenth of Nisan. He defended this practice in works that are now lost. His one surviving work is a Passover homily, which is characterized by highly rhetorical language. It includes a long paraphrase of the narrative on the first Passover in Egypt, with elements of midrash. In the second half of the sermon, he turns to the Crucifixion and strongly attacks the Jews for not accepting Christ.

Memar Markah "the word of [the Samaritan theologian] Markah," a Samaritan liturgical and theological writing that seems to date from about the fourth century C.E. Its contents are varied and consist of five homilies or sermons, based on specific themes of the Pentateuch, plus a sixth section that is a mystical interpretation of certain letters of the alphabet. The five homilies are built around the life of Moses and the events of the Exodus (the subjects of the first two homilies), Israel as a holy people, God's justice and mankind's sin, and the death of Moses. Within these broad themes, a huge number of subjects and biblical passages are discussed. *See also* MARKAH.

memra (Aram., from Heb.: *amar,* to speak, to say) Usually translated as "word," the term *memra* appears throughout the targums, but is unknown in rabbinic literature and other Jewish writings of the biblical period. It is usually associated with the name of God, either attached to the name, as in "the *memra* of the Lord," or replacing a reference to God. The targum to Isaiah 1:2 reads "they have rebelled against my *memra*" instead of the Hebrew text's "they have rebelled against me." It designates the active attribute of God—usually linked to commanding. Under that general rubric, it can be used to describe him speaking, creating, acting, punishing, or receiving worship. It does not constitute a separate entity, personality, or hypostasis.

men *see* GENDER ROLES, IN RABBINIC JUDAISM

Menahem *see* MENAHEM B. YOSE

Menahem, son of Judas the Galilean an early leader of the revolt against Rome in Jerusalem. He led a group to Masada and captured it in 66 C.E. Armed with weapons from Masada, he and his group returned to Jerusalem and took leadership over the rebel forces besieging the Roman garrison and Jewish leaders who had sought refuge in Herod's palace in the Upper City. Menahem took the palace and slaughtered those left there. When the fugitive high priest Ananias and his brother Ezechias were captured, Menahem executed them. According to Josephus, his brutal and high-handed leadership provoked an assassination plot by Eleazar ben Ananias. In the armed clash Menahem's forces were defeated. He escaped, but he was finally run down and executed.

Menahem b. Yose Tannaitic authority; a contemporary of Judah the Patriarch (late 2d c. C.E.); sometimes referred to simply as Menahem, without the patronymic

Menahem the Essene (Gr.: Manaemus) an Essene who predicted to Herod the Great when the latter was a boy that he would be king by God's favor, but would be punished in the end for injustice. During his reign (40–4 B.C.E.), Herod was assured by Menahem that he would reign for a long time. Because of these predictions, Herod treated all Essenes with honor.

Menahot (Heb., meal-offerings) Mishnah tractate on meal-offerings in the Temple. The tractate discusses improper intention and invalidating meal-offerings (chaps. 1–4); proper preparation of meal-offerings (chaps. 5–9); special meal-offerings (chaps. 10–11); and vows in connection with meal-offerings (chaps. 12–13).

Menander, Pseudo- In some Jewish writings, several verses are quoted and attributed to Menander, the famous Greek writer of New Comedy (fl. c. 300 B.C.E.); however, they seem to be Jewish pseudepigraphs. They speak out against having images of God and give various general moral exhortations.

Menelaus high priest who obtained the office in 172 B.C.E. by outbidding Jason at the court of Antiochus IV Epiphanes. He was the brother of Simon, the enemy of Onias III (2 Macc. 3:4, 4:1–4), and not a legitimate heir to the priesthood ("of the tribe of Benjamin"). He was responsible for the murder of Onias III; he conspired with his brother Lysimachus to rob the Jerusalem Temple; and he escorted Antiochus IV Epiphanes as the latter profaned and robbed the Temple (2 Macc. 5). He may also have collaborated in the transformation of the Temple cult (2 Macc. 6:1–11). According to 2 Maccabees 13:3–8, Menelaus was put to death at Beroea in 163 B.C.E. on orders from Antiochus V Eupator.

Men of the Great Assembly unidentified leaders of Israel in the Persian and early Hasmonean periods between the time of the classical prophets of ancient Israel and the first Pharisaic masters. This important link in the chain of tradition from Moses to the rabbis is recorded in the mishnaic tractate Abot (1:1). Tradition ascribes to them the enactment of festivals, prayers and blessings (especially the prayer of eighteen blessings), and the feast of Purim.

menorah (Heb., candelabrum) a stand that supports oil lamps or candles. A nine-branched menorah is used during Hanukkah; a seven-branched menorah was used in the ancient Temple. *See also* MENORAH, REPRESENTATION OF.

menorah, representation of The most popular motif in ancient Jewish art, the menorah (candelabrum) appears on coins, ceramic lamps, and decorating tombs and synagogues. It is considered the symbol par excellence of Judaism. The menorah is first mentioned in Exodus, where Moses is told to make a seven-branched candelabrum to put into the tabernacle. The description is unclear, but it appears it was to be made from one ingot of gold with six branches, three on each side curving upward from a central shaft that stood on some form of base. The shaft and branches were ornamented with knops and almond blossoms. The flowers which formed the uppermost cups of the branches served as the receptacles for oil. Solomon placed ten menorahs of a similar type in his Temple. All his menorahs and the later one that replaced them were lost when the Temple was plundered, first by Nebuchadnezzar and later by Antiochus Epiphanes. The Maccabeans, after their reconquest of Jerusalem, had a new golden menorah made in conformity to the biblical description. It was lit for the first time at the rededication of the Temple. The earliest known representation of the seven-branched menorah appears on a coin of Antigonus Mattathias (40–37 B.C.E.), the last of the Hasmonean kings. It is dated to the last year of his reign. The menorah is shown in a simplified form without the requisite knops and flowers and stands on what appears to be a tripod base. This latter detail, plus the fact that all the branches terminate at the same height, conforms to rabbinic descriptions of the Mosaic menorah and may be an accurate portrayal of the menorah that stood in the Hasmonean Temple. However, it differs somewhat in appearance from an image of a menorah scratched on plaster fragments found in an excavation of the Old City of Jerusalem that is dated to the reign of Herod (37 B.C.E.–4 C.E.), although it is believed that Herod continued to use the Hasmonean menorah. It was this menorah that was removed from the Temple by Titus's soldiers and carried by them in a triumphal procession depicted on the Arch of Titus in Rome. The base of the menorah shown on the arch is not a tripod as depicted on the coin and plaster fragments, but stands on an elaborate pedestal decorated with images of animals, suggesting it was added by the Romans to be make it easier to carry. The fate of the menorah is unknown. Tradition relates that during the sack of Rome in 410 C.E., the menorah was thrown into the Tiber River near where the modern synagogue now stands.

Following the ill-fated Second Jewish Revolt against Rome (the Bar Kokhba Revolt, 133–135 C.E.), the menorah became the most ubiquitous of Jewish motifs in Palestine. It was particularly popular for use in the synagogue despite the Babylonian Talmud's injunction forbidding Jews from making an exact copy of the Temple menorah. In fact, the appearance of a menorah is often the only means whereby a building can be identified as a synagogue. Three-dimensional, seven-branched menorahs were found in and around Palestinian synagogue sites, including a cast bronze replica from En Gedi and stone examples from Hammath-Tiberias, Eshtemoa, Maon, and Khirbet Susiya. A number of two-dimensional images of the menorah can be seen decorating synagogues' mosaic pavements, painted on walls, and in relief or incised on column capitals, doorposts, lintels, and chancel screens. Examples include capitals (Capernaum, Caesarea, Hammath-Tiberias); doorposts (Qisrin); lintels (Khirbet Shema, Nabratein, Japhia); wall painting (Rehov); mosaic pavements (Maon, Jericho, Maoz Hayyim); chancel screens (Hammath-Gadera, Horvat Qoshet). Torah shrines depicted in mosaic pavements are usually shown flanked by menorahs or have menorahs in the same panel, possibly a realistic rendition of their actual position in the synagogue. Examples can be seen at Hammath-Tiberias, Beth Shean, and Beth Alpha. At times the menorah is shown with more than seven branches and at times with less. It is unclear if this was done to conform to the talmudic prohibition forbidding exact replicas of the Temple menorah or due to artistic license. The majority of examples come from the Golan: Qisrin, Salokia, Apheca, Yahudiyya.

The origin of the seven-branched menorah is unknown, but its treelike form may be based on the ancient Mesopotamian tree of life. In antiquity, light and life were considered interchangeable: one could not exist without the other. Thus, the menorah, as a tree and symbol of life, became the bearer of lights. The seven lamps may represent the five planets known to the ancients, plus the sun and moon. The number seven has a magical significance in many ancient cultures because it consists of two groups of three, considered the most perfect of numbers as it is the only one with a beginning, middle, and end, flanking a single one, possibly within a Jewish context representing God the creator. Following the Temple's destruction and the two failed revolts against Rome, the menorah became both a religious and political symbol of Judaism and of the Temple that was to be restored in the messianic age. It remains a symbol of light, hope, and redemption of the Jewish people as seen in its representation on the emblem of the state of Israel.

menstruation   period of "uncleanness," in line with Leviticus 15, during which sexual relations are forbidden

mercenaries, Jews as   Various references indicate that some Jews participated as mercenaries in the Persian and Greek periods. To do so would have had certain religious ramifications, such as fighting on the Sabbath. For these reasons, Jews were generally exempted from military service in the Roman army.

mercy   compassion or forbearance shown particularly to an offender or to a person subject to one's power. The relationship between God and his people that is established through the covenant He made with them is called *hesed* in the Bible. It involves mutual trust and fidelity and is based on God's kind and continuing concern for his people. A related term is *raham,* which means compassion. *Hesed* and *raham* are often linked in the Bible, and in the Greek translation of the Bible (Septuagint), they are frequently translated as *eleos,* which means "mercy." The term appears in the Torah, Prophets, and Psalms. A repeated question is: why does God act in kindness, love, and compassion toward his people, even though they and their leaders are at times careless and disobedient? It is God's nature to be concerned, to forgive, and to restore and renew his people. But this is not just an emotion that God feels: it is an essential feature of the covenant relationship into which God entered with his people, even when their disobedience led to the division of Israel into the northern and southern kingdoms after Solomon's death. It is stated that even while Israel was under attack by neighboring nations (2 Kings 13:23), "the Lord was gracious to them [Israel] and had compassion on them; he turned toward them, because of his covenant with Abraham, Isaac and Jacob, and would not destroy them" (2 Kings 13:23). According to older English translations, that relationship is described in Genesis 24:27 as based on God's "mercy and truth," but the real meaning is "The Lord God of . . . Abraham . . . has not forsaken his steadfast love and his faithfulness toward my master [Abraham]." The same fidelity of God is evident toward Joseph (Gen. 39:21) and is of central importance when God establishes the covenant with Israel through Moses at Mount Sinai: "God shows his steadfast love to the thousandth generation of those who love him and keep his commandments" (Exod. 20:6). The same belief is repeated in Deuteronomy 5:10.

God's steadfast love and mercy are linked in the last words of David (2 Sam. 22:51), who is described as showing that same sort of generosity toward other humans, including Saul's son Jonathan (1 Sam. 20:8, 14) and Jonathan's crippled son, Mephibosheth (2 Sam. 9:7), and even to the young king of the Ammonites (2 Sam. 10:2). The theme of God's compassion and steadfastness toward his people is recurrent in the words of the prophets (Isa. 63:7; Jer. 16:5; Hos. 2:18; Zech. 7:9). Jeremiah declares he will boast only in God's steadfast love, not in human wealth, or might, or wisdom (Jer. 9:23). He asserts that it is because of God's steadfast love that his faithfulness to his people continues (Jer. 31:3).

This insight into the merciful and faithful nature of God and his dealings with humans is repeatedly asserted in the Psalms and is frequently linked with the continuing royal line of David as rulers of God's people. In Psalms 18:50 and 61:7, God's steadfast love will be given to the king and his descendants forever. This promise of God's faithful care of the nation Israel and its ruler is said to be conditional on their conformity to his "covenant and his decrees" (Ps. 25:10). Those who walk in God's ways without wavering will always have his gracious and steadfast love before their eyes (Ps. 26:10). This dependable mercy of God is evident in his willingness to forgive his people when they become disobedient (Ps. 86:5) and in the confidence that he is "merciful and gracious, and slow to anger" (Ps. 85:10).

In Proverbs, these paired qualities of mercy and faithfulness are said to be patterns for the way God's people live. They are to be bound around one's neck and written on the heart (Prov. 3:3) and are to be evident in the king's life and use of his authority (Prov. 20:28). Job says those who fail to manifest these qualities ("withhold kindness") are cutting themselves off from right relationship with the Almighty (Job 6:14).

The Hebrew Bible's depiction of God's mercy serves as the foundation for the rabbinic ideology, which frequently denotes God as Raḥmanah (the merciful) and which holds that just as God shows mercy towards humanity, so the people of Israel must be distinguished by their compassionate nature (B. Yebamot 79a). Mercy shown towards another person will be repaid by compassion from God (B. Shabbat 151a), who pardons the iniquities of people who themselves have pardoned the transgressions of others (B. Rosh Hashanah 17a; B. Shabbat 151b). People who exhibit such traits of mercifulness are presumed to be of the seed of Abraham (B. Betzah 32b).

The centrality of mercy in God's character is reflected in the thirteen attributes listed at Exodus 34:6, which define God as just, as well as merciful. Talmudic passages explain the possible contradiction between doing justice and showing mercy by arguing that while God initially engages in strict and truthful judgment, he ultimately acts upon his trait of mercy (B. Rosh Hashanah 17a). These same qualities of impartiality and compassion are expected of human judges (B. Sanhedrin 6b).

Meremar   *see* YEMAR

meridarch   *see* MEROS

merit   *see* ZEKHUT

merkabah   the chariot that bears God's throne, the Throne of Glory. The term is found as early as Ben Sira (49:8) and the Songs of the Sabbath Sacrifice from Qumran (4QShirShabb) to designate the wheeled vehicle seen by Ezekiel in his vision of the glory of God by the River Chebar (Ezek. 1:1–28). Though study of Ezekiel 1 and speculation on the mysteries of heaven to which it alludes—a body of lore known as the Account of the Chariot (Maseh Merkabah)—was declared esoteric by the Mishnah (Hagigah 2:1), circles of Merkabah mystics, called paradoxically "those who descend to the Chariot" (Yoredei Merkabah), flourished in the Talmudic period and left behind an extensive body of texts, the Hekhalot literature. In this literature "chariot" is not taken literally but defined as an elaborate structure of angelic hierarchies that support God's throne. *See also* OFANIM.

meros   (Gr., part, share, portion) frequently used to refer to a piece of property, especially a cleruchy or plot of land granted for service to the state. The word could also be applied to a district or province governed by a *meridarch*.

Meroth   *see* KHIRBET MARUS

Mesene   region in southern Mesopotamia, on the Persian Gulf; home to a Jewish population from the Parthian period and on. Talmudic authorities deemed Mesenean Jews to be of tainted genealogy (B. Kiddushin 71b; B. Yebamot 17a) and prohibited marriage with those of Apamea, a major city of the area (B. Kiddushin 71b).

Mesharshaya   Babylonian amora, best known for his statement: "When you want to go to learn before your master, first of all review your studies in the Mishnah, and then go to your teacher. And when you are in session before your teacher, watch the mouth of your teacher. . . . When you study any teaching, do it by the side of water. Just as water goes on and on, so may your learning go on and on. Stay on the garbage dumps of Mata Mehasia rather than in the palaces of Pumbedita;

eat a rotten fish rather than a bread pudding that breaks rocks" (B. Keritot 6a).

Mesopotamia, Jews in   *see* BABYLON, JEWS IN

messiah   (Heb.: *mashiah*)   **1.** in Second Temple literature, anointed one, a person designated by God for a special status or role. Kings were anointed with oil (1 Sam. 16:1–13), as were Israel's high priests (Lev. 8:1–13, cf. Lev. 4:3). "The anointed of YHWH" was a designation for Israel's king (1 Sam. 26:16). *Mashiah* alone never occurs in the Hebrew Bible, and the term should be translated rather than transliterated.

The exilic demise of the Davidic dynasty introduced some changes in the conception. Second Isaiah does not envision a restoration of the Davidic dynasty and calls Cyrus, king of Persia, YHWH's anointed one (Isa. 45:1). Third Isaiah is also silent about a Davidic king, and the prophet claims to have been anointed with God's spirit (Isa. 61:1). Zechariah, however, refers to Zerubbabel the Davidite and Joshua the high priest as God's anointed ("sons of oil," 4:14).

After the exile, the hope of a restored Davidic dynasty was nourished through the preservation and use of the royal Psalms (e.g., Pss. 45, 72, 89). Following the tradition in Psalm 89, the unnamed author of Psalms of Solomon 17 appeals to God's covenant with David, and employing phrases from royal oracles such as Psalm 2, Isaiah 11, and Ezekiel 34, he lays out a scenario for the restoration of the dynasty and details the activities of "the anointed of the Lord." Of special interest alongside the traditional kingly functions is this king's responsibility for the priestly function of purifying Jerusalem (Ps. Sol. 17:30).

Following the parallelism in Zechariah 3 (cf. Ecclus. 45:23–25), the priestly community at Qumran, smarting from what they perceived to be the pollution of the temple, awaited "the anointed ones of Aaron and Israel" (1QS 9:11; 1QSa 2:11–22). The Testament of Levi 14–18 details the sins of the Jerusalem priesthood and describes an eschatological priest, employing language from Isaiah 11.

In 1 Enoch 37–71, this same language and allusions to Psalm 2 are applied to a transcendent heavenly figure (1 Enoch 48:8–10, 49:2–3), who combines the features of the exalted son of man (Dan. 7:13), the exalted servant of YHWH (Isa. 49, 52:13–53:12), and the Lord's "anointed one" (1 Enoch 48:10, 52:4).

Other eschatologically oriented postbiblical Jewish texts make no reference to an anointed one, much less a future Davidic king. Most striking in this respect is the Wisdom of Solomon. Although it is ascribed to David's son and employs phrases from Psalm 2 (Wisd. of Sol. 4:18, 6:1), its protagonist is depicted in language and motifs drawn from Second Isaiah's servant songs. Most postbiblical passages drawing on Second and Third Isaiah are silent about a Davidic king.

Thus, postexilic Jews as a whole did not expect "the messiah," and those that did held divergent opinions about the anointed one or anointed ones. The New Testament proclamations about Jesus the Messiah (early called Jesus "Christ," a veritable surname) need to be read in this context. The variety of Jewish options warn against a facile conclusion that all Christians thought of Jesus as the son of David, although this interpretation occurs (Matt. 1–2; Rom. 1:3). The Epistle to the Hebrews emphasizes Jesus' priestly office, and Paul may imply this in his use of Psalm 110 (Rom. 8:34). Later church fathers interpreted Jesus' baptism as his priestly anointing, and the parallels between Mark 1:9–11 and Testament of Levi 18:6–7 are striking. The indentification of Jesus as the exalted son of man suggests that some claims about Jesus as Christ may reflect this form of messianic speculation (cf. Acts 2:36). Finally, the notion of a suffering and vindicated messiah (1 Cor. 15:3–4) could draw on the servant traditions as they are interpreted in the Wisdom of Solomon. In any case, the spectrum of Jewish messianic speculation and the similar variety in early Christian theology suggests a possibly important factor in first-century Jewish-Christian discussions about Jesus' identity and significance. *See also* ANOINTED; CHRIST; SERVANT OF THE LORD; SON OF GOD; SON OF MAN.

2. in rabbinic Judaism, eschatological king, to rule at the end of time. The messianic theme is of varying importance in diverse Judaic writings, episodic in writings concluded c. 200 C.E. (e.g., the Mishnah), but critical in documents put together after the Christianization of the Roman Empire in the fourth century C.E. (e.g., the Jerusalem Talmud, completed c. 400; Gen. Rabbah, completed c. 450; the Babylonian Talmud, completed c. 600). In constructing a systematic account of Judaism—that is, the worldview and way of life for Israel presented in the Mishnah—the philosophers of the Mishnah did not make use of the messiah myth in the construction of a teleology for their system. They found it possible to present a statement of goals for their projected life of Israel that was entirely separate from appeals to history and eschatology. Since they certainly knew, and even alluded to, long-standing and widely held convictions on eschatological sub-

jects, beginning with those in scripture, the framers of the Mishnah thereby testified that, knowing the larger repertoire, they made choices different from those of others before and after them. Their document accurately and ubiquitously expresses these choices, both affirmative and negative.

The Mishnah finds little of consequence to say about the messiah as savior of Israel, one particular person at one time, but manages to set forth its system's teleology without appeal to eschatology in any form. For the Mishnah, "messiah" is a category of priest or general. The messianic theme proved marginal to the system's program. By c. 400 C.E., by contrast, a system of Judaism had emerged in the Jerusalem Talmud in which the Mishnah, as foundation document, would be asked to support a structure at best continuous with—but in no way fully defined by the outlines of—the Mishnah itself. If the Mishnah provided a teleology without eschatology, the framers of the Jerusalem Talmud and related Midrash compilations could not conceive of any but an utterly eschatological goal for themselves.

Historical events entered into the construction of a teleology for the Jerusalem Talmud's system of Judaism as a whole. What the law demanded reflected the consequences of wrongful action on the part of Israel. Thus, again, Israel's own deeds defined the events of history. The failed messiah of the second century, Bar Kokhba, above all, exemplifies arrogance against God. He lost the war because of that arrogance. His emotions, attitudes, sentiments, and feelings form the model of how the virtuous Israelite is not to conceive of matters. The messiah, the centerpiece of salvation history and hero of the tale, emerged as a critical figure. The historical theory of this passage is stated very simply. In this view, Israel had to choose between wars, either the war fought by Bar Kokhba or the "war for Torah." "Why had they been punished? It was because of the weight of the war, for they had not wanted to engage in the struggles over the meaning of the Torah" (Y. Taanit 3:9 XVII). Those struggles, which were ritual arguments about ritual matters, promised the only victory worth winning. Then Israel's history would be written in terms of wars over the meaning of the Torah and the decision of the law.

The heart of the matter, then, is Israel's subservience to God's will, as expressed in the Torah and embodied in the teachings and lives of the great sages. When Israel fully accepts God's rule, then the messiah will come. Until Israel subjects itself to God's rule, the Jews will be subjugated to pagan domination. Since the condition of Israel governs, Israel itself holds the key to its own redemption: an act of humility and self-abnegation is what is required. Gentile kings are boastful; Israelite kings are humble. Thus, the messiah myth deals with a very concrete and limited consideration of the national life and character. The theory of Israel's history and destiny as it was expressed within that myth interprets matters in terms of a single criterion. Whatever others within the Israelite world had done or would do in the future with the conviction that at the end of time, God would send a (or the) messiah to "save" Israel, the concept of final redemption described above was a single idea for the sages of the Mishnah and the Talmuds and collections of scriptural exegesis. And that conception stands at the center of their system; it shapes and is shaped by their system. In context, the messiah expresses the system's meaning and thus makes it work. The rabbinic system, then, transformed the messiah myth in its totality into an essentially ahistorical force. If people wanted to reach the end of time, they had to rise above time, that is, history, and stand off to the side of great movements of political and military character. That is the message of the messiah myth as it reaches full exposure in the rabbinic system of the two Talmuds. *See also* ESCHATOLOGY.

messiah in the targums According to the Palestinian Targums to the Pentateuch, the messiah will come at the end of days, when the current world order will be changed. The messiah will fight and overcome all God's enemies, casting the wicked into Gehenna and placing the righteous into paradise (Eden). The messiah will spring from the tribe of Judah. The Targum to the Prophets further specifies that the messiah's origins are from the lineage of David and makes it clear that when the messiah comes, he will reestablish the Temple.

metallurgy the science and art of fashioning items from metals such as iron, bronze, gold, and silver. Simple jewelry and many small domestic tools were made of bronze. Despite this fact, almost no remains of bronze smelting installations have been uncovered, but numerous small slags have been found in many excavations. The finest metals, mainly gold and silver, were imported.

Iron was used for working and farming tools, weapons, and simple jewelry. Iron bracelets and rings have been found in many tombs from the Hellenistic, Roman, and Byzantine periods. Although many slags were found in excavations, no obvious remains of smelting installations were found. At four sites there is evidences of smithing.

At Masada and Herodium, two sites of the First Jewish Revolt, remains of smithing and weapon manufacturing have been uncovered and are believed to be connected to items the rebels left at the sites. At Betar, one of the main sites of the Second Jewish Revolt, a group of blacksmith tools were found, not in situ, together with small anvils. The tools are believed to be the remains of a portable mint of Bar Kokhba.

An entire blacksmith workshop was excavated at a late Byzantine Galilean site. In one of the rooms, a half storage jar that had been used as a furnace and was full of ashes was adhered to the packed soil floor. In the other room, a large ashlar had been used as the base for the anvil. About thirty iron tools were found all around the room and were divided into two groups—blacksmith tools and farming tools. Among the blacksmith tools were found three different types and sizes of anvils, three sizes of sledges, hammers, pliers, and chisels. The farming tools included picks, axes, hammers, and bidental hoes.

Although many jewels from many periods have been found all over the land of Israel, the remains of a possible jeweler's workshop was excavated at Beth Shean and dated to the late Byzantine or early Arab period. Broken jewels made of gold and bronze, together with two jugglets full of mercury, suggest jewelery making. *See also* JEWELRY.

metanoia (Gr., change of mind, or repentence) a term frequently used in reference to repentence of sin or evil. Thus, in both Jewish and Christian writings in Greek, it became an important theological concept relating to salvation.

Metatron archangel who plays an important role in Hekhalot mysticism. The name (also spelled Mitatron) may derive from the Greek *metathronos,* the one enthroned with God, or from the Latin *metator,* the title of the officer who went ahead of the Roman army to prepare the camp, hence, more generally, a forerunner. If the latter is correct, then the term may have first been applied to the biblical angel of the Lord who led Israel through the wilderness (Exod. 23:20). 3 Enoch designates him "the lesser YHWH," in contrast to God himself, "the greater YHWH," who withdraws from the world, leaving Metatron in charge. Metatron is, consequently, called the Prince of the World and he presides over the heavenly law court made up of the princes of kingdoms, the angelic representatives of the nations on the earth. He is sometimes identified with the archangel Michael (Israel's celestial representative). He also functions as the Prince of Torah, the Heavenly Scribe and the Heavenly High Priest, serving in the celestial tabernacle, the Tabernacle of Metatron. He has been compared to the Gnostic *demiurge* and to Christ—the latter parallelism being reinforced by the idea found in 3 Enoch that Metatron spent part of his existence incarnate on Earth as the patriarch Enoch. Some rabbinic authorities attacked the doctrine of Metatron as endangering the unity of God by implying that there are two powers in heaven. He is invoked in Jewish, Mandaean, and Islamic incantations. In the medieval Kabbalah, he is linked with the Shekhinah, the divine presence in the world.

metempsychosis (Gr., transmigration of the soul) A belief found in various religions (such as Hinduism), it was important in Pythagoreanism and Platonism. The concept is also found in the writings of Philo of Alexandria. According to Josephus, the Pharisees believed in it as well.

Methuselah son of Enoch (Gen. 5:21–27). He is best known for having lived longer than any human being, 969 years according to Genesis 5:27. In the literature ascribed to Enoch (1 Enoch and 2 Enoch), he is the recipient of the books of heavenly wisdom written by his father and hence the guarantor of this tradition (1 Enoch 81:5; chapters 72–82 in general; 91:1; perhaps "my son" in 105:2; chapters 106–107; and 2 Enoch 68–70, where he serves as priest).

meturgeman (or turgeman) translator. According to the Mishnah and other rabbinic texts, a *meturgeman* translates the text of the Hebrew Bible into Aramaic as part of a synagogue service. This translation is spoken either from memory or composed orally on the spot; the translation is not supposed to be read from a written text. Scholars sometimes use *meturgeman* to designate the author of a written targum. *See also* SCRIPTURE READING IN THE SYNAGOGUE.

Mezigah *see* CAESAREA IN CAPPADOCIA

mezuzah (Heb., doorpost) parchment containing the first two paragraphs of Shema, rolled tightly and placed in a case attached to the doorpost of one's home; *see also* MEZUZAH, AS AN ARCHAEOLOGICAL OBJECT

Mezuzah title of one of the so-called minor tractates of the Talmud. It is a collection of Tannaitic sources in two chapters, containing the rules for the writing, the type of parchment, and the placement of a *mezuzah* on a doorpost.

mezuzah, as an archaeological object a doorpost that had inscribed directly upon it a quotation from the book of Deuteronomy. The term *mezuzah* later came to be identified as an encased parchment scroll that contains one of these same citations from Deuteronomy, or the case that holds the scroll. This later understanding of *mezuzah* is how the term is used today, and these *mezuzah*s are common in almost all Jewish homes and worship centers. The *mezuzah* as an archaeological object is instructive in understanding how the transformation took place from the biblical understanding of the term as a literal doorpost to the modern usage as a container that holds a credo written on parchment.

One sees from the use of the word in Exodus 12:7 that the original meaning of *mezuzah* was simply a "doorpost" and not the parchment attached to the doorpost as is the modern practice. The term *mezuzah* took on the meaning of a kind of statement of faith attached to a doorpost, because two times in Deuteronomy the Israelites are commanded: "and you shall write them [the words of God] upon the *mezuzah*s [doorposts] of your house and your gates" (Deut. 6:9, 11:20). From this biblical evidence, it appears that originally the statements of faith were written on the doorposts themselves instead of on a piece of parchment that was placed inside a container, as is common today. Such a practice of writing on actual doorposts is confirmed and illuminated by several archaeological finds. One such inscription is actually found on a lintel from Palmyra, Syria. It dates from the third century C.E. and contained the text of Deuteronomy 6:4–9 ("Hear O Israel the Lord your God is one Lord . . .") on the actual lintel as opposed to a piece of parchment. The next development that can be identified archaeologically seems to be the practice of boring a cavity in the doorpost for the placement of an inscription with one of these citations from Deuteronomy. Such a cavity is found in a doorpost in the ancient synagogue of Caesarea. Though other extensive archaeological clues that illuminate more of this development are lacking, it seems that by the Middle Ages the term had taken on the modern meaning of a container that had this text from Deuteronomy 6:4–9 written on a piece of parchment or paper and that was fastened to the doorpost.

Micah, Targum to *see* TARGUM TO THE PROPHETS

Micah Commentary (Pesher Micah) tiny surviving fragments of a Hebrew composition (abbreviated as 1 QpMic) found in Cave 1, Qumran, in 1947 and published in DJD I. The surviving copy dates from the Herodian period; the work's date of composition is uncertain. The text is a continuous commentary on the Book of Micah, exhibiting the *pesher* form: quotation of biblical pericope, formulaic statement ("its interpretation is . . ."), interpretation based on events or personalities of the Qumran sect. Two figures that occur are the Teacher of Righteousness, the leader of the community and its inspired interpreter of scripture, and the Man of Lies, the leader of a rival congregation.

Michael (Heb., who is like God?) one of the four or, in some cases, seven holy ones (angels) who stand in God's immediate presence. Michael is mentioned in all lists of these angels in the pseudepigrapha (1 Enoch 20, 40) and Qumran scrolls (1QM 9:15–16). Along with Gabriel and Raphael, he is one of three who appear by name in canonical and deuterocanonical texts. In Daniel he is Israel's heavenly patron, serving as commander of the heavenly hosts (10:13–21) and as the nation's advocate at the great judgment (12:1). His name implies a challenge to his satanic opponent, who storms heaven and claims to be like God (Dan. 8:11; Isa. 14:14). In Revelation 12:7, he commands the heavenly army and, with a hint of his role as advocate, he drives Satan "the accuser" and his hosts from heaven.

middat Sedom (Heb., rule of Sodom) rabbinic description of an unfair or selfish principle, for example, the notion that "what is mine is mine and what is yours is yours" (M. Abot 5:10), which, while just, precludes charity. B. Baba Batra refers to *middat Sedom* in arguing that in a case in which there is no cost to himself, an individual must avoid selfishness or spitefulness by acting in a way beneficial to his associate.

Middle Aramaic *see* ARAMAIC, MIDDLE

Middle Platonism *see* PHILO; PLATONISM

Middot Mishnah tractate describing the layout of the Temple: watchposts and gates (chap. 1), the Temple Mount (chap. 2), the altar and porch (chap. 3), and the sanctuary and courtyard (chaps. 4–5)

Midrash exegesis of scripture or collection of such exegeses. Midrash compilations exhibit distinctive traits. Seen individually and also as a group, they intersect at a few places but not over the greater part of their territory, and they are not compilations but free-standing compositions. These documents emerge as sharply differentiated from one another and clearly defined, each through its distinctive viewpoint and particular polemic, formal, and aesthetic qualities. *Midrash* means "investigation," ordinarily, inquiry into the meaning of scripture. Midrash works so as to lead us into the world of the Hebrew Bible as that holy scripture enters into Judaism. It is how sages wrote with scripture. Through the workings of Midrash, the Hebrew Bible became the written half of the one whole Torah, oral and written, revealed by God to Moses Our Rabbi at Mount Sinai. Thus Midrash works in three dimensions: first, as explanation of meaning imputed to particular verses of scripture; second, as a mode of stating important propositions—syllogisms of thought—in "conversation" with verses or sustained passages of scripture; and, third, as a way of retelling scriptural stories in such a way as to impart to those stories new immediacy. The word *midrash* bears three meanings. First is the sense of Midrash as the explanation, by Judaic interpreters, of the meaning of individual verses of scripture. The result of the interpretation of a verse of scripture is called a Midrash exegesis. Second, the result of the interpretation of scripture is collected in Midrash compilations or a Midrash document. Third, the process of interpretation, for instance, the principles that guide the interpreter, is called Midrash method.

There are three types of interpretation of scripture characteristic of Midrash compilations. In the first, the focus of interest is on individual verses of scripture, and interpreting those verses, in the sequence in which they appear, forms the organizing principle of sustained discourse. The earliest compilations are organized mainly verse by verse, and in large measure they make their statements through comments on verses, saying the same thing in the same way about successive passages over and over again. These are the compilations that came to closure during the third century, as is shown by the frequent citation of the Mishnah and the Tosefta verbatim in those compilations. They are Sifra, to Leviticus; Sifrei to Numbers; and Sifrei to Deuteronomy. In the second type of interpretation, the center of interest is the testing and validating of large-scale propositions, which, through the reading of individual verses, an authorship wishes to test and validate. In that rather philosophical trend in rabbinic Midrash interpretation, the interpretation of individual verses takes a subordinate position—the appeal to facts of scripture in the service of the syllogism at hand. This form of writing with scripture so as to set forth a single, vast proposition, characterizes the second group of Midrash compilations, those associated with the Talmud of the Land of Israel. These are Genesis Rabbah, Leviticus Rabbah, and Pesikta deRab Kahana, all of which are believed to have come to closure between c. 450 and 500 C.E. The third approach focuses upon the reading of phrases or verses so as to make a single, remarkably cogent statement. Here the form is the same as before, but the result is not. Instead of relating a variety of things about many verses, the compilers of this third type of Midrash compilation really wish to say one thing in many different ways. This approach to Midrash compilation characterizes the documents associated with the Talmud of Babylonia. These are, in particular, Lamentations Rabbah, Esther Rabbah I (dealing with Esther 1–2), Song of Songs Rabbah, and Ruth Rabbah. A rough date for the conclusion of these compilations is c. 600 C.E.

All of these dates, approximate though they are, really are guesswork. The one thing that may be said for certain is that the first group is early; relative to that group, the second group is somewhat later; and the third group is the last in sequence. Nothing in any of the compilations plausibly permits us to date any document by reference to external events or evidence other than what the document itself gives us. But it is clear, in the unfolding of the Midrash compilations that form the other half of the Torah, oral and written, which, in secular language, comprises the classics of Judaism—the half focused upon scripture—we move from the exegesis of phrases to make a fresh point, through the reading of a variety of verses of scripture so as to form a proposition, to the compilation of readings of verses of scripture to make a single, stunning, and encompassing proposition.

Midrash Ahasweros   *see* ESTHER RABBAH I

Midrash Rabbah   compilation of Midrash collections devoted to the books of Genesis, Exodus, Leviticus, Numbers, Deuteronomy, and the Five Scrolls

Midrash Ruth   *see* RUTH RABBAH

Midrash Tanḥuma   Midrash compilation in which a rabbi, Tanḥuma, is often cited. A compilation of such Midrash exegeses, covering the whole of the Pentateuch, was printed under the title Midrash Tanḥuma by Salomon Buber in 1885. The earliest of the extant texts derives from the period after 800 C.E.

Midrash Threni   *see* LAMENTATIONS RABBAH

Migdal Eder   (Heb., tower of the flock) an undisclosed location between Bethlehem and Jerusalem, referred to once in scripture (Gen. 35:21) and mentioned at M. Shekalim 7:4 as an area in which cattle were grazed outside of Jerusalem

miggo   (Heb., in consequence of) In talmudic law, the term refers to (1) a principle of evidence holding that a deponent's statement should be believed on the ground that if he wished to lie, he could have invented a more advantageous lie than what he in fact said; and (2) a deed declared valid because the legal requirements needed to legitimate it could easily have been met or because one

aspect of those requirements indisputably has been met.

Migr.   *see* DE MIGRATIONE ABRAHAMI

mikdash   *see* SANCTUARY

Mikhwar, mountains of   a hill district in Transjordan, referred to with some frequency in the rabbinic literature. Its exact identity is unknown.

Mikra   (Heb.) designation of the Hebrew Bible, which Protestant Christians refer to as the Old Testament. In a Jewish context, the word "Mikra" is essentially interchangeable with "Holy Scriptures" and "Tanakh." *Mikra* can also refer to a specific biblical verse or passage as well as to the recitation of scripture or fixed prayers.

Mikvaot   Mishnah tractate on immersion pools. The tractate focuses on the kind of collection of water that serves to remove uncleanness (chaps. 1, 2–5); doubts in connection with immersion and immersion pools (chap. 2); the union of pools to form the requisite volume of water (chaps. 5–6); mixtures of water and wine, mud, and water in various locales (chaps. 7–8); and the use of the immersion pool and the problem of interposition between the flesh and the water (chaps. 8–10).

mikveh   (Heb.) immersion pool for ritual cleanness and baptism of converts, used for removing ritual uncleanness

milk and meat   "You shall not seethe a kid in the mother's milk" (Exod. 23:19, 34:26; Deut. 14:21) is taken to mean that cooking meat and milk together or eating them together is forbidden. All dairy products are considered milk. *See also* DIETARY LAWS.

min   (Heb.; pl., *minim*) a sectarian. In the rabbinic literature, the term usually applies to an apostate Jew, although it can signify as well a non-Jew who has rejected his people's gods (see, e.g., B. Abodah Zarah 65a). Understanding the term to refer specifically to Jewish-Christians, medieval censors often substituted it with the terms "Tzaduki" or "Kuti," which denote Sadducees. These substitutions remain in many contemporary printings.

mina   a unit of weight in the ancient Near East. Weights and measurements were not usually standardized; however, we have some information about them from archaeology. The *mina* was usually either fifty or sixty shekels, which would make it about 1.25 pounds (.5 kg) in Israel, based on the approximate weight of a shekel.

minhag   (Heb.) custom

minhah   1. afternoon prayer, recited at twilight
   2. meal-offering; *see also* MENAḤOT

minor, status of   Rabbinic Judaism deems a person a minor until the emergence of the first signs of puberty, estimated at the beginning of the thirteenth year for women and the beginning of the fourteenth year for men (Babli Niddah 52a). Prior to this age, the individual is in the same category as a deaf-mute or mentally incapacitated person, regarded as not responsible for his or her actions and exempt from ritual requirements.

Rabbinic law allows children over the age of six who understand business negotiations to sell movable property. Children are permitted to deal in immovables after the age of majority. This does not apply to inherited real estate, which they may not sell until they reach the age of twenty. A minor's testimony is not admissible in court, although in certain cases individuals who have reached the age of majority are permitted to testify regarding incidents they witnessed as minors (Babli Ketubot 28a).

Minor Prophets *see* PROPHETS

minyan *see* QUORUM

Miqra *see* MIKRA

miqvah *see* MIKVEH

Miqvaot *see* MIKVAOT

miracle an extraordinary event manifesting divine intervention in human affairs. The two most common biblical terms for the actions of God in the world and in human affairs are *peleh* and *mofet*. The first means an action that is so difficult as to be considered marvelous; the second means an act that fills the observer with wonder. These meanings are especially clear in Job, where God is said to do "great and unsearchable, marvelous things without number" (5:9), "things which we cannot comprehend" (37:5), "things too wonderful for me, which I did not know" (42:3). These terms are most frequently used in the Bible in accounts of God's actions in the events leading to Israel's liberation from slavery in Egypt in the time of Moses. Moses is told that God will strike Egypt's ruler, who otherwise would not let the people go (Exod. 4:20). God will perform many acts to convince Pharaoh. For example, Moses is to throw down his rod before the king, and it will become a serpent (Exod. 7:9). Even when God has done all the marvels, Pharaoh's heart is hardened and he refuses to release them (Exod. 11:10).

Moses' song after the successful crossing of the Red Sea recalls God's unique power and the wonder of God's action on behalf of his people (Exod. 15:11). When Israel becomes disobedient while still in the desert and God renews the covenant with Israel's people, He declares again that their relationship with Him rests on his incomparable actions on their behalf (Exod. 34:10). Again, in Deuteronomy 4:34, Israel is reminded of God's

unique activity in freeing and establishing his people. It is the recital of these marvelous divine acts that recur in the law (Deut. 7:18–19, 11:2–4), in the historical books (1 Chron. 16:12), and in the wisdom traditions (Wisd. of Sol. 19:8). They continue to be rehearsed from the time that Israel enters and settles in the Land of Canaan (Deut. 26:8, 29:3, 34:11–12), and in the hymns sung in the worship of YHWH (Ps. 78:43, 105:5, 27; 106:21, 135:9), as well as in the wisdom literature (Sir. 45:19) and the Prophets (Jer. 32:17–23).

In broader terms, it is God's "wondrous deeds" on behalf of his people that serve as a major theme in worship (Ps. 9:1, 86:10, 98:1; Isa. 25:1). God's amazing actions are also seen as taking place through Elijah, the prophet (Sir. 45:14). He continues to speak to and through the prophets by means of extraordinary events (Isa. 8:18). His actions on behalf of his people will be recognized as such only after the events, when they are recognized as God's work among them. In the later prophetic tradition, God's marvelous acts are foretold as happening in the future, when God fulfills his purpose for the renewal of his people (Joel 2:30; Dan. 6:27). It is essential that these deeds be acclaimed if the covenant people are to accept responsibility in that relationship (Isa. 29:13–14). But many will fail to understand God's work on their behalf to achieve his purpose. God's actions will be seen in the future to include severe punishment of idolaters, but also the preservation of his own people (Wisd. of Sol. 15:18–19:22).

The incomparable deeds of God are celebrated in Sirach 18:1–14. Looking back over the history of Israel, Sirach 44:1–50:24 describes the "famous men" through whom God has been at work to inform his people of his purpose for them and to shape the course of history so their destiny might be fulfilled. Examples of this perspective on the miraculous include the destruction of those in Israel who revolted against Moses and Aaron in the wilderness (Num. 16; Sir. 45:18–19) and the defeat of Israel's enemies through Joshua's leadership (Josh. 6–11; Sir. 46:2–8). The punitive actions Elijah carried out against the disobedient and rebellious element in Israel were accomplished "by the word of the Lord," although the prophet can be justly proud of his achievements (Sir. 48:1–4). Isaiah's ability to foresee the future was through "the spirit of might," and through God's power he was able to turn back the sun's movement and extend the king's life (2 Kings 20:10–11; Sir. 48:25).

God's mighty power on behalf of his faithful people is evident in the stories of Daniel and his companions, where natural powers and human capabilities are altered (Dan. 2:20–23). The faithful three who refuse to worship the golden image of the pagan king are thrown into the fiery furnace but are accompanied by one "like a son of the gods" and are preserved from the flames (Dan. 3). When Daniel violates the decree of King Darius by praying to the God of Israel, he is not devoured by the lions. Darius then acknowledges that the God of Daniel "delivers and rescues; he works signs and wonders." In 1 Enoch 46–48 there are descriptions of the amazing powers of the son of man, who removes kings from their thrones and destroys their kingdoms. In 4 Ezra 13, one like a human gathers the winds of heaven, carves out for himself a great mountain, and destroys his enemies by the flaming breath of his mouth. Operating through human agents, the marvelous powers of God are expected to work to accomplish the divine purpose for the world and for God's people. In Isaiah 35:5–6 there is a prediction that when God's renewal of the earth takes place, the blind will see, the deaf will hear, and the lame will walk.

Talmudic rabbis acknowledged that miracles occur and evidence God's action in the world. At the same time, they held that miracles were neither an appropriate foundation for faith, nor expected actions through which God could be depended upon to protect individuals or the Israelite people as a whole. This was especially the case insofar as contemporary generations were not as pious and worthy as earlier Jews (see, e.g., B. Berakhot 4a, 20a; B. Sanhedrin 94b). Accordingly, the rabbis held that one should not endanger him or herself in anticipation of a saving miracle (B. Taanit 20b; B. Ketubot 61b), and they considered human expectation of or demand for the miraculous to be folly (M. Abodah Zarah 4:7; B. Taanit 18b).

The rabbis believed the miracles described in the Bible to have been preordained, arranged by God at the time of creation, when, for instance, manna (consumed by the Israelites after the Exodus from Egypt) and the mouth of Balaam's talking ass were created (Mishnah Abot 5:6; see Exod. Rabbah 21:6). Miracles, therefore, did not actually interrupt the natural order; they were rather a part of that order, only appearing to people as extraordinary. In their own day, the rabbis saw as miraculous the wonders that occurred in daily life, for instance, in a person's recovery from an illness (B. Nedarim 41a) or even simply in people's having sufficient food (B. Pesahim 118a). Understood to result from divine providence, such everyday occurrences were viewed as greater miracles than the escape of

Hananiah, Mishael, and Azariah from the furnace (Dan. 3) or the parting of the Red Sea.

Mishnah a philosophical law code, completed c. 200 C.E. and promulgated by Judah the Prince in about the same year. The code contains six parts (divisions), comprising sixty-three tractates, concerning agricultural laws, festival and Sabbath law, family and personal status, torts, damages, and civil law, laws pertaining to the sanctuary, and rules of ritual cleanness. Through details of the law, a philosophical system of hierarchical classification of worldly things is set forth, showing that many things derive from one and one thing encompasses many; hence, the hierarchical unity of all being is set forth. The premise is that one God has generated many kinds and classes of things. The Mishnah classifies and compares, finding the right rule for each matter and each important situation, by determining whether one case is like another, or not like another. If it is like another, it follows the rule governing that other; if not, it follows the opposite of that rule. In this way, an orderly and logical way to sort out chaos and discover the inner order of being generates the balanced and stable, secure world described by the Mishnah. Historical events, when they enter at all, lose their one-time and unprecedented character and are shown to follow—even to generate—a fixed rule; events therefore are the opposite of eventful. This age and the age to come, history and the end of history—these categories play a very small role. Even the figure of the messiah serves as a classification; that is, designation or anointment distinguishes one priest from another.

The Mishnah focuses upon the sanctification of Israel; sanctification means, first, distinguishing Israel in all its dimensions from the world in all its ways and, second, establishing the stability, order, regularity, predictability, and reliability of Israel in the world of nature and supernature in particular at moments and in contexts of danger. Danger means instability, disorder, irregularity, uncertainty, and betrayal. Each topic of the system as a whole takes up a critical and indispensable moment or context of social being. Through what is said in regard to each of the Mishnah's principal topics, what this halakhic (legal) system as a whole wishes to declare is fully expressed. Yet if the parts severally and jointly give the message of the whole, the whole cannot exist without all of the parts, so well joined and carefully crafted are they all. This brings us to a rapid survey of the several parts of the system, the six divisions and their sixty-three tractates.

The Division of Agriculture treats two topics: (1)

producing crops in accord with the scriptural rules on the subject, and (2) paying the required offerings and tithes to the priests, the Levites, and the poor. The principal point of this division is that the Land of Israel is holy because God has a claim both on the land and on what it produces. God's claim must be honored by setting aside a portion of the produce for those for whom God has designated it. God's ownership must be acknowledged by observing the rules God has laid down for use of the land. In sum, the division is divided along the following lines: (1) rules for producing crops in a state of holiness—the tractates Kilayim, Shebiit, and Orlah; (2) rules for disposing of crops in accord with the rules of holiness—the tractates Peah, Demai, Terumot, Maaserot, Maaser Sheni, Hallah, Bikkurim, and Berakhot.

The Division of Appointed Times forms a system in which the advent of a holy day, such as the Sabbath of creation, sanctifies the life of the Israelite village through imposing on the village rules on the model of those of the Temple. The purpose of the system, therefore, is to bring into alignment the moment of sanctification of the village and the life of the home with the moment of sanctification of the Temple on those same occasions of appointed times. The underlying and generative theory of the system is that the village is the mirror image of the Temple. If things are done in one way in the Temple, they will be done in the opposite way in the village. Together the village and the Temple on the occasion of the holy day therefore form a single continuum, a completed creation, which is thus awaiting sanctification.

The Division of Women defines the women in the social economy of Israel's supernatural and natural reality. Women acquire definition wholly in relationship to men, who impart form to the Israelite social economy. The status of women is effected through both supernatural and natural, worldly action. What man and woman do on earth provokes a response in heaven, and the correspondences are perfect. Thus women are defined and secured both in heaven and here on earth, and that position is always and invariably relative to men. The principal interest for the Mishnah is the point at which a woman becomes or ceases to be holy to a particular man, that is, enters or leaves the marital union. These transfers of women are the dangerous and disorderly points in the relationship of woman to man, and therefore, the Mishnah states, to society as well. The formation of the marriage is discussed in Kiddushin and Ketubot, as well as in Yebamot. The rules for the duration of the marriage are scattered throughout, but derive especially from parts of Ketubot, Nedarim, and Nazir and from the paramount unit of Sotah. The dissolution of the marriage is dealt with in Gittin, as well as in Yebamot. We see very clearly, therefore, that important overall are issues of the transfer of property, along with women, covered in Ketubot and to some measure in Kiddushin, and the proper documentation of the transfer of women and property, treated in Ketubot and Gittin. The critical issues, therefore, turn upon legal documents—writs of divorce, for example—and legal recognition of changes in the ownership of property, for example, through the collection of the settlement of a marriage contract by a widow, through the provision of a dowry, or through the disposition of the property of a woman during the period in which she is married. Within this orderly world of documentary and procedural concerns a place is made for the disorderly conception of the marriage not formed by human volition but decreed in heaven, the levirate connection (marriage between the widow and surviving brother of a man who died childless). Yebamot states that supernature sanctifies a woman to a man under the conditions of the levirate connection. What it says by indirection is that man sanctifies too: man, like God, can sanctify the relationship between a man and a woman, and can also effect the cessation of the sanctity of that same relationship. Five of the seven tractates of the Division of Women are devoted to the formation and dissolution of the marital bond. Kiddushin, Ketubot, and Gittin treat what is done by man here on earth, that is, formation of a marital bond through betrothal and the marriage contract and dissolution of a marital bond through divorce and its consequences. Sotah is devoted to what is done by woman here on earth. And Yebamot, greatest of the seven in size and in formal and substantive brilliance, deals with the corresponding heavenly intervention into the formation and end of a marriage: the effect of death upon both the formation of the marital bond and its dissolution. The other two tractates, Nedarim and Nazir, draw into one the two realms of reality, heaven and earth, as they work out the effects of vows, perhaps because vows taken by women and subject to the confirmation or abrogation of the father or husband make a deep impact upon the marital life of the woman who has taken them.

The Division of Damages comprises two subsystems, which fit together in a logical way. One part presents rules for the normal conduct of civil society. These cover commerce, trade, real estate, and other matters of everyday intercourse, as well as mishaps, such as damages by chattels and persons, fraud, overcharges, interest, and the like, in that same context of everyday social life. The other part describes the institutions governing the normal conduct of civil society, that is, courts of administration, and the penalties at the disposal of the government for the enforcement of the law. The two subjects form a single tight and systematic dissertation on the nature of Israelite society and its economic, social, and political relationships, as the Mishnah envisages them. The main point of the first of the two parts of the Division of Damages is expressed in the sustained unfolding of the three Babas, Baba Kamma, Baba Metzia, and Baba Batra. It is that the task of society is to maintain perfect stasis, to preserve the prevailing situation, and to secure the stability of all relationships. To this end, in the interchanges of buying and selling, giving and taking, and borrowing and lending it is important that there be an essential equality of interchange. No party in the end should have more than what he had at the outset, and none should be the victim of a sizable shift in fortune and circumstance. All parties' rights to, and in, this stable and unchanging economy of society are to be preserved. When the condition of a person is violated, so far as possible the law will secure the restoration of the antecedent status.

The Division of Holy Things presents a system of sacrifice and sanctuary, addressing matters concerning the praxis of the altar and maintenance of the sanctuary. The praxis of the altar, specifically, involves sacrifice and things set aside for sacrifice and consequently deemed consecrated. This topic is covered in Zebaḥim and part of Ḥullin, Menaḥot, Temurah, Keritot, part of Meilah, Tamid, and Kinnim. The maintenance of the sanctuary (inclusive of the personnel) is dealt with in Bekhorot, Arakhin, part of Meilah, Middot, and part of Ḥullin. Viewed as a whole, the contents of this division's eleven tractates fall into three groups: (1) rules for the altar and the praxis of the cult, set forth in Zebaḥim Menaḥot, Ḥullin, Keritot, Tamid, and Kinnim; additional relevant material appears in Bekhorot and Meilah; (2) rules for the altar and the animals set aside for the cult, set forth in Arakhin, Temurah, and Meilah; additional relevant material appears in Bekhorot; (3) rules for the altar and support of the Temple staff and buildings, set forth in Bekhorot and Middot; additional relevant material appears in Ḥullin, Arakhin, Meilah, and Tamid. In short, this division speaks of the sacrificial cult and the sanctuary in which the cult is conducted.

The law pays special attention to the matter of the status of the property of the altar and of the sanctuary—both materials to be utilized in the actual sacrificial rites, and property the value of which supports the cult and sanctuary in general. Both are deemed to be sanctified, that is, "Holy Things."

The Division of Purities presents a very simple system of three principal parts: sources of uncleanness, objects and substances susceptible to uncleanness, and modes of purification from uncleanness. Thus it tells the story of what makes a given sort of object unclean and what makes it clean. The tractates on these several topics are as follows: (1) sources of uncleanness—Ohalot, Negaim, Niddah, Makhshirin, Zabim, and Tebul Yom; (2) objects and substances susceptible to uncleanness—Kelim, Tohorot, and Uksin; and (3) modes of purification—Parah, Mikvaot, Yadayim. Viewed as a whole, the Division of Purities treats the interplay of persons, food, and liquids. Dry inanimate objects or food are not susceptible to uncleanness. What is wet is susceptible, so liquids activate the system. What is unclean, moreover, emerges from uncleanness through the operation of liquids, specifically, through immersion in fit water of requisite volume and in natural condition. Liquids therefore deactivate the system. Thus, water in its natural condition is what concludes the process by removing uncleanness. Water in its unnatural condition, that is, deliberately affected by human agency, is what imparts susceptibility to uncleanness to begin with. The uncleanness of persons, furthermore, is signified by body liquids, or flux in the case of the menstruating woman (discussed in Niddah) and the zab (discussed in Zabim). Corpse uncleanness is conceived to be a kind of effluent, a viscous gas, which flows like liquid. Utensils for their part receive uncleanness when they form receptacles able to contain liquid. In sum, we have a system in which the invisible flow of fluidlike substances or powers serve to put food, drink, and receptacles into the status of uncleanness and to remove those things from that status. Whether or not we call the system metaphysical, it certainly has no material basis, but is conditioned upon highly abstract notions. Thus, in material terms, the effect of liquid is upon food, drink, utensils, and man. The consequence has to do with who may eat and drink what food and liquid, and what food and drink may be consumed in which pots and pans. These loci are specified by tractates on utensils (Kelim) and on food and drink (Tohorot and Uksin). The human being is ambivalent. Persons fall in the middle, between sources and loci of uncleanness, because they are both. They serve as sources of uncleanness. They also become unclean. The za<u>b</u>, suffering the uncleanness described in Leviticus, chapter 15, the menstruating woman, the woman after childbirth, and the person afflicted with the skin ailment described in Leviticus, chapters 13 and 14—all are sources of uncleanness. However, being unclean, they fall within the system's loci, its program of consequences. They make other things unclean and also are subject to penalties because they are unclean. Unambiguous sources of uncleanness never also constitute loci affected by uncleanness. They always are unclean and never can become clean: the corpse, the dead creeping thing, and similar things. Inanimate sources of uncleanness and inanimate objects are affected by uncleanness. Systemically unique, man and liquids have the capacity to inaugurate the processes of uncleanness (as sources) and also are subject to those same processes (as objects of uncleanness).

Misinai melody the oldest stratum of Ashkenazi synagogue music. It is putatively traced to Mount Sinai, but actually originates no earlier than the twelfth to the fifteenth centuries.

missionary literature literature written to propagate one's religion and perhaps even to gain converts. It has been argued that certain types of Jewish literature were written specifically with a gentile audience in mind, with more than one potential purpose. One type might be simply apologetic, intended to present Judaism in as good a light as possible. Another might, however, be aimed at the actual conversion of Gentiles to Judaism. It is much easier to identify the first type than the second. It seems fairly clear that some literature was written to present Judaism attracively to outsiders. A good example is Josephus's *Antiquities of the Jews,* in which Jewish history is presented as ancient and venerable, Jewish law is treated as modeled on a rational ideal, and the Jewish patriarchs appear in the recognizable guise of Hellenistic sages. The biblical text is sanitized so that several disreputable episodes are quietly omitted. A number of other writings, including some of the works of Philo, have been suggested as performing the same function. One of the principal works said to be aimed at conversion is Joseph and Asenath, which pictures the actual conversion of a non-Jew. *See also* PROSELYTIZATION.

Mithridates I Parthian ruler (r. 171–138 B.C.E.). Although not the first Parthian ruler, Mithridates I was the real founder of the Parthian Empire. He conquered the western reaches of present-day Iran, reaching Media in 155 B.C.E. and Seleucia in 141 B.C.E. By 139 B.C.E., Babylonia, Mesene, Characene, and Elymaeis were in his hands. Mithridates was part of a military aristocracy, and he established the Parthian policy of conciliating the various groups in the empire, including the Jews, and of not interfering with the religious life and cultures of the peoples they conquered.

Mithridates II Parthian ruler (r. 123–88 B.C.E.). Under Mithridates II, the Parthians definitively established their hold on Babylonia and expanded into central Asia. During his reign, the Parthians began to claim that they were descended from the ancient Achaemenids, and the rulers called themselves by the ancient title "king of kings." During his reign, Parthian architecture, as an amalgamation of Hellenistic and Iranian forms, began to develop. In addition, Seleucus of Seleucia, an important astronomer, and Apollodorus of Artemita, who wrote a history of Parthia, flourished.

Mithridates III Parthian ruler (r. 57–55 B.C.E.). When he was expelled by the Parthian nobility, he started a civil war. During the course of his revolt, he won over Babylonia, including Seleucia, before 55 B.C.E. However, Orodes I retook Seleucia and Babylonia and executed Mithridates III.

mitzvah (Heb., commandments) in the technical sense, scriptural or rabbinic injunctions; later, also used in sense of good deeds. Every human activity may represent an act of obedience to divine will.

mizbeaḥ *see* ALTAR

Mizpah alternatively, Mizpeh; the name of several biblical sites in and around the Land of Israel. The name means "watchtower"; in scripture and at M. Peah 2:6, it appears with the definite article. The most significant Mizpah (e.g., Josh. 18:26) was in the territory of Benjamin and is probably the modern Tell en-Natzbeh, 12 kilometers north of Jerusalem.

Moab land east of the Jordan River and Dead Sea; a neighbor of biblical Israel. The Moabites' eponymic ancestor was the son of Lot and his elder daughter (Gen. 19:30–38). Rabbinic texts are ambivalent about the Moabites: on the one hand, conscious of the continuing conflicts between biblical Israelites and Moabites but, on the other, cognizant that Ruth, the great-grandmother of King David, was a Moabite (Gen. Rabbah 51).

mobad chief of the magi. Ardashir I seems to have established a hierarchy of church officials: The magus was under the authority of the *herpat* (priest in charge of the sacred fire) and the *mobad,* headed at the top by the *herpatan herpat* (chief justice) and the *mobadan mobad* (high priest). Ardashir placed a *mobad* in each satrapy to foster the interests of the state religion. The Talmud indicates that under Ardashir, the *mobads* forbade those Jewish religious practices, such as the preparation of meat, the use of ritual baths, and burial of the dead, that offended the sensibilities of the followers of the Mazdean state church.

Modern Aramaic   *see* ARAMAIC, MODERN

Modiim   village in the district of Lydda, where the Maccabean revolt broke out; home of Mattathias the Hasmonean and his descendants. The village is about 15 miles from Jerusalem; in rabbinic times, it marked the boundary of the area deemed close to the holy city (M. Pesaḥim 9:2), within which individuals could be trusted regarding the purity of wine and oil (M. Ḥagigah 3:5). One Tannaitic authority is said to come from there, Eleazar of Modiim, a relative of Bar Kokhba.

moed   (Heb.) festival

Moed   the second division of the Mishnah, devoted to the rules of Temple sacrifice on Sabbath and festival occasions and laws pertaining to the home on those same holy days

Moed Katan   Mishnah tractate devoted to the intermediate days of a festival, with special interest in labor that may or may not be performed between the first and final festival days of Tabernacles and Passover (chaps. 1–2), commerce on the intermediate days of a festival (chaps. 2–3), and burial of the dead and mourning on the intermediate days of a festival (chap. 3)

mohel   (Heb.) ritual circumciser

money   a medium of exchange often used in standard weights and coinage. In the biblical period, silver appears to have been the most common currency. Rather than being coined, it was carried in unminted form and weighed out as required (see Deut. 25:13–16 and Lev. 19:36, which record warnings against false measures but not against adulteration of coins). Coined money came into use in the Persian period (see Ezra 8:27 and 1 Chron. 29:7, which refer to values of Persian coinage).

Rabbinic law reveals a continuing debate regarding the use of coins other than silver. In general, the rabbis retain silver as the primary coinage, allowing the use of gold or copper only in limited circumstances, for example, if they are to be exchanged for silver (M. Baba Metzia 4:1). Specific usages of gold coins are debated. While the House of Shammai prohibits a householder who needs to take second tithe to Jerusalem from exchanging silver *shekels* for gold, the House of Hillel permits it (M. Maaser Sheni 2:7). In this, the House of Hillel's approach may reflect an acceptance of the gold standard common in the Roman culture of the day.

In rabbinic economics, money functions as a means of exchange that facilitates sale and purchase of goods, that is, barter, but money is not viewed as itself a commodity that may be traded or invested for profit. All earnings from this latter use of money are deemed "interest," an inappropriate economic gain that is prohibited under rabbinic law.

In the rabbinic literature, the smallest copper coin is called a *perutah*. Eight *perutah*s are valued at an *issar*. Two *issar*s equal a *pondion* and two *pondion*s have the value of a *maah*, which is the smallest silver coin. Twelve *pondion*s equal a *denar* (also called a *zuz*) and two *denar*s have the value of a *shekel*. Two *shekel*s equal a *sela*. Less frequently mentioned are the *teresit*, equal in value to three *issar*s; the *asper*, five of which equal a *denar*; and the *tropaic*, two of which equal a *denar*. Twenty-five *denar*s have the value of one golden *denar*, and one hundred *denar*s equal a *mina*.

money changers   financiers and bankers in the Hellenistic and Roman periods who converted, for a premium of between 4 and 8 percent, various types of coinage to facilitate commerce. According to Mark 11:15, Matthew 21:12, and John 2:5, at the time of Passover, Jesus overturned the tables of the money changers, who would have been converting coinage into Tyrian silver didrachms, the currency accepted by the Temple (Exod. 30:13; Lev. 5:15, 27:25; Num. 3:47), and may have then been engaged in collecting the annual half-shekel tax (see M. Shek. 1:3). Debates continue on the symbolic meaning as well as the historicity of Jesus' action.

money lending   Biblical and rabbinic laws permit loans among Jews only where the lender charges the borrower no interest at all. The rabbis extended the prohibition of interest and increase to a variety of cases of commercial transactions where one party may derive some financial benefit from providing capital for the use of another party. The Mishnah (Baba Metzia 5) goes so far as to prohibit as interest the lending party receiving favors of any kind, even favorable statements, from a borrower. However, biblical and rabbinic law permitted a Jew to lend money to a Gentile and charge interest and to borrow from a Gentile and pay him interest. Jews could circumvent the prohibition of lending to one another with interest through the use of a Gentile as an intermediary in the transaction. Similarly, later when canon law imposed restrictions against usury among Christians in the Middle Ages, Jews were used as intermediaries. The stereotype of the medieval Jew as money lender has been exaggerated much beyond its historical fact and is a prominent theme in anti-Semitic writings from the Middle Ages to the present.

Monobazus II first-century-C.E. ruler of Adiabene. He was the brother and successor of Izates of Adiabene, who converted to Judaism. Monobazus also embraced Judaism. The Jewish sources credit Monobazus with using all of his resources to support the poor in a year of famine. They also emphasize his generosity to the people of Jerusalem and the Temple, his resources, and his wisdom. Josephus claims that he and his mother, Helena, had palaces in Jerusalem and that he buried his mother and his brother in a spectacular tomb in Jerusalem. Some of his family participated in the Palestinian Revolt against Rome in 66–73 C.E.

monogamy and polygamy The marriage of a man exclusively to one woman was the expected norm in Israelite and later rabbinic society. Polygamy was permitted but there is little evidence that it was practiced. Biblical sources provide a somewhat ambiguous model in this area. In its narratives, Adam had one wife, Abraham married his slave at the request of his wife, Isaac had one spouse, and Jacob was tricked into marrying two sisters who then asked him to marry their maids. The Israelite kings openly practiced polygamy but were castigated for it (Deut. 17:17). The prophets, priests, and other prominent biblical figures were monogamous. Social and economic obligations imposed on a husband to support each wife equally (Exod. 21:10) and to provide a marriage contract for each made monogamy more attractive. The obligatory polygamy imposed on a man whose brother died childless and which obligated him to marry as a *levir* his brother's wife was also rarely carried out in rabbinic times (M. Bekh. 1:7). Instead, more often the ritual of *ḥalitzah* was performed, freeing the woman from that relationship. Rabbenu Gershom b. Judah (d. 1028 C.E.) officially banned polygamy by decree for Ashkenazic Jews of France and Germany. *See also* MARRIAGE.

Monophysitism form of eastern Christianity. The doctrine holds that in the person of the incarnate Christ there is only a single, divine nature. This stands in opposition to the orthodox teaching, which holds that there is a double nature, divine and human, in Christ. Monophysitism became a distinct doctrine after the Council of Chalcedon, 451 C.E., which detailed the orthodox doctrine. The Byzantine emperors Zeno and Anastasius (474–518 C.E.) tried to appease the Monophysites, while Justin I and Justinian (518–565 C.E.) supported the Orthodox Christians. The Monophysites often accused their enemies, the Nestorians, of holding Jewish views on Jesus.

Mordecai, Dream of *see* DREAM OF MORDECAI

Moriah, Mount site in Jerusalem where Solomon built the First Temple (2 Chron. 3:1); associated in scripture and rabbinic literature with "the land of Moriah" (Gen. 22:2), where God sent Abraham to sacrifice Isaac. The holiest site in Judaism, Mount Moriah, represented by the Temple platform in the Old City of Jerusalem, currently is occupied by the El-Aqsa Mosque and the Dome of the Rock, from which, according to Muslim tradition, Mohammed ascended into heaven.

Moses the leader of Israel in Egypt and during the Exodus and wilderness wanderings. Exodus reports that Moses, along with all other Hebrew males, was supposed to be drowned in the Nile River, but his mother hid him in a basket in some rushes, where the pharaoh's daughter found him. She named him Moses (the biblical text derives his Egyptian name from the Hebrew word for "to draw out") and raised him in the palace. When he was forty years of age, he killed an Egyptian and fled to Midian to avoid punishment. There, he married a daughter of the priest Jethro and, while serving him as a shepherd, received the revelation of the divine name YHWH at the burning bush. On that occasion, the Lord commissioned him to return to Egypt and lead his fellow Hebrews from their servitude. After the ten plagues, he led the nation across the Reed Sea and to Mount Sinai (the location of the burning bush), where the Lord revealed to him the Ten Commandments and the many other instructions that were part of the covenant between God and his people. Moses served as the people's leader and frequent intercessor for forty years but was denied the right to enter the promised land because of a single act of disobedience. According to the story in Deuteronomy 34, he was allowed to view the land from a mountaintop but was not permitted to enter it. Deuteronomy 18 presents Moses as the model prophet: in each generation, it says, the Lord will raise up a prophet like him and use him as the divine mouthpiece. The later books of the Hebrew Bible (such as Ezra and Nehemiah) indicate that by then he was regarded as the author of much of the legal material now found in Exodus through Deuteronomy. Ezra was said to be a scribe who was an expert in the law of Moses (Ezra 7), and he was commissioned by the Persian king to implement that law.

Moses continued to play an important role for Jewish people after the biblical period. The laws that were disclosed to him served as the legal basis for Jewish life in the centuries of the Second Temple. Several books that were clearly written long after his time were attributed to him. Examples are the Book of Jubilees (c. 150 B.C.E.), the first witness to the belief that he had written not only the legal sections of Exodus and Deuteronomy but also the narrative parts of Genesis and Exodus, which claims to contain revelations from God to an angel, who in turn communicated them to Moses when he was on Mount Sinai, and the Testament of Moses, which contains his final, predictive address to Joshua before his death. The Dead Sea Scrolls, too, include some documents that are attributed to Moses' authorship, the Temple Scroll, for instance. In the scrolls, Moses is primarily associated with the law or teaching revealed to him in the biblical books Exodus, Leviticus, Numbers, and Deuteronomy. For the first-century-C.E. Jewish historian Josephus, Moses was the founder of the Israelite theocracy. Moreover, Josephus reproduced a story about Moses' successes as an Egyptian general before he led the people out of Egypt. The historian indicated that the parties of the Pharisees and Sadducees differed regarding the use of Moses' law: the Pharisees considered it and the traditional interpretations of it to be authoritative in legal matters, while the Sadducees believed that only what was written in that law could be employed for this purpose. Philo (c. 20 B.C.E.–50 C.E.), the Jewish philosopher from Alexandria, considered Moses a divine man possessed of supreme gifts—the perfect recipient for God's revelation of the highest wisdom.

Moses figures prominently in the New Testament as well. Matthew's gospel presents Jesus as parallel to Moses in several ways: their lives were endangered as infants; both were associated with Egypt and departed from it for the Land of Israel; both were in the wilderness (Moses was there for forty years, and Jesus was tempted for forty days); and both their stories feature inspired teaching from a mountain (Sinai for Moses, and the Sermon on the Mount for Jesus). Moses, with Elijah, appeared to Jesus on the mount of transfiguration (Mark 9 and parallels). Moses' name appears in Paul's letters when the apostle distinguishes his gospel of faith from the way of Moses' law (Gal. 3; 2 Cor. 3). Paul considered the law revealed to Moses to be associated with an old and now superseded covenant between God and his people. In Hebrews, Moses is contrasted with Jesus as a servant to a son

(chap. 3); later, the writer presents Moses as an example of faith, one who long before Christ suffered abuse for Christ's sake (chap. 11). The letter of Jude mentions an extrabiblical story about Moses' corpse (verse 9), and in Revelation 11 one of the witnesses who will be active at the end of time is described in language that reminds one of Moses.

Rabbinic Judaism primarily refers to Moses in his role as lawgiver, understanding him to have received both the written law, contained in scripture, and the oral law, embodied in rabbinic teachings, from God. In this thinking, Moses, called Moshe Rabbenu, that is, Moses Our Teacher, was the prototypical rabbi and foremost scholar of Torah. Central in rabbinic Judaism is the idea that even new interpretations of Torah embody truths that were revealed to Moses. This concept is highlighted in an account of Moses' being brought by God to the academy of Akiba, where Moses finds that he does not comprehend Akiba's teachings. His mind is set at ease only when Akiba proclaims that his teachings comprise laws he had received as a tradition from Moses at Sinai (B. Menahot 29b).

The rabbis viewed the life of Moses as the model for that of all great teachers. Like him, Hillel, Akiba, and Yohanan b. Zakkai lived 120 years. Moses was understood to have acquired from God forty-nine of the fifty gates of understanding (B. Nedarim 38a) and to have seen God as in a translucent mirror. In this way, Moses was above all other prophets, who saw God as though through dark glass (B. Yebamot 49b).

The rabbis heaped on Moses the highest praise, holding that the entire world was created only for his sake (Lev. Rabbah 36:4) and that, rather than die, Moses continues to stand and serve God as he did on Mount Sinai (B. Sotah 13b). At the same time, rabbinic texts are careful to depict Moses as a human being with human faults. Moses was not uniquely worthy of receiving the Torah. Yose holds that if Moses had not predated him, Ezra could have received it (B. Sanhedrin 21b). Moses' temper is said to have caused him to forget his wisdom (B. Pesahim 66b), and Moses made mistakes, although he admitted them without embarrassment (B. Zebahim 101a).

Moses died through a kiss of God, and God himself buried Moses in a grave prepared at the time of creation on the eve of the first Sabbath. Moses' tomb is opposite Beth Peor but cannot be located, since, wherever one stands, it appears to be elsewhere (B. Sotah 14a).

Moses, Apocalypse of   *see* ADAM AND EVE, BOOKS OF

Moses, Assumption of   a lost work that described Moses' assumption to heaven. It is attested by quotations in Jude, Clement of Alexandria, Origen, the Acts of the Council of Nicaea, and other Christian authors. Its name has been wrongly attached to the Testament of Moses.

Quotations of the Assumption suggest the following sketch of its contents. When Moses ascends Mount Nebo, Michael is sent to bury his body. Satan (Gr.: *ho diabolos*) opposes the burial, claiming to be the lord of matter and accusing Moses of being a murderer. Michael rebukes him, stating that God created the world and humans through the holy spirit, and accusing Satan of having provoked the sin of Adam and Eve. Joshua and Caleb watch as Moses, living in the spirit, ascends to heaven, while his dead body is buried in the recesses of the mountains.

The confrontation between Michael and Satan (cf. Jude 9) reflects Jewish traditions about the opposition of the two spirits and Satan's role as accuser (cf. Jub. 48:2) and employs wording from Zechariah 3:1–5. Satan's claim to be lord of matter parallels Luke 4:6 and adumbrates Gnostic views. The quotation in Jude indicates that the text was composed before the second century C.E. Moses' presence in the story of Jesus' transfiguration (Mark 9:1–8) may reflect knowledge of the tradition in the mid-first century C.E. *See also* MOSES, TESTAMENT OF.

Moses, Testament of   a rewritten version of Deuteronomy 31–34, cast in the genre of a testament. It is extant in a fifth-century Latin version that is poorly preserved on a single palimpsest which was first edited in 1861 under the incorrect name of The Assumption of Moses. This title was applied to the work because a series of patristic quotations from another text, The Assumption of Moses, also quoted this text, probably because the two separate works had been combined into one. The Latin translates a Greek version of a Hebrew or Aramaic original that was composed during Antiochus Epiphanes' persecution of the Jews (168–165) and revised in the first decade of the common era.

The heart of the Testament is a summary of Israelite history from the conquest to the time of Antiochus, structured according to the Deuteronomic historical scheme (sin–punishment–turning point–salvation), which is repeated in two cycles (chaps. 2–4, 5–10). The time of composition is indicated by unmistakable references to the 160s in chapters 5 and 8. The story of Taxo and his sons (chap. 9) also parallels contemporary martyr accounts. In his role as a catalyzer of salvation,

Taxo parallels the unnamed intercessor in the first cycle (4:1–4, possibly Daniel), but his action is radical. With an allusion to Deuteronomy 32:43, Taxo and his sons provoke their own deaths, appealing for God's vengeance (9:7). Chapter 10 describes the anticipated response to this prayer (v. 2) in the form of cosmic judgment, Israel's exaltation to heaven, and the destruction of its enemies. Much in the beginning and end of the Testament paraphrases Deuteronomy (cf. 1:1–11 with Deut. 31:7, 14; 9:7 and 10:2 with Deut. 32:43; 10:3 with Deut. 33:2; 10:7–8 with Deut. 33:27–29; 11:5–8 with Deut. 34:5–6). Details in chapter 10 also parallel apocalyptic predictions of the judgment in Daniel 12:1–3 and 1 Enoch 1:4–7.

The Testament was composed in some unknown group of pious Jews, who interpreted Antiochus's actions as punishment for the sins of their compatriots, which are described as pollution of the cult, gluttony, oppression of the poor, and religious hypocrisy (chaps. 5–7). Similar to the author of Daniel and different from the Hasmoneans, this author finds a solution not in human militant action, but in passive resistance of the martyrs. This ideology has some connections with 2 Maccabees, which recounts some of the same events; however, here salvation is not seen in accomplished historical events, but is anticipated in an imminent cosmic catastrophe.

By emphasizing the determined course of history (10:12–13, 12:4–5) and attributing the work's accurate detailed predictions of the present to a figure of antiquity, whose secret prophecy has been hidden until the latter days (1:16–18, 10:1; cf. Deut. 31:26, Dan. 12:4), the author adds credibility to his predictions of imminent salvation. Thus, like the almost contemporary pseudo-Mosaic author of Jubilees 23:16–32, this writer offers consolation and encouragement to his troubled readers.

An editor, writing in the difficult times after the death of Herod the Great, updated the text by interpolating chapter 6 with its references to the Hasmonean high priests, Herod and his sons, and the Roman intervention by Varus after Herod's death in 4 B.C.E., and thus reinterpreted chapters 9 and 10 as a scenario for current resistance and imminent salvation. *See also* MOSES, ASSUMPTION OF.

Moses Our Rabbi   representation of Moses as sage and rabbi, studying Torah as God's first disciple, teaching Torah to Joshua, his disciple, and onward through time

Moshe Rabbenu   *see* MOSES OUR RABBI

Most High   an epithet for God (Heb.: *elyon*, Gr.: *hypsistos*). El Elyon is an ancient Hebrew title for

God (e.g., Gen. 14:18–20, where Melchizedek is priest of God Most High, El Elyon). It was never a distinctively Israelite or Jewish title for God. It is also attested in the Sefire inscriptions from ancient Syria, and in the *Phoenician History* of Philo of Byblos, which refers to "a certain Elioun, called Most High." The Greek equivalent was widely used as a divine title by both Jews and Gentiles in the Hellenistic period. In Daniel 7:18 and 27, the Aramaic plural form *elyonin* is used in the expression "holy ones of the Most High." Some scholars have argued that it should be taken as an adjective in this case ("Most High holy ones"); however, *elyon* is not the usual Aramaic word for high, but an epithet for the deity. The plural, then, should be taken as a plural of manifestations, like the Hebrew word *elohim,* "god." A parallel expression using the singular, "holy ones of Elyon," is found in the Damascus Document from the Cairo Geniza (CD 20:8). *See also* GOD, NAMES OF.

mountains These typical features of Mediterranean topography were thought to be joining places between heaven and earth, or where subterranean springs welled up between heaven and the abyss. Because of its "proximity" to heaven, a mountain, especially a high mountain, suggested itself as the dwelling place of the deity, as a ladder on which God descended to earth, or at least a place where humans could most easily commune with God. Sacred mountains included Mount Cassius in Syria, Mount Hermon in Upper Galilee, the Lebanon and Anti-Lebanon ranges, Mount Gerizim, Mount Zion, and Mount Sinai. Hermon was where the rebel angels had descended from heaven to earth and where Enoch ascended to heaven. In the New Testament, Jesus is transfigured in glory on a "very high" mountain (quite possibly Hermon) (Mark 9:2–8) and commissions his disciples on a mountain in Galilee (Matt. 28:16–20). The cosmology of 1 Enoch 17–19 and 22–25 is populated with many mysterious mountains from which Enoch sees the mysteries of the universe. Sheol is said to be a great mountain (chap. 22), and God's mountain throne in the far northwest is flanked by seven small mountains (18:6–8; 24–25). *See also* HERMON, MOUNT; SINAI, MOUNT.

Mount Gerizim   *see* GERIZIM, MOUNT

Mount Hermon   *see* HERMON, MOUNT

Mount Horeb   *see* HOREB, MOUNT

Mount Moriah   *see* MORIAH, MOUNT

Mount Sinai   *see* SINAI, MOUNT

Mount Zeboim   *see* ZEBOIM, MOUNT

mourning   ritualized responses to death or to a crisis such as war and famine. Mourning rites encompass the mourner's clothing, diet, interpersonal relationships, and prayer. Genesis 50:10 (see also 1 Sam. 31:13; 1 Chron. 10:12 [with fasting]; Sir. 22:12) notes a mourning period of seven days. In the Life of Adam and Eve (Apocalypse of Moses), Michael tells Seth not to mourn more than six days. Sackcloth (the traditional garment for mourning), tearing clothes, and sprinkling ashes on one's head indicate mourning as well as repentance (Gen. 37:34; Jon. 3:6–8; 1 Macc. 2:14; 3:47; Matt. 11:21; Jos. Asen. 10). The Life of Adam and Eve 51, Mark 5:38, John 11:33, and many other texts note weeping. The Sentences of the Syriac Menander 458–474 instruct on the etiquette of mourning.

The talmudic rabbis formalized the rules for mourning, detailing activities permitted or forbidden of the mourner and setting out fixed periods within which mourning was to be conducted (see B. Moed Katan 22b–23a and the minor talmudic tractate Semaḥot). From death until the funeral, a period referred to as Aninut, the individual whose dead lies unburied before him was exempt from religious requirements, such as the recitation of fixed prayer and the donning of the prayer shawl and phylacteries. The individual additionally was prohibited from indulging in luxuries, such as drinking wine or eating meat (B. Berakhot 17b). After the funeral, during a seven-day period called Shiva (seven) or Avilut (mourning), mourners remained at home, sitting on low stools or on the floor, a common sign of mourning. During Shiva, they were prohibited from conducting business or doing other work, from bathing, cutting the hair, engaging in sexual relations, wearing leather shoes, or otherwise engaging in pleasurable activities. It was customary at this time for relatives and friends to visit and express condolences (B. Moed Katan 28b).

The prohibitions against cutting one's hair, getting married, and participating in joyous celebrations or social gathering continued for thirty days from burial (Sheloshim) and, in the case of the death of one's parent or spouse, for the entire year after the death. The prohibition against marriage was abrogated for a man with small children who needed to be cared for or for a man who had no children, in which case the obligation to procreate overrode the mourning ritual. In these circumstances, the mourner even could marry immediately following the death.

The rabbis viewed the thirty days after burial as an appropriate and sufficient period of grief, after which time the mourner was to return to his or her usual life. Excessive grief after thirty days was viewed negatively and understood potentially to cause the death of another, for whom the mourner would then need to continue to mourn (B. Moed Katan 27b). *See also* BURIAL.

MRI *see* MEKHILTA OF RABBI ISHMAEL

Mucianus, Gaius Licinius legate of Syria (67–69 C.E.). He became governor of Syria when Vespasian took charge of the Jewish war. When the Greeks prevented the Jews in Syria from receiving their refund of the oil tax and outlawed the observance of the Sabbath, Mucianus confirmed the Jewish right to receive the refund and to observe the Sabbath.

muktzeh (Heb., cut off) that which had not been planned for use on the Sabbath or a festival and therefore is forbidden for use or handling on those days. In the category of *muktzeh* are both items that have no permitted use on a holy day, for example, a tool or other implements associated with work and items, such as foods, that, while intrinsically permitted, had not been especially set aside or prepared for use on the holy day.

mumar *see* APOSTASY

Mundhir, al- ruler of Hira, capital city of the Lakhmid Arab vassal state, located on the Euphrates. The Persians placed al-Mundhir in charge of the western border of their kingdom. In the early 520s C.E., the Jewish rulers of Himyar sought his help against the Byzantines. It was a time of peace between Persia and Byzantium, and al-Mundhir refused to assist them. In 529, he invaded Syria, with Persian support, and Antioch. His war provided support for the Samaritan revolt against Justinian. There is no hard evidence that the Jews joined with the Samaritans during this revolt.

muqtzeh *see* MUKTZEH

murder the deliberate killing of another person, distinguished in biblical and rabbinic law from involuntary homicide (manslaughter). To be treated as murder, the homicide must have been premeditated and the result of malice (Exod. 21:14; Num. 35:20–21), unlike the case of manslaughter, in which the accused acted suddenly and without enmity (Num. 35:22–24). According to biblical law, one found guilty of murder is, after conviction, subject to death at the hands of the "avenger of blood" (Num. 35:21), who may carry out the sentence immediately. No other form of punishment is available; the execution of this sanction is left entirely in the hands of the kin of the individual murdered.

The rabbinic system recognizes a number of categories of homicide, only one of which is punishable by death at the hand of the "avenger of blood." Along with three categories of nonculpable homicide (resulting, for instance, from misadventure or accident), the rabbis define two categories of murder: culpable homicide, which is the result of criminal negligence, and felonious homicide, that is, murder. As in the biblical system, the rabbis define murder as the result of the perpetrator's premeditated, malicious action. In this circumstance, the accused is subject to trial and, if found guilty, is sentenced to execution by the sword (that is, decapitation). While, following the biblical view, the responsibility for the execution devolves first upon a relative of the deceased, if none is found or willing, the court itself assigns an executioner (Babli Sanhedrin 45b).

By contrast, a person who commits culpable homicide is exempt from criminal trial but is subject to death at the hand of the redeemer of blood. The act was intentional and therefore not in the category of nonculpable homicide, which would exempt the person from punishment. Since the act was not premeditated, however, the laws of felonious homicide do not apply, and the person cannot be brought to trial as a murderer. In the absence of alternatives, the rule of Numbers 35:21 applies: the redeeming relative of the deceased may kill this person at any time and in any place.

musaf (Heb., additional service) liturgy recounting the additional offerings presented in the Temple on the Sabbath, festivals, and holy days

Mut. *see* DE MUTATIONE NOMINUM

mystery (Heb./Aram.: *raz;* Gk.: *mysterion*) In Hebrew, *raz* is a Persian loanword meaning "secret." The word first appears in Daniel 2, in which Daniel interprets the "mystery" of Nebuchadnezzar's dream. This "mystery" cannot be found out through mere human effort, but must be revealed by God, "the revealer of mysteries" (Dan. 2:29). This notion of "mystery" as a special revelation by God to the chosen is used by the Qumran Essenes who produced the Dead Sea Scrolls. In the Qumran literature, the words of the prophets are "mysteries" (*razim*), and their correct interpretation can be obtained only through a special inspired knowledge given by God. The possessor par excellence of this special knowledge was the Teacher of Righteousness: "This concerns the Teacher of Righteousness, to whom God made known all the mysteries of the words of his servants the prophets" (1QpeshHab 7:1–5a). However, other members of the Community may also possess this special knowledge through the teachings of the sect; in the Community Rule it is stated that the "sons of light [the sect] faithfully conceal [from outsiders] the mysteries of truth." This information is corroborated by Josephus: the Essenes "conceal nothing from the members of the sect and report none of their secrets to others, even though tortured to death" (*War* 2.8.7).

This sense of mystery as concealed knowledge is also known in the Greek world, where *mysterion* refers to the practices, teaching, and implements of the mystery religions, such as those of Demeter at Eleusis, which flourished in the Graeco-Roman period. Thus, the Semitic and Greek streams of thought come together in early Christian literature, where the word "mystery" denotes the divine plan that is hidden from all except those who have the special knowledge or grace to perceive it; Romans 16:25–26 expresses this thought: "Now to God who is able to strengthen you according to my gospel and the proclamation of Jesus Christ, according to the revelation of the mystery that was kept secret for long ages but is now disclosed, and through the prophetic writings is made known to all the Gentiles. . . ." The Christian thus possesses the key to unlocking the "mysteries" of scripture: the revelation of God in Jesus Christ. In later usage, however, the word "mystery" came to refer to the practices of the Christian cult—the sacraments—in which God was revealed to the believer.

mystery religion, Judaism as Mystery religions were widespread in the Graeco-Roman world. They were characterized by secret rites of both initiation and worship, the goal of the religion ultimately being salvation. Judaism was primarily an ethnic religion and differed in many ways from the standard mystery religions, but there were certain characteristics they had in common that would make many outsiders lump them together. The practice of the Temple cult was off limits to Gentiles, which led it to be identified with the worship of Dionysus by some writers, such as Plutarch. Others even alleged secret, abominable rites, such as cannibalism and human sacrifice. As absurd as these allegations are, they arose in part because of the secrecy of the cult. Some scholars, however, have also suggested that Judaism was treated as a mystery internally, with a focus on initiation and esoteric knowledge, or *gnosis*. Although it is recognized that such writers as Philo used mystical language, this interpretation as a whole has not gained wide support. On the other hand, it has been argued that Gnosticism, with its focus on secret knowledge, originated in Judaism.

mysticism Though there is no general term for mysticism in the Hebrew Bible, there were individuals in ancient Israel whose spiritual life was marked by an intense desire for direct experience of the transcendent divine world and for communion, or even union, with God. Statements such as "taste and see that the Lord is good" (Ps. 34:8), or "as the hart pants for the water brooks, so pants my soul for you, O God" (Ps. 42:1), or "in your presence is fullness of joy, at your right hand are pleasures for evermore" (Ps. 16:11), can be seen as expressions of mystical longing. The Hebrew Bible contains some notable descriptions of theophanies that were granted to individuals: God spoke to Moses "face to face" (Exod. 33:11; Num. 12:8; Deut. 34:10; cf. Exod. 33:17–23); Isaiah saw God seated on his throne, surrounded by his angelic retinue (Isa. 6:1–5); Ezekiel had a vision of God's glorious chariot by the river Chebar (Ezek. 1:1–28). Mysticism in the Hebrew Bible is closely linked to prophecy in that both phenomena involve a direct experience of the divine. A distinction can, however, be drawn: in mysticism the experience remains essentially private and personal; in prophecy the experience validates a moral message that the prophet is expected to make public and is designed to reinforce the covenant between God and Israel.

Visionary accounts of the heavenly world are found also in apocalyptic literature of the Second Temple period: two early and influential texts are 1 Enoch 14:8–25 and Daniel 7:9–10. It is unclear to what extent these accounts reflect genuine psychological events or are literary constructions pieced together from elements drawn from earlier traditions. The latter suggestion is more likely: vision in apocalyptic literature in general seems to be used as a literary device to disclose information about the terrestrial and celestial worlds, or about the future. It may also be doubted whether there was genuine mysticism at Qumran. In the Songs of the Sabbath Sacrifice and other Dead Sea Scrolls, intense interest is shown in the angelic liturgy, but there is no indication as to how the esoteric knowledge of this liturgy was obtained. The point being made is fundamentally theological: the worship of the community on earth corresponds to and, perhaps, is validated by the worship of the angels in heaven.

The first clearly defined mystical movement in Judaism is attested in the Talmudic period (2d–9th cs. C.E.). The Hekhalot literature points to the existence of conventicles of mystics in both Palestine and Babylonia who met to study traditions about the heavenly world, some of them clearly derived from earlier apocalyptic movements. Behind the texts are real psychological events: they are full of magical techniques and incantations designed to assist the adept either to ascend to heaven to contemplate God's glory, to commune with the angels and to learn secrets, or to conjure powerful angels, such as the prince of the Torah (Sar Torah), down to earth to help him with his studies and to reveal the hidden meanings of scripture. This movement was regarded with some suspicion by the rabbinic authorities and its teachings were ruled to be esoteric (M. Ḥagigah 2:1). The impact of Islamic philosophical theology (the Qalam) on Jewish thought in the early Middle Ages seems to have brought Hekhalot mysticism as a living tradition effectively to an end. Influential thinkers, such as Saadia, clearly found its use of extreme anthropomorphic language about God hard to defend against the criticism of the Karaites. The literature of the movement was disseminated, however, to North Africa and Europe (it was being closely studied in Italy in the 9th c.), and, often radically reinterpreted, it formed a major source for later mystical developments among the Kabbalists of Provence and Spain and the Haside Ashkenaz of the Rhineland and northern France. *See also* KABBALAH.

myth a word used with a number of meanings in scholarship. It often occurs in Near Eastern studies in reference to stories that relate the activities of the gods (with "legend" being reserved for those stories about heroes and other human beings, even if gods are mentioned). Cultural and social anthropologists use it in a somewhat similar sense as a description of any stories of origins that explain how and why the world and society are the way they are. "Myth" is also used in theological and other contexts to denote a meaningful symbolic system. (None of these definitions has the common English meaning of "something untrue," since myths are regarded as true in a symbolic sense even if not literally.) Whether there is myth in the Hebrew Bible depends on one's definition, but there is certainly mythical language drawn from ancient myths about God's conquest of the monsters of chaos (e.g., Isa. 27:1, 51:9–11) known from myths elsewhere in the ancient Near East. Mythical language and imagery are also found in apocalyptic literature, in some cases with ancient roots. The Fragmentary Hellenistic Jewish writers, such as Artapanus, at times draw on myths from the Graeco-Roman world.

N

Naaneh Synagogue remains of a probable Byzantine synagogue found about 6 kilometers south of Ramlah. The town is not mentioned in the two Talmuds. A bronze plate about 49.5 centimeters in diameter was found here in the nineteenth century. It depicts a vine trellis with rosettes. Within one vine medallion is a seven-branched menorah with a horizontal crossbar joining the branches. A Torah shrine with a gabled roof is standing to the right of the menorah. Lulabs emerge from an amphora. Two squared capitals, perhaps from a synagogue, were found in the modern village. One is inscribed in Greek, "One God." Since this is a popular phrase in Samaritan contexts, it has been suggested that these are all remains of a Samaritan synagogue of the fifth or sixth century C.E.

Naaran Synagogue ancient synagogue site near Jericho at the Arab village of Ein Duk. Naaran is a biblical name (1 Chron. 7:28), but it is known to Josephus as Neara (*Ant.* 17.340). During the fourth century C.E., the Christian bishop Eusebius describes a Jewish settlement 5 Roman miles from Jericho, which he calls Noorath (Onomasticon 136:24). Variations on this name occur in other ancient sources.

The synagogue of Naaran is a basilica with square columns that divide the interior space into a nave with two side aisles and an aisle across the back. A large courtyard adjoins the synagogue on the north and west. Directly in front of the facade a small square pool occupied a rectangular courtyard with an entrance directly south into the narthex or roofed porch of the synagogue. The narthex was paved with a white mosaic, in the center of which is a depiction of a stylized, eight- or nine-branched menorah with twelve lamps surrounded by geometric and floral designs. An Aramaic inscription honors Phinehas ben Justa, the priest who donated the mosaic. A second inscription honors Rebecca, wife of Phinehas.

Those who entered the worship space, which measures about 15 by 21 meters, walked onto an exceptionally beautiful mosaic in three panels. The first panel is a series of octagonal spaces formed by wide braided ribbons; within each octagon is a bird or other animal. The central panel depicts a zodiac and the four seasons, and Helios rides his chariot in the central circle. The third panel represents Daniel with two lions right and left. Above and to the right of Daniel one reads in Hebrew "Daniel. Shalom." A dedicatory panel to the left of Daniel honors a certain Benjamin and all those who donated to "this holy place." Above Daniel and the two lions stands a Torah shrine flanked by two seven-branched menorahs. Two hanging lamps are suspended on chains from each menorah. Above the menorahs dedicatory inscriptions honor donors: Maruth, Ketin, Jacob, Ben Chrospedah. It is possible that there was an apse on the north wall. It is also possible that there was no column across the back, as the original excavators relied on what was known of other synagogues at the time (1921) for their reconstruction of the south end of the worship space.

A rectangular room about 9 by 13 meters opens

off the west side of the synagogue. Since it has no egress to the outside, its use is integral with the use of the synagogue. It may be a school or *beit midrash*.

The synagogue is understood today to date to the sixth century C.E. Its mosaic was badly defaced by those who were offended by the images but who left the Hebrew and Aramaic inscriptions.

Nabateans   a people who ruled the modern area of southern Syria, Jordan, and parts of the Negeb and the Sinai from the late fourth century B.C.E. until 106 C.E. The Nabateans are known for the massive archaeological remains found in their capital city of Petra, which is located in modern Jordan, about 80 kilometers south of the Dead Sea.

The Nabateans are not mentioned in the Hebrew Bible, despite a reference to the Ishmaelite clan of *nabayoth*. Though the modern spelling of Nabatea and the ancient Hebrew name are similar, there are significant differences between the Hebrew name and the spelling of the Nabateans found on Aramaic inscriptions, which make the identification of the two problematic. The notable differences are the absence of the letter *yod* from the Hebrew Bible name in the Aramaic version and the absence of the emphatic *t* in the Hebrew form. A Nabatean monarch (Aretas) is mentioned in 2 Maccabees 5:8. There is also a brief reference to the Nabateans in the New Testament (2 Cor. 11:32) in which Paul mentions a governor of King Aretas IV.

Linguistically, the root containing the name "Nabatea" (*nbt*), is found both in the southern and northern Semitic families, so the name itself provides little insight into the origin of this people. Affinities of later Nabatean culture suggest an origin from the north Semitic group—probably an Aramaic-speaking group. In spite of this probable Aramaic origin and in spite of the fact that Aramaic was used in their inscriptions as their lingua franca, their personal names and a fair number of Arabic inscriptions indicate that the native tongue of the Nabateans was a dialect of Arabic once they were established as a nation.

Though their origins are somewhat mysterious, some clarity can be found beginning around 312 B.C.E. from Greek records that describe the campaigns of Alexander the Great and mention that the Nabateans were in Petra. There are several ancient sources that shed light on the history of the Nabateans after they were established as a nation. The records of the Hasmoneans and Herodians relate some details of relations with the Nabateans. In addition, there are numerous Nabatean Aramaic inscriptions that provide further insight. The Naba-

tean king Aretas I (r.c. 170–160 B.C.E.) was the first king, and the Aramaic inscription "Aretas, King of the Nabateans" probably refers to him. Various Nabatean kings ruled the area until Cornelius Palma, the Roman governor of Syria, annexed Nabatea in 106 C.E. as the province of Arabia.

In general, the Nabateans had good relations with the Hasmonean and Herodian Jewish rulers. An exception is a conflict that arose when Herod Antipas divorced a Nabatean princess in order to marry his niece and sister-in-law, Herodias. There are also several cases where ambitious plans of one ruler or the other strained the relationship, but in general, the Jews and the Nabateans had cordial relations, for example, during the reign of Herod the Great. During Herod the Great's reign, Nabatea also flourished under Obodas III (30–9 B.C.E.) and Aretas IV (9 B.C.E.–40 C.E.), and Herod's mother (Cypros) was of Nabatean ancestry.

nabi   *see* PROPHET

Nabonidus, Prayer of   a first-person account of the sickness of Nabonidus, king of Babylon, his prayer, and his healing by a Jewish soothsayer. The Aramaic text is preserved in one Qumran manuscript, three pieces of which preserve parts of twelve lines.

Parallels to Daniel 4 enable us to reconstruct the story line; however, the Nabonidus fragments contain elements that are arguably more primitive than the Nebuchadnezzar story in Daniel 4 because they evidence accurate knowledge about historical facts that are obscured in the Daniel version. Nabonidus, not Nebuchadnezzar, was the father of Belshazzar (cf. Dan. 5:2). He, rather than Nebuchadnezzar, is known to have spent time away from Babylon (Dan. 4:31–33) in Teiman (4QPrNab 2), and he forsook the gods of Babylon (4QPrNab 7–8) for the worship of the moon god Sin.

Thus, although the Qumran manuscript dates from 50–1 B.C.E., it appears to preserve a form of the story in Daniel 4 that dates from the Persian period and derives from Babylonian Jewish circles. The story was revised in Daniel to refer to Nebuchadnezzar, the more familiar figure and a frequent stand-in for Antiochus Epiphanes. Belshazzar, who was his father's regent, is now said to have been present at the fall of Babylon (historical sources place Nabonidus on the scene). The gods of gold and silver, bronze, iron, wood, and stone, listed in 4QPrNab 7–8, but missing in Daniel 4, appear in Daniel 5:23 as objects of Belshazzar's worship (cf. the components of the colossus in Nebuchadnezzar's dream in Dan. 2:31–35). Thus the Prayer of Nabonidas preserves in an early form one of a series of stories about Babylonian monarchs who acclaim the true God, and it provides some insight into the complex history of the narratives collected in Daniel 1–6.

Nabratein *see* NABURAYA

Naburaya (also Niburayya, Niburayah; Arab.: Nabratein) Talmudic village and home of the fourth-century-C.E. sage Jacob, known in Jewish sources for his daring and unorthodox interpretations. The village itself is located around 4 kilometers toward the north of Safed in Upper Galilee and flourished in the Roman and Byzantine periods, though traces of Early Bronze, Iron II, and Hellenistic pottery were also found on the site. The site was occupied from the first century C.E. to the mid-fourth century, when it was abandoned. Resettled in the early sixth century, the village flourished until around 700 C.E., making it one of the important sites testifying to the continuation of Judaism throughout the Arab conquest. A twelfth-century-C.E. structure was also excavated on the site.

The existence of a Jewish synagogue on the site was long attested by the presence of a lintel there, whose secondary (added later) inscription bore the year 564 C.E. In fact, three synagogues existed on the same spot, demonstrating the long and complicated history of the site, whose remains were excavated in 1980 and 1981.

The earliest synagogue was built as a small broadhouse type of structure in the middle Roman period of the site (135–250 C.E.). The discovery of this type of synagogue, which is oriented toward Jerusalem by the long wall, represents the earliest broadhouse synagogue yet excavated in Israel. The synagogue interior contained two stone *bimah*s, or platforms, located on either side of the central doorway.

Around 250 C.E., the synagogue was rebuilt as a true basilical (columned hall) structure (Synagogue 2a) oriented on a north/south axis. The central aisle had three columns on either side dividing it from the side aisles. The building was lengthened, an exonarthex (exterior front porch) was added, and a permanent *aedicula* or Torah shrine was constructed on the western interior *bimah*. A fragment of the actual Torah shrine of Synagogue 2a, bearing a stone gable flanked by two lions, was discovered reused in the *stylobate* (column support) of the subsequently rebuilt Synagogue 2b. In 306, Synagogue 2a was destroyed by an earthquake; and the new structure (2b) was built on the same floor plan as the previous building, but at a higher level.

Sometime around 350 to 363 C.E., the synagogue

and village were abandoned, but around 500 C.E., the village was resettled and a much larger synagogue building was built (564 C.E.) directly over the remains of the earlier synagogues. It served the community until around 700 C.E., as attested by coins found in the latest floor of the structure. This last synagogue had a four-columned nave; and although no structural evidence for a *bimah* appeared, a broken, late Byzantine, burnished black ceramic bowl found in a nearby house carried a crude depiction of the Torah shrine of this last synagogue.

Naḥman *see* NAḤMAN B. JACOB

Naḥman b. Ḥisda Babylonian amora active in the late third and early fourth centuries C.E.; son of the head of the academy at Sura

Naḥman b. Ḥuna Babylonian amora active in the first half of the fifth century C.E.; during 452–455 C.E., head of the revived academy at Mata Meḥasia. It is unclear whether or not this is the same authority as the Naḥman mentioned without the patronymic in conjunction with Rabina and Ashi.

Naḥman b. Isaac Babylonian amora active in the mid-fourth century C.E. He studied under his uncle, Aḥa b. Joseph. He was head of the Kallah in the academy of Raba. After Raba's death in 352 C.E., he joined the academy at Pumbedita.

Naḥman b. Jacob leading Babylonian amora of the early fourth century C.E., usually cited simply as R. Naḥman, without the patronymic; born in Nehardea. His principal teacher was Rabbah b. Abuha. His marriage brought him into the family of the exilarch (B. Ḥullin 124a). In Nehardea, he held the post of dayyan (B. Erubin 34b).

Nahum, Targum to *see* TARGUM TO THE PROPHETS

Nahum Commentary (Pesher Nahum) The five fragments of this manuscript, representing seven damaged columns of writing, were found in Cave 4, Qumran, in 1952 and were published by J. M. Allegro in DJD V. The text, whose title is abbreviated as 4QpeshNah, is a running commentary on Nahum 1–3, making it one of the examples of a continuous *pesher*. It exhibits the *pesher* form: a citation of the biblical verse, followed by the phrase "its interpretation is," continuing with an interpretation concerned with contemporary events surrounding the sect. The date of the only manuscript is the late first century B.C.E., and the date of composition is approximately the same time.

The Nahum Commentary's importance lies in the fact that the commentary mentions two recognizable historical figures, the Greek kings Demetrius and Antiochus. Once these figures are identified, it becomes easier to interpret the symbolic names used by the commentary: the Wrathful Lion, the Seekers after Smooth Things, Ephraim, and Manasseh. As the Book of Nahum castigates its enemy Assyria and exults over its downfall, so the author uses Nahum to castigate the sect's enemies and gloat over their (coming) end. The identification of the figures, therefore, must be deduced from a knowledge of the enemies of the sect.

The Antiochus mentioned is Antiochus IV Epiphanes, the last Greek king to exercise sovereignty over Judah. Demetrius is associated with the Wrathful Lion, who "executes revenge on those who seek smooth things and hangs men alive" (a probable reference to crucifixion). The events seem best associated with the reign of Alexander Jannaeus (103–76 B.C.E.), when a revolt against him took place (93–88 B.C.E.) led by the Pharisees (evidently to be identified with the Seekers after Smooth Things). The Pharisees supported Demetrius III Eukairos (the commentary's Demetrius) against Alexander Jannaeus for a while, but then returned to Alexander, who punished them by crucifying hundreds of them (the reference to "hanging men alive"; cf. Josephus, *Ant.* 13:372–383 and *War* 1.90–98). If the Pharisees are the Seekers after Smooth Things, who are equated with Ephraim, then it is possible to identify Manasseh as the Sadducees, who suffered greatly in Pompey's conquest of Jerusalem in 63 B.C.E., the latest historical event alluded to in the commentary ("the coming of the rulers of the Kittim" [2:11b]). Thus the date of composition for the Nahum Commentary must be post–63 B.C.E. As the Book of Nahum rejoices over the fall of the enemy Assyria, so the Nahum Commentary ends by rejoicing over the imminent downfall of its enemies and the vindication of the sect.

Nahum of Gimzo Tannaitic authority of the late first and early second centuries C.E.; born in Gimzo (2 Chron. 28:18). Little is preserved of his teaching. According to B. Berakhot 22a and other sources, Nahum was a teacher of Akiba.

Nahum the Mede Tannaitic authority in Jerusalem during the period of the destruction of the Second Temple (M. Nazir 5:4). Few of his teachings have been preserved; according to Nathan (T. Baba Batra 9:1), Nahum was a judge of civil law.

Nain Roman Jewish village in the north central part of the Jezreel Valley. It is mentioned in Luke 7:11 as a locality where Jesus raised a young man from the dead; the young man was being borne on a bier in a funeral procession near the gate of the city. A village gate implies a city wall, and in fact the modern village of Nain, which lies north of the modern city of Afula on the slopes of the Hill of Moreh and not far from Mount Tabor, is ringed by the remains of a village wall. Nain was known to Origen of Caesarea about 200 C.E., and in Genesis Rabbah 98.12 it is known to be a Jewish village in the tribal territory of Issachar. Christian authors of the fourth and fifth century know of Nain and its location near Mount Tabor. An ancient cemetery of the Roman and Byzantine periods lies to the east of the modern village. A spring emerges from the ground to the northwest of Nain, and fragments of Roman sarcophagi from the cemetery are scattered about. The water from the spring collects in a basin 2 by 1.5 meters, perhaps from the Roman period. Pilgrim reports from as early as the fourth century locate a church in Nain, but its ruins have not been found. As yet no architectural fragments of an ancient synagogue have been found.

nakedness In ancient societies, clothing marked status, and so nakedness referred to a liminal, in-between state that could be either positive, denoting innocence (as in "naked but not ashamed," Gen. 2:25) or negative, denoting a state of shame and danger. In Revelation (3:17, 16:15, 17:15), to be without clothes is to be shamed, and throughout Second Temple literature there are countless exhortations to cover the naked (Tob. 1:17, 4:16; 2 Esd. 2:20; Test. Jacob 2:23, 7:25; Tes. Zebulon 7:1; 2 Enoch 9:1, 42:8; Matt. 25:36–44; James 2:15). As a source of danger, the nakedness of women is particularly troubling for a patriarchal society, so Reuben is said to have sinned when he saw his father's naked concubine (Test. Reuben 3:11–14; developing Gen. 35:22); the prophet Balaam suggests to the Moabites to send naked women to lead the sons of Israel astray (LAB 18:13); and the two elders sin when they see Susanna bathing. The Qumran covenanters also frowned on nakedness, enjoining a punishment of six months on unnecessary nakedness and of thirty days on nakedness resulting from poor attire (1 QS 7:12–14). In Jubilees, Adam's covering of his skin on expulsion from the Garden distinguishes humans from animals, and so the correct rule for humanity is not to uncover one's shame as the Gentiles improperly do (Jub. 3:26–31).

As a liminal state, nakedness is so disliked that Paul wants his heavenly body put over his earthly one (2 Cor. 5:3); Eve is described as having been clothed with righteousness before sinning (Life of Adam and Eve 20); and the blessed Rechabites are not really naked but covered with glory so that their private parts are not seen (Hist. Rech. 4:1, 12:1).

This same negative attitude toward nakedness is expressed in the rabbinic literature, which holds that God's desire that people not be naked is proved by the fact that the first man was created clothed (T. Berakhot 2:3). Performance of religious commandments while naked or even in the presence of naked people is prohibited (see, e.g., B. Berakhot 25b; B. Shabbat 14a; T. Berakhot 2:3). Despite their negative view toward physical nakedness, the rabbis see in nakedness both a positive and negative symbolic value. B. Berakhot 57a refers to one who, in a dream, is standing naked. If this is in Babylonia, the person knows that he is without sin. In the Land of Israel, however, this means that he is as one who has rejected the Torah and therefore stands naked of the fulfillment of religious duties.

name designation for a person or place. In the Hebrew Bible, names serve the normal purpose of identifying individuals, but in some cases the meaning of a name has special significance. Abram, for example, had his name changed to Abraham, which is explained as meaning that he would father a multitude of nations (Gen. 17). A large percentage of biblical and postbiblical Hebrew names contain a divine name as an element ("-iah," as in Jeremiah, is a shortened form of Yahweh; "-el," as in Daniel, is another word for God). The name of God took on special meaning in Deuteronomy and related literature in which the earthly sanctuary is identified as the place where the Lord makes his name dwell. His name was not to be taken in vain according to the Third Commandment. As the centuries passed, there developed a reluctance to utter God's name, especially the unique name YHWH. Various substitutes were introduced; the name Lord (*adonai*) is the most common. To have one's name written in the book of life is to be assured of eternal life (Rev. 13). "Name" has the sense of power or authority in those instances in which one blesses or curses in the name of another, or when one is baptized into the name of the Father, Son, and Holy Spirit (Matt. 28). According to Paul, Jesus was given the name above every name—apparently the name Lord (Phil. 2).

In rabbinic Judaism, too, a person's name represented his essence. People thus needed to be careful in choosing names of children, who the Talmud recommends should be named after the patriarchs but not after enemies of the Jews (B. Yoma 36b). Of all possible rewards, the crown of a good name is the best (M. Abot 4:13). In rabbinic practice, a person was called by his given name and patronymic. M. Gittin 9:8 refers to the use of family names, a practice that in Talmudic times apparently was not commonplace (B. Megillah 28a).

names, Graeco-Roman Jews have always taken names from their surrounding culture. This was also true in the Graeco-Roman world, where many Jews had Greek and occasionally Latin names; however, Jews can often be identified with fair probability or even certainty, despite having Greek names. Some names were evidently chosen because of closeness to Hebrew or Aramaic names, such as the name Simon, which closely resembles the name Shimon. There are also a few names that are purely Greek in form and origin but appear to have been taken only by Jews, such as the name Theodotus (God's gift).

naos (Gr., temple) term that usually referred to the main building of the Temple. The *naos* with the surrounding courtyard and outbuildings was usually called the *hieron*. Thus in Jerusalem the building with the Holy of Holies and the Holy Place would be the *naos*.

Narbata a Jewish area east of Caesaria. In 1 Maccabees 5:23, it is called Arbatta, from which Simeon evacuated Jews at the inception of the revolt. It appears in the Jerusalem Talmud as the site of an inn (Y. Berakhot 6:1, 10b).

Nashim the third division of the Mishnah, devoted to laws affecting women as they pass from the domain of the father to that of the husband (the marriage settlement, betrothal) and back (divorce), levirate marriage, the woman accused of adultery, and vows; *see also* GENDER ROLES, IN RABBINIC JUDAISM

nasi *see* PATRIARCH

Nathan the Babylonian Tannaitic authority of the mid-second century C.E. He moved to the Land of Israel in his youth and studied under Ishmael, Eliezer b. Hyrcanus, and others. During the Hadrianic persecutions, Nathan returned to Babylonia. Under Simeon b. Gamaliel, he was for a time vice president of the court. Along with Meir, he was removed from office as the result of a dispute.

natin (Heb., the donated one; pl., *netinim*) a descendant of the Gibeonites, whom Joshua dedicated to Temple service (Josh. 9:27). Treating them as comparable to bastards (*mamzerim*), rabbis excluded *netinim* from marriage into the Israelite people in perpetuity (M. Yebamot 8:3).

nations, seventy rabbinic enumeration of nations and languages of the world based on the biblical number of the grandsons of Noah (Gen. 10). Rabbinic sources say each nation is protected by its own angel, but God protects Israel (Gen. Rabbah 37); a sacrifice was offered on the festival of Tabernacles for each of the nations. Every judge of the

Sanhedrin ideally had to know the seventy languages (San. 17a).

Naveh Synagogue   ancient Jewish village and synagogue site at modern Nawa in southern Syria about 45 kilometers east-northeast of Tiberias in the territory of Batanaea. Batanaea was biblical Bashan, though it was called the "territory of Naveh" by some ancient Jewish authors (T. Shebiit 4:8). The town is called Naue or Neue by Greek authors (*Onomasticon* 136:12). It seems to have reached a peak in the fourth and fifth centuries.

Visitors to modern Nawa early in this century thought that they had located a synagogue building entered from its long side, therefore a broadhouse structure. They describe a niche more than two meters above the interior pavement with pillars on both sides. Above the niche a shell carved into one of the stones suggested a place for a Torah shrine. Other stones in secondary use in the modern village appear to have been taken from an ancient synagogue. For example, two lintels were decorated with inhabited meanders or repeated swastika patterns with figures in the space in the middle. One of these lintels is decorated with a seven-branched menorah at its center. A garland ornaments the central branch of the menorah. Another carved lintel in another house was decorated with a wreath around a shell. On either side of the wreath and shell stood two seven-branched menorahs. At least three other stones depicted menorahs, sometimes with lulabs and shofars. Researchers have found an ancient stone with a fragmentary Aramaic inscription built into the east wall of the modern mosque: ". . . bar Yudan . . . bar Ahawa . . . shrine." Scholars have noticed that these stones are decorated in much the same manner as the synagogue at Kefar Baram in Upper Galilee. A stone at Baram even bears the name "Eliezer bar Yudan," leading to speculation that this is the same man honored at both sites.

Nazarenes   term used in English for several related Greek and Semitic terms in Jewish and Christian literature. Most frequently in the Christian Gospels, the term refers to Jesus from Nazareth, the town (e.g., Mark 1:24; 14:67; 16:6; Matt. 2:23). But the term Nazoraioi or Nasraya (usually translated as Nazarenes) also came to be used for those who believed in Jesus as Messiah (Acts 24:5) and continued in Jewish and Syriac usage after the term "Christians" became standard in Greek.

Nazareth   the Jewish village of Jesus' youth, located in the Nazareth Hills in western Lower Galilee. According to Luke 1:26 and 2:4, it was where Mary and Joseph lived before Jesus' birth. It

is mentioned for the first time in the New Testament as the place of Jesus' education (Matt. 2:23; Luke 2:39). In the Roman and Byzantine periods Nazareth remained a Jewish city (Eusebius, *Onomasticon* 138). Nazareth became a place of Christian pilgrimage from the fourth century onward. In the sixth century Nazareth belonged to a territory called Helenopolis after Helen, mother of the emperor Constantine.

Excavations beneath the modern Church of Saint Joseph showed that there was village occupation at Nazareth from the period of the Israelite monarchy. Excavations beneath the Church of the Annunciation, however, showed that the period of continuous occupation began in the second century B.C.E. Nazareth was a small hamlet with many underground cisterns, granaries, and areas for storage and work. The location of the tombs of the first century B.C.E. to the first century C.E. disclose that the occupied area extended hardly 300 by 100 meters.

Further excavations directly beneath the proposed new Church of the Annunciation showed that there were three shallow caves in bedrock that were singled out for decoration by later Christian visitors. There had been a Jewish house on this spot, for a ritual immersion pool, or mikveh, was found just south and a little west of these caves. The mikveh was covered by a mosaic floor, presumably for a synagogue, in the fourth century. The mosaic was oriented north to south and included the raised bedrock and its caves. The excavators believe that this was a Jewish-Christian synagogue. About eighty architectural fragments, presumably from this synagogue, were found about 10 meters to the south beneath the floor of a fifth-century Byzantine monastery. They are carved in a form typical of the late Roman to Byzantine synagogues of the Galilee. In the fifth century C.E. the synagogue was destroyed to make way for the monastery. The chapel of the monastery incorporated one wall of the synagogue and incorporated the caves. One of the caves became honored as the Grotto of the Annunciation. There is no proposed date when the Byzantine monastery went out of use.

Nazir   Mishnah tractate on the Nazirite, with special attention to the vow that he or she takes (chaps. 1–4), the offerings presented by a Nazirite at the end of the period of restriction (chaps. 4–5), and the restrictions on the Nazirite concerning wine, haircuts, and corpse-uncleanness (chaps. 6–9); *see also* NAZIRITE

Nazirite   one who vows to abstain from wine, haircuts, and contracting of corpse-uncleanness, in line with Numbers 6

Neapolis modern Nablus on the west bank, a Roman city founded after the First Jewish Revolt in Samaria near the biblical city of Shechem. The city was founded in 72 C.E. as part of the Roman attempt to secure the area by ensuring that a major Roman population lived there. The city was long and narrow, built to fit in the narrow east–west valley that runs between Mount Gerizim on the south and east and Mount Ebal on the north and west. The walled city occupied about 250 acres. The earliest coins of Neapolis were minted in 82 C.E. They bear the head of the emperor Domitian and bear a Greek inscription: "The Autokrator Domitian, Caesar and Augustus." On the reverse is a laurel wreath with a Greek inscription inside: "Flavia Neapolis Samariae, year 11" (from the founding of the city). The inscription identifies it as a city of the Flavian emperors of the territory of Samaria. The city territory of Neapolis was considerable, extending from the Jordan River westward to the border with Antipatris. In the north its border was with Sebaste (the biblical city of Samaria), and to the south it bordered on the territory of Jerusalem, then known as Aelia Capitolina. Archaeological finds at Neapolis include a theater of the second century, an amphitheater of the third century and a hippodrome (horse track) of the second–third century, the city wall, a city gate at the foot of Mount Gerizim with a staircase that ascended the mountain, and an extensive cemetery. A Roman temple to Zeus was built on top Mount Gerizim. Neapolis seemed to be the Samaritan capital. From here two revolts of the Samaritans broke out against their Jewish and Christian neighbors in 485 and 529 C.E.

Nebuchadnezzar almost legendary Babylonian king who conquered Judea and exiled the Jews. He is mentioned frequently in extrabiblical early Jewish literature. Although a few of these sources devote significant attention to him, most that mention him do so only in passing. The sources that treat Nebuchadnezzar in detail tend to portray him as a model of the almost omnipotent monarch, as he is depicted in the biblical Book of Daniel.

Perhaps the most extended extrabiblical treatment of Nebuchadnezzar in early Judaism occurs in the book of Judith, which stresses that the Jews' resistance to Nebuchadnezzar was because of his threat, as absolute monarch, to impose worship of himself. Other significant references appear in Baruch 1:11–12; 4 Baruch 7:14, 24, 29; and Eupolemus, fragment 4 (39:4–5). Nebuchadnezzar also figures prominently in the section on Daniel in the Lives of the Prophets (chap. 4), a work that could be Jewish or Christian. This account, although based on Daniel 4, recounts many aggadic details not present there.

Nebuchadnezzar is not mentioned explicitly in the earliest, clearly Christian literature; he does, however, appear in rabbinic commentaries on the Bible.

necromancy a type of divination that works by calling on the dead for insight into the future. Although banned in biblical legislation, the practice continued to flourish. Thus Saul supposedly removed necromancers from the country, yet could easily find one to call up Samuel when needed.

nedabah *see* FREE-WILL OFFERING

Nedarim Mishnah tractate on vows. The tractate discusses the language of vows, euphemisms, and language of no or limited effect (chaps. 1–3); binding effects of vows (chaps. 4–8); absolution of vows (chaps. 8–11), for example, by a father for the daughter and by the husband for a wife (chaps. 10–11); and vows not subject to abrogation (chap. 11).

neder (Heb.) vow

neduniah *see* DOWRY

neeman (Heb., trustworthy one) in the Mishnah and later rabbinic literature, a person who follows rabbinic tithing requirements for all produce he grows, receives, sells, or gives away and does not accept hospitality from one who does not follow these rules (M. Demai 2:2). The *neeman* is contrasted with the *ḥaber* (associate), who also observes the laws of levitical cleanness.

Nefilim an obscure Hebrew term in Genesis 6:4 that Jewish tradition interpreted to refer to the giants begotten by the sons of God and the daughters of men (cf. also Numb. 13:33). Scholars disagree as to the relationship between the Nefilim and "mighty ones" (Heb.: *gibborim*) in Genesis 6:4. 1 Enoch 7:2 finds three classes of giants in the text, the third group evidently corresponding to "the men of renown" in Genesis 6:4 (the text of 1 Enoch 7:2 is corrupt). The Damascus Document 2:18–19 implies the name Nefilim when it applies the Hebrew verb *nafal* (to fall) to the sin of the giants and their fathers. Targum Pseudo-Jonathan on Genesis 6:4 identifies the Nefilim as the two angelic chieftains in 1 Enoch 6:4: "Samhazzai and Uziel fell from heaven and were on earth in those days." *See also* GIANTS; SHEMIḤAZAH; WATCHERS.

nega a skin blemish signifying that one is unclean, in line with Leviticus 13–14; *see also* NEGAIM

Negaim Mishnah tractate on the uncleanness signified by the skin ailment described in Leviticus 13–14. The tractate discusses marks of the skin ailment in general and the bright spot (chaps. 1–8), the boil and the burning (chap. 9), scalls (chap. 10), the bald spot on forehead and temple (chap. 10), garments and houses affected by the same marks (chaps. 11–13), and the process of purification of a person affected by the skin ailment (chap. 14).

Negeb the area of land south of the Judean hill country and northeast of the Sinai peninsula. This area extends in an inverted triangle from modern Beer Sheba and Arad down to Elat. Most, if not all, of the biblical references to the Negeb, however, seem to refer to only the northern area of this larger region around Beer Sheba and Arad (cf. Gen. 12:9, 13:1). The larger area was inhabited from the prehistoric period down through the early Arab period.

From the Persian period until the Byzantine period, the Negeb was primarily under Nabatean control. The question remains, however, just how early the Nabateans undertook extensive development of the Negeb. There are several sections from the Greek historian Herodotus that suggest that extensive development began early in the Persian period. Herodotus cites an admittedly less credible source describing the Nabateans as having constructed irrigation pipes made of ox hides. Herodotus is supplemented by the much more reliable source of Hieronymus of Cardia as told by Diodorus. Hieronymus describes the construction of great reservoirs in the ground for the collection of enormous amounts of rain water. Modern visitors to the Negeb during the rainy season can still see reservoirs from the Hellenistic and earlier periods collecting large amounts of water during the periodic thunderstorms.

The first positive evidence of the presence of the Nabateans in the Negeb is found in the Elusa inscription from the beginning of the first half of the second century B.C.E. Despite their presence in the Negeb, there is little in the way of archaeological building remains until the end of the first century B.C.E. Though puzzling, this fact is consistent with another description of the Nabateans in the Negeb by Hieronymus. He says, "It is their custom neither to sow grain, plant fruit-bearing trees, use wine, nor construct any house."

During the Middle Nabatean (Early Roman) period, the Nabateans were briefly expelled from the Negeb at the beginning of the first century B.C.E. They reconquered the Negeb, however, early in the reign of Obodas III (30–9 B.C.E.). Due to a large tariff imposed on Nabatean spice trade by Herod at this time, it seems that this reconquering might have taken place with the Judean monarch's blessing. In any case, the Nabateans established several new strongholds in the central Negeb region and in general strengthened the existing caravan trade routes.

The Nabatean power in the Negeb declined during the first century C.E., as did the rest of the Nabatean kingdom during the reign of Malichus II (40–70 C.E.). The succeeding monarch, Rabbel II (70–106 C.E.), instigated a period of growth. During this period, agriculture was developed in the Negeb and extensive terracing, which allowed for the collection of rainwater, was begun. This use of terrace farming continued down through the Byzantine and Arab periods, and many of these ancient terrace farms are still visible to the modern visitor.

negligence harmful neglect of responsibility resulting in a loss to another person through negligent lack of care, through loss of goods or animals caused by the dishonesty or lack of attentiveness of a bailee, or through a loss caused by a hired worker's poor workmanship or disregard for instructions of the employer. The most important category concerns accidents caused by lack of care, which are discussed in the first six chapters of M. Baba Kamma through reference to four types of negligence mentioned in scripture: (1) an open pit into which an animal falls and dies (Exod. 21:33–34); (2) a fire that spreads to a neighbor's fields (Exod. 22:5); (3) an ox that causes harm by goring (Exod. 21:28–32, 35–36); and (4) an ox that causes harm by trespassing on another's fields (Exod. 22:4). These primary categories yield derivative categories, for example, a knife or rock left where someone can be injured yields liability under the category of the open pit, and an animal's kicking, biting, or butting yields liability under the category of goring. In this way, the rules for all types of negligence are derived from the original scriptural categories.

Under rabbinic law, an individual is liable for damages only if the result of his actions could have been foreseen—for example, if he knew that his ox was a gorer or if the fire he made was spread by an ordinary wind, which he should have anticipated. But if an ordinary person would not have anticipated the damage—for example, if a fire was spread by an unusually powerful wind—the occurrence is treated not as negligence (*peshiah*) but as a mishap or accident (*ones*), and no liability is incurred. At the same time, an individual always is deemed to be aware of the consequences of his own actions, so that one always is liable for damage he causes directly. Only minors and people who are deaf and mute or mentally incompetent are exempted from liability under the laws of negligence, since they are deemed incapable of foreseeing the consequences of their actions.

Nehardea Babylonian town, located at the junction of the Euphrates and Malka rivers; seat of an important rabbinical academy. The city is believed to have been settled by Jews as early as the sixth century B.C.E.; in the century prior to the destruction of the Jerusalem Temple in 70 C.E., it was the collection site for the half-shekel offering and other donations for the Temple, which were transported from there to Jerusalem.

After the destruction of the Temple in 70 C.E., Akiba is said to have gone to Nehardea to intercalate the year, suggesting the importance of the city (B. Yebamot 16:7), which was the seat of the exilarch. Nehardea became particularly significant within rabbinic circles at the end of the Tannaitic period, when Samuel established the reputation of its academy, at which his father had taught, and which was second only to the academy of Rab (who for a time also was at Nehardea) at Sura, a short distance away. After Samuel's death in 254 C.E., Nehardea was destroyed, and its place of prominence was assumed by Pumbedita. Nehardea regained its stature under Nahman b. Jacob and, later, Dimi and Amemar. It continued throughout the Talmudic period as the site of an important rabbinical academy.

Nehar Pekod town with a Jewish population in Babylonia, in the district of Nehardea. Hananiah, the nephew of Joshua b. Hananiah, lived there after the Bar Kokhba Revolt and unsuccessfully attempted to establish an academy and a Sanhedrin (B. Berakhot 63a–b, B. Sanhedrin 32b). B. Hullin 127a speaks disparagingly of the city's inhabitants, in effect calling them thieves.

Nehemiah **1.** fifth-century-B.C.E. Jewish leader. Reliable information on Nehemiah is confined to the first-person narrative or memoir (Neh. 1:1–2:20, 3:33–7:5, 12:31–43, 13:4–31) and the third-person account in the same book dealing with several of the same incidents (Neh. 3:1–32; 11:1–2; 12:27–30, 44–47; 13:1–3). From these we gather that Nehemiah's mission to Judah occurred in the twentieth year of the reign of Artaxerxes I (445 B.C.E.) and that it lasted twelve years (Neh. 5:14), after which he was recalled to the imperial court and returned to Judah for another period of unknown length (13:6–7). His principal achievements as governor of the province were the rebuilding of the wall of Jerusalem (Neh. 2–6), the repopulation of the city (Neh. 11), dedication of the completed project (Neh. 12:27–43), rectification of social

abuses (Neh. 5), support and smooth functioning of the cult (10:1–38, 12:44–47, 13:10–14), measures to preserve the ethnic identity of the community (13:1–9, 23–31), and enforcement of the Sabbath law (13:15–22). Nehemiah was praised by Sirach (Sir. 49:11–13) and served as a role model for the Maccabees (2 Macc. 1:10–2:18). He is not prominent in rabbinic sources and is sometimes identified with Zerubbabel (e.g., B. Sanhedrin 38a).

2. Tannaitic authority of the mid-second century C.E.; a student of Akiba. His importance is indicated by B. Sanhedrin 86a's statement that Nehemiah stands behind all anonymous statements in the Tosefta. Nehemiah survived the Bar Kokhba Revolt and, at the end of the Hadrianic persecutions, was central in the renewal of rabbinic study.

Nehuniah b. Abin *see* HUNA B. ABIN

Nehuniah b. Hakanah a native of Emmaus; a Tannaitic authority at the end of the first century C.E., possibly a student of Yohanan b. Zakkai. B. Shebuot 26a states that Nehuniah b. Hakanah was Ishmael's teacher and taught him his hermeneutical principles.

neighbor someone in domestic proximity or, more generally, a member of one's tribe or people. Relationships with one's neighbors are detailed in biblical legislation. One is not, for example, to bear false witness against a neighbor or covet his wife or possessions (Exod. 20:16–17; Deut. 5:20–21). Epitomizing this legislation is Leviticus 19:17–18, "You shall not hate anyone of your kin in your heart, but you shall reason with your neighbor, lest you bear sin because of him. You shall not take vengeance or bear any grudge against the children of your own people, but you shall love your neighbor as yourself . . ." (see also Mark 12:31; Matt. 22:39; Luke 10:27; Rom. 13:8–10; Gal. 5:14; James 2:8). The neighbor is not only another member of Israel but may also be the sojourner, as Leviticus 19:33–34 indicates. Similarly, the parable of the good Samaritan (Luke 10:27–37) suggests that good neighbors are those who, regardless of national origin or enmity, help others. Testament of Isaac 5 discusses punishments of those who mistreat their neighbors and friends.

The rabbis were particularly concerned with the rights of neighbors on adjacent property or in abutting buildings. To prevent damage to a neighbor's property, rabbinic law controls, among other things, the digging of wells at the edge of one's field, the running of businesses or performance of other activities that cause disruptive noise, and the placement of ovens that create a fire hazard (M. Baba Batra 2:1–14). The importance the rabbis attributed to proper relationships with other people is indicated by the statement attributed to Hillel, which summarizes the entire Torah with the maxim "What is hateful to you, do not do to your neighbor" (B. Shabbat 31b).

Neilah closing service marking the end of Yom Kippur, recited at nightfall, when the fast ends

nekyia (Gr.) a ritual of necromancy; or, a human descent to the world of the dead. The word occurs mainly as a designation for Book 11 of Homer's *Odyssey*, in which Odysseus journeys to the land of the dead to learn his future fate from the shade of Tiresias.

Neofiti, Targum Having been miscataloged in the Vatican Library, Targum Neofiti was rediscovered there in 1957. The manuscript, technically known as Codex Neophyti 1, seems to have been copied in the early sixteenth century. The original targum was probably written sometime between 135 C.E. and the mid-fourth century. Targum Neofiti constitutes a complete, continuous translation of the Hebrew Pentateuch into Aramaic—apparently into the dialect of Jewish Palestinian Aramaic. This targum combines a word-for-word translation of the Hebrew text with additional material that ranges in length from a word or two to several paragraphs. In general, the additions follow the Palestinian Targum tradition and hence Neofiti can be classed as a Palestinian Targum. The manuscript itself contains later comments in the margins and glosses added between the lines.

Neofiti interlinear glosses the many notations written between the lines of the sixteenth-century codex of Targum Neofiti. These insertions, apparently done in the sixteenth century by several different scribes, usually correct the grammar of the Aramaic. The glosses often agree with the text found in Targum Onkelos.

Neofiti margins comments added into the margins of the sixteenth-century codex of Targum Neofiti. The comments were probably added in the seventeenth century. The different comments often correspond to a reading found in at least one of the Palestinian Targums to the Pentateuch or Targum Onkelos, but some provide readings otherwise unknown.

Neoplatonism *see* PLATONISM

Neo-Pythagoreanism *see* PYTHAGOREANISM

Nero Roman emperor (r. 54–68 C.E.). Nero's questionable claim as emperor led to the spread of stories about his miraculous birth. He arranged the assassination of his mother and, later, his wife. His extravagant lifestyle, vanity, suspicious nature, and sense of power made him unpopular. With the out-break of the war in Judea, he was forced to put Vespasian in charge of the Roman forces and Mucianus in Syria. There is no evidence that his persecution of the Christians in Rome in 64 included persecution of the Jews.

Nero redivivus (Lat., Nero resurrected) After the death of the Roman emperor Nero in 69 C.E., rumor had it that he had not actually died but was still alive and living secretly in the East. It was only a matter of time, it was said, before he gathered an army among the Parthians, the eastern enemy of Rome, and returned in triumph to take up his throne again. (No actual resurrection was envisaged until after the time of Nero's expected lifespan.) The legend is referred to in several Jewish apocalyptic writings and in Christian writings on the anti-Christ.

Nerva Roman emperor (r. 96–98 C.E.). When Domitian was assassinated without having named a successor, the Senate selected Nerva as the one who could promote its ideals and its interpretation of the constitution. However, he never gained the support of the military or of the Praetorian Guards. In 97 he adopted Trajan as his heir and gave him powers virtually equal to his own. He annulled Domitian's tax that was levied not only on the Jews but also on those who followed the Jewish way of life without formally becoming Jewish. His actions ended the practice of denouncing individuals who were following the Jewish way of life. He also put an end to the charge of impiety leveled against the Jews and recalled those individuals who had been unjustly banished, perhaps even Domitilla who had been exiled by Domitian for being Jewish.

neshekh *see* INTEREST

Nestorians a group of Christians who emerged in the fifth century and flourished in Syria, Mesopotamia, and Persia, especially in Edessa, Nisibis, and Seleucia. Nestorians, whose teachings were mistakenly attributed to the bishop Nestorius, emphasized the separation rather than the unity of the divine and human nature in Jesus Christ. They were accused by the orthodox of also affirming the presence of two persons in Jesus, a charge that seems mistaken. Members of this church wrote in Syriac, a dialect of Aramaic common in Syria, and were influenced by Antiochene theologians like Theodore of Mopsuestia. They developed their own ecclesiastical structures and were the dominant church in the Sassanid Empire, the context in which the Babylonian Jewish community flourished. Over the centuries, their missionaries established communities in India, Turkestan, Manchuria,

Siberia, and China. Communities of Nestorians still exist in Kurdestan and India.

Nestorius (c. 381–451) theologian and bishop of Constantinople (428–431). Embroiled in Christological controversies of the fifth century, he was removed as bishop and condemned as a heretic who affirmed that the human Jesus and divine Christ were two persons. He lived his last twenty years in exile. In retrospect, his teachings seem orthodox and the attacks of his opponents erroneous. The Nestorian churches of Mesopotamia and Persia were named after him, but he did not found them or inspire them by his teaching.

netilat yadayim (Heb.) hand-washing, not for hygienic purposes but to attain ritual cleanness prior to eating a meal

Netopha biblical town in the hills of Judah, near Bethlehem. In the rabbinic literature, Netopha is known as a place of olive production. It is referred to alternatively as Beth Netopha.

new heavens, new earth a phrase that seems to occur first in Isaiah 65:17 in reference to an ideal age, which God would inaugurate by intervening in world affairs. He would redeem his people, destroy their enemies, and renew heaven and earth. The theme becomes especially important in apocalyptic literature with regard to the "age to come."

New Moon When the Temple stood, this was a festival proclaimed by the Sanhedrin in Jerusalem after witnesses testified to observing the new moon. Bonfires were lit on hilltops to signal the event throughout the land. This is discussed in the mishnaic tractate Rosh Hashanah. After the calendar was fixed by calculation in the middle of the fourth century C.E., the new month was announced in the synagogue at the time of the Birkat haHodesh, the blessing of the month.

New Oil, Festival of a festival known only from the Temple Scroll from Qumran. It occurred fifty days after the Festival of New Wine.

New Testament a collection of writings that forms the second half of the Christian scriptures. Its three sections include twenty-seven books: the four Gospels and the Acts of the Apostles; twenty-one epistles written by, or ascribed to, Paul and others; and the apocalypse of John. These writings gradually gained authority during the second and early third centuries C.E. to the exclusion of other works ascribed to disciples of Jesus. In establishing its biblical canon, the church avoided two alternative possibilities. It rejected the view of Marcion, who denied the authority of the Hebrew Bible, but it insisted that the Hebrew Bible by itself was insufficient because it did not testify explicitly to Jesus. The term "New Testament" or "New Covenant" is first implied by Melito, bishop of Sardis (c. 180 C.E.), who refers to the Jewish canon as "the Old Testament" (Eusebius, *Eccl. Hist.* 4:26). The distinction asserts the superiority of Christianity over Judaism, employing the language of Jeremiah 31:31 as explicated in the Epistle to the Hebrews.

New Testament and targums *see* TARGUMS AND NEW TESTAMENT

New Wine, Festival of a festival known only from the Temple Scroll from Qumran. It occurred fifty days after the Festival of Weeks. *See also* SHABUOT.

Nezikin the fourth division of the Mishnah, devoted to civil law and damages

Nicanor Seleucid general sent by Demetrius I to support the high priest Alcimus against Judas Maccabeus. Judas defeated and killed him at Beth Horon, northwest of Jerusalem, in 161 C.E., thereby gaining control of Judea. This victory is celebrated on Nicanor's Day, on the thirteenth of Adar (March).

Nicolaus of Damascus Greek secretary and confidant of Herod the Great. After Herod's death in 4 B.C.E., Nicolaus composed a world history in 144 books. Although the work was a synchronic history of all nations, as had become common in the Graeco-Roman world, it seems to have been quite informative regarding Jewish history. It has not survived except in fragments but was heavily used by Josephus. Nicolaus was an important source because he evidently had access to court papers and reports not only about Herod and his rule but also about the reigns of the Hasmoneans. Our knowledge about the entire period of Hasmonean rule after Simon and of Herod's kingdom seems ultimately to depend on Nicolaus. Much of what remains of his history has come to us only indirectly through the accounts in Josephus's *The Jewish War* and *Antiquities of the Jews;* nevertheless, Josephus does occasionally quote him directly. We also have part of an encomium (speech of praise) to Augustus Caesar preserved separately, as well as one or two independent fragments on Jewish history. One of these concerns the dispute among Herod's sons before Augustus after Herod's death and gives us a better insight into Nicolaus's actual method of writing.

niddah (Heb.) menstruating woman

Niddah Mishnah tractate devoted to the uncleanness of the menstruating woman set forth in Leviticus 15. The tractate discusses the definition of unclean excretions (chaps. 2–5); rules applicable at various ages (chaps. 5–6); doubts in connection with unclean excretions (chaps. 6–9); and disputes of the Houses of Shammai on the same topics (chaps. 9–10).

Niger, Pescennius (in full, Gaius Pescennius Niger Justus) Roman official, born in 135 C.E. Of humble birth, he rose through military commands to equestrian status and enrollment, by Commodus, in the Senate. He was consul (190) with Septimius Severus and governor of Syria (191). Following Commodus's murder in December 192, Praetorian Guards first proclaimed Helvius Pertinax and then Didius Julianus emperor, but in June 193 the frontier legions began to put forth their own candidates and Niger was proclaimed emperor by the Syrian army and won support from Asia and Egypt. Meanwhile, Septimius Severus, saluted by the Danubian army as emperor, took control of Rome, and Niger attempted to consolidate his power in the east by taking control of Byzantium, from which he hoped to secure the route between Asia and Europe. Niger was defeated at Perintus, Cyzicus, and Nicaea. Finally, after being routed at Issus, in Cilicia, Niger broke for the Euphrates but was captured and executed in 194.

niggun (Heb., tune) the melody to which the Jewish liturgy is set; often, the melodic motif associated with a particular worship service, for example, the Sabbath niggun

Nihumai Saboraic authority; died in 506 C.E.; also referred to as Rihumai

Nimrin a location in Syria; the last station for messengers who traveled from the Land of Israel to proclaim the beginning of the new month (Y. Ketubot 2:7–8, 26d)

Ninth of Ab *see* AB, NINTH OF

Nisan seventh month of the Jewish calendar, corresponding to March/April. The full moon in Nisan is the first after the vernal equinox and marks the celebration of Passover.

Nisibis the modern town of Nesib in southern Anatolia; under Roman and then Persian rule, a trading city on the route from the Far East to the West. Josephus refers to the city's Jewish population and notes that Nisibis was a way station for pilgrims en route to Jerusalem. In the second century C.E., it became a center of Torah study when Judah b. Batyra attracted numerous scholars to the town, including some who came from the Land of Israel. By the third century, a growing Christian population had reduced the city's centrality within rabbinic circles.

nissuin *see* MARRIAGE

Nittai of Arbel *see* MATTAI OF ARBEL

Nizzana (or Nessana) ancient town of the central Negeb desert, 32 miles southwest of Beer Sheba.

The settlement was founded in the second century B.C.E. by the Nabateans. The town apparently was abandoned in the eighth century C.E.

At the eastern end of the acropolis stood a second-century-B.C.E. Nabatean fortress or temple. The structure, 27 by 25 meters in size, was defended by round towers on its southeastern, southwestern, and northwestern sides and by a slope to the south. A court measuring 8 by 8.5 meters stood in the building's center. Rounded buttresses and a supporting wall were added to the foundations when the north church was built (see below).

Most of the acropolis was occupied by a citadel, measuring 85 by 35 meters, built before the middle of the fifth century C.E. Two corner and two middle towers stood on the west side, two corner towers and one middle tower on the south, and one on the east. The main gate was located in the middle southern tower and a secondary gate was in the eastern.

In the fourth century C.E., the north church was constructed upon the foundations of the Hellenistic building and against the northern wall of the citadel. A monumental staircase led from the lower city to a gate in the southern end of the atrium. The atrium consisted of a paved east court with a cistern fed by underground channels, a colonnaded east gallery, and three rooms. Near the eastern end of the south court, two rooms held several burials. Greek inscriptions date the burials to 464 and 475 C.E. and mention Thoamos, a priest, and Paladius, a deacon. Other inscriptions refer to the rooms as a "holy place." Still others in the church mention Saint Stephen and the dedication of the building to saints Sergius and Bacchus.

The sanctuary itself was a long central nave ending in an apse and *bimah* (raised platform) in the east and a baptismal font in the west. The apse was flanked by two odd-shaped rooms. Nearby debris held the remains of a marble chancel screen. A block of limestone at the *bimah* was carved with grapevines and crosses. Crosses also decorated the nave. The entire north wall of the sanctuary served as the south wall of an adjacent chapel with flanking rooms east and west. A north court and gallery were added during the reign of Justinian. Several rooms adjoined the court and gallery on either side, and a well house stood to the north.

The south church was built on a hill south of the acropolis at the beginning of the seventh century C.E. Adjacent to the sanctuary in the north was a small paved atrium with a bench and cistern in the west and a colonnaded narthex on the east. Two adjacent rooms stood above a 2-meter-deep pit. The sanctuary, measuring 20.8 by 14.1 meters, had three apses, an altar, and a *bimah*. Two rows of six columns divided the sanctuary into a nave and two aisles, all paved with limestone.

South of the sanctuary was a chapel. Two rows of three columns supported the ceiling. A *bimah* and chancel screen stood in front of an apse, behind which was a room. An inscription on a column mentioning Mary, Mother of God, dates between 601 and 602 C.E. There were as many as three churches in the lower city, probably dating to the fifth and sixth centuries. One of these churches has been excavated.

Most important to the site are the Greek and bilingual Greek-Arabic papyri discovered in the north church. Literary papyri include a fragment of Virgil's *Aeneid* with a Greek dictionary to the work, a fragment of the Gospel of John, the Acts of Saint George, the apocryphal letters of Abgar to Christ with Christ's reply, and almost two hundred theological, legal, military, and business documents and fragments, dating from 512 to 689 C.E.

Noah the single righteous human being found on earth when God determined to destroy all living things because of their sin (Gen. 6–9). Preserved on an ark, together with his wife, his sons, and their wives, he became the patriarch of a new humanity, and all the nations are traced back to his three sons (Gen. 10).

The traditions in 1 Enoch that depict the flood as a prototype of the final judgment give a special place to Noah. In 1 Enoch 10:1–3 he is described as an eschatological prophet who receives the message of the coming judgment (cf. Isa. 26:20), but he is also a type of the righteous who will escape destruction in the judgment (cf. 1 Enoch 10:3 and 10:17). His role as patriarch in 10:3 (cf. 84:6) is described in language that is paralleled in the reference to Abraham in 93:5. In the story of Noah's birth in 1 Enoch 106–107 and the Genesis Apocryphon 2, the newborn Noah's radiant appearance leads his father to suspect that he has been conceived by an angelic father, but Enoch interprets Noah's appearance as a portent of his future role as the one who will renew humanity. Another narrative fragment in 1 Enoch 67 provides details about the construction of the ark. According to Jubilees 10 the angels gave Noah information about herbs and medicines that would ward off the illness brought on by the evil spirits that had proceeded from the dead bodies of the giants destroyed in the flood.

The reference to Noah as a "herald of righteousness" in 2 Peter 2:5 indicates knowledge of a tradition that described Noah as a prophet to his generation. Such a tradition is transmitted by Josephus (*Ant.* 1.3.1, sec. 74) and may be attested independently in 1 Clement 9:4. *See also* BIRTH, MIRACULOUS; FLOOD.

Noah, Books of traditions said to stand behind Noachic texts in 1 Enoch, the Genesis Apocryphon, and Jubilees. These traditions have been identified variously as the fall of the watchers (1 Enoch 6–11), the birth of Noah (1 Enoch 106–107, 1 Qap-Gen 2), the building of the ark (1 Enoch 65–67), other flood traditions (1 Enoch 54–55, 60, 68–69), and Noah's receipt of medical information (Jub. 10:1–16). The existence of a book or books of Noah seems quite possible. Jubilees 10:13 and 21:10 refer to such a book. The complex parallels in 1 Enoch 65–67, 83–84, 106–107, and the Genesis Apocryphon imply older Noachic traditions. However, the precise form, content, and date of such books or traditions cannot be determined with certainty.

Noah, representation of a minor motif in Jewish art, including images of Noah's ark. The ark, which was used to carry humans and animals to safety during the great flood, came to be understood as a symbol for salvation in general in early Jewish and Christian iconography. Noah's ark was one of the earliest representations from the Hebrew Bible that was adopted in both churches and synagogues. One example of a mosaic depicting Noah in the ark is from the synagogue at Jerash (Gerasa), which was converted into a Christian church.

In other instances, Noah in the ark seems to represent salvation in the afterlife. One example is seen on a coin of Apamea in Syria, dated 244 to 248 C.E. Noah is depicted with his wife emerging from a box, which is more in the shape of a sarcophagus than a boat. A dove is also portrayed next to Noah, and another dove flies overhead with an olive branch. In this instance, the symbolism of Noah's ark seems to have been converted to a sarcophagus, thus symbolizing victory over death. This same use of Noah's ark as a box (sarcophagus?) is found in a few synagogues and in the Christian Catacomb of Priscilla in Rome; its depiction in the catacomb is further evidence of its symbolic significance for salvation after death.

Noahides non-Jews who observe the seven laws that apply to the descendants of Noah (namely, all peoples). According to rabbinic authorities, these include the following prohibitions: idolatry, adultery and incest, bloodshed, blasphemy, robbery, social injustice, and eating the flesh of a limb cut from a living animal (T. Abodah Zarah 8:4–8).

nomos (Gr., law, or custom) term that was often used to translate the Hebrew word *torah* in the Septuagint. Although *nomos* overlaps *torah* and the English word "law" in meaning, it also has other connotations. An important additional concept was the idea of "custom" in a particular sense: the Greeks often considered their customs to be "natural law." Thus, obedience to the law meant more than honoring certain written regulations; it included an entire way of life. In Jewish writings in Greek, the term "the law" (*to nomos*) came to mean "Jewish religion."

notarikon (Heb., from Gr.: *notarikon*, shorthand) term used in rabbinic writings to refer to words in which each letter stands for a complete word, so that each word is an abbreviated sentence. Used as an exegetical device, a word from the Bible is interpreted as a phrase or sentence.

nous (Gr., mind) Although used generically, the word became a technical philosophical term, contrasted with such terms as *aisthēsis* (sense percep-tion), which it was supposed to govern. In Jewish writings, it is found especially in the works of Philo of Alexandria.

numbers, magic *see* GEMATRIA

Numbers, Targum to *see* PALESTINIAN TARGUMS; ONKELOS, TARGUM

Numenius Neo-Pythagorean writer from Apamea, in Syria, in the late second century C.E. Little is known of him apart from the fragments of his writings that have been preserved, but he seems to have influenced a number of important later writers, such as Porphyry. He admired eastern wisdom, including that of the Jews. One of his most famous statements is, "What is Plato but Moses speaking Attic [Greek]?" He also apparently made reference to the Pentateuch and Prophets, giving them an allegorical interpretation, and even seems to quote Genesis 1:2 on one occasion.

nusaḥ (Heb.) the "form" of a prayer. The term refers to either its wording or the musical system to which it is sung.

oath   an appeal to God as a witness to the truth of one's statement. Under talmudic law, oaths are admitted as probative evidence in civil but not criminal cases and when other sufficient evidence is unavailable. The oath is used by a defendant to deny a claim against him or her or, in certain cases, as a confirmatory oath made by a plaintiff to support his or her demand for payment from another. Such cases include those of a hired hand who claims not to have been paid, a shopkeeper who claims to have delivered goods and to be owed on account, and a victim of a theft who demands return of the stolen goods (M. Shebuot 7:1). In the absence of other evidence, an oath taken by such a plaintiff is sufficient to yield a judgment against the defendant, requiring him or her to pay the claim. Such a judgment, pronounced on the basis of an oath alone, is overturned if witnesses later come forward and testify that the oath was false. In such a case, any monetary judgment needs to be repaid to the defendant.

An oath generally is imposed only in a case of a valid claim indicating a set amount the defendant owes. Trustees, partners, or agents are an exception to this principle and may be required to take an oath even when no specific allegation has been made (M. Shebuot 7:8). Additionally, a plaintiff may demand that such individuals take an oath regarding all possible claims against them, arising from any matters concerning that same defendant.

Known or suspected liars, gamblers, usurers, and perjurers are disqualified from taking an oath (M. Shebuot 7:4), since their word cannot be trusted anyway. Minors and the deaf, dumb, or mentally incompetent also are excluded from oaths, for they are deemed unable to assess the truth of their own statements. M. Shebuot 6:5 states that oaths are not admitted in cases involving immovable property, slaves, or written deeds. Later talmudic law extended the use of oaths to such property as well.

Obadiah, Targum to   *see* TARGUM TO THE PROPHETS

Octavian   *see* AUGUSTUS CAESAR

Odenathus   ruler of Palmyra (r. 254–266 C.E.). After Shapur I rejected his offer of friendship in 260, Odenathus's troops harassed Shapur's forces. In 263, they crossed the Euphrates. Although Shapur expelled the Palmyrenes from central Babylonia, they held Mesopotamia until Aurelian destroyed Palmyra in 273. According to Sherira, Papa b. Nazer, who is identified with Odenathus, destroyed Nehardea and forced Samuel's students to establish their academy elsewhere. Nehardea was a center of activity for Jewish merchants, so the Palmyrenes, who lived by commerce and competed with Jewish merchants, would have benefited greatly from its destruction. Odenathus extended his rule over Palestine. Palmyra had a signicant Jewish population, and Christian sources claim that Zenobia, Odenathus's wife, favored Judaism; however, the Jews seemed to have regarded Odenathus as a Roman agent. The Palestinian Jews reviled him and rejoiced over his assassination.

Odes of Solomon   *see* SOLOMON, ODES OF

ofanim (sing.: ofan) one of the many orders of angels that make up the celestial hierarchies. The term, which literally means "wheels," is derived from the description of the chariot of God, the Merkabah, in the Book of Ezekiel (Ezek. 1:15–21, 10:9,16). The interpretation of the chariot's wheels as a class of angels is attested already in the Dead Sea Scrolls: in the Songs of the Sabbath Sacrifice (4QSirShabb) they are said to bless, and they stand in parallel to the cherubim (see also 1 Enoch 61:10). The synagogue prayerbook describes the ofanim and the holy hayot as singing the response to the seraphim in the performance of the celestial Kedushah.

Official Aramaic *see* ARAMAIC, IMPERIAL

Ohalot Mishnah tractate devoted to the uncleanness that is spread by a tent located over the body of a corpse, in line with Numbers 19. The tractate focuses on diverse modes of imparting uncleanness and sources of uncleanness in general (chaps. 2–3); tents as a medium for spreading corpse-uncleanness (chaps. 3–16); and sources of uncleanness analogous to corpse matter (chap. 16).

ohel (Heb.) tent; *see also* OHALOT

Oil, Festival of New *see* NEW OIL, FESTIVAL OF

oil, use in rabbinic period Olive oil was a primary commodity in Israel in rabbinic times, used for cooking, as a body lotion, for medicinal purposes, and for lamps. Oil was also derived from other animal, mineral, and vegetable sources, such as sesame seeds or nuts. In Babylonia, sesame oil was the most common. A special anointing oil was used for the ritual anointing of the high priest in the Temple (Lev. 8:12). Belief was widespread that the redeemer of Israel also would be anointed with oil (in Hebrew, *mashiah,* the source of the title "messiah"). According to the rabbis, when the Hasmoneans defeated the Hellenizers in the second century B.C.E., they found only enough pure oil for lighting the lamps in the Temple for one day, but it lasted miraculously for eight days. Accordingly, on Hanukkah, Jews celebrated this miracle by lighting oil lamps for eight days. The Mishnah (Shabbat 2) specifies which oil could be used for kindling the Sabbath lamp on Friday evening before sundown. In everyday use, olive oil commonly was perfumed with balsam, or sesame oil was mixed with extract of rose. A special blessing was recited upon using such oils. Anointing oneself with oil was prohibited on the Day of Atonement and the Ninth of Ab.

oil of life the source of life for humanity, whose sin condemns them to death. In the version of the Adam and Eve story in the Apocalypse of Moses and Life of Adam and Eve, the dying Adam sends Eve and Seth in search of the oil of life or oil of mercy that flows from an unnamed tree in paradise (Apoc. Moses 9:2–13:5; Life of Adam and Eve 26:1–42:1). The medicine is forbidden until the time of the resurrection of all flesh. Stories about the quest for this oil flourished in medieval times and are reminiscent of the Grail legends.

olah (Heb., burnt offering) an offering that is wholly burned up upon the altar fires in the Temple in Jerusalem, yielding no share of the sacrifice for either the officiating priest or the person in behalf of whom the offering is presented

Olam haBa *see* AGE TO COME

Olam haZeh *see* AGE, THIS

old age *see* AGE

Old Aramaic *see* ARAMAIC, OLD

Old Testament The earliest form of the Old Testament was created by the Christian church by combining the books of the Hebrew Bible with the books of the Apocrypha. When the Protestants broke with the Catholics, they removed the Apocryphal books, thus making the Protestant Old Testament the same as the Hebrew Bible. *See also* NEW TESTAMENT; TANAKH.

Old Testament Aramaic *see* ARAMAIC, BIBLICAL

olive leaves *see* LEAVES

olive's bulk (Heb.: *kezayit*) measure of food volume equal to a medium-sized olive. If one eats forbidden food in the volume of an olive's bulk, one incurs punishment; less than that is not culpable.

Omedim baShurah (Heb., standing in rows) a Tannaitic funeral custom, still followed today. Funeral participants arrange themselves in rows, so as to offer condolence to mourners as they pass through.

omer **1.** the first sheaf of barley cut in the harvest, offered on the second day of Passover, at which point the new crops of grain are permitted for use. The omer was offered in the Temple every day for forty-nine days, from the second day of Passover (the 16th of Nisan) until Pentecost; this was observed as a period of mourning.

2. a dry measure, comprising one and four-fifths of a kab

onaah (Heb., overreaching) a rabbinic economic term. In the purchase or sale of an article, the term indicates fraudulently deviating from the market price by at least one-sixth of the article's value.

On Abraham *see* DE ABRAHAMO

On Dreams *see* DE SOMNIIS

On Drunkenness *see* DE EBRIETATE

oneg Shabbat (Heb., Sabbath delight) engaging in activities of rejoicing on the Sabbath, taking pleasure in the Sabbath rest; singing, feasting, and relaxing on the Sabbath day

ones (Heb., forced) a rabbinic term for rape. Jewish sources extend the meaning to a circumstance for which a person cannot be held accountable, such as an act forced upon a person by threat of death, violence, or financial ruin, and to an unavoidable deterrent, such as a natural barrier, an illness, or an accident.

On Flight and Finding *see* DE FUGA ET INVENTIONE

On Husbandry *see* DE AGRICULTURA

Onias, Temple of *see* LEONTOPOLIS, TEMPLE AT

Onias II son of the high priest Simon I. As he was young when his father died, his uncle Eleazar and then his grandfather's brother Manasses at first substituted for him. Onias II was high priest around the middle of the third century B.C.E. Little else is known about him. He may have written to the Spartan king Areus (1 Macc. 12:19–23), but no certainty exists. In the legendary tale about the Tobiads, Josephus narrates how Onias refused to pay tribute to Ptolemy III (246–221 B.C.E.) out of stinginess, and so Joseph, son of Tobias, stepped in and became tax collector of Phoenicia (*Ant.* 12.4). Scholars have suggested political motives behind the refusal to pay taxes.

Onias III son of the high priest Simon II (Sir. 50:1–21) and the grandson of Onias II; Jewish high priest from 196 to 175 B.C.E. According to 2 Maccabees 3 and 4, Onias (Heb.: Honi or Yohanan) was the pious high priest who sought to dissuade Heliodorus, the emissary of Antiochus III, from robbing the Temple and then interceded with God for Heliodorus's life. He was removed from the high priesthood in 175 B.C.E. by his brother Jason and murdered in 170 B.C.E. by Andronicus, the deputy of the new high priest, Menelaus, at Daphne, near Antioch, in Syria.

Onias IV son of the high priest Onias III. According to Josephus (*Ant.* 13.62–73; cf. 12.387–88, 20.236), Onias IV fled to Egypt during the Maccabean wars. He requested from King Ptolemy VI Philometer (r. 180–145 B.C.E.) and Queen Cleopatra the authority to build a temple in Egypt, similar to the one in Jerusalem, at the site of an abandoned Egyptian temple in Leontopolis, in the Heliopolitan nome. Permission was granted and a temple and altar were built, with Onias serving as high priest. The date of Onias's migration to Egypt is disputed; some scholars say that he came to Egypt several years before he asked permission to build the temple and was already head of a Jewish military garrison at Leontopolis when the temple was requested. The temple would have been built

about 160 B.C.E. or even later. Onias IV and his sons served as generals in the military service of the Ptolemies and played a role in Egyptian political affairs. The Jewish military colony founded by Onias at Leontopolis ("the land of Onias") existed into the Roman period.

On Joseph *see* DE IOSEPHO

Onkelos Jewish proselyte at the end of the first century. He was wealthy and studied with both Eliezer b. Hyrcanus and Joshua b. Ḥananiah. The Babylonian Talmud (Meg. 3a) credits him with translating the Pentateuch into Aramaic, but this probably constitutes a confusion with the Palestinian Talmud's remarks concerning Aquila, who translated the Pentateuch into Greek (Meg. 1:11, 71c).

Onkelos, Targum As we now have it, this targum was probably composed in the third to the fifth century C.E. in a non-Palestinian (Eastern) form of Aramaic. Scholars think it was based on an earlier targum written in Palestine. Targum Onkelos is quite literal, containing only small amounts of additional material. By the time the Babylonian Talmud was written in the fifth century, Targum Onkelos constituted Babylonian Jewry's official translation of the Torah into Aramaic. As the Babylonian Talmud became authoritative among western Jews in the early Middle Ages, Targum Onkelos replaced the Palestinian Targums as the authoritative targum to the Pentateuch. This authoritative status led to the creation of a *masorah* for the targum to ensure that it would be accurately copied.

On Noah's Work as a Planter *see* DE PLANTATIONE

onomastica lists of names, often with other information, such as etymologies or equivalents in other languages. The term is derived from the Greek word *onoma* (name). Onomastica were sometimes used in exegeses using etymologies for those who were not bilingual, such as those by Philo of Alexandria.

On Providence *see* DE PROVIDENTIA

Onqelos *see* ONKELOS

On Rewards and Punishments *see* DE PRAEMIIS ET POENIS

On Sobriety *see* DE SOBRIETATE

On the Change of Names *see* DE MUTATIONE NOMINUM

On the Cherubim *see* DE CHERUBIM

On the Confusion of Tongues *see* DE CONFUSIONE LINGUARUM

On the Contemplative Life *see* DE VITA CONTEMPLATIVA

On the Creation of the World *see* DE OPIFICIO MUNDI

On the Decalogue *see* DE DECALOGO

On the Embassy to Gaius *see* DE LEGIATIONE AD GAIUM

On the Eternity of the World *see* DE AETERNITATE MUNDI

On the Giants *see* DE GIGANTIBUS

On the Life of Moses *see* DE VITA MOSIS

On the Migration of Abraham *see* DE MIGRATIONE ABRAHAMI

On the Posterity and Exile of Cain *see* DE POSTERITATE CAINI

On the Preliminary Studies *see* DE CONGRESSU QUAERENDAE ERUDITIONIS GRATIA

On the Sacrifices of Abel and Cain *see* DE SACRIFICIIS ABELIS ET CAINI

On the Special Laws *see* DE SPECIALIBUS LEGIBUS

On the Virtues *see* DE VIRTUTIBUS

Opf. *see* DE OPIFICIO MUNDI

oppression cruel and violent acts carried out by the powerful against the poor and powerless. That Jews in antiquity suffered such oppression cannot be doubted; however, the nature and extent of the oppression is difficult to determine when it is attested in polemical documents. A prime example of this is 1 Enoch 92–105 (cf. chaps. 6–11). That the author of this text and his sympathizers and followers suffered at the hands of the rich and powerful seems beyond dispute; otherwise the document would be pointless. Nonetheless, many of the specifics are uncertain, and one cannot be sure, for example, whether charges of killing (103:15) are technically justified or whether the author's rhetoric reflects the feeling that certain actions have led indirectly to death. In any case, the experience of oppression and injustice in these chapters is a challenge to the notion of God's power and justice and brings forth counterbalanced assertions that God's great judgment will set right the wrongs that these people perceive that they have experienced. *See also* PERSECUTION.

oracle an inspired utterance of a prophet in the name of a god. The Hebrew prophets delivered oracles, which are preserved in the prophetic books. In the Hellenistic world, oracles were delivered at shrines such as Delphi, and oracle-mongers made collections of oracles for various purposes. There also developed a tradition of literary oracles, which were not delivered under inspiration but composed as poetic works. In Hellenistic and Roman Judaism, however, prophecy declined in importance, and prophetic oracles were no longer collected. Josephus reports the activity of a number of prophets in this period, including one Jesus, son of Ananias, who delivered an oracle of woe prior to the fall of Jerusalem (*War* 6.300–309). Josephus also claims that an "ambiguous oracle," foretelling that a man from Judea would become ruler of the world, played a part in inciting the Jews to revolt against Rome (*War* 6.312). The prophecy found its fulfillment in the Roman commander Vespasian. The main collection of Jewish oracles from the Hellenistic and Roman periods is found in the Sibylline Oracles.

Oral Torah *see* TORAH, ORAL

ordination *see* HANDS, LAYING ON OF

Origen (c. 185–254 C.E.) Christian biblical exegete and theologian. He was born into a Christian family, probably in Alexandria. He received a good education in the Bible as well as in Greek classics. Origen was ordained a priest in Palestine on his way to Athens. The bishop of Alexandria, Demetrius, angered that Origen received ordination without his permission, had him exiled from Egypt and deposed from the priesthood. Origen moved to Caesarea where he had extensive contact with some Jews in the city. Origen comments on Jewish converts to Christianity and Christian converts to Judaism. He complains about Christian women who keep the Jewish Sabbath, frequent ritual baths, and prepare unleavened bread for Passover. Origen devoted considerable energy to studying the Bible. His *Hexapala* contains the whole Hebrew Bible in six columns, with the Hebrew text in Hebrew, the Hebrew text transliterated into Greek, and four well-known Greek versions, noting additions and lacunae in each text. It was designed to provide some knowledge of the Hebrew text to Christians who knew only the Septuagint and thus were at a disadvantage when discussing their interpretations of the Old Testament with Jews. He wrote a considerable number of commentaries to the biblical books, homilies, and brief exegetical notes on a wide range of biblical passages. In addition to these biblical works, Origen composed a large number of theological and philosophical works, often amply quoting scripture, the most famous being his *On First Principles* and *Against Celsus,* the latter being one of the most important apologetic works of early Christianity.

Origen, one of the greatest Christian biblical exegetes of antiquity and apparently the first to study Hebrew, was fascinated by the variant readings of the manuscripts in his attempt to discover the literal meaning of the biblical texts. However, he believed that the Holy Spirit was the author of the Bible, so that the Old Testament was merely a prophecy of Christ in which every detail had to be explored and exegeted. Addressing himself to Christians, Origen wrote positively about the Jews before Jesus' birth. The Jews had been a nation of philosophers; it was their rejection of Jesus and their failure to accept his teachings that resulted in their loss of wisdom and rejection by God. They did not recognize the truth about Jesus because they did not understand the true spiritual meaning of the Old Testament, which stated that with the appearance of Jesus the ritual law and Jewish control of the Holy Land were abrogated.

Orlah (Heb., uncircumcised) the tenth tractate in the Mishnaic Division of Agriculture (Zeraim), concerned with scripture's prohibition against eating fruit from trees in their first three years of growth (Leviticus 19:23). To allow observance of this commandment, the tractate's three chapters clarify what trees are to be classified as fruit trees, define what produce of such trees comprises their fruit, and indicate whether or not an old tree that is uprooted and replanted is deemed a new growth and thus again subject to the three-year restriction. Finally, several rules discuss conditions under which forbidden fruit, when mixed with permitted fruit, loses its forbidden status and may be eaten.

In their deliberations on these topics, Yabnean authorities are concerned with botanical characteristics of the tree and its fruit. Since a tree that is uprooted and replanted begins to grow anew, Yabneans deem it again to be subject to the three-year restriction. This is the case unless a root had remained in the ground at all times. Yabneans thus disregard the Israelite's own perception and intention, either to be planting the tree as a new growth or simply to be moving an old tree. Ushans, by contrast, judge matters in light of the intention of the individual who plants the tree. They hold that only a tree planted purposely for its fruit is in the first place subject to the restrictions of Orlah; if it is planted as a fence or for lumber, by contrast, it is not classified as a fruit tree at all. Then, even in its first three years of growth, one may eat its fruit.

While the particular laws given here are hardly unexpected, the tractate as a whole deserves note. Concerned primarily with basic matters of definition, the tractate's rules lack a narrow, generative issue such as stands behind the other tractates in the Division of Agriculture. Moreover, these rules on Orlah comprise only half of the tractate, with the rest dedicated to tangentially related matters, concerning the status of mixtures of forbidden and permitted produce. The existence of this tractate attests to the determination of the framers of the Mishnah to cover all topics of importance within

scripture's tithing law, in order to facilitate individuals' consumption of their food under the conditions mandated by the Bible. The tractate was created for this purpose and exists despite the fact that its authorities had little of interest to say on its topic.

Orosius, Paulus fifth-century-C.E. historian. Born in Spain, early in his life he moved to Hippo and met Augustine. Augustine sent him to Palestine where he met Jerome and became involved in the Pelagian controversy over free will, original sin, and God's grace. He returned to Hippo and wrote the earliest universal Christian history, which began with the creation of the world and moved to the events of 417. His chronology followed Eusebius and Jerome, while his account of Roman history drew on Livy, Tacitus, Justin, and Eutropius. The history was designed to show that the fall of Rome was not the result of its acceptance of Christianity, as the pagans were claiming.

orphan typically designated in the Bible as a fatherless child (Exod. 22:22; Deut. 24:17; Isa. 1:17; Job 31:21; see also 4 Ezra 2:20; Sib. Or. 2:76, 270–71). Orphans, along with the widow and the sojourner, symbolize those in need of divine protection. Scripture mandates the support of orphans (Deut. 24:17; Isa. 1:17; Job 31:21; see also 4 Ezra 2:20; Sib. Or. 2:76, 270–271), and often their care fell to relatives; for example, Mordecai raised his cousin Esther, and Tobit's grandmother instructed Tobit in the absence of his parents. James 1:27 defines pure religion as, in part, visiting orphans; such visiting is recorded in a heavenly manuscript, according to the Apocalypse of Zephaniah 7:5.

Orphic fragments quotations from alleged Orphic poems, cited by Aristobulus the Exegete. It is generally agreed that these are Jewish pseudepigraphs. They exist in different versions, which can be grouped into a shorter and longer recension. Other than knowing that they existed by the time of Aristobulus, no dating is possible. The main Jewish element is monotheism, though the longer version alludes to the "offshoot of the Chaldees" (probably Abraham), who understood the layout of the cosmos, and the "water-born" one who received the double law (Moses).

Orphism Greek religion or cult named for the legendary figure of Orpheus. Its development is disputed because most of the sources are late ones. According to Orphism, humans originated as follows: the Titans captured Orpheus and devoured him; Zeus struck them with lightning, and the first human arose from the ashes; thus, human nature has elements of both the Titans (evil) and Orpheus (good). The body was thought to be a detriment to the soul, giving rise to the cliche *sōma/sēma,* that is, "the body (*sōma*) is a tomb (*sēma*) for the soul." Orphism was influential on Plato. Some quotations are found in Jewish writings that are claimed to be Orphic fragments.

Oshayah   *see under* HOSHAYA

ossuary container normally made of soft limestone that held the bones of the deceased. Ossuaries seemed to be unique to the Second Temple period and were used only from the last quarter of the first century B.C.E. until the middle of the third century C.E. The development of ossuaries and their use sheds light on Jewish beliefs concerning resurrection in the Herodian period.

Throughout antiquity, it was common for one family to use and reuse a single burial cave for many generations. During the First Temple period, people took the decayed bones of their ancestors and moved them to the rear of the burial cave in order to make room for more recent burials. In the process, the bones inevitably became intermingled. This seems not to have been considered a problem when there was no belief in a physical, bodily resurrection. Early in the Hasmonean Period, a belief in the bodily resurrection developed in Jewish thought (cf. 2 Macc. 7). With this development, there seems to have arisen a concern for keeping the bones of one's ancestors separated. It is in this context that the practice arose of placing these bones in a special container or ossuary.

Ossuaries are known to have been constructed out of a variety of materials, but the most common was soft limestone. Several are known that were hewn from hard limestone, and some were made from clay, especially during the later period. Ossuaries are found throughout Judah, but their usage seems to have been concentrated in Jerusalem.

Ossuaries are known to have different types of decorations, but the meaning of these decorations is debated. Common motifs are geometric shapes, palm trees, and a pyramid-shape structure called a "nephesh." One school holds that these decorations relate Jewish beliefs in the types of things to be found in the afterlife. Others suggest that the ornamentation had no significance apart from aesthetic value. They point out that though almost all of the published ossuaries were decorated or had inscriptions, the majority of the known ossuaries (both published and unpublished) lack decorations. Thus, these scholars argue that the decorations were merely used for ornamental reasons. In further support of this interpretation, it is pointed out that many of the geometric images that in other cultures

did hold religious significance have been reproduced by artisans who merely altered the set geometric design to fit the artist's own particular style.

Probably the most famous group of ossuaries are those from the so-called Caiaphas's Tomb. This tomb is situated just south of Jerusalem in the modern suburb of North Talpiot. Several ossuaries discovered in this tomb bear Aramaic inscriptions mentioning both the names Qaifa (and the variant Qafa) and Yehosef. These are remarkably similar to the names of the high priest during the time of Jesus, namely, Caiaphas. The similarity of the names, in addition to the fact that the ossuaries seem to date from the time of Jesus, has led many scholars to conclude that this tomb actually belonged to the high priest during Jesus' day. *See also* OSSUARY DECORATIONS.

ossuary decorations decorative motifs used on the bone boxes manufactured for Jewish reburial practices in the Roman period. A wide variety of decorative motifs are present, but the most common motif features two rosettes in many variations on the long side of the ossuary with some other decorative element between the rosettes. For example, between the rosettes one may see a column, a third rosette, a vine trellis or garland, an amphora or other vessel, a lily, a palm frond, or a doorway (perhaps a Torah shrine). The motifs are usually carefully carved in low relief, revealing that they were realized by a practiced hand, that is, a professional artisan who specialized in the task. On occasion, the decoration is rendered by a decidedly unpracticed hand, which is usually interpreted as the work of the family, who perhaps were not able to afford decorations when they purchased the ossuary. Decorative motifs extend to the lid as well, usually simply repeating the two, sometimes three, rosettes on the body. Other types of decorations include a representation of the masonry of a wall, repeated moldings, and repeated floral motifs. These same decorations are found on coffins and sarcophagi.

Ostia Synagogue Ostia, the port 12 miles from Rome, had a synagogue from the first through fifth centuries C.E. The fourth-century synagogue had three entrance doors on the east and then a central gate with four pillars leading into the prayer room. A curved rear wall had a *bimah* (raised platform) against it, perhaps for the officials to sit on. A permanent apse for the Torah ark was added later on the east wall next to the entrance gate. Other community rooms were next to the prayer room, including a kitchen with an oven and a large room with wide benches around it.

ostracon (from Gr., sherd, or tile; pl., ostraca) the technical term in archaeology for a potsherd bearing an ink-written or incised inscription. The term is also sometimes applied to other inscribed hard materials, like stone or bone. In ancient Greece, voting on the expulsion of a political figure was carried out by means of potsherds (ostraca) on which the voter inscribed the name of the candidate for dismissal, thus the term "ostracism" for the procedure.

Ostraca have been found in excavations throughout the ancient world. Two of the oldest ostraca from Israel are dated to the sixteenth and seventeenth centuries B.C.E. and are inscribed in a proto-Canaanite pictographic script. The latest ages in which ostraca have been found date to the end of the Archaeological Period, that is, up to 1700 B.C.E.

Fired pottery is practically indestructible, but the use of broken pottery as a writing material was probably based more on the cheapness and availability of the substance than on a desire for permanence. In the 1930s Marston suggested that ostraca were in fact cheap and durable copies of documents originally inscribed on more expensive materials like papyrus or parchment—a suggestion revived by Yadin some fifty years later.

Sherds were generally squared off before they were inscribed with ink that was applied with a reed stylus. The ink was made from plant-derived carbon. The writing was generally executed by a skilled scribe, but occasionally it was done by an untrained person. Texts vary greatly in length, from a single letter to many lines comprising scores of words. The content is also extremely varied and includes missives, notifications, instructions, lists of names or commodities, receipts, literary texts, writing exercises, and so on. Ostraca have been found as components of well-arranged official or royal archives, as well as in the form of isolated pieces in private contexts.

Ostraca found in the area of ancient Israel described here constitute an important resource for the study of Hebrew script and its development in time. Of the two proto-Canaanite ostraca referred to above, one was found at Shechem in the Judean hills and the other at Gezer in the northern Shephelah (lowland) of Israel. A third proto-Canaanite ostracon is also known from Izbet Sarta, near Aphek of the Sharon. The latter bears an incised inscription of eighty-four letters in repeated alphabetical order and is dated to the twelfth century B.C.E. Among the better known ostraca from Iron Age 2 in ancient Israel (10th–6th cs. B.C.E.) is a group of 102 inscribed potsherds from the royal warehouses at Samaria, which was the capital of the northern kingdom of Israel. Most of the ostraca have short inscriptions of economic and administrative content, all identical in formula. They were written by skilled scribes and refer to settlements and regions in the country, as well as to contents of consignments dispatched to the royal warehouses in the city. These ostraca provide valuable linguistic, paleographic, administrative, and geographical information about the kingdom of Israel in the eighth century B.C.E.

The largest and most varied collection of ostraca from the biblical period found in a single site in ancient Israel comes from Tel Arad. Eighty-eight pieces, mostly dating from the seventh century B.C.E., were unearthed in this pivotal royal fortress in the Judean Negeb. A number of ostraca, discovered in one of the fortress rooms, evidently formed part of the archives of the commandant, Eliashib. The texts concern, *inter alia,* military matters, instructions for sending supplies to various places in the region, lists of commodities for distribution, lists of items stored in the fortress warehouses, and offerings made in the fortress temple.

In the last decade, one Edomite and about thirty Hebrew ostraca were found from the same period in another fortress, Horvat Uza, some 10 kilometers south of Tel Arad. Almost all bear lists of names, but one of them, a large bowl sherd, is inscribed in cursive Hebrew with a composition of rare literary content. The Edomite ostracon is textually the most complete found so far either in Israel or in Edom. This makes it a valuable source of information on Edomite script and language.

The reason that so many ostraca have been found at sites in the eastern Negeb is partly because the semi-arid climate of the region helps to preserve the ink-written inscriptions. Another reason is indicated by a study of all the inscriptions discovered so far in Israel, namely that in this period—the seventh to early sixth centuries B.C.E.—literacy was more widespread in the country than at any other time during the Iron Age.

Another group of ostraca that needs to be mentioned is the one known as the Lachish Letters. These are twenty-one Hebrew documents of important historical content dating from the end of the kingdom of Judah period, the early sixth century B.C.E. Discovered in the 1930s in the gate area of Tel Lachish, they comprise approximately one hundred lines of clear, legible script and provide dramatic testimony concerning the last events in the history of the kingdom.

The Persian period in Israel (5th–4th c. B.C.E.) is likewise rich in ostraca. These are invariably written in Aramaic—the administrative language of the Persian Empire and also the spoken idiom of the Jewish exiles in Babylonia. The ostraca have been found in most of the occupation strata from this period. Their contents are generally concerned with economic matters: consignment dockets of supplies or the distribution of commodities, storehouse inventories, and receipts. Outside the Land of Israel are the ostraca from the Jewish community in Elephantine in Upper Egypt.

Ostraca from the Roman period, a list of several hundred, part in Hebrew, part in Aramaic, were discovered in the excavations of the Masada fortress in the Judean–Dead Sea wilderness. Many of these bear only a single letter or word, indicating perhaps that they served as coupons for food rations that were distributed to the inhabitants of the fortress.

Ouranos (Gr., heaven) term used as the translation of the Hebrew *shamayim* in the Septuagint. By the Graeco-Roman period, it had come to be used as a substitute for "God." In Greek mythology, Ouranos is a god better known by his Latin name, Uranus, and is the grandfather of Zeus.

Our Targum The Babylonian rabbis called Targum Onkelos "Our Targum," thus indicating the official standing it had among Babylonian Jewry. Its translations of the Pentateuch into Aramaic were considered authoritative, even in matters of *halakhah*.

outer darkness the place of punishment for sinners (Matt. 8:12, 22:13, 25:30). The precise cosmological location is uncertain, but the expression denotes extreme distance from the inhabited world. Darkness is often associated with Sheol, the place of the dead and, later, the place of punishment, where, paradoxically, it coexists with fire (1 Enoch 103:7, 108:14). *See also* HELL.

outsider (Heb.: *aḥer;* pl., *aḥerim*) the "other"; "others"; sage(s) cited anonymously in rabbinic writings; occasionally a pseudonym for Meir; "others say" is cited for a dissenting view in a dispute. A legal saying assigned to "others say" may also stand for the consensus of opinion, hence, the decided law. In the Mishnah, *aḥer* (the other) may refer to the apostate Elisha ben Abbuyah.

Ovid (c. 43 B.C.E.–18 C.E.) Roman poet of the Augustan age. He is most famous for his writings on the subject of love: the *Ars Amatoria* (Art of Love), the love poems *Amores,* and the *Remedia Amoris* (Remedy for Love). There is also a collection of letters. There are only a few references to Jews in his writings. In suggesting places to look for possible female companionship, he twice mentions the seventh day of the Jews. Although he is not explicit, the context suggests that these are times when young women congregate together (perhaps even young unmarried Roman women, attracted by Sabbath day services).

ox a minor motif in Jewish art. The wild ox has been identified in the badly damaged mosaic floor of the synagogue of ancient Yaphia 3 kilometers southwest of ancient Nazareth. The animal in question faces left in a zodiac. It has a small head, is horned, and has cloven hooves. It is marked with a Hebrew word, but only the last three letters survive, -*rym,* therefore not to be read "bull" (*sur*). The excavator thought that each animal in this zodiac represented a tribe and that the wild ox therefore represented Ephraim, which ends with the three letters found.

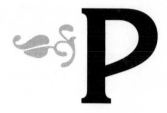

Pagan Martyrs, Acts of   *see* ACTA ALEXANDRINORUM

Pahat-Moab   in the books of Ezra and Nehemiah, the ancestor of a large Judean clan that returned with Zerubbabel from the Babylonian exile; at Nehemiah 10:15 (14), one of the chiefs who placed his seal on Nehemiah's covenant. The name means "governor of Moab."

paideia   (Gr., education; from *pais/paidos,* child) The theory of education was much debated in classical Greece, with many philosophical writings on the subject. Not much is known of Jewish education in the Graeco-Roman period; however, in the works of such writers as Philo of Alexandria, *paideia* is an important term. Philo himself evidently had an education that included a good deal of Greek literature and culture; nevertheless, he regarded education as primarily progress of the soul, interpreting his Jewish tradition in Platonic terms.

pairs   *see* ZUGOT

pakid   an official title used in the Community Rule of the Dead Sea Scrolls, meaning "officer in charge" of the "Many" (a technical term for the members of the Qumran sect). In 1QS 6:14 the *pakid* is responsible for the admission of new members to the sect, whom he examines for their fitness to join the Community. The *pakid* may possibly be the same person or officer as the *meḇaker,* (the overseer) or the *maskil* (the master).

Palestinian Jewish Aramaic   *see* ARAMAIC, JEWISH PALESTINIAN

Palestinian Talmud   *see* YERUSHALMI

Palestinian Targums to the Pentateuch   The targums belonging under the rubric of Palestinian Targums to the Pentateuch are: Targum Neofiti, the fragments of non-Onkelos continuous targums from the Cairo Geniza, the Fragmentary Targums, Targum Pseudo-Jonathan, and the Tosefta targums. The criterion that unites them under this rubric is that their nontranslation material—the additions—derives from the same source. Only Pseudo-Jonathan (which includes this source) derives a significant amount of its text from other sources. The Palestinian Targums can be divided into two stages by both their use of the source and their dialectal differences. The first stage consists of Targum Neofiti and the fragments of continuous targums from the Cairo Geniza. Both combined a literal translation with the additional material. They were written in Jewish Palestinian Aramaic between the early second and the mid-fourth centuries. By the seventh century, the use of the highly literal Targum Onkelos moved from Babylonia into the west, where Onkelos became the dominant targum among Jewry in Palestine and the eastern Mediterranean region. This inaugurated the second stage of the Palestinian Targums, which reacted in different ways to Targum Onkelos's new importance. The Fragmentary Targums excerpted nonliteral material from the Palestinian Targums of stage one, thus providing interpretive material to be used alongside the literal Onkelos targum. Pseudo-Jonathan reacted differently. It combined the Palestinian Targum source with Targum Onkelos's translation and a large amount of new additional material in an attempt to link Onkelos's authoritative standing with Palestinian traditions. The Tosefta targums provided a third reaction. They recast some of the larger additions of the Palestinian Targum source into a Targum Onkelos–like language and inserted them into Onkelos texts. The Palestinian Targums of stage two thus managed to accommodate themselves to Targum Onkelos's dominance and remained part of the interpretive tradition over the centuries. The targums of the first stage fell before Onkelos's competition and were lost, to be recovered only in modern times.

Palestinian Targum to the Prophets a translation of the prophetic books of the Hebrew Bible into Aramaic, done in Palestine in the first few centuries of the common era. There is some evidence that there may once have been a Palestinian Targum to the Prophets that contained large units of material added into the translation. The evidence is that some manuscripts of the known Targum to the Prophets preserve such additional material in their margins. Similarly, medieval scholars such as Rashi and Kimhi cite prophetic traditions in Aramaic designated as Targum Yerushalmi (i.e., Palestinian Targum) as do some manuscripts such as Codex Reuchlinianus. The best explanation for this material is that they once belonged to a complete Palestinian Targum to the Prophets, but during the early middle ages when the more literal Jonathan Targum to the Prophets became the dominant targum in the West, the aggadic material was extracted to preserve it alongside the newly authoritative translation, while the Palestinian Targum itself was lost.

palm a hardy tree found in Elim (Num. 33:9) and especially in Jericho, the "city of palms" (Deut. 34:3; Judg. 1:16, 3:13; 2 Chron. 28:15). The palm produces edible dates as well as leaves used for mats, baskets, and roofs. The leaves also provided a decorative motif in Solomon's Temple (1 Kings 6:29, 32, 35). In the Roman period, the region around Jericho was famous for its lucrative palm groves. John 12:13 explictly notes that palm branches were carried by those who greeted Jesus as he entered Jerusalem (the origin of Palm Sunday). *See also* LULAB; PALM TREE, REPRESENTATION OF.

palm branch *see* LULAB

palm tree, representation of a motif in Jewish art. The earliest Jewish context in which the palm tree appears is on the largest denomination of coins struck by the tetrarch Herod Antipas in 38 C.E. at Tiberius. On these coins, the palm tree is depicted with seven branches and two clusters of dates.

With the outbreak of the First Revolt in 66 C.E., new Jewish coins appeared. On coins of the fourth

year (69 C.E.), one type depicts a palm tree with seven or nine branches flanked by two baskets of dates. The inscription reads "for the redemption of Israel." On Roman issues called "Judea Capta," which were issued after the collapse of the First Revolt, Rome used the palm tree as the symbol for Israel. On one side of the palm tree sits a mourning female captive. On the other side stands a captive male wrapped in a cloak with his hands tied behind his back. These coins are inscribed "Judea," "Judaea Capta," "Judaea Devicta" (conquered), and so forth. A generation later, at the Jewish city of Sepphoris, coins were struck under the emperor Trajan (r. 98–117 C.E.) that depict a palm tree with fruit.

The next occasion of the minting of Jewish coins is during the Bar Kokhba Revolt of 132–135 C.E. The symbols on these coins include the palm tree. Certain small bronzes have a palm tree with seven branches on one side and two clusters of dates and a grape leaf on the other side.

Aside from coins, the palm tree appears as a Jewish symbol on ossuaries, on lamps, in tomb art, and on molded glass vessels of the Byzantine period. The palm tree is also well represented in synagogue art. For example, on the synagogue at Capernaum, palm trees with fruit are carved in high relief on lintels. A piece of gold glass (a glass disc with a picture engraved on gold foil embedded permanently in it) from Rome apparently shows the tent of meeting, surrounded by a curtain, with palm trees growing outside.

Palmyra ancient city located between Syria and Babylonia. In the first century B.C.E. it controlled the trade between Syria and Babylonia and policed the caravans that traveled from the Euphrates to Damascus and Emesa. It was probably annexed to Rome in 17 C.E., but it was not made a Roman colony until the early third century C.E. Under Zenobia and Ordenathus, Palmyra controlled Syria, Palestine, and parts of Babylonia, and it probably destroyed Nehardea, a center of Jewish merchant activity, at this time. Marcus Aurelian captured it in 273, and the Jews seem to have rejoiced at its fall from power.

Paneas city in the north of the Land of Israel; the modern Banias; identical with Caesarea-Philippi, referred to by Greek authors. Rabbinic sources know Paneas as the location of a cave deemed to be the source of the Jordan and, according to the Jerusalem Targum, sacred to Pan. *See also* CAESAREA-PHILIPPI.

Paneas, Battle of After several losses to the Ptolemaic forces in previous years, the Seleucid ruler

Antiochus III in 200 B.C.E. defeated the forces of Ptolemy V Epiphanes at Paneas (also spelled Panias; called Caesarea-Philippi in the Roman period), located north of Galilee. As a result of this battle, the Seleucids gained control of Palestine.

Panemos the name of a Macedonian month; appears in a number of Jewish sources, such as the writings of Josephus. Unfortunately, there was not a uniform usage; sometimes it corresponded to the Hebrew month of Sivan (May/June) and sometimes to the month Tammuz (June/July).

Papias Tannaitic authority active in the late first and early second centuries C.E.. In manuscripts and editions, his name sometimes is confused with that of Papos b. Judah.

Pappa Babylonian amora active in the early to mid-fourth century C.E.; the son of Ḥanan; generally referred to without the patronymic. A student of Abayye and Raba, Pappa founded the academy at Naresh, which he headed for nineteen years (B. Taanit 9a). A child of privilege, he was involved in a number of business ventures (see, e.g., B. Gittin 73a; B. Pesaḥim 113a). His legal opinions often come at the conclusion of talmudic arguments and are introduced by editorial language. He therefore is thought to have been involved in the editing of the Babylonian Talmud.

Pappa b. Ḥanan *see* PAPPA

Pappai 1. fourth-century-C.E. Babylonian amora; a student of Raba and the son-in-law of Isaac Nappaḥa. Along with his role as head of an academy, Pappai was a wealthy landowner.

2. fourth-century C.E. Palestinian amora; a student of Joshua of Sikhnin. He is known primarily for his several recorded exegetical comments.

Pappos b. Judah Tannaitic authority of the late first and early second centuries C.E. He was imprisoned with Akiba during the Hadrianic persecutions (B. Berakhot 61b).

papyri All Jewish papyri were found in the Judean Desert, where the dry and stable weather kept the papyri in reasonable condition. The papyri belong to a period between the first century B.C.E. and second century C.E. They were found in caves that were used by fugitives of the First and Second Revolt and can be divided into two main groups: (1) private archives of wealthy families; and (2) administrative and strategic orders of Bar Kosiba, the leader of the Second Revolt.

Among the first group we can ascribe fragments that deal mainly with purchasing goods, lands, or property. Most of them are title deeds; some are marriage or divorce contracts. To this group belongs the archive of Babata, a Jewish woman

who collected her private documents from 93 to 132 C.E. The documents were written mainly in Greek, Aramaic, and Nabatean.

The second group are letters that were written by Simon Bar Kosiba or his clerks. Some of the letters deal with the movement of forces and supplies, others with religious matters, and some deal with direct orders from the commander to his officers and soldiers. The papyri provide for the first time the commander's name and reveal much about his attitude toward his people and his world.

parables (Heb.: *mashal;* Gr.: *parabole*) instructional narratives, metaphors, or similes, which appear throughout Mediterranean and Egyptian literature of antiquity. Like the Buddhist *koan,* they are enigmatic; like jokes, they lose their impact if they are not grasped without explanation. Several with political import appear in Hebrew narrative, including the Parable of Jotham (Judg. 9:8–15); Nathan's Parable of the Ewe-Lamb (2 Sam. 12:1–4), and Isaiah's Song of the Vineyard (5:1–4). The Parables (or Similitudes) of Enoch (1 Enoch 37–71) recount the seer's tour of the cosmos and heavenly throneroom and his description of the eschatological judgment and judge.

The parables attributed to Jesus in the synoptic Gospels use mundane images to prompt new perceptions of daily life and to describe the "Kingdom of God." Among the more famous are two unique to Luke: the Good Samaritan (10:29–37) and the Prodigal Son (15:11–32). Gospel tradition claims that the parables were intended to fulfill prophecy (Matt. 13:34–35, citing Ps. 78:2) as well as to confound the listener (Matt. 13:10–17, citing Isa. 6:9–10). Indeed, parables can evoke a multiplicity of interpretations. Some prompt allegorical readings (Matt. 13:18–23 and Mark 4:14–20 provide such an interpretation of the Sower, but the correspondence between elements in the parable and elements in daily life is inconsistent); others refocus priorities (e.g., the Pearl of Great Price, Matt. 13:45–46); still others question one's present worldview without providing an alternative (e.g., the Unjust Steward, Luke 15:1–8). Several of the parables of the Gospel of Thomas recapitulate synoptic versions; however, they lack the synoptics' allegorical explications.

In the rabbinic literature, parables most frequently appear in exegetical contexts. The parable sheds light on God's actions, described in a biblical verse, by comparing them to the actions of an earthly king. Through parables, the rabbis depicted God as a three dimensional figure, a king who like other kings judged his subjects, argued with the members of his court, fought and killed his enemies, and worked to assure justice for all people. While using images intelligible to a nation familiar with the ways of earthly kings, the rabbinic parables ultimately define the unique power and place of God who, as the king of kings, created and rules over the entire world.

paradise the home of the first human beings (Gen. 2–3) and the place of intermediate rest or eternal bliss for the righteous. *Paradeisos* is a Greek loan word from a Persian expression denoting a walled park or garden. The Septuagint translates the Hebrew *gan eden* (garden of delight, or garden of Eden) as *paradeisos tēs tryphēs* (garden of delight). Later usage converts *paradeisos* into a technical term or proper noun, "Paradise" or "The Garden." The idea that this garden was created before the world is reflected in the Life of Adam and Eve 25–28, where Adam, cast out of the garden, is taken up to the garden's polar opposite, "the paradise of righteousness," where God is enthroned. 2 Corinthians 12:2–4, with its reference to the praise of the angelic choruses, suggests that paradise is the location of God's throne and places it in the third heaven.

In many Jewish and Christian texts, paradise has eschatological functions. According to 2 Esdras 7:36, the entries to hell and the paradise of delight stand opposite one another, and Revelation 2:7 places the tree of life in "the paradise of God" (cf. 1 Enoch 25:1–6). The present existence and significance of paradise are indicated in Luke 23:43, where Jesus promises the dying thief that they will be together "today" in paradise. 2 Enoch 8–10 locates paradise, the place prepared for the suffering righteous, in the third heaven, evidently opposite the place of torment (cf. 2 Esdras 7:36). Testament of Levi 18:10–11 promises that the righteous will return to paradise. *See also* EDEN.

Parah Mishnah tractate devoted to the preparation of purification water described in Numbers 19, through the burning of a red cow and the mixture of its ashes with running water. The red cow is defined (chaps. 1–2); the rite is described in a narrative (chap. 3); and the conduct of the rite is then set forth in laws (chap. 4). Subsequent chapters discuss the purity of utensils used in the rite (chap. 5); mixing the ash and the water (chap. 6); drawing the water (Chaps. 6–8); water used for the rite (chaps. 8–9); uncleanness and the purification rite (chaps. 9–11); hyssop used for sprinkling the purification water (chaps. 11–12); and the rules of sprinkling the water (chap. 12).

Paraleipomena Jeremiou *see* JEREMIAH, PARALEIPOMENA OF

paralysis found in the scriptures and later Jewish literature as (1) a characteristic of imperfect humans and animals; (2) a metaphor for fear and uncertainty; and (3) an evil that will be overcome when God fulfills his purpose for the creation. Lame and handicapped animals are not to be presented as offerings to God (Lev. 21:18; Deut. 15:21). Drooping hands and paralyzed knees are caused by wives who do not make their husbands happy (Sir. 25:23). When God brings his fierce judgment on the evil nations of the world, they will be overcome with paralysis (Jer. 46:16, 50:16, 16, 43; Ezek. 7:27). But the signs of God's renewal of the creation will include the transformation of the crippled and the lame so that they can walk (Isa. 35:3–6). The early Christians claimed that this began to happen when Jesus and his followers healed paralytics (Matt. 9:2; Luke 5:18, 7:1–10, 13:10–17; Acts 3:10).

pareve neutral, being neither dairy products (milk, cheese, and the like) nor meat

Paris Targum *see* FRAGMENTARY TARGUMS

parokhet (Heb., curtain) often refers to the veils that in the Second Temple demarcated the Holy of Holies (M. Shekalim 8:4–5; M. Yoma 5:1), as well as other special areas. B. Ketubot 106a states that thirteen such curtains were found in the Temple.

parousia (Gr., presence, or appearance) in a religious context, often used in reference to a hidden divinity's making itself felt. In Jewish writings, it is used especially of the eschatological advent of God; in Christian writings, it refers to the return or manifestation of Christ.

Parthians a people of southwest Asia in what is today part of Iran. The people whom the Greeks and Romans called Parthians were originally semi-nomads who filled the political vacuum in Mesopotamia after the defeat of the Achaemenids (Persians) by Alexander the Great in 330 B.C.E. The founder of the Parthian dynasty was Arsaces (hence the name Arsacids for the subsequent ruling family), who defeated the Seleucid satrap in 247 B.C.E. The Parthians were not Persians but adopted the Persian ways and organized their territory into satrapies. They became a powerful force in the east, driving the Seleucids out of Mesopotamia and invading Syria more than once. Therefore they had a common enemy with the Jews in the second century B.C.E. In subsequent centuries the Parthians, who had made Ecbatana their capital, were a strong military presence in the Middle East, controlling the trade routes and frustrating Rome's expansionist desires. The fact that a large colony of Babylonian Jews lived peacefully within their territory meant that good relations were maintained with the Jews in Palestine. Thus when the young Herod the Great sought to establish himself in Palestine under the aegis of the Romans, the ousted branch of the Hasmoneans was able to call on Parthian support against him. This was gladly forthcoming; a Parthian army invaded Palestine in 40 B.C.E. and Antigonus II, grandson of Alexander Jannaeus, was enthroned as king in Jerusalem. With Roman support Herod was able to oust Antigonus by 37 B.C.E. and claim the kingdom that the Roman Senate had conferred on him three years earlier. Herod was quick to establish good relations, however, appointing a Babylonian Jew, Hananel, as high priest. In the period between the destruction of the Jerusalem Temple and the fall of the Arsacids in 230 C.E. there are indications within the rabbinic corpus that Jews repeatedly supported the Parthians in resisting the efforts of various Roman emperors against the Parthians, especially those under Hadrian, Trajan, and Caracalla.

partnership   joint ownership, especially of land. Laws regulating these are addressed in the Talmud division Nezikin. Rabbinic authorities declared that capital investment may be treated like a business partnership (Aram.: *iska*) to avoid the charge of usurious lending against the investing party. This serves as the basis for later rabbinic authorities to allow most commercial and banking transactions.

Parush   (pl., Perushim) separatist, abstainer; *see also* PHARISEE

Passover Chronicle   an anonymous Byzantine world chronicle extending from Creation to c. 630 C.E. It is generally dated to the seventh century C.E. Its name comes from the Christian Easter cycle rather than the Jewish Passover; Greek Christianity uses the word *pascha* (Passover) for Easter. It makes use of a variety of sources, including the Hebrew Bible and some Jewish writings, and contains a number of midrashic elements. For example, the kings of Chaldea are said to be the *nefilim* who were the progeny of the fallen angels and women. This probably represents an interpretation of 1 Enoch.

Passover Narrative   *see* HAGGADAH OF PASSOVER

Passover Seder   (Heb.: *seder shel pesaḥ*) meal eaten at home on the eves of the first and second days of Passover, commemorating the Exodus from Egypt; *see also* HAGGADAH OF PASSOVER

Paternus Clementianus, Claudius   *see* CLAUDIUS PATERNUS CLEMENTIANUS

patience, human   *see* ENDURANCE

patience of God   the view that God is patient, long-suffering, and slow to anger. God's patience is a divine attribute that is attested in almost every layer of biblical and extrabiblical Jewish tradition. In the Bible, the usual expression is "slow to anger," normally occurring as part of the formula [God is] gracious and merciful, slow to anger, and abounding in steadfast love" (Exod. 34:6 et pass.).

The notion of God's patience occurs frequently in intertestamental literature, where it is often invoked in a prayer or encomium to God, as in Prayer of Azariah 1:19, the Wisdom of Solomon 15:1, and the Prayer of Manasseh 7. Ben Sira explains that God's patience is a consequence of the ephemeral nature of human life (18:11) and warns that humans should not try to take advantage of this attribute (5:4). 2 Maccabees 6:14 claims that God shows patience longer for other nations than for Israel. Eschatological descriptions of the day of judgment hold that this day is to take place either when God's long suffering is truly manifest (2 Bar. 24:2) or when God's patience is "withdrawn" (4 Ezra 7:33).

God's patience is also an important theme in rabbinic literature. The tractate Yoma in the Babylonian Talmud (69b) states that God's long suffering toward the ungodly and his hesitancy to destroy them is one expression of his greatness (cf. Deut 10:17). In Kohelet Rabbah on 7:15, Ra<u>b</u> Yoshiyya enumerates some of the reasons for God's patience toward the ungodly: so that they might repent, keep the commandments, and beget righteous children.

Ra<u>b</u> Ḥanina, in tractate Taanit of the Jerusalem Talmud (65b), opposes the notion that God's long suffering expresses indulgence, stressing that God will eventually receive his recompense. In Seder Eliyyahu Rabbah 24 (135), God's patience is held up as a model for the behavior of humans toward one another.

In early Christian literature, the patience of God is usually evoked together with a warning of the negative consequences that will result if a person does not repent (Rom. 2:4, 9:22; 1 Pet. 3:20; 2 Pet. 3:9–15).

patriarch   (Heb.: *nasi*) Roman-recognized Jewish ruler of the Jewish community in the Land of Israel, beginning after the destruction of the Temple in 70 C.E. and continuing to the abrogation of government authorization by the Romans in 429 C.E.

Patricius   leader of a Jewish revolt against Gallus Caesar in 351 C.E. Mentioned only by non-Jewish sources, the revolt began in Sepphoris. After the revolt's initial success, the inhabitants of Tiberias and Lydda joined in. Aurelius Victor states that the rebels established "a kind of kingdom." The disturbance remained in the Galilee and did not affect Jerusalem. While the rebels attacked Hellenes and Samaritans, they did not trouble the Christians. The revolt may have reflected economic tensions, for Tiberias, Sepphoris, and Lydda were Jewish industrial centers. The Romans easily defeated the rebels near Acre, sacking Sepphoris and destroying many villages.

patrios politeia (Gr., ancestral constitution) term often used in Greek debates as a slogan of those advocating a return to the old values in the Greek world. It has been suggested that when Hecataeus described the Jewish state of his own time, he used such a model.

Paulinus prefect of Egypt, 73 C.E. Vespasian had ordered that the Jewish sanctuary in Leontopolis be demolished because he feared that it would become a center for anti-Roman activity in Egypt at the time that the Jews of Palestine were revolting against Rome. Lupus merely closed the entrance to the Temple itself but allowed access to the area around it. In the summer of 73, Paulinus took further action; however, he also avoided demolishing the sanctuary. He prevented access to the Temple's precinct and he stripped the Temple itself of its internal furnishings and treasures.

Paul the Apostle *see* SAUL OF TARSUS

Paulus Alexandrian citizen. The longest extant chapter of the Acts of the Alexandrian Martyrs is entitled "Acta Pauli et Antonini." It describes Hadrian's presiding over a disputation between Jews and Greeks from Alexandria. Paulus and Antoninus were the leaders of the Greeks. One of the issues brought to the emperor dealt with a theatrical pantomime of a king. Although the text is poorly preserved at this point, Paulus has an edict of Lupus read, which orders that the character be brought forth "for him to make fun of." Some have speculated that the Greeks had staged a farce ridiculing the messianic nature of the Jewish revolt in North Africa in 115–117 C.E.

peace *see* SHALOM

Peace Blessing *see* BIRKAT SHALOM

peace offering votive offering in the Temple, yielding meat for the priest and the person who presents the offering

peacock a minor symbol in Jewish art thought by some to represent immortality. It appears in the art of synagogues, lamps, and in tombs. In ancient Greece there were two usages for images of peacocks. The first was purely decorative without sym-

bolic meaning. The second arose out of the identification of the peacock as the bird symbolizing the empress, as the eagle symbolized the emperor. With the connection to the empress, the peacock came to be identified with the goddess Hera, or Juno. This identification was combined with an Indian tradition that those who ate the flesh of a golden peacock would neither grow old nor die, and the peacock came to represent immortality in general by the second century C.E.

It is still somewhat of a mystery as to how and why this pagan symbol for immortality came to be adopted by Jews. Nonetheless, placement of peacocks in synagogues from Isfiya in Palestine and the Hamman-Lif in North Africa show that the bird did come to play a prominent symbolic role of immortality for Jews. The same holds true for Jewish burials, where peacocks were not uncommon. One particularly clear use was the flanking of a menorah by two peacocks on a tombstone from Priene in southern Turkey. It is also interesting that peacocks were adopted by early Christians.

peah (Heb.) the corner of the field, to be left for the poor, in accordance with Leviticus 19:9, 23:22

Peah Mishnah tractate on the rules of gifts to the poor. The tractate discusses the corner of the field (chaps. 1–4); gleanings to be left for the poor (chaps. 4–5); the forgotten sheaf (chaps. 5–7); grape gleanings and the defective grape cluster to be left for the poor (chap. 7); and general rules governing gifts to the poor and poor man's tithe (Deut. 14:28–29; chap. 8), covering when the poor may glean, claims of the poor to produce, and the minimum requirement of poor man's tithe.

peasants term from agrarian, aristocratic society, referring to farmers who own or rent small plots of land but who lack significant political, financial, and social power and influence. In ancient society, peasants made up about 90 percent of the population. They usually lived at or close to a subsistence level, though some might acquire larger holdings. In the Near East they most often occupied small villages or towns from which they walked to their plots of land. They paid taxes to the government or rent to the landowner in the form of produce. Thus, their surplus produce supported the governmental, military, bureaucratic, and educational activities of the upper classes. For the most part, peasants were illiterate or had limited literacy and lived according to customs, traditions, and laws deeply rooted in local society.

Pella city on the Jordan River, 8 miles below Beth Shean; known as early as the nineteenth century B.C.E. from Egyptian Execration texts, under the name Pi-hzi-lim. It is not mentioned after the thirteenth century B.C.E. until the Hellenistic period, when it first appears under the name Pella. The city was destroyed by Alexander Yannai (Josephus, *Ant.* 13:397) and rebuilt by Pompey. During Titus's siege of Jerusalem, that city's Christian community moved to Pella.

Pentateuch the first five books of the Hebrew Bible or Old Testament: Genesis, Exodus, Leviticus, Numbers, and Deuteronomy. They are occasionally referred to as the Torah. They were written around the time of the Babylonian exile, probably between the seventh and fifth centuries B.C.E. These five books were the earliest to be canonized. They have formed the central texts for synagogue worship for two millennia. *See also* TANAKH; TORAH.

Pentateuch, Samaritan the five books of Moses that form the entire canon of the Samaritans. It is written in the Samaritan script, a form of the old, or paleo-Hebrew script used in Israel during the monarchy. Its text type has similarities to both the traditional Jewish, or Masoretic, text and the Septuagint but is generally classified in its own right as a third text type. Its differences from the other texts are important ones to textual critics, though the layman reading a translation of most passages would notice few if any differences. The main differences concern conflated passages, such as Exodus 9:6. In the Samaritan version, this verse repeats virtually the entirety of verses 1–5 to show that all happened exactly as predicted.

The Samaritan Pentateuch seems to be derived from an earlier text type that some label the "Old Palestinian," now known from some of the Qumran manuscripts. At some point, however, a few verses in the Samaritan Pentateuch were changed to bring them into line with Samaritan theology (especially Exod. 20:17, 24; Lev. 26:31; Deut. 5:21, 11:30, 27:4). The changes relate mainly to Gerizim and the place that God would choose when Israel came into the land.

Pentecost *see* SHABUOT

peot (Heb., corners) Leviticus 19:27 forbids removing hair at corners of the head, meaning not to cut earlocks.

Peqiin (or Pekiin) small Galilean village in Upper Galilee west of Meiron. The ancient name of the village was likely Baca. Several carved stones have been found in the village that are surely from an ancient synagogue. One stone depicts in low relief a frieze of a grapevine with grapes. The second may be from an arch. In low relief one sees a seven-branched menorah about 27 centimeters high with an etrog and lulab to the left and an incense shovel and shofar, or ram's horn, to the right. The menorah stands on three legs. A third stone depicts the facade of a Torah shrine carved in relief on a stone about 46 by 30 centimeters. The shrine shows two spiral-fluted columns with a double-leaf, paneled door between the columns. Above the door is a shell in the bottom center of the pediment. The pediment is decorated with a rope molding at the bottom and repeated design (egg and dart) on the top. The ancient synagogue has not been located or excavated.

perfect *see* BLAMELESS

Peripatetics a philosophical school founded by Aristotle (384–322 B.C.E.) that focused mainly on literary criticism and moralistic discourse. Aristotle himself inquired into most areas of study—logic, metaphysics, ethics, biology, physics, rhetoric, and drama—but the later Peripatetic school was much narrower in its interests, though it continued Aristotle's emphasis on an empirical approach. This was partly because Aristotle's main writings were lost for a period of time, and their rediscovery led to a revival. Although not as popular as Platonism and Stoicism, the Peripatetic school influenced those philosophical traditions. Aristobulus the Exegete is said to have belonged to this school.

Peritios the name of a Macedonian month; appears in a number of Jewish sources, such as the writings of Josephus. Unfortunately, there was not a uniform usage; sometimes it corresponded to the Hebrew month of Tebet (December/January) and sometimes to the month of Shevat (January/February).

Peroz Sassanid ruler (r. 459–484 C.E.) He fought the Hephthalites and dealt with revolts in Iberia and Armenia. While he quelled the revolts, he was killed in his second war against the Hephthalites. Later Jewish sources refer to persecutions under Peroz, and the Talmud calls him "Peroz the Wicked." He forbade the observance of the Jewish Sabbath, closed schools, abolished the Jewish court system, and executed leading rabbis and the exilarch. Some sources claim that he closed synagogues and seized Jewish children. Hamza Isfahani claims that in 468 he ordered the killing of half the Jews of Isfanhan because they had flayed two magi alive.

persecution affliction for reasons of religion or race. In antiquity the persecutor of the Jews par excellence was Antiochus IV. Evidently in response to a revolt that was related to their piety for the Torah, Antiochus proscribed observance of the Torah, forced Jews to violate its commandments, for example, by participating in pagan rituals and eating forbidden foods, and threatened with death persons who refused to comply and those who possessed copies of the Torah. No event in Israelite history except the exile spawned the volume of literature that witnesses to these events (Daniel; the Testament of Moses; 1, 2, and 4 Maccabees; 1 Enoch 85–90; and Jubilees). The motto of pious Jews in this period was, in effect, "We would rather die than transgress the laws of our forebears" (1 Macc. 2; 2 Macc. 7; Test. Moses 9). Reaction to the persecution took the alternative forms of passive resistance (Test. Moses 9; 2 Macc. 7), refusal to defend oneself on the Sabbath (1 Macc. 2:29–38), and militant action against the Syrians (1 Macc. 2–9; 1 Enoch 90:9–13). Those who eschewed militant activity awaited divine vindication (Test. Moses 10; Dan. 11–12; 2 Macc. 7).

There is also some evidence that, on occasion, Jewish authorities persecuted other Jews, although the details are not always clear. The Qumran commentary on Habakkuk describes a confrontation between the Wicked Priest and the Teacher of Righteousness (1QpHab 11:4–8), and Alexander Jannaeus is said to have crucified a whole multitude of his enemies (Josephus, *Ant.* 13.14.2, sec. 380). The apostle Paul refers to punishment "at the hands of the Jews" (2 Cor. 11:24), presumably because of his convictions, though the details are uncertain. The Gospel of Mark also alludes to some such punishment, although the extent of such activity cannot be determined (Mark 13:9).

Such texts as Mark 13:9, 1 Peter, Revelation, perhaps Hebrews 10:32–39, and the correspondence between Pliny and Trajan indicate that Christians also suffered for their faith at the hands of Gentiles and gentile leaders during the closing years of the first century, although the extent of such persecution during this period has often been exaggerated. *See also* ANTIOCHUS IV EPIPHANES; OPPRESSION.

Persia Indo-European empire bordering on the western border of India and the eastern frontier of Rome, extending from the Tigris-Euphrates to India and into central Asia. The empire was governed in biblical times by successive dynasties: a Persian dynasty from the province of Fars, in the southwestern corner of present-day Iran; the Parthian dynasty, from the province of Parthia, in the northeast of the empire; and the Sassanids, another Persian dynasty from Fars.

Persian period the period from 539 B.C.E. to 332 B.C.E., when Palestine was under the rule of the Persian Empire. In 539 B.C.E. when Babylon fell to Cyrus, the Achaemenid king of Persia (r. 559–530 B.C.E.), Persia was raised to the position of world empire, which encompassed the whole Near East. In contrast to the Assyrians and Babylonians, how-

ever, who had based their rule on large-scale deportations of peoples and a reign of fear, Cyrus from the outset adopted a much more lenient policy, which included resettling exiles in their homelands, reconstructing their temples, and in general presenting himself to the conquered as a liberator. This policy gained him the good will of almost the entire ancient world.

Within the framework of this policy, Cyrus issued a proclamation to the Jewish exiles in Babylon urging them to return to Jerusalem and rebuild the Temple there. The first Jews to return from Babylon were headed by Sheshbazzar, "the prince of Judah" (apparently Shenazzar, the son of Jehoiachin, the former king of Judah).

Cyrus was succeeded by his son, Cambyses II (r. 530–522 B.C.E.), whose chief accomplishment was the conquest of Egypt and its annexation into the Achaemenid kingdom in 525 B.C.E. He gathered his troops in Acco (Strabo, XVI.2.25; Diodorus Siculus, XV.41.3) and achieved victory with the help of Arabian-Qedarite tribes, who supplied the Persian army with water during their advance across the Sinai Desert. In the spring of 522 B.C.E., when Cambyses was still in Egypt, a revolt broke out in Persia. The king set out to suppress it but died on the way home.

The death of Cambyses was followed by a series of revolts in Persia and a power struggle for the throne, which was finally won by Darius I (r. 522–486 B.C.E.), also a member of the Achaemenid royal family. Darius extended the empire to hitherto unknown frontiers by annexing parts of India and eastern Europe. During the rest of his reign, he waged wars mainly on the western border, in Anatolia and Greece. In 512 B.C.E. he crossed the Bosphorus and conquered Thrace.

Of major importance for the future of the Persian Empire was the rebellion of the Greek cities of Anatolia and Cyprus in 499 B.C.E. Although it was put down harshly, it brought about a major confrontation between the Persians and the Athenians. The hostilities continued over a long period of time and ended in the complete routing of the Persian army at the battle of Marathon in 490 B.C.E. This was the Persians' first serious defeat.

In the early days of Darius's reign, there was a steady increase in the stream of people returning to Palestine from the Babylonian exile. Some historians consider that one of the reasons for the great numbers of returning exiles was the great turmoil in Babylon caused by the revolts of Nebuchadnezzar III (522 B.C.E.) and Nebuchadnezzar IV (521 B.C.E.), which were suppressed with great cruelty, and by the economic crisis which followed in their wake. The repatriates may also have been encouraged by Darius's new imperial organization. It can be assumed that Judah was made an independent state (*medinah*) for the short period during which Zerubbabel, the son of Shealtiel and the grandson of Jehoachin, served as governor (*pehah*) of the province by Darius's appointment. In any event, the Bible records that 42,360 persons returned to Judah from Babylon in those days.

Zerubbabel began to rebuild the Temple and developed commercial relations with the Phoenicians, who supplied him, as they had Solomon, with cedars of Lebanon, through the port of Jaffa, for the construction of the Temple. For some unknown reason, the governor, the last of the Davidic line, disappeared suddenly, only a short time after construction work began. How the Jewish community was governed thereafter is unknown.

In 480 B.C.E. Xerxes, Darius's son and heir, undertook an expedition against the Greeks and suffered major defeats in the famous battles of Salamis and Mycale. The Greek campaign ended when the Persian fleet was totally destroyed in the battle of Eurymedon. The Persians were evidently driven out of the area of the Aegean Sea.

In Palestine, conditions changed when Artaxerxes attained the throne. A new wave of Jews from Babylon left to resettle in Palestine. This time they were headed by a strong religious and political leadership. According to the Bible, Ezra the priest and scribe came from Babylon in the seventh year of the reign of Artaxerxes (458 B.C.E.). Artaxerxes appointed him to repair the Temple and to establish the laws of the Torah as the religious and social authority of the Jewish community. Some time later, Artaxerxes accepted the appeal of a court official, Nehemiah, the son of Hacaliah, and appointed him governor of Jerusalem. It appears that Nehemiah at this time also reestablished the state of Judah as an independent political unit.

By these and other actions, Ezra and Nehemiah laid the foundation for the future way of life of the Jewish people. They also, however, provoked the final division between the Jews and the Samaritans, the latter abandoning the center at Jerusalem and establishing a separate temple on Mount Gerizim.

On the death of Artaxerxes I, a crisis arose within the empire. It ended when Darius II seized the throne (423–404 B.C.E.). Artaxerxes II Memnon (r. 404–358 B.C.E.) succeeded to the throne after the death of Darius II. His rule was challenged by his younger brother, Cyrus, who raised an army and marched to Babylon. They met in the battle at Cunaxa, where Cyrus was killed. This war is described vividly in the Anabasis of the Athenian writer Xenophon.

During the reign of Artaxerxes II, the process of the disintegration of the Persian Empire began. During the war between the two brothers, the Egyptians again rose in rebellion, headed by Pharaoh Armyrteus (r. 404–399 B.C.E.) of the twenty-eighth dynasty from Sais. This time they succeeded in throwing off the Persian yoke for some sixty years (until 343 B.C.E.).

Shortly after their successful rebellion, the Egyptians, aided by the Athenians and Cypriots, set out on an expedition against the Persians. The route of their campaign was through the Sinai desert and the coastal plain of Palestine. It appears that they gradually occupied this territory. In 385 B.C.E., when Abrocamus was the satrap of Abar Nahara, peace was concluded with Athens and the Athenians withdrew their armies. Abrocamus expelled the Egyptians and Cypriots from Phoenicia and Palestine by 380 B.C.E.

One year later, Pharnabazus, satrap of Cilicia, began mustering mercenaries in Acco for a fresh attack on Egypt. By 375 B.C.E. he had assembled three hundred ships, about twelve thousand Greek mercenaries, and a large number of native soldiers. Even before it engaged in its first battle, logistic problems and disease had decimated the force and it was thoroughly routed by the Egyptians (Isaeus Nicostrat, 7).

From 366 to 360 B.C.E. the whole of the Persian Empire was endangered by what is generally known as the revolt of the satraps. In 360 B.C.E., when Pharaoh Tachos came to the throne, he assembled a large Egyptian army as well as Greek mercenaries and renewed the Egyptian occupation of the coastal plain of Palestine and Phoenicia. Persian rule, however, was gradually restored to Abar Nahara, as one by one the rebels surrendered or were captured.

In 358 B.C.E. Artaxerxes died and the throne was inherited by Artaxerxes III Ochus, who reigned until 336 B.C.E. After putting down the satraps' revolt, the new king set out to conquer Egypt. His failure was the signal for the rebellion of the towns of Phoenicia led by Tennes, king of Sidon, with the aid of Pharaoh Nectanebo II (r. 359–341 B.C.E.).

At the beginning of 345 B.C.E. Artaxerxes assembled a huge army in Babylon and marched against Sidon. The inhabitants of the town made preparations for a lengthy siege, but their leaders betrayed them to the enemy and the whole town was razed to the ground (Diodorus, XVI.45.1–9). In 332 B.C.E.

the entire Persian Empire fell into the hands of Alexander the Great and the Macedonian armies, thus starting the Hellenistic age.

Administrative organization. During the Persian period. Palestine was included in the territory of the satrapy of Abar Nahara (Ezra 4:10, 11), a term derived from the Assyrian administration (ebir-Nari), established in the days of Esarhaddon or even much earlier (compare 1 Kings 4:24). Pseudo-Scylax refers to the area as Coele Syria, which is a translation of the Aramaic term Kol Suria, an early name for the interior of Syria. At that time the country was already divided into designated political units.

It has been suggested that Palestine was divided at that time into three types of political entities: (1) national states, that is, units whose borders coincide with the various ethnic elements dwelling in the country, such as Judah and Samaria, Megiddo, Ashdod, and the Edomite province around Hebron, as well as Ammon and Moab; (2) the Phoenician commercial cities along the coast; and (3) the tribal system of the Arabs. M. Avi-Yonah was of the opinion that Acco and Gaza were ruled directly by the Persians.

While the existence of national states (*medinoth*), headed by governors (*pahot*), is certain from both written as well as archaeological sources, it appears that the Arab settlement was basically tribal, while that of the Phoenicians was urban. Nevertheless, it is difficult from the standpoint of the Persian satrapal organization to accept Avi-Yonah's proposal that free Phoenician cities existed in Palestine, which were under self rule. The king of Sidon, for example, was himself known to be governed directly by a resident Persian satrap (Diodorus, XVI.41:5). His palace was excavated and found to be built in a pure Achaemenid style and he had his own Persian garrison troops. If the king of Sidon was under direct Persian control, the entire concept that the coastal cities in Palestine enjoyed political independence under the supervision of this king becomes doubtful. It does seem as though these cities did possess commercial freedom. Moreover, in another contemporary source, the inscription on the saracophaeous of Eshmunazar II, king of Sidon from the late sixth or early fifth century B.C.E., the region indicated coincides perfectly with the boundaries of the Assyrian-Persian province of Dor.

The same seems to have been the case in the southern region of Palestine, the area personified in the Bible by Geshem the Arabian. In recent excavations, a number of military fortresses have been unearthed, for example, at Tell Jemmeh, Tell el-Fara (south), Beersheba, Arad, Kadesh-Barnea and Tell el-Kheleifeh. Ostraca found at some of these sites indicate the presence of garrison troops. Two ostraca from Arad even designate the unit by name, "degel" (standard), which is the name of a Persian military unit also mentioned in Elephantine Papyri. This entire area was probably under the direct rule of a Persian governor.

In summary, Palestine in the Persian period was apparently organized into a number of provinces or states (*medinoth*). Each unit was ruled by a dynasty of governors (*pahot*), generally of a local family: Jews in Judah, Samaritans in Samaria, and Arabs in the south. These governors had small courts, imitating those of the satraps, and they stood at the head of small administrative organizations. They were probably in charge of small military garrisons and were allowed to keep official stamps of the state in their possession. They also seem to have been permitted to strike the small silver coins, which are now known as "Palestinian coins." Thus far, the inscriptions of four of the provinces are clearly legible: Samaria, Judah, Ashdod and Gaza.

Archaeological research. The study of the material culture of Palestine in the Persian period has been of great value in understanding the transition of the country's culture from its age-old eastern tradition to the new, western Greek concept. It reveals that the country was divided into two regions at the beginning of the Persian period: one in the mountainous area of Judea and Transjordan (and to a lesser extent, also Samaria), and the other in the Galilee and the coastal area. The border between these two cultural areas is at times very sharp, almost like a border dividing two countries.

An analysis of the culture of these two regions demonstrates that the mountain culture remained basically eastern in character. It is made up of local cultures which continue the Israelite tradition and eastern influences (Assyrian, Babylonian, Persian and Egyptian). In the coastal culture, on the other hand, which is basically western in nature, eastern Greek, Cypriot, and Athenian elements can be observed. It is therefore probable that the Greek material culture considerably preceded the Macedonian conquest. At the same time, there is no doubt that this was exclusively an external conquest, that is to say, Greek cultural products were used without acquiring the significance they had in their native land. They were adapted to local traditions and customs. It appears that the main bearers of this new culture in Palestine were the Phoenicians and only in the Hellenistic period the Greek soldiers and settlers.

In any case, by the third century B.C.E., the entire country became completely Hellenized. The most important contribution to this final step had been made by Ptolemy II Philadelphus, in whose time many new towns had been built or rebuilt, both on the coast as well as in the internal parts of the country, along the Greek polis concept. The entire local administration and the internal division had been changed into the Greek-Hellenistic one, modeled first on the Egyptian-Ptolemaic system.

Pesah *see* HAGGADAH OF PASSOVER

Pesahim Mishnah tractate devoted to Passover. The tractate discusses preparation for Passover, such as removing leaven and avoiding that which ferments (chaps. 1–4); slaying and eating the Passover offering on the night of the fourteenth of Nisan (chaps. 5–9); and the Passover Seder (chap. 10).

peshat (Heb.) the literal meaning of a passage of scripture or a rabbinic text, in contrast to *derash,* a homiletical interpretation. In the Talmud itself, *peshat* refers to the interpretation recognized as authoritative. Current usage derives from Rashi, the first exegete carefully to distinguish literal from homiletical meaning.

pesher (pl., *pesharim;* Heb., interpretation) a specific method of biblical interpretation characteristic of the Dead Sea Scrolls. The *pesher* has a distinctive form: a citation of a biblical passage, followed by some form of the word *pesher,* and concluding with an interpretation concerning people and events connected with the Qumran Community. The Qumran sect believed its tradition of interpretation to be inspired, based on the special revelation given to the Teacher of Righteousness. The outstanding characteristic of this interpretation is its historical-eschatological nature, related to the sect's belief that it was at the center of events leading to the eschaton.

There are three types of *pesharim:* continuous, thematic, and isolated. Continuous *pesharim* are running commentaries on whole biblical books, mostly prophetic; examples are the Habakkuk Commentary and Nahum Commentary. These *pesharim* often contain allusions to people and events in the community's life that are useful for reconstructing a history of the sect. Thematic *pesharim*—for example, the Florilegium and the Pesher on Melkhzedek—are collections of interpretations of biblical passages gathered around a common theme. These texts are helpful in reconstructing the ideas of the sect. Finally, the isolated *pesher* occurs within another, larger work, and the biblical passage chosen depends on the context of the larger work. For example, the Damascus Docu-

ment contains *pesharim* on Zechariah 13:7 and Amos 5:26–27. These isolated *pesharim* are used to illustrate a specific point within the larger document. *See also* DAMASCUS DOCUMENT; FLORI LEGIUM; HABAKKUK COMMENTARY; NAHUM COMMENTARY.

Pesher to Habakkuk *see* HABAKKUK COMMENTARY

Peshita a translation of the Hebrew Bible (Old Testament) into Syriac, a dialect of Aramaic. The Peshita was used by Syriac-speaking Christians, primarily in Syria, but in other parts of the Eastern Mediterranean region as well. The origins of the Peshita are a matter of controversy, but translations of some books were in circulation by the early fourth century C.E. (both Ephrem and Aphrahat refer to them). The earliest manuscripts date from the fifth century, while the earliest complete manuscript is the Ambrosianus from the seventh century. Since the nineteenth century, scholars have debated the relationship between the Peshita and Jewish traditions and targums. While different books of the Peshita (especially those of the Pentateuch) reveal some acquaintance with Jewish traditions and translations, the exact nature of the shared material and its place in the Peshita's manuscript development remain unclear.

Pesikta deRab Kahana Midrash compilation of twenty-eight *piskaot* (explications of propositions). Each *piska* refers to a base verse, which generates the *piska*'s unifying theme and proposition. The compilation is organized around the synagogue liturgy and expounds the readings of scripture for various holy days or special Sabbaths. Like Leviticus Rabbah, its closest companion and model, Pesikta deRab Kahana formulates propositions, which are demonstrated over and over again through the discussion of specific verses of scripture. In many cases, a single verse stands at the head, which sets the tone; then all the other verses that are read and expounded are brought into relationship with that verse—and with the message of the holy occasion on which that verse is read in synagogue worship. Thus, the various verses of scripture are chosen on account of their affinity with a liturgical occasion of the synagogue, which is identical to a holy day, and the organizing text, which has told our authorship what topic it wishes to take up and therefore also what verses of scripture (if any) prove suitable to that topic and its exposition, is the life of synagogue prayer on special occasions. In the pages of Pesikta deRab Kahana, therefore, scripture speaks to an occasion in the liturgical life of the worshiping community of Israel.

Pesikta deRab Kahana follows the synagogal lections from early spring through fall, in the Western calendar, from late February or early March through late September or early October, a period of twenty-seven weeks, approximately half of the solar year and somewhat more than half of the lunar year. On the surface, the basic building block is the theme of a given lectionary Sabbath—that is, a Sabbath distinguished by a particular lection or portion of scripture that is read in the synagogue, besides the everyday cycle of scripture readings—and not the theme dictated by a given passage of scripture, let alone the exposition of the language or proposition of such a scriptural verse. The topical program of the document may be defined very simply: expositions of themes dictated by special Sabbaths or festivals and their lections. The single definitive trait of Pesikta deRab Kahana derives from its fundamental principle of organization and topical selection, for the document's framers have chosen as the program of their twenty-eight *piskaot* the interplay of an occasion and a lection for that occasion. There is, then, a three-dimensional construction, made up of (1) the occasion, (2) the base verse, and (3) the intersecting verse, which now sheds light on both the base verse and the occasion. In other words, the framers draw together lessons for various liturgical moments of the synagogue, and they identify a verse of the Pentateuch pertinent to each moment. They then undertake to explain that verse by appealing to some other verse, one not found in the Pentateuch. Many of the *piskaot* refer to a key verse, the base verse. The base verse generates the unifying theme and proposition of the *piska*. The compilers make their way through the liturgical year, beginning in December, with Hanukkah, the first liturgical event after the holy season of Tishrei, then moving on to the Sabbaths prior to Passover and ending with the conclusion of the penitential season (the Days of Awe) of Tishrei, the month corresponding to September–October.

Pesikta Rabbati compilation of twenty-eight *piskaot* (explications of propositions) in the model of Leviticus Rabbah and Pesikta deRab Kahana, formed by imitation, without real comprehension, of the intersecting verse–base verse form and the exegetical form. Each syllogism is presented in a cogent and systematic way. Each *piska* contains an implicit proposition, and that proposition emerges from the intersection of an external verse with the base verse that recurs through the *piska,* and then is restated by the systematic dissection of the components of the base verse, each of which is shown to say the same thing as all the others. Pesikta Rabbati goes over precisely the same liturgical calendar as Pesikta deRab Kahana, in pretty much the same way. While Pesikta deRab Kahana exhibits remarkably coherent discourse, in which a single implicit premise comes to diverse expression, Pesikta Rabbati does not. It is not so much a propositional statement as a collage, with discrete items linked to a common and shared theme.

Petra (Gr., rock) city located about 80 kilometers south of the Dead Sea; the Nabatean capital from the first half of the second century B.C.E. until the annexation of Nabatea in 106 C.E. by the emperor Trajan. From that point on, the city served as the capital of the Province of Arabia and as a major trading post. It was damaged by a severe earthquake in 363 C.E., and it became less important when the Province of Arabia was divided in two. Petra then became the capital of the southern province (Palaestina Tertia).

Though there are signs of habitation at Petra from prehistoric times through the Iron Age, Petra is known for its Nabatean heritage. Literary sources and various small finds, consisting mainly of pottery, point to the beginning of a Nabatean occupation since the Early Nabatean period (Hellenistic period). Only several buildings have been identified with this early period. The important finds include several incense altars, some small figurines, coins, and Nabatean painted pottery. In general, however, the finds are not as extensive as from the Middle Nabatean period.

Most of the extant architectural remains at Petra come from the Middle Nabatean (Roman I) period which ran from the first quarter of the first century B.C.E. to the middle of the first century C.E. The principal discoveries include houses, a theater, a colonnaded street, a monumental gateway, a bathhouse, and several temples.

One of the oddities about Petra is that few "normal" houses have been found. Petra seems to have been a royal dwelling with few signs of dwelling places for the common people and attendants who must have been present. It seems that the majority of these servants dwelled in neighboring Gaia to the east or in tents. There are limited signs of houses beginning at the end of the first century B.C.E. These were mostly erected with ashlar and contained plastered walls that might have been incorporated into the defense systems. These houses only cover a limited area, though, so they leave many unanswered questions about how the people of Petra actually lived.

The theater was located to the south of the town above the southern bank of the Wadi Musa. The seats of the theater were cut into sandstone and consisted of three tiers. The stage is really more of a *scaena frons* with three entrances than a conventional building. Though the structure is labeled a theater, scholars debate whether its function was for entertainment or a cultic purpose. The presence of seats cut into the sandstone makes it similar to other Graeco-Roman theaters used for entertainment, but an entertainment center so far from the city is unusual. Some scholars posit that the theater structure, therefore, was used for cultic or funerary practices. The theater seems to have been destroyed by an earthquake in 363 B.C.E.

The colonnaded street served as the main street of Petra and bisected the town. The street ran along the southern bank of the Wadi Musa and was approximately 6 meters wide and was steeply sloped. In many places the pedestals which flanked both sides of the streets were preserved and many were found in situ.

At the westernmost end of the colonnaded street, a monumental gateway was found. Though this gateway was located at the end of the street, it seems that it was built after the street because excavations show that during its construction part of the street had to be removed and then was later repaired. The gateway itself consists of four piers that form three openings. The outer two openings are 2 meters wide and the central opening is 3.5 meters wide. On the western side of the gateway there are four columns on high pedestals, while on the eastern side there are half columns on top of half pedestals. The arch that must have completed the top of the gateway was not preserved. The entrance was flanked by images of deities and floral reliefs. Next to the gatehouse there is a bathhouse. A parallel structure at Seeia suggests that this bathhouse was sacred and served a cultic function.

The Qaṣr Bint Farum Temple is located to the west of the gatehouse. It was situated upon a high podium (36 m × 36 m), and on the inside, the roof has a height of about 23 meters at its highest point. A pair of columns decorate the facade of the temple, and the vaulted entranceway contains another four columns. Like other Nabatean buildings, the temple contained walls that have a rubble core set in mortar. Wooden beams were also added, presumably to add strength in case of an earthquake. The placement of the tripartite gate and an inscription of Aretas IV that was found in a forecourt of the temple suggest an early date. The Northern Temple (or the Temple of the Winged Lions) is located about 100 meters north of the *via sacra* area. The site, originally identified as a gymnasium, is spectacularly decorated and many human and animal bones were found inside. This temple has been dated to the first century C.E.

Some of the most famous finds from Petra are the tombs. There are basically two types: shaft tombs that were cut into horizontal rock platforms, and tombs dug into the vertical rock walls of the canyons surrounding the wadi. Petra is perhaps most famous for this second type of tomb, which transformed the natural cliffs surrounding the city into spectacular monuments. To construct these tombs, the facade of the cliff was first smoothed, and then this smooth facade was carved, often with much ornamentation. Some of the more famous tombs include the Khaznet Farun, which is a two-storied monument. The lower story contains six pillars and is detached from the rock by a large incision. The upper story contains three pavilions. Another famous tomb is the Ed-Deir, which also contains six pillars in the lower story and three pavilions in the upper story. Impressive, but less spectacular tombs include the Pylon tombs, the stepped tombs, the Proto-Hegr tombs, the Hegr tomb, and others.

Petronius, Publius governor of Syria, appointed by the Roman emperor Gaius in 39 C.E.; he remained in office until 41 or 42. After Jamnian Jews destroyed an altar to the emperor, Gaius ordered a statue of himself made in Sidon and set up in the Jerusalem Temple. Petronius, knowing that this would provoke conflict, temporized and finally advised the emperor to rescind his order. The emperor's order to Petronius to commit suicide was abrogated by the emperor's assassination.

Pharisee (from Heb.: *parush,* separatist) member of an ancient Judaic sect teaching that the oral Torah was revealed at Sinai along with the written Torah and was preserved among prophets and sages down to the Pharisaic party. The Pharisees espoused prophetic ideals and translated them to the everyday life of Jewry through legislation. The Pharisees' distinctive beliefs, according to Josephus, were (1) immortality of the soul, (2) existence of angels, (3) divine providence, (4) freedom of will, (5) resurrection of the dead, and (6) oral Torah. Their distinctive practices, according to the Mishnah and certain passages in the Gospels, of Mark and Matthew, were observation of ritual purity even at home, not only in the Temple; faithful giving of tithes and offerings from food; and careful observance of the holiness of the Sabbath day. The Pharisees formed a Judaic religious system, defined by practices and laws that either were interpreted and obeyed by the group in a way different from that of other groups or from that of common society at large, on the one hand, or were observed only by the group, on the other. In the latter category are the purity laws, which play so large a role in the Pharisaic corpus.

One primary mark of Pharisaic commitment was the observance of the laws of ritual purity outside of the Temple (everyone observed them inside the Temple). Eating one's secular, that is, unconsecrated, food in a state of ritual purity as if one were a Temple priest in the cult was one of the two significations of party membership. The manifold circumstances of everyday life required the multiplication of concrete rules. Representative of the other category may be the laws of tithing and other agricultural taboos. Pharisees clearly regarded the keeping of the agricultural rules as a primary religious duty. The agricultural laws, just like the purity rules, in the end affected table fellowship, namely, what one might eat. Since food that had not been properly grown or tithed could not be eaten, and since the staple of the diet was agricultural products and not meat, the centrality of the agricultural rules is in no small degree due to precisely the same consideration: what may one eat, and under what circumstances? When one reviews the substance of the laws, one finds that they pertain either directly or ultimately to table fellowship, involving preparation of food; ritual purity (either purity rules directly relating to food or purity rules indirectly important on account of the need to keep food ritually clean); and agricultural rules pertaining to the proper growing, tithing, and preparation of agricultural produce for table use. All agricultural laws concern producing or preparing food for consumption, ensuring either that tithes and offerings have been set aside as the law requires or that the conditions for the nurture of the crops have conformed to the biblical taboos. The taboo against milk with meat is applied to chicken and cheese. The laws of ritual cleanness apply in the main to the preservation of the ritual cleanness of food, of people involved in preparing it, and of objects used in its preparation. Secondary considerations include the ritual pool. These matters took on practical importance in the lives of Pharisees in regard to the daily preparation of food. They took effect in the lives of all Jews only in connection with visiting the Temple. And they governed the lives of the priests in the cult itself. Laws regarding the Sabbath and festivals furthermore pertain in large measure to the preparation and preservation of food on festivals and the Sabbath. The ritual of table fellowship also included blessings and rules of conduct at meals.

Pharsalus, Battle of Julius Caesar, aided by Mark Antony, defeated Pompey and his eastern allies at Pharsalus, in Thessaly, in 48 B.C.E. Pompey fled to Egypt and was assassinated by his own men. His partisans and sons fought against Caesar until Caesar's own assassination in 44 B.C.E.

Phasael son of Antipater the Idumean; brother of Herod the Great. He was made governor of Jerusalem by his father, Antipater, in the mid-40s B.C.E. and was appointed tetrarch by Mark Antony in 42 B.C.E., after his victory at Philippi. He was captured by deceit by the Parthians when they invaded in 40 B.C.E.; he committed suicide while in captivity.

Pheroras son of Antipater the Idumean; brother of Herod the Great. He was made tetrarch of Peraea by Herod the Great with the permission of Augustus Caesar in 20 B.C.E. Pheroras supported Herod's son Antipater in his successful plots to have his half-brothers, Alexander and Aristobulus, executed and in his unsuccessful attempt to succeed Herod. In 5 B.C.E. Pheroras died of poisoning.

Philadelphia (Rabbath-Ammon) ancient city located in present-day Amman, Jordan. Archaeological data show that Philadelphia has been settled since the Neolithic period. Inhabitation continued throughout the Chalcolithic, Bronze, and Iron ages. During the Iron Age (and probably during the earlier periods as well), the city was called Rabbath-Ammon and served as the capital of the Ammonite kingdom. It is referred to in the Hebrew Bible in association with the battle the Israelites fought against Og, king of Bashan (Deut. 3:11) and as the place where King David sent Uriah the Hittite to his death (2 Sam. 11:14–21). Archaeologically, the Iron Age city produced two important inscriptions from the ninth and seventh centuries, respectively.

During the Hellenistic period, the city was renamed Philadelphia in honor of Ptolemy II Philadelphus, the Greek ruler of Egypt (r. 285–247 B.C.E.). In 218 B.C.E., it was captured by Antiochus the Great, and the city remained a part of the Nabatean kingdom until c. 63 B.C.E., when the Roman ruler Pompey conquered the region. In 106 B.C.E. the city was transferred to the Roman province of Arabia, and it continued to be prosperous throughout the second century C.E.

Roman Philadelphia consisted of two separate entities: the citadel (or upper city) and the lower city. The remains of the citadel have not been well preserved because of modern and medieval construction. In fact, the citadel is situated in the center of modern Amman. Archaeological investigations have permitted a general, if sketchy, reconstruction of the history of the citadel. The citadel served as the defense center of the city from the Bronze Age through the Iron Age. During the Roman Period, the fortifications also appear to have been impressive. Parts of a Roman wall were found surrounding the entire upper city, and there was a major wall separating the acropolis from the lower city. At the northernmost part of the citadel, there is evidence of two large towers built with ashlar masonry.

One of the principal parts of the acropolis during the Roman period was the Temple of Hercules. Today only part of the podium, the bases of several columns, and some architectural decorations are extant, but the remains and earlier descriptions of the temple suggest that it consisted of a cella surrounded by a row of columns. The temple was located at the southeastern part of the citadel on what was considered a sacred rock, suggested by a fragmentary inscription mentioning the Ammonite deity Milkom.

Several archaeological trenches dug on the citadel point toward domestic occupation in the upper city throughout the Hellenistic and Roman periods, but modern buildings prevent extensive investigations into the specifics of domestic life. The occupation in the acropolis seems to have been intense during the Byzantine-Umayyad period (6th-7th cs. C.E.). A Byzantine church and an Umayyad palace are among the chief discoveries.

The lower city was extremely well preserved up until the beginning of the twentieth century, and even today many parts of the city are extant. Architecturally, the lower city is constructed along two colonnaded streets. One runs along the southern foot of the acropolis, while the other runs along the western end of the citadel. Today, modern Amman covers these two colonnaded streets, but they were visible and documented in the early part of the twentieth century.

One of the principal discoveries still extant in the lower city is the large theater, which was situated south of the colonnaded street on the southern side of the citadel. The rows for the seats were built in a partly natural depression on a hillside. The seats of the theater themselves are distinguished from what is found at Petra. They are built of stone instead of being hewn out of rock. There is also another small theater facing west that was built adjacent to the larger one. The small theater, unlike the larger one, was built on a level surface.

Other important discoveries in the lower city include the propylaeum and the nymphaeum. The proplyaeum was located just north of the colonnaded street and south of the acropolis wall. The building contained three square doorways, and its pillars were decorated with Corinthian capitals. Investigations have shown that visitors to the cultic area in the acropolis of the upper city would have passed through the propylaeum and gone up a series of stairs to the acropolis. Unfortunately, none of the stairs are extant.

The nymphaeum was located in the western part of the lower city and faced north. It was composed of a central wall with a series of connected niches. The building had a facade two stories high and should be compared with nymphaea from Gerase, Beth Shean, Side, and Aspendos.

Another important archaeological feature of ancient Philadelphia is its tombs. Burial tombs were discovered from the earliest periods of occupation and provide valuable clues to life during the entire history of Philadelphia. From the Nabatean period, an important tomb dating from the first century B.C.E. was discovered near the base of Jebel Amman. It was originally a Late Bronze Age tomb, which was reused during the Nabatean period. Principal finds include two Hellenistic lamps and one Herodian lamp, a *terra sigillata* bowl, several Nabatean bowls, and glass bottles. Just a few meters from this grave, a Roman burial cave was found with three sarcophagi, lamps, and pottery characteristic of the second century C.E. Two other Roman burial caves have been discovered in various parts of ancient Philadelphia that produced a large amount of pottery and jewelry, as well as several sarcophagi. One of these caves contained two decorated sarcophagi with designs of garlands and rosettes. Bones belonging to a male and a female were found inside each of the sarcophagi, and four lamps and a juglet were found on the floor adjacent to the sarcophagi. In addition, silver and bronze jewelry was found inside the sarcophagus with the female's bones. These items are extremely important in helping scholars understand burial customs during the Nabatean period.

philanthropia (Gr., love of mankind) a technical term used in reference to those who performed acts of charity or public works; a trait normally expected of rulers. It is important in the writings of Philo of Alexandria, who puts it alongside justice in establishing social relations.

philanthropy (Heb.: *tzedakah*) charity; literally, righteousness manifested in charity. Acts of righteousness in general were defined as help to the poor in particular; funds for the poor were called "funds for righteousness." The poor had a right to support, and everyone owed them proper assistance, with dignity and respect. A poor person could demand support in the language, "Acquire merit through me," meaning, carry out an act of righteousness through which you will personally be recognized as having done what the law does not require but does reward—an act of grace.

philhellene (Gr., lover of [things] Greek) a title given to certain Oriental individuals or rulers because of their favor toward Greek culture. These included the Hasmonean ruler Aristobulus I, according to Josephus.

Philip, son of Herod son of Herod the Great and Cleopatra of Jerusalem. After his father's death, he was appointed by Augustus as tetrarch of Batanaea, Trachonitis, Auranitis, Panias, and Ituraea in 4 B.C.E. He married Salome, daughter of Herod son of Herod, and Herodias, granddaughter of Herod. (The Gospel of Mark [6:17] mistakenly identifies him, instead of Herod son of Herod, as the first husband of Herodias.) He rebuilt Panias as Caesarea Philippi and Bethsaida as Julias. His rule was generally peaceful until his death in 34 C.E.

Philip of Macedon (382–336 B.C.E.) Macedonian king (r. 359–336 B.C.E.); father of Alexander the Great. He united upper Macedonia with lower Macedonia, and then through skillful diplomacy and new military tactics conquered the surrounding areas south and east of Macedonia, eventually defeating the Athenians at Chaeronea in 338 B.C.E. After his death his son Alexander led a united Greece in a war that led to the demise of the Persian Empire and the ascendancy of a Hellenistic empire.

Philippi, Battle of In 42 B.C.E. at Philippi, Mark Antony and Octavian defeated Cassius and Brutus, two of the assassins of Julius Caesar, who had gathered an army in the east and were challenging the Roman Senate's condemnation of their act. Both conspirators committed suicide. Antipater and Herod the Great had supported Cassius, but after the Battle of Philippi, Herod appeared before Antony in Asia Minor and won his favor. Herod and his brother Phasael were subsequently appointed tetrarchs over Jewish territory.

Philo (15 B.C.E.–50 C.E.) Hellenistic Jewish philosopher, often referred to as Philo of Alexandria or Philo Judaeus. He is the most important representative of Hellenistic Judaism, the Greek-speaking and Greek-influenced variety of Judaism that flourished in Alexandria from 200 B.C.E. to 100 C.E. Philo was born into a wealthy and distinguished Alexandrian family. His brother Alexander was alabarch, a leading Jewish official. His nephew Tiberius Julius

Alexander apostatized from the Jewish religion and became governor of Egypt. The Jewish historian Josephus tells us that Philo was "held in the highest honor" in the Jewish community and was "not unskilled in philosophy." The only event in his life that is known is his leadership of an embassy of Alexandrian Jews who appeared before the emperor Gaius Caligula in 39 C.E. to protest against anti-Jewish mob violence in their city. Vivid descriptions of this event and its social context are given in Philo's treatises *In Flaccum* and *Legatio ad Gaium*. The background to Philo's writings and thought is at all times the precarious situation of the Jewish community in Alexandria, sandwiched between the educated Greek upper class and the volatile native Egyptian population.

Nearly fifty works written by Philo are still extant. The majority of these concentrate on the interpretation of the Law of Moses (or Pentateuch), as found in the Septuagint translation (Philo knew no Hebrew). These treatises can be divided into three lengthy series: (1) the Allegorical Commentary; (2) the Exposition of the Law; and (3) Questions and Answers. In the Allegorical Commentary, Philo gives a very detailed and complex exegesis of Genesis 1–17. Through the use of the exegetical technique of allegory, he interprets the early history of humankind and the wanderings of the patriarch Abraham in terms of the moral life and religious quest of the soul. The Exposition of the Law is a more varied work, containing biographies of the patriarchs and an explanation of the Decalogue and the other ordinances of the Mosaic law, with emphasis on both literal observance and symbolic interpretation. The third series, imperfectly preserved in an Armenian translation, poses questions and gives answers on the text of Genesis and Exodus; most of the (usually) short chapters contain literal followed by figurative (or allegorical) exegesis. Philo also wrote a number of purely philosophical treatises and some apologetic works in defense of Judaism. In one of these he mentions a Jewish community of male Therapeutae and female Therapeutrides, who led an ascetic life of contemplation in the countryside outside Alexandria. (The community may have been related to that of the Essenes.) The church historian Eusebius later misinterpreted these ascetics as early Christians.

Philo's thought is centered on scripture, which he interprets in a consistently philosophical manner, exploiting his considerable knowledge of Greek philosophy. By means of allegorical and symbolic interpretation Moses is presented as the lawgiver, prophet, and philosopher par excellence, who is the source of all later philosophy. For this reason, Philo concentrates on the Pentateuch and seldom refers to the rest of the Bible. His apologetic motives are clear: in his Alexandrian context Philo is eager to show that Jewish culture is not inferior to Hellenism. In practice, however, it emerges that his thought is heavily influenced by Greek philosophical ideas. His greatest debt is to Plato and to the interpretation of Plato's thought known as Middle Platonism. Stoic and Pythagorean ideas are also used, but are placed in a Platonist framework and used to expound scriptural texts.

The focus of Philo's thought is primarily theological. God as revealed in the Bible is identified with Being (derived from the divine self-disclosure in Exod. 3:14). In his essence, He is nameless and unknowable. Humans can only know *that* He is, not *what* He is. Highly influential is Philo's doctrine of the divine Logos, which builds upon Hellenistic Jewish concepts. The Logos can be thought of as the aspect of God that stands in relation to created reality, and thus makes the divine being known to humankind. But Philo often talks about the Logos as if it were an entity that had a separate existence from God himself, that is a divine hypostasis, or self-subsistent entity. Philo is the first author to give an extended commentary on the Mosaic account of the Creation, whose interpretation he regards as fundamental to a deeper understanding of the law. The goal of human existence is to gain knowledge of and communion with God, to be gained through contemplation of both the created order and study of the law. Through contemplation, the soul can reach a state of "sober intoxication" (a phrase first found in Philo) and ultimately attain to an immortal, nonmaterial existence.

Despite his strong concern for the fate of the Jewish people, eschatology in Philo is primarily personal rather than nationalistic or apocalyptic. This is consistent with a marked tendency toward universalism in his thought. Although the source of the highest wisdom is the divine revelation through Moses, Philo allows for the possibility that some glimpses of the truth can be gained independently, for example, in the efforts of the Greek philosophers. He insists, however, that the whole world would stand to gain from a deeper acquaintance with the Jewish law.

Philo is important in the history of Judaism because he exemplifies a striking variety of prerabbinic Judaism, whose concern with the problem of assimilation to a dominant (Hellenistic) culture is remarkably parallel to the situation of many Jews in the nineteenth and twentieth centuries. After the fall of Jerusalem in 70 C.E. and the catastrophe that struck the Jewish community in Alexandria in 115–117 C.E., this form of Judaism died out. The rabbis wholly ignored Philo's writings, either because they disapproved of his views or because they were not interested in philosophy. His works survived on account of their popularity in the Christian tradition, where they were eagerly read by Clement, Origen, Ambrose, and other patristic authors. In medieval manuscripts, Philo is sometimes called "the Bishop." In Jewish circles, Philo was rediscovered by Azariah dei Rossi in the sixteenth century, and since then has regained his rightful place in Jewish thought.

philo-Judaism a coined word meaning "friend/lover of Judaism." Some Graeco-Roman writers, especially in the early Greek period, show considerable sympathy for and even admiration of the Jews. They include such writers as Hecataeus of Abdera and Numenius. *See also* JUDAISM IN GREEK AND LATIN SOURCES.

Philo of Byblos (c. 65–140 C.E.) Greek writer from Phoenicia. In his *History of Phoenicia,* he claims to be quoting from the ancient writer Sanchuniathon. Evaluating this claim is difficult because his work is known only from fairly extensive quotations in Eusebius, but the portion of the text that is extant contains an important description of many aspects of Canaanite religion. On the other hand, the work itself is clearly Hellenistic, showing the influence of Greek myth and legend. Thus, the contribution—and even the existence—of Sanchuniathon is uncertain.

philoroman (Gr., lover of [things] Roman) term used in reference to Eastern individuals and rulers who sought to ingratiate themselves with the Romans. For example, Agrippa I included the word *philokaisar* (friend of Caesar) on some of his coins.

philos (Gr., lover [of something], or friend) Like the English word, the term could be used generically; however, it also had a technical connotation with reference to the Friends of the king, that is, advisers and officials of the court. The related word *philia* means "love" or "friendship," and the root *philo* is also frequently found as an element in Greek names.

philosophy The encounter of Jews and Judaism with Greek philosophy began in the Hellenistic period, in the course of which the number of Jews living in the Graeco-Roman world greatly increased. The relationship of Jews to the Greek philosophical tradition must be understood within the larger context of Jews trying to interpret their own cultural and religious traditions while living in the larger Graeco-Roman world. There was almost always an apologetic motive involved. Jews tried to show that their own beliefs and traditions were compatible with the best Greek philosophy and indeed were superior to it. In fact, it was alleged, the Greeks even derived their philosophy indirectly from Moses.

Sometimes this was reflected in the use by Jewish writers of popular Greek philosophical ethics (e.g., Sybilline Oracles, Pseudo-Phocylides, 4 Maccabees). At other times Jewish writers tried to provide a deeper, more philosophical understanding of their beliefs and traditions. The two Greek philosophical schools most congenial for this effort were Stoicism and Middle Platonism (the Platonic tradition between 80 B.C.E. and 220 C.E.). This effort began as early as the middle of the second century B.C.E. with Aristobulus and the Letter of Aristeas. Aristobulus, although sometimes referred to as a Peripatetic, was rather more eclectic. He tried to show, through the use of an allegorical style of interpretation rooted primarily in Stoicism, that the apparent anthropomorphisms in the Bible (speaking of God's "hands," "feet," or "voice") were actually ways of using the language of appearances to point to deeper realities. Similarly, the Letter of Aristeas tried to show that the various purity regulations of the Mosaic law were primarily intended to point to deeper ethical truths.

The two most important works of Greek-speaking Judaism to deal with the Greek philosophical tradition were the Wisdom of Solomon and the works of Philo of Alexandria. The Wisdom of Solomon probably comes from Alexandria and was written in the first century B.C.E. While showing a wide knowledge of Greek philosophical ideas, the author of the Wisdom of Solomon tried to integrate them into a context that demonstrated the superiority of Jewish beliefs and traditions as well as of the history of Israel. The most sustained effort to interpret Judaism in a way that showed both its compatibility with and its superiority to the best of Greek philosophy is found in the works of Philo of Alexandria, who wrote in the first half of the first century C.E. Although influenced by both Stoicism and emerging Middle Platonism, the worldview of Philo's interpretations was that of Middle Platonism. This affected his conception of reality as divided into the intelligible and the sensible worlds, his view of the Logos of God as a kind of intermediate reality between God and the created world, and his view of the goal of the human soul as the achievement of a "likeness to God." Given the complexity of his biblical interpretations, Philo may have been part of an already developed tradition of interpretation, which he both carried on and significantly developed. The interpretations of Philo became immensely influential on early Christian writers beginning with Clement of Alexandria in the late second century C.E. *See also* PHILO; SOLOMON, WISDOM OF.

Philo the Elder writer known only in fragments from Eusebius, who took them in turn from Alexander Polyhistor. Only twenty-four lines in all are preserved, and these are often in obscure Greek with rare words. A further problem is that of textual corruption. This has made the understanding of the poem very difficult; however, recent study suggests that the author had a Greek education and followed Hellenistic epic models. Two of the fragments concern Abraham and one concerns Joseph. Only one work seems to be in question, though, with the title *On Jerusalem*. Although it has been suggested that the author was a Samaritan, this seems unlikely in view of the mention of Jerusalem. The Jewish identity of the author is reasonably certain. Three of the fragments concern the water system of Jerusalem. These may be of significance for archaeology, since they seem to show the existence of a double pool. If this is identical with the double pool of Bethesda, Philo would help to date its construction. The obscurity of the language makes it difficult to be certain, however. His praise of Abraham and Joseph seems extravagant, but was wholly in keeping with the literary conventions of the age.

Phineas Israelite priest; son of Eleazar the son of Aaron (Exod. 6:25). His zeal in killing an Israelite man and a Moabite woman engaged in sexual intercourse stayed the wrath of God against Israel and established a covenant of "perpetual priesthood" (Num. 25). Winning one's priestly credentials through zeal against idolaters and promiscuous sinners occurs elsewhere in the Bible and Jewish literature (Exod. 32:25–29; Jub. 30), and the tradition that Elijah was Phineas redivivus (LAB 48) may derive from a perceived connection between Numbers 25 and 1 Kings 18:40. The story in Numbers 25 serves as an archetype for 1 Maccabees 2:23–26, which legitimizes the Hasmonean high priesthood on the basis of a similar action by Mattathias, which, it is implied, began the process of turning back God's wrath against hellenizing Israel (1 Macc. 1:64).

phoboumenoi tou theou *see* GOD-FEARERS

Phocas emperor of the Eastern Roman Empire (r. 602–610 C.E.). Apparently, in 610 he ordered the

Jews in Antioch, Palestine, and Alexandria to be forcibly baptized; however, he does not seem to have baptized the Jews of Europe. It appears that baptism became a political matter and a sign of fidelity to the emperor. He engaged in the last war between Rome and Persia. By 609, the main Persian army was advancing on Antioch. At the same time, a revolt broke out in Constantinople, which led to Phocas's being deposed and executed.

Phocylides, Pseudo- author of a Greek didactic poem from the late Second Temple period (ca. 100 B.C.E.–50 C.E.), attributed to a Greek poet from Miletus of the sixth century B.C.E. The poem was popular in the Middle Ages and early Renaissance, but its authenticity became suspect in the seventeenth century and it is now generally recognized as a Jewish composition.

The poem consists of 230 hexameter verses in the Ionic dialect, purporting to convey "counsels of God with his holy judgments." These counsels, often inspired by the Decalogue and the admonitions of wisdom and prophetic literature, inculcate fundamental values such as sexual restraint, honesty, and honor of God and parents. The poem exhorts the listener to justice, mercy, self-control, and moderation, and warns against vices such as greed and envy. Beyond such general admonitions, it gives special attention to the importance of labor and diligence (ll. 153–74), appropriate sexual behavior and the management of domestic affairs (ll. 175–227). Embedded within the moral instruction is a reflection on human destiny that affirms the immortality of the soul (ll. 97–115).

The purpose of the poem has been variously described. The absence of any polemic against idolatry is striking, as are the numerous parallels to Greek gnomic wisdom. The poem clearly attempts to effect some accommodation with Hellenic culture. It may have been an educational exercise, although a more serious apologetic purpose is likely. The poem in fact illustrates a claim frequent in Jewish apologetic literature of the Hellenistic period, that the best in Greek culture was compatible with the Torah.

phoenix mythic bird in antiquity believed to live to a great age and to generate from its corpse a worm that grew into a new phoenix. According to 3 Baruch 6:2–12, the phoenix flies alongside the sun, protecting the earth from its heat.

phoros (Gr., tax, or tribute) term often used generically for all sorts of taxes; however, it also had the connotation of "tribute," which implied foreign subjugation. Judea paid tribute when under Persian, Seleucid, and early Roman rule.

phronēsis (Gr., practical wisdom) one of the four cardinal virtues widely referred to in the Graeco-Roman world. Philosophical wisdom was highly prized in learned circles, but this was usually called *sophia*. *Phronēsis* had more to do with practical or administrative skills.

phylactery *see* TEFILLIN

physician The Hebrew word translated as "physician" derives from the verb meaning "to heal." The first reference to physicians in the Bible, in Genesis 50:1–14, has nothing to do with healing, however. Those physicians, in the service of Joseph, are ordered by him to embalm the body of his father, Jacob, so that it can be carried back for burial in Canaan. The operation takes forty days, and the body is subsequently taken there. Two other biblical passages depict physicians in a directly negative way: Job denounces his friends who offer him useless advice, calling them "worthless physicians" who "whitewash with lies"; and in 2 Chronicles 16:11–14, Asa, the king of Judah, is criticized for his futile turning to physicians for help, instead of looking to the Lord to heal him. He soon dies and is buried in a tomb in the city of David.

In the prophetic Book of Jeremiah, the prophet asks why the health of God's people has not been restored: "Is there no balm in Gilead? Is there no physician there?" (8:22). He compares the futility of Egypt's attempt to withstand defeat at the hands of Nebuchadnezzar of Babylon with having "used many medicines in vain" (46:11). In Jeremiah 51:8 the prediction of the destruction of Babylon mentions the useless attempt to heal "her wound."

However, in the Hellenistic period (Sir. 38:1–15) there is a call to honor physicians, since the ability to heal comes from God, who created medicines and who works through physicians. Ben Sira describes the medicinal benefits of various trees. Success lies in the hands of the physician when he prays to the Lord for success in diagnosis and prescription so that human life may be preserved. This development in Judaism clearly reflects the rise of medicine under Hippocrates, who formulated a theory of the medicinal value of natural substances. Ben Sira, however, considers the ultimate source of healing to be God, who works through medicines and physicians. In his description of the Essenes, Josephus (*War* 2.136) tells us that they study ancient writings to foster the welfare of body and soul, and their study includes investigation of the medicinal properties of roots and stones. In describing the Therapeutae (which means "healers"), Philo of Alexandria reports that they cure the soul as well as the body, and that through worship they are attuned to the natural laws immanent in the created order and are thus able to effect cures.

Like the Hellenistic writers, Talmudic rabbis generally viewed physicians favorably. Their ability to heal was held to derive from God (B. Berakhot 59a; B. Baba Kamma 85a), and the herbs they use as medicines were said to grow through divine command (Gen. Rabbah Parashah 10). Sages were admonished to live only in towns served by a physician (B. Sanhedrin 17b). Doctors had an important role in the rabbinic court, serving as expert witnesses (B. Sanhedrin 78a; B. Gittin 12b) and determining the number of lashes a convicted criminal could withstand as punishment (B. Makkot 22b). Physicians were paid according to their skill, the best of them collecting large fees. An injured person had the right to quick and appropriate medical attention, paid for by the one who had caused the injury. For this purpose, a physician willing to work for free could be rejected as worthless (B. Baba Kamma 85a). The Talmud contains numerous references to specific medical procedures and methods.

Alongside this positive perspective, rabbinic writings reveal a very negative attitude towards physicians. This was possibly a result of the rudimentary nature of the physician's art and the likelihood that, even with the best medical attention, many patients did not recover. Thus even the best of physicians is said to be doomed to Gehenna (M. Kiddushin 4:14; see also Abot deRabbi Nathan 36); one should avoid living in a town of which the head is a physician (B. Pesahim 113a); and physicians' abilities are compared unfavorably to those of sages (B. Ketubot 74b).

physiognomy the alleged art of determining character from physical appearances. Although such pseudoscientific theories as phrenology (determining character from bumps on the head) are recent developments, the idea that one's physical appearance is a clue to character is an ancient one. Greek writings as early as Aristotle suggest a connection between climate and both physical and mental characteristics. A physiognomic text from Cave 4 of Qumran uses the shape of the thighs, fingers, toes, and so on as a clue to how much the person shares in the "realm of light" and the "realm of darkness."

physis (Gr., nature) term that became very important in philosophical discussion in the Graeco-Roman world. It surfaces in such Jewish writers as Philo of Alexandria and Josephus. Part of the debate centered on the question of which things occurred "by nature" and which by mere "convention." Those things that were only convention had no particular authority and could be rejected. Very important were those things "by nature," however, which in Jewish texts took on the imperative of divine authority.

piety an attitude and a mode of life that recognize the divine's purity and power, as reflected in the order of the universe and, for Jews, as seen in precepts of the law of Moses. The messianic king whose coming is announced by the prophet Isaiah (9:1–7; 11:1–5) will have the wisdom and understanding to fulfill his role through the "Spirit of the Lord," which will "rest upon him" (11:2). This is described as "the spirit of wisdom and understanding, the spirit of counsel and strength, the spirit of knowledge and piety." "Piety" is then linked with "the fear of the Lord."

In the Septuagint, the term "pious" is rare in the writings of the prophets, although Isaiah 26:7 reports that "the way of the pious is smooth" and Isaiah 33:5–6 says that "the holy God who dwells in the heights will fill Zion with justice and righteousness," which is to be "conveyed by the law", through which will come "the treasures of our salvation: wisdom, knowledge, and piety toward God." It is in the wisdom traditions of Israel that the term "pious" is widely used. Proverbs 1:7 in the Greek version adds to the declaration "Fear of God is the beginning of wisdom" the assertions that "understanding is good for all who perform wisdom" and that "piety toward God is the beginning of perception."

In Sirach there is a close link between wisdom and piety. What God grants to the pious will endure and have lasting success (Sir. 11:17). The pious are the beneficiaries of divine rewards (11:22), and He rewards good deeds done to the pious (12:2, 4). However, the pious are to have no close relationships with the impious (13:17), and the latter will not get away with their acts of thievery (16:13) and their false oaths (23:7–12). The pious patience will be rewarded, and their discourse is always wise, while that of fools keeps changing like the phases of the moon. Those who take delight in the mishaps that befall the pious will be caught in a trap and consumed with pain until they die (27:29). Gossip and slander will bring disaster on the unwise, but will never gain control over the pious (28:22). Just as good is the opposite of evil, and life is the opposite of death, so the sinner is the opposite of the pious (33:14). The readers of Sirach are urged to maintain close association with the pious, "whom you know keep the commandments" (37:12). It is to them that God has granted true wisdom (43:33). Similarly, following a report of King Josiah's reforming of Israel's worship of God (2 Kings 23), in 1 Esdras 1:23 Josiah's uprightness in the sight of the Lord is said to be the result of his heart being "full of piety."

The Letter of Aristeas, written in the second century B.C.E. to show the compatibility of the Jewish scriptures and (Hellenistic) philosophy and to claim divine approval for the translation of the Bible into Greek, describes a conversation between the king of Egypt who had commissioned the translation and the Jewish translators. The king asks, "What is the essence of piety?" to which the man questioned replies: "The realization that God is continually at work in everything and is omniscient, and that man cannot hide from him an unjust deed or evil action. For as God does good to the whole world, so you by imitating him would be without offense" (210). That perception matches well with the statement of the Roman Stoic philosopher Epictetus, who lived in the late first and early second century C.E.: "In piety toward the gods . . . the chief element is this: to have correct opinions about them, as existing and as administering the universe well and justly, and to have set yourself to obey them and to accept everything that happens, and to follow it voluntarily in the belief that it is being carried out by the highest intelligence" (Encheiridion 31). Epictetus goes on to say that one should never blame the gods for difficulties or apparent disasters, but anyone who takes care to "control both desires and aversions" is also being "careful about piety." At the same time, the pious individual should be bringing offerings to the gods.

Philo of Alexandria, whose interpretations of the Bible are shaped largely by Greek philosophy (Platonic and Stoic), declares that only fools are unmoved by fear of the gods. He asserts (in *On the Unchangeableness of God* 69), "I observe that all the exhortations to piety in the law refer either to our loving or fearing the One who is. So for those whose conception of the One who is involves no such factor as human parts or passions, but who choose instead to love him, they honor him in a manner suitable to God and for his sake alone. It is others who fear God."

In his *Against Apion* (II.16), Josephus praises Moses who, in spite of his spectacular successes in leading his people and their dependence upon him and obedience to him, refused to seize power as a monarch. Instead he felt obligated to live a life of piety and to provide an abundance of good laws for his people. This was the most effective way of showing his own virtue and of guaranteeing the welfare of those whose leader he had become. He was convinced that God was his leader and counselor and that it was God who had guided all that he did and thought. What was essential was that this perception be communicated to the entire community. Josephus sees piety to be based on a personal relationship with God and expressed in terms of the laws that are to shape the life of God's people.

By far the most extensive treatment of piety appears in the Fourth Book of Maccabees. Probably written in the first half of the first century C.E., its author announces at the outset that the "philosophical subject" that he proposes to discuss is whether "pious reason" is the absolute master of the passions (1:1). The greatest of the virtues is "intelligence." Reason is master over the passions opposing gluttony and lust, but reason can also overcome the passions hindering justice and courage (1:4). Conformity to the law, even if it could be proved not to be of divine origin, is so strong that nothing can undermine Jews' commitment to the piety that is in accord with the law (5:16–18) and that enables them to "reverence highly the only living God" (5:24). That commitment will not wane as old age comes (5:31). No amount of argument will divert the author from his commitment to "true piety" (5:38). Even under torture, Eleazar refuses to change his position and asserts that the children of Abraham must be ready to "die nobly for the sake of piety" (6:22). It is "pious reason" that is master of the passions" (6:31), and it was Eleazar's rational powers that enable him to "steer the ship of piety on the sea of the passions" (7:1), guided as it was "by the rudder of piety" (7:3). It was piety alone that enabled this old man to despise the fatal torments he experienced, and younger men follow his example by remaining faithful until death for the sake of their piety (9:6–7). Only in this way can they fight for true religion (9:24). In spite of excruciating torture, they remain true to their "ancestral religion" (9:29). The sons all refuse to obey the king's order for them to defile themselves. As he is being tortured, the sixth son declares that he is suffering for the sake of piety, and that religious knowledge is unconquerable (10:20–21). The youngest son asserts that by their noble deaths his martyred brothers have fulfilled their piety toward God (12:14).

A hymnlike passage (4 Macc. 13:1–27) declares that it is "pious reason" that has enabled them to remain true to their commitment. These brothers, with their common origins in one family, grew and gained strength from a common nurture and discipline in the law; sharing the same virtues and growing up in the common life of righteousness, they loved one another and shared a zeal for goodness that served to confirm their common commitment to true piety. Through this piety they were able to endure the suffering and death they all experienced. Their unity in life and death was for the sake of piety (14:4). Their mother, who had watched the ghastly deaths of her seven sons, loved piety more than the lives of her offspring or her own life. This piety preserves the faithful to eternal life according to God's word (15:1–3), and the mother's fear of God (15:8) kept her from yielding to the king's command that she and her sons abandon their purity in accord with the law (15:13). It was pious reason that gave her the courage to persevere (15:23) and that subdued all her fiery emotions (16:4).

Use of the word piety in the New Testament is limited to some references in the Book of Acts and in later letters attributed to Paul and Peter. For example, there is mention of a Gentile who believed in the God of Israel (Acts 10:2, 7) and Paul refers to the Athenians' worshiping a God they do not know (Acts 17:3). In later letters attributed to Paul, piety refers to the Christian religion in general: "The mystery of our piety" (1 Tim. 3:16) describes the career of Jesus as the Christ. Piety is to be one of the moral qualities that are the goal of members of the community (1 Tim. 6:11). In 2 Timothy 3:12 there is a warning that all who seek to live lives of piety will be persecuted. Titus 1:1 declares the effort in Paul's name to "further the faith of God's elect and their knowledge of the truth which accords with piety." The Hellenistic abstract notion of piety clearly influenced Judaism and Christianity in the Graeco-Roman period.

In the rabbinic literature, piety is defined by a complex of religious, social, and human qualities understood to represent exacting adherence to the terms of God's covenant with the Jewish people, as defined by rabbinic law and theology. Beyond simply going to the house of study, the pious person consistently practiced what he learned there (M. Abot 5:14). Without expectation of a worldly reward, such a person gave all that he had for the benefit of others (M. Abot 5:10). Judah the Patriarch defined piety with the maxim: "What is the straight path a person should choose for himself? Whatever is an ornament to the one who follows it, and an ornament in the view of others. Be meticulous in a small religious duty as in a large one, for you do not know what sort of reward is coming for any of the various religious duties. And

reckon the cost of carrying out a religious duty against the reward for doing it, and the reward for committing a transgression against the cost for doing it. And keep your eye on three things, so you will not come into the clutches of transgression: Know what is above you: an eye that sees, and an ear that hears, and all your actions are written down in a book" (M. Abot 2:1).

Perfect piety was the goal of rabbinic learning and practice, and a number of rabbinic masters are referred to with the appellation "the pious." The rabbis however were clear that, because of human nature, achieving absolute piety was nearly impossible. They interpreted the use of the word "iniquity" in Psalm 51:5 ("Behold, I was brought forth in iniquity, and in sin did my mother conceive me") to indicate that even the most pious person could not exist without a certain sinful side to his nature (Lev. Rabbah 14:5).

pig *see* PORK

Piga *see* PUGA

pikuaḥ nefesh (Heb., saving a life) in rabbinic Judaism, the concept that saving an imperiled individual—either oneself or someone else—supersedes all other obligations. Death or martyrdom is to be preferred only as an alternative to committing murder, idolatry, or an unlawful sexual act (B. Sanhedrin 74a–b).

Pilate, Pontius prefect of Judea (26–36 C.E.). According to Philo, the first-century Jewish philosopher, who says he is quoting a letter of Agrippa I, Pilate was unbending, harsh, greedy, and cruel. Josephus, the Jewish historian, relates three confrontations between Pilate and the Jewish population of Judea that support that view. Soon after Pilate took office he had his legions bring their military standards, which included images of the emperor Tiberius, into Jerusalem. This practice was offensive to the people and had been avoided by his predecessors. The leaders and people protested to him in Caesarea and continued their protests even when threatened with death. Finally, Pilate backed down. Later he used funds from the Temple treasury to build an aqueduct to Jerusalem. Faced with a protesting mob in Jerusalem, he had his soldiers (in disguise) mingle with the crowd and club them into submission at a prearranged signal. Late in his term of office Pilate mounted votive shields carrying the name of Tiberius on Herod's palace, his residence when in Jerusalem. The people and leaders of Jerusalem sent a petition to Tiberius, who ordered them removed to the Temple of Augusta in Caesarea. In addition, the Gospel of Luke alludes to an incident involving "Galileans whose blood Pilate had mingled with their sacrifices" (13:1). The New Testament accounts of Pilate's sentencing of Jesus to execution by crucifixion for suspicion of sedition fit well with what other sources say about him. Pilate was finally recalled to Rome by Tiberius because he had routed a group of Samaritans and executed their leaders when they gathered at Mount Gerizim in the hope that a prophet would produce the Temple vessels. Pilate did not arrive in Rome until after Tiberius's death in 37, and the final disposition of the charges against him is not known.

pilgrimage (Heb.: *aliyah laregel*) making trips to Jerusalem on the pilgrim festivals, which were Tabernacles, Passover, and Pentecost. The piety of Israel in the Land of Israel entailed pilgrimages to the Temple on festivals in celebration of nature and in commemoration of historical events. Specifically, the encounter with God and the yearning for salvation at the end of time came to a climax in the coincidence of those turnings in the natural year, spring and fall, identified at the natural year's beginning and end and explained in all forms of Judaism as celebrations of great events in the life of historical Israel. At these intense moments of heightened reality during the natural year, scripture required a pilgrimage to the Temple. Accordingly, in theory at least, "all Israel," or as many as could make it, assembled in the holy place, the Temple in Jerusalem. They then together celebrated the passage of the natural year, on the one hand, and the past and future of the people, on the other. In the dimension of the future, of course, messianic hopes were associated with the pilgrim festivals, particularly Tabernacles and Passover. The pilgrim festivals, joined in sectarian doctrine to the moment at which the Messiah would come (Christ at Passover; in the sages' later writings, the Messiah at Tabernacles), drew the nation to the Temple in Jerusalem.

These festivals found their first definition in scripture. Passover came in the spring. Tabernacles came in the fall. The festal season began at Passover, on the fifteenth of Nisan (the month corresponding to April). That marks the first full moon after the vernal equinox. The festival continued for seven days, with a further festival coming fifty days after the beginning of the first. This second festival was Pentecost (Heb.: Shabuot). The corresponding high point of the year in the autumn, Tabernacles (Heb.: Sukkot), came to its climax on the first full moon after the autumnal equinox—the fifteenth of Tishrei, that is, the first full moon after September 21. However, the holy season began two weeks

earlier, on the eve of the first of Tishrei, and ended a week later, on the twenty-first of Tishrei. The opening of the holy season of autumn, the first of Tishrei, with the celebration of the New Year, followed by the Day of Atonement on the tenth of Tishrei, marked (as is still the case) a penitential season of repentance, fasting, and charity. Pilgrim festivals thus celebrated in particular the sun's movement around the earth relative to that of the moon (and thus the seasons of the land). Especially important were dramatic shifts in the pattern of the rains in the Holy Land itself. The fall festival marked the beginning of the autumnal and winter rains, on which the life of the Holy Land depended. The spring festival marked the end of the rainy season. Scripture identified the Passover with the liberation of Israel from Egypt and the beginning of the life of the people. As indicated, the autumnal season focused upon the moral condition of individuals and of the people as a whole. In the pilgrim festivals the affairs of the individual, the people, and the natural and supernatural world all reached a climax in a massive and impressive celebration in the cult.

While the Mishnah and Talmud speak of the obligation to make the festival pilgrimage, to offer the required sacrifices, and to make a freewill offering, a variety of classes of individuals are exempted (see M. Hagigah 1:1; B. Pesahim 8b), giving the overall impression that the trip was viewed as an important religious responsibility but not an absolute requirement. Accordingly, while some reports describe participation by whole towns or by large numbers of people from many cities (Josephus, *War* 2.515; Acts 2:1–10; B. Megillah 26a; B. Pesahim 64b), it was hardly the case that everyone in the diaspora or even in the Land of Israel went.

The practice of pilgrimages to Jerusalem continued after the Temple's destruction in 70 C.E. The Talmud reports the sadness of those who saw Jerusalem's ruins and speaks of those who abstained from wine and meat on that occasion (see, e.g., B. Moed Katan 26a; B. Shebuot 20a).

pillars in Jerusalem a reference to James, Cephas (Peter), and John as the leaders of the Christian community in Jerusalem (Gal. 2:9). The metaphor derives from the broader image of the church as a building and specifically as God's temple (cf. also Rev. 3:12), and it is related to Peter's prominent function as "the rock" on which Jesus is said to have built his church (Matt. 16:16–19).

pilpul dialectical reasoning in study of oral law

Pinhas *see* PINHAS B. HAMA

Pinḥas b. Ḥama Palestinian amora of the fourth century C.E.; a member of a priestly family; referred to in the Jerusalem Talmud and Genesis Rabbah as R. Pinḥas, without the patronymic. He was a contemporary of Yose, with whom he appears in dispute, and teacher to Ḥananiah, who transmits many of his legal statements.

Pinḥas b. Yair Tannaitic authority of the late second century C.E., known for his piety and ability to work miracles; a son-in-law of Simeon b. Yoḥai. Pinḥas is cited primarily in exegetical comments and is recalled for his activities in redeeming captives, from which work even natural disasters did not stop him (B. Ḥullin 7a–b).

pirka (Aram., period) used in the talmudic literature in reference to study sessions (e.g., B. Pesaḥim 100a) or lectures held in different locations at fixed periods (e.g., B. Ketubot 62a). The latter allowed individuals to study rabbinic lore without leaving home.

Pirke Abot *see* ABOT

pit (Heb.: *bor* and *shaḥat,* from verb *shuaḥ*) commonly used in the Bible and the Qumran scrolls as a metonymy for the grave, or Sheol, or the place of eternal damnation. The noun *shaḥat* is perhaps used with an eye toward the Hebrew verb *shaḥat,* "to destroy."

piyyut *see* SYNAGOGUE POETRY

Plant. *see* DE PLANTATIONE

platform (Heb.: *dukhan*) place in the Temple on which Levites sang psalms while the animal sacrifices were offered and priests stood to recite the priestly benediction. In synagogue liturgy, *dukhan* gained the sense of the act of bestowing.

Platonism philosophical school founded by Plato (429–347 B.C.E.) and referred to as the Academy, which taught the reality, not of the material world of sense perception, but of the invisible world of forms, accessible to logic. The school continued formally until Justinian closed it in the sixth century C.E., though its influence continues to the present day. According to Platonism's teachings, the goal of life was that the soul would become free from being reborn into the material world (*metempsychosis*). Not long after Plato's death, Platonism became dominated by Skepticism, which emphasized the human mind's inability to determine truth and reality. However, in the Roman period this was succeeded by Middle Platonism and Neoplatonism, which returned to the central core of the Old Academy (original Platonism), though these later developments also included significant influence from Stoicism. A distinction between Middle Platonism and Neoplatonism is not clearly established among

scholars, and although it is agreed that Philo of Alexandria was significantly influenced by Platonism, some (but not all) consider him an important representative of Middle Platonism.

pleasure (Heb.: *ratzon;* Gr.: *eudokia*) the special favor or delight that God bestows on the chosen. An especially important text is Isaiah 42:1, "Behold my servant whom I uphold, my chosen one, in whom my soul delights; I have put my spirit upon him." 1 Enoch 49:3–4 applies the text to the chosen one or "son of man," who is also God's anointed one (48:10). Mark 1:11 uses this language with reference to Jesus, who is depicted as Messiah and servant. At Qumran "the chosen of his good pleasure" and "the sons of your good pleasure" are technical expressions for members of the Dead Sea community (1QS 8:6; 1QH 11:9). In Luke 2:14 the plural expression denotes God's people who will be blessed through the birth of Jesus the Messiah. *See also* CHOSEN ONE; CHOSEN ONES.

Pliny the Elder (23/24–79 C.E.) Roman writer. His father was wealthy enough to educate Pliny and to allow him to embark upon an equestrian career at about the age of twenty-three. He served for the next twelve years with troops on the Rhine. He had no official posts under Nero, but returned to prominence when Vespasian became emperor. He served in Germany with Titus and held a number of procuratorships. At this time he wrote his *Natural History,* which he dedicated to Titus. He died observing the eruption of Vesuvius in 79. The *Natural History* contains a paragraph on the Essenes in his discussion of Judea.

Plotina wife of the emperor Trajan (r. 98–117 C.E.). A papyrus fragment, probably fictional, records that she sided with the Jews over the Alexandrians when they sought Trajan's aid in solving a dispute. There is no other evidence that Plotina favored the Jews or of a dispute in Alexandria between Jews and Greeks during Trajan's reign.

Plutarch (c. 45–125 C.E.) Greek writer and priest of Delphi. He was unusual in living and working on mainland Greece, which had become a backwater, more or less, in the Greek cultural world. Plutarch's two main writings are the *Parallel Lives,* in which he compares the lives of the major figures of Greek and Roman history, and the *Moralia,* which consists of treatises on all sorts of subjects, from literary criticism to moral and ethical conduct to philosophy and religion. It is especially in the *Moralia* that he makes several important references to Jews. One of these is a description of the Sukkot celebrations in the Jerusalem Temple, but from the point of view of an outside observer and nonparticipant. In some of his symposium literature, he discusses the Jewish concept of God. He also identifies Judaism with the worship of Dionysus, as did some other writers. The value of Plutarch is that he gives the perspective of a trained and curious observer, interested in philosophical inquiry, but not necessarily a Jewish sympathizer. Although he considered Judaism a superstition, he felt the same about other non-Greek religions.

pneuma (Gr., spirit, or wind) term that can refer to the physical wind, but which often means the individual spirit or life of a person. It can also be used in reference to God's spirit. In the Septuagint, it is the usual translation of the Hebrew *ruah*.

poetry Much of our understanding of the forms and conventions of Hebrew poetry has been developed from the study of the poetry in the Bible, especially the older poems (Exod. 15, Judg. 5, Hab. 3) and poems composed over many centuries and collected in the biblical psalter. However, religious poetry continued to be written throughout the Second Temple period, and we are able to see elements of both continuity and change in terms of style, topics, forms, and usage.

Many of these poetic compositions are preserved in the Apocrypha and Pseudepigrapha, and thus often are available only in translation into Greek, Latin, Ethiopic, and other languages. Although a close study of poetic forms is more difficult in translation, many of the features of parallelism, balance, repetition, strophic divisions, and imagery are still recoverable. There are a variety of types: hymnic songs of praise, modeled very closely on biblical psalms (the Songs of the Three Jews), victory songs (Jdt. 16), wisdom poems (Bar. 3:9–4:4, Sir. 24), poems of consolation (Bar. 4:5–5:8), lamentations (1 Macc. 1:36–40; 2:7–13; the lament of Seila; LAB 40.5–7), and euologies (1 Macc. 3:3–9; 14:4–15). Some of the poetry of the New Testament, particularly the Magnificat and the Benedictus in Luke 1, was translated from a Semitic original or at least written in a very Semiticized Greek and exhibits many of the same features.

From the Dead Sea Scrolls, we now have a much larger corpus of poetry in Hebrew and Aramaic. Although many manuscripts are too fragmentary to recover the poetic structures with any certainty, the Thanksgiving Scroll from Cave 1 at Qumran preserved over thirty poems, some of them virtually complete. Although sometimes these have been evaluated solely in terms of the conventions of the biblical psalms and found wanting, recent scholarship has been more sensitive to the way that these poems reflect different and developing poetic con-

ventions. Certainly the basic poetic line tends to be longer than in the biblical psalms, often nine to thirteen syllables; sometimes there is a "double line" that cannot be divided into shorter cola because of its grammatical structure. There is parallelism, but it is quite fluid, with more complex patterning spread over a series of bicola and tricola (two- or three-line units); sometimes, however, the parallelism is internal within a line. Tricola are very frequent, but exhibit considerable variation; the second and third lines can be synonymous, or both infinitive clauses. A distinctive feature is the way nouns, infinitives, and prepositional phrases are used in a listlike fashion; this is not so much a prosaic feature but points to similar usage in later Hekhalot poetry. Most of the poems can be divided into strophes, although the precise points of division are not always certain; often new units are indicated by the personal pronoun (first or second person), an interrogative, the conjunction *ki*, or the repetition of similar language or grammatical structure at the beginning and at the end to form an inclusio. The vocabulary of the Hodayot is rich, with a surprising number of words not attested in the biblical psalter. Images are complex and often developed over an extended series of cola or a whole strophe. Although in only one case is there an extended quotation from a biblical psalm, the poems "sound biblical" because of the extensive reuse of biblical metaphors and standardized phrases; these are not mechanically quoted but rather reworked in a fresh and creative way.

Our corpus of poetry in Aramaic is much smaller and the conventions still less well understood. One of the most interesting examples is the lengthy poem in Genesis Apocryphon 20:2–8a, which describes Sarah's beauty in a style reminiscent of the Song of Songs and later Arabic *wasf* poetry.

poetry in Greek Although Jews are not known for their poetry in Greek, Jewish authors did write some poetic works, and part of these survive. A number of the Fragmentary Hellenistic Jewish writers produced poetry, including Ezekiel the Tragedian, Philo the Elder, and Theodotus. Also extant are anonymous verses ascribed to Homer, Sophocles, Pythagoras, Orpheus, and Menander. These are known only in isolated verses and fragments, but we also have complete poems in Pseudo-Phocylides, some of the Sibylline Oracles, and the Wisdom of Solomon.

Poimandres a writing in the Hermetica, a collection of late Egyptian religious writings in Greek. Poimandres is a Gnostic writing with many Jewish traditions (e.g., literary dependence on 2 Enoch has been argued) and is thought by some to be an example of Jewish Gnosticism.

polis (Gr., city) In ancient Greece, the polis was a city-state, comprising a major city, along with its territory and smaller towns and villages. There were only a few thousand citizens, with the bulk of the population made up of slaves or foreign noncitizens. The citizens governed the city-state, though there was not a uniform system of government. Sparta, for example, was governed by a dual kingship. Athens, though, was famous for a democatic form of government in which the citizens met in a large assembly to vote on laws and policies. Some cities had a representative council (*boulē*) or perhaps a council of elders (*gerousia*). In the Hellenistic period, Greek cities were founded all over the ancient Near East. Unlike the kingdoms of classical Greece, they were not autonymous entities but were ultimately under the control of the ruling power; however, they did have certain rights of self-government and were treated as semi-autonomous. The form of government varied, though many followed the Athenian model. At the heart of each city was the gymnasium. Noncitizens were not allowed a part in the government, though ethnic communities might be allowed to form a *politeuma* (governing body). *See also* HELLENISTIC REFORM.

politeuma the governing structure of ethnic and other communities in Greek cities. Though the Greek city (polis) was self-governing, this privilege applied only to citizens. In most Greek cities, there were relatively few citizens. Many of the inhabitants were slaves or temporary residents; most cities, however, also had a large population of permanent residents who were not citizens. In many cities, large resident ethnic communities had arisen. Because of their common background and customs, such communities were often allowed to organize into a *politeuma,* which was a semi-autonomous body within the city. It could elect or appoint its own officials and have its own form of government. It could enforce its own laws (within certain limits) on the members of the community and hold sessions of its own courts to try offenders. Naturally, the members of the *politeuma* had to obey the laws of the city as well, and laws could not be passed that conflicted with the city laws. The officials of the community could also be held accountable to the city government for actions of the community. Otherwise, the *politeuma* had a good deal of independence.

political theory, rabbinic the set of rules about who may legitimately do what to whom. The Mishnah sets forth a view of power and of the disposi-

tion of power in society that is fundamentally political. But the political theory of Judaism works out an essentially theological problem, which is the distribution of responsibility and power. What makes matters political is that the system treats violence as legitimate when exercised by proper authority. Indeed, it specifies who may impose his will through coercion. That defines within the framework of the faith a political structure and system that are integral to its religious plan for the social order. To the sages of Judaism, represented by the Mishnah, the separation of power in the form of legitimate violence from power in other forms, supernatural ones, for instance, proves implausible. To them, as in the Graeco-Roman philosophical tradition in political theory, politics forms a component of the social order. Power is not to be separated from other critical elements of that same order. Politics and power cannot be treated as an independent topic of inquiry, for in antiquity, what we say about politics forms a chapter in a larger statement within our theory of the social order. Politics, then, is subordinated, contingent, instrumental. Treating politics as limited to the use of violence to achieve one's will proves a distinctively modern reading of matters. The task undertaken by the political myth of Judaism is not only to make power specific and particular to cases. It is especially a labor of differentiation of power, indicating what agency or person has the power to precipitate the working of politics as legitimate violence at all. When, therefore, one understands the differentiating force of myth that imparts to politics its activity and dynamism, one shall grasp what everywhere animates the structures of the politics and propels the system. Appealing to a myth of taxonomy, the system accomplishes its tasks by explaining why this and not that, by telling as its foundation story a myth of classification for the application of legitimate violence. The myth appeals in the end to the critical bases for the taxonomy, among institutions, of a generalized power to coerce. The encompassing framework of rules, institutions, and sanctions is explained and validated by appeal to the myth of God's shared rule. That dominion, exercised by God and his surrogates on earth, is focused partly in the royal palace, partly in the Temple, and partly in the court. The issue here is the differentiation of power, which is to say, which part falls where and why? The political myth of Judaism explains who exercises legitimate violence and under what conditions, and furthermore specifies the source for differentiation. The Judaic political myth comes to expression in its details of differentiation.

Pollion Pharisee and teacher of Samaias. He advised the people of Jerusalem to admit Herod the Great and the Roman general Sosius in 37 B.C.E. Because Herod favored him, he and his disciples were exempted from the oath of loyalty in 20 B.C.E. He is often identified with the rabbinic figure Abtalion.

Polybius (c. 200–120 B.C.E.) Greek historian. In 168, he was one of the Greek persons of eminence taken to Rome as a hostage. He spent many years there under the patronage of the Scipio family and came to admire the Romans and their rise to power. His *Histories* give the story of Rome's ascent to become the most important power in the Mediterranean. In doing so, the work provides important background for Jewish history during the Ptolemaic, Seleucid, and early Maccabean periods. Although the extant history says little about Palestine directly, it does make explicit references to Judea when it mentions the taking of Jerusalem by Antiochus III in 200 B.C.E. and Antiochus IV's plundering of the Temple. Polybius is considered one of the best historians of antiquity, perhaps second only to Thucydides. Unfortunately, only books 1–5 (covering c. 250–215 B.C.E.) are complete, with the rest known only to a lesser or greater extent in a medieval epitome (summary) and fragments; however, in antiquity when the entire work was still known, it served as an important source for other writers, such as Livy.

polygamy *see* MONOGAMY AND POLYGAMY

pomegranate a motif in ancient Jewish art, perhaps connected with the biblical view that the pomegranate is a symbol for the fertility of the land (Num. 13:23). The pomegranate played a role in the biblical period, and it continued to be used on coins, glass, sarcophagi, ossuaries, in synagogue art, and in tomb art. For example, on bronze coins of John Hyrcanus I (135 B.C.E.), one sees on the reverse double cornucopias with a pomegranate between horns. The pomegranate was used again on silver coins of the First Revolt (66–74 C.E.). On the reverse one sees within the inscription "Jerusalem the Holy" (or "Jerusalem is Holy") three pomegranates on one branch. In Jewish art that features the agricultural richness of the land, pomegranates are likely to be found. For example, the pomegranate appears frequently on the friezes of the synagogue at Capernaum, but also on a fragment of the marble screen from the synagogue of Hammath-Tiberias. The pomegranate is found in the repeated design of the mosaic floor of the synagogue at Hammath-Gader across the Jordan, but also in the mosaic floor of the synagogue at Beth Alpha near Beth Shean. The pomegranate is a feature of the mosaic floor from Isfiya on Mount Carmel. In tomb art, including sarcophagi, the pomegranate is prominent, though not always modeled realistically.

Pompeius Falco *see* FALCO, QUINTUS POMPEIUS

Pompeius Longinus *see* LONGINUS, GNAEUS POMPEIUS

Pompeius Trogus Greek historian who flourished in the early first century C.E. His *Histories* formed a world history from earliest times to Augustus. Unfortunately, his work as such has survived only in fragments. What we know of it comes primarily from an epitome (abridged version) by the Roman writer Justinus, who wrote around the third century C.E. The work helps to fill in our knowledge of Persian, Ptolemaic, and Seleucid history and thus serves as background to the history of Judea during these periods. Only a few passages give direct references to Judea or Judaism. He shows a detailed knowledge of some parts of the Pentateuch, along with a good deal of muddle. He makes Abraham a king of Damascus, followed by Israel, who had ten sons. One of these sons, Joseph, was sold into Egypt, where he became the first to establish the science of interpreting dreams. His son was Moses, but he was expelled along with many who had leprous and other diseases. Moses led the expelled to his ancestral home, Damascus. The Sabbath arose as a celebration for surviving seven days without food in the desert. Pompeius also mentions the Dead Sea and some of the natural products of Palestine.

Pompey (106–48 B.C.E.) Roman general and member of first triumvirate (60 B.C.E.). Gnaeus Pompey, known as "The Great," came to prominence through military prowess in the turbulent period of the late Republic in Rome. After assisting Crassus in bringing the slave war to an end, he had himself appointed consul and in 67 extracted from the Senate extraordinary powers against the pirates who had infested the Mediterranean and damaged Roman trade links with the East. He was victorious within a period of three months. After defeating Mithridates, king of Pontus, he organized his territories into the provinces of Bithynia-Pontus and Syria. At this point he was invited to intervene in the affairs of the Jews in order to settle the dispute between two rival Hasmonean claimants. In 63 B.C.E. he captured Jerusalem, entered the Temple there, but did not rob it of its treasures as Antiochus IV had done a century earlier. He then settled the Jewish question by dismantling the Hasmonean state, appointing Hyrcanus as high priest and ethnarch, and restoring independence to the Greek cities of Palestine. Pompey joined Caesar and Crassus as a member of the first triumvirate in 60 B.C.E. that marked the transition from republican to imperial rule, but after the death of Crassus in 53, he became embroiled in a struggle for sole power. He was defeated by Caesar at Pharsalis in Greece in 48 B.C.E. and died soon afterwards in Egypt. Pompey was an able general, who after his early years of flouting the Senate's position because of his military prowess adopted a constitutional stance against Caesar's ambitions.

Pontius Pilate *see* PILATE, PONTIUS

poor those lacking food, shelter, and/or sufficient land for farming, as well as those suffering social injustice (e.g., Isa 32:7; Amos, pass.). The existence of the poor is permanent (Deut. 15:11, paraphrased in Mark 14:7, Matt. 26:11, and John 12:8, where Jesus defends the woman who spent money on anointing him rather than on the poor), as are the commands to improve their lot. Only if the people obey their God and follow all the commandments will there be no poor (Deut. 16:4–5). Not only are the poor protected by heaven (Isa. 29:19; Ps. 10, 12, 68; Ps. Sol. 5, 15), those with greater assets are required to aid them (Exod. 23:11; Lev. 19:9–10; see also Josephus, *Ant.* 4.8.21; Philo, *Virt.* 17). The poor's care is also mandated by 2 Enoch 63; Pseudo-Phocylides 10; Testament of Jacob 7 and throughout the Testament of Job. Ahikar claims there is nothing more bitter than poverty (105; also Sentences of Syriac Menander 427–432). However, some wisdom literature attributes poverty to the failure to heed instruction and to laziness (Prov. 13:18, 20:13). The Gospel of Luke places particular emphasis on responsibility to the poor (4:18–21 and 7:22 citing Isa. 61:1; see also Matt. 11:5). Paul seeks from his Gentile congregations a collection for the "poor," i.e., the church members, in Jerusalem (Rom. 15:26; Gal. 2:10; 2 Cor. 8–9; also Cor. 16:1-4). The Testament of Isaac 14 offers instructions for how the poor are to mourn. The designation "poor" applies also to those who abandon social prestige for religious asceticism or who lack spiritual goods. "Congregation of the poor" appears in the Qumran Scrolls (e.g., 4QpPs37 3:10). Matthew 5:3 speaks of the "poor in spirit." The Jewish-Christian Ebionites likely took their name from the Hebrew *ebionim* (the poor).

In Judaism, support of the poor is viewed as an act of religious righteousness (*tzedakah*), incumbent upon all people of means. Judaism recognizes that God, as ultimate owner of the land, is entitled to a portion of all that the land produces. According to scripture, God designates parts of his share for the poor, the widow, the orphan, the Levite, and the stranger. Accordingly, in providing for the poor, Israelites not only carry out the will of God but actually act on behalf of God, distributing God's share of the earth's produce to those God designated for its benefit.

The fundamental rabbinic elements of support for the poor derive from scripture, which assigns to the poor that which grows in the corner of a field (*peah;* Lev. 19:9, 23:22), gleanings (*leket;* Lev. 19:9, 23:22), forgotten sheaves (*shikhah;* Deut. 24:19), a tithe in each third year (*maaser ani;* Deut. 14:28–29), separated grapes (*peret;* Lev. 19:10), defective clusters (*olelot;* Lev. 19:10; Deut. 24:21), and all of the produce of the Sabbatical year (Exod. 23:11). The Mishnah tractate Peah details the rule for distribution of that which grows in the corner of the field, gleanings, and forgotten sheaves. The Mishnah's central principle is that the farmer may play no active role in identifying which specific produce is to be set aside for the poor. Rather, this happens accidentally, when the farmer leaves some grain unharvested, drops a few stalks in the field, or forgets to collect some of his sheaves. Since in rabbinic Judaism, that which happens unintentionally is associated with the will of God, the Mishnah's view of the payment of poor-offerings suggests its recognition of the poor's direct claim upon God for support.

Already in Talmudic times, the development of a cash economy and the inaccessibility of farmland to most poor people necessitated a type of support for the poor not clearly defined by scripture. Responding to this need, Talmudic Judaism developed an intricate system of charity and expected all members of the community actively to ensure that the poor were fed and clothed. Charity was collected and dispersed through a community chest, to which all people of means were expected to contribute and from which anyone in need could take. Anonymous gifts were deemed particularly meritorious (B. Ketubot 67b), and emphasis was upon providing a means for the poor to return to self-support (B. Shabbat 63b).

poor man's tithe a tenth of the crop, to be distributed among the local poor in the third and sixth years of the Sabbatical cycle

pork As pork was a highly prized food in the Mediterranean world, the Jews' refusal to eat it came to symbolize their sense of separation from the gentile world. So the martyr Eleazar was asked to eat pork and, on his refusal, was executed (2 Macc. 6:18; 4 Macc. 5:2). To defile the Temple at Jerusalem, swine and other unclean beasts were offered in sacrifice (1 Macc. 1:47). Pigs are used as a code word for the unclean world in Mark 6:11–13 and Luke 15:15. Attempts by Gentiles to explain why Jews do not eat pork are found in Plutarch's *Dinner Conversations* 4.5. *See also* FOOD TABOOS.

porneia (Gr., fornication) term specifically applied to prostituion but also used broadly for any kind of unlawful sexual activity. It was usually the generic word, whereas other terms were used for more specific sexual misdeeds (e.g., *moicheia* for adultery).

Porphyry Greek writer and Neoplatonist philosopher from Tyre in the third century C.E. One of his writings was an attack on Christianity, called *Against the Christians;* unfortunately, it is known only from quotations, especially in the commentary on Daniel by Jerome. Here his ideas are particularly interesting because he anticipated modern biblical criticism by arguing that Daniel 7–12 was actually written in the second century B.C.E., not the sixth. Despite his opposition to Christianity, he makes a number of positive references to Jews and Judaism. He regards Judaism not only as superior to Christianity but also as one of the ancient religions (along with those of the Phoenicians, Assyrians, and Egyptians) with a correct view of God. He justifies the Jewish abstention from pork on the ground that many different peoples have food taboos. Other laws of the Pentateuch about animals are also quoted with approval, such as not taking both parent birds and their offspring. In one long passage, he paraphrases Josephus at length on the Essenes, evidently seeing them as a fascinating philosophical group, much as Josephus did.

portents signs or phenomena that were interpreted as indications of the future, usually of disaster. It was a common belief in antiquity that God would send such signs to herald coming troubles. It was common for even the most sober historian to mention them as, for example, before the fall of the Temple.

Posidonius of Apamea (c. 135–50 B.C.E.) Greek writer and polymath. His works, preserved only in fragments, mention Jews directly only a couple of times, once in reference to bitumen collection from the Dead Sea. Josephus accuses Posidonius of anti-Semitic views, seeming to imply that the story of Apion about a Greek imprisoned in the Temple in preparation for human sacrifice came from him, but the fragmentary nature of the text makes it difficult to be certain about his real views. He also wrote a history, which has perished but which Josephus may have used, either directly or indirectly.

Post. *see* DE POSTERITATE CAINI

pottery objects made of clay, usually turned on a wheel, and fired in a kiln. The most important

archaeological evidence for indicating dating, trade and commerce, and regional patterns of interaction of people depends on the controlled recovery and study of pottery found on an archaeological site. The reason for this lies in a series of truisms well known to professional archaeologists, but little understood by nonpractitioners of field work.

Pottery is made of clay, almost always during the biblical period formed on a wheel, which, when fired in a kiln, retains its visual qualities and shape permanently. Fired clay, then, is virtually indestructible. Its manufacture or use on a site leaves a permanent record as either whole vessel forms, usually found only in shipwrecks, tombs, cisterns, and upon the floors of buildings that experienced the kind of instantaneous destruction represented by fire or earthquake, or as broken shards. Examination of the various whole-vessel forms in any given age make the study of even broken and partial pottery pieces (sherds) identifiable and, therefore, of paramount scientific importance.

It is mostly the small broken pieces of a pot that are recovered in excavations of sites and structures. The most important pieces of a broken vessel are the rims, handles, and bases because these are the indicators that enable the archaeologist to "read" the pottery, that is, to recognize and classify the vessel type and date. It is the very uselessness of a broken vessel to ancient peoples that makes ceramic evidence the most reliable dating and commerce indicator in assessing a site's history. Coins had an inherent, continuing value based on the metal in the coin. The value of ancient coinage was based on the amount of metal in the coin itself and not in any modern concept of the "promise" of a mint or government to "redeem" a coin for an agreed upon amount of real money. Thus inhabitants, subsequent "campers" on a site, and later treasure hunters search out and remove most of this kind of evidence from an archaeological site long before the professionals arrive to excavate scientifically and record carefully all evidence on the site.

Types of pottery. Pottery is classified according to two differing types, based on the quality of the clay used to manufacture a pot and on its function in the daily life of its users: crude ware and fine ware. As the names suggest, crude ware is made from roughly prepared clays with a high content of gritty particles and is used in the kitchen (cook pots, casseroles, pitchers, jugs and jars) and for large storage and shipping amphorae. Fine ware is made from carefully prepared, well-fired clays and is used to manufacture the fancy black and red, slipped tableware so loved by Mediterranean peoples throughout the entire historical period under consideration.

Crude ware vessel forms tend to continue the same shapes and types for long periods of time, often up to a hundred years. This is due to several factors. Local cuisines remain stable and require storage and cooking in the same kinds of vessels. People learn to cook from their primary families and want the same kinds of utensils which were employed when they learned to cook. The easily recognizable standardized shapes of large storage and shipping vessels termed amphorae served to advertise both the type of contents (wine, fish sauce, oil) and frequently the place and company of manufacture. In a famous Roman literary banquet scene called *Trimalchio's Feast,* the guests at the party realize that their host has served them an inexpensive wine and kept the best wine for himself when they see the shape of the amphora from which their host's wine is drawn. The long continuance of crude ware vessel forms diminishes somewhat their value for precise dating when such vessels and their shards are found with no dateable coins.

Fine ware pottery shapes, however, change more quickly, since these kind of dishes are less determined by daily function and are more subject to changing fashion. Thus, the recovery of fine ware forms can aid in giving more chronological precision to excavation, since the longest most shapes perdure is c. fifty years (with many characteristic shapes and types in use for only around twenty-five years). In Israel, despite occasional false reports to the contrary, such as the alleged find of fine ware manufacturing kilns from the Herodian period at the northern Negeb site of Oboda, all fine wares are imported from outside the country. Most came from Greece, Italy, Gaul (France), Egypt, Cyprus, Asia Minor, and North Africa (primarily Carthage), depending on what archaeological period is under excavation. The sole exception to this is probably Judaean, locally manufactured fine ware of the Byzantine period called "Judaean sigillata." Precisely because fine tableware is imported, it serves as evidence of trade links between sites in Israel and other Mediterranean areas.

Moreover, the Institute of Archeometry of the Hebrew University Institute of Archaeology in Jerusalem has perfected over the last twenty years a process involving the neutron activation of sherd samples found on sites. By breaking the shard down under neutron bombardment into its trace elements, it is possible to match the trace elements of the clay in the shard with the "print" of clay beds in Israel, to locate the sources of the clay, and also to classify the pots into "pottery families."

Such new "families" of clays and pottery types have enabled researchers like D. Adan-Bayewitz to track the sales routes of itinerant pottery peddlers in Roman Galilee. While clay bed "prints" are not available for the entire Mediterranean, we do know what clays are "foreign" to Israel. Thus, we know at least when we are dealing with pottery that has come from outside the country.

Whether one is considering crude or fine ware pottery, however, the shapes or forms of individual vessel types do evolve over time. It is this kind of variance in shape that enables the archaeologist to trace the evolution, and hence, the chronological sequence of a particular kind of pot. For example, the rims of cooking pots become progressively higher or lower over time, or the bodies become more globular or squat. Lips of vessels tend to evert and droop over time or to gradually lift. Handles that were once functional can, over time, become small, vestigial lumps of clay that appear exactly where a handle would have been placed on an earlier vessel of the same type.

In the light of the crucial importance of pottery for determining the chronological horizons and sequencing of a site, it is necessary when using an archaeological report to make sure that the pottery found in excavation has been catalogued, described and studied in the publication, and that section drawings (profiles) of the individual sherds or pots have been published. Otherwise, readers are dependent solely on the word of the excavator, whose dating results cannot be checked by comparing pottery from one site to that recovered from the same time period on other sites.

Some indicator vessels for the Persian through the Byzantine periods. The least published and studied pottery of all the periods is that of the Persian period. Discussions even continue among scholars as to whether this period should better be seen as the very end of the Iron Age. Hence, it is sometimes called Iron III. One of the sure signs of a Persian occupation on a site is the large white, slipped bowl which appears on sites the length and breadth of the country. In the 1977 excavations of the synagogue of Gush Halav, the excavators were stunned to discover that this much-surveyed, single-period site was in reality a tel with a long occupational history, thanks to the presence of this Persian-period form among the late Roman-period shards. Recent study of the

Persian-period sites across the entire country has also revealed a pervasive early contact between Israel and Greece. To date, not a single Persian-period site has been excavated on which some examples of pottery imported from Greece has not been found. Thus, the beginning of extensive trade and commerce between Israel and the Hellenic world, which historians reserved to the period after Alexander the Great's Conquests, has now been pushed back several centuries in time.

The Hellenistic period saw the introduction of a series of black-slipped and red-slipped fine ware dishes manufactured in the eastern Mediterranean. Earlier attributions of these dishes to local imitations of western pottery have now been set aside. Tel Anafah and Samaria-Sebastia have produced the best published collections of such pottery. Also, among the favorites of the Hellenistic age were imported amphorae from Rhodes and Kos and large, rounded, high-rimmed cookers with large handles attached from lip to shoulder.

The Herodian period saw, as one could expect from the close ties established between the house of Herod and the emperors at Rome, an influx of western "terra sigillata," which means signed earth. This designation was made by the potter's stamp or name on the bottom of plates, cups, and dishes. Such high-gloss and beautifully manufactured red ware was imported from Italy primarily, as were the numerous large wine amphorae imported from the countryside around Rome. Caesarea Maritima has produced the best corpus of these latter vessels. The large ovoid storage jar with ring handles right at the break between the shoulder and the wall of the vessel were common in Judaea and were the hiding vessels for the Qumran scrolls.

By the time of the Bar Kochba Revolt (132–135 C.E.), imported fine pottery ceased to be a factor on sites in Palestine. Local wares, except for a small dribble of fine wares in seaports like Caesarea Maritima, supplied the need for cups, bowls, and juglets. The sites of Capernaum and Meiron provide the best examples of preferred vessels for the second and third centuries. Cooking pots with everted and grooved rims and jars with everted rims open the period, but in these early deposits, we see the first examples of what is the best indicator of Galilean manufacture and occupation—the Galilean bowl. This exterior-ridged, open bowl continued in use and development in the Galilee and parts of the Golan for nearly two hundred years. Though the rim development and precise datings of this had been known for over a decade,

thanks to careful recovery in excavations of shards with coins, it was not until the 1980 excavations at Naburiya that examples preserved from rim to base were first discovered.

Pottery from the Byzantine period, roughly from the late-third to mid-fourth centuries (c. 640 C.E.), represents the best archaeological look at Israel's trade links with the wider Mediterranean world and at its own highly developed, locally made, regional ceramic products.

Imported pottery to the end of antiquity. After nearly a century and a half hiatus of imported fine wares, in the closing decades of the third century and the opening of the fourth, imported red ware bowls begin to appear on sites in the interior of the country. Small North African bowls lead the way, followed in the middle of the century by Cypriot red slip ware bowls, so termed because of visual similarity to much earlier products made in Cyprus, although the manufacturing place of these has not yet been found. By the opening decade of the fifth century, the third kind of late fine ware appears on sites across the country. This type will become the predominant imported pottery for the whole north of Israel until the Arab conquest. It is called Phocaean red slip ware, formerly "late Roman C ware."

These three imported fine wares are found in all regions of the country, but differences in distribution allow us to draw some conclusions about trade influences. In the north the predominance of Phocaean ware indicates extensive trade links to Asia Minor. In the northern Negev, the predominance of African red slip ware indicates primary trade with North Africa, which was interrupted in the fifth and early sixth centuries by the Vandal conquest of North Africa. Also, the predominance in the Negeb of red ware manufactured in Egypt and its appearance in only small numbers at seaports like Caesarea Maritima underscores that region's trade links to the south.

Regional crude ware pottery. If imported pottery helps us track the differences in international trading patterns for the various regions of the country, the advances that have been made in understanding regional pottery tastes help us to trace the independence and complexity of the various regions and subregions of the Holy Land. The surest way to know the place of manufacture of a pot is to find the kiln site that made it. By no means have all the regional kilns operating in late antiquity yet been found. At this stage of discovery and research, we do know that each region probably had its own preferred pottery factory or factories. In the north, the Galilean bowl was a locally distributed, hence manufactured, product. The extensive excavations in Jerusalem and environs indicate local Judaean production of both crude and fine ware vessels, Judaean sigillata. A storage and shipping amphora found all over the south and erroneously known as the Gaza jar was made in Ashkalon. The large, bag-shaped, black-ribbed northern amphora, decorated with paint dribbling down it, was probably made and used in the north coastal plain. The brittle red-brown cookers of the Golan region must have been locally manufactured. The soft, flaky, brown amphorae found throughout the Negev must have been produced in or near one of those desert cities.

Thus, the scientific recovery and publication of pottery constitutes one of the most important pieces in reconstructing the history, commerce, and daily life of people in ancient Israel.

powers, of God   *see* DYNAMEIS

praefectus   *see* PREFECT

Praem.   *see* DE PRAEMIIS ET POENIS

praetor   Roman chief magistrate with a rank just below that of consul. Originally, the praetors were mainly concerned with military affairs, but as time passed they took on the function of judges in judicial matters. The power of the office declined during the early Roman Empire.

prayer   words of address to God. In the broadest sense, prayer includes any type of address (praise, thanksgiving, blessing, lament, petition) whether in prose or poetry, by the individual or the community, in spontaneous one-time-occasion words or in set predetermined formulas. However, often a distinction is made between formal poetic texts that were originally rooted in the Temple and cultic realm (particularly the collection of 150 psalms in the Psalter) and prayers that are compositions in prose, almost always containing an element of petition. It is the latter that will be the focus here.

The Hebrew Bible provides the precedence for both the practice of prayer in all times, places, and situations of need, and for examples of various forms of prayer. About one hundred prose prayers are found, ranging from the simple direct petitions ("Lord, heal her," Num. 12:13), to longer more formally developed prayers combining elements of praise and petition (1 Kings 8:22–53; 1 Chron. 29:10–19), and extended prayers of historical remembrance and repentance (Neh. 9; Ezra. 9).

The literature of the Graeco-Roman period continues and expands this tradition, with the composition of many new prayers in Hebrew, Greek, and Aramaic. In addition, there are numerous references to people praying, even when the exact words are not given (e.g., the prayer of the scribe in Ecclus. 39:5, 6; prayer before battle in 1 Macc. 5:33 and 2 Macc. 10:26–27; the custom of prayer three times a day in Dan. 6:10). Biblical models are followed for how a prayer should be structured, though there is a notable increase in prayers that begin with blessing formularies.

In almost every narrative work from this period, the main character prays at crucial moments in the action; examples include the prayers of all the leading characters in the Book of Tobit (3:2–6, 11–15; 8:5–6, 15–17; 11:14–15), Judith (9:1–14, and 13:4–5 and 7, which continue the biblical pattern of the short petition), the priests Simon and Eleazar (3 Macc. 2:2–20, 6:2–15), and the convert Asenath (Joseph and Asenath 12–14, 21:11–21). These prayers provide a religious and pietistic dimension to the narrative and often serve as vehicles for the author's theological views.

In addition, prayers were added to biblical works that lacked them, for example, the prayers of Mordecai (13:8–18) and Esther (14:1–19) preserved in the Greek version of Esther, and the Prayer of Azariah and the Song of the Three Children added to Dan 3:23. The Prayer of Manasseh fills in the missing prayer of penitence which is only referred to in 2 Chronicles 33:10–13, 18–19. In works that retell the biblical stories with expansions, amplifications, and additions, prayers are often added. For example, in retelling the biblical story from Adam to Saul, the Book of Biblical Antiquities adds some twenty-five short prose prayers and four psalms; Genesis Apocryphon adds the prayer of Abraham when Sarah is taken from him (20:12–16); Jubilees adds prayers of Moses (1:19–21), Noah (10:3–6), and Abraham (12:19–21, 22:6–9).

In addition to these literary prayers, most scholars have presumed that some type of set, formal prayer was part of the developing institution of the synagogue in the pre-70 period, though no such collections of prayers had survived. Recently, in Cave 4 at Qumran, various collections of set prayers have been recovered, though all are in a very fragmentary form. There are prayers for morning and evening of each day of the month (4Q503), prayers for each day of the week (4Q504–6), and prayers for feasts (specifically the Day of Atonement and First Fruit, 4Q507–9). On the basis of the language, the very early date of some of the copies, as well as the calendar presumed in the daily prayers, these should not necessarily be seen as composed specifically by the Qumran Community, but may give us a glimpse into patterns of prayer that were developing more widely in Second Temple Judaism. The prayers are short, with opening and concluding formulas ("Remember, O Lord," "Blessed is the God of Israel"); that is, we can see the beginnings of certain features of later synagogal prayer, but there is little standardization at this stage.

Prayer of Manasseh   *see* MANASSEH, PRAYER OF

Prayer of Nabonidus   *see* NABONIDUS, PRAYER OF

prayer shawl   (Heb.: *tallit*) four-cornered cloth with fringes (Num. 15:38) worn by adult males in the morning service

preaching   delivering a sermon; urging acceptance or abandonment of an idea or course of action. The terms that came to be associated with preaching in later Judaism and early Christianity are used in the older scriptural traditions to refer to messages communicated by human sources or messages from God that are, or are thought to be, good news. Sometimes the communication is about a past event and at other times it predicts the future. But in each case, what is at stake is the fate of either a leader of God's people or of one of their enemies or even of the people as a whole. In the older Semitic and Greek sources, the term is used for the proclamation of a military victory. But in the historical books, the proclamation involves the divine action behind human events, reports of which can be heard by some as bad news and by others as good news. For example, in 1 Samuel 3:8–9, the report of the killings of Israel's first king, Saul, and his sons is heard by the Philistines as good news. The messengers who thought that David would consider the report of the deaths of Saul and his sons as good news were, in fact, killed by David, who was deeply grieved by the news. Similarly, the Cushite who thinks that David will be happy to hear the news of the death of his rebellious son, Absalom, finds that the king is overcome with grief. When, however, David has messengers proclaim that Solomon is to be anointed by the priests to succeed him as king, the news is welcomed by the people, whose rejoicing resounds as a roar through the city of Jerusalem (1 Kings 1:32–48). The Samaritan lepers who planned to defect to the Aramaeans who were besieging Samaria find that they had all fled when God had caused them to hear the sounds of chariots, horses, and a great army (2 Kings 7). The lepers then report this "good news" to the Samaritans (7:9).

In the Prophets, however, the message that God sends through these chosen instruments is regarded as not merely providing information but also as assuring that what God has spoken concerning his purpose for his people will surely come to pass. In Joel 2 the prophet portrays God conveying his message to the world as an army chief would do: "Blow the trumpet in Zion . . . Let all the inhabitants of the land tremble" (2:1), and when "the Lord utters his voice . . . numberless are those who obey his commands" (2:11). They all will know "that I the Lord, am your God, and there is no other" (2:27). When Jeremiah is commissioned by God to speak to the people of Judah, he is told "You shall speak whatever I command you" (Jer. 1:7). The message to be proclaimed by the prophet is often tragic, as when he announces that the city of Jerusalem will fall to the Babylonians and only those inhabitants who surrender to them will survive (Jer. 21:8–10). It is the false prophets who preach peace (Jer. 28), but Babylon's ultimate doom as the work of God is also proclaimed (Jer. 51:6–10).

The prophetic tradition and the psalms from the period during and after Israel's return from exile in Babylon proclaim the glorious future of the people of God. God's preservation of his people and his deliverance of them from the powers of evil are announced (Ps. 40:9). The armies of the enemies of Israel are to be defeated (Ps. 68:11). This message of the divine restoration of God's people is to be told, not only to God's people, but among the nations of the world (Isa. 40:9). At the same time, the rulers of those nations hostile to Israel will be brought under divine judgment, but God's people will rejoice at the deliverance that God will achieve in their behalf (Isa. 41:27). The chief bearer and instrument of this good news will be a messenger anointed by God to bring assurance of divine justice for the poor and oppressed and of vengeance on those who oppose God's purpose (Isa. 61:1–3). The news proclaimed in this prophetic tradition is of judgment on the rulers of the nations and of deliverance for God's people (Isa. 41:27). Messengers are to bring good news of peace and liberation through God's establishment of his rule in the world. These events will be seen by all the nations of the world (Isa. 52:7–10).

In his *Antiquities,* Josephus tells of the good news about the fall of Jericho to the Israelites (5.24), of the message to Manoah's wife that her son (Samson) will defeat the Philistines (5.277), of Herod Agrippa's joy at the news of the death of the emperor Tiberius (18.229), and of the Roman general Vespasian's hearing the good news of his having been acclaimed as emperor by the people of Rome (4.656). In the first-century-B.C.E. Psalms of Solomon, Solomon hears the message that God is watching over Jerusalem and Israel and that throngs will gather there to praise God (11:2). Josephus also notes that human messengers should be swift in bringing good news, just as Hermes, the messenger among the Greek gods, is.

Rabbinic sermons took the form of homilies, sometimes offered in synagogues but more frequently given in the school or in other private settings, including funerals, weddings, rabbinical ordination ceremonies, or other occasions. The rabbinic literature refers to a meturgeman (translator) or amora (speaker, lecturer), who would stand at the side of the preacher and repeat his words so that the gathered audience could hear (see, e.g., B. Ḥagigah 14a, B. Moed Katan 21a). Homilies focused upon the interpretation of scriptural passages, with a special interest, presumably, in the lectionary selection appropriate to the particular week. Some modern scholars have argued that rabbinic Midrash actually preserves the texts of sermons that were given orally in synagogues or the schools. The technical complexity and scholarly construction of these texts makes it almost certain, however, that they are literary creation not originally intended for oral delivery.

While Philo and Paul speak of preaching in the synagogue, rabbinic texts reveal little about how common such preaching was. The Torah, read in Hebrew, was simultaneously translated into Aramaic, and this periphrastic translation may have served as a rudimentary homily as well. But especially in the first centuries, synagogues were not under rabbinical control, and the rabbinic sermon does not appear to have been a fixed element of the worship service.

predestination determinism; the belief that all or some occurrences are fixed or defined by God (or the gods) before they happen. The Hebrew Bible offers no systematic presentation of this belief or the consequences of it. Several passages and motifs do, however, serve as the bases for later developments of such thinking. The story of the ten plagues in Egypt refers repeatedly to the pharaoh's stubbornness in refusing to release Israel and to the fact that that response was caused by God's hardening his heart (Exod. 6–11). Some sections in Isaiah 40–55, praise the Lord as the one who knew long ago what would happen. Foreknowledge of this kind could easily lead to the belief that He had also determined what would happen from the beginning. Later, the different Jewish groups developed various positions on the matter. The first-century-C.E. Jewish historian Josephus distinguished the Pharisees, Sadducees, and Essenes on several teachings, among which was fate. According to him, the Essenes attributed all events to fate; the Pharisees believed some events were predetermined and others were not; and the Sadducees rejected the notion of fate altogether and held individuals responsible for their actions. Some texts among the Dead Sea Scrolls express the Essene position on predestination. The Manual of Discipline says that God established the design of everything before it occurred; all happens according to his predetermined plan. All individuals fall under the power of light or darkness in line with that divine blueprint (cols. 3–4). Jubilees finds the history of Israel, its apostasy and eventual return, already recorded on heavenly tablets (Jubilees 1).

Among early Christian texts, similar thoughts are found. In Acts 2:23, Peter proclaims that Jesus was handed over to those who crucified him by the plan and foreknowledge of God. But Paul is the writer who comes closest to treating the issue and its implications in a more systematic way. He deals with the complex of questions while treating the problem of the changed place of Israel in God's plan (Rom. 9–11). From Malachi, he quotes the statement that God loved Jacob but hated Esau—a decision made before they were born. Yet he defends the deity from the charge of injustice by asserting his right and power to act according to his will. To the objection that God ought not therefore to find fault with those whose actions he predestined, he responds that humans are not in a position to argue with their Maker. Moreover, they do not see the full breadth, splendor, and mystery of his plan. Two later (c. 100 C.E.) Jewish pseudepigrapha—4 Ezra and 2 Baruch—wrestle with the same sorts of problems but do so in connection with the soul-searching evoked by the sack of Jerusalem, the burning of the Temple by a pagan foe (Rome), and the resulting suffering of the elect Jewish people. The protagonists, each in his own way, present probing questions about justice, but in the end the books encourage human submission to the inscrutable ways of God, who alone understands all. There remains a future relation between the Lord and his chosen people.

The rabbinic literature presents a largely deterministic point of view, expressed in the statement of Ḥanina that "A person does not hurt his finger on earth unless it has been decreed from above (B. Ḥullin 7b). The Talmud comparably reports that when the impoverished Eleazar b. Pedat questioned how long he would suffer, God responded that, since his poverty was predetermined, in order to improve Eleazar's situation, God would have to overturn the entire world (B. Taanit 25a).

Despite this deterministic point of view, the rabbis imagined the existence of free will and understood people to be responsible for their actions and fate. Akiba expressed this in the paradoxical maxim, "Everything is foreseen, yet free choice is given" (Mishnah Abot 3:15). Similarly, the Talmud notes that "All is in the hands of Heaven except for the fear of Heaven" (B. Megillah 25a; B. Berakhot 33b; B. Nidah 16b). The rabbis here distinguish between material existence, in which everything is predetermined, and spiritual life, in which people have the choice of abiding by or rejecting God's will.

prefect Roman military term used for the commander of various types of units, such as the ala or cohort, and then for other officials. From the time of Augustus, the term was used for officers of equestrian rank. Under Augustus, Tiberius, and Caligula (31 B.C.E.–41 C.E.), the governors of Judea were called prefects (not procurators, as Josephus and Tacitus imprecisely claim).

presbyteros (Gr., elder) term used generically to refer to someone physically older; also used to refer to one superior in rank. It also took on a technical meaning in some circles, used with reference to community officials or religious figures (hence the English "presbyter" and its modification, "priest").

price controller *see* AGORANOMOS

pride defined in this context as inordinate self-esteem; an impression of superiority; arrogance. Psalms 73:2–9 presents a vivid, detailed portrait of those who are proud: they are arrogant, prosperous, sound of body, free from strife and struggle, and scoffing and malicious toward God. But God will bring destruction upon them (73:19), and this is what they deserve (Ps. 94:2). It is these wicked nations who are the enemies of God's people (Ps. 17:10), and who speak about them with insolence and contempt (Ps. 31:18), but God will repay them in an appropriate way (31:23). He will protect his own from being trampled by their proud opponents, and they will be crushed (Ps. 36:11–12, 86:14). That day of vindication of the faithful and punishment of the proud is predicted by the prophets (Isa. 2:12). God says through the prophet, "I will punish the world for its evil, and the wicked for their iniquity; I will put an end to the pride of the arrogant, and lay low the insolence of the tyrants" (Isa. 13:11). The humiliation of Nebuchadnezzar, after he boasts of his accomplishments in building Babylon, leads to his contrition and

acknowledgment of God's sovereignty (Dan. 4:28–37). The arrogance of Antiochus Epiphanes in desecrating the Jerusalem Temple and requiring all his Jewish subjects to sacrifice pigs (1 Macc. 1:20–50) leads to his defeat and the triumph of the obedient within Israel. It is the insolent, scornful, and contemptuous who are to fall under the rebuke of God (Ps. 119:21–23).

In the Testaments of the Twelve Patriarchs there are solemn warnings against acting out of pride and false self-esteem: "Do not pursue evil impelled by your lusts, by the arrogance of your heart, and do not boast of the exploits and strengths of your heart, and do not boast of the exploits and strengths of your youth, because this too is evil in the Lord's sight" (Test. Jud. 13:2). The Letter of Aristeas warns against "being carried away by wealth and glamour" and "having overweening or unworthy ambitions" (211). In the Sibylline Oracles (8.168) the Persians are denounced: "In return for overbearing pride, all their arrogance will be destroyed." Josephus reports that Nero, on hearing of the initial successes of the Jewish revolutionaries against Vespasian was filled with alarm, but "felt that the majesty of the empire obliged him to treat bad news with lofty disdain and to appear superior to all eventualities" (*War* 3.1.2). Tobit's solemn pronouncement is that "in pride there is ruin and great confusion" (Tob. 4:13).

Like the biblical and Hellenistic literatures, rabbinic texts contain stern warnings against arrogance. God cannot live in the same world as the arrogant, whom he will destroy (B. Sotah 5b). The arrogant will be brought low and at the end of time will have not part in the resurrection of the dead (ibid.; B. Erubin 13b). God himself acts with humility, for he appeared to Moses in a lowly bush and caused his presence to rest on Mount Sinai rather than on a taller mountain (B. Sotah 5b). God's humility is a model for people, who will be rewarded for emulating this trait: "Who will inherit the world to come? One who is meek and humble, who bends when he comes and bends when he goes out, who always is studying the Torah, but does not take pride in himself on that account" (B. Sanhedrin 88b).

priest (Heb.: *kohen*) a hereditary class of male cultic functionaries found in the Bible. Priests conducted sacrifices and other rituals at holy places throughout the land and finally in the sacred areas of the Temple. They also instructed the people in the laws, customs, rituals, and traditions of Israel. The biblical accounts of Levites and priestly families testify to a long, complex development of the priesthood and to a series of struggles for dominance among families and sanctuaries. In the exilic period (586 B.C.E. on) a sharp division emerged between priests and Levites, and the postexilic period saw a conflict for power between them. The priests, tracing their lineage to Aaron and Zadok, one of David's priests, became dominant and Levites were reduced to subordinate roles in the Temple. Priests performed the sacrificial rituals and administered the Temple, while Levites took charge of singing and music, preparations for sacrifice, custodial care of the Temple, and so forth. Priests were expected to remain holy and ritually pure, marry only Jewish women who were virgins or widows, and to be without physical blemish. They were organized into twenty-four divisions (courses), which rotated service at the Temple. Priests were supported by sacrificial offerings brought to the Temple. Many of them lived in town and villages in Judea. After the destruction of the Temple by the Romans in 70 C.E., the Temple sacrifices and rituals ended, resulting in a gradual diminishing of priestly power and influence in favor of the emerging rabbinic movement. *See also* LEVITES; PRIESTS, CHIEF.

priesthood, unfit male (Heb.: *hallal*) offspring of a priest and a woman whom he is prohibited by the Torah from marrying, for example, a divorcee. Such an offspring is a profaned priest, that is, the offspring of a priest who does not possess the sanctity of the priesthood.

Priestly Benediction technically, the blessing of the Israelites by the priests (from Num. 6:24–26, "The Lord bless you and keep you . . . "). In the Second Temple period, it became part of the daily sacrifice. By extension, it entered the synagogue service as the final blessing of the Tefillah, and was expanded to include a lengthier prayer for peace (Birkat Shalom), recited by the prayer leader (who need not claim priestly lineage). On holidays, among some Jews, it is expanded further, as all descendants of the temple priests stand and bless the people in an extended ritual. *See also* DUKHENEN.

priestly courses, the twenty-four the divisions or "courses" of the priests and the Levites, according to which these priests and their families performed specific tasks in the Temple. Fragments of inscriptions mentioning these courses have been found in synagogues from Caesarea and Ashkelon. The origin of this practice of dividing the functions of the priests is attributed to King David (cf. 1 Chron. 23:1ff). In 1 Chronicles 24:7–18 the names of the priestly families who were arranged into twenty-four divisions, or courses, are detailed. Liturgical poems from Palestine, dating from the sixth and seventh century C.E., also preserved these courses for each priestly family, as well as specifying the new locality of these families following the destruction of the Temple. Archaeological remains have now authenticated this reconstructed list from the liturgical poems. Fragments of the seventeenth through the twentieth courses from the Caesarea Synagogue should be dated to the third or fourth century C.E. and contain the same family names as found in 1 Chronicles 24:7–18, as well as the new localities postulated from the liturgical poems. The finds from the synagogue in Ashkelon are even more fragmentary, but they too are consistent with this reconstruction. Thus it appears that it may have been a common practice in synagogues after the destruction of the Second Temple to keep a remembrance of the priestly duties and their new localities either in poetry or in a memorial inscription.

priestly rations *see* HEAVE-OFFERING

priests, chief English translation of the term used to designate the priestly aristocracy during the late Second Temple period. The chief priests appear to have been, in effect, the ruling aristocracy of Judea (and at times of other territories such as Galilee and Perea) under Herod and the Roman governors. By the time of Nehemiah, the Zadokite priestly aristocracy, centered in the office of high priest, had become the rulers of Judea and, in effect, the (Persian, later Hellenistic) imperial officials in charge of tax collection and social order. The Hasmonean family simply replaced the Zadokites as the rulers of Judea, but vastly expanded the territory controlled by the Jerusalem Temple/high priestly government. Herod reduced the powers of the chief priests and appointed new men to the high priesthood. From Herod to the Great Revolt, four prominent families of chief priests dominated affairs in Jerusalem, their members alternatively occupying the offices of high priest, captain, and treasurers of the Temple. Headed by the high priest, who was usually appointed (and periodically deposed) by the Roman governor, the chief priests collected the tribute and maintained control of Judea and Samaria—and exerted what influence they could elsewhere—under the watchful eye of the Roman authorities.

principalities and powers (Gr.: *archai kai exousiai*) a class of heavenly beings possessing unspecified power. The word pair occurs in early Jewish literature only in 1 Enoch 61:10. Perhaps they are the angels whom YHWH has put in charge of the nations (Ecclus. 17:17). 1 Enoch 89:59–90:19 depicts these angelic patrons as evil forces. Paul claims that Christ will triumph over the malevolent ruling spiritual powers (1 Cor. 15:24). The passage may allude to the son of man's receipt of authority and kingship over the nations in Daniel 7:14. *See also* ANGEL.

private domain the property of a household, distinct from all other households. On the Sabbath it is forbidden to carry an object from private domain to public domain.

PRK *see* PESIKTA DERAB KAHANA

Probus abbreviation of the tractate *Quod Omnis Probus Liber Sit* (Every Good Man Is Free) by Philo. The tractate considers the Stoic belief that only the wise person is truly free, whereas all others are slaves to their desires and passions. Philo refers to the Essenes to illustrate his point.

proconsul (Lat., in place of a consul) Proconsulship was a form of authority given to an official of consular rank (usually an exconsul) who held the *imperium*. Such individuals often became governors of provinces, after the term of office as consul had ended, and needed such authority. *See also* IMPERIUM.

procurator in Roman law, an authorized agent for another; in the imperial period, an agent of the emperor; from the mid-first century C.E., the equestrian governor of a minor province, such as Judea. Despite statements to the contrary by Tacitus and Josephus, inscriptions show that Pontius Pilate and other early first-century governors up to the time of Agrippa I were called prefects, not procurators.

progymnasmata (Gr., preliminary exercises) a stage in formal schooling in the Graeco-Roman world, with the exercises forming the first stage of training in Greek rhetoric. The literary forms used for the student exercises included such genres as the *creia*.

promise Biblical views of God are bound up with God's making promises to Israel, and God's faithfulness in keeping these promises is axiomatic. Especially noteworthy are the covenantal promises to Abraham in Genesis 12:1–3, 15:1–6, and 17:1–8, whose fulfillment is either narrated in the text or presumed. Although Israel's prophets doomed the people to exile, they promised a return to the land, and some predicted a restoration of the Davidic dynasty. The Jewish writers of the Persian and Graeco-Roman periods wrestled with the fact that these promises were only partially fulfilled or not fulfilled at all (see Ecclus. 36:11–17). Typical of the Christian tendency to interpret the Hebrew Bible in light of the coming of Jesus, Paul sees the promises to Abraham and his offspring fulfilled in Christ and in those who believe in him, who are said to be the true descendants of Abraham (Gal. 3:16–29). Not surprisingly, the New Testament depicts Jesus as one who made trustworthy promises (Mark 13:30–31). When the return of Christ failed to materialize, Christian apologists found it necessary to argue against "scoffers," who pointed out this fact (2 Pet. 3:1–10). Strikingly, the New Testament, as finally compiled, ends with the promise, "I am coming soon" (Rev. 22:20). *See also* PROPHECY, FULFILLMENT OF.

pronoia *see* PROVIDENTIA

property Like other legal systems, rabbinic law divides property into two types, immovables (Heb.: *karkaot,* grounds) and movables (Heb.: *mitaltelin,* those that can be carried). Slaves are included in the former category, while bonds and demands upon other individuals belong in the latter. The distinction between these categories is significant, since under rabbinic law, a properly written and attested bond automatically represents a lien on all of the debtor's immovable property. Upon death, such immovables are subject to seizure by the decedent's creditors. The same is not the case for chattels or demands, which, through the talmudic period, were not subject to seizure for payment of a debt, whether in the debtor's lifetime or after death. The situation changed only in the Middle Ages, when, as a result of almost universal Jewish landlessness, all goods, money, and effects were made liable for a decedent's debts.

Like Roman law (but unlike English common law), for purposes of inheritance rabbinic law does not distinguish between movable and immovable property (see M. Baba Kamma 8). Comparably, a gift made in apprehension of death, if death indeed ensued, is deemed equally valid for the transfer of real property and chattels or demands. This is under the theory that the words of one lying sick take the place of the deed through which real property usually is transferred, the act of pulling (*meshikhah*) used in the transfer of chattels, or the meeting of the creditor, debtor, and proposed assignee needed to transfer a monetary claim.

The principle of *onaah* (overreaching) allows a sale or purchase of chattels to be set aside in a case in which it turns out that the purchase price was one-sixth above or below the market value (M. Baba Metzia 4:1–9). This rule does not apply to real estate or slaves, which rabbinic law deems to have no set market value. In light of this understanding, rabbinic law holds even the smallest piece of property to be of inestimable worth, sufficing to secure a loan of any amount (M. Shebiit 10:6). Sales of immovables are rescinded only upon proof of a claim of actual fraud or other error.

property, rabbinic law for lost Return of lost property to its rightful owner is an important biblical obligation spelled out in four chapters of the Mishnah and Talmud (Baba Metzia 1–4). Specific rules are set forth for determining which objects are subject to identification and return. Failure to attempt to return a lost object to its owner is deemed theft and is subject to punishment.

prophecy, fulfillment of the notion that current events realize predictions made by God's ancient prophets. Although the prophets' primary function was to speak in the name of God, much that they said related to future events. According to Deuteronomy 18:20–22, the sign of a true prophet was the fulfillment of the prophet's words. This notion must have run into a great deal of trouble in the postexilic period. Figures like Isaiah, Second and Third Isaiah, Jeremiah, Ezekiel, Zechariah, and Haggai had forecast glowing scenarios about a return of the twelve tribes, a new exodus and new covenant, the restoration of the Davidic dynasty, a new creation, and a glorious existence on the mountains of Israel, with Zion dominating the nations.

Although empirical reality surely caused "cognitive dissonance," postexilic Jewish sages preserved the ancient prophetic oracles, expecting their promises to be fulfilled. Jewish texts from the Graeco-Roman period widely attest this belief, although it must be emphasized that many other Jewish texts totally omit reference to the prophets.

In the wisdom tradition, Ben Sira interprets (Third) Isaiah as one who "revealed what was to occur to the end of time" (48:25), and he preserves a prayer imploring God to "fulfill the prophecies . . . and let your prophets be found trustworthy" (36:15–16). The author of Tobit believed that all the prophetic words "would come to pass in their times" (14:4).

In the apocalyptic corpus, texts like Jubilees 23 and the Testament of Moses, following a tradition already evident in the early postexilic works of Ezra and Nehemiah, read Deuteronomy 28–32 as a prophecy par excellence that laid out a scheme of sin-punishment-repentance-salvation to be fulfilled in Israel's history. Current disasters located the nation in the sin part of the cycle and called for acts of repentance that would bring eschatological blessing.

The writers of the Qumran commentaries (Heb.: *pesharim*) made a science out of the study of prophecy. Like Ben Sira, they believed that the prophets spoke about the last times, and like the author of the Testament of Moses, they saw themselves living at the eschaton. What was written in the prophets pertained to them, the eschatological community of the chosen, and God had revealed to the "Teacher of Righteousness" all the secrets of the prophets. Their commentaries explicate in detail how prophecy is fulfilled in the events of their community.

The author of the Psalms of Solomon 17 expected that the Davidic oracles in Psalm 2, Isaiah 11, and Ezekiel 37 would be fulfilled when the scion of David appears to deal with Israel's Roman oppressors, and he wove allusions to these texts into a lengthy description of that king's activities.

The early church arose from an eschatologically oriented sector of Judaism and, like the Qumran sect, it understood itself to be the community of the chosen. To a degree that is unparalleled in extant Jewish literature (except some Qumran texts), the writings of the New Testament read the Hebrew Scriptures as prophecy from start to finish and appeal to it as documentation for their claims about Jesus the Messiah.

Understanding the words of the prophets to have originated in the revelation at Sinai (B. Megillah 2b), the rabbis believed that prophetic utterances accurately predicted what had happened in the past and also indicated what would occur in their own day and in the messianic future. Prophetic passages buttressed rabbinic dogma concerning proper behavior (Mishnah Abot 3:17), showed how people could bring about the coming of the messiah (Y. Taanit 1:1), explained what would happen at the time of the final judgment (B. Rosh Hashanah 17a), and proved that, at the end of time, all nations and kingdoms would be gathered together in Jerusalem (Abot deRabbi Nathan 35, end). As in the New Testament, prophetic texts also explained specific occurrences of the rabbis' own day, for instance, the destruction of the Second Temple (B. Menahot 53b). To indicate that a particular incident fulfilled a prophecy, the rabbis used the formula "This occurred to carry out that which is said . . .," followed by the appropriate scriptural verse. The same expression appears at Matthew 1:22 and 21:4, where Jesus' actions are explicitly associated with prophetic statements. *See also* SCRIPTURAL INTERPRETATION.

prophet (Heb.: *nabi*) popular figure who uttered oracles or led a movement. Continuing in the traditions of earlier Israelite prophets, at least two types of popular prophets were active in late Second

Temple times. Among the literate groups, the "righteous teacher" who founded the Qumran Community is portrayed as a new Moses, who received instruction from God for Israel (CD 1; 1QpHab 7–8). Among the ordinary people in Judea and Samaria in the mid-first century C.E., several popular prophets emerged, promising new acts of redemption patterned after paradigmatic events of Israel's beginning. Theudas led his followers to a new exodus or wilderness journey, and a prophet from Egypt led followers to expect the walls of Jerusalem to fall like those of Jericho (*Ant.* 20.97–98). A Samaritan prophet led followers up Mount Gerizim in anticipation of recovering sacred objects of the tabernacle (*Ant.* 18.85–87). The followers of all such movements were slaughtered by Roman troops. Other prophets simply delivered oracles of salvation or doom. Most reminiscent of the classical prophets was Jesus, son of Hananiah, a latter-day Jeremiah who pronounced prophetic laments over Jerusalem for several years prior to the Jewish revolt and Roman destruction of the city (*B.J.* 6.300–309). John the Baptist appears to have been a similar type of popular prophet, appearing in the wilderness and baptizing people into a new covenantal relationship with God and each other through the water, like a new Moses.

Rabbinic Judaism held that prophecy came to an end with Haggai, Zechariah, and Malachi. From that time onward, divine communication took the form of dreams or visions. The rabbinic authorities recognized the availability of "heavenly echoes," deemed to convey supernatural counsel, but these were accorded no normative authority.

prophetic reading   *see* HAFTARAH

Prophets   (Heb.: *nebiim*) a Jewish division of the Hebrew Bible, containing the books of Joshua, Judges, 1 and 2 Samuel, 1 and 2 Kings, Isaiah, Jeremiah, Ezekiel, and the twelve Minor Prophets. The Minor Prophets are Hosea, Joel, Amos, Obadiah, Jonah, Micah, Nahum, Habakkuk, Zephaniah, Haggai, Zechariah, and Malachi. Some of these books, such as Hosea, are probably the oldest in the Bible. They received a sacred, or canonical, status shortly after the books of the Pentateuch (Torah).

Prophets, Lives of the   (Vitae Prophetarum) an ancient anonymous work comprising a series of short narratives describing, in some cases very briefly, the lives and deaths of twenty-three Hebrew biblical "prophets." Although the Lives has traditionally been interpreted as a Jewish writing of about the first century C.E., recent research has opened the possibility of its having a Christian origin, perhaps as late as the fourth century. The

work seems to have been written in Greek, in or around the Land of Israel.

This work's individual sections may not have all been written by the same author, and the work probably went through stages of editing, expansion, or abbreviation before reaching the forms found in the present manuscripts. These extant manuscripts also show the work's varying recensions, which differ not only in their details about individual prophets but also in which prophets they include.

The Lives is attested in numerous Greek manuscripts, which divide into four main recensions. The recension usually regarded as the most original, labeled the "anonymous" recension, is represented by the oldest manuscript of the work, from the sixth century. The other recensions are the "longer Epiphanian," best known in a thirteenth-century manuscript; the "shorter Epiphanian," in a tenth-century manuscript; and the "Dorothean," in a thirteenth-century manuscript.

The most original recension covers, in order, the three "major prophets," Daniel, the twelve "minor prophets," and the seven biblical prophets to whom no currently surviving biblical writings are attributed—Nathan, Ahijah, Joad, Azariah, Elijah, Elisha, and Zechariah, son of Johoiada.

Although several of the prophets receive only short notices, the notice always includes at least the prophet's place of birth, place and manner of death, and place of burial. Typically, however, more detail about the prophet is given. This material tends to be information not found in the biblical account of the prophet. It includes other types of aggadic narrative, which are often esoteric or exotic tales of the prophet's activities and powers. Their characteristic concerns are nonbiblical prophecies made by the prophets, "mysteries" associated with them, and subject of prophetic martyrdom.

The Lives is perhaps the earliest extensive extant witness to a Jewish or Christian concern for cataloging the births, lives, deaths, and burials of biblical "saints" systematically. It therefore set the tone for, and probably had a profound influence on, later hagiographical tradition, especially in Christianity.

prosbul   a legal formula designed to circumvent the Sabbatical-year cancellation of loans made between Israelites (see Deut. 15:1–2). Before 70 C.E., Hillel instituted preparation of the *prosbul*, a document that turned the debt over for collection by a court (M. Shebiit 10:2). Since on the basis of Deuteronomy 15:2–3, it was understood that private, but not public, loans are released in the seventh year, this allowed collection of the debt during the Sabbatical year. Yabnean authorities held that only secured loans could be turned over to the court (M. Shebiit 10:6–7). Since a creditor in a secured transaction held a claim upon the security, he could be understood already to have been repaid. The court simply presided over the exchange of the security for cash. Rabbinic authorities were, however, extremely lenient in establishing a minimal required value of the security. They even allowed the creditor himself to assign property to the borrower and then to use that same property as security to allow preparation of a prosbul. *See also* SHEBIIT.

proselytization   the process of making converts to a religion. Judaism has never been a proselytizing religion in the way that Christianity has; rather, Judaism was usually an ethnic religion, centered on the people of Israel. Nevertheless, the idea that outsiders could become a part of Israel has evidently existed in Israelite religion from an early time. Various passages in the Hebrew Bible assume this (e.g., Deut. 21:10–14; Ruth). On the other hand, apparently the choice was not open to all, and some ethnic groups were excluded (Deut. 23:3–6).

In the Graeco-Roman period, there is evidence of many converts to Judaism, as well as of sympathizers, or God-fearers. Josephus mentions an occasion in 19 C.E. when a large number of Jews were expelled from Rome for proselytizing activity. Josephus puts the blame on four "rogues"; however, other sources suggest that attempts at conversion were much more widespread and brought the wrath of Tiberius down on the head of the Jewish community. On the other hand, those who have argued for a widespread Jewish "mission" in the first century C.E. have not been very persuasive. The occasional convert and the persistent attempts at conversion by some Jews is not the same as a mission of proselytization.

The question of the process of conversion is not a simple one. Circumcision seems to have been an absolute requirement for males. The one exception mentioned by Josephus concerned the king of a country in unusual circumstances. Whether a ritual bath (baptism) was required is uncertain before 70 C.E., even though rabbinic sources make it a requirement. *See also* CONVERSION; GOD-FEARERS.

proseuchē   (Gr., prayer, or praise [of god]) This became the term for a synagogue, that is, a place of prayer, during the diaspora. It is normally thought that a *proseuchē* and a synagogue (Gr.: *synagogos*) were the same, but some think the difference in terminology indicates other differences as well.

prostitution   (Heb.: *zenut*) sexual intercourse for payment. The rabbis prohibited prostitution, seeing it as a social ill so serious that, in their understanding, it was one of the causes of the destruction of the Jerusalem Temple in 70 C.E. (M. Sotah 9:13, 15). Rabbinic law encompasses under the concept of *zenut* not only prostitution but any sexual act outside of the context of matrimony, even if no payment is involved. In line with this attitude, the rabbis frequently criticized Roman culture for promoting licentiousness (B. Pesahim 113b; B. Shabbat 33b). Rabbinic literature refers to Jews taken captive and forced into prostitution, of Jewish men who acted as pimps, and of women who considered engaging in prostitution for economic reasons (Y. Taanit 1:4, 64b).

protrepticus   *see* LOGOS PROTREPTICUS

Prov.   *see* DE PROVIDENTIA

proverb   a concise observation about an aspect of daily life, phrased in poetic form. The biblical word for proverb, *mashal*, covers a wide range of sayings such as taunt, riddle, mocking word, dark saying, despite its essential meaning of "likeness," hence simile. The earliest proverbs, traditional sayings, circulated orally among the populace and lacked poetic parallelism (cf. Jer. 31:29; Ezek. 18:2). The simplest form of proverb in the book of Proverbs, the saying, has two stichs, the second expressing either virtually the same thing or exactly the opposite, except when the observations are additive (synonymous, antithetic, and synthetic parallelism, respectively). Variations of these forms include numerical sayings ("Three things . . . four"), "better than" sayings, and simple declarations ("There is . . ."). Many of these sayings lack any religious or educational purpose ("The poor must entreat; the rich answer curtly"). More developed proverbs, instructions, use imperatives to compel assent and to dictate conduct. They do so positively by exhortation and negatively by threat. This instructional literature, consciously artistic, tended to expand into paragraph units, particularly in Proverbs 1–8 and in Ecclesiasticus. The proverb in both forms, saying and instruction, was widespread in the ancient Near East, collections of varying length having survived from Sumer, Assyria, Babylonia, and Egypt, as well as Aramaic sayings of Ahikar. One Egyptian instruction, Amememope, influenced Proverbs 22:17–24:22, where ten sayings link the two works literarily.

Proverbs, Targum to   a highly literal translation of the Book of Proverbs into Aramaic, with very little additional material. Linguistically, this targum mixes Aramaic forms known from the Palestinian Targums to the Pentateuch, the Babylonian Talmud, and Targum Onkelos. Its wording is quite close to that of the Peshita to Proverbs, although it is not clear whether the targum derives from the Peshita, or vice versa. In its current form, the targum probably stems from the early Middle Ages.

providence God's benevolent guidance of the world. It comes from the Latin noun *providentia,* which derives from the verb *provideoe* (to see ahead, to have thought for). The Greek equivalent is *pronoia,* from the verb *pronoeisthai.* In the Graeco-Roman world, both Platonic and Stoic philosophers had doctrines of providence or fate. There is no equivalent term in the Hebrew Bible, but there is certainly the belief that God benevolently guides the world and especially the history of Israel (e.g., Deut. 32:7–43; 2 Kings 19:25–28; Job 10:12; Ps. 74:12–17; Isa. 44:6–8). Both the Pharisees and the group at Qumran (e.g., 1QS 3:13–4:26) had beliefs in providence. The term itself is found in a number of Jewish documents written in Greek (e.g., Wisd. of Sol. 14:3; 3 Macc. 4:21; 4 Macc. 17:22). The emphasis is often on God's care of those who are devoted to and suffer for the sake of God. The concept is also important for the first-century-C.E. Jewish writer Josephus (e.g., *Ant.* 1.13.2, sec. 225, 2.5.1, sec. 60, 11.5.7, sec. 169). Philo of Alexandria (first century C.E.) devoted a whole treatise to the doctrine of providence (*De Providentia*). The use of the term in these documents is influenced in various ways by Greek discussions of providence. These concepts were also taken up by Christian writers from the second century C.E. on.

providentia (Lat., providence) The word is similar to the Greek *pronoia* (foreknowledge); both of these imply the direction of the world by God according to moral standards, rewarding the good and punishing the evil (as opposed to *tychē,* which means "fate").

psalms term used to refer to poetic compositions collected together in the biblical Book of Psalms and, by extension, to other compositions and collections which are modeled on the biblical psalms. Although there is considerable difficulty in defining the term in a technical sense, "psalm" is often used interchangeably with "hymn" and "song."

The biblical psalms were composed over many centuries as poems of praise and lament. Many were originally for use in the Temple, to be sung by the Temple singers. Some seem more suitable for private mediative use (Ps. 119), and the Bible itself assumes the psalms can be used by individuals in times of need outside the Temple (e.g., 1 Sam. 2; 2 Sam. 22; Jonah 2).

The 150 psalms in the Massoretic psalter and the 151 psalms in the Greek psalter are probably only a selection from a much wider collection. Other collections of psalms are found among the manuscripts in the Dead Sea Scrolls, though it is very difficult to know if these were considered as psalters per se or as collections of prayers. For example, 11QPs^a contains some forty biblical psalms, plus the previously unknown Hymn to the Creator, the Plea for Deliverance, the Apostrophe to Zion, two psalms previously known only from later Syriac translations, and Psalm 151 (known from Septuagint manuscripts).

There are a number of different collections made up totally of nonbiblical psalms. The very fragmentary manuscripts 4Q380 and 4Q381 are a collection of over a dozen psalms ascribed to various kings of Judah and perhaps some prophets (Obadiah); it is very difficult to place these precisely in terms of date, purpose, or author, although they certainly attest to a continued practice of psalmic composition in the postexilic period. In contrast, the Hodayot, or Thanksgiving Psalms (1QH), are a collection of over thirty poems of thanksgiving that are distinctive in both vocabulary and theme, with a strong emphasis on salvation, knowledge, predeterminism, and union with the angels; these are compositions of the specific sectarian group that wrote many of the Qumran documents. Another collection is the eighteen Psalms of Solomon, which reflects more of the political situation in the first century B.C.E. (Ps. Sol. 2) and the expectations for a Davidic messiah (Ps. Sol. 18).

In this period, individual psalms came to be included in many different types of compositions; for example, among the wisdom discourses of Ben Sira there is a psalm praying for the eschatological gathering of the people (36:1–22) and a psalm of thanksgiving for deliverance from death (51:1–12). Some psalms probably had a prior, perhaps liturgical, existence and were secondarily added to narrative works (Tob. 13; Jdt. 16). Certain themes reoccur, for example, praise of Jerusalem (Tob. 13; Bar. 4:36–5:9; Ps. Sol. 11; Apostrophe to Zion in 11QPs^a and 4QPs^f) and praise of God's creation (e.g., Ecclus. 42:15–43:33; 1QH i). A special category of psalms were composed to "terrify and frighten" the demons (4Q510; 4Q511; 11QapPs^a). Other psalms have been called "autobiographical psalms" because the "I" of the psalm is a specific biblical character (e.g., David in Ps. 151 and 2Q22) or a specific figure (the Teacher of Righteousness in 1QH 2:1–19, 4:5–5:4, 5:5–19) quite unlike the more general "I" of the biblical psalms.

One of the most distinctive characteristics of this psalmody is the reuse of biblical language, sometimes by actual quotation of a biblical verse, but more often in an anthological style in which biblical words and phrases are reworked and recombined into a new composition. It is very difficult to know if and how these psalms functioned liturgically in the life of a community; it is generally assumed that most were literary compositions. *See also* DAVID; HODAYOT; SOLOMON, PSALMS OF.

Psalms, Targum to a generally literal translation of the Book of Psalms, with only a few additions inserted into the translation. This targum shares many similarities with the rabbinic Targum to Job, including a linguistic mix that combines elements of Eastern and Western forms of Aramaic. This suggests a composition dating from the early Middle Ages, although some scholars have argued for a date as early as the first century.

Psalms of Solomon *see* SOLOMON, PSALMS OF

Pseudepigrapha (Gr., spurious writings) texts composed under a pseudonym. Pseudepigraphy was a common phenomenon in the ancient world, intended to invest one's writing with verisimilitude and with the authority of an ancient figure (often one from the distant past). A number of writings, or parts of them, in the Hebrew Bible and the New Testament are pseudonymous, either because they were composed as such or because they were incorporated into the writings of named persons. In Judaic studies, "Pseudepigrapha" is used most narrowly and technically to refer to noncanonical writings ascribed to prophetic and patriarchal figures from biblical history. Among these are some texts, originally anonymous, that became pseudonymous because a scribe added a title or superscription or copied them into a manuscript that included the writings of a named person.

The first English collection of Pseudepigrapha, edited by R. H. Charles, included: Books of Adam and Eve; the Letter of Aristeas; 2 and 3 Baruch; 1, 2, and 3 Enoch; 4 Ezra (2 Esdras); the Martyrdom of Isaiah; the Book of Jubilees (ascribed to Moses); the Assumption (really Testament) of Moses; the Sibylline Oracles; the Psalms of Solomon; the Testaments of the Twelve Patriarchs; and several other nonpseudonymous texts that served the editor's purpose. More recent editors (H. F. D. Sparks and J. H. Charlesworth) have expanded the corpus to include other valuable pseudonymous works ascribed to such persons as Abraham, Elijah, Jeremiah, Job, and Zephaniah.

All of the writings collected as Pseudepigrapha have been preserved by Christian scribes in translations often twice removed from the original language of composition. In some cases, Christian editing, interpolation, and recomposition are evident, and occasionally a text may be a Christian composition that draws on Jewish traditions. Nonetheless, used cautiously, the Pseudepigrapha are a valuable resource for the student of postbiblical Judaism. Fragments of the original Hebrew or Aramaic texts or sources of a few of the Pseudepigrapha (1 Enoch, Jubilees, Testaments of the Twelve Patriarchs) provide some control for our use of the translations.

The term "Pseudepigrapha" is problematic because it focuses on only one feature of these texts, a feature found in biblical texts and in writings of the Apocrypha such as Tobit and the Wisdom of Solomon, and because the edited collections include nonpseudepigraphic works. Study of the Pseudepigrapha should be carried out in conjunction with work on the late biblical texts, the Apocrypha, and the Qumran scrolls and with an eye toward the light that the Pseudepigrapha can shed on the history of the Christian scribes and communities that preserved them.

Pseudo-Eupolemus *see* EUPOLEMUS, PSEUDO-

Pseudo-Hectaeus *see* HECATAEUS, PSEUDO-

Pseudo-Jonathan, Targum a complete, continuous targum rendering the Hebrew Pentateuch into Aramaic. This targum was written, perhaps in several stages, sometime between the mid-fourth century and the ninth century C.E. Pseudo-Jonathan combines a fairly literal translation with a large amount of additional material, producing a text that is twice as long as the original Hebrew. The translation is quite close to that of Targum Onkelos, whose wording and dialect it often follows. Many of the additions follow the rubric of the Palestinian Targums, although the majority of the additional material either reflects the influence of rabbinic midrashim or stands independent of any known source. The language of the text reflects this composite nature; it adheres to no single dialect, but seems to constitute a mixture of Eastern and Western Aramaic elements. In the earliest references to this text, it is called Targum Yerushalmi, or the Targum of Jerusalem.

Pseudo-Longinus *see* LONGINUS, PSEUDO-

Pseudo-Menander *see* MENANDER, PSEUDO-

Pseudo-Philo *see* BIBLICAL ANTIQUITIES, BOOK OF

Pseudo-Phocylides *see* PHOCYLIDES, PSEUDO-

psyche (Gr., soul) There were a variety of views of what this constituted in the Graeco-Roman world. The original view was probably that the *psychē* was simply the life of the person. A very early concept, found in Homer, is that the soul leaves the body at death and continues in some sense to live on. Nevertheless, it is not a person, since to be a real person also requires a body and perhaps other components. The shades, or souls, in the underworld were only shadows of the living individuals. Some traditions in Greek developed a different idea, however, with the soul being the whole person and the body only an unnecessary and even undesirable appendage. The important thing was the immortal soul, which might be returned to earth in another body at death (*metempsychosis*) or perhaps escape the material cycle and remain an incorporeal soul. *Psychē* is the normal translation of the Hebrew *nefesh* (life, body) in the Septuagint, where it does not imply immortality or a separate existence. *See also* METEMPSYCHOSIS.

Ptolemais *see* ACRE

Ptolemy, celebration of delivery from Jewish festival supposedly celebrated in Graeco-Roman Egypt. 3 Maccabees recounts that Ptolemy IV had all the Jews assembled into an arena with the aim of having them trampled by elephants. However, God delivered them on a succession of occasions, once even by having the king oversleep. Finally, they were released, and a holiday was declared to be celebrated from year to year. Persecution of the Jews at such an early time is unknown, and the story may have arisen in Roman times, when persecution did occur. *See also* PTOLEMY IV PHILOPATOR.

Ptolemy, son of Abubus son-in-law of Simon the Hasmonean; appointed governor of the plain of Jericho. He sought to win the kingdom for himself and so invited Simon and his sons to a banquet, got them drunk, and killed them, except for John Hyrcanus (c. 134 B.C.E.; 1 Macc. 16 and Josephus, *Ant.* 13, secs. 228–235). He was thwarted in his plans to gain control and was forced by Hyrcanus to flee to Philadelphia in the Transjordan.

Ptolemy I Soter (c. 367/366–283 B.C.E.) friend of Alexander the Great who fought with distinction in Alexander's campaigns and later wrote a history of Alexander. He became satrap of Egypt in 323 B.C.E., declaring himself king in 304. In the wars among Alexander's successors, he endeavored to obtain control over Syria and Palestine and finally did so in 301 B.C.E. Traditions about his relations with Judea show him both as ruling Jerusalem harshly and also as so benevolent to Jews that some preferred his rule to that of other Greek overlords. He laid down the main lines of

Ptolemaic administration of Egypt, founded the great museum and library at Alexandria, fostered the cult of the god Sarapis, and commissioned the Egyptian priest Manetho to write, in Greek, a history of Egypt.

Ptolemy II Philadelphus (308–246 B.C.E.) son of Ptolemy I. He was made joint ruler with his father in 285 B.C.E. and succeeded to the throne in 283. Philadelphus encouraged the scientific and cultural developments begun by his father, but his engagement in competitive dynastic wars—the First and Second Syrian Wars, the Chremonidean War—would cause severe fiscal problems for his successor. From his reign, the Zenon Papyri provide some evidence for the economic conditions in Syria and Palestine. The Letter of Aristeas portrays Philadelphus as friendly to the Jews, freeing enslaved Jews and promoting the translation of the Hebrew Scriptures into Greek (the Septuagint).

Ptolemy III Euergetes king of Egypt (r. 246–221 B.C.E.). His marriage to Berenice II united Cyrene to Egypt; the Third Syrian War to avenge the murder of his sister Berenice, alluded to in Daniel 11:7–9, saw him retain control of Judea and also of the port of Seleuceia-in-Pieria. Euergetes is the ruler mentioned in the Tobiad romance wherein the high priest refused to pay taxes, but Joseph, son of Tobias, saved the day. Josephus (*Ant.* 12.4) mentions that Euergetes offered sacrifice in Jerusalem. Inscriptions from this period show the existence of Jewish *proseuchai* "prayer places" in some towns of Lower Egypt.

Ptolemy IV Philopator king of Egypt (r. 221–204 B.C.E.). He successfully defended Ptolemaic possessions in Coele Syria from an invasion by Antiochus III, winning a decisive battle at Raphia, although late in his reign (207/206) the Thebaid Delta seceded from his rule. The Book of 3 Maccabees is set during the reign of Philopator. This narrative describes how Ptolemy's life is saved by a renegade Jew just before the Battle of Raphia. After the battle, Philopator visits neighboring cities, but becomes infuriated when not allowed to enter the sanctuary of the Temple at Jerusalem. He is deterred only when thrown into a faint by God; nevertheless, he returns to Egypt bent on revenge. He decrees that all Jews must either participate in the worship of Dionysus and become citizens of Alexandria, or be branded with an ivy leaf, the emblem of Dionysus. The Jews are finally saved, Philopator repents, and he orders that the Jews be protected. The Jews institute a seven-day festival at Ptolemais to commemorate the event. *See also* PTOLEMY, CELEBRATION OF DELIVERY FROM.

Ptolemy V Epiphanes king of Egypt (r. 204–181/ 180 B.C.E.). He was five years old when Ptolemy IV, his father, died in 204 B.C.E. Antiochus III and Philip V of Macedon conspired against the young king to seize his overseas possessions. Antiochus III gained possession of Syria and Judea. Later Antiochus made an alliance with Ptolemy V by giving his daughter in marriage (Dan. 11:13–18). Ptolemy finally took control of the rebellious Delta in 184/183, but died in 181/180 at age 28.

Ptolemy VI Philometer (186–145 B.C.E.) Egyptian boy-king, at first very much under the influence of his advisers when he came to the throne in 180 B.C.E. Egyptian preparations for recapturing Phoenicia and Syria ended when Antiochus IV Epiphanes attacked in 169 and became master of Egypt except for Alexandria. Philometer struggled for power with his younger brother, Ptolemy VIII Euergetes, and his sister-wife, Cleopatra II. He was driven from Alexandria to Rome in 164 B.C.E., but returned in 163; it was decided that Philometer should rule Egypt and Euergetes the western half of the kingdom, Cyrenaica. Philometer, meddling again in Coele Syria, first supported Alexander Balas's claim to the Seleucid throne but later switched sides to Demetrius II; he was eventually killed in a victorious battle against Alexander Balas (1 Macc. 11:13–18; see 1 Macc. 10:1–11:7 for the role of Jonathan Maccabeus). Onias IV is said to have fled to Philometer for refuge and to have built in Leontopolis a temple similar to the one in Jerusalem (Josephus, *Ant.* 13, secs. 62–73), and Josephus states that Philometer placed his entire army under the command of two Jewish generals, Onias and Dositheus (*Against Apion* 2.49). Fragments exist of a work by a Jewish writer, Aristobulus, who may be dated to Philometer's reign and who is also mentioned in 2 Maccabees 1:10. The Jewish Sibylline Oracles, Book 3, may date to Philometer's reign.

Ptolemy VII (VIII) Euergetes (also called Physcon) younger brother of Ptolemy VI. He co-reigned with his brother from 170 to 164 B.C.E., was sole ruler from 164 to 163, became king of Cyrene from 163 to 145, and returned to Egypt in 145. He married his brother's wife, Cleopatra II, in 144 and then seduced and married his niece, Cleopatra III, in 142. Cleopatra II successfully led a revolt in 132, but Ptolemy recaptured Alexandria in 127 and peace returned after 124, lasting till Ptolemy's death in 116. Josephus relates how the Jewish general Onias defended Cleopatra II; consequently, Physcon sought to massacre all the Jews in Alexandria, but was prevented from so doing and the Alexandrian Jews inaugurated a feast (*Against Apion* 2.50–56). The story is similar to that of 3 Maccabees.

Ptolemy VIII (IX) Soter II (also called Lathyros; 142–81 B.C.E.) eldest son of Ptolemy VII Euergetes and Cleopatra III, and co-regent with his mother from 116 B.C.E. Lathyros sent six thousand soldiers to help Antiochus IX Cyzicenus against John Hyrcanus's siege of Samaria (Josephus, *Ant.* 13.10). Cleopatra III temporarily drove Lathyros out of Egypt to Cyprus in 107 B.C.E. From there he continued to support Cyzicenus; he eventually invaded Syria and fought and defeated the Jews under Alexander Jannaeus (Josephus, *Ant.* 13.12). He returned as ruler to Egypt in 89/88 B.C.E.

Ptolemy XII Auletes son of Ptolemy Lathyros; succeeded to the Egyptian throne in 80 B.C.E. and cultivated relationships with Rome, bribing Caesar in 59 B.C.E. to uphold his claim to recognition by the Roman Senate. The extortions to raise this money led to his being expelled by the Alexandrians in 58 B.C.E.; he was restored to power in 55 by the Roman general Gabinius, who was helped by Antipater. The colophon at the end of the Greek Additions to Esther may suggest that the translation of Esther was brought to Egypt during Auletes' reign in 78 B.C.E.

Ptolemy the Geographer Greek writer from Alexandria in the second century B.C.E. He is known mainly for his *Geography,* which is important because of its discussion of Palestine and information on various geographical sites. He also wrote the *Tetrabiblios,* a work on astrology, which divided the world into regions and considered the characteristics of the people as determined by geography and the stars. From this he concluded that the Jews have various negative traits, including unscrupulousness, cowardliness, servility, and godlessness, though they are also bold.

publicans (Lat.; Gr.: *telonai*) tax-farmers; groups who purchased the right to collect taxes for Greek city-states and for the Roman Republic. Their activities were curtailed under the Principate of Augustus (31 B.C.E.–14 C.E.). In Syria and Palestine, either local leaders, such as the high priests and Herod the Great, or officials directly responsible to the Roman governor were responsible for collecting taxes, especially the personal head tax (a sort of poll tax) and the land tax. Others may have purchased the right to collect various indirect taxes, such as tolls on goods. The New Testament speaks of "publicans" (ASV translation of *telonai*), who were probably toll collectors at commercial centers, such as Capernaum and Jericho (Mark 2:14; Luke 19:2), and testifies to their unpopularity. During the Second Temple period, representatives of the priests and Levites collected "tithes," a second set of taxes for the Temple and priesthood.

public domain   marketplaces, public squares, and streets, where everyone has an equal right to walk. On the Sabbath it is forbidden to carry an object from private domain to public domain, or for more than four cubits within the public domain.

Publicius Marcellus   *see* MARCELLUS, GAIUS QUINCTIUS CERTUS PUBLICIUS

Puga   name of river in the Land of Israel (M. Parah 8:10; B. Sanhedrin 5b), perhaps equivalent with the biblical river Pharpar (2 Kings 5:12); also the name of a place (T. Terumot 1:15; T. Yebamot 6:8). In manuscripts, the name appears alternatively as Piga.

punishment, forms of   Rabbinic law imposes punishments of fines, for unintentional ritual violations; imprisonment, for recidivism (M. Sanhedrin 9:5); flogging, for intentional ritual violations, perjury, and other offenses (M. Makkot 1:1); exile, for manslaughter (M. Makkot 2:1); and execution, for homicide.

Within the talmudic system, flogging, in particular, takes the place of the Bible's ubiquitous divine punishment of extirpation (*karet*). M. Makkot 3:15 makes clear that anyone who undergoes the judicial punishment of flogging is exempt from further divine punishment.

While hesitating ever to impose the death penalty (M. Makkot 1:10), rabbinic law recognizes its applicability in cases called for by scripture. Where scripture does not indicate the method of execution, the rabbis assign one of the four biblical methods. Stoning, considered the most severe punishment, was applied in eighteen circumstances, including bestiality, blasphemy, cursing a parent, idolatry, and witchcraft. Strangulation, deemed the mildest form of execution, applied in five cases, including false prophecy and kidnapping. The other methods are burning, applied in ten cases of inappropriate sexual activity, and decapitation, applied in cases of communal apostasy and murder.

purification of the Temple   Judas Maccabeus's restoration of the furnishings and rituals of the Jerusalem Temple in late 164 B.C.E., marking the achievement of the immediate goal of the uprising led by Mattathias of Modein and his five sons. The account in 2 Maccabees 10:1–8 stresses the theme of purification ("they purified the sanctuary" [10:3]). In this account, Judas and his followers take away the remnants of foreign worship and restore the proper forms of Jewish worship; pray that the defilement of the Temple may never happen again; celebrate a festival patterned on the Feast of Tabernacles for eight days, beginning with the twenty-fifth of Kislev (November/December), and decree that the whole nation of Jews should observe these days every year. The account in 1 Maccabees 4:36–61 emphasizes the theme of (re-)dedication, thus giving the name Hanukkah (from Heb.: *ḥanak,* dedicate) to the feast: "So they celebrated the dedication of the altar for eight days" (4:56). Judas and his men chose "blameless priests," dismantled the defiled altar, built a new altar, and restored the sanctuary, according to Exodus 25–27. Their celebration began on the twenty-fifth of Kislev in 164 B.C.E. and lasted for eight days. The provision for the annual celebration of Hanukkah— the commemoration of a recent event—was ironically closer to Hellenistic than to biblical custom.

purification water   the water prepared in accordance with Numbers 19 to remove corpse-uncleanness, prepared by mixing the ashes of a red cow with running water

Purim   festival celebrated on the fourteenth and fifteenth of Adar, commemorating the victory of Jews over their enemies, recorded in the Book of Esther

Pythagoreanism   a philosophy or perhaps more of a religious movement or cult founded by Pythagoras (fl. 525 B.C.E.). Like many cult figures, the historical Pythagoras is not easily accessible behind the legend. Mathematics was evidently very important to him, and he is alleged to have discovered the formula for working out the area of a triangle. Similarly, music and the relationship between music and mathematical proportions was of considerable interest. He is said to have worked out the relationships that produced the "music of the spheres," the music allegedly produced by the heavenly bodies as they moved through the heavens. Some of his other beliefs were in the area of religion. He believed in an ascetic life-style and held that the soul was the person trapped in a body. At death, the soul would migrate to another body, though this could be an animal, not necessarily another human being. Platonism was very much influenced by Pythagoreanism, especially in the areas of mathematics and the soul. Josephus compares the Essenes to the Pythagoreans, perhaps because of the ascetic life-style and certain beliefs (though he does not give detailed reasons). *See also* METEMPSYCHOSIS; PLATONISM.

Q

q *for Hebrew words beginning with the letter* Q, *see also under* K

qaddish *see* DOXOLOGY

Qadosh Qodashim *see* HOLY OF HOLIES

Qahat, Testament of an Aramaic composition, surviving in one fragmentary copy, found in Cave 4, Qumran, in 1952. Published in 1991 by E. Puech, the manuscript is dated c. 100 B.C.E. and was probably composed in the second century B.C.E.; its title is abbreviated as 4QTQah. An example of the "testament" genre (e.g., the Testaments of the Twelve Patriarchs), the work is an admonition from Qahat, Moses' grandfather, to his son Amram, instructing him to honor the heritage of the fathers (Abraham, Isaac, and Jacob) and to obey the "prescriptions of Abraham" and the "ordinances of Levi" (probably the Torah).

Qatsrin modern village in the Golan Heights about 1½ kilometers northeast of the Sea of Galilee that incorporated parts of an ancient Jewish village, mainly of the Byzantine period. Excavations uncovered remains dating from the Middle Bronze Age to the present, with a flourishing of settlement and construction in the Early Byzantine to Early Arab periods. Parts the village have been reconstructed. The village was constructed on an "organic" plan. That is, houses were built as needed, usually as additions to existing houses or house complexes. Most houses were built as needed, usually as additions to existing houses or house complexes. Most houses were built next to an outdoor courtyard and consisted of a common room separated from a storage area by an interior wall pierced by openings (a

"window wall"). A bedroom or loft was constructed over the storage area in the second story. Some houses had indoor kitchens or small storage spaces. As nuclear families expanded into extended families, additional houses were constructed directly onto existing houses, resulting in crowded blocks of houses with shared walls. Construction was of basalt, a local volcanic stone.

Qatsrin Synagogue ancient synagogue excavated at Qatsrin in the Golan Heights. Building remains in the village reveal that life continued from the third or fourth century C.E. to the eighth century C.E. The first synagogue built at Qatsrin was almost square, 15.2 by 15.3 meters. The floor was hard plaster and was carved with shallow grooves to mimic stone slab pavers. There are remnants of an original door at the northern edge of the floor. A low bench lined the northern wall. Columns were in two rows of three. Some architectural fragments found in the village may have come from this synagogue, including a doorjamb carved with a seven-branched menorah and a cornice fragment bearing a Hebrew inscription. The second building, erected apparently in the sixth century C.E., was larger, about 18 by 15.4 meters. The entrance was reconstructed in the south wall and is well preserved. It is complete, with a cornice bearing an egg-and-dart design and a lintel carved with a wreath, a Hercules knot, two pomegranates, and two amphorae.

The worship space is divided into a nave and two aisles by columns. Inner walls were plastered, whitewashed, and in some places painted with red bands. At the south end of the building was the Torah shrine on top of a raised platform, or *bimah*. The *bimah* was approached by two stone steps that extended from the last two columns in both rows and extended across the nave. A two-tiered bench lined all four walls. Two rows of four columns supported a tiled roof and divided the inner space into two aisles and a nave. The style of the column capitals is a variation on the Ionic style that is peculiar to the area of the Golan Heights. A pair of small pilasters, one of which was used in part of a later wall, may be remnants of the Ark of the Law. Fragments of mosaics indicate mosaic floors were used in the worship space. A doorway in the southeast leads to a small attached room. A hoard of 180 coins, found between the bottom bench and wall, date the construction of the second building to the early sixth century C.E. A similar hoard of 82 coins, found underneath a floor near the Ark of the Law, date some repair work and renovation to the seventh and eighth centuries C.E.

Qatsyon Synagogue   possible ancient synagogue in Upper Galilee about 9 kilometers north-north-west of modern Tsfat (Safed). In the late nineteenth century explorers thought that they had discovered either a pagan temple or possibly a synagogue. They described a building oriented to the south, that is, to Jerusalem, surrounded by a colonnade and associated with a pool. Inside the building was found a six-line Greek inscription: "For the salvation of the Roman Caesars, Lucius Septimius Severus Pius Pertinax Augustus and Marcus Aurelius Antoninus and Lucius Septimius Geta, their sons, by a vow of the Jews." To the left one reads "and Julia Domna Augusta" and to the right "and the legions." The inscription dates between 196 and 198 C.E., when Caracalla held the title Caesar but not yet the title Augustus. The consensus of scholarship today is that this represents a commendation of Caesar's family by the Jewish community in lieu of a votive offering. There is no consensus that the building is a synagogue.

Q.E.   *see* QUAESTIONES ET SOLUTIONES IN EXODUM

Q.G.   *see* QUAESTIONES ET SOLUTIONES IN GENESIN

Qinneret   *see* GALILEE, SEA OF

Qisrin   *see* QATSRIN

Quadratus Bassus   *see* BASSUS, GAIUS JULIUS QUADRATUS

Quaestiones et Solutiones in Exodum   the treatise *Questions and Answers on Exodus* by Philo of Alexandria; its title is abbreviated as *Q.E.* The style of this work takes the form of a question about a biblical passage, followed by Philo's answer. He usually gives the literal meaning first and then follows it with the allegorical meaning.

Quaestiones et Solutiones in Genesin   the treatise *Questions and Answers on Genesis* by Philo of Alexandria; its title is abbreviated as *Q.G.* The work is styled in the form of a question about a biblical passage, followed by Philo's answer. A literal meaning is usually given first, followed by an allegorical interpretation.

quaestor   (Lat.) term usually used in reference to a treasury official, though at times a quaestor might also have military functions. The office was usually taken by young Romans of the nobility (normally around age thirty) on their way up through the ranks of the administration.

Quartodecimans   a Christian movement of the first and second centuries C.E. that celebrated the death and resurrection of Christ on the fourteenth of Nisan, instead of the usual Easter celebrations. A number of important early Christians of the second century were said to be Quartodecimans, including Polycarp, Polycrates, and Melito. Some early traditions suggest that the apostle John was also of this persuasion. This suggests that the movement may represent an earlier practice of the Jesus movement. However, apart from the calendar used, the group seems to have had little in common with Judaism. The eucharist celebrated seems to have been no different from that of other Christians and apparently did not represent a form of Jewish Christianity such as the sect of the Ebionites. According to some testimonies, the Quartodecimans actually began their celebration a day later than did the Jews and were at pains to be still fasting when the Jews were celebrating the Passover meal. From the information preserved, there seems a concern on the part of some of this group not to appear to be Jewish. Melito, for example, makes harsh accusations against the Jews in his pascal address.

Queen of the South   the Queen of Sheba, who visited Solomon to listen to and test his wisdom (1 Kings 10:10). In Matthew 12:42 and Luke 11:31, this Gentile's willingness to seek out Solomon and the repentance of the Ninevites in the Book of Jonah are contrasted with "this generation" of Jews who would not listen to Jesus' words.

Quietus, Lucius   consular legate of Syria-Palaestina from 116 C.E. until shortly after Trajan's death. He was appointed legate of Judea as a reward for his service in the Parthian War and his suppression of a revolt in Mesopotamia. Dio refers to a revolt against Trajan in 116 in Armenia, Mesopotamia, and perhaps Adiabene. In his *History,* Eusebius claims that Trajan sent Quietus to the area because the emperor feared that the Jews would attack the local inhabitants. Quietus was ordered to expel the Jews from Mesopotamia, and Eusebius states that he massacred a number of the inhabitants of the area. In his *Chronicle,* Eusebius writes that Quietus's arrival was in response to a Jewish uprising. Several Jewish sources mention "a war of Quietus." Although the rebels enjoyed initial success, Quietus's arrival turned the tide of the war. He took Nisibis, destroyed Edessa, and captured Seleucia, all of which probably had significant Jewish populations.

Quietus, War of   *see* TRAJAN, WAR OF

Quinctius Certus Publicius Marcellus   *see* MAR-CELLUS, GAIUS QUINCTIUS CERTUS PUBLICIUS

Quinta   an otherwise-unknown Greek translation of the Hebrew Bible (or portions of it) known from Origen's *Hexapla.* It forms an extra column in the Psalms but is absent from most of his work, so it may have been done for only some books. It generally agrees with the *kaige.*

Quirinius, Publius Sulpicius   a Roman of senatorial and consular rank who was appointed legate of Syria by Augustus in 6 C.E. He carried out a census in Palestine, referred to by Josephus and the Gospel of Luke 2:1, which produced unrest. He also appointed Ananus, son of Seth, to the high priesthood (6–15 C.E.).

Quis Rerum Divinarum Heres   the treatise *Who is the Heir of Divine Things* by Philo of Alexandria; its title is abbreviated as *Heres.* The treatise is an allegorical exegesis, with few digressions, of Genesis 15:2–18, in which Abraham offers a sacrifice and is promised an heir. Every small detail of the text is considered significant.

Qumran   the Judean wilderness site associated with the finding of the Dead Sea Scrolls, located on the northwest shores of the Dead Sea and south of Jericho. It may be the "city of salt" of Joshua 15:61–62. Although an Israelite farmstead was found at Qumran dating from the eighth to the sixth centuries B.C.E., the main occupation at Qumran began sometime between 154 to 134 B.C.E., or during the reigns of the Jewish kings Jonathan Maccabaeus (152–142 B.C.E.) and Simeon Maccabaeus (142–134 B.C.E.). This is phase Ia. In this period the round Israelite cistern was reused and the new occupants dug two more nearby.

In the next phase, called Ib by the archaeologists, Qumran assumed the complete form familiar to tourists. Perhaps during the reign of John Hyrcanus I (134–104 B.C.E.) the buildings were greatly enlarged. The occupants constructed a massive main building with a tower, a central courtyard, a meeting room, and a dining hall with connected pantry. A potter's shop was constructed on the west side with two kilns and arrangements for preparing clay and manufacturing pots. To the west, a second courtyard building was constructed with storage rooms around it. Cisterns and workshops stood between the west building and the main building. Northwest of the tower was a large courtyard with a ritual bath in its northwest corner. Here and there among the ruins, archaeologists recovered caches of uneaten ritual meals with sheep, goat, calf, or cow bones and broken associated dishes. There was no provision for living within the buildings, except perhaps for two rooms connected with the meeting room (locus 1). An elaborate water system brought water in from the Wadi Quman to the west in an aqueduct resting directly upon the ground. The aqueduct fed the complex of eight cisterns and ritual baths for which Qumran is famous. At the entry point of the aqueduct there was a settling basin for the water. Great care was lavished upon the ritual baths, complete with small, clay and plaster markings on the steps to distinguish a path for descending into the water from the path for exiting from the water. Such care suggests a strong commitment to ritual bathing and perhaps other rites of cleansing the person. This era of occupation ended with an earthquake in 31 B.C.E. The earthquake damaged the tower, brought down the ceiling of the pantry on the assembled dishes, smashing them in place, collapsed the western cistern, and damaged the corner of the second building. An associated conflagration burned extensively and left thick layers of ash and burned soil in open areas near the buildings.

The ruin was left abandoned for a period. The water system continued to function and brought in a layer of pure silt that was deposited on top of the ash, burn, and debris from the earthquake and the conflagration. Shortly afterward, perhaps with the accession of Herod Archaelaus as tetrarch of Judea in 4 B.C.E., the site was reoccupied in what is known as phase II. The new occupation continued the usages of phase Ib. The walls were strengthened where they had been damaged, and the tower was reinforced with a buttress around its lower story. A few rooms went out of use, but in the main the occupation continued along the lines of phase Ia. Ritual meals continued as before with the burial of the bones and dishes. The potter continued manufacturing pottery at the site. There was a kitchen with five ovens, a flour mill, and a baker's establishment. In the collapse from the upper story of one of the rooms of phase II, the archaeologists found a long table with low benches, two shorter tables, also with low benches, and three ink wells. This room was dubbed the "scriptorium," or scribal space, by the archaeologists.

This is the period of major activity of the occupants, whom the archaeologists identify with the Essenes mentioned in Josephus and in other ancient sources. The assumption is that this is a mainly celibate sect of Jewish men who attempted to live ritually pure and pious lives apart from other men. Their cemetery to the east contained 1,100 graves, all oriented north to south. It indicates something of the length of occupation and the continuity of occupation, as all were buried with the same customs. A small settlement exactly parallel to Qumran was found at Ein Feshkah, a few kilometers south of Qumran. This ruin had been occupied in exactly the same periods as Qumran, and presumably by the same people.

Phase II was destroyed in June of 68 C.E. by the Roman army under Vespasian. The army occupied Jericho at this time, two years into the First Revolt against Rome. The latest coins of phase II are four Jewish coins of year three of the revolt, a year which began in March or April of 68 C.E.

Phase III of Qumran is the period when a small Roman garrison occupied the site. In this occupation, the soldiers built rooms here and there from the actual debris of the site, on top of the rubble of the destruction they had performed. The soldiers used only one cistern, filling in the others with rubble. The garrison was withdrawn after the fall of Masada in 73 C.E. A few rebels associated with the Bar Kokhba Revolt of 135 C.E. camped at the site but built no permanent structures.

Qumran caves 1, 2, 3, and 11 lay far north of Qumran. Caves 4 and 5 were found on the next projecting terrace to the immediate west of Qumran. Qumran cave 6 was found in the cliff face just west of Qumran. On the same terrace as the ruin of Qumran were found Qumran caves 7 to 10, all of which contained scroll fragments. *See also* DEAD SEA CAVES; DEAD SEA SCROLLS.

Qumran Aramaic   *see* ARAMAIC, JEWISH LITERARY

Qumran Scrolls   *see* DEAD SEA SCROLLS

Quod Deterius Potiori insidiari solet   the treatise *The Worse Attacks the Better* by Philo of Alexandria; its title is abbreviated *Quod Det.* This work is an allegory on Cain and Abel, contrasting the love of self and the sophist (represented by Cain) with the love of God (represented by Abel).

Quod Deus immutabilis sit   the treatise *On the Unchangeableness of God* by Philo of Alexandria; its title is abbreviated as *Quod Deus.* An allegorical exegesis of Genesis 6:4–12 that continues the treatise *De Gigantibus,* this work attempts to refute the idea apparently expressed by the text that God might change his mind.

Quod Omnis   *see* PROBUS

quorum   (Heb.: *minyan*) number needed for quorum for worship; ten people (males in Orthodox Judaism, males or females in other forms of Judaism) required for the recitation of public prayer or public reading of the Torah

R

Rab *see* ABBA ARIKHA

Raba Babylonian amora of the first half of the fourth century C.E.; a student of Naḥman b. Jacob and Joseph. His full name was Raba b. Joseph b. Ḥama. He became head of the academy at Meḥoza and is known for his legal disputes with Abayye, which form a significant aspect of talmudic dialectic. Except in several instances, the decided law followed Raba's opinion.

Rabba *see* AḤA B. ABBUHA

Rabba b. Ḥana *see* RABBAH B. ḤUNA

Rabba b. Ulla *see* ABBA B. ULLA

Rabbah b. Avuha Babylonian amora active at the end of the second century C.E.; a student first of Rab and then at Nehardea, under Samuel. Later, he was a judge and head of the academy at Meḥoza.

Rabbah b. b. Ḥana Babylonian amora of the early fourth century C.E.; the son of Abba b. Ḥana. He is known for his accounts of his sea voyages.

Rabbah b. Ḥuna Babylonian amora of the early fourth century C.E.; in the Jerusalem Talmud, called Abba b. Ḥuna. After Ḥisda's death, he was head of the academy at Sura. He died in Babylonia but was buried in the Land of Israel (B. Moed Katan 25b).

Rabbah b. Naḥmani Babylonian amora of the late third and early fourth centuries C.E.; born of a priestly family that traced its lineage to Eli. At Sura, he studied under Ḥuna; at Pumbedita, he studied under Judah b. Ezekiel. It is unclear whether or not, for a time, he studied in Palestine under Yoḥanan (B. Nedarim 59a). His was regarded as an expert in the laws of ritual purity (B. Baba Metzia 86a). For twenty-two years he was head of the academy at Pumbedita.

Rabbah b. Shila Babylonian amora active in the late third and early fourth centuries C.E.; a contemporary of Ḥisda. He reports that Ḥisda's ban on the butchers of Ḥutzal has been ineffective. His activities as a civil judge are frequently mentioned.

Rabbah Tosfaa one of the last Babylonian Amoraic authorities, active in the middle of the fifth century C.E.; a student of Rabina. He followed Mar b. Ashi as head of the academy at Sura, holding that position from 468 through 474 C.E. The name Tosfaa (the amplifier) may have been intended to characterize his talmudic activity.

Rabbai Savoraic authority or possibly a gaon, active at Pumbedita in the mid-sixth century C.E.

Rabban title of honor, meaning "lord"

Rabbana honorific title (our rabbi), applied to a number of Babylonian authorities, in particular, to Ashi

Rabban Uqba *see* MAR UKBA II

Rabbat Moab Synagogue a building located 20 kilometers east of the southern quarter of the Dead Sea, which can possibly be identified as an ancient synagogue that was used from the second half of the fourth century C.E. until sometime in the fifth century C.E. The building has been identified as a synagogue because of its westerly orientation toward Jerusalem and because of a seemingly exaggerated statement by the fifth-century monk, Bar Sauma, who claims to have destroyed a synagogue at Rabbat Moab. The possibility should not be ruled out, however, that the building functioned as a Byzantine church instead of a synagogue.

Rabbenu   title of honor, meaning "our lord"

rabbi   my lord, or my master; title of honor, generally associated with a master of the Torah. The rabbi functioned in the Jewish community in ancient times as judge and administrator. But he lived in a society in some ways quite separate from that of Jewry as a whole. The rabbinical academy was a law school. Some of its graduates served as judges and administrators of the law. However, the rabbinical school was by no means a center for merely legal study. It was, like the Christian monastery, the locus for a peculiar kind of religious living. Only one of its functions concerned those parts of the Torah to be applied in everyday life through the judiciary. In ancient, medieval, and modern times these activities and institutions remained remarkably stable. The school, or *yeshiva* (Heb., session), was a council of Judaism, a holy community. In it, men learned to live a holy life—to become saints. When they left, sages continued to live by the discipline of the school. They invested great efforts in teaching that discipline by example and precept to ordinary folk. Through the school, classical Judaism transformed the Jewish people into its vision of the true replica of Mosaic revelation.

The schools, like other holy communities, imposed their own particular rituals, intended, in the first instance, for the disciples and masters. Later, it was hoped, all Jews would conform to those rituals and so join the circle of master and disciples. As with study, the schools' discipline transformed other ordinary, natural actions, gestures, and functions into rituals—the rituals of "being a rabbi." For example, everyone ate, but rabbis did so in a "rabbinic" manner. In other words, that which others regarded as matters of mere etiquette—formalities and conventions intended to render eating aesthetically agreeable—rabbis regarded as matters of "Torah," something to be *learned*. It was "Torah" to do things one way, and it was "ignorance" to do them another way (though not heresy, for theology was not the issue). The master of Torah, whether disciple or teacher, would demonstrate his mastery not merely through what he said in the discussion of legal traditions or what he did in court but also by how he sat at the table, by what ritual formulas he recited before eating one or another kind of fruit or vegetable, by how he washed his hands, and so on—by performing all mundane acts according to "Torah."

The personality traits of ordinary men might vary, but those expected of and inculcated into a sage were of a single fabric. The central human relationship in the schools was between the disciple and the master. Long ago, it was taught that the master took the place of the father. The father brought the son into this world; the master would lead him into the world to come. Whatever honor was due the father was all the more owed to the master. But the master did not merely replace the father. He also required the veneration and reverence owed to the Torah. The extreme forms of respect that evolved over the centuries constitute the most striking rituals attached to "being a rabbi." If study was an act of piety, then the master was partly its object. This is not to suggest that the master, though a saint, was regarded divine in any sense. But the forms of respect reserved for the divinity or for the Torah were not too different, in appropriate circumstances, from those owed to the master. The forms of respect for the master constituted part of the ritual of being a rabbi. The service of the disciples of the sages separated the true sage from the merely learned man. It had earlier been taught that if one had studied scripture and the Mishnah but did not attend upon disciples of the sages, he was regarded as a boor (am haAretz). To this epithet a fourth-century rabbi added: "Behold, such a one is a magus," and the talmudic discussion then cited a popular saying: The magus mumbles and does not know what he is saying, just as the tanna (the professional memorizier and reciter of the Mishnah) who has not attended on the sages recites and does not know what he is saying" (B. Sotah, 22a). The sage claimed to see no difference between a learned Jew and a learned Zoroastrian except that the disciple served the sages. That service—meaning not merely personal attendance but also imitation and study of the master as much as of the Torah—constituted a vital part of Torah study. The master exemplified the whole Torah, including the oral part of it. Scripture and Mishnah, written and oral Torah, meant little without observation and imitation of the sage. The whole Torah was not in books or in words to be memorized. Torah was to be found in whole and complete form in the master. That is why the forms of respect for the master were both so vital and so unique to the mythic life of the schools. What made a man into a rabbi was study of the Torah as a disciple with a master of the Torah. This was regarded in Judaism in ancient times (and is still regarded today) as the principal purpose of life; in the words of Rabban Yoḥanan ben Zakkai: "If you have accomplished much in the study of the Torah, do not take pride on that account, for it was to that end that you were created."

All the great saints and heroes of Israel, both in the times of ancient Israel and later on, were regarded as rabbis. The rabbis taught that the "whole Torah"—oral and written—was studied by David, augmented by Ezekiel, legislated by Ezra, and embodied in the schools and by the sages of every period in Israelite history from Moses to the present. It is a singular, linear conception of a revelation preserved only by the few, pertaining to the many, and in time capable of bringing salvation to all. The Torah myth further regards Moses as "our rabbi," the first and prototypical figure of the ideal Jew. It holds that whoever embodies the teachings of Moses, "our rabbi," thereby is himself a rabbi and conforms to the will of God—and not to God's will alone, but also to his way. In heaven, God and the angels study the Torah, just as rabbis do on earth. God dons phylacteries, as does a Jew. He prays in the rabbinic mode. He carries out the acts of compassion called for by Judaic ethics. He guides the affairs of the world according to the rules of Torah, just as does the rabbi in his court on earth. One exegesis of the Creation legend taught that God had looked into the Torah and therefrom had created the world. The myth of Torah is multidimensional. It includes the striking detail that whatever the most recent rabbi is destined to discover through proper exegesis of the tradition is as much a part of the way revealed to Moses as is a sentence of scripture itself. It therefore is possible to participate even in the giving of the law by appropriate, logical inquiry into the law. God himself, studying and living by Torah, is believed to subject himself to these same rules of logical inquiry. If an earthly court were to overrule the testimony, delivered through miracles, of the heavenly one, God would rejoice, crying out, "My sons have conquered me! My sons have conquered me!" Moses, "our rabbi," is the pattern for the ordinary sage of the streets of Jerusalem, Pumbedita, Mainz, London, Lvov, Bombay, Dallas, or New York. And God Himself participates in the system, for it is his image that, in the end, forms that cosmic paradigm. The faithful Jew constitutes the projection of the divine on earth. Honor is due to the learned rabbi more than to the scroll of the Torah, for through his learning and logic he may alter the very content of Mosaic revelation. He *is* Torah, not merely because he lives by it, but because at his best he forms as compelling an embodiment of the heavenly model as does a Torah-scroll itself. Learn-

ing by rabbis thus finds a central place in a classical Judaic tradition because of the belief that God had revealed his will to mankind through the medium of a written revelation given to Moses at Mount Sinai, accompanied by oral traditions taught in the rabbinical schools and preserved in the Talmuds and related literature.

The texts without the oral traditions might have led elsewhere than into the academy, for the biblicism of other groups yielded something quite different from Jewish religious intellectualism. But belief in the text was coupled with the belief that oral traditions were also revealed. In the books composed in the rabbinical academies, as much as in the Hebrew Bible itself, was contained God's will for humanity. The acts of studying, memorizing, and commenting upon the sacred books are holy. The reason is that when the faithful Jew studies the Torah, he hears God's word and will. The study of sacred texts therefore assumes a central position in Judaism. Other traditions had their religious virtuosos, whose virtuosity consisted in knowledge of a literary tradition; but few held, as does Judaism, that everyone must become such a virtuoso. Traditional processes of learning are discrete and exegetical. Creativity is expressed not through abstract dissertation, but rather through commentary upon the sacred writings, or, more likely in later times, commentary upon earlier commentaries. One might also prepare a code of the laws, but such a code would represent little more than an assemblage of authoritative opinions of earlier times, with a decision being offered upon those few questions the centuries had left unanswered. The chief glory of the commentator is his *ḥiddush* (novelty). The *ḥiddush* constitutes a scholastic disquisition upon a supposed contradiction between two earlier authorities chosen from any period, with no concern for how they might in fact relate historically, and upon a supposed harmonization of their "contradiction." Or a new distinction might be read into an ancient law, upon which basis, ever more questions might be raised and solved. The focus of interest quite naturally lies upon law rather than theology, history, philosophy, or other sacred sciences. But within the law it rests upon legal theory, and interest in the practical consequences of the law is decidedly subordinated.

What makes a person into a rabbi, therefore, is study, and one central ritual of the Judaic tradition, therefore, is study. Study as a natural action entails learning of traditions and executing them—in this context, in school or in court. Study becomes a ritual action when it is endowed with values extrinsic to its ordinary character—that is, when it is set into a mythic context. When a disciple memorizes his master's traditions and actions, he participates in that myth. His study is thereby endowed with the sanctity that ordinarily pertains to prayer or other cultic matters. Study loses its referent in intellectual attainment. The act of study itself becomes holy, so that its original purpose, which was mastery of particular information, ceases to matter much. What matters is piety—piety expressed through the rites of studying. Repeating the words of the oral revelation, even without comprehending them, produces reward, just as imitating the master matters, even without really being able to explain the reasons for his actions. The separation of the value, or sanctity, of the act of study from the natural, cognitive result of learning therefore transforms study from a natural to a ritual action. That separation is accomplished in part by myth and in part by the powerful impact of the academic environment itself. A striking illustration of the distinction between mere learning and learning as part of ritual life derives from the comment of Mar Zutra, a fifth-century-C.E. Babylonian rabbi, on Isaiah 14:5, "The Lord has broken the staff of the wicked, the scepter of rulers." He said, "These are disciples of the sages who teach public laws to boorish judges" (B. Shabbat, 139a). The fact that the uncultivated judge would know the law did not matter, for he still was what he had been—a boor, not a disciple of the sages. Mere knowledge of the laws does not transform an ordinary person, however powerful, into a sage.

Learning carried with it more than naturalistic valence, as is further seen in the saying of Amemar, a contemporary of Mar Zutra: "A sage is superior to a prophet, as Scripture [Ps. 90:12] says, And a prophet has a heart of wisdom" (B. Baba Batra, 12a). The sense is that what made a prophet credible was his knowledge of wisdom, and wisdom, in sages' speech, stood for Torah-learning. What characterized the prophet was, Amemar said, sagacity. Since the prophet was supposed to reveal the divine will, it was not inconsequential that his revelation depended not upon gifts of the spirit but upon learning. The talmudic rabbis' emphasis on learning as a ritual act ought not to obscure their high expectations of actual accomplishment in learning. While they stressed the act of study without reference to its achievement, at the same time they possessed very old traditions on how best to pursue their task. These traditions included much practical advice on how to acquire and preserve learning.

No role whatever was assigned to women, who could not become rabbis; only in the last part of the twentieth century has women's right to become rabbis been recognized. They did not study in the schools, and the life of Torah effectively was closed to them. On the other hand, mothers would encourage their sons to study Torah. Rabina, a late fourth-century master, explained how the merit of study of the Torah applied to womenfolk. Women, he suggested, acquire merit when they arrange for their sons' education in scripture and the Mishnah and when they wait for their husbands to return from the schools. Since that return was often postponed by months or even years, it was no small sacrifice. But the schools were entirely male institutions, and no equivalent religious life was available for women. It is only in our own day that women have entered the world of Torah-study in the ways in which men have carried on that enterprise.

rabbinic literature   *see* LITERATURE, RABBINIC

Rabin   *see* ABIN

Rabina I   Babylonian amora; died c. 422 C.E.; a student of Raba and frequently cited in conjunction with Naḥman b. Isaac, Aḥa b. Raba, and Ashi. Many of his statements involve relations with non-Jews and other practical aspects of life in Sassanid Babylonia.

Rabina II b. Ḥuna   Babylonian amora active in the late fifth century C.E.; the nephew of Rabina I; during 474–499 C.E., head of the academy at Sura

Rabina of Amutzya   Saboraic authority; died c. 506 C.E. The details of his life and work are not known.

raca   (Gr.: *raka*; probably from Aram.: *reka*, Heb.: *rekah*, empty one) term of contempt suggesting something like empty-head or numbskull. Matthew 5:22 sets it in parallel to "Fool!" as part of one of the "antitheses" in which Jesus cites a commandment (against murder) and then demands more radical behavior (do not be angry or insult another).

Rachel   Jacob's wife, Leah's sister and rival, and Joseph's mother, who died giving birth to Benjamin. Her story is expanded by Jubilees, Demetrius the Chronographer, and the Testaments of the Twelve Patriarchs. According to Matthew 2:18, she weeps for the children killed by Herod's soldiers and thereby fulfills Jeremiah 31:15.

Rafid   (Raphid) a possible synagogue site of the Roman or Byzantine period in the Golan Heights (though some have suggested that the ruins are Christian). In the nineteenth century, it was reported that a large building was found with decorations on the stones carved in low relief. An apse was also reported. A lintel stone presents two birds holding the ribbons of a wreath in their beaks. A second lintel was decorated with three simple circles. A doorpost, on the other hand, was decorated with an equal-armed cross. Since the ruins are dated to the second century, and the cross does not emerge on Christian buildings until the fourth century, this need not be a church. On the other hand, there is nothing in the ruins that identifies them as unambiguously Jewish. Only excavation will tell.

Rafram I b. Pappa Babylonian amora; a student of Ḥisda at Pumbedita in the fourth century C.E. Following Dimi, he became head of that academy.

Rafram II Babylonian amora active in the mid-fifth century C.E.; during 433–443 C.E., head of the academy at Pumbedita; referred to at B. Bekhorot 36b as Rafram of Pumbedita

Rahab harlot in Jericho who sheltered in her house the men whom Joshua sent to spy in the city (Josh. 2). The story attributes to her genuine belief in the invincible power of the God of Israel (2:8–14), and she makes a covenant of mutual protection with the spies. Rahab's active faith is cited in the catalog of heroes and heroines in Hebrews 11:31, while James 2:25, following his own emphasis, focuses on the deed that embodied her faith. In Matthew 1:5 she is mentioned along with Tamar, Ruth, and Bathsheba as a forebear of Jesus the Messiah. This noteworthy group of women prefigure Mary the mother of Jesus, who is under considerable suspicion in Matthew 1:18–19.

Rahba Babylonian amora active at Pumbedita in the fourth century C.E.; a student of Judah b. Ezekiel. His name is a contraction of the title Rab and the personal name Aḥba.

rain The uncertainty of the water supply in the Land of Israel meant that, in biblical and rabbinic culture, drought was dreaded. Rain was seen as a gift from God, who offered abundant rain as a reward for the Israelites' faithful observance of the commandments (see, e.g., Deut. 11:13–14). Iniquity, by contrast, was punished by God's withholding of rain (Deut. 16:15). Malakhi 3:10 clearly expresses the connection between the observance of agricultural laws and the rains: "Bring the full tithes into the storehouse, that there may be food in my house; and thereby put me to the test, says the Lord of hosts, if I will not open the windows of heaven for you and pour down for you an overflowing blessing."

In line with Deuteronomy 11:14 and Jeremiah 5:24, which refer to early and late rains, the rabbis speak of the first rains, called *yoreh,* which come in the autumn (in the month of Ḥeshvan or, alternatively, Kislev), and the second rains, called *malkosh,* in the spring (in the month of Nisan). This distinction reflects the importance for agriculture not simply of appropriate quantities of rain but of rain at the right times of the year. The rabbis view prayer as a viable means of assuring such rain. From December through the end of the rainy season in the spring, a petition for rain is included daily in the eighth of the Eighteen Benedictions (M. Berakhot 5:2). Additionally, during the period of the later rains, the second benediction of the Amidah, concerning the resurrection of the dead, is expanded with a declaration that God "causes the wind to blow and the rain to fall." The rainy season as a whole is introduced with a special appeal for rain, inserted in the Musaf prayers on Shemini Atzeret, understood as the day on which God judges the people by determining whether or not to provide rain (M. Rosh Hashanah 1:2). This liturgical poem petitions God for rain by recalling the significance of water in the lives of the patriarchs, Moses, Aaron, and the people of Israel. God is asked to provide rain for the sake of his people, who were redeemed from slavery in Egypt by going through water and who, as martyrs for God's name, have had their blood spilled like water.

Mishnah Taanit (chap. 1) describes a sequence of public fasts declared in the case of a drought. If rain does not fall by the seventeenth of Marḥeshvan, individuals undertake three fasts during the daylight hours. After the beginning of Kislev, the court decrees additional sequences of three and then seven fasts. With each series of fasts, additional activities are restricted, including, initially, work, bathing, and sexual relations. The failure of these fasts to bring rain leads to a period of national mourning, during which commerce, building, planting, engagements, marriages, and greetings are prohibited.

Mishnah Taanit 3:8 recalls the story of Honi the Circle-maker who, because of his special relationship to God, was able to compel the production of rain. Honi refused to move from a circle he drew on the ground until God provided the amount and sort of rain needed by the people. The rabbis reject such activity as an inappropriate coercing of God, which cannot be successfully undertaken by most people, who do not have Honi's stature before the deity.

Ramah Synagogue a possible synagogue site in Lower Galilee about 3 kilometers north of Sepphoris. Josephus knew of a Galilean village named Ramah, the home of two of the defenders of Yodfat against the siege of the Romans in 66 B.C.E. An Aramaic inscription cut in stone has been found at Ramah that says, "Blessed be for good Rabbi Eliezer bar Theodoro who built this house as a hospice." The name Eliezer of Elazar is very common among rabbis and others of the Roman and Byzantine periods, so it is impossible to say which Eliezer this is. On the other hand it attests to a hospice. In other inscriptions from other localities, including Jerusalem, hospices are associated with synagogues. A lintel that is said to have come from Ramah is decorated with a repeated square pattern around its edges, then depicts a wreath in the center with two *nike*s (victories) or genii on either side.

Ramat Aviv Synagogue   ancient Samaritan synagogue found on the slope of a hill north of Tel Aviv near the entrance of the HaAretz Museum. The site is in part of the ancient city of Appolonia. Only one row of columns and the south wall of an east-west building have so far been recovered. Originally two rows of columns divided the interior space into nave and two aisles. There appears to be an opening to the east, but it is not clear if this is the main entrance. The interior space would be about 6.7 meters long, but the width is unknown. A colorful mosaic covered the floor of the entire building in antiquity, but only about one-third was recovered. The design consists of geometric patterns and repeated images of plants and flowers. A Greek inscription set in a mosaic medallion reads: "Blessing and Peace on Israel and on the place, Amen." The word "place" or "Holy Place" is often a term for "synagogue" in ancient inscriptions. A longer Greek inscription reads: "In the rule of count Urbicus, as an offering of . . . son of Agatheus for the salvation of his most God-loving children, the structure with light chamber [?] is [dedicated] to the Lord." A third inscription in Samaritan script has not been published. The structure is sixth-century or Late Byzantine, judging by the pottery and a single bronze coin.

Ramat Bene-Anat   *see* BETH RAMAH

Rami b. Abba   Babylonian amora active in the fourth century C.E.; often mentioned with Eleazar b. Pedat and Ḥiyya II; father-in-law of Ashi. His name is a contraction of R. Ammi.

Rami b. Ḥama   Babylonian amora of the third century C.E.; a student of Ḥisda, whose daughter he married. He was a junior contemporary of Raba, who, after Rami's premature death, married his widow. At B. Berakhot 47b, Raba states that Rami's death resulted from Rami's ill-treatment of Manasseh b. Taḥlifa.

rank   (Heb.: *bet maamad,* place of standing) technical term found in sectarian manuscripts of the Dead Sea Scrolls that designates the location of each individual member in the Community's hierarchy. The hierarchy of the sectarian community reflected in the texts, most clearly in the Community Rule, is based on the structure of the camp of Israel in the wilderness—portrayed particularly in the Book of Numbers—that was laid out in units of "thousands, hundreds, fifties and tens" (cf. Exod. 18:21, 25; Deut. 1:15). Likewise, the Qumran Community envisaged a hierarchy in which each member was enrolled by tribe and then ranked in units of thousands, hundreds, fifties, and tens. Therefore, according to 1QS 6:22, all new members are registered in order of rank, and at the annual Covenant Renewal ceremony, all the members enter according to their rank: "The Priests shall enter first, ranked one after another according to the perfection of their spirit; then the Levites, and thirdly, all the people one after another in their Thousands, Hundreds, Fifties and Tens, that every Israelite may know his place in the community of God according to the everlasting design. No man shall move down from his place nor move up from his allotted position" (1QS 2:19–23). This hierarchical structure is also envisioned for Israel in the eschatological age (cf. 1QS^a 2:12–17, 1QM 3–4). This hierarchy, in units of thousands and hundreds, is an idealization, since the Community at Qumran never numbered over two hundred at any given time, and Josephus reports only four thousand Essenes living in Judah in the Second Temple period.

ransom   the price paid to free a war captive, slave, or debtor. In Hebrew, the word for ransoming a slave or debtor is from *kpr,* which is also the root of the Hebrew word for atonement or expiation. In Greek, it is associated with the word root meaning "release" (*apollyo*), and thus with the English word "redemption," which also pertains to being released or bought freedom. Some other words are used for ransom and redemption as well. In this entry, emphasis will be on the metaphor of paying a price, which is connoted by the English word "ransom."

Postbiblical usage generally continues biblical usage. In the Bible, one ransoms or redeems a first-born ass with a sheep (Exod. 34:20) and a brother's possessions with money (Lev. 25:25). In the Letter of Aristeas, the ransom or redemption (*apolytrosis*) of Jews brought to Egypt, perhaps as captives, is sought and obtained (Let. Arist. 12, 33). God also redeems Israel from the house of bondage in Egypt

(Deut. 7:8). In 4 Maccabees, the martyrs Eleazar and the mother and her seven sons conceive of their deaths as a ransom (*antipsychon*) for the nation (6:27–29, 17:21). In the Dead Sea Scrolls, God's saving activity is sometimes described with the word *kpr,* but the metaphor of paying a ransom is not prominent in these documents. In the New Testament, the death of Jesus, like that of the Maccabean martyrs, is understood as a ransom. Jesus is said to have "given his life as a ransom [*lytron*] for many" (Mark 10:45) and to have given himself to redeem or ransom believers from iniquity and purify a people for himself (Titus 2:14). Cultic imagery merges with ransoming in the claim that Jesus' blood, not silver or gold, ransomed gentile believers from their futile ancestral ways (1 Pet. 1:18–19). Paul speaks of Christians as slaves of Christ, bought for a price (1 Cor. 6:20, 7:23), an ironic reversal of slavery and redemption terminology.

Rabbinic literature uses the term *pidyon shevuim,* or redemption of captives, to refer to payment of a price for the release of a prisoner or kidnapped person. Talmudic rabbis considered captivity to be the worst possible punishment (B. Baba Batra 8a–b) and accordingly deemed the ransom of Jewish captives to be one of the most important communal obligations, taking precedence even over feeding or clothing the poor. Ransom of captives was underwritten with public funds, even those collected for other purposes, including the construction of a synagogue (B. Baba Batra 3b). To discourage would-be captors, rabbinic law precluded payment of more than the usual value of a captive or slave (B. Gittin 45a). The law requiring ransoming of a captive was relaxed in the case of individuals who, for financial reasons, had allowed themselves to be taken captive a number of times (B. Gittin 46a). M. Horayot 3:7–8 provides an order in which captives are to be ransomed when sufficient funds are not available to ransom everyone: priest, Levite, Israelite, *mamzer, natin,* proselyte, freed slave. According to M. Horayot, a man takes precedence over a women; and a sage, even if he is a mamzer, takes precedence over all other categories.

rape sexual intercourse with a woman against her will. Biblical and rabbinic law distinguish rape from seduction, in which the woman improperly was caused to consent to intercourse. Intercourse with a woman in a place in which, even if she called out, no help could have come is presumed to be rape unless witnesses testify to the contrary (Deut. 22:25–27). In a town, where cries for help would have brought assistance, an absence of witnesses to her crying out leads to a presumption of seduction. Intercourse with a female minor always is deemed rape, as is intercourse that began forcibly but ended with the woman's consent.

In rabbinic law, rape of a minor is penalized with a fine of fifty shekels of silver and compensation for pain, suffering, shame, and blemish (cf. Deut. 22:28–29). For an adult, payment is made only for pain and suffering. A seducer of an adult is exempt from financial liability.

Raphael (Heb., God has healed) one of four, or in some cases, seven holy ones (angels) who stand in God's immediate presence. He is mentioned in all lists of these angels in the Pseudepigrapha (1 Enoch 20, 40) and the Qumran scrolls (1QM 9:15–16), and is he is one of three who appear by name in canonical and deuterocanonical texts. In the Book of Tobit he is the divinely sent healer and the opponent of the demon Asmodeus. According to 1 Enoch 10:4 he heals the earth from the plague caused by the rebellious watchers, and in 1 Enoch 22, with a different play on his name, he is in charge of the shades of the dead (Heb.: *refaim*).

Raphia, Battle of The Seleucid ruler Antiochus III, known as Antiochus the Great (r. 223–187 B.C.E.), pushed the Ptolemaic forces out of Palestine during 220–218 B.C.E. In 217 B.C.E., Ptolemy IV Euergetes (r. 221–204 B.C.E.) defeated Antiochus at Raphia, on the northernshore of the Sinai peninsula, and forced him to give up his gains in Palestine.

Rautah and Fanutah the coming time of "Divine Favor" and the current period of "Divine Disfavor" that will be replaced in the Samaritan scheme of history. The idea is akin to the apocalyptic present evil age and the redemptive age about to come, and the similar notion of two ages described by the Qumran Community. For the Samaritans, the original period of Divine Favor was present when the Holy Tabernacle was on Mount Gerizim. That period ended when the Jews withdrew and Eli moved the sanctuary from Gerizim to Shiloh. The subsequent secession of the Northern Kingdom by Jeroboam I and the establishment of a sanctuary at Bethel further justified God's anger. God turned away (hence, *fanutah,* to turn away) and left Gerizim, initiating the period of Divine Disfavor. God instructed the priest Uzzi to put the holy vessels and garments into a cave and seal it. The cave subsequently disappeared to await the Rautah, or return of God's favor, when God will return to his tent on Mount Gerizim. Originally the idea of a Taheb, or prophet like Moses, and that of a Second Kingdom, were independent from the notion of the Rautah, but in time the three concepts merged into a single vision of hope for the future.

rebiit *see* LOG

reconciliation Greek term (*katallagē; [apo] katallassein*) for which there is no Hebrew or Aramaic equivalent. Etymologically, atonement (at-one-ment) means reconciliation, but this meaning is obsolete, since "atonement" is now used as the equivalent of "expiation." The Septuagint uses a cognate, *dialassein,* to speak of the Levite's reconciling his concubine to himself, where the Hebrew has him cause her to return to himself (Judg. 19:3). In 2 Maccabees, people pray that God will be reconciled (1:5, 8:29), knowing that after chastening for sins, God will be reconciled to his servants (7:33); after God is reconciled, the Temple is restored to its former glory (5:20). In 3 Maccabees, persecuted Jews pray to God, who is easily reconciled (5:13). Josephus speaks of God's being reconciled with Saul (*Ant.* 6.143) and says that God lets himself be reconciled to those who repent (*War* 5.415). In the New Testament, Paul uses the same language to say that Jesus' death reconciles sinners throughout the world with God (Rom. 5:10–11, 11:15; 2 Cor. 5:18–20). The same expressions are used of humans' reconciliation to one another (Sir. 22:22, 27:21; Matt. 5:24; 1 Cor. 7:11).

The concept of reconciliation appears in the rabbinic notion that a person's sins against another individual will be forgiven by God only after the wrongdoer has reconciled with ("gained the good will of") the one whom he has harmed (M. Yoma 8:9). Reconciliation does not appear in rabbinic descriptions of the process by which people atone for sins against God, which involves rather expiation and repentance.

redemption the process of paying a price to regain land, houses, or persons (Lev. 25). In the Bible, the firstborn son is owed to God and must be ransomed or redeemed (Exod. 13:1–16). "Redemption" also refers to God's deliverance of Israel or of the needy from trouble (Pss. 25:22, 72:14) or of sinners from their sins (Pss. 19:15, 78:35). In Hebrew, several word roots are used (*g'l; pdh; kpr*); in Greek, words from the word root meaning "release" ([apo]lyo) are used.

These usages continue in the literature of the Second Temple period. Israel goes into exile when it neglects God, who had redeemed it (Pss. Sol. 9:1). God redeems or delivers Israel (Sir. 50:24) and does so through the prophets (Sir. 48:20, 49:10). The Gospel of Luke, dependent on the Septuagint, speaks of God's redeeming Israel (1:68), of those who look forward to the redemption of Israel (2:38), and of Jesus as the one who was going to redeem Israel (24:21). The Hymns from Qumran articulate a confidence that God grants the community deliverance (*pedut*) from enemies (1QH 2:32, 35). In the War Scroll, God saves and is faithful to the people of his salvation (1QM 1:12–13, 14:5). Acts of the Apostles says that God sent Moses as a deliverer or redeemer to Israel (Acts 7:35). Redemption terminology is also used in the New Testament as an explanation of the effects of the death of Jesus. Sinful humans are justified by God through the redemption which is in Christ (Rom. 3:24), and God is said to have made Christ the believer's sanctification and redemption (1 Cor. 1:30), which is forgiveness of sins (Col. 1:14).

Rabbinic usage of the term redemption matches what is found in the Hebrew Bible. The rabbis provide rules for the redemption of prisoners and of the firstborn of sons and beasts; they discuss as well the redeemer of blood, who brings to justice a relative's murderer, and the redeemer whose duty it was to espouse the wife of a deceased relative and raise a son in that person's name. Most central in the rabbinic literature is the term's association with messianic redemption, reflected in the designation of God in the Amidah as the "redeemer of Israel." The use of the term redemption to mean "salvation" reflects the rabbinic characterization of the messianic age as the time when God will return the Jewish people to the land of Israel from exile, a return equated with the redemption and bringing home of captives. *See also* ESCHATOLOGY; SALVATION.

red heifer animal that is burned and whose ashes are used in preparation of purification-water, as described in Numbers 19; *see also* PARAH

Rehov Synagogue a Byzantine period synagogue found about 6 kilometers south of Beth Shean in the Jordan Valley. The building is entered from the north through a narthex that was added after the founding of the building. The synagogue is oriented north to south. The main hall is a basilica in plan and measures about 19 by 17 meters. There appears to have been a narrow door in the southwest that opened into the west aisle. The colorful mosaics of the side aisles have been destroyed except for their borders. The aisle mosaic was replaced during the life of the building with geometric patterns. It is possible that the original mosaic had images, but the nave mosaic is completely missing. Piles of stone cubes (tesserae) to build a new mosaic were left when the building went out of use. At the south end of the prayer hall there stood a *bimah* (raised platform), which was added in the second phase of the building. A chancel screen enclosed the *bimah,* which was quite tall at 90 centimeters. It was approached by three steps from the north. A niche was cut into the east corner, perhaps as a *geniza,* or storeroom. The *bimah* underwent modification and enlargement in the third phase of the building.

The artistic decoration of the building is modest. A relief of a lion within a medallion, perhaps part of a lintel, was found near one of the entrances. On the other hand, the building had many inscriptions. For example, the excavators have mentioned lists of donors, halakhic regulations, benedictions, and other texts relating to synagogue worship. Two names so far published from these are Agrippa and Yitzhak. The largest synagogue inscription ever found in Israel was found in the floor of the narthex. It is in Hebrew and Aramaic and is 365 words long. Most of the text is reproduced in Sifre Deuteronomy 51. There is new material in the opening paragraph and part of the final paragraph. In the opening paragraph cities of Samaria are listed, and the list in the Rehov mosaic pavement includes cities not known in the Tannaitic sources. In the final paragraph there appears a detailed description of the gates of Beth Shean and its vicinity. This is also the first time that a text from rabbinic sources has appeared in a synagogue. It is important for comparative textual studies, but it is also instructive to see it enshrined in a building used for worship, which suggests that it was a living text, consulted for its list of fruits and vegetables forbidden and permitted and the regions where cities were declared exempt from these ordinances. The city list from the area of Sebaste (biblical Samaria) includes Dothan and Ibleam, which we know from the Bible, but also Yazit, Yehudit, and others known from the Samaria Ostraca. Others in the list are yet to be identified. The excavator assigns a date from the fourth to the seventh century C.E. for the building. The inscription must date to the seventh century. A huge earthquake shook this area and destroyed Beth Shean in 747 C.E. It is tempting to see the demise of Rehov at the same date.

Reichsaramäisch   *see* ARAMAIC, IMPERIAL

Rekam Geah   a location in northern Sinai; the biblical Kadesh Barnea, where the Israelites camped prior to their entry into Canaan. T. Sheḇiit 4:11 lists Rekam Geah as a location within the Land of Israel, among the sites on the land's southern border.

Rekem   a location in the area of Benjamin (Josh. 18:27); also the ancient name for Petra. The rabbinic literature uses the name to refer to the latter site. At M. Gittin 1:1, Gamaliel treats Rekem as a

border area, documents from which require special authentication.

religio licita   (Lat., permitted religion) Although it is debated among classical scholars whether this specific term was used in Roman law, it is an expression often found in scholarly writings, and the concept certainly applied to Judaism, where religious rights were generally respected.

religious rights of Jews   Under Greek and Roman rule, Jews generally had a right to practice their religion without hindrance, for by its nature, polytheism was tolerant of other gods and beliefs. The Hellenistic kingdoms and the Romans normally allowed the native peoples—including Jews—in the lands they ruled to carry on their beliefs, customs, and religion as long as they paid the required tribute and did not rebel. Although some Greek and Roman writers made disparaging comments about Judaism—picturing the Jews as peculiar or even misanthropic—the state did not attempt to force religious ideology on those under their control.

The Jews were even given certain special considerations because of their religion. Naturally, these considerations varied according to time and place and depended on which empire held sway over them at a particular time. In certain circumstances, however, Jews were even given exemptions from going to court on the Sabbath. They usually had the freedom to celebrate their annual holidays in group gatherings. Under Roman rule, synagogues were usually exempt from the frequent prohibitions against associations, or *collegia.*

The one major exception to tolerance was the persecution of Jews under Antiochus IV. This persecution was a traumatic event because it was completely unprecedented, and it was not repeated until the Roman Empire became Christianized. For a period of about three years under Antiochus, Judaism was officially prohibited on pain of death. This prohibition still lacks a clear explanation, but already before his death in 164 B.C.E., Antiochus relented and once more legalized the normal practice of Judaism.

The only other major example of apparent government-sponsored persecution was Caligula's attempt to place a statue of himself in the Temple. Although this attempt is often presented as merely a capricious action on the part of Caligula, who had megalomaniacal delusions, recent study suggests something quite different. It is now thought that Caligula was far from mad (although not always an astute ruler), and that his attempt to place his statue in the Jerusalem Temple was, in fact, due to Jewish intolerance of pagan altars in a non-Jewish part of Palestine. Caligula had clearly miscalculated in proposing to desecrate the Temple and subsequently found it necessary to withdraw his order, but his motives were evidently political, not religious.

remembrance-verses (Heb.: *zikhronot*) prayers on theme of God's remembering his mercy and covenant, in New Year Additional Service, joined with revelation-verses (Heb.: *shoferot*) and sovereignty-verses (Heb.: *malkhuyot*). The main theme of the remembrance-verses is: "Remember unto us . . . the covenant and lovingkindness and the oath that You swore to our father Abraham at Mount Moriah, and remember the binding with which our father Abraham bound his son Isaac . . . so may your compassion outweigh your anger against us. . . ."

Remiel *see* JERAHMEEL

remnant what remains when the larger part of an entity is removed or destroyed; in the Bible, the fraction of a group or nation that survives a time of trial. In Genesis, for example, "remnant" is employed for those who will endure the famine in Egypt because of the wise policies that Joseph put in place. The concept appears more frequently in the prophetic books. There, the general thought is that when God, through foreign conquerors, punishes the people of Israel or Judah for their habitual violation of his will, most will be deported or killed but a small part of the nation will survive the disaster. Amos spoke of a city from which a thousand residents marched out but only a hundred returned (5:3); that is, the Lord would punish Israel severely but he would not destroy it completely (9:1–8). Isaiah resorted to a remnant theology more frequently: the dross will be smelted away (1:26), but whoever is left will be called holy (4:2–4). The concept was so central to his message that he incorporated it in the name of one of his sons, Shearjashub (lit., a remnant will return; 7:3). After the restoration of some Judeans to their homeland (from 538 B.C.E. on) for the purpose of rebuilding Jerusalem and the Temple, they understood themselves to be the remnant about which the earlier prophets had spoken (in Haggai, Zechariah, Ezra, and Nehemiah). The perception by a Jewish group that it was only a part, not the whole, of what once had been is expressed in later literature as well. Jubilees 23 predicts that the decisive change toward the better will come about in the latter days only through a small group. The Qumran scrolls contain frequent references to this community, which had separated itself physically from the rest of Israel, as a remnant living in the wilderness,

where they were preparing for the coming of the Lord. The Damascus Document, a central text of the group, speaks of the original members as a remnant raised up by God (cols. 1–2), and the War Scroll uses this language for God's people in the last times (cols. 13–14). One of the poets who wrote the Thanksgiving hymns looks to a day, after the uproar of the nations subsides, when God will raise survivors among his people, a remnant that belongs to him (col. 6). A remnant theology reemerges in the New Testament. In Romans 9–11, where Paul speaks about God's election and rejection of the Jewish people but also about his plan to save all Israel, he cites passages from the Hebrew Bible in which a remnant is mentioned. From these passages, he concludes that it was not the complete nation of Israel that God intended to save, but only those who believed his promises.

The conception of the surviving Jews as a remnant of the people of Israel does not yield significant theological discussions in the rabbinic literature, though the idea does appear in interpretations of scriptural passages that include the term and, much less frequently, in rabbinic statements that allude to such biblical usage. Mishnah Berakhot 4:4 states that one who enters a place of danger should offer a short prayer for God to "save his people, the remnant of Israel." This passage reflects Jeremiah 31:7, which refers to God's saving of the remnant of Israel. According to Lamentations Rabbah 2:3 and Ezekiel 9:8, which questions whether or not by destroying Jerusalem, God intends to obliterate all of the remnant of Israel, the term refers in particular to the death of the righteous.

repentance (Heb.: *teshubah;* literally, returning) turning from evil against heaven or against another individual and turning to good deeds. To return to the right path and obtain forgiveness and peace, one prays, sacrifices, fasts, mourns, confesses, and—when applicable—makes restitution. The Septuagint usually translates *shuv* and its cognates as *espistrepho* (conversion). The more common Greek term for repentance is *metanoia*.

At Qumran, repentance consisted of confession (offering of the lips) and acceptance of suffering (1QS 8–9), but it was not accompanied by Temple sacrifice. John the Baptist's preaching of repentance for the forgiveness of sins was eschatologically motivated: "Repent, for the kingdom of heaven is at hand" (Matt. 3:1–6; Mark 1:4–5; Luke 3:3); its sign is baptism. The Gospels depict Jesus as also teaching repentance within an eschatological context (e.g., Matt. 4:17; Mark 1:15). Paul rarely addresses repentance (Rom. 2:4; 2 Cor. 7:9–10).

While rabbinic Judaism does not believe that people are by nature sinners, it accepts as an inevitable part of life the tendency to stray from divine law. The process of repentance, through which the sinner atones for past actions and returns to proper modes of behavior, thus is a central aspect of religious and social life. Repentance is listed as one of the seven things God made before creation (B. Pesaḥim 54a; B. Nedarim 39b). Sincere repentance is seen as equivalent to the rebuilding of the Jerusalem Temple and restoration of the sacrificial cult (B. Sanhedrin 43b). It represents the most direct and efficacious manner of placating God and assuring God's continued protection.

In rabbinism, repentance is a precondition of atonement (*kaparah*), which designates the actual forgiving of sin by God. The Day of Atonement, which annually provides an opportunity for forgiveness by God, is significant only insofar as it marks the conclusion of the process through which people repent and correct their ways. The Day of Atonement is efficacious only if the individual has already repented. Thus Mishnah Yoma 8:8 states: "Death and the Day of Atonement atone when joined with repentance. Repentance [by itself] atones for minor transgressions of positive and negative commandments. And, as to serious transgressions, [repentance] suspends the punishment until the Day of Atonement comes along and atones."

Repentance entails confession of the sin before God and formulation of a resolve not to commit the same sin again. In the case of a sin against another person, repentance is possible only after full restitution or correction of the wrong deed has been made and a pardon from the other person has been obtained. In scripture's system, repentance is followed by an expiatory offering. After the destruction of the Temple and the cessation of the sacrificial cult, the rabbis found a replacement for this offering in charitable deeds. Rabbinic authorities viewed repentance and charity together as a person's greatest advocates before God (B. Shabbat 32a).

Forgiveness is available to all who repent, and the hand of God is continually stretched out to those who seek atonement (B. Pesaḥim 119a). Recognizing the dramatic change of behavior and intense commitment to God's will that stand behind true repentance, rabbinic authorities praise those who have sinned and repented even beyond those who have never sinned (B. Berakhot 34b: "In a place in which those who repent stand, those who are completely righteous cannot stand"). Repentance always is possible, even on the day of death. The only requirement is that the desire to repent be serious and that the individual forsake his sinful ways (M. Yoma 8:9: "One who says, 'I shall sin and repent, sin and repent'—he is given no chance to do repentance. If he says, 'I will sin and the Day of Atonement will atone'—the Day of Atonement does not atone"). Repentance thus is not accomplished through a linguistic formula or through simple participation in a rite of expiation; it depends, rather, upon a true change in the life of the one who seeks atonement. *See also* ATONEMENT; FORGIVENESS.

Resh Galuta   *see* EXILARCH

Resh Lakish   *see* SIMEON B. LAKISH

reshut haraḇim   *see* PUBLIC DOMAIN

reshut hayaḥid   *see* PRIVATE DOMAIN

resistance to rulers   Living under the rule of foreign governments, Jews found themselves not infrequently faced with laws that conflicted with the Torah and rulers who insisted that these laws be obeyed. Much early Jewish literature describes or prescribes forms of resistance to these laws and rulers. Such resistance could take one of two forms.

During the persecution by Antiochus IV, Mattathias the Hasmonean and his sons led an armed revolt against the Syrian king, making common cause with the Hasidim, "a company of mighty warriors." The paradigm was the biblical institution of holy warfare. 1 Maccabees celebrates this revolt as the justification for the Hasmonean high priesthood (2:23–26, 5:62). Passive resistance was also an option. According to 1 Maccabees 2:29–38, certain Jews died a violent death because they would not defend themselves on the Sabbath. In the Testament of Moses 9–10, Taxo and his sons allow themselves to be slaughtered in order to trigger the avenging wrath of God against their enemies. Although 2 Maccabees acknowledged the success of Judas's military activity, it ascribes this victory to the innocent deaths of the martyrs (6:18–8:4). Daniel 11:34 and 12:1 downplay the importance of the Hasmoneans and await judgment through the activity of the great prince Michael.

Restitutus, Titus Aelius   procurator of Syria-Palaestina. A fragment of a dedication names him as procurator of Palestine. The exact dates of his tenure are unknown, but it was likely in the last quarter of the second century C.E. Nothing else is known of his career.

restoration   the return from the Babylonian exile in the early decades of Persian rule, the rebuilding of the Jerusalem Temple (completed 515 B.C.E.), and the establishment of a Jewish commonwealth in the province of Judah (Yehud) under priestly and lay leadership. During the period from the fall of Jerusalem (587 B.C.E.) to these events, hopes were entertained in prophetic circles for a restoration of twelve-tribal Israel on its own land (e.g., Isa. 43:3–7, 49:8–13; Jer. 31:7–9; Ezek. 20:33–38, 36:24–28; Mal. 4:6; cf. Sir. 48:10), an aspiration expressed vividly in Ezekiel's vision of the valley of dry bones (Ezek. 37:1–14). For some, these expectations focused on the restoration of the Davidic dynasty (Jer. 23:5–6, 30:8–9, 33:14–26; Ezek. 34:23–24, 37:24–25; Isa. 55:3), represented in the decades after the return by Zerubbabel, grandson of the exiled king, Jehoiachin (Hag. 2:20–23; Zech. 3:8–10, 6:9–15), and on Zion as the center of the world (Isa. 60–62). In some circles, the eschatological perspective was enlarged to take in the restoration of the entire cosmos, with the creation of new heavens and a new earth (Isa. 65:17, 66:22–23). *See also* EXILE, RETURN FROM.

resurrection the raising of the dead, at the end of the age, either to new life as a reward for righteousness, or to punishment for one's sins. Early on, the notion is driven by a concern to affirm God's justice in an unjust world. The righteous are vindicated for the just conduct that caused their death or are recompensed for a life devoid of deserved blessing; the wicked are raised to receive the punishment that they unjustly eluded in this world. Later, resurrection and its consequences pertain to larger numbers and, finally, to all of humanity.

A resurrection from Sheol is attested first in Isaiah 26:19 (for the righteous) and Daniel 12:2 (for some righteous and some of the wicked). 2 Maccabees 7 envisions a physical resurrection in which the divine Judge recreates the bodies of the martyrs who have been unjustly killed because of their fidelity to the Torah. In 1 Enoch 102, the spirits or souls of the righteous come to life from the gloom of Sheol. In 2 Baruch 49–51, all the dead are raised to the bodies they previously had, so that they can be recognized, and then they are transformed to heavenly glory or disfigured. With the exception of 2 Esdras 7:76–99, Jewish texts do not provide details about the state of human beings between death and resurrection.

New Testament belief in resurrection is governed by the conviction that God has raised Jesus from the dead, thus vindicating him for his unjust death. Accounts of the empty tomb imply a resurrection of Jesus' body. Stories about appearance of the risen Christ are more ambiguous, asserting, at once, his physicality and his extraordinary ability

to penetrate closed doors, appear and disappear suddenly, and be mistaken for someone else.

Jesus' resurrection has broader implications than simply his vindication vis-à-vis an unjust death. It marks the inauguration of the new age. Jesus' resurrection appearances have the quality of epiphanies or angelophanies, in which a transcendent Jesus commissions his disciples, like the biblical prophets, for divine, eschatological tasks. The early credal formula "the God who raised Jesus from the dead" (Rom. 4:24) imitates the biblical expression "the God who brought Israel up from Egypt," thus identifying Jesus' resurrection as a new act of salvation transcending the Exodus. In a similar vein, the apostle Paul sees the resurrected Christ as the prototype for a new humanity that will be transformed into the image of the New Adam (1 Cor. 15). In its setting of persecution, the Apocalypse of John returns to the original Jewish notion that resurrection is vindication for those whose faithfulness to God brought on their death (Rev. 6:9–11, 20:4–6).

In rabbinic Judaism, resurrection, *teḥiyat haMetim,* refers to the concept that on the Day of Judgment God will bring all dead back to life. Developed from postbiblical Israelite and Graeco-Roman thought, the rabbinic doctrine of resurrection took firm hold with the ascent of Pharisaism after the destruction of the Second Temple in 70 C.E., in particular with the decline of the Sadducees, who had rejected the notion of resurrection (see Acts 23:8, Matt. 22:23).

The centrality of resurrection in rabbinic thought is indicated by M. Sanhedrin 10:1. The first of those who have no portion in the world to come are those who deny the origin in the Torah of the belief in resurrection of the dead. Later sources report disputes not over the fact of resurrection but concerning its mechanics. B. Rosh Hashanah 16b–17a, for instance, presents a compendium of materials concerning the Day of Judgment. Here the Houses of Hillel and Shammai agree that, in the end, the thoroughly wicked will be consigned to Gehenna while the thoroughly righteous will have eternal life. Under dispute is the fate of middling people. The Shammaites hold that they will rise only once they have been sent to Gehenna and screamed in supplication to God; the Hillelites argue that, in his mercy, God immediately will grant them eternal life. Other talmudic texts describe the process of resurrection, stating that it will be in the nature of the growth of a grain of wheat (B. Sanhedrin 90b; B. Ketubot 111b). B. Berakhot 60b describes resurrection as the reuniting of the soul with the dead body. Some sources hold that a small, incorruptible part of the body, or even a small amount of rotted flesh, will serve as the material from which a new body is fashioned.

The doctrine of resurrection has a prominent position in the liturgy, forming the focus of the second benediction of the Amidah, recited in all worship services. This prayer proclaims that God kills, makes alive, and causes salvation to spring forth; he makes the dead live and keeps faith with those who sleep in the dust. It concludes by praising God as one who resurrects the dead. *See also* AFTERLIFE; LIFE, ETERNAL.

retribution distribution of rewards and punishments in this world or in the world to come. According to the Tanakh, divine retribution occurs in this world: the righteous will prosper, and the wicked will wither; the apparent prosperity of the wicked will not endure. Even the Book of Job, which explores the suffering of the righteous, concludes with assurances of Job's redoubled prosperity following his trial; other biblical passages questioning the seeming good fortune of the wicked imply that they will ultimately receive their just deserts. In the Talmud, the concept of retribution becomes more complex. The rabbis believed in "measure for measure"—that people are justly compensated for their deeds in this world. But the rabbis spiritualized the concept of retribution: "The reward of a good deed is a good deed, and the wages of sin is sin." Their examination of the problem of the suffering of the righteous also led them to extend the doctrine of retribution to the world to come: imbalances in rewards and punishments in this world will be compensated for in the next.

Reuben b. Istrobeli Tannaitic authority active in the second century C.E., in Hadrianic and post-Hadrianic times. His father's name may have been Aristobulus, and there is speculation that Reuben spent time in Rome. His name appears at times without the patronymic, for example, at T. Shebuot 3:6, where Reuben appears in debate with a gentile philosopher.

Reuchlinianus, Codex a manuscript in the Badische Landesbibliothek in Karlsruhe, Germany. This 1105 C.E. copy contains a Masoretic Hebrew text of the Former and Latter Prophets as well as Jonathan's Targum to the Prophets. It also contains some eighty or so targum *toseftot,* which may be remains of a Palestinian targum to the Prophets.

revelation (Mattan Torah) the giving of the Torah, the concept that, at Sinai, God communicated to Moses laws and ideologies intended to govern the Israelites' individual and communal existence. Rev-

elation is central in Judaism, comprising the physical act through which God called upon Israel to be his covenanted people. The entirety of Jewish religious and social practice is thus held to have its source in Moses' encounter with God at Sinai. Both the individual believer and the people in their social and political life look to God's revelation as the event defining their nature and giving direction and purpose to their lives. A Jew who denies that the Torah derives from revelation loses the possibility of life in the world to come (M. Sanhedrin 10:1). One who deems so little as a single law not to derive from God is called a despiser of the Torah (B. Sanhedrin 99a).

Revelation involves God's revealing of himself and his teachings to the revelation's recipients. In line with this, scripture routinely introduces an act of revelation with the passive form of the verbal root *raah,* signifying "to be seen" (see, e.g., Gen. 12:6–7 and numerous other instances in which the Lord "appears" to Abraham or to another Israelite progenitor). Rabbinic Judaism, however, refers to revelation in different terms. It sees the period of God's physical participation in revelation to have ended with the prophets, having reached its apex long before in the events at Sinai. In the rabbinic view at Sinai, God transmitted to Moses the entirety of the divine law, encompassing the content of both prior and subsequent acts of communication with human beings (see Exod. Rabbah 29:6, which holds that all later prophecies were revealed to Moses at Sinai). When rabbis speak of revelation, Mattan Torah, they therefore refer to this event in particular. They place other acts of revelation within a hierarchy of importance reflecting the way in which God revealed himself. At the top is the revelation to Moses, who beheld God as in a translucent mirror (B. Yebamot 49b). Below are other forms of revelation, for example, to the prophets who saw God as though in a dark glass (B. Yebamot 49b), or to other individuals who saw God in dreams.

Most important, the rabbis hold that in their own period revelation occurs through the rabbis' own manipulation and interpretation of the laws and knowledge received at Sinai. In this process of revelation, God no longer needs physically to reveal himself to any person. Indeed, even though such an appearance might occur in which God actively reveals the correct law through a heavenly voice (*bat kol*) or by disrupting the natural order, such divine intercession is rejected as immaterial to the determination of the law (B. Baba Metzia 59a–b). Such determinations are viewed as in the hands of the rabbis alone. The rabbis' own intellectual deliberations and legal discussions, that is, reveal aspects of the divine will that are of equal authority as that which God himself made known in his appearance at Sinai. In this way, the rabbinic theory of revelation holds that statements and principles expressed by rabbis who lived in the first six centuries C.E. preserve teachings that derive from God's original contact with Moses.

To sustain this theory, the rabbis develop a concept of revelation entirely unanticipated by scripture. They propose that Moses actually received the revelation in two distinct parts: the written law, embodied in the text of the Pentateuch, and an oral law transmitted only by word of mouth. While the written component of the revelation was made accessible to all of the people of Israel, the oral part was transmitted only to successive generations of sages: from Moses to Joshua to certain elders to the biblical prophets and, ultimately, into the hands of the rabbis themselves. In this perspective, while comprising an essential part of the revelation, the oral law was known to and understood by the rabbis alone. Only beginning in the second century C.E., to assure that this law would not be lost as a result of war, national strife, or other physical or intellectual calamity, did the rabbis begin to codify and preserve it in written form. The oral Torah thus was encompassed first by the Mishnah and completed in the third century C.E. Then by the subsequent documents of rabbinic Judaism, concluding with the Babylonian Talmud, completed in the sixth century C.E.

The notion of the closed transmission of an esoteric revelation functions polemically within rabbinic Judaism. The rabbinic claim to possess an otherwise unknown component of God's revelation legitimates rabbinic authority and promotes acceptance of rabbinic leadership. Through this notion of revelation, the rabbis claim to be direct successors to Moses, referred to as "our rabbi," and thus designated as the first rabbinic sage. In this view, only under rabbinic leadership can the Jewish people correctly observe God's will. Since the written Torah, which is available to all of Israel, contains only half of God's revelation, access to it alone does not provide all of the information needed properly to observe the law. Correct observance is possible only under rabbinic guidance.

The concept of revelation described here is uniquely rabbinic. Other postbiblical Jewish writings know nothing comparable. For instance, Josephus' description of the Pharisees, whom the later rabbis understood to be the direct recipients of the oral revelation, says nothing about their knowledge of revealed or even inherited traditions. In *The Jewish War* (1:97), Josephus says only that the Pharisees are "considered the more accurate interpreters of the laws." In the *Antiquities* (13:171), Josephus adds that the Pharisees preserve and follow certain traditions developed in accordance with their distinctive philosophical doctrine. He does not suggest that they have legal or exegetical dicta passed down by tradition and derived ultimately from divine revelation.

The nature and content of the documents of rabbinic Judaism confirm the perception suggested by Josephus that what the rabbis came to call the product of revelation in fact is the result of arguments and discussions among rabbinic sages of the first centuries. During the period following the destruction of the Jerusalem Temple in 70 C.E., rabbinic sages studied and interpreted scripture and worked out a program of ritual and legal practice that eventually would shape Judaism according to the rabbis' own ideals and aspirations. At the end of the Mishnaic period, these rabbis increasingly came to consider the results of their deliberations to be part of a divinely revealed oral law. From the content of the principles, rules, and issues at play in the rabbinic documents, however, it is apparent that this oral Torah is substantially the product of the rabbis' own day and of their own distinctive attitudes and philosophies.

This is not to say that traditions regarding ritual practice and the meaning of scripture did not exist in late antiquity. The point, rather, is that, so far as the literary evidence indicates, the rabbis did not simply preserve traditions already understood to be revealed by God to Moses at Sinai. Rather the Mishnah and other rabbinic writings are the independent intellectual and literary creations of rabbinic circles. Only within the theological construct of rabbinic Judaism, which understands the product of rabbinic interpretation and legislation to equal divine law, do the rabbinic documents come to be characterized as products of the revelation at Sinai.

Revelation, Book of also called the Revelation to John, the only apocalypse in the New Testament, written in Greek by an otherwise unknown Christian prophet who presents himself as John. In Christian tradition the author was identified with the apostle John, son of Zebedee, a disciple of Jesus. Revelation is usually dated around 96 C.E., at the end of the rule of the emperor Domitian.

In style and content, Revelation has many similarities to apocalypses (e.g., Dan. 7–12, 1 Enoch,

4 Ezra), and it makes direct use of Daniel. Similar to other apocalypses, Revelation is a visionary account of transcendent, divine reality, portrayed in both spatial (heavenly) and temporal (eschatological) terms. The book begins with a commissioning vision (chap. 1), in which the exalted Jesus appears to John, a prophet exiled to the island of Patmos because of "the persecution," and commands him to write letters (see Rev. 2–3) to seven churches in western Asia Minor (modern Turkey). The central theme of the book—the tension between God's kingship in heaven and the resistance to his rule on earth—is introduced in Revelation 4–5: through an "open door" (4:1) the seer glimpses God on his heavenly throne, adored by the heavenly host, and attended by Jesus, the "Lamb who was slain," also called the triumphant "lion of Judah." The rest of the book serves to resolve this tension through a series of visions depicting the "eschatological woes" by which God will punish evildoers, the second coming of Jesus (as a great warrior), the last battle against Satan and his armies, final judgment, and the establishment of the new Jerusalem, where God will dwell with his people, and where evil, suffering, and death will be no more (chaps. 6–22).

Revelation is unique among the apocalypses in that it is not ascribed pseudonymously to a figure from the remote past, such as Adam, Enoch, Ezra, or Daniel. Also unique are the seven letters, which assign praise and blame to the various churches, warn them of the coming judgment, and promise rewards to those who remain faithful. Both letters and visions reflect tensions between the Christian faith and the dominant Graeco-Roman culture. Drawing on imagery from the Tanakh (Old Testament) the author portrays Rome as a beast empowered by Satan to make war on God's elect (chaps. 13 and 17). The city of Rome is described as the "whore of Babylon" (chap. 17). Although written well before the official, widespread persecution of Christians by the Roman state, the book reflects some specific cases of Christian martyrdom (e.g., 6:9–11), and the author says he was in exile because of his faith (1:9). He is concerned to sharpen his readers' awareness of the essential conflict between the Kingdom of God and the kingdom of Caesar and to warn them to avoid any association with Roman civic religion. Specifically, the book warns against Christian participation in the worship of the emperor (chaps. 13 and 17), which, though not official Roman policy, was practiced in the eastern provinces at the end of the first century.

Revelation achieved canonical status as the last book of the New Testament only after considerable debate, and Christian attitudes toward the book have continued to vary, with some (e.g., Luther) regretting its place in the canon. It has been particularly popular among certain Christian groups (e.g., millennialists) that emphasize the imminence of the eschaton.

Revolt Against Rome, Great a war initiated in Jerusalem in 66 C.E. It involved widespread destruction and death throughout the country, especially in Judea and Jerusalem. The war concluded with the destruction of Jerusalem and its Temple by the Roman army in 70 C.E. Most information about the war comes from *The Jewish War* and the *Vita* written by the Jewish historian Josephus, who was a participant first on the Jewish and then on the Roman side. The causes of the Judean uprising against the Romans were multiple, including resentment of foreign rule, inept governance by the Roman procurators in the fifties and sixties C.E., heavy taxation, resentment of the common people against the governing classes in Jerusalem, and conflict among rival factions of priests and wealthy families. Earlier in the first century C.E., the Roman authorities and the population of Judea had clashed a number of times over economic and religious matters. A series of popular leaders claiming to be prophets, Davidic messiahs, and others arose and led short-lived disturbances.

Early in 66 a long-lasting dispute between the Jewish and gentile communities in Caesarea became violent, and the procurator Florus (64–66) did little to settle it. In the summer of 66 Florus demanded a large sum of money from the Temple treasury, an act which caused great resentment among the people and a series of violent clashes with Roman soldiers in Jerusalem. In the end, the people destroyed the bridge connecting the Antonia Fortress with the Temple, and Florus withdrew from Jerusalem. Despite efforts at conciliation by the established Jewish leaders and King Agrippa II, Eleazar, a revolutionary aristocrat who was son of the high priest Ananias, succeeded in stopping the daily sacrifices offered for the welfare of the emperor. With the symbol of submission to the empire gone, Jerusalem factions for and against revolt clashed violently. The Antonia Fortress was captured and the high priest and other leaders were besieged in Herod's palace. The palaces of Agrippa, Bernice, and the high priest in the Upper City (the western hill) were burned along with the archives that recorded debts. Menahem, son of Judas the Galilean, armed with weapons from Masada, led the attack that took the palace, but not the towers. The high priest Ananias and his brother were killed. Subsequently Eleazar's faction killed Menahem and most of his supporters and then treacherously slaughtered the small Roman garrison in the towers when they marched out under truce.

In the fall of 66 the Roman governor in Syria, Cestius Gallus, led an expedition that captured some Judean villages but was not strong enough to take Jerusalem. As Cestius withdrew from Jerusalem toward the coast of the Mediterranean, his forces were routed in the valley of Beth Horon, as the Seleucid forces had been routed by the Maccabees two centuries earlier. Knowing that further Roman response was inevitable, the governing classes in Jerusalem regained some control of society by agreeing to supervise defense plans for the country. High-ranking priests and aristocrats divided up responsibility for fortifying numerous cities and towns, storing supplies, and recruiting armed forces. Their efforts, however, were marked by factionalism, competition for power, and a lack of centralized planning. Josephus was placed in command of Galilee, the first place likely to be attacked by the Romans. He testifies to a population divided between allegiance to Rome and Jerusalem and riven by factional disputes between him and John of Gischala, who suspected Josephus (possibly correctly) of seeking accommodation with the Romans. Attempts by the Jerusalem leadership, at John's instigation, to remove Josephus from command failed. In 67, the Roman general and future emperor Vespasian arrived to lead the Roman forces. Sepphoris, Tiberias, and Gischala submitted to the Romans, and Jotapata and Gamala were conquered after sieges. By the fall, all of Galilee was in Roman hands. Josephus was captured and ingratiated himself with Vespasian, while John of Gischala fled with his forces to Jerusalem.

During the next spring (68 C.E.), Vespasian captured the cities and towns of Judea and prepared to besiege Jerusalem. But the emperor Nero died in June, and during the next year three men became emperor and were assassinated in turn. Finally, in 69 Vespasian was proclaimed emperor by the armies in the East and by the end of 69 was accepted by the whole empire. Vespasian went to Rome and left the war in Judea in the hands of his son Titus.

During this struggle over the succession to the imperial throne, Roman operations in Judea were restricted to capturing a few fortresses and controlling Simon bar Giora's roving groups of insurgents. This did not, however, improve Jerusalem's chances

for survival, because several groups within the city fought each other so ferociously that they weakened its defenses. The leadership and defenders killed one another, destroyed the food supplies, and divided the city so that no unified preparation for siege could be made. Armed groups were loyal to their own leaders rather than to the city or national government. The original group of Zealots were led by Eleazar ben Simon. They united with and broke off from another group of resisters who came to Jerusalem with John of Gischala. The Idumeans, too, came to Jerusalem to help the Zealots, who controlled the Temple Mount against the traditional leaders. Then, when the Idumeans broke with John of Gischala in 69, they, the people, and the high priest Matthias invited into Jerusalem Simon bar Giora, who had gathered a large group of dispossessed Judeans. They had controlled and plundered parts of Judea and Idumea until driven out by the Romans. Simon gained control of most of the Upper City and part of the Lower City by the spring of 69 and became the most powerful leader in Jerusalem. When Titus, the son of Vespasian, began the siege of Jerusalem in early 70, the factions within Jerusalem finally coordinated their efforts at defense. Even then, John of Gischala managed to assassinate Eleazar ben Simon and unite the two factions of Zealots under his command.

Titus first fortified his camps and turned back several dangerous sallies by the defenders of Jerusalem. Then Titus attacked the northern walls, which lay on level ground. The first two walls fell in less than a month, but the Antonia Fortress and the Temple Mount, itself a fortification, took several more weeks to fall and the fortifications in the Upper City took another month. The walls, fortifications, and Temple were burned or torn down, except for Herod's three towers and part of the wall, which then became a Roman army camp. Thousands were killed and the leadership of Judea was destroyed. Simon bar Giora, John of Gischala, and seven hundred young men were marched in a triumphal procession in Rome, after which Simon was executed and John imprisoned for life. Thousands others were sold into slavery and Judea was turned into a senatorial province occupied by its own legion. Worship at the Temple and relatively autonomous local rule had ended in Judea. During the next three or four years the fortresses at Herodium, Macherus, and Masada were captured by the Roman procurators who took office after the war. At Masada, the Sicarii, led by Eleazar ben Jair, committed suicide along with their families to avoid capture by the Romans.

revolutionary parties a term sometimes used by modern scholars to describe rather diverse anti-Roman Jewish groups, especially in the first century C.E. Groups that have been variously included under this rubric are the Zealots, the Sicarii, and the Fourth Philosophy. Although they helped instigate riots and eventually even a full-scale revolt, in many cases their activities were mainly directed at "collaborators" (i.e., upper-class Jews). In antiquity, the term "bandit" or "brigand" (Gr.: *lēstēs*) was often used for them, even though they were not always bandits in the conventional sense.

reward and punishment divine retribution for the righteous and the wicked. The notion that YHWH is the judge who rewards and punishes the nation and individuals in it is commonplace in the Hebrew Bible. Deuteronomy 28 presents a list of such rewards and punishments, enacted in this world, as the blessings and curses of the covenant. The two-ways text incorporated into the Qumran Community Rule reflects the influence of covenant theology and presents lists of virtues and vices and their this-worldly and future rewards and punishments (lit., visitation; Heb.: *pekudah,* 1QS 4:2–14). Similar notions of reward and punishment regularly occur in other Jewish texts of the late Second Temple period, either with or without explicit reference to the covenant. Christian theologians have often alleged that such a belief in divine reward and punishment is typical of "late Jewish legalism," which has been overcome in the New Testament, and especially Pauline, belief in divine grace. In fact, as Deuteronomy shows, divine reward and punishment of one's deeds is essential to the notion of covenant in the Hebrew Bible. Moreover, Paul and most other New Testament writers depict God as the rewarder and punisher of human deeds. *See also* JUDGMENT, DIVINE.

rewritten Bible modern scholarly term used to designate various writings that loosely follow the biblical text but also contain many expansions and interpretations. Examples include Jubilees, Pseudo-Philo, the Genesis Apocryphon, the *Antiquities of the Jews* of Josephus, and the Targum Pseudo-Jonathan.

ribit (Heb., usury) any fee for lending money, including fees in kind, such as free rent, and fees in personal services. Usury is absolutely forbidden in transactions between Israelites, but permitted between Israelites and Gentiles; Israelites may pay interest to Gentiles or collect it from them.

righteous Gentiles (Heb.: *ḥzasedei ummot ha-Olam*) non-Jews who, because of their righteous behavior, have a place in the world to come. The concept appears first at Tosefta Sanhedrin 13:2, where Joshua distinguishes "Gentiles who forget God" (Ps. 9:17), who are doomed to Sheol, from Gentiles who do not forget God, who, like righteous Israelites, have a portion in the world to come. The concept of righteous Gentiles occurs in some midrashic texts but is significantly elaborated only by medieval Jewish philosophers. Maimonides applies the term to non-Jews who accept the seven Noahide commandments out of a belief in their divine origin. Other medieval thinkers explicitly equate righteous Gentiles with Israelites, who are worthy of all of God's mercies. In modern times, the term "righteous Gentiles" has been applied to non-Jews who protected Jews from the Nazis.

righteousness the most frequent translation of two Hebrew nouns from the root *tzdk* (*tzedek* and *tzedakah*) and of the Greek word *dikaiosunē.* These terms have a much broader range of meaning than the English "righteousness": other senses include "justification," "justice," "rescue," and "innocence." As with *mishpat* (justice, order) and *ḥesed* (grace), the root *tzdk* is used in relation to the covenant between God and Israel (Hos. 2:18–20, Jer. 9:24). Most generally, righteousness refers to the order that results when the stipulations of the covenant are observed. As a description of God, righteousness designates his covenant loyalty (Ps. 4:1), his righteous judgments (Ps. 9:8), his acts of vindication and salvation (Deut. 9:4–6; Hos. 10:12; Mic. 6:5), as well as the ordered life that he wills and works to establish (Isa. 11:1–2). Applied to human beings, righteousness characterizes obedience to God's commandments (Ps. 15:2, 18:20–24, Ps. 119, Ezek. 18:5–9) and the establishment of God's order in society (Isa. 5:15–16, 32:1, Jer. 22:3). The king, as the special representative of God, is to rule the people with righteousness, delivering the poor and the oppressed (Ps. 72). The ideal Davidic king who will rule with righteousness figures in prophetic hopes for the future: "In those days and at that time I will cause a righteous Branch to spring up for David; and he shall execute justice (*mishpat*) and righteousness (*tzedakah*) in the land" (Jer. 33:15, cf. Isa. 9:7 and 11:4–5).

In the Psalms and Isaiah 40–66 *tzdk* refers most often to God's saving action; it is used in parallel with "salvation" (the root *ysh*). While this sense cannot be conveyed by the English term "righteousness," it is closely related to other meanings of the Hebrew term, especially to the sense of the order demanded and established by God. Thus, in the Psalms of lament an individual prays to God to act in accordance with his righteousness, that is, to deliver the petitioner from a state of disorder and suffering (Ps. 71:4, 88:12–13). In Isaiah 46:13, *tzedakah* refers to God's deliverance of Israel from exile in Babylon: "I bring near my deliverance (*tzedakah*), it is not far off, and my salvation (*teshuah*) will not tarry; I will put salvation in Zion, for Israel my glory" (cf. Isa. 45:8; 51:5; 54:14, 17).

The root *tzdk* (with its Greek translation *dikaiosunē*) is used frequently in the literature of early Judaism (2d c. B.C.E.—2d c. C.E.). In many texts it has a moral sense, usually associated with fulfilling the commandments: "For none that do evil shall be hidden from your knowledge, and the righteousness of your devout is before you, Lord" (Ps. of Sol. 9:3). 1 Maccabees 2:29 reports that when the Seleucid ruler Antiochus Epiphanes ordered the Jews to abandon their law, "many who were seeking righteousness and justice" fled to the desert, in order to remain faithful to the Torah. Philo of Alexandria, drawing on Greek philosophy, presents *dikaiosunē* as the first of the four cardinal virtues (*Abr.* 27, 56; *Leg. All* I.63; cf. 4 Macc. 1:16–18). The Dead Sea Scrolls use *tzdk* in most of its biblical senses. Particularly noteworthy are texts in the Community Rule (1QS) and the Damascus Covenant (CD), which use the root *tzdk* to speak of God's saving action (cf. Psalms and Isaiah): "And the priests shall recount the righteous acts (*tzedakot*) of God in his mighty works and proclaim all the favors of (his) mercy toward Israel" (1QS 1:21–22; cf. 11:14–16, which speaks of God's deliverance of the individual from his sinful ways). Several of the Scrolls refer to the founder of their community as the Teacher of Righteousness (CD 1:11–12, 1QpHab 11:4–6)

In the New Testament, righteousness (Gr.: *dikaiosunē*) is especially prominent in two of Paul's letters, Galatians and Romans. In Romans 3:21–26, Paul characterizes the essence of the Christian message: "But now, outside the law, the righteousness of God has been revealed, attested by the law and the prophets, the righteousness of God through faith in Christ Jesus for all who believe" (3:21, cf. 1:17). As in the Dead Sea Scrolls, righteousness here designates God's saving action which rescues human beings from sin. Paul also speaks of the righteousness of human beings, by which he means a restored relationship with God, made possible only by believing in Jesus Christ (Rom. 4:3, 1 Cor. 1:30). In this sense the Greek *dikaiosunē* is usually translated as "justification," a term which assumed particular importance in the Reformation. Despite his background as a zealous observer of the law, Paul sees the righteousness

appropriated by faith in Jesus as separate from, and even antithetical to, the righteousness which comes from obedience to the commandments of Torah (Rom. 10:3–13, cf. Gal. 3:5). Other New Testament texts portray righteous observance of the commandments in a positive light (Luke 1:6, 2:25). In the Gospel of Matthew, Jesus is presented as telling his disciples: "Unless your righteousness exceeds that of the scribes and the Pharisees, you will not enter the kingdom of the heavens" (5:20). *See also* JUSTIFICATION.

righteous one (Heb.: *tzadik;* Gr.: *dikaios*) one who is upright in God's eyes by virtue of fidelity to the covenant and its obligations. The righteous person is not sinless, but seeks to be faithful and makes appropriate reparations for unwitting sins. The Psalms of Solomon 3 provides a classic description of the righteous one, contrasting that person's conduct with that of "the sinner." The righteous one stumbles (sins), but awaits God's deliverance. The righteous one does not let sins accumulate, but atones for them through fasting and rituals of self-abasement. The sinner, by contrast, is not concerned about these matters. The Psalms of Solomon employ the term "the pious one" (Gr.: *hosios;* Heb.: *ḥasid*) as a veritable synonym for "the righteous one," and along with other texts (e.g., 1 En. 92–105) regularly juxtapose "the righteous" and "the pious" with "the sinner" and "the wicked" or "the lawless" (Gr.: *anomoi*).

The term "righteous one" is used in a more restricted, but heightened way, with reference to one whose devotion to God leads to suffering or even death in behalf of the Torah. Often such a person is a teacher or leader of the community. The Wisdom of Solomon 2 and 5 explicates the case of such a righteous one, employing language and motifs from the servant poem in Isaiah 52–53 (cf. Isa. 53:11). This tradition is modified in 1 Enoch 37–71 where a transcendent figure described as "son of man," "the chosen one," "the righteous one," and God's "anointed one" is portrayed through traditions drawn from the Deutero-Isaianic servant poems, biblical oracles about the Davidic king, and Daniel 7. As "the righteous one" (1 Enoch 53:6, 38:2), he is the champion of "the righteous," who cry for vindication because their blood has been shed (1 Enoch 47:2–4).

The New Testament uses "the righteous one(s)" in all of these senses. The Gospels regularly depict Jesus' ministry as being directed toward sinners (e.g., tax collectors and prostitutes) rather than the righteous, and Luke, who highlights this activity, quotes Jesus making a distinction between "sinner who repents" and the "righteous who need no repentance" (Luke 15:7; cf. Mark 2:17). The contrast is that of the Psalms of Solomon 3. The righteous as the martyred spokespersons of God awaiting vindication are referred to in Matthew 23:34–36, as well as in Revelation 6:9–11 (cf. 1 Enoch 47:2–4).

Jesus' preeminent status as the righteous one is indicated in several New Testament texts that refer to his innocent death (Luke 23:47; Acts 3:13–14, 7:52; 1 Peter 3:18; cf. Acts 22:14 of his exaltation). *See also* SERVANT OF THE LORD; SON OF MAN.

right hand of God the place of honor in the heavenly throne room. In Psalm 110:1, YHWH invites the Davidic king, also said to be a "priest forever after the order of Melchizedek" (v. 4), to sit at YHWH's right hand. The oracular form in verses 1 and 4 is reminiscent of Psalm 2, where YHWH seats the king on his throne on Zion and declares him to be "my son" and YHWH's anointed one, who rules over the nations in YHWH's behalf. The wording of Psalm 110:1 and 4 appears with some frequency in the New Testament. Mark 14:62 conflates language from Daniel 7:13 and Psalm 110 to describe Jesus' exaltation and future coming as "son of man" and God's anointed one. Paul employs Psalm 110:1 to describe Jesus' exaltation (Rom. 8:34), and his reference to Jesus' intercession may imply the priestly functions mentioned in Psalm 110:4. Jesus' heavenly high priesthood is explicit the Epistle to the Hebrews, which quotes Psalm 110:1 and 4 twelve times (Heb. 1:3, 13; 8:1; 10:12; 5:6, 10; 6:20; 7:3, 11, 15, 17, 21). The psalm was obviously an important and formative text in the early church's interpretation of Jesus' identity and functions. *See also* MESSIAH.

Riḥumai *see* NIḤUMAI

rinceau *see* VINE SCROLL

rite of removing the shoe (Heb.: *ḥalitzah*) rite described in Deuteronomy 25:9–10, by which the relationship between a childless widow and her surviving brother-in-law is severed. The surviving brother-in-law having refused to marry his childless brother's widow, the widow publicly removes the man's shoe. *See also* LEVIR.

ritual slaughterer (Heb.: *shoḥet*) one who is qualified properly to slaughter an animal and who is knowledgeable concerning the defects (e.g., in the brain, windpipe, esophagus, heart, lungs, or intestines) that disqualify use of the meat because the animal would have died naturally of these defects

robbers *see* BANDITS; ROBBERY

robbery the unlawful seizure of another person's property through an open and often violent act.

The Torah explicitly prohibits not only robbery but also theft, the unlawful seizure of another person's property by stealthy means. According to the rabbis, the Eighth Commandment prohibits the capital offense of kidnapping; theft and robbery of money or goods are noncapital offenses. Many rabbis included in robbery the borrowing of an item without the owner's consent. Certain items that the owner would not want to keep are excluded from this category; a tailor, for example, may keep thread left over from a commissioned suit. Thieves and robbers are required to return stolen property to the owner; they must compensate the rightful owner for any damage sustained by the property while it was in their control, but they are entitled to compensation for any improvements to the property while it was in their possession. If the stolen item has been lost or destroyed while it was in their possession, they must make monetary compensation to the owner. An owner's claim on property lapses if he despairs of having it returned to him; while the robber then gains title to the property, he must still pay the original owner for its value at the time of the robbery.

robes a common eschatological metaphor with various meanings. In the ancient world, formal investiture could accompany and signify an important change of status (Gen. 41:42; Esther 6:6–11). The point is explicit in Psalms of Solomon 2:19–21 and 11:7, which play on the imagery of Isaiah 52:1–2. That the body is a garment to cover the "nakedness" of the soul seems to be implied in 2 Corinthians 4:16–5:4, where Paul, mixing the metaphors of tent and clothes, hopes to have an immortal body placed over his present body before he is unclothed through death. Reinterpreting Isaiah 52:1, the author of 1 Enoch 62:15–16 describes the resurrection as investiture with glorious garments that will not wear out. Several early Christian texts extend this imagery by describing the heavenly body as a garment (Rev. 6:11, 7:9–14; Matt. 22:11–12; Ascension of Isaiah 9:1–26). The Ascension of Isaiah 9:9 contrasts the garment of the flesh with the higher, heavenly garment, recalling Paul's notion of an immortal body, also described as a heavenly building that replaces the earthly tent (2 Cor. 5:1–2). Since the heavenly body is likened to Christ's (1 Cor. 15:42–54; Phil. 3:21), the imagery may be related to Christological speculation that saw Jesus' incarnation and exaltation as the Savior's divestiture and reinvestiture (Asc. Isa. 9:13–18; Acts of Thomas 108–113).

rock (Heb.: *sela, eben*; Aram.: *kefa*; Gr.: *petra*) bedrock or a large rock, a symbol for stability that is sometimes employed in the metaphorical complex that describes the religious community as a building. Isaiah 28:16–17 provided the exegetical basis for a series of related texts that employ this metaphor. The Qumran Hodayot 6:26 does not explicate what the rock is. In Matthew 16:16–19, the "rock" (Gr.: *petra*) is Simon, who is nicknamed Peter (Gr.: *petros*). In both 1 Peter 2:6–8 and Acts 4:11–12 references to passages about a rock are ascribed to Peter.

Matthew 7:24–27 employs the rock image for another purpose. People who hear Jesus' words and either do them or do not do them are likened to two men who build their houses, respectively, on rock and sand and who survive or do not survive the storm of the judgment. The comparison is reminiscent of Isaiah 28:16–18. Abot deRabbi Natan 24 ascribes a similar comparative parable to Elisha ben Abuyah (1st–2d c. c.e.), in which the foundational stones of a well-built house are likened to the good works that derive from the study of the Torah. *See also* BUILDING.

romance   a genre of Greek and Roman literature usually consisting of a prose tale of adventure or love. Some romances, called novels, were stories about the adventures of a man and his espoused who are kept apart or whose love is tested by a series of adversities, which they overcome and "live happily ever after." Others are tales of the adventures of a famous figure, such as the Alexander romance. A Jewish writing that might be classified under this heading is Joseph and Asenath; however, the stories of the patriarchs in the Fragmentary Hellenistic Jewish writers and in Josephus have romantic elements.

Roman Empire   The transition from republic to empire in the first century B.C.E. was due to the increasing influence of successful military leaders who gradually usurped political power from the Senate, the traditional guardian of Roman *imperium*. Octavian, the adopted son of Julius Caesar, emerged as sole ruler in 31 B.C.E., following a period of civil wars that had lasted almost thirty years. The period had been marked by triumvirates or alliances of various generals.

At its peak the empire extended from Britain in the west to the Euphrates in the east and from the Rhine and Danube in the north to the deserts of Arabia and Sahara in the south. Thus the Romans could speak of the Mediterranean as "our sea." The provincial system was maintained and developed with a clear distinction between the imperial provinces, where the appointments were the preserve of the emperor, and the procuratorial ones of lesser importance, whose governors theoretically were appointed by the Senate and did not have a legion stationed there. In addition, client kings such as the Herods of Judea were used to maintain order and enforce Roman law while respecting local tradition.

In theory Roman law applied equally throughout the empire, although the rights and privileges of citizens differed from those of noncitizens, as Paul illustrates in his appeal to Caesar in Acts of the Apostles 25:11. Citizenship was hereditary for freeborn males, but it could also be granted either to individuals or whole provinces for services rendered to Rome. Gradually the distinction was whittled away and then abolished in the early third century, only to be replaced by another one based on property, which had its own potential to incite social unrest.

All power resided with the emperor, but many emperors did consult the Senate, whose decisions, like the decrees of the emperor, had the force of law. Judicial power was given to the Senate, which acted like a supreme court, although the emperor reserved the right to try any case himself. In addition to the Senate and the imperial council (*consilium*), the imperial household, consisting of various personal friends and advisers as well as slaves and freedmen, was also highly influential. The administration of the provinces improved considerably under the empire because of direct imperial control of appointments to the more important or difficult provinces and through control of the taxation system following the abolition of the hated *publicani* or tax-farmers. Despite the fact that governors enjoyed full *imperium* (ruling authority) in their provinces, they were subject to rigorous control from the center. Pliny's letters to Trajan, when the former was governor of Bithynia, document this clearly.

When possible emperors usually appointed their sons, either natural or adopted, as successors. Thus in theory the principate was hereditary, though there were several interruptions. In 69 C.E., the year of the three emperors, the Julio-Claudian line came to an end, replaced by the Flavians on the appointment of Vespasian, then engaged in quelling the troublesome Jewish revolt in Palestine. Again in 193 C.E., with the death of Commodus, a period of internal turmoil followed in which a soldier, Septimius Severus, eventually established a new dynasty with a strong military emphasis, rather than the civil constitution that had prevailed since Augustus. The third century was a period of decline for the empire generally with barbarian tribes threatening on the borders and civil strife at the center. Diocletian (r. 284–305), a strong military man, emerged as the leader and divided the empire in two. He appointed two vice-regents or caesars, Constantius in the west and Galerius in the east, thus establishing what he hoped would be a proper mode of succession. However, with Diocletian's death turmoil once more ensued until Constantine, the son of Constantius, defeated Maxentius, his rival in the west, at the battle of the Milvian Bridge in 312. Later in 324, Licinius, the caesar in the east, was forced to surrender to Constantine, who thus established himself as the sole ruler of the empire. He moved the seat of government from Nicomedia to Byzantium, which he reestablished as New Rome, but which soon came to be called Constantinople in honor of its founder. It remained the capital of the Eastern, or Byzantine, Empire until it was captured by the Ottomans in 1453. For a time the Western Empire survived the onslaught of the barbarians despite Rome being sacked by the Visigoths in 410. By the end of the fifth century, however, an Ostrogothic kingdom was established in Italy and the centralized authority that was Rome had come to an end. However, many of its customs and institutions, as well as its language, were to endure through the Roman church and its missionary activity among the new peoples who eventually would constitute the Holy Roman Empire.

Roman period a conventional designation for a time period used by scholars of ancient Palestine to denote the period of Roman hegemony over the area called Palaestina. The period is ordinarily taken to run from 37 B.C.E. to 324 C.E. according to standard references in the field, though not without some adjustments. The date 37 B.C.E. is the year when Herod the Great began his rule as a client king for the Romans. Many researchers take the beginning of Roman rule to extend from the coming of Roman legions to Jerusalem under Pompey, therefore 63 B.C.E. The end of the period could be argued to extend to 363 C.E., or the great earthquake so destructive in Palestine in that century. The period is typically divided into three subperiods called Early Roman (or Roman I or Herodian) from 37 B.C.E. to 70 C.E. Middle Roman from (Roman II) from 70 C.E. to 180 C.E., and Late Roman (Roman III) from 180 C.E. to 324 or 363 B.C.E. The Roman period is preceded by the Hellenistic period and followed by the Byzantine period.

Rome The city of Rome emerged from a synoecism of various smaller settlements that can be traced in the Tiber Valley as far back as the ninth century B.C.E. These settlements occur at a point where the river meanders through a deep trough,

one half to one and a half miles wide, cut in the soft tufa rock. This valley is surrounded by steep cliffs, giving rise to Rome's famous seven hills: the Capitoline, Palatine, Aventine, Caelian, Esquiline, Viminal, and Quirinal. The beginnings of the city proper coincide with the draining of the marshy area at the foot of the Capitoline by a canal, the *cloaca maxima* (still in use today), making possible the development of a central marketplace or Forum, probably in the sixth century B.C.E. when the cave burials cease. In the period of the kings the Capitoline was designated a sacred acropolis, the Campus Martius as royal gardens, and a bridge over the Tiber replaced an earlier ford. Walls on the Viminal together with the cliffs gave the city a strong fortress-like character in this earliest period.

During the Republican period (c. 500 B.C.E. on) these areas of public space were further developed, and the Palatine became a residential area. Gradually the city attracted more and more residents as Rome's influence increased, and by the third century B.C.E. it had become crowded with high tenements overlooking narrow streets. In 378 B.C.E. a city wall was built encircling the four designated regions into which Rome had been divided for administrative reasons. Temples and other public buildings were added and aqueducts built to meet the increasing demand for water. Various important political figures such as Sulla in the second century B.C.E. and Pompey and Caesar in the first century B.C.E. all contributed to the public buildings of the city as part of their wider political agendas.

This same trend was continued in the first two centuries of the common era. Older buildings were rebuilt and enlarged and new ones added, such as the Forum of Augustus and a mausoleum in the Campus Martius, and the city was reorganized into fourteen different regions. Gradually the residential quarters of the Palatine had to make way for magnificent public buildings, such as Nero's Golden House, described by Suetonius. This was facilitated by the great fire for which the early Christians had to pay the price of popular suspicion. The Via Sacra leading to the Capitoline was also part of Nero's reconstruction, comparable in elegance to the great colonnaded streets in the cities of the Roman east. Triumphal arches celebrating famous victories abroad, such as those of Titus and Septimius Severus, still stand today at either end of the Forum, showing how no expense was spared in adorning imperial Rome through public monuments and other buildings. Under the Flavians the Colosseum, the Fora of Vespasian and Trajan—

showing strong Syrian influences in its architectural style—and various bathhouses, which were such an integral part of Roman life, were all added. So crowded in fact was the city that later emperors such as Caracalla, Diocletian, and Constantine had to find suitable sites well outside the recognized center for their bathhouses. The continued expansion of the city during the imperial period is indicated by the need for new walls by Aurelian (r. 270–275 C.E.).

Rome, Jews in From at least the second century B.C.E., Jews lived in Rome and the Roman authorities had official contact with the Hasmoneans rulers in Judea. In the first part of the first century B.C.E., Cicero refers to Jews sending money to Jerusalem. When Pompey conquered Jerusalem in 63 B.C.E., he brought many Jewish prisoners to Rome as slaves, some of whom eventually gained their liberty. The trial of Flaccus, the anti-Jewish governor of Alexandria, in 59 B.C.E. attracted a crowd of Jews. An embassy of Judean Jews to Rome after the death of Herod in 4 B.C.E. was supported by a crowd of eight thousand Roman Jews. Roman authors often took notice of the numerous and influential Jewish community, both positively and negatively. In the first century C.E., members of the Herodian family spent time in Rome. Agrippa I was an influential friend of the Emperor Tiberius and Nero's wife Poppaea was attracted to Judaism. Literature of the period also refers to Jewish slaves and beggers. The poor quality of some Jewish inscriptions in Rome suggests that many Jews were poor and uneducated. The Jewish community was expelled from Rome under Tiberius in 19 C.E. and probably also under Claudius in the 40s. The Jewish community lived originally in Trastevere, a quarter on the far bank of the Tiber River. During the imperial period they spread to other parts of the city. Several Jewish catacombs (burial areas) have been found along with numerous inscriptions. The inscriptions indicate that there were eleven synagogue communities in Rome and that Jews lived there for centuries. *See also* EXPULSIONS OF JEWS FROM ROME.

rosette a major motif in Jewish art, simply inscribed in stone or other media by inscribing circles and arcs with a compass. The rosette normally has six petals, for that is the division of the circle by its own radius. A double rosette has twelve petals. Double rosettes commonly appear on ossuaries with some other artistic motif centered between the two rosettes. Rosettes also occur on lamps, plates, sarcophagi, and in tombs, and it is above all a motif in tomb art. Rosettes on sar-cophagi and sarcophagi lids may have four, six, or twelve petals. Occasionally a sarcophagus will be found with two round raised surfaces that were never finished. These might have been shaped into rosettes at the request of the purchasing family, but apparently sometimes not. In synagogue art rosettes appear on friezes in the Chorazin and Capernaum synagogues alongside flowers, circlets, stars, and other simple geometric shapes. On a lintel from Horvat Amudim there appeared a floral rosette in the two outside panels on either side of a wreath. Other rosettes in relief decorate stones from the large synagogue at Kefar Baram, and a seven petal rosette appears on the base of the menorah in the wall paintings at Dura-Europos. Thus the rosette appears to have wide use in Jewish art, but it is not clear if it bears any special meaning.

Rosh Hashanah **1.** New Year, celebrated on the first day of Tishrei (month corresponding to September)

2. Mishnah tractate on the celebration of the New Year, the designation of the new month throughout the year, and testimony as to the appearance of the new moon (chaps. 1–3) and the sounding of the shofar (ram's horn) on the New Year (chaps. 3–4)

Rosh Ḥodesh *see* NEW MOON

Rosh Yeshivah head of talmudic academy

Ruaḥ haKodesh *see* HOLY SPIRIT

Rufinus (345–410 C.E.) monk, historian, and translator, born near Auileia in northern Italy. He attended school in Rome, where he befriended Saint Jerome. He translated into Latin works by Origen, Basil, Gregory of Nazianzus, and Eusebius. He produced original commentaries on the Bible and Christian works. He indicates that Julian called the Jews to Antioch in 362 C.E. to discuss the rebuilding of the Jerusalem Temple. He states that the Italian Jews believed that the Messiah had come, and he records the ingathering of Jews in Jerusalem. He also discusses the earthquake and fire that ended the rebuilding of the Temple.

Rufus, Quintus Tineius consular legate of Syria-Palaestina (c. 131–134/135 C.E.). He was the legate during the Bar Kokhba War. Passages in Jewish literature mention that Rufus or Hadrian destroyed the Temple and plowed up the Temple Mount. It is unclear if the Jews had started to rebuild the Temple under Simon Bar Kokhba or whether these texts refer to a further desecration of the Temple Mount. Jewish sources associate him with a decree against circumcision, but their accuracy is questionable. Several texts record disputations between

Rufus and Akiba in which the former exhibits familiarity with the Torah and Judaism; however, the authenticity of these encounters is doubtful. One source records that Rufus's wife was so disturbed by Rabbi Akiba's ability to respond to her husband's challenges that she sought to seduce the rabbi but failed. According to the story, she eventually converted to Judaism and married Akiba.

ruler cult   *see* CULT, RULER

ruler of this world   a designation for evil spirits (1 Cor. 2:6, 8) or their chief, whom God permits to hold sway until the end of the age (Jub. 10:8–9, 1QS 3:20–23). The singular figure is identified with Belial (Mart. Asc. Isa. 2:4, 4:2), the devil (Luke 4:6, Assum. Moses), and Sammael (2 Cor. 4:4).

Rum Bet Anat   *see* BETH RAMAH

Ruth, Targum to   The Targum to Ruth is moderately expansive, interweaving sections of literal translation of the Book of Ruth with sections of additional material. The targum probably stems from the early medieval period. Some of its additions parallel material in other rabbinic literature, especially Ruth Rabbah.

Ruth Rabbah   compilation of comments on the Book of Ruth, compiled c. 500–600 C.E. The compilation deals with (1) Israel and God, with special reference to the covenant, the Torah, and the land; (2) Israel and the nations, with attention to Israel's history, past, present, and future, and how that cycle is to be known; (3) Israel on its own terms, with focus upon Israel's distinctive leadership; and (4) the Book of Ruth in particular. The document presents only one message, concerning the outsider who becomes the principal, the messiah out of Moab; this miracle is accomplished through mastery of the Torah. The compilation sets forth the following principles: (1) Israel's fate depends upon its proper conduct toward its leaders. (2) The leaders must not be arrogant. (3) The admission of the outsider depends upon the rules of the Torah. These differentiate among outsiders. Those who knows the rules are able to apply them accurately and mercifully. (4) The proselyte is accepted because the Torah makes it possible to do so, and the condition of acceptance is complete and total submission to the Torah. Boaz taught Ruth the rules of the Torah, and she obeyed them carefully. (5) Those proselytes who are accepted are respected by God and are completely equal to all other Israelites. Those who marry them are masters of the Torah, and their descendants are masters of the Torah, typified by David. Boaz in his day and David in his day were the same in this regard. (6) What the proselyte therefore accomplishes is to take shelter under the wings of God's presence, and the proselyte who does so stands in the royal line of David, Solomon, and the messiah. Ruth the Moabitess, perceived by the ignorant as an outsider, enjoyed complete equality with all other Israelites, because she had accepted the yoke of the Torah, married a great sage, and produced the messiah-sage David.

Rutilius Lupus   *see* LUPUS, MARCUS RUTILIUS

Sabbath   (from Heb.: *shabbat,* to cease)   **1.** in Second Temple literature, the day of the week on which one rests from work. Observance is attributed to two sources: the divine rest on the seventh day of Creation (Gen. 2:1–3; Exod. 20:8–11; etc.) and the lesson taught by Egyptian slavery (Deut. 5:12–15). The Torah provides some legislation, such as insisting that one's servants and animals are provided rest (e.g., Exod. 23:12). Later material notes the Sabbath was celebrated as a festival, with Temple visits, songs, and special food. Emphasized by the exilic and postexilic writers (Isa. 56:2–7, 58:13–14; Jer. 17:19–27; Ezek. 20:12–24; Neh. 13:15–22), the Sabbath, like circumcision and diet, provided a means of maintaining community identification (Exod. 31:12–17). Sabbath reading of scripture in synagogues is well attested in first-century-c.e. sources (Luke 4:16; Acts 13:14–15, 15:21, etc.), but the practice may have originated in the early postexilic period: Josephus and Philo both locate the origin of the custom with Moses. The Dead Sea Scrolls (see 4QShirShabb; 4Q403) speak of Sabbath celebration with song; cosmological speculation; and various restrictions, such as on walking certain distances (CD 10:21; see also Acts 1:12 on "a Sabbath day's journey"), eating food prepared on the Sabbath (CD 10:22), and rescuing an animal in a pit (CD 11:16–17). Jubilees, which insists that Sabbath celebration is only for Israel, shares with the scrolls many of the laws and attitudes concerning Sabbath activities (2:17–33, 6:34–38, 50; see also 2 Bar. 84). Aristobulus associates the Sabbath with Wisdom.

The text of 1 Maccabees 2:39–41 recounts how the Hasmoneans came to advocate self-defense on the Sabbath rather than to accept slaughter (see also Josephus, *Ant.* 12.6.2). The Gospels depict Jesus as preaching in synagogues on the Sabbath (Luke 4:16) but rejecting certain popular directives regarding Sabbath observance (for example, Mark 3:1–5). Jesus' rationale, shared by Jewish teaching, is "the sabbath was made for people, and not people for the sabbath" (Mark 2:27). Their desire for self-identification, the tradition of Jesus' Sunday resurrection, and the increasingly gentile church's disinterest in Jewish Sabbath ritual led Christians eventually to designate Sunday as their day of worship. The Hellenistic Synagogal Prayers (part of the Apostolic Constitutions) may contain portions of Jewish Sabbath hymns (e.g., 5:1–3).

2. in rabbinic Judaism, the seventh day of the week, on which God rested from the activities of Creation (Gen. 2:1–3), commemorated in Judaism through rest and cessation of work. The rabbis deem observance of the seventh day to be a fundamental element of Judaism, equivalent to all other precepts combined (Exod. Rabbah 25:12). While the Sabbath is referred to in scripture alongside the other, annual festivals—New Year, the Day of Atonement, and the pilgrim festivals of Tabernacles, Passover, and Pentecost—in the rabbinic period, it attained a special place as a weekly observance that in the absence of the cult, could continue as a family holiday practiced in individual homes.

Scripture provides only a limited description of Sabbath observance, for instance, forbidding agricultural labor even at the time of plowing or the harvest (Exod. 34:21), prohibiting trade on that day (Amos 8:5), and forbidding even discussion of one's business (Isa. 58:13). Within rabbinic Judaism, through analogy and extension of biblical prohibitions, the list of prohibited activities, as well as the description of expected or required behaviors, grew increasingly detailed. The result was a system of law that, in the rabbis' own description, hung like a mountain from a strand of hair, containing an inordinate number of rules, based on a small biblical foundation (M. Ḥagigah 1:8).

At the center of rabbinic Sabbath law lies the enumeration of thirty-nine categories of prohibited labor. The list derives from Exodus 35, which, after speaking of the prohibition of work on the Sabbath, uses the same word, "work," in a list of the tasks performed in building and outfitting the wilderness tabernacle. Cataloging the labors specified or implied in this passage yields an inclusive list of categories of prohibited Sabbath work (M. Shabbat 7:2). In rabbinic law, each category is subject to further expansion through the delineation of derivative varieties of forbidden labor. In some interpretations, this yields as many as 1,521 forbidden activities (Y. Shabbat 7:1, 9b–c).

In keeping with Exodus 16:29, the rabbis prohibit travel on the Sabbath beyond a distance of 2,000 cubits from one's town. Additionally, activities that fall under no other category may be prohibited simply because they are not in keeping with the ideal of Sabbath rest (M. Besah 5:2). Sabbath (and almost all other) observance is, however, set aside when a human life is endangered. Whatever is necessary to save a life is to be done, even if this requires transgressing the prohibition against working on the Sabbath or some other holy day.

Alongside determining what is prohibited on the Sabbath, rabbinic authorities develop a system of requirements and practices that recognize the sanctity of the Sabbath day and promote its celebration in a positive way, in particular, through indulgence in food and drink. Three meals are to be eaten on the Sabbath (B. Shabbat 118a), and the Sabbath table is to be as lavish as one's means permit. To ensure that they have an appetite for the Sabbath meals, people should eat sparingly on Friday (T. Berakhot 5:1). To enhance enjoyment of the food, certain methods allow it to be kept warm for Sabbath consumption (M. Shabbat 3 and 4).

The Sabbath is welcomed through the housewife's lighting of a lamp on Friday afternoon before dusk (M. Shabbat 2:6). After sundown, the master of the house recites a sanctification (*kiddush*) comprising a blessing over wine and a blessing of the day, which sets the Sabbath apart from the preceding weekday. Sabbath meals include two loaves of bread, corresponding to the double portion of manna collected for the Sabbath (Exod. 16:22–26). On the Sabbath, one should wear special clothes, walk in a distinctive manner, and even use special speech (B. Shabbat 11a–b).

Sabbatical year the seventh of every seven years, observed by leaving fields fallow and their crops ownerless and by forgiving debts

Saboraim (Heb., those who render decisions) rabbinical authorities active in Babylonia between the Amoraic and Gaonic periods. Neither the exact nature of Saboraic activity nor the dating of the Saboraic period is certain. Sherira dates the Saboraim from the death of Rabina (according to B. Baba Metzia 86a, the last amora) in 499 C.E. through the death of Gada and Simuna in 540 C.E. Ibn Daud dates this period from the death of Mar Joseph in 502 C.E. through the death of Sheshna in 689 C.E. The extant lists of individual Saboraim are confused and of little help in ascertaining the exact period. This may reflect the only gradual realization of the rabbis that a shift in authority had occurred.

Sherira and other medieval sources hold that the Saboraim both explained that which the Amoraim had left unclear and completed the earlier work, for example, by deciding the law in cases previously subject to dispute. They did not, however, function as independent authorities adding to the corpus of learning and authoritative exegesis of the Mishnah, already contained in the talmudic literature. According to some sources, the Saboraim additionally were responsible for completing the redacting of the talmudic text, which had been begun late in the Amoraic period. Since little evidence of the Saboraim's literary product exists, and since passages defined by Sherira as Saboraic are similar in style and argumentation to Amoraic passages, the character and extent of the Saboraim's work remains subject to dispute.

sackcloth and ashes The donning of a black garment of goat's hair or camel's hair was a ritual act of mourning that might be in response to death (Gen. 37:34), personal loss (2 Sam. 3:31), or national disaster (Lam. 2:10; Jdt. 4:10). It might also constitute a ritual of formal repentance (Jonah 3:5–8; Matt. 11:21). The "sack" in sackcloth derives from the transliteration of the Hebrew *sak* in the Greek and Latin translations of the Bible. In connection with the ritual of putting on sackcloth, or apart from it, one might also cover oneself with ashes or dust or lie in them (Esther 4:1–3; Job 42:6; Joseph and Asenath 10:8–15).

Sacr. *see* DE SACRIFICIIS ABELIS ET CAINI

sacrifices and offerings those items that a person gives from his or her possessions as an act of worship. In the Apocrypha, pious characters, such as Tobit (chap. 1) and Judith (chap. 16), make and commend appropriate sacrifices, although in Judith one hears an echo of the prophetic theme that love is greater than sacrifice and offering (16:16). Ben Sira teaches that sacrifices from lawbreakers are unacceptable and that virtuous deeds also qualify as sacrifices (34:18–35:12). The Books of Maccabees describe the time when such cultic acts as sacrifices to the God of Israel were prohibited and replaced by pagan ones (from 167 to 164 B.C.E.). The original Hanukkah marked the rededication of the altar to proper use. Even the authors of the Dead Sea Scrolls, who apparently did not participate in the Temple cult, preserved detailed rules about sacrifices and how and when they were to be offered (the Temple Scroll is an example). The community regarded itself as an atoning sacrifice for the nation's sin; its prayers were an acceptable fragrance to God (Manual of Discipline 8–9). Sacrifices and offerings are mentioned several times in the New Testament (e.g., when Mary brought the appropriate one after Jesus' birth [Luke 2:24]). Jesus assumes the Temple cult but teaches the superiority of love (Mark 12:33). He himself is presented as the sacrificial Passover lamb, slain for his people. In Hebrews, his sacrificial death once and for all puts an end to the need for the continual Temple offerings. In Judaism, animal and grain sacrifices and offerings ended with the destruction of the Temple in 70 C.E.

In the Division of Holy Things (Kodashim), the mishnaic rabbis presented detailed descriptions of the proper conduct of the Temple cult and of the rules for offering all of the Bible's sacrifices. Rabbinic Judaism was shaped by the model of the Temple cult. A central element of the liturgy was prayers for the rebuilding of the Temple and the reestablishment of animal sacrifice, seen by the rabbis as the signifiers of the messianic age. At the same time, after the destruction of the Temple, the rabbis developed a sophisticated system of social and ritual practice they understood to replace sacrifice as concrete means of expiation and union with God. At the center of this system were deeds of loving kindness, seen as a mode of atonement that replaced sacrifices (Abot deRabbi Natan 4; see Hos. 6:6). This same concept is expressed in a range of activities the rabbis hold to be comparable to sacrificial practice: the humble are accounted by God as though they had offered all of the prescribed sacrifices (B. Sotah 5b); the recitation of the liturgy and donning of phylacteries are equivalent to building the altar (B. Berakhot 15a); proper consumption of food at the home table has the same expiatory impact as sacrifices (B. Berakhot 55a); bringing joy to a bridal couple is comparable to offering a thanksgiving offering (B. Berakhot 6b); and those who study Torah are as beloved by God as those who burned incense on the altar (B. Menahot 110a).

sacrilege use for secular purposes of what has been consecrated; *see also* MEILAH

Sadducees a group of the Second Temple period drawn from the governing classes of the wealthy and priests, according to Josephus. Not all priests and aristocrats should be conceived of as Sadducees, however. The name Sadducees is Greek and is derived either from the Hebrew name of the priestly line of Zadok or from the Hebrew for "righteous ones." Though no writings from this group have survived, Josephus and the New Testament report that the Sadducees favored a traditional interpretation of the Bible and Jewish customs and thus rejected the more recent belief in an afterlife and the apocalyptic version of divine intervention in human life, as well as innovative, Pharisaic interpretations of Jewish law. They competed with the Pharisees for the favor of the rulers, such as John Hyrcanus, in order to have their teachings enforced as law. They may have been a subgroup of the priestly and governing classes, with a program for living Jewish life that sought to avoid the excessive Hellenization of others of their class. In the Mishnah and Tosefta, the Sadducees appear as opponents of Pharisaic rulings on purity and civil law. In the Midrash and Talmuds, they are often treated anachronistically as heterodox because they deny the existence of an afterlife or oppose Pharisaic and rabbinic teaching. Many pejorative talmudic references to the Gentiles or heretics may have been changed to references to the Sadducees by censors. The Sadducees are related to the Boethusians in rabbinic literature.

Sadok the Pharisee *see* TZADDOK THE PHARISEE

Safed city of Upper Galilee, of that name today, situated on the south end of Mount Canaan; likely named Sepph or Seph in the Roman period. Seph stood on a high hill 11 kilometers northwest of the Sea of Galilee and could be easily seen from its shores. This was a village known to Josephus in the first century as Seph, a village which he claims to have fortified against the Roman attack of 66 C.E.

(*War* 2.20.6, p. 573). His verb means "build walls," so presumably he is claiming to fortify it against Roman siege engines. In his *Vita* he omits the name of Seph. According to the Yerushalmi, Seph or Sepph was a way station in the signaling stations for communicating to the Jews of Babylon that holy days had ensued in Jerusalem (Y. Rosh Hashanah 58A). After the destruction of the Second Temple in 70 C.E., Seph became one of the villages of Galilee in which the priestly courses settled. In the case of Seph it was the priestly course of Yachin-Pashur (Mishmarot 12).

Safsaf a small village in Upper Galilee in the Roman period, also known as Saphsopha (willow). The village is mentioned once in Y. Temurah 46b, but with no illumination about the village. In the former mosque of the village, decorated stones were found that are possible synagogue remains. The lintel stone, for example, depicted two bulls' heads on either side of a wreath in the center. The ribbons of the wreath extended with vine tendrils to form a border. Above the lintel stood a shell carved in stone. Voussoirs or wedge-shaped stones from an ancient arch stood above the shell, forming an arch with a vine scroll on the inner band of the arch and tendrils on its outer band. Two other voussoirs were built into the wall of the mosque. These two were decorated in concentric moldings. It is possible that the stones did not originate at Safsaf, since no traces of buildings of the ancient world are yet found there. On the other hand, the ancient villages of Gush Ḥalab (Greek: Gischala) stood only 1 kilometer to the north. Gush Ḥalab had two synagogues, and one of them may have been destroyed in the earthquake of 1853 that completely destroyed the modern village.

sage *see* RABBI

saints *see* HOLY ONES

Salathiel the Greek form of the Hebrew name Shealtiel. The most significant occurrence of this name outside the Jewish scriptures is in 4 Ezra 3:1, where Salathiel is given as an alternative name for Ezra, the narrator and hero of the apocalypse. Salathiel appears in genealogies of Jesus in Matthew 1:12 and Luke 3:27.

Salbit Synagogue Samaritan synagogue in the Arab village of Salbit or Salebi, biblical Shaalbim (Josh. 19:42) about 25 kilometers west by northwest of Jerusalem in ancient Samaria. The ancient village overlooked the Ayalon Valley. The synagogue building contained a prayer hall about 14.5 by 8 meters. The whole was paved with a mosaic with no indication of columns to hold up the roof in the style of a basilica. The lower of two mosaic pavements in the prayer hall had a central, rectangular panel which measured 6 by 3.2 meters. It was decorated in interlaced circles surrounded by a frame of small triangles. A circular medallion about 1.45 meters in diameter dominated the center with its Greek inscription, of which only two lines have survived. Only a small part can be read: ". . . of the posses[ion]," perhaps referring to dedicating the property. Below the Greek inscription stand two menorahs, each with seven branches, and between them seems to stand a stylized representation of Mount Gerizim, the mountain holy to Samaritans. To the north of the large panel a Hebrew inscription in the Samaritan alphabet reads: "The Lord [the holy name is spelled out] shall reign for ever and ever" (Exod. 15.18). Another damaged Samaritan inscription of three lines was found south of the central panel. It cannot be read. The upper mosaic floor, lying 15 to 28 centimeters above the first, is in even more fragmentary condition than the lower floor. The design is of floral and geometric patterns. The date of the synagogue is not fixed. A date in the late fourth century C.E. is reasonable for the lower floor, while the upper floor could be any time during or after the six century C.E.

sale, talmudic law of transfer of real estate was effected by payment of money, by deed, by *seisin* (assertive action), or by symbolic transfer of a cloth (also called acquisition by reciprocal exchange). Personal property (chattel) was acquired by taking hold of the object (by lifting it, drawing it toward oneself, or effecting a symbolic transfer), by taking it into one's domain, or by the symbolic transfer of a cloth.

Salome **1.** sister of Herod the Great. She conspired against Herod's favorite wife, Mariamme; denounced her second husband, Costobar, to Herod; slandered two of Herod's sons, Alexander and Aristobulus, who were executed in 7 B.C.E.; and supported another of Herod's sons, Antipater. After Herod's death she received several cities. When she died in 10 C.E., she bequeathed her property to the Roman empress Livia.

2. daughter of Herodias, the granddaughter of Herod the Great, and Herod, son of Herod the Great. She first married her uncle Philip, the son of Herod the Great and the tetrarch of Bananeia and Paneion. After his death in 33/34 C.E., she married Aristobulus, son of Herod of Chalcis. The gospels refer to a dance she did for Herod Antipas, the second husband of her mother, Herodias, and her request for the head of John the Baptist.

Salome Alexandra *see* ALEXANDRA, QUEEN

salvation divine deliverance from trouble or danger. The Hebrew Bible and Jewish and Christian tradition regularly depict the God of Israel as one who rescues the covenant people. Thus "salvation" has justifiably become a central category in theological vocabulary. However, the manner in which "salvation" is construed has often oversimplified the breadth of biblical and postbiblical tradition.

Two misimpressions prevail in particular. First, for reasons inherent in the New Testament, Christians usually construe salvation as deliverance from sin and its consequences: guilt and divine condemnation. In fact, the Hebrew Bible and much postbiblical tradition employ the Hebrew root *ysh* and the Greek verb and noun *sōzō/sōtēria* (save, salvation; rescue; deliver[ance]), as well as a number of other terms and metaphors, to denote a range of divine activity that includes rescue from one's enemies, healing from illness, and deliverance from death, in addition to forgiveness of sin and release from its consequences. Moreover, the portrayal of a rescuing, vindicating God occurs quite apart from the use of expressions meaning to "save" and "deliver." Second, much that is defined as "salvation" does not involve God saving anyone from anything. Rather, God is bestowing on the covenant people the blessings that they have been promised, without any sense that they have hitherto been deprived of these things. There are two exceptions in this connection. The righteous may cry out for deliverance from unjust persecution or oppression or for rescue from undeserved illness and premature death. Following the prescription of Deuteronomy 28–30, the receipt of covenantal blessings may be sought by a sinful people who repent and ask for deliverance from the curses of the covenant.

Development in Jewish religion. The conception of salvation and the nature of its mechanisms changed in Jewish religious thought and practice as the ancient world and the historical circumstances of the Jews changed. Exile from the Land of Israel required substantial adjustment. Political and social changes within Israel were factors, as was the development of an eschatological or an apocalyptic dualistic world view. In these and other respects, early Jewish literature provides an indispensable tool for understanding differences between the Hebrew Bible and the texts of rabbinic Judaism and early Christianity.

Salvation from sin and Its consequences. In preexilic Israel, the sacrificial system was the major prescribed mechanism to remove the guilt and impurity incurred by transgression of the Torah. With the Babylonian destruction of Judah's cultic center and exile from the land, sacrifices were no longer possible. Late exilic and postexilic texts attest some new ways for dealing with sin.

Following Second Isaiah's cue that Israel has paid double for its sins (Isa. 40:2), Tobit 11:15, 13:2, 5, 9, 2 Maccabees 6:12–17, and Psalms of Solomon 7:8–10 and 13:9–10 interpret Israel's suffering at the hands of their enemies as God's way of scourging and disciplining the covenant people, so that they may repent and receive mercy. Suffering could also serve the cultic functions of purification and the wiping away of transgressions (Ps. Sol. 10:1–2, 13:10).

In analogy to Second Isaiah's portrayal of the servant's suffering for others (Isa. 52–53) and drawing on parallel notions in Greek religious thought, 2 Maccabees 7 and 4 Maccabees understood the martyrs' innocent deaths in behalf of the Torah as a means of cleansing the nation and propitiating God's wrath.

More generally, righteous deeds, especially almsgiving and fasting along with self-humiliation, cleanse from sin and expiate for it (Tob. 12:9–10; Ecclus. 35 [Gr. 32]:1–2; Ps. Sol. 3:8). The origin of these practices as expiatory rituals is not clear. They may have arisen where access to the cult was not possible because of distance from Jerusalem, disruption of the cult, or the perception that the cult was ineffectual. Nonetheless, Ben Sira's reference to such a function for deeds of kindness indicates that the notion flourished among persons who had access to the Temple and believed in its efficacy (see Ecclus. 51). After the destruction of the Temple in 70 C.E., the notion took on new viability (see Abot deRabbi Natan 4).

Prayers of repentance—widely attested in such texts as Ezra 9, Nehemiah 9, Baruch 1:15–3:8, Daniel 9, the Prayer of Azariah, the Prayer of Manasseh, and 4QDib Ham—constitute another ritual for dealing with sin, which is first clearly attested in the postexilic period.

Taking a completely different tack, 1 Enoch 10:20 finds the pollution of the land to be so complete that it posits a high-priestly figure (Michael) as the necessary agent for a universal purification similar to the flood.

Salvation from one's enemies. The Hebrew Bible frequently depicts God rescuing Israel or individual Israelites from their enemies. The Exodus is prototypical in this respect, and references to "the God who brought Israel up from the land of Egypt" are widespread. The historical scheme in the latter chapters of Deuteronomy allow for

God's deliverance from Israel's captors when the people have repented, and Second Isaiah, especially, interprets the return from Babylon as a second Exodus. Rescue from unjust persecution is the topic of the Psalms of individual lament and individual thanksgiving.

This topic recurs many times in the literature associated with Israel's major crises in the Graeco-Roman period: the persecution by Antiochus IV Epiphanes; the invasion by Pompey; the Roman destruction of Jerusalem in 70 C.E. Many of these texts have an eschatological orientation and employ the scheme of Deuteronomy 28–30 and 32 to explain present suffering and to posit imminent deliverance (Jub. 23; Test. Moses). The means of salvation vary. In Jubilees 23, repentance based on a proper understanding of Torah leads to a change of situation (vv. 23–27). In Testament of Moses 9, the obedience of Taxo and his sons involves their innocent death. Daniel 10–12 does not emphasize the Deuteronomic scheme, but like Testament of Moses 10, it envisions the intervention of a high angel. In all of these cases, salvation is final and cosmic and involves a qualitative change in the world and the shape of human life. In other texts generated in response to Antiochus' persecution, salvation takes place within history and through human agents. In 1 Maccabees the family of Mattathias brings "salvation" to Israel through their militant struggle with the Syrian armies (5:62) and especially through the leadership of Judas, Israel's "savior" (*soter*, 9:21). Second Maccabees, on the other hand, sees the deaths of the martyrs as instrumental in turning God's wrath to mercy (7:1–8:5) and facilitating the victories of Judas.

Healing and rescue from death. Early Jewish texts exhibit a variety of nuances about this traditional aspect of God's saving activity. Ben Sira attests the development of "medical science" in the Graeco-Roman world and sees physicians and pharmacists as agents of God's healing (Ecclus. 38:1–8). Within its apocalyptic world view, 1 Enoch attributes illness to the activity of the evil spirits of the dead giants (15:11), but Shemihazah the chieftain of the rebel angels who fathered the giants is also responsible for revealing magical medicine: charms and the cutting of roots (8:1). According to the Book of Jubilees, which employs traditions from 1 Enoch, the angels of God's presence provide Noah with pharmaceutical information to help him and his children deal with sickness of demonic origin (10:10–13). In the Book of Tobit, sickness caused by the activity of demons can be healed through angelic intervention, and Raphael appears

in human form to serve as physician, magician, and exorcist. In Genesis Apocryphon 20 Abraham's intercession exorcises an evil spirit that causes impotence.

Salvation as revelation. A substantial part of the Hebrew Bible is devoted to the activity of the prophets, who brought the people the divine message, either that they needed to change their ways to save themselves from present or imminent disaster, or that God was about to act to enact such deliverance. In such cases, revelation was intimately bound up with salvation, either to facilitate it or to encourage the people to take heart as it approached.

Revelation was an important mechanism of salvation also in Judaism of the Graeco-Roman period. Transcendent agents might transmit such information. According to Jubilees 4:15, in primordial times God had sent angels to earth to instruct them in righteousness. In apocalyptic thought, angels mediated heavenly mysteries, and the apocalyptic seer encouraged his community through information received from the appearance of such an agent or during the course of heavenly journeys, often in the company of angelic interpreters. This knowledge about imminent judgment and salvation from persecution or oppression enabled the members of the community to endure and not lose faith (1 Enoch 104:4–6). According to Daniel 12:3, the wise teachers of the Torah led many in Israel to righteousness. At Qumran the revelation of the true interpretation of the Torah facilitated the obedience that delivered the members of the community from the sphere of death that enveloped Israel (1QS 5:17–11; QH 3:19–23), and the revealed interpretation of the prophets indicated history was rapidly moving to its consummation and the moment of salvation (1QpHab 7:1–4). In all cases, revealed knowledge was constitutive of the eschatological community of the elect.

The New Testament. The unique dynamic of early Christian views of salvation is their attachment of Jewish notions of salvation to Jesus of Nazareth. This christological orientation, rather than the specific mechanisms of salvation, distinguish it from Judaism, although the differences are substantial and the emphases noteworthy.

This is especially clear in New Testament views about sin and forgiveness. In Jewish texts about the effective death of the martyrs (2 Maccabees and 4 Maccabees), these deaths are followed by the purification of the Temple and the restoration of the cult. For Paul (Rom. 3:24–25) and the author of Hebrews, Jesus' expiatory death has had a permanent effect in dealing with sin, and the Jerusalem cult is now irrelevant and unnecessary. The Eucharist effects participation in the results of Jesus' death and in the new covenant established by the shedding of his blood (1 Cor. 11:24–25). Paul's scheme, however, is much more comprehensive (Rom. 6–8). Sin is a power, the equivalent of the evil spirit or evil inclination, which dominates all members of the human race. However, as the New Adam, Jesus the incarnate son of God has initiated a new race from which sin is purged and the righteousness that leads to eternal life is possible through the prompting of the spirit of the risen Lord.

The construal of salvation as rescue from one's enemies is much less frequent in the New Testament than in the corpus of Jewish texts. Where suffering is mentioned, it is usually a function of one's following Jesus (Mark 8:34–36, 13:9–10). This is especially the case in Revelation (Rev. 6:9–11). In both instances the exalted Jesus, as son of man and messiah, will deliver the elect at the end time.

In the Gospels as in 1 Enoch, Jubilees, and Tobit, demons are largely the source of illness, and much of the gospel narratives is devoted to stories that depict Jesus as the divinely sent healer and exorcist. Mark and John indicate some similarity between Jesus the son of God and Raphael the heavenly being who appears in human form in the Book of Tobit.

The notion of salvation as revelation is a central New Testament concept. The author of Revelation presents his apocalyptic message specifically in order to encourage the churches in Asia Minor to endure and thus attain salvation from persecution and the result of that salvation, eternal life (Rev. 1–3). The scheme of salvation in the Fourth Gospel turns on its claim that Jesus, heavenly Wisdom, has descended into the dark cosmos, bringing the revelation that enables those who believe in it to escape the power of the devil and attain eternal life (John 1:1–18). A similar view of Jesus as heavenly wisdom or wisdom's agent governs the christology of the sayings material in the Synoptic Gospels (the so-called Q source; e.g., Matt. 11:25–30).

Thus in diverse ways, the New Testament uniformly focuses on Jesus as the eschatological agent of divine salvation. That salvation takes many forms and responds to different kinds of trouble and danger; however, it does seem to be the case that the New Testament—more than the Jewish texts—emphasizes salvation from sin and its consequences. Identifying the reasons for this special focus is an interesting challenge for historians of religion in the Graeco-Roman period.

Within rabbinic Judaism, salvation refers to an individual's place in the world to come. This salvation, promised to the Israelites as a nation, is assured to all but the most recalcitrant sinners, for instance, those who deny the resurrection of the dead or who claim that the Torah does not derive from God (M. Sanhedrin 10:1). At the same time, the rabbis propose that through meticulous observance of the law and repentance of sins Jews must individually earn their personal portion in the coming world. In response to his students' question of how to accomplish this, Eliezer says, "Be attentive to the honor owing to your fellows, keep your children from excessive reflection and set them among the knees of disciples of sages, and when you pray, know before whom you stand" (B. Berakhot 28b). At the heart of this rabbinic notion of salvation is the understanding that God fully forgives the sins of those who atone, desiring that His children will be delivered from the ills of current life and will experience the blessings of God's salvation. *See also* ESCHATOLOGY; KNOWLEDGE.

Sama b. Judah Saboraic authority; died 594 C.E. The details of his life and work are unknown.

Sama b. Raba Babylonian amora at the conclusion of the Amoraic period; head of the academy at Pumbedita, 449–476 C.E.

Samaias (also Sameus, Samaeus) a disciple of Pollion the Pharisee. In 47–46 B.C.E. Herod the Great was charged with illegally killing the Galilean bandits of Ezekias, but he appeared with his bodyguards and intimated the Sanhedrin. In addition, Hyrcanus, the high priest, was ordered by Sextus Caesar, the governor of Syria, to acquit Herod. Samaias rebuked the Jerusalem Sanhedrin when it refused to stand up to Herod, predicting that Herod would rule and would punish its members and Hyrcanus, the high priest (Josephus, *Ant.* 14.172–74; elsewhere, this rebuke is attributed to Pollion [*Ant.* 15.3–4, 370]). Samaias later advised the people of Jerusalem to admit Herod when he besieged it with the Roman general Sosius. For this reason, he and the Pharisees won Herod's favor and did not have to take an oath of loyalty. He is often identified with the rabbinic figure Shemayah.

Samaria, archaeology of the excavation and survey of the part of ancient Palestine bounded on the west by the coastal plain, on the east by the Jordan Valley, on the north by the Jezreel Plain, and on the south by Judea. The major cities of the region of Samaria before and during this period were Samaria (later Sebaste) and Shechem (later Neapolis). After the exile, and well into the Persian period, the number of sites in Samaria dropped considerably in the south. Most of the population moved near the Mediterranean coast, probably because the coastal cities were economic centers during the Persian period. Shechem appears to have remained mostly in ruins during the Persian period.

During the Hellenistic period, population increased again, particularly in southern Samaria. Samaria and Shechem were rebuilt as Macedonian cities at the beginning of the period. The Hellenistic city walls of Samaria have been found. They are 4.2 meters thick at the base and enclose an area of about 230 by 120 meters. Also at Samaria during the third century B.C.E., the locals built a temple for the worship of Isis. Building stones of this temple were found under a later temple. Isis is attested to by a Greek inscription dedicated to her and Serapis, her consort. Early in the second century B.C.E., the Seleucids built a Greek city on top of Mount Gerizim just south of Shechem. Both Shechem and Samaria were destroyed by John Hyrcanus II in 108 B.C.E. Western Samaria thrived during the Hellenistic period, with farms, rural oil, wine presses, and widespread terracing of fields.

At the very beginning of the Roman period, or in 63 B.C.E., the invading Roman general Pompey annexed the region of Samaria to Syria. In 57 B.C.E. the Roman governor Gabinius rebuilt the city of Samaria. When Herod the Great gained control of the area, he continued the Romanization of the city and renamed it Sebaste in honor of Caesar Augustus (Sebaste is the Greek word for Augustus). The city wall was strengthened with towers, and the gate contained two round towers. By the second century C.E., the city had a colonnaded street down its center, the cardo maximus, the tops of the columns of which can still be seen emerging from the ground for a total of 800 meters. Herod also built a temple to Augustus, an Augusteum, which stood on a rectangular platform 83 by 72 meters. North of the Augusteum there stood a temple to the Mediterranean goddess Korē, only the foundations of which have been uncovered. Also at Sebaste a stadium or hippodrome, a theater, a forum, a public basilica, and numerous tombs were built. The stadium was connected with the worship of Korē and was first built by Herod the Great. In the second century C.E. the stadium was rebuilt in Corinthian style. By 225 C.E. a theater had been built at Sebaste large enough to seat perhaps 3,000 visitors. The market place or agora was surrounded by roofed porticoes on all four sides. Beside the agora stood a basilica 68 meters long by 32.6 meters wide. It may originally have been built by Gabinius or Herod the Great in the first century B.C.E. An aqueduct brought water to the city from the hills to the east.

During this period the number of settlements reached close to its zenith, with hamlets, villages, towns, and cities dotting the landscape. Umm Rihan, the modern name for an ancient village in northern Samaria, a Roman town of significance, had existed in the Persian and Hellenistic periods. The existence of a Latin inscription suggests that it was settled by Roman veterans and possibly Samaritans. The town has about one hundred houses covering 9 to 10 acres. The town includes streets, defense towers at its entrances, public areas, public baths, shops, and several oil and wine presses. In addition, there were several hundred field towers in the vicinity of the Roman town. These were largely abandoned in the second century C.E. After the destruction of Jerusalem, Shechem was rebuilt and refounded in 73 C.E. as Neapolis, a new city of the Flavian emperors. The region of Samaria was divided for administrative purposes into the city territories of Sebaste and Neapolis. In the third century C.E., Neapolis was further granted the title of "colony."

Neapolis was a wholly Roman city. It contained a theater, an amphitheater (circus) connected to a hippodrome or stadium, a city wall with round towers, a large water system on the south side, and courtyard houses. A long, colonnaded street ran east and west. A mosaic from a third-century house is often considered to be one of the finest ever made in Israel. The area of the city within the walls was about 250 acres.

In the Byzantine period, occupation in Samaria reached its height, though cities settled by Samaritans thinned out. Christian monasteries are especially strong in the Byzantine period in southwestern Samaria. On the other hand, Samaritan synagogues have been excavated in at least three Byzantine towns in Samaria. In 484 C.E. the Samaritans in Neapolis rose up in revolt against their Christian and Jewish neighbors, but principally against the emperor Zeno. This resulted in the destruction of many Samaritan villages and towns. Zeno built an octagonal church on top of the remains of the Samaritan city on Mount Gerizim, the former focus of Samaritan worship. Both the church and the ruins of the town beneath have been excavated. Samaritans broke out in revolt anew in 529 C.E., this time against the newly crowned emperor Justinian. This revolt was also brutally suppressed, including the destruction of Samaritan synagogues and towns. *See also* SAMARITANS.

Samaria, Persian province of   After the Assyrian conquest of Samaria (722 B.C.E.), the city and territory became a province within first the Assyrian and then the Babylonian Empire. Its provincial status remained unchanged after the conquest of Babylon by the Persians (539 B.C.E.). While Judah was probably not administered from Samaria under the Persians, the Samaritans, under the leading family of the Sanballats, bitterly opposed the establishment of a quasi-autonomous province in Judah, especially during Nehemiah's administration.

Samaritan, Anonymous   *see* EUPOLEMUS, PSEUDO-

Samaritan Aramaic   *see* ARAMAIC, SAMARITAN

Samaritan Chronicles   a series of recitations of Samaritan history, which have considerable authority in the Samaritan community. Although most of them have names, they are also given numbers by scholarly convention. The list is as follows: Chronicle 1 (Asatir), Chronicle 2, Chronicle 3 (Tolidah), Chronicle 4 (Samaritan Book of Joshua), Chronicle 5 (Shalshalat), Chronicle 6 (Abul Fath), and Chronicle 7 (the Adler Chronicle). The chronicles are of various types. Several of them make use of the Samaritan succession of high priests as the backbone of the work. This sort includes the Adler Chronicle, the Tolidah, and the Shalshalat. Others are somewhat different. The Samaritan Book of Joshua is very much parallel to the Book of Joshua in the Hebrew Bible. Chronicle 2 is more of a narrative in form, similar to Samuel or Kings. The Asatir is a paraphrase of Genesis in Aramaic similar to the Targums. The Samaritan Chronicles often have sections that have a parallel in Jewish history. For example, the sect is alleged to have begun in the time of Eli, when the true priesthood remained with Ithamar (i.e., the Samaritans) but the Jews followed the false high priest (Eli).

Samaritan diaspora   the movement of Samaritans out of Samaria, particularly the immediate area of Mount Gerizim. The earliest account of a Samaritan diaspora is in 2 Kings 17, which describes the Assyrian victory over Samaria (the Northern Kingdom of Israel) in 722 B.C.E. Its inhabitants were dispersed throughout the Assyrian empire.

The Samaritans are probably a remnant of only a small portion of the Northern Kingdom, and their real split with the Jews does not come until centuries later. Samaritan troops were garrisoned in Egypt by Alexander, initiating a long-term Samaritan community in Egypt. By the second century B.C.E., Samaritans had communities in Rhodes, Athens, Sicily, and Delos. They moved to the Palestinian coastal cities in the Roman period and, according to Justin Martyr, also lived in Rome. The Samaritan leader, Baba Rabbah, moved to Constantinople in the third or fourth century C.E., and by the fifth century, Samaritans were found throughout Italy and had a synagogue in Rome where they were generally prosperous. In the sixth century, Pope Gregory the Great prohibited the Samaritans from holding Christian slaves. In the East, Samaritans worked the silver mines of Persia and Armenia, and settled in Arabia and the islands of the Red Sea.

Beginning in the thirteenth century, the Samaritan diaspora, traced through the colophons (notes) in surviving manuscripts of the Pentateuch, shifted between Egypt and Damascus, depending on the changing political climate. In the sixteenth century a one-way exodus toward Nablus began, and at the beginning of the twentieth century a tiny community of fewer than two hundred Samaritans clung to the foot of Mount Gerizim. At the end of the twentieth century there were two major communities of Samaritans, one at Nablus and one in Holon, a suburb of Tel Aviv. The population of each was less than three hundred.

Samaritans   a small religious group unique in having survived from biblical times to the present day. Currently, there are some five hundred Samaritans, some living at their ancestral site near Nablus, in the West Bank territory, and others living at Holon, near Tel-Aviv. Their history, though often troubled, has been unbroken for over more than two thousand years.

It is unlikely, despite appearances, that there are any references to the Samaritans in the Hebrew Bible. Many English translations use the word at 2 Kings 17:29, but it is very doubtful whether the reference is to Samaritans in the later sense, and other versions (e.g., the NIV) use "people of Samaria." The difference is an important one: the Samaritans, properly so called, were a religious group, who rejected Jerusalemite hegemony and claimed that their ancestral site of Mount Gerizim, above Shechem, was the place on which God should be worshiped. That is quite different from a general reference to the people of the northern kingdom at large, who might better be described as "Samaritans."

Of the origin of the Samaritans as defined above, we know little for certain. From the second century B.C.E. onward, there are clear references to them; before that, everything is somewhat obscure. There are, broadly speaking, four theories as to their origin. The first, held by the Samaritans themselves, dates their division from the Judahites at the end of the Judges period, during the judgeship of Eli, regarded by the Samaritans as an impostor whose claims were rejected by the true believers. A second view, widely held in Judaism and propagated by Josephus, associates the Samaritans with the foreign settlers brought into the country by the Assyrians when they overran the northern kingdom of Israel in the eighth century B.C.E. These settlers are called "Kutheans" in 2 Kings 17:30, and this word is used in Jewish sources in a dismissive way to refer to the Samaritans. This theory, like the first, is unlikely to be historically accurate; just as the first view can be considered as anti-Jerusalemite polemic from the Samaritans, the second view is anti-Samaritan polemic from a Jerusalemite viewpoint.

The remaining theories have more to commend them historically. The third view regards the Samaritans as having retained some of the distinctive characteristics of northern Israelite belief. Not all the inhabitants of Israel were exiled by the Assyrian conquerors, and it is maintained that some of those who remained were the ancestors of the later Samaritans, who hoped to maintain the political and religious traditions of their inheritance. This is an innately plausible view, weakened only by our lack of detailed knowledge of the characteristic features of northern Israel's worship and understanding of God. (Such knowledge as we have comes to us from hostile sources in the books of Kings.) Because of this ignorance, and because of the custom of referring to a Samaritan schism, a fourth view has been put forward by some scholars, who have sought for a specific event that led to a breach between those centered on Jerusalem and those who wished to retain the traditions associated with Mount Gerizim. It is doubtful whether such a quest is justified; some have seen the unacceptable marriage described in Nehemiah 13:28 as a possible occasion of such a breach, but in the Bible it has no direct Samaritan reference; this is only supplied by Josephus (*Ant.* 11.302), who places the event a century later than Nehemiah, in the time of Alexander the Great. In the present state of our knowledge, therefore, the third of these four theories may seem the most plausible, but it is important to recognize that if either of the last two theories is broadly correct, there will be no direct references to Samaritans in the Hebrew Bible.

Such references can first be found clearly in the Apocrypha. Two passages in particular demand attention. The closing chapters of the Book of Ben Sira, or Ecclesiasticus, include a gratuitous condemnation of "the foolish people that dwell in Shechem" (Ecclus. 50:26), a reference that suggests that division between the rival sanctuaries of Jerusalem and Mount Gerizim had reached an acute stage at that time (2d c. B.C.E.). In another polemical aside, the author of 2 Maccabees implies that the Samaritans had not shown the same zeal in defending the law as had the faithful in Jerusalem, but had allowed their temple to be given a Greek dedication by the Hellenistic rulers of Palestine (2 Macc. 6:2). Again this is hostile polemic; we have no means of knowing the underlying circumstances.

When we turn to the New Testament the situation is somewhat clearer. The translation of John 4:9 is disputed (RSV: "Jews have no dealings with Samaritans"; NEB: "Jews and Samaritans do not use vessels in common"), but whether the reference is specifically to ritual cleanliness or to a more general hostility, the divisions between the two communities are by this time marked. A similar picture is given by the two references in the Gospel of Luke (10:29–37; 17:11–19): in each case, the behavior of a Samaritan is commended and used to highlight Jewish failings.

The other relevant New Testament material is found in the Acts of the Apostles and can be used to illustrate a question that caused much dispute. Were the Samaritans to be regarded as part of the overall Jewish community or not? They had much in common, particularly in their veneration for the Torah (the Samaritans, like some other Jewish groups, regarded only the Torah as "holy scripture") and in their punctiliousness in observing the requirements of ritual cleanliness. However, they rejected the claims of Jerusalem, its Temple, and its priesthood. Josephus resolved the problem by attacking the Samaritans, asserting that they claimed to be Jews when it suited them and rejected the link when things were going badly for the Jewish community, but this only provides further illustration of the ambiguity of the relation. It is shown again in Acts. Stephen's speech in Acts, chapter 7, has so much in common with Samaritan rejection of the Jerusalem Temple for it to have been seriously suggested that Stephen was of Samaritan origin. In Acts, chapter 8, we find a difficulty already noted in the Hebrew Bible: it is not clear whether the journey of Philip (8:5) is specifically to the Samaritans or simply to Samaria. This chapter is also important as providing the earliest references to Simon Magus (8:9–24), who later came to be identified as a leading Samaritan Gnostic. But to explore this theme is to go beyond the biblical period, at the end of which it is clear that the Samaritans were a well-established group, part of the larger spectrum of Judaism, but rejecting and being rejected by those aspects of Judaism that were tied specifically to the cultic observance of Jerusalem.

Samaritan targums In late antiquity, the Samaritans lived throughout the Eastern Mediterranean, with their strongest concentrations between Cairo and Damascus. Their scripture was limited to the Pentateuch. Over the centuries, three different Samaritan targums were composed to it; all three stand independent of the rabbinic targums and the Peshita. The first Samaritan targum was written around the fourth century C.E. in a dialect similar to that used in Targum Neofiti (Jewish Palestinian Aramaic). The second Samaritan targum was composed a century or so later in a dialect similar to that used in the Palestinian midrashim and the Palestinian Talmud. The third Samaritan targum was composed between the fourteenth and the sixteenth centuries, after Arabic had replaced Aramaic as the everyday language among Samaritans. The Aramaic of this targum consisted of a blend of Aramaic and Hebrew, with some Arabic influences. The Samaritan targums are quite literal, with only a few additional elements, and their translations were occasionally shaped to incorporate Samaritan aggadic and legal exegesis.

Sammael name for the chief of the evil spirits, derived from the Semitic roots *sama/sema* (blind) or *sam/samma* (poison), combined with the angelic suffix, *'el*. The first meaning appears in two Gnostic texts, which translate the name "god of the blind" (Hyp. Arch. 87:3, 94:25) and "the blind God" (Orig. World 103:18) and accuse him of erring. The former suggests a background in which Sammael blinded people and led them astray (cf. Mart. Asc. Isa. 1:8, 11; 2:1; 5:15–16; 11:10, 14). Sammael's activity as the poisoning angel relates to his role as the angel of death (Tg. Ps.-Jon. Gen. 3:6; 3 Bar. 4:8 [Greek]), and the name is suggested in Testament of Abraham 16–17 (A) and B. Abod. Zar. 20b. Sammael is also the accusing angel (*satan*; Exod. Rab. 18:5), and all three roles are combined in Deuteronomy Rabbah 11.

Samuel early Babylonian amora, born in Nehardea and active from the end of the second through the mid-third century C.E.; head of the academy at Nehardea; also known as Mar Samuel and Samuel Yarhinah. Samuel is frequently in dispute with Rab, after whose death he became the preeminent authority of his day. Samuel appears to have had close relations with the exilarchate (see Y. Taanit 4:2, 68a) and was involved in astronomy (B.

Berakhot 58b). He is known for his statement, "the law of the state is the law," which required Jews to observe the laws even of a non-Jewish government.

Samuel's teachers are unknown. B. Baba Metzia 85b's statement that Samuel cured an eye ailment of Judah the Patriarch has led some scholars to suggest that he studied with Judah in the Land of Israel. But this claim is poorly supported, insofar as Samuel neither reports any laws that he heard directly from Judah nor refers to any practices that he learned in Judah's household. Others claim that Samuel studied in the Land of Israel under Hanina b. Hama. This is based upon the two rabbis' implementation of similar medical cures and their identical use of drawings of a palm branch as their signatures (Y. Gittin 9:9, 50d). The same parallels can be found, however, among other authorities in distant settings, leaving this evidence as well to be judged as inconclusive.

Little is known of Samuel's personal life. He appears to have been wealthy, employing household servants (B. Niddah 47a) and tenant farmers (B. Baba Kamma 92a). His fields had been left to him by his father (B. Hullin 105a). Samuel's sons died as children (B. Shabbat 108a), and two of his daughters were taken captive and later ransomed in the Land of Israel (B. Ketubot 23a).

Samuel stands at the beginning of the postmishnaic period, transmitting Tannaitic traditions in Babylonia while, at the same time, presenting his own interpretations and laws. The hundreds of sayings attributed to him in the Babylonian Talmud, along with those of a few contemporaries, represent the earliest stratum of what would become the Babylonian Talmud. Evaluation of Samuel's statements suggests that in their earliest form, they were short comments that circulated along with the particular mishnaic passages to which they pertained. In the later development of talmudic argumentation, these statements were often expanded and set within the larger talmudic dialectic. The process of formulation and redaction of the Babylonian Talmud thus obscured Samuel's own work of composing a commentary on the Mishnah.

Samuel, Targum to *see* TARGUM TO THE PROPHETS

Samuel b. Abbahu Babylonian amora active in the fourth century C.E.; referred to at B. Hullin 59b in a controversy concerning the use of a Circassian goat for food

Samuel b. Ammi Palestinian amora, active in the late third and early fourth centuries C.E. Only a few of his exegetical statements are extant.

Samuel b. Ḥofni gaon of the academy at Sura from 997 C.E.; died 1013 C.E.; descended from scholars at Pumbedita. He was a prolific writer, but most of his works are no longer extant. He prepared the first introduction to the Talmud, which summarized its basic principles; parts of this introduction have been found in the Cairo Geniza.

Samuel b. Isaac Palestinian amora of the fourth century C.E.; a student of Ḥiyya b. Abba; the father-in-law of Hoshayah II. He also spent time in Babylonia, with Ḥuna. He was a teacher of Jeremiah, who transmits many of his statements.

Samuel b. Naḥman Palestinian amora of the late third and early fourth centuries C.E. A native of Lydda, he visited Babylonia several times, once on a mission to enact in Babylonia the intercalation of the calendar (Y. Berakhot 2:1, 2d) and again to argue on behalf of a youth who had committed a political crime (Y. Terumot 8:10, 46b). He studied with Jonathan b. Eleazar and Joshua b. Levi.

Samuel b. Yose be Bun also referred to as Samuel b. Yose b. Abin/Abun; a Palestinian amora active in the mid-fourth century C.E. Very little of his teaching has been preserved.

Sanballat I an opponent of Nehemiah. He is referred to as Sanballat the Horonite (Neh. 2:10, 19; 13:28), so he probably was from Beth Horon, northwest of Jerusalem; the name is Babylonian in origin (*sin-uballit,* the god Sin has given life). He may have been governor of the province, but this is not stated explicitly. Sanballat was the bitter opponent of Nehemiah's program of rebuilding the defenses of Jerusalem and setting up a quasi-autonomous province of Judah (Yehud). Two of his sons, Delaiah and Shemaiah, are mentioned in a letter from Elephantine (408 B.C.E.), and two papyri discovered in Wadi ed-Daliyeh mention a Sanballat who was governor of Samaria toward the end of Persian rule (cf. Josephus, *Ant.* 11.302–25), suggesting that the family maintained control of the province for at least a century.

sanctify God *see* GLORIFY, MAGNIFY, SANCTIFY GOD

sanctuary (Heb.: *mik dash*) the holy place; refers only to the Temple in Jerusalem. The sanctuary is the place in which the offerings were burned upon the altar and raised to heaven through the smoke of the altar fires; a place to be kept clean of the sources of uncleanness listed in Leviticus, chapters 11–15; and a place in which only appropriate persons, that is, priests (Heb.: *kohanim*) and Levites (Heb.: *leviim*), carry out the rites.

sanhedrin name for a Jewish administrative body

Sanhedrin Mishnah tractate devoted to the organization of the Israelite government and court system and the punishments administered to those convicted by the courts of having committed various crimes. The first five chapters describe the court system, covering various kinds of courts and their jurisdictions, the heads of the Israelite nation and courts, and the procedures of the court system in property and capital cases. Chapters 6 through 11 set forth rules on the death penalty, which is administered through stoning, burning, decapitation, and strangulation. How these penalties are administered is described, and the classifications of sins or crimes punished by each is specified. Extra-judicial penalties administered by Heaven are spelled out: all Israelites share in the world to come except those who deny that the Torah teaches the resurrection of the dead. Both Talmuds devote important and lengthy expositions to this tractate.

Sarah (Heb., princess) name of both Abraham's wife, Isaac's mother (Gen. 11, 12, 16), and the heroine of the Book of Tobit. Galatians 4:21–31 (see also Rom. 9:6–9) compares Sarah—the free matriarch, representative of heavenly Jerusalem, and mother of Isaac and the children of promise—to the slave Hagar, whose children of the flesh are enslaved by Mosaic law. For Hebrews 11:11, Sarah exemplifies faith by trusting that she would conceive after menopause (see Rom. 4:19, from Abraham's perspective). In 1 Peter 3:6, she is the model of an obedient, subordinate wife. Her story is particularly expanded in the Testament of Abraham.

The second Sarah (in the Book of Tobit), also unable to conceive and in conflict with her servants (Tob. 3:8–9), is plagued by the demon Asmodeus until her prayers—which parallel those of Tobit—are answered by Tobias. Perhaps reflecting the tradition of the "fall of the watchers," the angel Raphael avoids her company.

sarcophagus large stone coffin, usually decorated, and most commonly of the Roman period. Sarcophagi are well known in Roman period sites in the eastern Mediterranean, as they were customary for persons of means. The sarcophagus was normally interred in a family tomb, perhaps with other sarcophagi. Sarcophagi were most commonly manufactured at a central place, then sold either with completed decorations or with certain elements left "blank" for the family to complete with a hired artist. Others were clearly completed by the family, as they bear all the marks of a popular art by an unpracticed hand. A famous example of one of the fine sarcophagi is from Ashkelon. It is likely from the third or fourth century and depicts the battle between Greeks and Gauls, perhaps Greeks and Trojans, in fine white marble. Other favorite motifs include a battle between Greeks and the Amazons. Other sarcophagi may be completely undecorated. For example, the second-century-C.E. mausoleum or burial monument from Capernaum in Galilee was found to contain three completely plain sarcophagi.

In the cemetery of the Jewish town of Beth Shearim in western Galilee, many sarcophagi were apparently decorated by the families that used them. Sarcophagi are generally more massive than receptacles for the dead made of other materials, because of the greater density of stone and because of the larger dimensions. For example, sarcophagus 87 from catacomb 20 at Beth Shearim (in which no less than 125 sarcophagi were found) was 2 meters by 87 centimeters by 61 centimeters, not counting the lid. Even larger sarcophagi are known at Beth Shearim and elsewhere, some of them approaching 7 tons in weight. Lids of sarcophagi were typically carved to resemble a roof with *acroteria*, or rounded projections, on each corner. The "shell" sarcophagus from Beth Shearim, catacomb 20, is carved everywhere in low relief. In the center of the long side of the lid between the two acroteria is a rounded projection with a shell carved into its hollow. Thus, its name. On the long side of the sarcophagus, on the side facing out from the wall, there appears a flat, rectangular panel surrounded by a repeated geometric pattern on the bottom and by wreath and garland at the ends. The rectangular in the center features what appears to be two Torah shrines, that is, a shell carved above two columns. The one on the left has an eagle with spread wings between the columns, while the one on the right has a feline, perhaps a lioness, between the columns. Four different decorations embellish the top edge of the rectangle, including two lions facing a bull's head between them. All the carvings are finished in primitive style. The eagle sarcophagus from Beth Shearim features not only an eagle but also, on the long side, two lions face one another, again with a bull's head between them. The same motif appears on the lion sarcophagus, also from Beth Shearim, which appears to depict a chalice between the lions. Smashed fragments of marble sarcophagi abound at Beth Shearim, surely broken by looters of much later periods. Some betray traces of elaborate decoration in high relief in motifs borrowed from Roman art, including the war of the Greeks with the Amazons (an Amazonomachy). On the wall of catacomb 20 at Beth Shearim is painted an inscription in Hebrew: "These sarcophagi, the inner and the outer, are of Rabbi Aniana and of . . . the holy ones, the sons of . . . ." All the inscriptions on the sarcophagi are in Hebrew.

Sometimes the name of the deceased appears on the side of the sarcophagus, presumably so that family members who entered the tomb at a later date for a new burial could locate family members. In catacomb 20 at Beth Shearim, twenty of the sarcophagi are inscribed with a family member's name. Other sarcophagi in fine marble feature carvings in high relief of war scenes and other popular motifs. The white marble sarcophagi with such scenes have been traced to Attica in Greece and to the island of Marmara in the Dardanelles. A second famous sarcophagus from Ashkelon depicts in high relief the rape of Proserpine. A fragment of a sarcophagus from Beth Shearim depicts Lydda and the swan. *See also* SARCOPHAGUS DECORATIONS.

sarcophagus decorations   Jewish symbols found on ancient stone coffins (sarcophagi) that exhibit both Jewish and Graeco-Roman symbols of death, the afterlife, and salvation. Relatively few sarcophagi have been discovered in Palestine compared to the vast number of ossuaries. This is probably merely a matter of the added expense of constructing and storing a sarcophagus that held the entire body. Ossuaries were more convenient both in terms of money needed for construction and in terms of storage because they only held the bones after the body had decomposed. In light of the small numbers of sarcophagi found in Palestine, conclusions concerning Jewish decorations must be supplemented by Jewish burials from outside Palestine.

A central question concerning sarcophagus decorations from Jewish burials is the need to explain the presence of extensive Hellenistic symbols and relatively few traditional Jewish symbols. In contrast to the paintings and epithets found in Jewish and Christian burials in Rome, where the bones are found behind simple stone slabs, the rooms with the elaborate sarcophagi exhibit extensive pagan borrowing. The same phenomenon is found on sarcophagi from Palestine. This fact has caused some scholars in the past to argue that these sarcophagi were actually not Jewish. More recently, it has been argued that since only the Jewish upper class could have afforded the construction of sarcophagi, Hellenistic influence was much more extensive among the Jewish upper class.

The sarcophagi from the Catacomb Randanini in Rome are important in identifying both traditional Jewish and Hellenistic symbols with Jewish burials. Two rooms in the Catacomb Randanini are especially filled with Hellenistic symbols. Both rooms have ceiling decorations which have been labeled the "dome of heaven." In these ceilings, a central circle serves to symbolize salvation. Other symbols of Hellenistic origin, representing the afterlife or immortality, include a winged victory crown, a libation offering flowing from a cornucopia, peacocks, birds, the sign Pisces, a Cupid figure, and Pegasus.

In spite of these so-called pagan symbols, fragments of sarcophagi from this catacomb exhibit traditional Jewish symbols along with traditional Hellenistic symbols. One sarcophagus fragment from the Jewish Catacomb Randanini contains a representation of the four seasons with Dionysian wine pressing. In addition, there are a pair of victories which hold up a shield between them. A lighted menorah is depicted on the shield, however, instead of the portrait of the deceased or a symbol of hope as would be expected from other "pagan" burials. Another sarcophagus fragment from this same catacomb contains completely Jewish symbolism, including two palm trees which could be seen to symbolize the tree of life. In light of these symbols, which definitely point to Jewish burials, one should interpret the other burials and symbols from the same catacomb as Jewish even if the use of pagan symbolism is difficult to understand.

The suggestion of wealthier Jews being more Hellenistic because the expensive sarcophagi exhibit pagan symbols is possible. One can also postulate that more humble burials did not use elaborate decorations of either type because of the cost involved. The lack of these symbols in burials where sarcophagi are not present does not sway the interpretation in either direction.

Sardis, Jews in   Sardis, in Lydia, about sixty miles from the western coast of Asia Minor, was a major city from the sixth century B.C.E. until its destruction in the seventh century C.E. It is possible that Obadiah 20, which refers to an exilic community of Sepharad, speaks of Sardis because a Lydian-Aramaic inscription gives Sardis that name. According to documents preserved in Josephus, the Jewish community was already established in the first century B.C.E. and successfully defended its rights and privileges. The recently excavated synagogue in Sardis, the largest yet found, testifies to the size, influence, and prosperity of the Jewish community in Sardis from at least the third century C.E. A basilica in a large Roman public complex was taken over for a synagogue, probably in the third century, and underwent several renovations over the years. A forecourt (31 × 25 ft.) had a central fountain and a colonade around the sides. Three doors

in the east wall led into a main hall (75 × 25 ft.). Between the door at the east end were two Torah shrines and on the west wall an apse. A large table and two reused lion sculptures along with mosaics on the floor and other decorations on the walls graced the interior. Over eighty inscriptions have been found, some recording donations by community members who held municipal offices. The building, its frequent renovations, and the inscriptions all testify to a well-established, prosperous, and influential Jewish community in a major city of Asia Minor.

Sariel   (Heb., prince of God) one of four holy ones (angels) who stand in God's immediate presence according to 1 Enoch 6–11 and 1QM 9:15–16. In 1 Enoch 10:1 he is God's messenger to Noah. In the Ethiopic version of 1 Enoch he is confused with Uriel, and in 1 Enoch 40:9 he is replaced by Fanuel.

sarx   (Gr., flesh) Although it is used generically, it also became a philosophical and theological term to designate the desires and appetites of the flesh and thus usually had a negative connotation. The view in the Graeco-Roman world was that a person's desires should be controlled by the mind (Gr.: *nous*). *See also* NOUS.

Sasa   Jewish village in the western side of the territory of Sepphoris, but so near the border that there were doubts in the rabbinic sources whether it belonged to Sepphoris or to Acco-Ptolemais (T. Gittin 2:3). Sasa was far enough into the hills to be included in Upper Galilee, though it lay just south of the Roman track from Tiberias to Acco-Ptolemais. The site has never been excavated, though a column base discovered in the ruined village in the nineteenth century was said to resemble those of synagogues. In 1334 a Jewish traveler reports that a synagogue stood in the village, perhaps the building to which this column base belonged.

Sassanids, Jews under   the period of the Persian dynasty, ruling Iran from 224 to 651 C.E., that claimed Sasan, a Zoroastrian priest who served at the Istakhr temple, as its founder. In 224 Sasan's grandson Ardashir became the first Sassanid ruler. The Jews were not enthusiastic about the new dynasty, for it set out to establish a state-church which would serve as the empire's unifying force. Ardashir's government was determined to cancel the traditional prerogatives that the Parthians had granted to the Jewish community and to control the activities of the Jewish courts. The Babylonian Talmud records Rab's lamenting upon the Ardavan's death and numerous complaints about the new situation that even led to the destruction of synagogues. The situation changed when Shapur I took the throne in 241, for shortly thereafter Samuel's dictum that "the law of the government is the law" accepted the authority of the Sassanids and recognized the legitimacy of their courts and laws. This political decision seems to have resulted in the Sassanids' allowing the rabbis to maintain their control over the daily lives of the Jews in both religious and nonreligious matters as long as they were deemed unimportant by or in agreement with Sassanid policy according to the Persian authorities. The rabbinic texts naturally indicate that the rabbis were the primary Jewish authority, even though the Persians recognized the exilarch as the official Jewish representative. The period from the death of Shapur I in 272 to the advent of Shapur II in 309 witnessed the succession of weak leaders who constantly fought wars with Rome and who lost significant amounts of territory. However, the rabbinic sources take only slight account of the political and military unrest or the frequent military invasions of the empire. They do not indicate that Jewish settlements were destroyed, that the Jews suffered greatly at this time, or that their way of life was notably disturbed. The Jewish sources almost ignore the threat posed by Kartir's religious reforms. From the point of view of the Jewish documents, the most pressing issue was the new tax structure and its system of penalties. Many Jews seem to have lost their property or were sold into slavery in order to meet their tax obligations.

Shapur II (309–379) was an exceptionally gifted politician, administrator, and soldier. He was able to regain the territory that his predecessor's had lost, defeating several Roman armies. He is credited in some texts with creating a Mazdean state-church; however, we have no evidence that he persecuted the Jews, although he did persecute Christians whom he probably connected with his western enemies. The only rabbinic stories that point to the government's persecuting Jews revolve around cases of tax evasion. The Talmud contains five stories about Ifra Hormizd, Shapur's mother, who they claim supported the Jews at her son's court. The few rabbinic stories about Shapur II picture him as curious about some Jewish practices and respectful of others. The rabbinic texts indicate that Jewish life prospered during his administration under the leadership of the rabbis who attempted to disengage themselves from the exilarch's authority. When Shapur II died in 379/380, the Persian Empire was at peace on its western and eastern frontiers and secure under a strong centralized government. This was the state of affairs when Yazdagird I gained the throne in 399. Both the later Persian and rabbinic traditions picture Yazdagird as friendly toward the Jews. The former claim that the emperor had a Jewish wife, and the latter suggest that women in Yazdagird's harem supported the Jewish community and that the exilarch and the emperor were on good terms.

The fifth century was a time of external threat by the Hephthalites and internal instability. Late Jewish sources claim that Yazdagird II (438–457) and Peroz (459–484) issued decrees against Sabbath observance, closed Jewish schools, and abolished the Jewish court system, placing Jews under Persian rather than Jewish law. In addition, the emperors are accused of executing leading rabbis and exilarchs. These activities parallel the emperors' persecution of Christian institutions and holy men. Under Kavad I (488–531) and Khusro I (531–579) the empire again became strong and united. Kavad undertook the reconstruction of the domestic economy and the strengthening of the traditional nobility. Khusro revamped agriculture, reorganized the empire's communication system, and created a new tax system which guaranteed him a steady revenue. He also brought an end to the threat of the Hephthalites. Our sources about the Jewish community at this time are late, but they do not indicate that the Jews suffered under these emperors. Some claim the exilarch and the rabbis founded an independent Jewish state, but if they did, it was short lived. Jewish sources suggest that under Khusro II (591–628) and his successors, the situation of the Jews worsened. They describe the period as a time of persecutions; therefore, it is doubtful that the Jews mourned the passing of the Sassanids and the arrival of the Muslims.

Satan (from Heb., adversary) a member of the heavenly court whose primary adversarial function is to accuse in legal dispute. The noun usually appears with the definite article, indicating a role rather than a personal name. In Zechariah 3 he and the angel of YHWH dispute Joshua's fitness for the high priesthood. In Job 1–2 accusation leads to testing; the prosecutor attempts entrapment. In 1 Chronicles 21:1 satan, rather than God, incites David to sin (cf. 2 Sam. 24:1). The role of the accusatorial adversary is widespread in later literature, even where the title "satan" is not present, and his malevolent intentions predominate (cf. Jub. 1:20, 17:15–18:12, 48:1–12). In general, however, "satan" is relatively infrequent as a designation for the chief evil spirit.

In the New Testament, however, the Greek *satan(as)* and the normal translation of the Hebrew, *diabolos,* predominate. The surprising frequency of *satan(as)* suggests that the title had become a veritable proper name, although the word usually appears with the definite article. Most New Testament passages depict this figure as a tempter rather than an accuser, but the old meaning appears in Revelation 12:10 in a version of the myth recounted in Isaiah 14 and the Life of Adam and Eve 12–17.

Satanael name for the leader of the fallen angels in 2 Enoch. In chapter 18 he is the counterpart of Shemihazah, the chief of the watchers according to 1 Enoch 6–11. In 2 Enoch 31, he is identified with the tempter of Eve, and his story parallels the Life of Adam and Eve 12–17.

satrapy a division of the Persian Empire, governed by a satrap, that formed the basic administrative unit. Within his satrapy, the satrap governed with a great deal of autonomy. Herodotus states that the empire was divided into twenty satrapies by Darius I, though the exact number may have changed through history. Satrapies were subdivided into provinces (called medinahs or eparchies) and smaller units. With the Greek conquest, the larger satrapies did not usually remain intact (though Egypt became the Ptolemaic Empire), and the administrative units tended to be the smaller ones.

Saul of Tarsus usually known as Paul (after the Greek form of his name), the apostle Paul, or Saint Paul; a Jew of the first century C.E. who became the most influential early Christian missionary. At least seven of his letters are preserved in the New Testament (Romans, 1 and 2 Corinthians, Galatians, 1 Thessalonians, Philippians, Philemon), and his ideas played a formative role in the development of Christian theology. Knowledge of Paul's life derives from his letters (written in the 50s) and from the Acts of Apostles (c. 90), over half of which is devoted to an account of his missionary journeys. Paul describes himself as a "Hebrew of the Hebrews," a Pharisee of the tribe of Benjamin, who was "blameless" in regard to the Torah (Phil. 3:5–6; cf. Gal. 1:13–14). Initially repelled by the Christian preaching of a crucified and resurrected messiah, Paul sought to destroy the church (Gal. 1:13) until a vision of Jesus on the road to Damascus convinced him that he was called to be Jesus' apostle (missionary) to the Gentiles (Gal. 1:15–17; cf. Acts 9). From his base at Antioch in Syria, he journeyed around the Mediterranean world, preaching about Jesus and founding churches in Asia Minor (modern Turkey) and Greece. Paul aroused animosity, not only among Jews but also among many Jewish Christians, by his radical position on the place of Torah in the new Christian faith. Arguing that observance of the Torah played no positive role in Christian salvation, he vigorously opposed Jewish Christian missionaries who attempted to impose Torah observance on his gentile converts (Gal.; Rom. 3–4). Although his views resulted in some tensions with the first Christian community in Jerusalem (cf. Gal. 1–2; Acts 15), Paul championed Christian unity, and as a sign of this he traveled to Jerusalem to deliver a gift of money collected in his mostly gentile churches. On this last visit to Jerusalem, Paul was arrested; he appealed to the emperor and was taken by ship to Rome (Acts 21–28). Acts breaks off the story with Paul under house arrest in Rome; according to Christian tradition, he died during the persecution of Nero in 64 C.E.

The teaching contained in Paul's letters has had enormous influence on Christian theology. Paul says little about the life and teachings of Jesus but focuses on his death and resurrection, which he views as the central act in God's plan for the salvation of all people, both Jews and Gentiles (1 Cor. 15, Rom. 3:21–26). Sharing the perspective of apocalyptic thinkers who contrasted the present evil age to the salvific "age to come" (cf. 2 Esdras 7:112–113), Paul views the death and resurrection of Jesus as the breaking in of the new age, which will be consummated in the final victory over the powers of evil and death at the second coming of Jesus, an event that Paul expects in his own lifetime (1 Cor. 15:19–58). Paul's articulation of salvation in Christ as "justification (appropriated) by faith," apart from the works of the law (Rom. 3:21) was particularly emphasized by Luther and the Protestant Reformation.

savior *see* SALVATION

scales and weights instruments for measuring, which epitomize the notion of justice and fairness; false scales and weights symbolize injustice (Prov. 20:10, 23; Mic. 6:11). The weighing process became a metaphor for the process of justice, whether human (1 Enoch 95:6) or divine (Dan. 5:27). *See also* BALANCE, JUDGMENT.

school (Heb.: *beit midrash,* house of study) rabbinic center for study and prayer. Through the Talmudic period, the school, under exclusive rabbinic control, was distinct from—and, according to some authorities, holier than—the community-run synagogue. B. Megillah 27a reports an amoraic discussion concerning the permissibility of turning a synagogue into a school or vice versa. The underlying premise, supported through a citation of the Tannaitic authority Joshua b. Levi, is that the school, where Torah is exalted, had a higher status.

In general, rabbis held that activity in the school was an essential element of piety. Those who went directly from the synagogue to the school were deemed worthy of the divine Presence (B. Berakhot 64a). Wives were praised for waiting up for husbands who returned home late from the school (B. Berakhot 17a).

The first known appearance of the term *beit midrash* occurs at Ben Sira 51:23: "Draw near to me you who are untaught and lodge in my school." The term and its Aramaic equivalent, *bei midrash,* occur numerous times throughout the rabbinic literature, describing a rabbinic culture in which participation in rabbinical study was the society's highest value. According to B. Ketubot 105a, in Jerusalem alone, there were 394 courts and synagogues and an equal number of schools.

The terms *beit midrash* and *bei midrash* occur in rabbinic sources deriving from both Babylonia and the Land of Israel. The Babylonian usage of these terms, however, occurs almost exclusively in reference to rabbinical institutions in the Land of Israel or in interpretations of verses of scripture. For their own institutions, Babylonian authorities used the term *bei rabbanan* (house of our rabbi/master) or *bei rab* (house of the rabbi/master), to which the name of a specific Amoraic authority often was attached. This terminology reflects the fact that, during the Talmudic period, the large Babylonian academies that would develop in the gaonic period did not exist. The Babylonian school, rather, consisted of a circle of disciples gathered around particular rabbinic master. These circles lacked the formalized institutional culture that would allow them to continue after the death or retirement of that master. Instead, upon the master's death, the circle would disband, and its students would search for a new teacher or would themselves take on students of their own. Rabbinical schooling in Babylonia thus differed from that in the Land of Israel, where formal rabbinical institutions appear to have existed in the Talmudic period. Called *betei midrash,* these schools were equipped with their own staffs and set curriculums and had corporate identities that transcended the particular masters who taught in them in any particular period.

In the post-Talmudic period, words that in the Talmud designated rabbinical courts—the Hebrew word *yeshivah* and its Aramaic equivalent, *metivta*—increasingly were applied to formal academies of higher rabbinic learning. Such academies were separate from the *beit midrash,* which remained open to all men who wished to study. In medieval times, the *beit midrash* often was merged with the synagogue, though it retained its distinctive character as a place for study of rabbinic texts and discussion of Jewish law, in which prayer was a secondary activity.

sciatic nerve in the back of the hip, understood to be the "hollow" of the thigh, put out of joint by the messenger of God who wrestled with Jacob on the evening before Jacob's reunion with Esau (Gen. 32:24–30). As a result of this belief, the sciatic nerve is not eaten and must be removed from all meat slaughtered and consumed under the Jewish dietary laws.

scribes (Heb.: *sofer, soferim;* Gr.: *grammateus, grammateis*) literally, those who can write; more broadly, those who are literate. In ancient Near Eastern and Graeco-Roman society about 90 percent of the population were illiterate, mostly engaged in farming. Thus, those who were literate, the scribes, served in specialized roles as administrative and financial officials, educators, religious functionaries, and so on. The imperial courts in Egypt and Mesopotamia had elaborate systems of scribal training and administration. These patterns were probably imitated in Israel from the time of Solomon on. The chief scribe at the Jerusalem court was a high cabinet officer concerned with finance, policy, and administration (2 Kings 22; Jer. 36:10). Scribes such as Baruch were also associated with the prophets (Jer. 36:32). The development of biblical literature during the Babylonian exile and the proliferation of extrabiblical Jewish literature during the Persian and Greek periods indicate intensive activities of professional scribes among prophetic priestly, apocalyptic, and governing groups. In postexilic Israel, Ezra the Scribe was a community leader, learned in the law (Ezra 7:6), who was given wide authority over the Jewish community by the Persian king (Ezra 7:21–26). Levites also served as scribes (1 Chron. 24:6) and teachers (Neh. 8:7–8). In the Graeco-Roman period, a group of scribes sought reconciliation with the high priest, Alcimus (I Macc. 7:12–14), and Eleazar, a leading scribe, died for the law (2 Macc. 6:18). Scribes appear in the writings of Josephus as lowly village copyists, high Jerusalem officials, and members of the council. In the Gospels, scribes appear with the Pharisees as a group opposed to Jesus of Nazareth. They are best understood as low-level village officials and teachers who were the first to come into conflict with Jesus. Rabbinic literature refers sporadically to scribes (*soferim*) as early authoritative teachers of various rulings and biblical interpretations. The "words of the scribes" are premishnaic traditions, which are less authoritative than scripture. Because their writings do not form a coherent body of teachings, the term *soferim* probably refers to a variety of learned scholars and teachers in the Hellenistic period about whom little is known. In the Talmuds, scribes appear in several roles. They are skilled copyists of Torah scrolls, which have by then become an object of veneration in the Jewish community. Local scribes continue as literate functionaries who write letters and documents. Some scribes are teachers and interpreters of scripture, but generally the rabbis take over these functions of scribes. In diaspora synagogues, the scribe (Gr.: *grammateus*) sometimes appears as an official subordinate to the leader (*archon*).

scribes, words of the laws assumed to derive from ancient scholars and educators, held to comprise the foundation of the oral law later codified in the rabbinic literature. The exact significance of the designation "words of the scribes" is difficult to ascertain, since in the rabbinic literature, the term "scribes" refers to authorities from a variety of historical periods, not from a discernible social, academic, or political class. Gamaliel refers to his fellow scholars as "scribes" (B. Sotah 15a), suggesting that the term simply denotes legal authorities. By contrast, M. Sotah 9:15 and Leviticus Rabbah 9:2 suggest that the scribes are less learned than rabbis.

Scriptores Historiae Augustae a series of biographies of the Roman emperors in Latin, extending from Hadrian in the early second century C.E. to Numerianus in the late third century C.E. The work is anonymous and claims to have been written by half a dozen authors, but some scholars think there was only one; it was probably composed in the fourth or fifth century C.E. The reliability of the information varies considerably, and the work contains some alleged documents that are now considered suspect, if not outright forgeries. The biography of Hadrian is one of the few sources on the Bar Kokhba Revolt and also seems to be more generally reliable than some of the other biographies. Nevertheless, the statement that the Jews revolted at the time of the Bar Kokhba uprising because they were forbidden to "mutilate their genitals" (usually interpreted as a reference to circumcision) is a controversial one and rejected by many scholars. If such a decree was issued (and some doubt this), it was more likely a consequence than a cause of the revolt. The Life of Hadrian also gives a brief statement that Palestine was included in the 115–117 C.E. revolt, though there is no other evidence of this.

scriptural interpretation 1. *In the Second Temple period and the New Testament.* The systematic and careful study and exposition of sacred written tradition, well known from the rabbinic writings, has its roots at least in the Hellenistic period, although it is uncertain exactly when collections of written texts began to have canonical authority. Ecclesiasticus is the earliest testimony to a collection of written Israelite sacred traditions that approximates the Hebrew Bible. Writing in the first decades of the second century B.C.E., Ben Sira recounts the accomplishments of Israel's "famous men," in the following order: the Pentateuch; the Former Prophets; Isaiah, Jeremiah, Ezekiel, and the Twelve; and Zerubbabel and Joshua (Ecclus. 44–49). Two generations later, Ben Sira's grandson refers to "the Law and the Prophets and the other books of our fathers" (Ecclus. prologue).

Ben Sira refers explicitly to the detailed study of the collection. The scribe who is learned in the study of the Law of the Most High, seeks out the wisdom of all the ancients and is concerned with prophecies (39:1–3). The verb "search" is used twice of the process (39:1, 3; Gr.: *ekzētō* = Heb.: *darash*). Study presupposes prayer, which results in revelation and inspired teaching, or illumination (vv. 4–8; cf. 24:32–34). Ben Sira's association of Torah and wisdom is noteworthy in two respects; he sees the Mosaic Torah as the embodiment of heavenly wisdom (24:1–29), and the teaching in his book is not in the form of halakhic exposition, but of proverbial instruction.

The Book of Jubilees provides a witness to the study of Scripture almost contemporary with Ben Sira. The book is itself an aggadic elaboration on Genesis 1–Exodus 12, with interpolations into the Pentateuchal narratives that highlight the author's particular understanding of specific laws. The setting for this interpretation is the religious crisis of the Hellenistic period, which, in the author's view, has led to the serious troubles of his own time. The situation is alleviated when the younger generation "begin to study the laws, and to *seek* the commandments, and return to the path of righteousness" (23:26). The process of seeking or searching is necessary and crucial, because Israel's failure properly to understand and observe the Torah is the cause of its suffering the curses of the covenant.

Like Ben Sira's scribe, the Qumran Community (and its sectarian predecessors?) engaged in the interpretation of the Torah and the Prophets. "The searcher of the Torah" (Heb.: *doresh hattorah*) came to Damascus and dug "the Well" of the Torah for the "converts of Judah" (CD 6:2–11), persons who sought how properly to act during the time of

Israel's wickedness. Opponents of the community are called facile interpreters, literally "seekers of slippery things" (Heb.: *dorshe habalaqot;* 4QpNah 1:2, 7; 2:2, 4; 3:2, 6–7; 1QH 2:32; CD 1:18). Detailed interpretation of prophecy is attested throughout the commentaries (Heb.: *pesharim*), and the process is tied to revelation received by the Teacher of Righteousness (1QpHab 7:4).

Running through all of these texts is the notion of interpretation as "seeking" or "searching" for what is not obvious. For Ben Sira, it is part of the scholar's search for the wisdom that is not easily accessible (cf. Bar. 3:14–4:4). In bad times, this search for the right interpretation of the Torah is a strategy to obtain the covenantal blessing (see also Bar. 3:9–14), and sometimes it involves a kind of sectarianism that damns the other's interpretations.

Interpretation of scripture took many forms: aggadah; commentaries and other ad hoc *pesharim* (e.g., in the Damascus Document); compilations of laws (e.g., CD 9ff.); halakhic exposition of biblical narrative (Jubilees, Temple Scroll); a proverbial exposition of the Torah (Ecclus. 3:1–16). We have only a few hints of the precise setting and "mechanics" of interpretation. Ben Sira invites his readers into his house of study (51:23; Heb.: *beit midrash*). His reference to prayer in chapter 39 is paralleled in Daniel 9, where Daniel's penitential prayer is answered by the appearance of an angel, who interprets Jeremiah's prophecy to refer to seventy weeks of years. It is unclear what role such "revelations" played in the interpretation of the traditional written texts.

It should not be supposed that in all cases "scripture" was limited to the emerging canon of the Hebrew Bible. 1 Enoch is a developing collection of revelatory traditions, each building on and interpreting the other. The Book of Jubilees, although it is an interpretation of Genesis 1–Exodus 12, is presented as itself a sacred tradition dictated to Moses by the angels of God's presence, and the Damascus Document cites it as authoritative (CD 16:2–4) The Temple Scroll seems also to claim to be authoritative Torah.

The New Testament witnesses to a sophisticated process of Jewish scriptural interpretation, but the emphasis falls on the prophets rather than the Torah. John 5:39 highlights this situation. Jesus' response to the Jews in John 5:39 employs technical terminology: "You search the scriptures, because you think that in them you have eternal life; and it is they that testify to me." His opponents seek life in the Torah, but he is incarnate wisdom, and the ancient texts, *qua* prophecy, speak about

him. Paul employs techniques reminiscent of rabbinic exegesis in his eschatological arguments against the ongoing viability of the Torah in the Epistles to the Galatians and the Romans. Matthew is more conservative about the Torah (chaps. 5–7), and his highly polished eschatological interpretation of prophecy has parallels at Qumran.

2. *In Greek.* In one sense, it is wrong to make a distinction between exegesis in Greek and that in other languages such as Hebrew and Aramaic, for, in theory, the same sorts of methods and forms might be used, whatever the language. Nevertheless, certain types of interpretation tend to predominate in works by Jewish exegetes writing in Greek. Generally, such exegetes have used forms better known in Greek literature than in Hebrew and Aramaic literature.

The first Greek interpretation of the Hebrew Bible was the translation known as the Septuagint. All translations represent interpretations to some extent, and the Septuagint, despite being a fairly literal rendering, imported Greek forms into a Semitic book. It thus provided two important contributions: (1) it made the biblical text available in Greek for those who could not use the original or who found a Greek text easier for their purposes, and (2) it began the interpretive process and smoothed the way for Greek-speaking Jews to carry out their exegesis.

The main forms of interpretation are usually known and used in commentaries and writings in more than one language. Nevertheless, some types tend to be more common in Greek-language interpretation. These include allegory (e.g., Philo of Alexandria), apologetic historiography (e.g., Josephus), and arithmology. On the other hand, "rewritten Bible," etymology, and chronography are found in various languages. Much more Midrash is found in Hebrew and Aramaic, but see the Midrash on the ten plaques in the Wisdom of Solomon 15–19 as an example in Greek. In addition to Philo and Josephus, other major interpreters include the Fragmentary Hellenistic Jewish writers.

The format of the writings that contain biblical interpretation varies considerably. The strict commentary form, with a verse-by-verse exposition, is best exemplified by Philo, who often makes use of it (though in some of his treatises, he ranges quite widely from the passage being expounded). A favorite method of exposition is to retell the biblical story or some part of it. Josephus does this in the first half of the *Antiquities,* which is primarily a paraphrase of the biblical text but with significant additions, omissions, and changes. Eupolemus tells the story of the Israelite kings; similarly, Artapanus reinterprets the story of Abraham and Moses. Sometimes the writer will draw on explicitly Greek literary models. For example, Ezekiel the Tragedian produced a version of the Exodus but in drama form, a literary genre not known in the ancient Near East. Josephus presented such biblical figures as Moses and Solomon as models of the Hellenistic sage. In each case, the familiar biblical story is developed to give a new meaning to contemporary readers.

3. *In rabbinic Judaism.* The Hebrew word for biblical interpretation, Midrash, applies to the interpretation of scripture in general; when Midrash produces a rule, it is called Midrash halakah; when it produces a theological or ethical point, it is Midrash Aggadah. Much biblical interpretation takes place through translating scripture in a freehand way, imputing meanings through the way in which verses are rendered into another language. In ancient Judaism, this was called Targum, which means translation, in particular, into Aramaic, the language of Jews in the Land of Israel and Babylonia. A translation into Greek, called the Septuagint, accomplished the same goal. Accepted rules of exegesis governed the reading of scripture. Seven of these rules are attributed to Hillel; thirteen, to Ishmael. In rabbinic Judaism, compilations of interpretations of verses of scripture were made, called Midrashim. The Mishnah's character itself defined a principal task of scriptural exegesis in rabbinic Judaism. Standing by itself, providing few proof-texts to scripture to back up its rules, the Mishnah bore no explanation of why Israel should obey its rules. Brought into relationship to scripture, by contrast, the Mishnah gained access to the source of authority that is by definition operative in Israel, the Jewish people. Accordingly, the work of relating the Mishnah's rules to those of scripture got under way alongside the formation of the Mishnah's rules themselves. It follows that explanations of the sense of the document, including its authority and sources, would draw attention to the written part of the Torah. We may classify the Midrash-compilations in three successive groups: exegetical, propositional, and exegetical-propositional (theological).

Exegetical discourse and the Pentateuch. One important dimension, therefore, of the earliest documents of scriptural exegesis, the Midrash compilations that deal with Leviticus, Numbers, and Deuteronomy, measures the distance between the Mishnah and scripture and aims to close it. The question persistently addressed in analyzing scrip-

ture is, Precisely how does a rule of the Mishnah relate to, or rest upon, a rule of scripture? That question demanded an answer, so that the status of the Mishnah's rules, and, right alongside, of the Mishnah itself, could find a clear definition. Collecting and arranging exegeses of scripture as these related to passages of the Mishnah first reached literary form in Sifra, to Leviticus, and in two books, both called Sifrei, one to Numbers, the other to Deuteronomy. All three compositions accomplished much else. For, even at that early stage, exegeses of passages of scripture in their own context and not only for the sake of Mishnah exegesis attracted attention. But a principal motif in all three books concerned the issue of Mishnah-scripture relationships.

A second, still more fruitful path in formulating Midrash clarifications of scripture also emerged from the labor of Mishnah exegesis. As the work of Mishnah exegesis got under way, in the third century C.E., exegetes of the Mishnah and others undertook a parallel labor. They took an interest in reading scripture in the way in which they were reading the Mishnah itself; that is to say, they began to work through verses of scripture in exactly the same way—word for word, phrase for phrase, line for line—in which, to begin with, the exegetes of the Mishnah pursued the interpretation and explanation of the Mishnah. Precisely the types of exegesis that dictated the way in which sages read the Mishnah now guided their reading of scripture as well. And as people began to collect and organize comments in accord with the order of sentences and paragraphs of the Mishnah, they found the stimulation to collect and organize comments on clauses and verses of scripture. This kind of verse-by-verse exegetical work got under way in the Sifra and the two Sifreis, but reached fulfillment in Genesis Rabbah, which, as its name tells us, presents a line-for-line reading of the book of Genesis. Characteristic of the narrowly exegetical phase of Midrash compilation is the absence of a single, governing proposition, running through the details. It is not possible, for example, to state the main point, expressed through countless cases, in Sifra or Sifrei to Deuteronomy.

From exegesis to proposition. A further group of Midrash compilations altogether transcends the limits of formal exegesis. Beyond the two formal modes of exegesis—search for the sources of the Mishnah in scripture, and line-by-line reading of scripture, as of the Mishnah—lies yet a third, an approach we may call "writing with scripture," that is, using verses of scripture in a context established by a propositional program independent of scripture itself. To understand it, we have to know how the first of the two Talmuds read the Mishnah. The Yerushalmi's authors not only explained phrases or sentences of the Mishnah in the manner of Mishnah and scripture exegetes; they also investigated the principles and large-scale conceptual problems of the document and of the law given only in cases in the Mishnah itself. In other words, they dealt not only with a given topic, a subject and its rule and the cases that yield the rule, but with an encompassing problem, a principle and its implications for a number of topics and rules.

This far more discursive and philosophical mode of thought produced for Mishnah exegesis sustained essays on principles cutting across specific rules. Predictably, this same intellectual work extended from the Mishnah to scripture. Exegesis of scripture beyond that focused on words, phrases, and sentences produced discursive essays on great principles or problems of theology and morality. Discursive exegesis is represented, to begin with, in Leviticus Rabbah, a document that reached closure, people generally suppose, sometime after Genesis Rabbah, thus about 450, and that marked the shift from verse-by-verse to syllogistic reading of verses of scripture. It was continued in Pesikta deRab Kahana, organized around themes pertinent to various holy days through the liturgical year, and Pesikta Rabbati, a derivative and imitative work.

Typical of discursive exegesis of scripture, Leviticus Rabbah presents not phrase-by-phrase systematic exegeses of verses in the Book of Leviticus, but a set of thirty-seven topical essays. These essays, syllogistic in purpose, take the form of citations and comments on verses of scripture, to be sure. But the compositions range widely over the far reaches of the Hebrew scriptures, while focusing narrowly upon a given theme. They moreover make quite distinctive points about that theme. Their essays constitute compositions, not merely composites. Whether devoted to God's favor to the poor and humble or to the dangers of drunkenness, the essays, exegetical in form, discursive in character, correspond to the equivalent, legal essays, amply represented in the Yerushalmi. The framers of Pesikta deRab Kahana carried forward a still more abstract and discursive mode of discourse, one in which verses of scripture play a subordinate role to the framing of an implicit syllogism, which predominates throughout, both formally and in argument.

Saying one thing through many things. "Writing with scripture" reached its climax in the theological Midrash compilations formed at the end of the development of rabbinic literature. A fusion of the two approaches to Midrash exegesis, the verse-by-verse amplification of successive chapters of scripture and the syllogistic presentation of propositions, arguments, and proofs deriving from the facts of scripture, was accomplished in the third body of Midrash compilations: Ruth Rabbah, Esther Rabbah I, Lamentations Rabbah, and Song of Songs Rabbah. Here we find the verse-by-verse reading of scriptural books. But at the same time, a highly propositional program governs the exegesis, with each of the compilations intended to prove a single, fundamental theological point through the accumulation of detailed comments.

Halakhah and Aggadah, Mishnah and Midrash in a single definitive document. The Talmud of Babylonia, or Babli, which was the final document of rabbinic literature, also formed the climax and conclusion of the entire canon and defined this Judaism from its time to the present. The Talmud of Babylonia forms the conclusion and the summary of rabbinic literature, the most important document of the entire collection. One of its principal traits is the fusion of Mishnah and scriptural exegesis in a single compilation. The authors of the units of discourse collected in the Talmud of Babylonia, or Babli, drew together the two, up-to-then distinct, modes of organizing thought, either around the Mishnah or around scripture. They treated both Torahs, oral and written, as equally available in the work of organizing large-scale exercises of sustained inquiry. Thus we find in the Babli a systematic treatment of some tractates of the Mishnah. And within the same aggregates of discourse, we also find (in somewhat smaller proportion to be sure, roughly 40% to 60% in a sample made of three tractates) a second principle of organizing and redaction. That principle dictates that ideas be laid out in line with verses of scripture, themselves dealt with in cogent sequence, one by one, just as the Mishnah's sentences and paragraphs come under analysis, in cogent order and one by one.

4. *In translation literature.* During the period immediately following its formation, the Hebrew Bible was little more than an idiosyncratic religious document of an internationally powerless region. As long as the Hebrew Bible existed only in Hebrew, few people outside of Palestine could read it. But beginning in the third century B.C.E., the Hebrew Bible was translated first into Greek and later into Aramaic. The Greek version (the Septuagint) made the Bible available to people throughout the eastern Mediterranean region, while the Aramaic versions (the targums) rendered it accessible to people throughout the Syrian and Mesopotamian worlds. Suddenly the Hebrew Bible could be read in the local languages of people from Athens to Babylon. Of course, it was Jews in these regions who formed the primary audience for these translations, but Christians also used them, especially the Septuagint.

The texts of the Septuagint and the targums differ from the Hebrew Bible. As all scholars of translation know, translation involves interpretation. Although the amount of interpretation contained in these translations varies from passage to passage and from book to book, any interpretation alters the text's meaning. Since all biblical translations present passages that differ from the original, they ultimately constitute a different text. While the notion that translation involves interpretation constitutes a commonplace, a fuller understanding of its implications for the study of biblical interpretation requires us to evaluate different types of interpretation within the translations and to examine the nature, interrelation, and impact of translation and interpretation. In basic terms, translation is the act of recreating a text composed in one language (the source language) in another language (the target language). Scholars usually classify translations as literal or paraphrastic—a distinction that goes back to the time of Cicero and Horace, when translations were designated as either *verbum e verbo* (word for word) or *sensus de sensu* (sense for sense). Both types of translation aim to render a text's meaning in another language, literal translation, by reproducing the meaning of each word, paraphrastic translation, by rendering the meaning of each phrase or sentence. Both processes necessarily introduce some interpretation into the translated text.

Considered in more general terms, translation transforms a text composed in one culture (the source culture) into another culture (the target culture). Because of the language difference, a text's source culture is rarely identical to the target culture. Even when the two cultures are similar, that similarity often masks important differences, since a history of language difference also entails a history of separate cultural development. To bridge this difference, translators often alter the text in ways that make the translation understandable to the target culture, but that change the original meaning. Translators usually accomplish this alteration either by rewriting the text so that the translation no longer matches the original or by adding material to or subtracting material from the translation. These differences—interpretations—have often been designated "paraphrase." But this designation is incorrect, for the differences change meaning rather than attempt to reproduce it. For example, although Targum Neofiti has often been termed paraphrase, it actually combines a highly literal translation—not just word-for-word but often morpheme-for-morpheme—with large amounts of additional material. Even as the targum's writer translates literally, he or she brings in additions that recast the targum—the translation—in the light of the religious world of its translators. This difference between the original text and the translation constitutes interpretation.

Because they stem from the target culture's view of the Hebrew Bible, interpretations in biblical translation neither appear randomly nor incorporate random material. The study of interpretive material in translations thus leads to the scholarly understanding of the religious and mythic beliefs of the target culture as well as the translation process. Two central questions help focus that analysis. First, where does the translator place interpretations in the translation? Second, what inspires the interpretation placed by the translator into the translation? Both questions direct us to specific differences between the source text and the target language and culture. Both enable modern scholars to understand the translation's purpose and the makeup of the culture and religion for which the translation was produced.

The first question—where do interpretations occur in a translation?—guides scholars to locations in which the source text, language, or culture differs from the target language or culture. In some places, textual and linguistic features of the source text force interpretation into the translation because the features do not translate into the target language. For example, some words in the source language have multiple meanings. If the target language represents those meanings by different words, the translator must choose among them or provide an interpretation that includes them all. In addition, some words, phrases, or other semantic units lack any equivalent in the target language, and the translator must provide an interpretation.

Other language differences between the source text and the target language encourage, but do not force, a translator to interpret. The most obvious of these constitute puns, analogies, metaphors, and idioms. These linguistic features depend on a difference between the surface meaning (which usually can be translated) and a deeper meaning. The deeper meaning often defies easy translation, and the translator must choose to ignore it or to find a semantic or rhetorical analog in the target language. Poetry likewise provides strong encouragement for interpretation, since its dual play of semantics and form defies easy rendering into another language. In the targums, for example, the poetic sections frequently contain large amounts of interpretation. Textual problems also encourage interpretation in translation. The appearance in the source text of inappropriate words, scribal or copyist errors, missing words, or unfinished sentences often brings on interpretation. In addition, geographical terms often receive interpretation, particularly ones that no longer have any identification in the translator's world. For example, Targum Neofiti consistently translates the place name Kadesh-barnea as Reqem de-Gaya.

Cultural differences between the worlds of the source text and the target culture also encourage the translator to incorporate interpretation into translation. Sometimes ordinary words appearing in the source text have taken on important symbolic or theological meaning in the target religion and culture. For example, the word "Torah" in the Hebrew Bible simply refers to a law or a set of laws. By contrast, in rabbinic Judaism, Torah became a central sacred category, identifying scripture and its authoritative interpretation as well as the holy way of life based on it. This new meaning of Torah encouraged the targums' rabbinic translators to emphasize the new meaning when the word appeared in the text. Another occasion for interpretation derives from theological dissonance between the source text and the target religion. A religion rarely wishes its central beliefs refuted by its own sacred texts, so translators modify the text to fit their understanding of it. For instance, in the biblical story of Balaam (Num. 22–24), Balaam appears as a neutral character. Since rabbinic Judaism views Balaam as evil, the (rabbinic) translator of Targum Pseudo-Jonathan recasts the story to portray Balaam as utterly wicked. Another impetus to interpretation lies in the behavior of important ancestors recorded in the biblical narrative. Sometimes the behavior appears inconsistent with a translator's standards of religious or moral behavior. This behavior is often changed or justified by the translator. When Rachel steals her father's idols (Gen. 31:19), for instance, Targum Pseudo-Jonathan makes its clear that she does this to prevent her father from worshiping them, not so that she can worship them.

Not all of the interpretations placed into a translation stem from the difference between the source text and the target culture. Sometimes translators bring their own agenda to their work, one that often has little to do with the accurate translation of the original text. For instance, many of the targum translators believed that God should not be represented in anthropomorphic terms, and they used a number of strategies to avoid the impression that God could talk, hear, stretch out an arm, or perform other human acts.

The issue of the translator's agenda brings us to our second question in the analysis of interpretation in translation, namely, what inspires the content of interpretations inserted into a translation? The answer is that the contents derive from the theological, religious, and cultural beliefs of the target culture. Indeed, the interpretations stem directly from the target culture—Judaism—and cannot be predicted on the basis of the biblical text alone. The interpretations thus provide a window into the religious world of of the Jewish translator behind each translation.

The penetrating nature of these two questions can be demonstrated in a single example. The Hebrew text of Genesis 4:7 provides a clear rationale for interpretation. In English, the passage, where God speaks to Cain after rejecting his sacrifice, reads, "If you do well, will you not be accepted? And if you do not do well, sin is lurking at the door; its desire is for you, but you must master it" (NRSV). Although the English translators have glossed over some of the problems in this verse, scholars have long recognized the original Hebrew of this verse as difficult to understand, let alone translate. It contains several noun/pronoun referent problems, grammatical inconsistencies, and unusual syntax. It is not surprising that these difficulties have brought about interpretation in the targums.

Targum Neofiti renders Genesis 4:7 by adding several theological concepts foreign to the verse and even to the Book of Genesis. The targum reads, "Surely, if you make your work in this world to be good, you will be remitted and pardoned in the world to come; but if you do not make your work in this world to be good, your sin will be kept for the day of great judgment; and at the door of your heart your sin crouches. Into your hand, however, I have given the control over the evil inclination and you shall rule it, whether to remain just or to sin." Neofiti explains the passage by introducing several theological concepts important in rabbinic Judaism. These include the distinction between this world and world to come and the idea that actions in this world lead to reward in the next. The notion of the Great Judgment Day also appears, as well as the rabbinic concept of the evil inclination. None of these notions are native to the Hebrew text, but they stem from the religious world of the translator. In this way, interpretations that originate in the target culture become part of the translated sacred text.

The ramifications of interpretation as translation are far-reaching. The translation of a sacred text is a powerful act; once accepted, the translation replaces the original document. For religious believers who do not understand the language of the sacred text, the translation and its message takes on the status of the original. The interpretations themselves become sacred and reinforce the target culture's own beliefs. A clear example of this phenomenon is the almost exclusive use of the English-language Bible by American Christians and Jews. The translation provides the basis for communicating the divine revelation and its meaning. Indeed, the communication of meaning constitutes the translation's greatest impact. Since translations interpret their original text as well as provide faithful renderings, the interpretations acquire the same status as the rest of the translation: they become holy. Since those who use the translation cannot differentiate between faithful rendition and interpretation, the interpretation's meaning becomes the meaning of the sacred scripture.

The Septuagint and the targums functioned in the same way. For Jews who could not understand Hebrew, these translations replaced the original sacred text; the translation's meaning became the Bible's meaning. Some Jewish authorities recognized that the interpreted translation was being substituted for the holy original and took steps to prevent it. The steps they took were ultimately unsuccessful. In contrast to the interpretive translation of the Septuagint, Aquila produced an extremely literal Greek translation. Unfortunately, its literalness distorted the Greek so much that it could be understood only by people who knew the original Hebrew text. The substitution was also recognized by rabbinic authorities, who took two different steps to combat it. Some rabbis attempted to ban translation. They accomplished this by designating Jews who performed different types of translation as sinners. According to Tosefta Megilla 3:41, Rabbi Judah held, "He who translates a verse just as it is presented in scripture—lo, such a one is a deceiver, but the one who adds to what is written, lo, this person is a blasphemer." The widespread use of translations shows that this attempt to stifle translation never succeeded. Other rabbis attempted to structure scripture reading in the synagogue service so that the sanctity and importance

of the original Hebrew text was paramount and the translation clearly appeared in a lesser status. But although the rabbis may have been successful in preventing the translation from being seen as sacred, they could not prevent the translation's meaning from replacing that of the Hebrew text. As long as the average Jew could not distinguish between straight translation and interpretation, the translation served as the vehicle for the interpreted meaning of the divine revelation.

In sum, the ultimate result of interpretation in the translation of sacred scriptures is that the interpretation becomes part of the sacred text. For those who can understand only the targum, the interpretation no longer stands apart from the sacred text as a separate entity—a product of the text—but now functions as the original text. As part of the sacred text, it will now become the basis for future interpretation.

scripture a written phrase, document, or set of documents that is regarded by a religious community as possessing doctrinal significance or authority, or as being "inspired." In a Jewish context, "scripture" normally refers to the Hebrew Bible or some part of it; early Christians extended the phrase to refer to certain authoritative Christian writings.

It is not surprising that the term "scripture," with the connotations indicated above, does not occur explicitly in pre-exilic or exilic Jewish biblical writings, since at this stage there was evidently not yet a "scriptural self-consciousness." In fact, one of the few biblical references of potential significance for the idea of "scripture" occurs in the Septuagint of Ezra 6:18, which states that the returned exiles, in setting up the Second Temple, proceeded "as it is written in the scripture of the book of Moses." Here, as often elsewhere, it is difficult to determine whether the Greek (or Hebrew) words used for "scripture" denote an "authoritative" or "holy" piece of writing, or simply a piece of writing.

With the passage of time in the Second Temple period, certain Jewish writings—portions of what today is known as the Hebrew Bible—were accorded a special, authoritative religious status. It is usually thought that this status was given first to the Torah, then to the "prophets," and finally to certain other "writings." Especially the Torah and the prophets came to be viewed by many Jews of the Second Temple period as not only authoritative but also as inspired repositories of perfect truth that derived directly from God. This understanding of "scripture" is generally prevalent in late Second Temple and subsequent Judaism.

An early noncanonical Jewish usage of the term appears in 1 Enoch 104, where Enoch, giving advice and admonition to his children, predicts that sinners will "invent fictitious stories and write out my scriptures on the basis of their own words" (104:10), whereas "to the righteous and wise shall be given the scriptures of joy" (104:12). The Letter of Aristeas (mid-second century B.C.E.) refers to ordinances that "have been made in scripture" (168) and introduces a biblical citation with the phrase "so we are exhorted through scripture" (155).

It is in Jewish and Christian writings of the first century C.E. and later that the term "scripture" (Gr.: *graphe*) first appears on a consistent basis with its traditional meaning. Both Philo and Josephus regularly use the Greek term to indicate either an individual biblical passage or work, or the Jewish sacred literature as a whole. 4 Maccabees 18:14 prefaces a quotation of Isaiah with the phrase "he reminded you of the scripture of Isaiah. . . . ." The Testament of Zebulon uses "it is written in the scripture of the law of Moses" (3:4) to introduce a reference to Deuteronomy and prefaces an eschatological prediction with the words "In the scripture of the fathers I came to know . . ." (9:5). Likewise, rabbinic literature regularly uses "scripture" or "the holy scriptures" to refer to parts or the whole of the Hebrew Bible.

Earliest Christianity was a form of Second Temple Judaism, and many early Christian thinkers evidence the widespread contemporary Jewish view of the Torah, prophets, and other writings as divinely inspired repositories of truth. This attitude is implied, for example, in some of the sayings attributed to Jesus. In post-Resurrection Christian tradition, the main focus of such a view was to show that the person and actions of Jesus, his messiahship, and various other points of Christian doctrine were already present in "scripture," and thus had been divinely preordained. On the other hand, as "Christianity" grew increasingly distinct from "Judaism," there was also a tendency for Christians to deemphasize the salvific significance of Jewish "scripture." Such an attitude is also suggested in various sayings attributed to Jesus, especially Matthew 5:21–48 and its Lukan parallels.

Virtually every attested phase of early Christian literature bears witness to the classical Jewish notion of "scripture" as a repository of divine truth. In standard rabbinic fashion, Paul appeals to "scripture" to prove many of his theological points. Favorite Pauline expressions for introducing scriptural-proof texts are "the scripture says" (e.g., Rom.

9:17, 11:2) and "what does the scripture say?" (Rom 4:3; Gal. 4:30). In Galatians 3, Paul personifies "scripture": "And the scripture, foreseeing that God would justify the Gentiles by faith, preached the gospel beforehand to Abraham" (3:8). In keeping with normative early Christian Christology, Paul interprets Jesus' person and actions as being "in accordance with the scriptures" (1 Cor. 15:3–4).

The idea of "scripture," and its authority and fulfillment, are especially prominent in the canonical New Testament Gospels, which together use the term more than twenty-five times. One important motif is Jesus' charge that his Jewish opponents, who claim to base their belief in scripture, have missed its which essential points, which support his own attitudes (e.g., Mark 12:24 and parallels; John 5:39). Jesus is depicted as claiming that his own actions and fate conform to and "fulfill" scriptural models. In Mark 14:49 and parallels, for example, Jesus surrenders to the Jewish mob with the words "but let the scriptures be fulfilled," presumably referring to his impending passion. The narrator of the Gospel of John also frequently points out that one or another of the events that he is describing occurred "that the scripture might be fulfilled" (e.g., 7:38, 13:18).

The Book of Acts confirms the idea that the theme of Jesus' fulfillment of scripture was one of the central messages of early Christianity (e.g., 8:35, 17:2) and further extends the theme of scriptural fulfillment to the activities of the early church (1:16).

Several noteworthy points appear in the later letters of the New Testament and in other, noncanonical, early Christian literature. These sources show that, at a relatively early stage, the term "scripture" began to be applied not only to the teachings of Jesus but also to the writings of Paul. In 2 Clement 2:4, a saying of Jesus is labeled "scripture." 2 Peter 3:16 states that "there are some things in [Paul's writings] hard to understand, which the ignorant and unstable twist to their own destruction, as they do the other scriptures." 1 Timothy 4:13 recommends the "public reading of scripture" in Christian meetings; it is unclear whether this refers to "Jewish" or specifically "Christian" scripture.

scripture reading in the synagogue The Hebrew Bible was regularly read in synagogues as early as the first century C.E., but it was not until the end of the second century that we learn any details about how that reading was practiced. The Mishnah rules that scripture should be read on Monday, Thursday, and the Sabbath. The emphasis is on readings from the Torah, but a few passages from the Prophets (*haftarah*) may also be read. The readings should be read by four to seven different people, with each saying a blessing afterward. Each person should read at least three verses, and each passage should be translated into Aramaic by a second person. Additional readings were added on festivals (e.g., Sukkot, Passover, and the Day of Atonement). By the seventh century C.E. or so, the Torah had been divided into fixed readings; in Palestine, the readings covered the Torah in three years (Triennial Cycle), while in Babylonia, they took only one year (Annual Cycle). There is also evidence that readings from the Writings were interspersed with those from the Prophets.

scroll   *see* BOOKS AND SCROLLS

Scroll of Esther   the biblical Book of Esther, read in the synagogue at Purim

Scythopolis   *see* BETH SHEAN

sea   (Heb.: *yam*) a powerful symbol of danger and chaos in ancient Near Eastern thought. Reflecting the experience of travel on the stormy Mediterranean, Canaanite religion personified the sea as the god Yam, who, along with Mot (death), was the opponent of Baal. Such a mythic antagonism lies behind Isaiah 51:9–10, where YHWH's opponent, the sea dragon Raha<u>b</u>, is defeated in the crossing of the sea during the Exodus. Recalling the Canaanite motifs, Daniel 7 depicts the sea as the source of the four great beasts which represent the empires that oppose Israel and are overcome before the appearance of "one like a son of man," the heavenly patron of Israel, who, like Baal, rides to his enthronement on a cloud chariot. Such texts as Psalm 107:23–32, 1 Enoch 101, and Mark 4:35–41 focus on the fearful, destructive power of the sea and on God's ability either to tame it or to use it to punish sinners. According to Revelation 21:1, when heaven and earth are created anew, the sea will no longer exist, because the forces of chaos and death have been finally and completely tamed.

seah   (Heb., dry measure) measure of volume of dry produce, yielding 2 hin, 3.5 omer, 6 kab, 12 log

seal   a device that identified and authenticated ownership, authorship, or manufacturer. The term could refer either to an impression or to the instrument that made it. The content of documents was authenticated by seals that indicated authorship and secured the document from tampering. In Isaiah 8:16–21, sealing a scroll until a later time symbolizes the belief that its contents will remain unfulfilled until that time. A similar notion occurs in apocalyptic literature in Daniel 12:4 and in Revelation 22:10, where the seer is forbidden to seal the

prophecy because the time is near. The progressive breaking of the seven seals in Revelation 5–9 dramatizes the unfolding of the prophecies in the book of human deeds. The idea of a seal can also be used figuratively to refer to something that confirms or attests authenticity (1 Cor. 9:2; Rev. 9:4). In this sense, it is employed of circumcision (Rom. 4:11) and of Christian baptism (2 Clem. 8:6). In the Paraleipomena of Jeremiah 6:25, "the sign of the great seal" refers either to circumcision or Christian baptism. *See also* SEALS AND BULLAE.

seals and bullae   The seal is an instrument for making an impression, in lieu of a signature, on an ancient document or on a wet pottery vessel before it is fired, or on other media; the impression itself (bulla; pl., bullae) was usually made on a ball of wet clay on the document. Thus if the document is destroyed in a conflagration, the impression, or bulla, will survive. Seals were signs of personal ownership in the ancient Near East and were used long before the biblical period. A seal is usually carved from stone or even semiprecious stone. It depicts various deities, people, animals, plants, and even geometric designs. From the Iron Age particularly, the name of the owner was inscribed in Hebrew retrograde, so that it could be read properly on the impression or bulla. Seals with Hebrew names are well known. The script in the Persian period especially begins to be the square Aramaic script, replacing the more ancient Phoenician one. The seals of the Persian period are often cone shaped with an octagonal base and with a hole at the top to allow hanging from a cord. Human figures, usually understood to be priests, decorate these seals. The most famous of these seals bear place names: Yahud (Judea), Ha Ir (the city, that is, Jerusalem), and Yerushalayim or Jerusalem. It is thought that these seals were not for personal ownership but for identification of jars for tax purposes and pertaining to the First Temple.

From the Hellenistic period, seals begin to take on a characteristic Hellenistic or Roman form. Hellenistic seals in the shape of scarabs are well known. Two Hellenistic bullae from Jerusalem bear Hebrew inscriptions: "Yehonathan the king" and "Yonathan High Priest Jerusalem M." These are interpreted to refer to Alexander Jannaeus, the Jewish king who called himself by both these titles on his coins. In this period seals appear on imported wine amphora and attest to the contents. In the Roman period seals are most often found on pottery vessels and on documents. On pottery vessels the seals identify the large pottery-producing sites of Italy (Arretium, Puetoli), Egypt (Alexandria), Asia Minor, and Gaul. Seal impressions appear on the handles of jars and identify the Roman consul under whose rule the jar was produced as a standard measure. Roman military kilns also produced bricks, roof tiles, and clay pipes with seal impressions identifying the legion, for example, the "Tenth Legion, the Fretensis" (X Leg Fr and variations). Roman period document seals, on the other hand, have been found in the Judean Desert Caves actually on documents. In these cases, the document was rolled and folded after the witnesses had affixed their signatures, then the document was tied with a palm fiber string. A wet clay ball was formed on the knot and then the clay ball was sealed. The seal attested that the contents of the document were not tampered with. These particular seal impressions, or bullae, show various decorations, such as a bearded man wrestling with a lion, an olive branch, a vine leaf, and a pomegranate. A group of seals from the Roman city of Mampsis in the Negeb date between 106 to 140 C.E. and are stamped with the names of other cities: Petra, Characmoba (biblical Kiriat Moab), and Rabbathmoba (Rabbath of Moab). In the center of each seal is a god or goddess (Tyche as Arabia, Tyche as Antioch on the Orontes, or Ares-Mars). Other seals have signs of the zodiac with their Hebrew names in Greek letters.

In the Byzantine period seals with Christian motifs come to dominate, but others are known, including Jewish seals and Gnostic seals. Wooden seals for marking bread and even cheese are known with Jewish symbols. Other such symbols appear on seals mounted as rings and carved in semiprecious stone, such as carnelian.

Sebaeus Armenian historian. He records that in 614 C.E. the Jews joined the Persians invading Palestine and fought the the Christians in Jerusalem. The Persians besieged Jerusalem, destroyed the churches outside the city walls, plundered the city, burned the Church of the Holy Sepulcher, and put the Jews in control.

sebara in talmudic argumentation, a conclusion reached through reasoning; frequently contrasted with that which is known through tradition, as, for example, at B. Baba Batra 77a: "Is this [known] through tradition [*gemara*] or through logical inference [*sebara*]?"

Sebaste the biblical city of Samaria, renamed by Herod the Great in honor of the emperor Augustus (Greek Sebastos, feminine Sebaste). An accidental discovery of papyri in a cave in the Wadi ed-Daliyeh near Samaria proved to be of the fourth century B.C.E., or just before the time of Alexander.

These were invaluable documents of elite citizens of the city who had fled during an uprising. They record marriages, divorces, manumission of slaves, buying and selling of property, loans, and transfer of slaves. The city of Samaria became Hellenized when Alexander the Great settled Greek veterans who took local wives there. Later, Samaria was conquered and destroyed when John Hyrcanus I took the city and began the process of the conversion of its inhabitants to Judaism. The Roman governor Gabinius engaged in construction in the city, according to Josephus (*War* 1.166), about 55 B.C.E. When Herod befriended Augustus, the latter gave it to Herod the Great.

Herod set out to build the city anew as a showplace to rival the other royal cities of Palestine. The city wall and gate were already impressive and had been built in the Hellenistic period. The gate towers, for example, were round and measured 13.8 meters in diameter and stood on square platforms. The platform and staircase of Herod's temple to Augustus has been found. The temple was fully 24 by 33.5 meters and stood on a platform nearly 5 meters high which was about 74 by 95 meters in extent. A small Hellenistic temple to the goddess Korē already stood north of the Augusteum. Herod also built a Hippodrome or stadium in the northeastern part of the lower city. The forum or agora, the major regional market place, stood east of the highest part of the city or the acropolis. Near the forum stood a Herodian basilica, traces of which have been found. Herod may have built the aqueduct, but Severus may have also rebuilt it.

In later centuries, Sebaste continued to be embellished. Under the Roman emperor Septimius Severus it received the title of colony (Colonia Lucia Septimia Sebaste) and all the rights and privileges of a colony. For example, Septimius Severus probably rebuilt the Augusteum after it was destroyed sometime after the rule of Herod the Great. Septimius Severus also added to the city gate and possibly the city walls. Severus honored the city with a great cardo, or colonnaded street, that stretched nearly a kilometer through the city. The cardo measured 12 meters wide with shops and houses on either side, and some of its columns are still erect in the olive groves around the ruins. Severus may have built the theater of the city. The Mishnah mentions the "gardens of Sebaste" in contrast to the "sands of Mahoza" (M. Arakhin 3:2).

Second Temple see TEMPLE, SECOND

second tithe a tenth of the crop, to be taken to Jerusalem and eaten there

seder **1.** order

> **2.** a division of the Mishnah
>
> **3.** the Passover home service; *see also* PASSOVER SEDER

Seder shel Pesaḥ *see* PASSOVER SEDER

Sefer, Waters of location corresponding to Ein Girpah; referred to at T. Sheḇiit 4:11 as demarcating a border area of the Land of Israel

Sefer haRazim (Heb., book of mysteries) an early work of Jewish mysticism, detailing prayers and sacrifices to be offered to pagan and Jewish deities in magical ceremonies, including an invocation of Helios in Greek, transliterated into Hebrew script. Authored by a Jew, the book is written in Mishnaic Hebrew and has a close philological relationship to the language of the magic bowls of the period. On the basis of content and style, the work probably belongs to the Talmudic period, although it possibly contains Graeco-European magical texts from as late as the eighth century. The work includes deliberations on angels and the seven heavens, and about thirty sets of instructions for those seeking to know the future, influence people in power, bring enemies to ruin, be healed, speak with the moon and stars, and fulfill other, similar desires.

The work originally was known from references scattered throughout the Sefer Raziel. It has been reconstructed, apparently in its entirety, by Mordecai Margalioth on the basis of fragments from the Cairo Geniza and Hebrew, Latin, and Arabic manuscripts. The relatively short book now contains about eight hundred lines, divided into seven chapters. While composed in Hebrew, it is replete with transliterated Greek, representing the technical terms of Greek magic. The book includes the names of about seven hundred angels and, following its chapters on the lower six heavens, contains a chapter on the seventh heaven, dealing with God's throne and the throne of great light. Like the magic bowls, this work sheds light on the extent to which the mystical and magical doctrines of the Hellenistic world were familiar to and accepted by the Jews of the Talmudic period.

Sefer Tehillim *see* TEHILLIM

Sefer Torah (Heb., scroll of the Torah) the title of one of the so-called minor tractates of the Talmud. A collection of tannaitic sources in five chapters, which are also found in tractate Soferim, it contains rules for writing, writing materials, and translating the Torah, as well as special precautions for writing and erasing the name of God.

Sefer Yuḥasin *see* YUḤASIN

Sefirah (Heb., counting) a season in the Jewish calendar. It is the same as the Omer, but also called Sefirah, because of the practice of counting the days and the weeks (see Lev. 23:15–16) from the time of the Exodus (Passover) until the reception of Torah at Mount Sinai (Shaḇuot). It thus features a daily liturgical counting ritual in the synagogue. *See also* LAG BAOMER.

sefirat haOmer the counting of the omer in the Temple; *see also* OMER

Seganzagel *see* ZAGNAZGAEL

sela a weight equal to 48 duponia, that is, 1 sacred or 2 common shekels. In the rabbinic literature, the term also is used in general to refer to a coin, without specific interest in its value or weight.

Seleucus I Nicator (c. 358–281 B.C.E.) one of Alexander the Great's generals. After Alexander's death, he obtained the satrapy of Babylonia in 321, but he was driven out by Antigonus in 316 and fled to Egypt. In 312 he regained Babylon as well as Media and Susiana, and from this date the Seleucid era begins (Oct. 312 in Macedonian calendar, April 311 in Babylonian). The Seleucid dynasty was to last till 64 B.C.E. After the Battle of Ipsus in 301, he received Syria, claimed Coele Syria, and finally won Asia Minor in 281. He was assassinated as he attempted to claim Macedonia. Seleucus founded several great cities including Antioch, where he settled many Jews, probably retired soldiers.

self-righteousness a religious disposition that focuses on the rightness of one's relationship to God, especially as this is established through proper adherence to God's will. The term is particularly used in Christian circles with reference to the attitude attributed to the Pharisees in such texts as Luke 18:9–14, "They trusted in themselves that they were righteous and despised others." Self-designations like "the chosen," "the pious" (ḥasidim), and "the righteous" sometimes do intend a comparison with others who do not meet these qualifications. However, self-righteousness is the potential shadow side of *any* religion that prizes righteous conduct, and it can also appear in systems that contrast orthodoxy (one's claim to have right doctrine) with heterodoxy (labeling as spurious the doctrine of those with whom one does not agree). The stereotype that the Pharisees were generically self-righteous is difficult to sustain or falsify since most of our evidence about first-century Pharisees comes from their opponents, the writers of the New Testament. In any case, Christian theologians, sometimes guided by an anti-Jewish agenda, have generally ignored contemporary Jewish texts that criticize other Jews for playing the hypocrite (Ps. Sol. 4) or "righteously" calling down God's wrath on sinners (Test. Abr.). *See also* ANTI-JUDAISM, CHRISTIAN; HYPOCRITE.

Selihot penitential prayers, recited before New Year

Semahot a minor rabbinic tractate on death and mourning, published with the Babylonian Talmud; euphemistically titled Joys, though also known as Ebel or Ebel Rabbati, that is, Mourning. Absent from the Talmud's Munich manuscript, Semahot appeared in the first printing of the Babylonian Talmud (Venice, 1523). The earliest references to it are by Franco-German scholars of the eleventh century C.E. Contrary to medieval commentators, it is not clear whether references at B. Moed Katan 24a and 26b to a tractate on mourning attest Semahot in particular.

Scholars place the final redaction of Semahot in the mid-eighth century C.E. Since it is in Mishnaic Hebrew and the latest rabbis it cites are third-century-C.E. contemporaries of Judah the Patriarch, it may contain earlier material. Its fourteen chapters discuss the legal status of a dying man, treatment of corpses of suicides or those who were executed, burial practices, and the laws that apply to mourners in the first seven and thirty days after burial. Chapter 8 contains a detailed martyrology.

semikhah *see* HANDS, LAYING ON OF

Sempronius Senecio *see* SENECIO, LUCIUS SEMPRONIUS

senatus consultum technical term for a decree of the Roman Senate. It was not unusual for a foreign state or kingdom to make a special request to the Senate, and a *senatus consultum* might be issued in response. One of the best known on behalf of the Jews is in 1 Maccabees 8:22–32.

Seneca the Younger (d. 65 C.E.) Roman orator and philosopher. He is known as being the tutor and adviser to Nero for the first part of the latter's reign, but was eventually forced to commit suicide by the emperor. Only a handful of references to Jews are found in his many writings. These show a negative attitude toward Judaism, especially the Sabbath, though he allows that at least the Jews know the origin of their rites. He also mentions the practice of lighting lamps on the Sabbath. His views probably represent a general animosity toward foreign religions, not Judaism in particular.

Senecio, Lucius Sempronius procurator of Judea, early second century C.E. Virtually nothing is known about him. The cursus-inscription that mentions his procuratorship identifies his post as "Judaea," which implies that he was in office before Hadrian renamed the province in 135.

Senoftha location corresponding to Sephina; the most northern location referred to at T. Shebiit 4:11 as demarcating a border area of the Land of Israel

Sepphorean log *see* LOG

Sepphoris Jewish city in Upper Galilee, first referred to during the reign of Alexander Yannai (Josephus, *Ant.* 8.12, 5). Later the city was controlled by Herod the Great. A rebellion after his death led to the city's destruction by Varus, who sold Sepphoris's inhabitants into slavery (ibid., 17.10, 9). Rebuilt by Herod Antipas, who made Sepphoris the capital of Galilee (ibid., 18.2, 1), it remained a Roman city with a mixed population until after the Bar Kokhba Revolt. Then the large number of Jewish residents revived the Jewish city council. Judah the Patriarch made Sepphoris the seat of the patriarchate and Sanhedrin, a status it retained through the period of his grandson, Judah II. Little is known of the subsequent history of the city.

Sepphoris, archaeology of the survey and excavation of the ancient city of Sepphoris (Heb: Tsippori; Gk: Diocaesarea) in Lower Galilee. Excavations first took place at Sepphoris in 1931 by the University of Michigan. Local workers cut a long trench east of the citadel or fortress on top of the hill and a second northwest of the citadel. The first trench disclosed a large theater seating four thousand that the excavators thought was built by Herod Antipas. A very large cistern was discovered south of the citadel and a large wall, perhaps a defense wall, also south of the citadel and around the acropolis of the city. The excavators identified a Roman and Byzantine structure in his second trench as a church, though others proposed later it was to be understood as a Roman villa. Various rescue operations and accidental discoveries of Greek inscriptions at Sepphoris were published from this time forward, but the next systematic work was initiated from 1975–1985 by Haifa University, on whose behalf the cisterns of Sepphoris were surveyed and the aqueduct was traced. Tel Aviv University cleared the reservoir about one Roman mile east of Sepphoris in 1993 and 1994. These researches added to and greatly clarified the extent of the aqueduct, which extended several miles eastward to er-Reina and Mashhad. The aqueduct entered the reservoir for storage, then conducted water to the city in a lead pipe and tunnel. A large pool is part of the water system near the eastern extent of the city.

In 1983, new excavations were initiated at Sepphoris by the University of South Florida. The foundations of the citadel or fortress were excavated and shown to have been built in mid-fourth century C.E. The erection of the first phase of the citadel coincided with destruction of all structures in the vicinity of the citadel and the filling in of the theater, presumably as a result of Gallus's Revolt in mid-century, followed by the earthquake of 363 C.E. The University of South Florida excavations at Sepphoris also reexcavated the church and showed that it was a villa with *mikvaot,* or Jewish ritual baths, beneath the floors, therefore built and lived in by Jewish families. Up to ten underground chambers beneath the villa were used for storage, work spaces, and ritual baths. A building south of the villa was excavated and was found to contain a series of pools in use from the late first to the middle of the fourth century C.E. It may have been a common ritual bath for the community. Finally, a large Roman building on the east side of the site was excavated. It measured about 40 by 60 meters in extent and contains about 800 square meters of mosaics. The central two carpets are a series of medallions containing fish and birds in fine work with brilliant colors. The second carpet contains geometric designs. The side rooms on the south contained mosaics predominantly in colored geometric designs, but also at least one featured a duck in green tessersae (the stones of the mosaic). The west end of the building went out of use as a beautiful basilica type structure in mid-fourth century C.E. At the east end, on the cardo or colonnaded street, a bath and a glass industrial area were in use from the fifth through the early seventh century C.E. A cache of gold jewelry was found in the glass industrial area in a clear sixth century C.E. context.

Beginning in 1985 a joint project of the Hebrew University and Duke University excavated the Jewish Quarter west of the citadel, finding homes and shops with ritual baths beneath the floors. A spacious villa with a beautiful mosaic featuring Dionysius was found south of the theater. South of the citadel this team also found a huge sixth-century Byzantine building, used perhaps for grain storage. Duke University continued in the Jewish Quarter, while Hebrew University also excavated on the east and northeast side of the hill of Sepphoris, disclosing houses and shops predominantly of the Byzantine period and a fine synagogue mosaic of the Byzantine period showing a zodiac, menorahs, and with dedicatory inscriptions in Aramaic, Hebrew, and Greek. Excavation shows that Sepphoris was a vigorous city from the Roman through the Byzantine periods, only declining in the Arab periods to a large village.

Septuagint oldest Greek translation of the Jewish scriptures, originally produced for the Jews of Egypt in the pre-Christian era; its title is abbreviated as LXX. It contains three types of material: (1) translations of the books in the Hebrew canon of scripture; (2) translations of Hebrew or Aramaic books outside this canon, and sometimes no longer extant in the original language, including Judith, 1 Maccabees, 1 Esdras, Ben Sira (Sirach, or Ecclesiasticus), Tobit, Psalms of Solomon, and Psalm 151; and (3) other noncanonical material, not found in Hebrew or Aramaic, including the Wisdom of Solomon, 2–4 Maccabees, and additions to the books of Esther, Daniel, and Jeremiah.

The term Septuagint is from the Latin for "seventy" and arose from an account of the origin of the Greek translation of the Torah, given in the so-called Letter of Aristeas. This work purports to tell how the king of Egypt, Ptolemy II Philadelphus (r. 285–247 B.C.E.), wished to acquire the law books of the Jews for his library. Seventy-two elders, six from each tribe of Israel, were sent by the high priest in Jerusalem to work on the translation and finished it in seventy-two days. It was approved by the Egyptian king and by the local Jewish population, and a curse was pronounced on anyone who tried to alter the text in any way. This story was embellished over the years, probably in order to defend the Septuagint against detractors or rival versions. In the mid-first century C.E., Philo stressed its divine inspiration, and some church fathers knew a miraculous version: although the seventy-two translators were divided up into thirty-six separate pairs, each pair came up with an identical translation of the entire Old Testament. Such a version of the story was necessary to prove that the Septuagint was as inspired as the Hebrew Bible and more authoritative than later Jewish Greek revisions.

In fact, the Septuagint took form over many years, section by section, in various places and through different translators. It is more than likely that the Torah was the first part to be translated, as being of fundamental importance to Judaism, and that the translation was carried out in Egypt, where there was a very large Jewish community, principally in Alexandria. These Jews had little or no knowledge of Hebrew and required a version in Greek for synagogue and study purposes. Probably Isaiah was also translated there, since it, too, has many linguistic parallels with Egyptian Greek papyri. The rest of the Latter Prophets probably followed, then parts of the Former Prophets, and lastly the Writings. Sirach, the translation of the

Book of Ben Sira, can be dated by his preface to the years after 132 B.C.E. Since this preface also mentions existing translations of "the Law, the Prophets and the rest of the Writings," we can be fairly sure that most of the Septuagint was in existence by this date.

Somewhat ironically, it was the Church where the Septuagint had the most profound influence; Greek-speaking Christians adopted it as holy scripture at a very early date. In the Greek New Testament, most citations of the Jewish Scriptures are in the form found in the Septuagint, and though the same is true for the first-century Jewish Greek writers Philo Judaeus and Flavius Josephus, the Septuagint fell out of favor among Jews as its importance grew among Christians. It was translated into Latin for Christians further west, though this Old Latin version was eventually superseded by Jerome's Vulgate, which was a translation of the Hebrew text current in his day; Jerome himself challenged the miraculous details in the story of the origins of the Septuagint, preferring the "Hebrew truth." The Septuagint text was also the main influence on many other ancient translations, such as the Coptic, Ethiopic, Gothic, Slavonic, Georgian, Armenian, and Arabic versions.

Even before the Church took it over, there was some Jewish dissatisfaction with the Septuagint as a version, particularly if we understand the Letter of Aristeas as a defense of its authority, cursing those who tampered with it. In addition, there had developed in Palestine a Hebrew text of scripture that differed from the one underlying the Septuagint. Fragments of a Greek scroll of the Minor Prophets, discovered at Qumran in 1952 and 1961, reflect a mid-first-century C.E. revision toward the Palestinian Hebrew text then current. This revision is very closely related to the one called Theodotion, one of the three named Jewish revisions of the Septuagint, the others being Aquila and Symmachus.

Christians, too, became aware of the discrepancies between the Septuagint and the Hebrew Bible. Although there was a strong tendency to explain these differences by accusing the Jews of having altered the Hebrew text, some scholars accepted that it might be the Septuagint that needed revision, since the Greek manuscripts themselves often differed from one another to some degree. In the mid-third century C.E., Origen in particular saw that the differences between the two versions, which were often substantial, greatly hindered Christians in their disputations with Jews. These two factors, the desire for a standard text of the Septuagint and the need to know exactly where and why the Greek and Hebrew diverged, led to Origen's monumental work, the Hexapla. The Hexapla not only enabled comparison of the Septuagint with the Hebrew and with the versions of Theodotion, Aquila, and Symmachus, but introduced an edited Septuagint text, with marks showing additions and omissions. Though the Septuagint column of the Hexapla suffered in transmission, as copyists tended to leave out some or all of the markings, manuscripts stemming from it display some revision toward the Hebrew text. Other groups of manuscripts have also undergone revision, those of the Lucianic or Antiochene recension, for example, showing some stylistic revision of the Greek. Such revisions make reconstruction a frustrating task for modern scholars who would like to get as close as possible to the original Septuagint, both for its own sake and also to give a clearer indication of the Hebrew text used by the Greek translators.

seraphim   (from Heb.: *saraf,* to burn) six-winged attendants at God's throne, probably with fiery, serpentine bodies (Isa. 6:1–7, cf. Num. 21:6; Isa. 14:29). 1 Enoch 61:10 and 71:7 list them with the cherubim and ofanim. *See also* ANGEL; CHERUBIM; OFANIM.

Serekh haYaḥad   *see* COMMUNITY RULE

Seron   Seleucid general; referred to as "commander of the Syrian army" in 1 Maccabees 3:13. He led an army against the forces of Judas Maccabeus in 166–165 B.C.E. In the narrow pass at Beth Horon, Judas's forces routed the Syrian army.

serpent   snake. In Genesis 3, the serpent deceives Eve into eating the forbidden fruit (cf. LAB 13:8; Jub. 3:17–25). As a result, God decrees eternal enmity between humans and snakes. Later tradition identifies the serpent with Satan (*Vita* 33:3; Rev. 12:9; *Lives* 12:13; Apoc. Moses 16:5). Sibylline Oracles 1:38–64 emphasizes the serpent's craftiness (cf. Gen. 3:1; Matt. 10:16; Rev. 2:9). In *Vita* 37–39, the serpent (Satan) attacks Adam's son Seth, the image of God (cf. Gen. 5:1, 3).

Serpents are venomous creatures (Ps. 58:4; Eccl. 10:8, 11; Amos 5:19; Sir. 12:13, 21:2, 25:15; Matt. 7:10) that are sometimes instruments of divine punishment (Isa. 14:29–30; Jer. 8:17; 1 Cor. 10:9; Wisd. 16:5; 3 Bar. 4–5). Protection from serpents indicates divine favor (Deut. 8:15; Mark 16:18; Luke 10:19). When God uses serpents to punish the people, Moses fabricates a bronze serpent to heal them (Num. 21:4–9; cf. John 3:14). This incident is an etiological explanation of an idolatrous bronze serpent in the Temple that was called Nehushtan, which Hezekiah destroys (2 Kings 18:4).

Ancient Near Eastern myths contain a serpentine monster, called Leviathan or Rahab in the Bible, who represents chaos opposed to divine order. Creation involved the conquest of this monster, which will be definitively defeated in the future. Revelation develops the eschatological implications of this imagery (12:9, 14, 15, 20:2). *See also* LEVIATHAN; SNAKE.

servant of the Lord a multivalent biblical term whose usage in Second Isaiah is crucial in Jewish texts and formative for early christology. The servant of YHWH in Isaiah 40–55 denotes both Israel, God's chosen one (42:1–4; cf. 41:8, 43:10), and a figure with a mission to Israel (49:1–7). Depicted in personal terms, the servant has features and functions traditionally ascribed to the king and to Israel's prophets. He is the executor of God's justice (42:1, 4), whose speech is provided by God (49:2; cf. Isa. 11:3–4), and he is exalted in the sight of the kings and the nations (49:7, 52:13–15). He is also the suffering and vindicated prophet (50:4–9, 52:13–53:12). In this capacity, he is persecuted (50:6–9, 53:5–7a) and put to death (53:7b–9). Although his suffering and death are perceived as divine punishment, his prophetic activity and his death benefit others (53:10–12).

Third Isaiah is the earliest interpreter of Second Isaiah's servant. Faced with a nation that as a whole he could not describe as God's servant, he distinguished the servants and chosen ones from the rebels who have forsaken God (Isa. 65:1–15). Haggai and Zechariah, Third Isaiah's contemporaries, may draw on the kingly dimension of the servant's description, as they refer to Zerubbabel as God's servant and chosen one (Hag. 2:23; Zech. 3:8).

Taking up the prophetic aspect of the servant's work, Daniel 12:3 promises heavenly exaltation to "the wise" (Heb.: *maskilim;* cf. *yaskil,* Isa. 52:13), the suffering teachers, who, by their knowledge of God's will, "bring many to righteousness" (cf. Isa. 53:11; cf. Dan. 11:32–33) during the persecution by Antiochus IV Epiphanes. Wisdom of Solomon 2 and 5 explicates this interpretation in a description of the persecution, exaltation, and vindication of the righteous one, the wise spokesman of the Lord that shapes language and motifs of Isaiah 52–53 with narrative elements from the traditional genre about the persecuted and exalted court sage (cf. Gen. 37–45; Dan. 6). The teacher in the Qumran Hodayot 7:10–12 and 8:36 describes his mission in the words of Isaiah 50:4. 2 Maccabees 7 employs servant motifs, referring to the seven brothers' deaths in behalf of Israel and to their vindication through resurrection. In 1 Enoch 37–71, the chosen one is a transcendent figure, God's anointed one, the protagonist of the suffering righteous and the judge of their persecutors. Targum Pseudo-Jonathan of Isaiah 52:13 also distinguishes between the glorious servant, God's militant anointed one, and suffering Israel whom he delivers.

Although scholars dispute the extent of Second Isaiah's influence on New Testament christology, certain connections seem probable. Early creeds and an early hymn have been shaped by the pattern of the suffering and exaltation/vindication of the servant (Rom. 4:25; Phil. 2:6–11). The gospel narratives about Jesus' passion and death employ the genre of the persecuted and vindicated courtier, especially as it has been shaped in the Wisdom of Solomon (Matt. 26–28; Mark 14–16; Luke 22–24; John 12, 19–20), and Jesus' announcements of the son of man's death and resurrection reflect the persecution-vindication pattern (Mark 8:31, 9:31, 10:33–34; cf. Acts 2:36, 3:13–15). Some references to Jesus' death for others may also interpret Isaiah 53 (e.g., Mark 10:45, 14:24; Rom. 4:25; cf. Isa. 53:11–12) in light of motifs in classical Greek thought. Paul applies Isaiah 50:8–9 to the suffering and vindication of God's chosen ones (Rom. 8:31–34). *See also* CHOSEN ONE; CHOSEN ONES; RIGHTEOUS ONE; SON OF MAN.

servants *see* SLAVERY

service (Heb.: *abodah*) narrative of the Temple rite on the Day of Atonement paraphrasing Leviticus 16, recited in the Additional Service at synagogue worship on the Day of Atonement; more generally, divine worship

Seth third son of Adam and Eve (Gen. 4:25). Genesis 5:1 recalls humanity's creation in God's image, and Genesis 5:3 declares that Seth is Adam's image, implying that the divine image is transmitted through him. In Jewish tradition, Seth represents righteous humanity and is the mediator of esoteric revelation. In Life of Adam and Eve 25–29, Adam gives Seth secret knowledge, including information about history, eschatology, and Adam's ascent to heaven (cf. Test. Adam 3). In Apocalypse of Moses 10:3 and 12:1, Seth is the image of God. Seth sees Adam's reception by God in heaven when Adam dies (Apoc. Moses 35–36). When God comes to the earthly Paradise to bury Adam's body, only Seth stays awake to hear the promise of resurrection (Apoc. Moses 38:4). In Life of Adam and Eve 50:1–2, Adam tells his children to write what Eve and he have said on two tablets, one stone and one brick. Stone resists water, and brick resists fire. Josephus (*Ant.* 1.2.3, secs. 68–71) says that Seth and his progeny knew astrological wisdom and wrote it on two steles, one stone and the other brick, to resist water and fire. Josephus emphasizes the righteousness of Seth and his descendants (see also 1 Enoch 85). Sethian Gnosticism sees Seth as the progenitor of the perfect humans, the Gnostics. A number of Gnostic treatises are attributed to him: Paraphrase of Seth, Second Treatise of the Great Seth, and Three Steles of Seth. The only mention of Seth in the New Testament is in Luke's genealogy of Jesus (Luke 3:38).

seudah shel mitzva a banquet in fulfillment of a religious duty, for example, a wedding banquet, which is part of the marriage rite

seven a sacred, special, and symbolic number in the ancient world. References to seven-day periods can be found in cuneiform texts from the twenty-third century B.C.E., and the notion of seven planets was widespread in antiquity. The number seven is so frequently used to refer to so many different things that often it is difficult to define its specific significance. In part it appears to denote completeness, perfection, or consummation. In any case, when the number seven or seventy occurs in a text, one must be cautious about taking it as a literal enumeration of the objects or persons described.

Seven Blessings (Heb.: *sheba berakhot*) the seven blessings recited over a cup of wine at a wedding ceremony. They are as follows: "[1] Praised are You, O Lord our God, King of the universe, Creator of the fruit of the vine. [2] Praised are You, O Lord our God, King of the universe, who created all things for your glory. [3] Praised are You, O Lord our God, King of the universe, Creator of Adam. [4] Praised are You, O Lord our God, King of the universe, who created man and woman in his image, fashioning woman from man as his mate, that together they might perpetuate life. Praised are You, O Lord, Creator of man. [5] May Zion rejoice as her children are restored to her in joy. Praised are You, O Lord, who causes Zion to rejoice at her children's return. [6] Grant perfect joy to these loving companions, as You did to the first man and woman in the Garden of Eden. Praised are You, O Lord, who grants the joy of bride and groom. [7] Praised are You, O Lord our God, King of the universe, who created joy and gladness, bride and groom, mirth, song, delight and rejoicing, love and harmony, peace and companionship. O Lord our God, may there ever be 'heard in the cities of Judah and in the streets of Jerusalem voices of joy and gladness, voices of bride and groom, the jubilant voices of those joined in marriage under the bridal canopy, the voices of young people feasting and singing.'

Praised are You, O Lord, who causes the groom to rejoice with his bride."

Seventeenth of Tammuz (Heb.: *sheba asar be-Tammuz*) fast day commemorating five catastrophes: Moses' breaking the first tablets of the Torah; the cancellation of the daily whole offering; the breaching of the city wall of Jerusalem by the Romans; Apostemos's burning the Torah; and setting up an idol in the Temple

Seventh of Adar anniversary of the birth and the death of Moses

seventh year *see* SABBATICAL YEAR

Severus governor of Palestine, around 310 C.E. The Acta Martyrum, a source of questionable historical value, mentions Severus as governor of Palestine. The text states that he was responsible for a martyrdom under Maximian, presumed by scholars to be Galerius Maximian, who was chosen Caesar of the East by Diocletian in 293.

Severus, Gaius Julius legate of Palestine (155–161 C.E.). The position in Palestine was his first provincial office, other than serving in two Roman legions. His father had held posts under Hadrian and Antonius Pius. His parents seem to have been descendants of several eastern client princes, including Herod the Great.

Severus, Lucius Septimius Roman emperor (192–211 C.E.). He was born in North Africa in 145 or 146. Upon becoming emperor, he disbanded the Praetorian Guard and created a new guard in which any legionary could serve. His claim to be emperor was challenged by Pescennius Niger, the governor of Syria who was proclaimed emperor by his forces. After defeating his challenger, he divided Syria into two provinces, Coele and Phoenice, in order to prevent further disturbances. Eusebius and Orosius both mention a Jewish and Samaritan war, for which Caracalla was awarded a triumph, but no other Roman or Jewish sources mention it. It is possible that the Jews in specific localities sided with Niger against the emperor. Dio refers to a brigand Clausius who caused trouble in Palestine and Syria. Although there is no evidence that he was Jewish, the Babylonian Talmud does refer to two rabbis aiding the Roman authorities in capturing some brigands, much to the dismay of their fellow Jews. Parthia had supported Niger, so the emperor moved against Vologases IV. In 197 he took Ctesiphon from Parthia, and in 199 he annexed the kingdom of Osroene and Mesopotamia for the Roman empire.

The emperor remained in Syria and Egypt for the next two years. The emperor undertook a program of urbanization in Palestine, founding the city of

Lucia Septimia Eluetheropolis on the site of Beth Gabra between Jerusalem and Gaza and Lucia Septimia Severa Diospolis on the site of Lydda. Under Severus, Jews were allowed to serve on local councils and hold magistracies, but they had to perform only those duties that did not conflict with their religion. The Historia Augusta states that Severus, "under heavy penalty," prohibited people from becoming Jews. Although this statement is not collaborated by any legal texts or other writers, it is in line with the policy inaugurated by Antonius Pius of accepting Judaism as licit religion for the Jews but opposing Gentiles from adopting the religion. The passage implies that Severus applied the ruling to women as well as men, and it seems also to prohibit non-Jews from adopting Jewish practices as well as converting. The ambiguous nature of the text does not allow us to ascertain what sort of penalties were applied to those who violated the edict. If there was a ban on conversion, the Jewish and Christian writers suggest that it was not strictly adhered to, for they both mention converts to Judaism at this time.

Severus Alexander Roman emperor (r. 222–235 C.E.). In 230 the Persians invaded Mesopotamia, and in 231 the emperor and his mother left Rome for Antioch to regain Mesopotamia. At this time Furius Timestheus, procurator of Palestine, was ordered to collect the remainder of the *annona* for support of the emperor's military expedition. Under the Severian emperors the *annona* had become a regular tax, and it appears that it had not been successfully collected. Severus Alexander's campaign was not totally successful, but he did manage to regain Mesopotamia. The Scriptores Historiae Augustae states that he continued the Jews' privileges enacted by his predecessors.

sexuality Concerns with and about sexuality and the desiring/desired body permeated the literature of the ancient world: sexual metaphors shape theology (e.g., Hosea) and poetry (Song of Solomon); discussions of restraining sexuality and containing desire pervade wisdom literature (e.g., Ben Sira) and epistles (1 Corinthians); expressions of sexual allure and its dangers accompany depictions of personal relationships (e.g., Testament of Reuben). Although it is a scholarly commonplace to contrast the more ascetically inclined or spiritual Graeco-Roman and later Christian traditions with the more earthy, carnal emphases of Judaism, both categorizations are reductive and misleading. Some Jews practiced celibacy (e.g., the Therapeutae, perhaps some Essenes, Paul); some Christians preached the value of marriage and children (e.g., the pastoral

Epistles). Both groups were influenced by Hellenism and so by the Platonic distinction between the spiritual and the corporeal, and both found differing means to address it. Moreover, it appears neither group viewed sexuality as an autonomous category; rather, the management of desire is not separable from structures of power.

In the biblical tradition, women are occasionally depicted as suggesting sexual availability to allure men (Tamar [Gen. 38]; Ruth 2; Judith, perhaps Jael [Judg. 4–5]; etc.). Generally, physical expressions of love were to take place within marriage; rape, incest, adultery, and fornication are all condemned. A man's sexuality was his own to control; a woman's sexuality was the responsibility of her father or guardian to protect and the property of her husband to utilize. To prevent abuse of the system, the woman was granted specific conjugal and economic rights. While children were desired, they were not the focus of all depictions of sexuality and marriage. The most notable celebration of sexual love apart from procreation is the Song of Solomon. In both Jewish and Christian traditions, however, the Song is allegorized and so spiritualized into representing the love of God for Israel or of Christ for the Church.

The sexuality of the deity remained veiled throughout antiquity. Although humankind was created in the image of God, male and female (Gen. 1:27), and although ancient Near Eastern, Greek, and Roman gods frequently displayed sexual desires and prowess, the sexuality of the biblical God beyond the use of masculine grammatical forms remained virgin territory (e.g., Ezek. 1:27).

Complicated also is the sexuality of that first human created in Genesis: For Philo, the first Adam was a spiritual androgyne (cf. Empedocles, Plato's *Symposium*); Genesis 2 then introduces woman, sexuality, and the consequent fall from bliss. Philo's distinction between spirit and corporeality is Platonic, and its incarnation for him is also expressed in the practices of the celibate Therapeutae.

Desire assumes a dualistic form in Ben Sira, the Testaments of the Twelve Patriarchs, 1QS, and elsewhere: the evil inclination vies with the good (see also Deut. 30:15ff.; Josh. 24:15; Jer. 21:8–14). Woman often represents the threat of sexual desire: the Testament of Reuben exhorts its listeners to "guard against sexual promiscuity, and if you want to remain pure in your mind, protect your senses from women" (6:1). Her unconstrained sexuality symbolizes unfaithful Israel (Hosea; Isa. 3:16–4:1) and idolatrous Rome (the Whore of Babylon in

Rev. 17), and these woman-identified communities are then according to prophetic discourse punished by sexual humiliation and rape (Isa. 3:17; Ezek. 23; Rev. 2:22). Positively channeled, desire is devoted to (female) Torah and Wisdom (cf. Prov. 8:1–9:12; Wis. 10:1–11:26).

In Matthew 19:12, Jesus states that some make themselves eunuchs for the Kingdom of Heaven. Jesus' own sexuality is not explored in canonical texts, but the majority of church documents suggest he was a virgin as was his mother (cf. Matt 1; Luke 2). Paul recognizes the power of sexual desire and emphasizes physical mutuality in marriage, yet he prefers the gift of celibacy (1 Cor. 7).

Rabbinic Judaism provides a detailed system of laws permitting sexual relations only within legitimate marriages. These laws develop scripture's precepts, which range from general prohibitions against lewdness and immodest conduct to specific mandates against homosexuality, adultery, pederasty, incest, and other sexual practices deemed deviant. Underlying the rabbinic treatment of this topic is the perspective that within marriage sexual intercourse is a positive and natural aspect of human conduct. Sexual intimacy is neither sinful nor shameful. At the same time, the rabbis are conscious of the potential of the sex drive to lead the individual into sin. Therefore, while celibacy is discouraged, a person's ability to control the sexual urge is viewed as an aspect of piety. Rabbinic law holds that any breach of the rules of sexual conduct comprises a serious threat to the structure of society and is to be punished severely. Prohibited unions are a particular concern, seen both as threatening normative society and as violating the order of creation. Bestiality, for instance, comprises an illegitimate commingling of beings that God created as distinct, and homosexuality threatens the integrity of the distinction made by God at the time of creation between male and female. Accordingly, through the legislation on sexual relations, the rabbis attempt to support and maintain what they view as the God-given order of creation.

The rabbis read Exodus 21:10's statement that a wife has marital rights to imply a husband's duty to have sexual relations with her. M. Ketubot 5:6 details this obligation and states that a man's vow not to have sexual relations with his wife is valid for no more than two weeks, according to the House of Shammai, or, according to the House of Hillel, for only one week. The same passage details the minimum frequency with which men must fulfill their sexual duty: rabbinic disciples may leave their wives for thirty days and workers for one week. In Eliezer's view, those of independent means who do not work must have sexual relations every day; workers, twice a week; ass drivers, once a week; camel drivers, once in thirty days; and sailors, once in six months. According to M. Ketubot 5:7, either a husband or wife who refuses to perform normal marital duties is subject to a monetary penalty.

Mishnah Ketubot 5:6 makes clear sexual relations are a central aspect of the relationship between husband and wife. The rabbinic legal system assures that within this setting intercourse occurs only within strict parameters established by rules of purity that preclude intercourse during menstruation (see Lev. 19:19, 20:18). Scripture punishes violation of this precept with karet, to be cut off from the people. According to Mishnah Makkot 3:1, this act, as well as sexual intercourse with relatives, is punishable by flogging. Other sexual offenses—adultery, incest, sodomy, bestiality, and homosexuality—are capital offenses under biblical and rabbinic law. Their perpetrators are to be stoned to death (M. Sanhedrin 7:4). Likewise, upon marriage, a woman who is found not to be a virgin, having consented to intercourse with a seducer, is punished along with her lover by stoning. *See also* ADULTERY; BETROTHAL; CELIBACY; FORNICATION; HOMOSEXUALITY; INCEST; MARRIAGE; VIRGIN.

shaatnez (Heb., mingled stuff) Deuteronomy 22:11's term for a mixture of wool and linen, which Israelites are prohibited from wearing. The earliest rabbinic discussion of the prohibition occurs at M. Kilaim 9:1–10, which defines what constitutes a garment or type of cloth subject to the restriction.

Shabbat **1.** the Sabbath, the seventh day, commemorating the day on which God rested after the six days of Creation

2. Mishnah tractate on the observance of the Sabbath. The first fifteen chapters discuss general principles of Sabbath observance (chap. 1); preparing for the Sabbath, with special reference to light, food, and clothing (chaps. 2–6); and prohibited acts of labor on the Sabbath (chaps. 7–15). Chapters 16 through 24 discuss other taboos associated with the Sabbath, for example, the taboo against fire; circumcision on the Sabbath; permitted procedures in connection with food for human beings and beasts; and seemly and unseemly behavior on the Sabbath.

Shabbat haGadol (Heb., the great Sabbath) refers to the Sabbath before Passover. It probably gets its name from the *haftarah* (the prophetic lection) of the day, Malachi 3:23, promising the coming of the "great and terrible day of the Lord." It is not mentioned in early Jewish sources but is cited in John 19:31 and other early Church documents.

Shabbat haḤodesh (Heb., Sabbath of the month) one of four Sabbaths designated by special Torah lections. It falls on the Sabbath prior to the month of Nisan and features Exodus 12:1–20, which advocates preparation for Passover.

Shabbat Ḥazon (Heb., Sabbath of the vision) the Sabbath preceding the Ninth of Ab. It features the *haftarah* reading of Isaiah 1, which envisions Jerusalem's destruction.

Shabbat Naḥamu (Heb., Sabbath of comfort) the Sabbath following the Ninth of Ab. It features the *haftarah* reading of Isaiah 40, which urges comfort for Israel despite the Temple's fall.

Shabbat Parah (Heb., Sabbath of the heifer) one of four Sabbaths designated by special Torah lections. It falls at the beginning of the period leading up to Passover (but before Shabbat haḤodesh) and demands the reading of Numbers 19:1–22, an account of sacrificial cleansing, that is, cultic purification of the Temple before Passover, which was interpreted as signifying a spiritual preparation for the Passover feast.

Shabbat Shekalim (Heb., Sabbath of the shekels) one of four Sabbaths designated by special Torah lections. It falls roughly two weeks prior to Purim and features the reading of Exodus 30:11–16, an account of the annual shekel tax for the ancient Temple.

Shabbat Shuḅah (Heb., Sabbath of return) the Sabbath falling between Rosh Hashanah and Yom Kippur. It features a call to repentance, especially through its *haftarah* reading of Hosea 14:2–10 (vv. 1–9 in translation), which begins, "Return, O Israel, unto the Lord."

Shabbat Zakhor (Heb., Sabbath on which to remember) one of four Sabbaths designated by special Torah lections. It falls immediately before Purim and recollects Purim's archenemy, Haman, in the Book of Esther, by the recitation of Deuteronomy 25:17–19, which urges Jews always to remember Amalek, an Israelite foe traditionally identified as Haman's ancestor.

Shabbos *see* SHABBAT

Shaḅuot (Heb., weeks) the festival of Pentecost, called in the Bible Ḥag Shaḅuot (Feast of Weeks, Exod. 34:22; Deut. 16:10), Ḥag haKatzir (Feast of the Harvest, Exod. 23:16), and Yom haBikkurim (Day of Firstfruits, Num. 28:26). The rabbinic name for the festival is Atzeret (M. Rosh Hashanah 1:2; M. Ḥagigah 2:4), a term which in scripture designates the day following the festival of Tabernacles (Lev. 23:36; Num. 29:35), and which generally is

translated as "solemn assembly." As suggested by the Pesikta deRab Kahana 192a–193a, it appears that rabbis viewed Pentecost as a conclusion to Passover.

Pentecost is celebrated in the Land of Israel on the sixth of Sivan; in the diaspora, it is celebrated on the seventh as well. It is one of the three biblical pilgrimage holidays and marked the conclusion of the barley harvest (Passover) and the beginning of the midsummer wheat harvest. Leviticus 23:15–16 describes the festival as follows: "You shall count from the day after the sabbath, from the day that you brought the sheaf of the wave offering. Seven full weeks shall they be, counting fifty days to the morrow after the seventh sabbath. Then you shall present a cereal offering of new grain to the Lord." The "sheaf of the wave offering" refers to the sheaf waved on the day after the "sabbath" of the festival of Passover. Taking the reference to designate a Sabbath literally, the Sadducees understood Pentecost always to fall on a Sunday. The Pharisees, by contrast, understood "sabbath" to mean, simply, "day of rest" and, in this context, to refer to the first day of Passover. In their view, which has become normative, Pentecost falls on the fifty-first day from the first day of Passover.

In scripture, Pentecost occasioned the bringing of firstfruits to the Temple sanctuary and a declaration of God's role in taking the Israelites from Egyptian bondage and giving them a land flowing with milk and honey (Deut. 26:1–11). In M. Bikkurim, this ceremony is understood to take place anytime between Pentecost and Tabernacles and to be accompanied by a large celebration, in which pilgrims gather in the towns of their district and go as a group with their ripe produce to Jerusalem. There they are greeted by levitical singing and celebration.

In rabbinic interpretation, the festival of Pentecost also took on a meaning totally absent from scripture. Leviticus 19:1 states that the Israelites came into the wilderness of Sinai on the third new moon after they left the land of Egypt. Beginning in the second century C.E., rabbis associated the arrival at Sinai with Pentecost and hence deemed Pentecost to commemorate God's revealing of the Torah. In the liturgy, Pentecost is referred to as "the occasion of the giving of our Torah." This transformation is in line with a larger process evident in rabbinic times as well as in the Bible itself, in which agricultural holidays were associated with historical and religious events in the life of the Israelite nation.

shaḥarit (Heb.) morning service; dawn. This service comprises psalms of praise (pesukei deZimra), the recitation of the Shema, with blessings for Creation and revelation recited beforehand and a blessing for redemption recited afterward; the Eighteen Benedictions; and the Aleinu prayer. On Mondays and Thursdays, the Torah-portion for the week is read in part; on Sabbaths and festivals, the Torah-lection for those occasions is read in full. Morning worship is required in Judaism every day of the year; it normally takes place soon after dawn, since the Shema is recited at early light. But the morning Prayer (the Eighteen Benedictions) may be recited until midday. The afternoon prayer may be recited until the evening. The evening prayer has no fixed time. One may stand to pray only in a solemn frame of mind. The Mishnah teaches that the early pious ones used to tarry in meditation for one hour before they would pray, "so that they could direct their hearts to the Omnipresent."

Shahrbaraz Persian general, whose name means "wild boar." After taking Damascus in 613 C.E., he sacked Jerusalem in 614, with Jewish help. Defeated by the Byzantine emperor Heraclius in 622, he returned to Persia. In 629, after seeking Roman support, he captured Ctesiphon, but was assassinated soon thereafter.

shalom (Heb., wholeness, completeness; peace) From this root idea comes a wide range of meanings in the Hebrew Bible. *Shalom* characterizes a cessation of hostilities between nations (Josh. 10:1) as well as their safety, security, and prosperity (Lev. 26:6; Ps. 122:7; Deut. 23:6). An individual's personal welfare or health can be referred to as *shalom* (Isa. 38:17; 1 Kings 22:17), and thus the term came to be used as a greeting or as a farewell (Judg. 6:23; 1 Sam. 15:9). For individuals and nations, *shalom* depends on righteousness (Ps. 85:10; Isa. 32:17); consequently, the wicked have no *shalom* (Isa. 48:22). In the Septuagint, "shalom" is usually translated mechanically by the Greek *eirene,* which has the usual meaning of a nonwarring state between nations. Thus, the lexical range of *eirene* is expanded to that of *shalom* in Jewish-Greek literature and in the New Testament. In much of this literature, the notion of *shalom/eirene* can have eschatological significance. *Shalom* is anticipated as integral to the eschatological time (Ps. 85:8–10; Isa. 55:12), and Ezekiel describes a covenant of *shalom* that will usher in a time of blessing and security (34:25–31).

The rabbinic literature extols peace among people as the greatest possible blessing, which encompasses all other blessings (Lev. Rabbah 9:9; Mishnah Uksin 3:12). Achieving peace is the purpose of the entire Torah (B. Gittin 59b). Acts that bring peace between people have both a concrete benefit in this world and bring a reward from God in the world to come (Mishnah Peah 1:1). For the sake of peace, behaviors that might otherwise be forbidden are permissible, for example, assisting Gentiles who do not follow Israelite agricultural rules or lending domestic items to Jews who might use them illicitly (Mishnah Shebiit 5:9). To assure peace, even truth may be sacrificed (B. Yebamot 65b). Hillel defines the heart of Judaism with the maxim, "Love peace and pursue it" (M. Abot 1:12).

Shalshalat one of the Samaritan Chronicles, also known as Chronicle 5. It is made up mainly of a list of high priests, along with lengths of office. These are correlated with various world eras. In its present form it extends from Adam to the nineteenth century. The name Shalshalat derives from the Hebrew word meaning "chain."

Shamhazai According to Targum Pseudo-Jonathan's account of Genesis 6:4, Shamhazai (also known as Shemyazza and Semyaz) is an angel who lusted after human women and fell to earth with Azael. The Babylonian Talmud (Nid. 61a) states that Shamhazai is the grandfather of the wicked kings Sihon and Og. The First Book of Enoch indicates that Shamhazai is punished along with the other fallen angels.

Shammai first-century Pharisaic sage; colleague of Hillel

Shammai, Houses of *see* HILLEL AND SHAMMAI, HOUSES OF

Shapur I Sassanid king (r. 241–272 C.E.). Shapur I was successful in regaining most of the territory that the Achaemenids had held in the west. He easily subdued the Armeanians and conquered Hatra in the east. In the west he took Nisibis in 238 after a prolonged siege, but he held the city for only a short time. After a period of peace with the Romans, Shapur again moved west sometime between 253 and 256, retaking Nisibis, Carrhae (Harran), Edessa, and Antioch. He attempted to place his own candidates on the Roman throne in 260, after retaking Edessa and Antioch. For ten years, 263–273, Shapur faced the threat of Odenathus and Zenobia in Palmyra until they were destroyed by the Romans. Shapur reversed Ardashir's policies of persecuting other religions and attempting to forcibly unify the empire under a pure Zoroastrian state-church. Although Shapur was more tolerant and supported Mani's attempt to bring together Christianity, Buddhism, and the Iranian religions into one cult, his plans were foiled by Kartir's execution of Mani. Shapur and Samuel worked out an agreement by which the

Jews recognized the legitimacy of the Persian government and its legal system, while the government allowed the Jews to govern their own affairs as long as the Persians deemed them unimportant and in conformity with Sassanid policy. This allowed the rabbis to create a Jewish community that was fairly independent of the Sassanids in its daily way of life.

Shapur II Sassanid king (r. 309–379 C.E.). Shapur II was an extremely able leader, administrator, and soldier. Through diplomatic means he was able to gain possession of Nisibis and to dominate Mesopotamia, Armeania, and the Caucasus. Although he often faced superior Roman armies, in the end he was able to convince his foes to give him what he wanted. The rabbinic sources indicate that the Jewish communities suffered along with the rest of the country; but it does not appear that the Jews were singled out by either the Roman or Persian forces. Later Iranian sources credited Shapur with establishing a Mazdean state-church and with producing scriptures in order to ensure orthodoxy. It appears that in the 340s he began a rather extensive period during which the Christians were persecuted. The rabbinic sources paint a flattering picture of Shapur II. They describe his curiosity concerning some Jewish practices and his general support of the Jews. However, Shapur's many wars forced him to amass a considerable amount of money, and the talmudic stories focus on his policy of taxation and the penalties suffered by Jews who attempted to evade their financial responsibilities toward the government. The Talmud also contains five stories about Ifra Hormizd, Shapur's mother, which describe her as a friend of the Jews and one who supported them in government circles.

Shapur III Sassanid king (r. 383–388 C.E.). Shapur III gained the throne when his father Ardashir II was deposed in 383. He continued his father's policy concerning Armeania, accepting its partition with Byzantium. The Arabic historians call him "the warlike" because he apparently attacked an Arab tribe.

Sharon, Plain of the coastal plain of ancient Palestine from Joppa north to Mount Carmel. The name may mean "forested country." Its two main port cities in the biblical period until the construction of Caesarea by Herod the Great at Strato's Tower were Joppa and Dor (Dora). In the Persian period the whole of the Sharon was formed into a single Persian province named after its northern port, Dor or Duru. From literary sources in the fourth century B.C.E. it is possible to deduce that Tyre and Sidon controlled the coastal cities of Duru alternately from the middle of the fourth century B.C.E. Sidon controlled the city of Dor, and the next city south, name unknown, was controlled by Tyre. South of Strato's Tower was ancient Arsuf, which presumably belong to Tyre. The next city is Joppa, which belonged to the territory of the city of Azotus or biblical Ashdod.

Following the death of Alexander the Great, rule of Palestine passed first to his successors in Egypt, the Ptolemies. The old Persian province of Duru was revived as a hyparchy (a Greek name for a political entity ruled by a hyparch or viceroy) with two Hellenistic cities, Corcodilonpolis and Bucolonpolis. The capital of the province was probably Strato's Tower and Dor became a royal fortress and emporium. By 129 B.C.E., the Jewish king John Hyrcanus I had added Apollonia in the Sharon Plain to his kingdom. In 104 B.C.E., the new Jewish king Alexander Jannaeus (104–76 B.C.E.) deposed a certain Zoilus who ruled in Dora and Strato's Tower, and thereby annexed the main part of the Sharon to his kingdom under the Greek name of Paralia, meaning seacoast.

With the coming of Rome in 63 B.C.E. the Roman general Pompey recognized the separate character of the Sharon and kept it independent in three city territories: Dor, Strato's Tower, and Apollonia. Under Herod the Great, the Sharon was added to his domain, except for Dora (Dor), which was maintained as an independent city. Dor remained independent until the outbreak of the first revolt against Rome in 66 C.E. The Roman general Vespasian relied on the coastal road to move his troops from Caesarea to Dor to his headquarters in Acco-Ptolemais. Dora remained independent of Palestine after the revolt through the Bar Kosiba Revolt. It was only from the time of the eastern emperor Diocletian (284–305 C.E.) that Dor is to be found listed as a city of Palestine. Therefore, during the Byzantine period Dor and the rest of the Sharon belonged to the Byzantine province of Palestina Prima.

Shavei Zion modern name for an ancient village site about 6 kilometers north of Acco on the Mediterranean coast. Shavei Zion is best known for its sixth-century-C.E. Byzantine church, but it is also important for an underwater shipwreck site of the fifth century B.C.E., or the Persian period. The cargo of this ship was hundreds of terra cotta figurines of the goddess Tanit, a Phoenician-Punic deity. She is depicted with her right arm raised in benediction, her head covered, fully draped, and her left arm folded against her chest. Other items in the cargo include an elephant's tusk, amphorae (perhaps for wine), bowls, and juglets. Analysis of the clay of the figurines showed that they were manufactured on the Palestine coast between Sidon and Achzib, apparently for export to Tanit cultic centers to the west. These finds illustrate the common appellation of the northern coast in this period as "Phoenician." Another shipwreck site about one kilometer north of Acco revealed a load of amphorae with wine of a variety of grape known to be used for raisin wine. This shipwreck is dated to about 500 B.C.E., the Persian period.

She̲ba asar beTammuz   (Heb., the 17th of Tammuz) one of several fast days on the traditional Jewish calendar associated with events leading to the destruction of the First and Second Temples, and understood as derived from Zechariah 8:19. In traditional circles, it introduces three weeks of mourning behavior (e.g., weddings are forbidden), culminating in the Ninth of A̲b.

She̲ba Berakhot   *see* SEVEN BLESSINGS

She̲bat   fifth month of the Jewish calendar, corresponding to January/February

She̲bat, Fifteenth of   *see* FIFTEENTH OF SHE̲BAT

she̲biit   *see* SABBATICAL YEAR

She̲biit   Mishnah tractate on conduct of farming before, during, and after the Sabbatical year. The tractate discusses the sixth year of the Sabbatical cycle (chaps. 1–2); the Sabbatical year itself (chaps. 3–9), covering field labor that may or may not be done and permitted and forbidden uses of produce grown in the Sabbatical year; and the release of debts at the end of the Sabbatical year and the prosbul, the document that allows the lender to assign his debts to the court in order to avoid remitting them in the Sabbatical year (chap. 10). *See also* PROSBUL.

She̲buot   Mishnah tractate elucidating the issues of Leviticus, chapters 5 and 6, concerning those who are liable to present a sin-offering. The tractate discusses the uncleanness of the cult and its Holy Things and the sin-offerings (chaps. 1–2); oaths in general, the rash oath, and the vain oath (chap. 3); the oath of testimony (Lev. 5:1) (chap. 4); the oath of bailment (Lev. 6:2ff.) (chap. 5); the oath imposed by the judges (chaps. 6–7); and oaths and bailments (chap. 8).

Shechem   city located in the pass between Mount Ebal and Mount Gerizim 2 miles east of what is now Nablus. It was called Shechem, meaning shoulder, because of its placement relative to Mount Ebal and Mount Gerizim. Tell Balata was identified as Shechem by Hermann Thiersch in the twentieth century. It was excavated by Ernst Sellin, G. Welter, and Hans Steckeweh, respectively (German Archaeological Institute); then by George Ernest Wright and B. W. Anderson; and subsequently by R. Boling, J. Seger, and W. G. Dever (Drew University, McCormick Theological Seminary, and the American Schools of Oriental Research). A survey of the Shechem region was conducted by E. F. Campbell, Jr.

Shechem was abandoned during the Persian period. In 331/330 B.C.E., it was reoccupied by the Samaritans, who had been expelled from Samaria as punishment for the revolt of their mercenaries against Alexander the Great. In addition to the archaeological data from Tell Balata, the Samaria papyri found in Wadi ed-Daliyah are informative about the Samaritan occupation of Shechem. During the period of Samaritan inhabitation, Shechem became a flourishing city that remained politically significant until John Hyrcanus destroyed it around 107 B.C.E. Ben Sira's reference to the Samaritans, whom he dogmatically deems a senseless, nonpeople living at Shechem, is an ideologically oriented reflection from the Jerusalemite rivals and enemies of the Samaritans.

After Shechem was destroyed by Hyrcanus, an insignificant village was established on its site. This village remained in existence throughout antiquity, although there is some question about its name. In late antiquity, Neapolis and Shechem were identified as one and the same place, but they were also identified as different. Perhaps this confusion emanates from Josephus's statement that Vespasian built Flavius Neapolis just slightly west of ancient Shechem in 72 C.E.

sheep, shepherd   In both a literal and figurature sense, sheep and shepherds appear frequently in the Hebrew Bible and in subsequent Jewish and Christian writings. The sheep was one of the most commonly kept animals in the Near East, and it also figured prominently in the Jewish sacrificial cult. Its nonaggressive nature, defenselessness, and constant need of supervision, together with its dependence on the vigilant shepherd, made the sheep an apt metaphor in various contexts.

The most common usage of sheep and shepherd imagery in early Jewish literature is that of the people of Israel as a flock of sheep and of God as the protective shepherd. In some passages, the human rulers of Israel are also depicted as "shepherds" of the people. Ezekiel (chap. 34) attacks contemporary leaders as evil and irresponsible shepherds who have led the people astray. The "Animal Apocalypse" in 1 Enoch 85–90 also employs sheep-shepherd imagery to portray relations between the Jewish people and their leaders.

Sheep and shepherds also figure prominently in early Christian literature, mainly in a metaphorical sense. Here the main theme is that of Jesus as a shepherd and of his followers, or all of humanity, as sheep. This image is especially highly developed in John 10.

Shefar Am Jewish village in Lower Galilee in the city-territory of Sepphoris and about 12 kilometers to the west of Sepphoris. This village was known to the rabbis as the seat of the Sanhedrin for a time after the Bar Kokhba War (T. Mikvaoth 6.2). It is not mentioned in Josephus or other first-century sources. Many tombs north and south of the town were discovered there in the nineteenth century. One of them is decorated on its facade with a grape vine trellis. Small figures of birds are to be found here and there in the trellis. Effaced Greek inscriptions were found on either side of the door. The tomb featured a vestibule with lions on either side carved in low relief. It is noticed that the tombs of the Early and Middle Roman periods resemble Jewish tombs from other sites, including tombs with rolling stone doors. On the other hand, the Byzantine tombs often have Christian crosses in them. It appears that the village became Christian in its later history.

Shehehiyanu *see* BIRKAT HAZEMAN

shehitah (Heb.) Jewish ritual slaughter, required to prepare animals or birds for use as food. According to rabbinic law, the animal must be killed with a single, swift cut across the its throat, severing the trachea, esophagus, jugular veins, and carotid arteries.

Sheiltot Aramaic expositions by Aha of Shabha (Israel, 8th c. C.E.) of biblical and rabbinic moral precepts organized around the weekly Torah readings and based on the Talmud and Midrash. Aimed at a popular audience rather than only at sages, the material was cited widely by the geonim and medieval rabbinic commentators.

Shekalim Mishnah tractate on collecting and using the half-shekel collected from all Israelites to support the daily whole offerings for collective atonement presented in the Temple in Jerusalem. The tractate discusses collecting the shekel (chaps. 1–2); using the shekel for Temple offerings for the altar (chaps. 3–4); and the Temple administration and its procedures (chaps. 5–8).

shekel a unit of weight in the ancient Near East (known in Aramaic as *tekel,* as in Daniel 5). Like most weights and measures, it was never standardized over the region, but archaeological remains indicate that it was slightly less than half an ounce (roughly 10 g) in Israel, with variations.

shekhinah (Heb.; Aram: *shekhinta*; from the verbal root *sh-kh-n,* to dwell, or to reside). In the targums and in rabbinic literature, the word *shekhinah* at first appears to be used as a circumlocution to avoid the use of anthropomorphisms; for example, Genesis 9:27 says, "let him [God] dwell in the tents of Shem," which Targum Neofiti renders as, "may the Glory of his *shekhinah* dwell in the midst of the tents of Shem." But it means more than that, for wherever it appears, *shekhinah* designates the attribute of God's presence, often to specify his presence in the Temple or the Tabernacle. The destruction of the Temple in 70 C.E. led to the idea that God removed his presence—his *shekhinah*—to the heavens. Later, in the Babylonian Talmud, it was also suggested that God's *shekhinah* went into exile with Israel.

Shela Babylonian amora active at the beginning of the third century C.E.; head of the academy at Nehardea. His authority and renown were diminished when Ra*b* returned to Babylonia from the Land of Israel and, in a number of recorded instances, disapproved of Shela's rulings (B. Yoma 20b; B. Ye*b*amot 121a).

Sheliah Tzibbur (Heb., agent of the congregation) technical term employed for the leader of public worship. Theologically, the person is charged with representing the community's prayers to God.

shelihut *see* AGENCY

shell (or scallop shell) a major motif in Jewish art, often incorrectly called a conch in reference works. This shell, however, is an artistic convention, not an attempt to produce an accurate picture of the shell of a sea creature. The same shell was a minor decorative element in Graeco-Roman art, but it became conventional in some surprising contexts in Jewish art of the Roman and Byzantine periods. For example, the shell appears as the central decoration on a lamp of the second or third century C.E. Here it appears to be a simple artistic convention exactly as in Roman art, even if the tomb in which it was found was Jewish. The shell appears above all in synagogue art where it is the central decorative element within the pediment of the Torah shrine or aedicula. This pattern was borrowed directly from Graeco-Roman art where a shell above two columns forms the frame for a niche in which a statue appears, as at Caesarea Phillipi-Panias. This pattern of scallop shell within a triangular pediment and above two or four columns is so common in synagogue art that it serves as a kind of marker for the investigator. When this pattern appears on sarcophagi in Beth Shearim, for example, the viewer knows immediately that this is a Jewish motif and that what is depicted is like a Torah shrine. This is the case even with the windows of the Capernaum Synagogue, which appear to have been built after this pattern. In later Byzantine mosaics depicting the Torah shrine, the shell is reduced to a generic figure and is not produced with care, but it is recognizable. Otherwise the shell appears in the center of a wreath or within a circlet of acanthus leaves, but it is simply filling space with an artistic motif.

Shema   proclamation of unity of God: "Hear O Israel, the Lord our God, is the one God" (Deut. 6:4–9, 11:13–21; Num. 15:37–41)

shemad   *see* APOSTASY

Shemayah   prerabbinic sage of the first century B.C.E.; in the chain of tradition at M. Abot 1:1–18, listed along with Abtalion as a pair, directly preceding Hillel and Shammai. Shemayah is quoted as saying: "Love work. Hate authority. Don't get friendly with the government" (M. Abot 1:10).

Shemihazah   (Heb., he has seen my name) one of the two chieftains of the rebellious watchers in 1 Enoch 6–16. The tradition builds on the story in Genesis 6:1–4 and describes a revolt of heavenly beings who bring evil to earth by revealing magic, medicine, and astrology and by mating with women and begetting giants whose bellicose deeds decimate the earth and humanity. Shemihazah, his associates, and their progeny are judged at the time of the Deluge. The story in 1 Enoch may parody claims that gods had fathered the successors of Alexander the Great.

Shemini Atzeret   eighth day of solemn assembly (Num. 30:35); last day of Sukkot. This is a holy day in itself.

shemoneh esrei   the Eighteen Benedictions; *see also* AMIDAH

Shemot Rabbah   *see* EXODUS RABBAH

Shemuel   *see* SAMUEL

Sheol   the underworld, the place of the dead. The word is widely supposed to derive from Hebrew *shaal,* "to ask, inquire," perhaps referring to the practice of necromancy or the notion of calling the dead to account. In biblical texts, Sheol is the land of dust, darkness, forgetfulness, where the "shades" of the dead (*refaim*) are gathered (Isa. 14:8–20, 26:19, 38:10–20; Ps. 88:3–12), although there is a tendency to associate the place with premature or evil death. Sheol is sometimes combined with "destruction" (*abaddon*) and "the pit" (*shahat, bor*), and "death" (*mavet*) is sometimes a metonymy for it. Second Temple Jewish texts continue biblical usage, but indicate some tendency to see Sheol as

a place where distinctions are made between the righteous and the wicked (1 Enoch 22) and everlasting punishment is exacted (1 Enoch 103:5–8, contrast 102:5). Playing on the notion that death and life are spheres that permeate into the present existence of the wicked and righteous respectively, one Qumran psalmist thanks God for deliverance from the pit (*shahat*), Sheol Abaddon (1QH 3:19). The normal Septuagint translation of Sheol is Hades, the classical word for the underworld. In the New Testament, Hades designates both the place of the dead (Rev. 1:18) and the place of fiery punishment (Luke 16:23).

Sher, Tower of   location referred to at T. Shebiit 4:11 as demarcating a border area of the Land of Israel; possibly the Tower of Satraton (Sharshon)

Sherira, ben Hanina Gaon   (c. 906–1006 C.E.) medieval Jewish scholar. He followed his father and his grandfather, R. Judah, as head of the academy at Pumbedita. He became head of the academy when he was seventy. Sherira's personality and scholarly reputation helped to reestablish Pumbedita's prestige, and students came from all over the world to study with him. Sherira helped to establish the Babylonian Talmud as the central document in the Jewish world. He composed a large number of responsa on religious practices and commentaries to some of the talmudic tractates. The *Igeret Rab Sherira Gaon,* written in 987, traces the history of rabbinic institutions and documents from Moses to his own time.

Sheshet   Babylonian amora of the late third and early fourth centuries C.E.; taught in Nehardea and Mahoza and founded the academy at Shilhe; known for his focus upon legal precedent. Sheshet was sickly and blind (B. Pesahim 108a; B. Berakhot 58a), but with the aid of a reader (B. Sanhedrin 86a), he became one of the leading scholars of his day.

Shezur   town in the Galilee, west of Kefar Anan; in the rabbinic literature, known primarily as the home of Simeon Shezuri

Shiba   (Heb., seven) seven days of mourning following the burial of a close relative

Shikhin   village of Lower Galilee famous in the Talmuds for its hard clays and for the vessels that the potters manufactured there. Shikhin was known to Josephus as Asochis, a Greek form of the name. He says that Shikhin (Asochis) lies "a little way" from Sepphoris (*Ant.* 13.12.5 or 338), and elsewhere says it was down the hill from Sepphoris (*Vita* 45, p. 233). The rabbis often mention Shikhin in the same breath as Sepphoris, which implies that they were close together. The rabbis also preserve the memory that Shikhin was a pottery-making center (B. Shabbat 120b). In field survey it was possible to locate the site of ancient Shikhin 1.5 kilometers north-northwest of Sepphoris on the south edge of the Beth Netopha Valley. Pottery wasters found at the site confirm that pottery was manufactured there, and the remnants of a great pit confirmed the mining of clay at the site. Neutron activation analysis of the wasters from the pottery-manufacturing process confirmed that they are of the same clays as the storage jars that are found all over Galilee, but whose origin has not been known. The site was an Iron Age village, but principally a Jewish village in the Roman and Byzantine periods.

Shikmona site of ancient Sycaminum or Sycamina (Sycamore), a coastal city west of Mount Carmel. In the fifth century B.C.E. Strabo mentions Sycaminopolis in Phoenician territory, but says that only the name survives. By the fourth century C.E. a Christian pilgrim from Bordeaux knew Sycaminum as a place to overnight near Mt. Carmel. By the sixth century, the Piacenza Pilgrim knew that Sycamina was a Jewish town one-half mile straight across the sea from Acco-Ptolemais, but six miles by land. Archaeological investigations at Shikmona do indeed reveal a gap in settlement during the earliest part of the Persian period, but the site is repopulated in the early sixth century B.C.E. Two intersecting, well-paved streets with three-roomed houses on both sides of the streets were discovered. One entered an unroofed courtyard from the street into each house. One such house had a room for the sale of perfumes. During the fourth century B.C.E. a fortress was hastily built. The storage jars found in its basement had Phoenician inscriptions. This fort and its scattered houses suffered a violent end, evidently in the wars between Alexander's successors. A new fortress was built in the Hellenistic period. Now the language on storejars shifted to Greek. One bore the seal of the overseer of markets of the year 131 B.C.E. This fortress was destroyed in 130 B.C.E. during the reign of the Jewish king John Hyrcanus I. During the second half of the first century C.E. a Roman fort was built at Shikmona that was used until the middle of the third century C.E. This structure provided a core around which the Jewish town gradually grew, though by the Byzantine period Christians also lived there. The houses of the Byzantine period featured mosaic floors in geometric patterns and walls decorated with frescoes. There were also shops and artisan's quarters and at least one church. A synagogue has not been found.

Shikmonah *see* SIMEON OF SHIKMONAH

Shiloh a Hellenistic, Roman, and Byzantine period village that occupied the ancient site of biblical Shiloh (Josh. 18:1) about 30 kilometers north of Jerusalem. Although there are scant traces of Persian pottery at the site, it is only possible to show that Shiloh was actively reoccupied from the Hellenistic period. In the Roman period the village extended from the top of the hill down the north slope, but it is in the Byzantine period that Shiloh had its maximum population, judging from the size of the site. Shiloh had become a place of Christian pilgrimage with no detectable Jewish presence. Two Christian churches dominated the site in the fifth and sixth centuries C.E.

Shimon *see under* SIMEON

Shinena *see* JUDAH B. EZEKIEL

shofar ram's horn, sounded during the period of the high holy days, from a month before New Year until the end of Yom Kippur

Shofarot a liturgy with biblical passages concerning the ram's horn, contained in the third section of the core liturgy of the additional prayer for the New Year. It expresses the Rosh Hashanah themes of revelation and redemption. The shofar is sounded at the conclusion of this section, just as it is done at the conclusion of the two preceding liturgical divisions, the Malkuyyot and Zikronot. The passages of scripture include three from the Torah, three from the Writings, and three from the Prophets, with one final verse from the Torah: "On the morning of the third day there was thunder and lightning, as well as a thick cloud on the mountain, and a blast of the shofar so loud that all the people in the camp trembled" (Exod. 19:16); "As the blast of the shofar grew louder and louder, Moses would speak and God would answer him in thunder" (Exod. 19:19); "When all the people witnessed the thunder and lightning, the sound of the shofar, and the mountain smoking, they were afraid and trembled and stood at a distance" (Exod. 20:18); "God has gone up with a shout, the Lord with the sound of a shofar" (Ps. 47:5); "With trumpets and the sound of the shofar make a joyful noise before the King, the Lord" (Ps. 98:6). "Praise the Lord! Praise God in his sanctuary; praise him in his mighty firmament. Praise him for his mighty deeds; praise him according to his surpassing greatness! Praise him with shofar sound; praise him with lute and harp! Praise him with tambourine and dance; praise him with strings and pipe! Praise him with clanging symbols; praise him with loud clashing cymbals! Let everything that breathes praise the Lord! Praise the Lord!" (Ps. 150:1–6); "All you inhabitants of the world, you who live on the earth, when a signal is raised on the mountains, look! When a shofar is blown, listen!" (Isa. 18:3); "And on that day a great shofar will be blown, and those who were lost in the land of Assyria and those who were driven out to the land of Egypt will come and worship the Lord on the holy mountain at Jerusalem" (Isa. 27:13); "Then the Lord will appear over them and his arrow go forth like lightning; the Lord God will sound the shofar and march forth in the whirlwinds of the south. The Lord of hosts will protect them." (Zech. 9:14–15); and "Also on your days of rejoicing, at your appointed festivals, and at the beginnings of your months, you shall blow the trumpets over your burnt offerings and over your sacrifices of well-being; they shall serve as a reminder on your behalf before the Lord your God: I am the Lord your God" (Num. 10:10). The liturgy concludes with the blessing formula, "Blessed art thou . . . who listens to the sound of the shofar blast of his people Israel with mercy," after which the shofar is sounded.

shohet   *see* RITUAL SLAUGHTERER

showbread   bread of the presence; the twelve loaves of unleavened bread that, in accordance with Leviticus 24:5–9, were displayed in the Temple sanctuary, symbolizing the covenant between God and the tribes of Israel. M. Menahot presents a complete picture of the rules regarding the production and display of the showbread. According to the Mishnah, the showbread was not required to be waved or brought near to the altar. It was deemed to belong to the priests alone, so none of it was burned on the altar. The loaves were kneaded one by one, and then baked in a double mold. Upon removal, they were placed in a second mold, so that their shape would not be spoiled. The showbread loaves were 10 handbreadths long and 5 handbreadths wide and had horns seven fingerbreadths long.

show-fringes   (Heb.: *tzitzit*) knots that are attached to the corners of a garment, to serve as reminders of God's commandments

Sibylline Oracles   attested from the fifth century B.C.E. in the Greek-speaking world. The phenomenon seems to have originated in Asia Minor and it spread westward to Italy, where there was a famous shrine at Cumae. The sibyl was always depicted as an aged woman, uttering ecstatic prophecies. By the Hellenistic period, several areas of the eastern Mediterranean laid claim to a sibyl, and sibylline oracles proliferated as literary productions.

The standard collection of Sibylline Oracles has twelve books, numbered 1–8 and 11–14. Two manuscripts were combined. (Books 9 and 10 duplicated material in other books.) The main Jewish oracles are found in Books 3–5. They date from the mid-second century B.C.E. to the early second century C.E. Jewish oracles can also be identified in Books 1–2 and in Book 8, but these have been reworked by Christian editors. Books 11–14 may also be Jewish, but these are from a later period, extending down to the seventh century C.E., and are almost exclusively concerned with political history.

The most characteristic feature of the Sibylline Oracles is the prediction of woes and disasters to come upon humanity. Books 3–5 bear considerable similarity to apocalypses of the historical type. Like the apocalypses, they speak of successive kingdoms, often divided into schematic numbers (four or ten), and "predict" events after the fact. They differ from the apocalypses in the manner of revelation, as they contain no visions or heavenly journeys. Only Sibylline Oracle 4 expects the resurrection of the dead. Oracles 3 and 5 are closer to the Hebrew prophets than to the apocalypses in this respect. The Oracles are always written in Greek hexameters, and so are distinctively a product of Greek-speaking Judaism.

Book 3 is a loose collection of oracles, covering a range of about two hundred years. The main corpus, in verses 97–294 and 545–808, was composed in Egypt in the middle of the second century B.C.E. This is shown by the fact that the turning point of history is expected in the reign of the seventh king of Egypt from the line of the Greeks (vv. 193, 318, 608), either Ptolemy VI Philometor or his short-lived successor Ptolemy VII Neos Philopator. Philometor was especially favorable to the Jews. He gave Onias IV, the high priest who had fled from Jerusalem at the time of the Maccabean revolt, land to build a temple at Leontopolis in Egypt. Onias was also a general in Philometor's army. The Jewish philosopher Aristobulus was allegedly a teacher of Philometor. The sibyl speaks of "a king from the sun" who will bring peace to the earth by the counsels of God (vv. 652–656). The expression "a king from the sun" is an allusion to Egyptian mythology, where the king was regarded as an incarnation of the sun-god Re. The Ptolemies used the old Pharaonic titles with reference to themselves. It appears, then, that the sibyl looked to the Ptolemaic line for a savior king. The political oracles, however, are accompanied by strong propaganda for Judaism.

Idolatry is denounced repeatedly, as are adultery and homosexuality. The sibyl calls on the Greeks to send gifts to the Jerusalem Temple and sacrifice to the true God.

Later additions to Book 3 also have a strong political interest. Oracle 3:350–380 speaks of a lady who will exact vengeance on Rome on behalf of Asia. The lady should be identified as Cleopatra. Another oracle in verses 63–74 speaks of the coming of "Beliar from the Sebasteni." The reference is to Nero, from the line of Augustus, who was regarded as Beliar incarnate. Some other oracles are more spiritual in nature and denounce idolatry (3:1–45).

Oracle 5 represents a later stage of the Egyptian Sibylline tradition, from around the time of the great diaspora revolt of 115–117 C.E. There is no longer any hope for a benevolent gentile ruler. The oracles repeatedly refer to the legend of Nero's return, and portray Nero as a virtual antichrist. The Oracles denounce Egypt, but are much more vehement against Rome. Twice, in verses 256 and 414, the sibyl speaks of a "man from heaven" as a savior figure, but the dominant tone of these oracles is pessimistic.

Book 4 stands in a somewhat different tradition. It builds on an oracle that divided history into four kingdoms and ten generations, but then extends this oracle to include Rome, which is not fitted into the numerical sequence. The latest event to which the oracle refers is the eruption of Vesuvius in 79 C.E. This oracle has a number of distinctive theological features. In marked contrast to the other Sibylline books, it declares that God "does not have a house, stone set up as a temple" (v. 8). To avoid disaster people should refrain from violence, "wash your whole bodies in perennial rivers" (v. 165), and supplicate God. It is, apparently, a rare witness to the Jewish practice of baptism in an eschatological context. It ends with a prediction of conflagration and resurrection.

The Sibylline Oracles originated as an attempt to express Jewish religious values in a Greek medium. They also lent themselves to political propaganda. By the time Oracle 5 was written, hopes for rapprochement between Judaism and the Greek-speaking world had declined severely, at least in Egypt. The Sibylline tradition was taken up enthusiastically in Christianity, however, and continued to flourish down to the Middle Ages.

Sicarii (Lat., dagger men) Jewish assassins who murdered their opponents in Jerusalem, especially during festivals. They arose during the procuratorship of Festus (52–60). The historian Josephus lumped them together with the bandits and others whom he blames for the civil unrest that caused the war with Rome. Under the procurator Albinus (62–64), the Sicarii opposed the high priest Ananias and kidnapped members of his family and faction to get their own members out of jail. They played a prominent role at the beginning of the war against Rome in 66 when, under the leadership of Menahem, son of Judas the Galilean, they captured the fortress at Masada. Then they returned to Jerusalem, heavily armed, to take over leadership of the people's uprising against the Romans and Jewish governing class. In the conflicts among Jewish revolutionary groups, Menahem and the Sicarii were defeated by the forces of Eleazar ben Ananias, another leader of the revolt, and most of the rebels, including Menahem, were killed. A few escaped from Jerusalem under the leadership of Eleazar, son of Jair, and spent the rest of the war in Masada. Three years after the destruction of Jerusalem and the Temple, the Romans besieged the Sicarii at Masada and in the spring of 74 took the fortress. According to Josephus, all the defenders, except seven who hid themselves, committed suicide rather than risk capture by the Romans. Over six hundred Sicarii had escaped to Alexandria where they assassinated some of the leaders of the Jewish community and resisted Roman rule. The Alexandrian Jewish council of elders and community, however, turned them over to the Romans, who tortured them. They died as they had lived, refusing to submit to Caesar.

sick, visiting It is a deed of charity in rabbinic practice to visit the ill to alleviate their isolation and suffering. Rabbis emphasize that the act is an imitation of God himself, who visited Abraham when he was ill after his circumcision (Gen. 17:26–18:1). Each person who visits a sick individual takes a portion of his illness, according to a more mystical rabbinic view of this obligation (Ned. 3qb).

Siddur Jewish prayer book for all days except holy days. The Siddur (Heb., order) contains the order of service for the morning, afternoon, and evening worship on weekdays, the Sabbath, and festivals, and also deals with rites of home and family, including Grace after Meals, the Wedding Service, and other liturgies. All morning and evening services follow a single paradigm of prayer (Heb.: *matbea shel tefillah*): the recitation of the Shema ("Hear O Israel, the Lord our God, the Lord is one") followed by the Prayer (the Eighteen Benedictions), and then the Aleinu prayer ("It is incumbent upon us to praise the Lord of all being"). The afternoon service omits the Shema, and the Sabbath service adds a liturgy for the proclamation of the Torah and also an Additional Service (Mussaf).

Sidon   port city, north of Tyre, in Lebanon. After 111 B.C.E., the city was autonomous of Seleucid rule; in 64 B.C.E. its autonomy was recognized by Pompey as well. Evidence of inscriptions and references in the New Testament (e.g., Matt. 11:22; Mark 7:24) suggest a large Jewish population in this period. Josephus (*War* 2:479) states that in 66 C.E., so many Jews dwelled in Sidon that gentile Sidonians were afraid to attack them, in contrast to what occurred in other Greek towns.

Sifra   commentary to the Book of Leviticus, written by sages, probably between 250 and 350 C.E. Sifra consists of a systematic commentary on the verses of Leviticus, explaining the sense of scripture and showing the relationship between the rules of the Mishnah on the topics covered by the book of Leviticus and the laws of that book; the main point is that the rules of the Mishnah derive from the laws of Leviticus. For sizable passages, the sole point of coherence for the discrete sentences or paragraphs of Sifra's authorship derives from the base-verse of scripture that is subject to commentary. A sizable proportion of Sifra consists simply in the association of completed statements of the oral Torah with the exposition of the written Torah, the whole re-presenting as one whole Torah the dual Torah received by Moses at Sinai. Without the Mishnah or the Tosefta, Sifra's authorship would have had virtually nothing to say about numerous passages of the book of Leviticus. Sifra re-presents the written Torah—the Book of Leviticus—in topic, in program, and in the logic of cogent discourse, and within that rewriting of the written Torah, it re-presents the oral Torah—the Mishnah and the Tosefta—in its paramount proposition and in many of its substantive propositions. In order to do so, the authorship constructed through its document, first, a sustained critique of the Mishnah's *Listenwissenschaft,* and then, a defense of the Mishnah's propositions on the foundation of scriptural principles of taxonomy, in particular, hierarchical classification.

Sifrei Bamidbar   *see* SIFREI TO NUMBERS

Sifrei Devarim   *see* SIFREI TO DEUTERONOMY

Sifrei Qatan   *see* SIFREI ZUTTA

Sifrei Shel Panim Aḥerim   *see* SIFREI ZUTTA

Sifrei to Deuteronomy   verse-by verse commentary to the Book of Deuteronomy, written c. 250–350 C.E., often citing passages of the Mishnah and the Tosefta. In this commentary, sages maintained that Israel stands in a special relationship with God, defined by the contract, or covenant, that God made with Israel. The covenant comes to particular expression, in Sifrei to Deuteronomy, in two matters: first, the land, and second, the Torah. Each marks Israel as different from all other nations, on the one hand, and as selected by God, on the other. In these propositions, sages situate Israel in the realm of heaven, finding on earth the stigmata of covenanted election and concomitant requirement of loyalty and obedience to the covenant. First comes the definition of those traits of God that the authorship finds pertinent: God sits in judgment upon the world, and his judgment is true and righteous. God punishes faithlessness. Second, the contract, or covenant, produces the result that God has acquired Israel, which God created. The reason is that only Israel accepted the Torah, among all the nations, and that is why God made the covenant with Israel in particular. Why is the covenant made only with Israel? The Gentiles did not accept the Torah, Israel did, and that has made all the difference. Israel recognized God forthwith; the very peace of the world and of nature depends upon God's giving the Torah to Israel.

Sifrei to Deuteronomy also presents an account of the structure of the intellect. The explicit propositional program of the document is joined by a set of implicit propositions, which have to do with the modes of correct analysis and inquiry that pertain to the Torah. The systematic and orderly character of scripture is repeatedly demonstrated, with the result that out of numerous instances, we may on our own reach the correct conclusion. Two implicit propositions predominate. The first, also stated in Sifrei to Numbers and in Sifra, is that pure reason does not suffice to produce reliable results. Only through linking our conclusions to verses of scripture may we come to final and fixed conclusions. The implicit proposition, demonstrated many times, may therefore be stated very simply. The written Torah is the sole source of reliable information. Reason undisciplined by the Torah yields unreliable results. The second of the two recurrent modes of thought is the demonstration that many things conform to a single structure and pattern. We can show this uniformity of the law by addressing the same questions to disparate cases and, in so doing, composing general laws that transcend cases and form a cogent system.

Sifrei to Numbers   a commentary to the Book of Numbers, written c. 250–350 C.E., by sages in the Land of Israel. The document presents exegeses of verses in Numbers both in terms of the theme or problems of the verse—hence, intrinsic exegesis—and in terms of a theme or polemic not particular to the verse—hence, extrinsic exegesis. The document explicates the role of scripture in syllogistic composition. Scripture supplies hard facts, which, properly classified, generate syllogisms. By collecting and classifying facts of scripture, therefore, we may produce firm laws of history, society, and Israel's everyday life. The fallibility of reason unguided by scriptural exegesis is emphasized. Scripture alone supplies a reliable basis for speculation. Laws cannot be generated by reason or logic unguided by scripture. Scripture stands paramount, logic, reason, and analytical processes of classification and differentiation, are secondary. Reason not built on scriptural foundations yields uncertain results. The Mishnah itself demands scriptural bases.

Sifrei Yerushalmi   *see* SIFREI ZUTTA

Sifrei Zutta   a midrashic compilation on the Book of Numbers, distinct from the better known Sifrei to Numbers. The document was well known in the medieval period, when it was cited under a variety of names, including Baraita deSifrei, Sifrei Qatan, Sifrei Yerushalmi, and Sifrei Shel Panim Aherim. These names distinguished Sifrei Zutta from the other Sifrei to Numbers.

Subsequent to the medieval period, Sifre Zutta disappeared; no complete text of it is extant. The current compilation is reconstructed from *geniza* fragments and citations in other midrashic works, especially the Yalkut Shimoni, which identifies Sifrei Zutta as one of its sources.

The standard edition is that of H. S. Horovitz, who in 1917 published a critical edition of Sifrei Zutta and Sifrei to Numbers. Along with the critical apparatus, his work includes an introduction and notes to each text. Recognizing that the content of Sifrei Zutta is largely conjectural, Horovitz clearly distinguishes his sources: *geniza* fragments, citations indicated by the compiler of Yalkut Shimoni as deriving from Sifrei Zutta, and passages from such documents as Midrash haGadol, which appear to belong in a midrash on Numbers but which are not specifically marked as belonging to Sifrei Zutta. In 1930, J. N. Epstein published another substantial manuscript fragment.

In light of the lack of a complete manuscript, the contents and extent of the original text are unknown. It appears as though Sifrei Zutta, like Sifrei to Numbers, was composed chiefly of an exposition of the legal sections of Numbers, that is, chapters 5–35. Its language is Mishnaic Hebrew but includes numerous Greek words and uses a unique style and terminology. Sifrei Zutta cites rabbis unknown in other documents and also gives laws different from those found in the Mishnah.

Sifrei Zutta appears to have been compiled around the same time as were the Sifra and other Sifrei texts, the late fourth century C.E. On the basis of authorities sited, Epstein held that Sifrei Zutta was compiled in the Galilee; Lieberman, by contrast, found a close connection with rabbis in Lydda. Lieberman additionally held that Sifrei Zutta was earlier than all other legal midrashic compilations.

Sigibert III   Visigoth king of Austasia (r. 632–656). His father, Dagobert, appointed him ruler of Austasia, while giving Neustria and Burgundy to another son, Clovis. In 634 C.E., Heraclius asked him to force the Jews in his realm to be baptized. After Dagobert's death in 639, Sigibert was unable to rule effectively.

sign, miracle as   extraordinary event that points to a larger meaning. The basic meaning of "sign" as a pointer to a more basic reality fits the biblical usage. One of the most common signs in scripture is the complex of acts by which God achieved Israel's liberation from slavery in Egypt in Moses' time. These consist primarily of the contrasting experiences of different peoples, in which the Israelites were given special opportunities while the Egyptians suffered difficulties; for example, the plagues that struck the Egyptians but from which the Israelites were delivered (Exod. 8:23, 10:1–2, 11:9–10). As important as these events were in themselves, they pointed to the more basic factor of Israel's special relationship with God and his unique purpose for them as his covenant people. That theme appears in Exodus 7:3; Deuteronomy 4:24, 6:22, 7:19, 11:3, 26:8, 29:3; Joshua 24:5; Nehemiah 9:10; Psalms 78:43, 105:27, 135:9; Jeremiah 32:20–21; and Baruch 2:11. Other signs, such as the change of Moses' rod into a snake (Exod. 4:8–28) and the coming and disappearance of a skin disease (Exod. 7:9), attest God's choice of leaders. Yet in spite of all these signs, some of the people did not believe God was supporting them (Num. 14:11, 22).

Another variety of sign is the visible symbol of a special relationship: the rainbow as sign of the covenant with Noah (Gen. 9:12–13); circumcision as sign of the covenant with Abraham (Gen. 17:11); blood on the door as the sign of covenant participation (Exod. 12:13); wearing a phylactery as a sign of the covenant (Deut. 6:8, 11:18); taking the stones from the Jordan as a sign of God's deliverance of his people (Josh. 4:1–7); the growth of crops and Hezekiah's recovery from sickness as signs that God will restore Israel (2 Kings 19–20).

Signs are also requested to prove God's present or future support. Gideon's request for a sign that it is God who is leading him results in the consummation by fire of his offering of meat and cakes (Judg. 6). Joel sees signs of the coming Day of the Lord (Joel 2:31). Isaiah sees a sign of God's continuing and renewing purpose for his people in the conception and birth of a child to a young woman (Isa. 7:10–14). Isaiah's condition of being without shoes or clothes is a sign of the judgment God is going to bring on Israel, and the transformation of natural growth on the earth is a sign of its renewal by God (Isa. 20:3, 55:13). In the wisdom tradition, God is asked to provide signs and wonders so that his purpose can be known in advance (Wisd. of Sol. 8:8; Sir. 36:6). In the apocalyptic writings, God sends cosmic signs to warn the wicked and to reassure the faithful remnant of his people.

Talmudic rabbis are ambivalent whether signs, ranging from dreams to unexpected natural occurrences, have symbolic value to indicate the will of God or to predict the future. In nonlegal contexts, signs generally are taken seriously as indicators of divine will or attitude. Thus one who, in Babylonia, dreams of standing naked knows that he or she is without sin (B. Berakhot 57a). Similarly, Mishnah Yoma 6:8 reports on a crimson thread tied to the door of the sanctuary that turned white upon the scapegoat's arrival at the wilderness on the Day of Atonement, signifying God's acceptance of the goat as atonement for the nation's sins.

While accepting such interruptions as meaningful of the natural order, the rabbis rejected God's ability through miracles to indicate the correct law and so to interfere in the processes through which rabbis in their own schools would evaluate and articulate proper practice. This idea is expressed powerfully at B. Baba Metzia 59a, where Eliezer's legal argument is supported by God, who rips a carob tree from its place, causes a stream of water to flow backward, begins to topple the house of study, and finally states explicitly that in all matters the law agrees with Eliezer. God's miraculous intercession is rejected. The law has been given into human hands and through reason alone may be evaluated and applied. Miraculous signs are accepted as indicators of God's will, but so far as the rabbis are concerned, such signs have no determinative force at all.

signs, eschatological extraordinary events on earth and in the cosmos that were believed to signify the nearness of the eschaton. Biblical texts about "the Day of the Lord" or its like offered much material for such speculation: darkness, earthquakes, and cosmic disintegration (Amos 5:18–20; Zeph. 1:7–18; Joel 2:30–31; Isa. 24, 34). Among its descriptions of the end, 1 Enoch refers to war and the disintegration of family loyalties (99:4–5, 100:1–4). 2 Esdras 5:4–13 and 7:39–42 describe the general dissolution of the cosmic order. In Mark 13, Jesus' prediction of events expected to happen at the time of the Temple's destruction includes a range of traditional portents: false prophets and messiahs, persecution, wars, earthquakes and famines, family disintegration, and cosmic dissolution. Only the last of these, which immediately precedes the coming of the son of man, is a true sign, and the chapter in general warns against trusting in signs. This point is underscored in Luke's rewriting of this chapter (Luke 21). Traditional material about eschatological signs plays a major role in the description of the end in Revelation 6 and 8. *See also* ESCHATOLOGY.

Silva, Lucius Flavius governor of Judea, 72/73 C.E. Early in 73 Silva set up his headquarters just northwest of Masada and stationed several smaller camps around the mountain to cut off possible escape routes. He constructed an earthen ramp to bring the troops up to the fortress to destroy it.

Simeon b. Azzai usually simply Ben Azzai, without the honorific Rabbi; an eminent Tannaitic authority active in the late first and early second centuries C.E. Ben Azzai was known for his dedication to his studies (M. Sotah 9:15), which kept him from marriage (B. Ketubot 63a). He is listed as one of the four sages who engaged in mystical speculation ("entered paradise," B. Hagigah 14b), which led to his death. Elsewhere, he is said to have been martyred in the Hadrianic persecutions (Lam. Rabbah 2:2).

Simeon b. Eleazar Tannaitic authority in the second century C.E.; a contemporary of Judah the Patriarch and student of Meir; a resident of Tiberias. He is cited infrequently in the Mishnah, but in the Talmuds, he transmits numerous statements in Meir's name. His name more frequently appears in midrashic compilations.

Simeon b. Gamaliel I grandson of Hillel, president of the Sanhedrin in the decades prior to the destruction of the Jerusalem Temple in 70 C.E., a leader of the First Revolt against Rome. He is referred to by Josephus (*Vita* 38:189–194), who praises his leadership and intelligence and calls him a person of considerable political genius. Two legal opinions of Simeon b. Gamaliel I are preserved, in each of which he shows a concern for the impact of the law on the common people. He ruled that no law involving a public matter should be imposed without the people's concurrence (T. Sanhedrin 2:13), and at a time at which the price of birds for sacrifice went up considerably, he ruled that women obligated to bring five bird offerings need bring only one (M. Keritot 1:7). Mishnah Abot 1:17 quotes his saying: "All my life I grew up among the sages, and I found nothing better for a person than silence; and not the learning is the main thing but the doing; and whoever talks too much causes sin."

Simeon b. Gamaliel II   patriarch in the first half of the second century C.E.; the father of Judah the Patriarch. Following the Bar Kokhba Revolt, he survived the Roman persecution of the patriarchate by concealing himself. At the end of the persecution, he was appointed patriarch at Usha, with Nathan the Babylonian serving as head of the court. His name is associated with hundreds of rules in the Mishnah, Tosefta, and Talmuds.

Simeon b. Ḥalafta   a Tannaitic authority at the end of the second century C.E., at the nexus between Tannaitic and Amoraic authority; a student of Meir. He is known primarily for his scriptural interpretations, and is the subject of numerous stories regarding miracles involving him (e.g., Ruth Rabbah 3:4).

Simeon b. Judah   Tannaitic authority active in the first half of the third century C.E.; the younger son and student of Judah the Patriarch

Simeon b. Lakish   important Palestinian amora, active in the third century C.E.; in the Babylonian Talmud, cited as Resh Lakish. In his youth he participated in gladiatorial contests (Y. Terumot 8:5, 45d). At the academy at Tiberias, Yoḥanan encouraged him to study Torah, and he married Yoḥanan's sister (B. Baba Metzia 84a).

Simeon b. Manasiah   Tannaitic authority of the late second and early third centuries C.E.; a contemporary of Judah the Patriarch; cited primarily in the Talmuds (cf. M. Ḥagigah 1:7)

Simeon b. Nanas   Tannaitic authority active at the beginning of the second century C.E.; a contemporary of Akiba; usually referred to simply as Ben Nanas.

Simeon b. Nathanael   Tannaitic authority of the second half of the first century C.E.; a student of Yoḥanan b. Zakkai (M. Abot 2:8). A priest, he married the daughter of Gamaliel I (T. Abodah Zarah 3:19). Few of his sayings are preserved.

Simeon b. Pazzi   Palestinian amora of the second half of the third century C.E.; infrequently cited in the Talmuds, but better known in midrashic documents

Simeon b. Shetaḥ   prominent Pharisaic scholar of the first century B.C.E., active during the reigns of Alexander Yannai and Salome Alexandra, who was Simeon's sister (B. Berakhot 48a). Mishnah Abot 1:8 lists him along with Judah b. Tabbai as a pair. At Tosefta Ḥagigah 2:8, the later Tannaitic authority Judah holds that Simeon was patriarch and Judah b. Tabbai was *ab beit din*.

Apparently as a result of Simeon's relationship with the queen, he was able to effect a reconciliation between Yannai and the Pharisees, whom Yannai previously had persecuted and exiled. Simeon accordingly is recalled for having restored the Torah to its former glory (B. Kiddushin 66a). With the Pharisees' return to power, the Sadducees lost their leading position in the Sanhedrin.

Among his many legal rulings, Simeon b. Shetaḥ is known for reducing the number of divorces by ruling that all of a man's property is subject to seizure for payment of his wife's marriage contract (*ketubah*). Additionally, in a period in which education still was seen as the obligation of the father, he is remembered for ordering the establishment of communal schools.

Simeon b. Tarfon   Tannaitic authority who was active at the end of the first and beginning of the second centuries C.E. He is known exclusively through four exegetical comments, all found at B. Shebuot 47b.

Simeon b. Yehosadak   Palestinian amora of the first half of the third century C.E.; of a priestly family; the teacher of Yoḥanan; generally referred to simply as Simeon

Simeon b. Yoḥai   important Tannaitic authority active in the mid-second century C.E., in the Mishnah always referred to simply as Simeon, without the patronymic. Ordained by Judah b. Baba, he was one of the five students of Akiba who revived rabbinic learning after the failed Bar Kokhba Revolt (B. Yebamot 62b). Later tradition assigns to him authorship of all anonymous statements in Sifra (B. Sanhedrin 86a) as well as of the Zohar, such that he is a central figure in mystical lore.

During the Hadrianic persecutions that followed the Bar Kokhba Revolt, Simeon fiercely opposed Roman rule and culture. B. Shabbat 33b reports that, as a result of derogatory statements against the Roman people, he was sentenced to death and was forced to flee with his son to a cave, in which they hid for twelve years. Whether or not Simeon subsequently participated in rabbinic leadership at Usha is unclear (see B. Berakhot 63b and Song Rabbah 2:5).

Along with his many legal dicta recorded in the

Mishnah, Simeon is known for his homiletical remarks. Among these are his statement that the messiah will come after the Jews correctly observe two sabbaths (B. Shabbat 118b) and his comment that one who breaks off from study to observe a tree or natural phenomenon deserves death (M. Abot 3:7).

Simeon b. Yose b. Lakoniah Tannaitic authority; a contemporary of Judah the Patriarch (late 2d c. C.E.); the brother-in-law of Eleazar b. Simeon, whose son he instructed. He is known through a small number of legal and exegetical statements preserved in the Talmuds and midrashic compilations.

Simeon b. Zoma Tannaitic authority of the second century C.E., known as the last of the authoritative interpreters of the Bible (M. Sotah 9:15); generally referred to simply as Ben Zoma. He is known for the proverb: "Who is a sage? He who learns from everybody. . . . Who is strong? He who overcomes his desire. . . . Who is rich? He who is happy in what he has. . . ." (M. Abot 4:1). Ben Zoma engaged in mystical speculation (T. Ḥagigah 2:5), and the Talmud lists him as one of the four who, as an aspect of their mystical study, "entered paradise" (Y. Ḥagigah 2:1, 77b).

Simeon haPakoli Tannaitic authority of the late first and early second century C.E.; mentioned only once in rabbinic sources. B. Berakhot 28b holds that in the presence of Gamaliel II, at Yabneh, he determined the organization of the Eighteen Benedictions.

Simeon Hatimni a Tannaitic rabbi from the generation of Yabneh. He was a contemporary of Akiba and Judah b. Baba, and is cited in the Mishnah and Midrash.

Simeon of Shikmonah Tannaitic authority; a student of Akiba; from a town in the area of Mount Carmel. Three exegetical comments of his are preserved in Sifrei Numbers.

Simeon of Timna Tannaitic authority and member of the Sanhedrin in the second century C.E.; from a town near Bet Shemesh. In Tannaitic texts, he holds discussions with Akiba and Joshua; later tradition held that he knew "seventy languages" (B. Sanhedrin 17b), denoting a special status within the members of the court.

Simeon the Just high priest at the time of Alexander the Great; referred to by Josephus as Simeon I, son of Onias I (*Ant.* 12:157; cf. Y. Yoma 6:3, 43c–d, and B. Menaḥot 109b, which hold he was the father of Onias I). He is mentioned at M. Abot 1:2 as one of the last survivors of the Great Assembly. He is credited with the statement: "On three things does the world stand: on the Torah, and on the Temple service, and on deeds of loving kindness."

simḥah (Heb.) celebration

Simḥat Torah (Heb., rejoicing over the Torah, rejoicing of law) **1.** the second day of Shemini Atzeret, following Tabernacles, on which the Torah-reading cycle is completed; celebrated with song and dance

2. the completion of the cycle of reading the Pentateuch in the synagogue

Simlai b. Abba Palestinian amora of the third century C.E., from Nehardea; later active first in Lydda, and then with Yannai in Sepphoris. His statements are transmitted by Tanḥum b. Ḥiyya.

Simon slave of Herod the Great in Perea, who claimed kingship and led a band of brigands after Herod's death in 4 B.C.E. He was one of a series of royal pretenders. He plundered and destroyed the palace in Jericho and other royal residences. He was pursued and killed by Roman infantry.

Simon, son of Boethus Alexandrian priest appointed high priest by Herod the Great in 24 B.C.E. so that the latter could marry Simon's daughter, Mariamme, as his third wife. Simon was removed from the high priesthood in 5 B.C.E., when Mariamme was discovered plotting with her stepson Antipater over the succession to Herod's throne.

Simon, son of Mattathias Maccabean leader; the second son of the priest Mattathias of Modein. He succeeded his brothers Judas and Jonathan, and served as leader in Israel from 142 to 134 B.C.E. His exploits are described chiefly in 1 Maccabees 13:31–16:22 and Josephus's *Antiquities* 13.213–29. According to 1 Maccabees 13:42, Simon (surnamed Thassi) combined in his own person the religious ("the great high priest"), military ("commander"), and political ("leader of the Jews") leadership. Simon captured the citadel at Jerusalem (the Akra), renewed diplomatic relations with the Romans and Spartans, achieved further stability and independence for his people (against the background of Seleucid instability), and won military victories over the forces of Trypho and Antiochus VII. He (or his brother Jonathan) may have been the "Wicked Priest" who is criticized in some Qumran scrolls. His benefactions on Israel's behalf are recounted in an "official" decree presented in 1 Maccabees 14:27–45. In 134 B.C.E., Simon was killed at a banquet at the stronghold of Dok, near Jericho, by his son-in-law Ptolemy, the son of Abubus. He was survived and succeeded by his son John Hyrcanus I. Though Simon stressed the traditional values of the Maccabean movement, he was also open to Hellenistic and other foreign influences.

Simona Saboraic authority; head of the academy at Pumbedita; a contemporary of Eina, head of the academy at Sura. According to Seder Tannaim veAmoraim, these individuals mark the end of the Saboraic period.

Simon bar Giora a native of Gerasa whose patronymic means "son of a proselyte." At the beginning of the war against Rome in 66–70 C.E., he led armed forces against the Romans. He then gathered a group of revolutionaries and raided the toparchy of Acraba (between Jerusalem and Shechem) until routed by the forces of the high priest Ananus. He then joined the Sicarii occupying Masada for a time, but soon withdrew into the hills where he could take a more active role in the war (68 C.E.). He was physically powerful and daring and attracted a large number of followers. He over-ran southern Judea and Idumea, where he collected a wealth of supplies in preparation for an attack on Jerusalem. After an indecisive battle with the Zealots, he destroyed many towns in Idumea and then again threatened Jerusalem. In the spring of 69, the Idumeans, the high priest Matthias, and the people invited Simon and his forces into Jerusalem as a counterforce to John of Gischala and his Zealots, who ruled the city by terror. Simon quickly dominated the Upper City and a large part of the Lower City and became its most powerful leader. Nevertheless, civil war within the city between Simon and John continued to the detriment of the population.

When Titus besieged Jerusalem in the spring of 70, Simon's forces defended the Upper City. After the Romans captured and burned the Antonia Fortress and Temple Mount in August, they attacked and occupied the Upper City in September. Simon and some of his followers took miners into the underground passages in the hope of tunneling out of the city. When his supplies ran out, however, he had to emerge and was captured. As the senior commander in Jerusalem, Simon was taken to Rome, displayed in Vespasian's and Titus's triumphal procession, and then executed.

Simon Magus Samaritan magician and convert to Christianity who tried to buy an apostleship (Acts 8). No further reference is made to him until Justin Martyr, well into the second century C.E., by which time he is alleged to be the author of a Gnostic system. The connection between Simon, Samaritanism, and Gnosticism is still debated.

Simon the Essene according to Josephus, a skilled interpreter of dreams, as were other Essenes. In 6 C.E. he interpreted Archelaus's dream of ten ears of wheat being eaten by oxen as a prediction that Archelaus's rule would soon end, as it did.

sin a moral or ritual offense against God. Up to fifty Hebrew words are used for various types of sins in hundreds of cases. Though modern Western thought limits sin to intentional moral infractions, in antiquity a wide variety of unintentional infractions against divinely sanctioned norms were considered sins. The awareness of sinfulness that permeates the Bible and later Jewish literature testifies to the complexity of maintaining a proper relationship to the divine ritually, morally and in purity matters.

The most common root from which words for sin, guilt, punishment, and sin-offerings are derived is *ḥt'*, which, like the Greek *hamartia*, means "to miss, be in error, be deficient," and is used with a wide range of meaning. Another root, *psh'*, means "rebellion" or "transgression" and is used for deliberate sin. A third term, *awon*, meaning "iniquity" and then "guilt, punishment," is almost always used of moral guilt in relation to God. In addition numerous terms describe sinners, for example, committers of "wicked" and specific sins.

In Second Temple Judaism, biblical usage continues. In addition, the term "sinner" is often used to designate Gentiles (Jub. 23:23) and Jews who do not keep the law or assimilate to the ruling empire (1 Macc. 1:34, 2:44; Pss. Sol. 1ff.). Jewish reformist groups often called opponents who disagreed with their way of life and interpretations of the law sinners (1 Enoch 82:4; 1 QS 5:7–11). Many writings, especially apocalyptic works, have an intense sense of sin and of the corruption of humanity, a condition that can be only corrected by divine intervention and the final destruction of the wicked. The Gospels and other New Testament writings see sin as an endemic problem, which requires divine intervention through Jesus and his death. The Qumran Community sees two spirits, one of good and one of evil, at work in humans, and exhorts its members to repent and live according to the covenant, in contrast to the men of falsehood, who walk in the way of wickedness. Paul envisions sin as a transcendent, enslaving power, from which Jesus gives freedom. Early sections of 1 Enoch trace human sin to its cosmic origins in the fall of the angels who corrupted humans.

These judgments of sinfulness within the Jewish and gentile worlds are combined with a strong exhortation to repentance and reform based on an accurate understanding of the covenant and law that enshrine God's will. In some works, such as the Testaments of the Twelve Patriarchs, the influence of Hellenistic groups of virtues and vices may be seen in lengthy exhortations to good behavior and against wickness. In others, such as the Dead Sea Scrolls, the biblical notions of holiness and purity retain their importance. Works from the diaspora often contrast the sins of the Gentiles with the righteousness of a faithful Israel (Jos. As.; Wisd. of Sol.).

In rabbinic Judaism, sin refers to an act that violates the stipulations of the covenant with God, set out in rabbinic law. To refer to sin, the rabbinic literature most commonly uses the term *averah*, from a root meaning "to pass over." This term closely parallels the idea of transgression of God's will, and rabbinic interpretation plays upon its relationship to the concepts of passing forth or making public. B. Sotah 3a states that, although a person might sin in private, God will make the matter known in public.

The rabbinic literature distinguishes sins of omission, in which the individual fails to do what he should, from sins of commission, in which he does that which is expressly prohibited. Sins of commission generally are considered more serious, since they involve a conscious act on the part of the individual. The most severe sins are murder, idolatry, and sexual impropriety. These are the only sins that one must not commit even under duress, when the alternative is being killed (B. Sanhedrin 74a).

The rabbis hold that people have an inclination to engage in wrong actions. This inclination, the *yetzer haRa* (see Gen. 8:21), is recognized as an aspect of the human condition, a temptation to which all people are subject. This inclination is not, however, equivalent to the Christian concept of original sin. According to rabbinic Judaism, people do not have an inherited, corrupt nature; rather, they are subject to temptation, a heinous force that must constantly be fought. While the rabbis are clear that the reason for the existence of death is Adam's sin and that all people thus suffer for that first misdeed, the proximate cause of one's death is one's own actions. Death was instituted with Adam, but one dies as a consequence of one's own sins (Tanhuma Bereshit 29; Tanhuma Ḥukkat 39).

One consequence of sin is its growing power over the sinner, leading one who at first commits a minor infraction to greater and greater offenses, culminating with idolatry (B. Shabbat 105b). Committing one transgression inevitably leads to committing another, just as performance of one religious duty leads to the performance of another (M. Abot 4:2). While at first sin may be called a passerby, it later is

viewed as a guest and, finally, as a member of the household (B. Sukkah 52b).

Though rabbinic authorities see the temptation toward sin as a force that must consistently be fought, some recognize in this temptation one of life's motivating powers. Babylonian Talmud Yoma 69b relates that, when the men of the great synagogue succeeded in capturing the *yetzer haRa* for three days, they discovered that during that time no productive activity took place. Similarly, Genesis Rabbah 9:7 states that were it not for the *yetzer haRa*, people would not be motivated to engage in business, marry, raise a family, or construct a house. This view seems to hold that human productivity is a positive result of people's need constantly to rise above their tendency towards evil. This is accomplished through recognizing the ever-present eyes and ears of God (M. Abot 2:1) and, above all, through study of Torah and practice of the law (B. Sotah 21a). The rabbis hold that knowledge of Torah is the single greatest antidote against the temptation to sin. This idea is made concrete in the belief that upon a person's entry into a house of study, the inclination to sin dissipates completely (B. Kiddushin 30b). *See also* RIGHTEOUSNESS; SINNERS; TEMPTATION.

Sinai, Mount a mountain that today is commonly thought to be the Mountain of God. In fact, the biblical mountain is sacred space, and it may not be possible to locate it in the real world. Nevertheless, Sinai is accorded a physical location in the biblical text. It is a wilderness (Exod. 19:1, 2a) located in some proximity to the wilderness of sin (Exod. 16:1). *See also* HOREB, MOUNT.

Sinai Pericope the segment of the Pentateuch in which there is a theophony and in which the Deity concludes a conditional covenant with the sons of Israel. The Sinai Pericope extends from Exodus 19:2b through Numbers 10:11. The entire Sinai Pericope is paralleled, but not duplicated by the D segment of Deuteronomy, in which the sacred mountain is Horeb, rather than Sinai.

sinners (Gr: *hamartōloi*) a generic designation for persons whose way of life places them outside the covenant or the realm of God's blessing and salvation. Psalms of Solomon 3 offers a classical description of the sinner in contrast to the righteous. The latter attends to his or her relationship with God, making amends for sins committed through ignorance. The sinner, who has no concern about this relationship, allows sins to pile up. The respective fates are eternal life and destruction. A similar contrast between the righteous and sinners, also called "unjust" (Gr.: *adikoi*) and "lawless" (Gr.: *anomoi*), appears in 1 Enoch 92–105, where the author's opponents both oppress the righteous and adhere to wrong interpretations of the Torah. Yet another meaning of "sinner" applies generically to Gentiles, who have no access to the Torah and who oppose Israel (Ps. Sol. 2:1, of Pompey).

The Gospels, especially Luke, regularly depict Jesus as a friend and companion of "sinners" and as the object of criticism from the righteous, notably the Pharisees and scribes. Paul believes that all humanity stands under God's indictment and thus applies the term "sinner" to both Jews and Gentiles (Rom. 5:8). The more restricted use with reference to Gentiles appears in Galatians 2:15 but is immediately undercut in verse 17.

sin-offering an offering of either a bull or a goat for expiation of and purification from sin. It is also offered for purification even when no sin is being expiated. It must be the first sacrifice offered and the priest must eat it in the Temple on the day that it is offered. The purificatory nature of the offering is addressed in the Babylonian Talmud, where one who has given birth must bring a sin-offering. The Temple Scroll and the Mishnah are in disagreement about which animal is to be sacrificed for purification from sin vis-à-vis purification without any implication of sin.

Sirach, Wisdom of a collection of proverbial sayings and didactic essays from a single author, Joshua ben Sira, writing about 180 B.C.E., probably in Jerusalem. The book consists of fifty-one chapters (and a prologue composed by Ben Sira's grandson in Egypt, the translator of the work from Hebrew into Greek). Sirach has survived in two major Greek manuscript traditions, although large portions of the book also exist in Hebrew. Two themes run through the teachings from first to last, the fear of God and the Torah, which is specifically identified with the earlier Mosaic legislation.

Sirach marks a decisive transition within wisdom literature, the move to identify wisdom as Torah and to incorporate sacred Yahwistic narrative into the wisdom corpus. It does the latter in two ways: first, by frequent reference and allusion to events narrated in Israelite historiography; and second, by introducing a special section on national heroes, "Now let us praise famous men." Sirach also carries one step further the tendency in the latest collection of Proverbs, 1–9, to discuss topics at some length; the second century work has extensive treatments of themes like shame, honor, daughters, vocations, begging, and death.

Priestly interests permeate the book, concluding with an elaborate description of the contemporary high priest, Simon, as he celebrated a holy day at the Temple in Jerusalem. Sirach urged the Jewish people to support their priests and expressed complete faith in the sacred dice, Urim and Thummim (Exod. 28:30; Lev. 8:8). Like later Sadducees, Ben Sira dismissed the notion of life after death and treated the subject with humor: "Mine today, yours tomorrow." He distinguished, however, between a normal death and an unwelcome one brought on by difficult circumstances.

Although Hellenistic influence has been suspected in Sirach, the evidence is not strong. It uses the epithet, "He is the all," and Greek arguments for divine justice, namely that God punishes evil persons by psychic distress and that the universe reinforces good but combats wickedness. The praise of famous men resembles encomiastic literature somewhat, although decisive differences exist.

Sirach depicts the sages at worship. Only one prayer occurs in Proverbs (30:7–9), none in Job unless self-imprecations count. Ben Sira mentions prayer often, actually including two substantial prayers in his book, one in each half (22:27–23:6 and 36:1–17). The final chapter comprises a thanksgiving hymn (51:1–12) and an invitation to enroll in his academy (51:23–30). Ben Sira abandoned the old idea that people earned what came their way; now they must rely on divine compassion. He also departed from earlier universalism, opting for nationalistic fervor.

Misogynistic ideas are prevalent in the book, whether caustic descriptions of daughters' conduct or the attribution of evil's origin to Eve. Ambiguous views about physicians stand alongside one another, the defense of their trade as well as a relic of the notion that sickness is punishment for sin. Rhetorical devices, particularly refrains, mark the teachings, as do occasional poetic images of exceptional power ("Like a wedge between stones, greed lies between buying and selling"). Polemic against sectarian mysteries warns of unbridled thoughts, noting that even wisdom, like her name, withholds her insights, despite an elaborate presentation of personified wisdom descending from God's presence to reside in Jerusalem as the Law of Moses.

Sivan ninth month of the Jewish calendar, corresponding to May/June

Skepticism philosophical system arising out of Platonism that flourished from the third century B.C.E. to the third century C.E. It was characterized by logical skepticism about the possibility of certainty in knowledge. One of its goals was *ataraxia* (calmness of mind). Most members of this school argued that one should suspend judgment and refuse dogma. However, it also became clear that absolute skepticism was impractical, and the philosopher Carneades developed a theory of probability that made it possible to conduct ordinary and intellectual life without abandoning the doubts about certainty.

S.L.   *see* DE SPECIALIBUS LEGIBUS

slaughter, rules of   *see* KOSHER

slavery   From the second millennium B.C.E. to the first millennium C.E., slavery and other types of forced labor were common throughout the Mediterranean world. Ancient Judaism was no exception. From Abraham to David and successive kings, from the Temple cult to the returnees from the Babylonian exile, ancient Israelites kept slaves. Jews living outside the Land of Israel also held slaves; legal documents from the third century B.C.E. to the third century C.E. found in Egypt, Greece, Asia Minor, and Italy indicate that Jews in these regions owned slaves. Furthermore, the late Roman Empire explicitly regulated the ability of Jews to own slaves, especially Christian slaves. While this evidence consistently points to the practice of slave-holding among ancient Jewry, it does not indicate that any Jewish society ever became dependent on slave labor. Unlike societies such as Sparta or Egypt, slavery never shaped the economic practices or social structure of Jewish society. The few times when the number of slaves increased—as under Nehemiah (Neh. 5:1–13)—it met strong opposition from the authorities. Slave-holding was sanctioned and practiced, but slaves never became a major source of labor.

In the millennium and a half before the rise of Islam, Jews often discussed regulations concerning slaves and their proper treatment. The Pentateuch alone contains three sets of laws concerning slaves, while several important rabbinic texts contain legal and theological discussions of slavery. Despite this wealth of material, little knowledge exists about Jewish practices of slavery. On the one hand, scholars possess little evidence revealing whether or not Jewish slavery laws were practiced. On the other hand, where scholars have found evidence of Jewish slave-holding, there is little to indicate any specifically Jewish practices. This leaves modern scholarship unable to describe any distinctively Jewish slave-holding practices. The only distinctively Jewish aspects of slavery appear in the legal discussions and rulings.

The history of Jewish legal and theological thought concerning slavery follows one main track:

the systematization of the pentateuchal laws about slavery. This approach to the Pentateuch's slavery rules begins within the Pentateuch itself. It is picked up in the rabbinic period in the commentary to Exodus—the Mekhilta of Rabbi Ishmael—and the Talmuds. Only one Jewish document provides a scheme of slavery that ignores this systematization process—the Mishnah.

The Pentateuch contains three different sets of regulations concerning slaves, and some isolated, individual rules. The first set of laws, Exodus 21:1–11, refers to two different types of slaves, a male Hebrew slave and a female Hebrew slave. The male slave is an indentured servant, who serves six years. During his servitude, his master may provide him with a slave-wife. At the end of his enslavement, he may choose to become a permanent slave through a rite of ear piercing. The female slave, by contrast, serves as a concubine or wife for the master or his son. She remains permanently enslaved unless her master mistreats or rejects her.

The second passage, Deuteronomy 15:12–18, develops from the one in Exodus. It essentially joins the male and female slaves into one category, that of the six-year indentured servant. The concubine/marriage role of the female slave has been eliminated, as has the master's ability to provide the male slave with a wife. Both male and female may choose to become permanent slaves by having their ears pierced. But if the male slave chooses to leave after six years, his Jewish master is directed to provide him with livestock and other resources to begin an independent life.

Leviticus 25:39–46, the third pentateuchal passage concerning Jewish slavery, describes different kinds of slaves. As in the other passages, the Hebrew slave essentially corresponds to an indentured servant, but here he or she must serve until the Jubilee year, which comes once every fifty years. This passage also describes non-Hebrew slaves, who possess the status of mere chattel. As property, they may be bought, sold, or willed to their owner's heirs. While the passage emphasizes that Hebrew slaves should not be treated in a disrespectful manner, no such strictures protect the non-Hebrew slave.

The Covenant Code in Exodus contains a few individual laws about slaves. One of these, Exodus 21:26–27, rules that the master who puts out a male or female slave's eye or tooth must free the slave. Another, Exodus 22:1–4, states that any thief (presumably an Israelite) who cannot pay restitution shall be sold as a slave.

While modern scholarship treats these different sets of laws as independent, the authors of most rabbinic texts understood the laws to comprise a single, integrated system of slavery. The most elaborate depiction of this system appears in the Mekhilta of Rabbi Ishmael (Nezikin) and the Babylonian Talmud (Kiddushin 14b–25b), although the Tosefta and the Palestinian Talmud have similar portrayals. At the most fundamental level, these documents distinguish between Hebrew slaves and Canaanite (i.e., non-Hebrew) slaves. The Mekhilta and the Babli further subdivide male Hebrew slaves into those who were sold by the court for committing theft and those who sold themselves out of poverty. The slaves in the former category served for only six years. During their enslavement, they could be given Canaanite slave women as wives. When these male slaves went free, their masters were required to provide them with the means for starting their free life. Although these slaves could choose to become permanent slaves by having their ears pierced, the authors of the two texts redefined "permanent" as the time until the next Jubilee year. By contrast, those who sold themselves served until the Jubilee but could not agree to become permanent slaves. Their masters were not permitted to give them wives and were not required to support the freed slaves at manumission.

According to the Mekhilta and the Babli, Jewish females could become slaves only if, as minors, they were sold by their fathers for the purpose of marriage (not concubinage). They could not sell themselves or be sold by the court. They became free at puberty if they had not already been redeemed or espoused to the master or his son. The Babli and the Mekhilta classed Canaanite slaves of Jews as property; they could be bought and sold and passed on to their owner's heirs at the owner's death. Apart from their master deciding to manumit them, Canaanite slaves could attain freedom only if the master accidentally or intentionally caused them to loose a major organ, such as an eye or a tooth. This route to freedom, according to the Mekhilta and the Babli, was closed to Hebrew slaves.

The Mishnah constitutes the only rabbinic text with a system of slavery that ignores these biblically based categories of slavery. Of the Mishnah's 129 passages concerning slaves, 123 of them work out a system of slavery independent of the pentateuchal passages, and only six use the Pentateuch's categories. The Mishnah's main system ignores the slave's ethnic background. Anyone who became a slave lost all legal recognition of his or her ethnicity and became a chattel slave. Release from slavery—which was possible but never required—placed the slave into the category of freed slave; it did not return the slave to his or her former Israelite status, as was the case in the Pentateuch-based systems. While enslaved, these slaves were defined as mere property. Although they worked for the master, he was responsible for their actions only when they carried out his specific instructions. The Mishnah's scheme was not carried forward into later rabbinic texts. The Tosefta—the earliest text based on the Mishnah—essentially ignored the Mishnah's system of slavery; its authors began to reinterpret the Mishnah's slavery passages as part of the pentateuchal scheme of Hebrew and Canaanite slaves.

sleep a metaphor for death, but also for lack of knowledge and moral alertness. The natural image of sleep for death occurs in Job 3:13, 14:12, and Jeremiah 51:39 and 57. Daniel 12:2 describes resurrection as awakening from sleep in the land of dust (Sheol). 1 Enoch 100:5 employs an expression attested in Classical Greek literature (Homer, *Od.* 1:364) as an image for death. The protected, untroubled rest of the pious is likened to sleeping "a sweet sleep."

In a totally different usage, though also with reference to the eschaton, a number of New Testament texts liken unpreparedness, moral laziness, and carelessness to sleep (Matt. 25:5; cf. 26:36–46; 1 Thess. 5:5–10; Rev. 3:3). The image has roots in the Hebrew Bible (Isa. 56:10–11; Ezek. 33:7). In Gnostic texts, sleep and drunkenness are images for the human condition and its lack of the knowledge necessary for salvation.

snake a minor motif in Jewish art, primarily of the Roman and Byzantine periods. Snakes are not depicted very realistically, so it is impossible to come to any conclusions about their species. A possible snake's head appears in the earlier mosaic floor at Beth Alpha. In the synagogue art of the Golan Heights, one sees eagles with snakes in their beaks. These are now understood to be Harrier eagles, which have been observed attacking snakes in the Golan Heights. For example, on the lintel stone of the School of Rabbi Eliezer ha-Kappar at Dabura there appear two snakes whose bodies become ribbons at the end of the central wreath. Their heads are in the beaks of the eagles. On the other hand, the snake or winged serpent is well known on Jewish amulets, particularly in forms evidently borrowed directly from Graeco-Roman magical practices. This borrowing is particularly clear in the case of the chicken-headed god with the body of a man and two snakes for legs. Finally there is the snake or two snakes entwined around the winged staff, called the caduceus. The caduceus is associated the Hermes and Asklepios in Greek mythology, but it appears on Jewish coins, namely, on coins of Herod the Great and on city coins of Sepphoris during the reign of the emperor Trajan. In these cases it appears that the Jewish ruler and the Jewish city of Sepphoris chose a symbol from the repertoire of those representing Roman authority.

Sobr.   *see* DE SOBRIETATE

Sodom and Gomorrah   From the destruction of their wicked populations because of their general evil and sin as well as their treatment of Lot, his family, and his visitors (Gen. 18:20–32, 19:1–29), Sodom and Gomorrah are evoked in warnings against sin (Deut. 29:23; Amos 4:11; Isa. 1:9–10 [cited in rom. 9:29]; Jer. 49:18; Sir. 16:8; Test. Abr. 6:13; 3 Macc. 2:5; Matt. 10:15; Luke 10:12; 2 Pet. 2:6; Rev. 19, 20; Greek Apoc. Ezra 7, etc.), violations of hospitality customs, lack of reason, and, particularly, sexual crimes (Jub. 13, 16, 22; Jude 7, etc.). According to the Martyrdom of Isaiah 3:10, under King Manasseh Jerusalem was like Sodom and its princes like the people of Gomorrah.

Rabbinic writings attribute the destruction of Sodom and Gomorrah to their citizens' failure to care for the poor or, alternatively, to share their possessions (M. Abot 5:10). While, for twenty-two years, God warned the cities of their impending doom, the citizens did not repent. These people have no share in the world to come (M. Sanhedrin 10:31). The rabbis compare the sins of the Israelites that led to the destruction of Jerusalem to those of Sodom and argue that, despite the fact that Jerusalem was left standing, God had punished the two cities equally (B. Sanhedrin 104b).

Soferim, Massekhet   (Scribes) a minor talmudic tractate covering the rules for the copying of holy books and the regulations for the public reading of scripture. The tractate appears to derive from about the mid-eighth century C.E. It lacks a consistent topical organization. The presence of considerable material of concern to leaders of prayer and not to scribes suggests that it has been substantially altered by later interpolations.

Three main topical divisions of the tractate can be discerned. Chapters 1–5 concern the rules for copying Torah scrolls, including a discussion of the materials to be used, a determination of who is fit to perform the task, and rules for the spacing of letters, lines and columns, and for rolling and unrolling a scroll in liturgical use. These discussions are the earliest in the tractate and appear separately as an independent minor tractate enti-

tled Sefer Torah. Chapters 6–9 provide Masoretic rules, including discussion of Masoretic textual and orthographic variants and the use of capital letters and other special markings. Chapters 10–21 are of less uniform composition and appear to derive from a later period. This is the case especially for chapters 16–21, which contain passages from the Babylonian Talmud. Chapters 10 through 15 include regulations for the public reading of the Torah and for other liturgical functions, defining the requisite number of persons who must be present, indicating the order of the reading and the method for correcting errors made by the reader, and listing rules for the reading of specific passages, for example, the Decalogue. Chapters 13–15 concern the copying and reading of the hagiographa and the Scroll of Esther. Chapters 16–21 conclude the tractate with a variety of rules for specific liturgical circumstances, such as the psalms for festivals and the order of prayers for the anniversary of the destruction of Jerusalem.

sojourner   (Heb.: *ger toshav;* Gr.: *paroikos* or, in Septuagint, *proselytos*) resident alien or person having no tribal or ethnic connection to the population with whom the person lives. The sojourner has both specific legal responsibilities to (Exod. 12:49; Num. 15:16) and special protection within the covenant community. This benevolence springs partially from Israel's own experience (Exod. 22:21, 23:9; Lev. 19:33–34; Deut. 10:19) and in part from the association of the sojourner with those needing special support, such as widows (Deut. 16:11–12). According to Ephesians 2:19, those within the "household of God" are no longer sojourners but fellow citizens. For 1 Peter, the Christian is a sojourner among and alien to those who are part of the present social structure (2:11).

The category of resident alien is not significant within rabbinic law, which instead provides considerable legislation controlling Jewish interaction with the non-Jews who lived in close physical and economic relationship to the Jewish community but who did not exist as part of that community.

solar calendar   *see* CALENDAR

Solomon   son of David and third king of Israel; ruled for about forty years in the mid-tenth century B.C.E. He organized the royal court and administration, built the Temple, engaged in large building programs, established widespread international relations, and built up international trade (1 Kings 1–11). The Bible blames his many political marriages for the split of the kingdom after his death, but in fact the northern tribes threw off what they saw as the oppressive rule of the Davidic dynasty.

Because Solomon needed large numbers of wise men to carry on his affairs, he probably established scribal schools. The Bible attributes to him various sorts of wisdom: administrative skill, encyclopedic knowledge, mastery of proverbs, and the ability to solve riddles. Tradition concentrates primarily on such wisdom. Several later sources attribute to him extensive knowledge of demons and even describe him as an exorcist (Josephus, *Ant.* 8.2.5, secs. 42–49; Test. Sol.). Josephus also sees him as a solver of riddles (*Ant.* 8.5.2, secs. 148–49). Several sapiential works are ascribed to Solomon: sections of Proverbs (1:1, 10:1, 25:1), the Wisdom of Solomon, Ecclesiates (also called Kohelet). The Song of Songs is attributed to him, perhaps because of his reputation for composing songs. It is unclear why the Psalms of Solomon bear his name. The New Testament remembers Solomon's glory (Matt. 6:29) and his wisdom (Matt. 12:42).

Treating Solomon extensively, the rabbinic literature takes up the biblical theme of his wisdom. While viewing Solomon positively for this trait, it ultimately sees him as an example of a person whose rationality leads to sin. Solomon thus substantiates the rabbinic notion that strict adherence to the law is the only assurance of piety. Solomon, by contrast, believed that because of his wisdom he would not be induced to sin. He therefore felt free to transgress biblical commandments, including the ones against marrying many wives and amassing horses and wealth (Deut. 17:16–17; B. Sanhedrin 21a).

The result was devastating. Solomon's marriage to the daughter of Pharaoh caused the building of the city of Rome, in the rabbis' day the great oppressor of the Jews. This happened because, after the wedding, the angel Gabriel stuck a reed in the sea; around it a sand bank formed, on which Rome was later built. Additionally, Pharaoh's daughter led Solomon to worship idols and, by making him sleep late in the morning, caused him to prevent the offering of the daily sacrifice, which could not be performed since Solomon had the Temple keys under his pillow (Lev. Rabbah 12:5).

The result of Solomon's sins was the loss of his throne, his wealth, and even his wisdom. While at first he had ruled over the creatures of the upper world, he later ruled over the creatures of the lower world. Next he ruled only over Israel and, yet later, over Jerusalem alone. By the end of his life, he ruled only over his own house and, finally, over only his staff or, alternatively, his pitcher (Song of Songs Rabbah 1:10). Traveling as

a beggar in atonement for his sins, he wrote Ecclesiastes, which refers to his previous life as king of Israel. This work is contrasted with his other compositions: Song of Songs, written in his youth, and Proverbs, written in his middle age (Song of Songs Rabbah 1:10). Had it not been for Solomon's construction of the Temple, which he made more elegant than his own palace and which he had completed in about half the time, he would have been listed among the sinful kings of Israel (Song of Songs Rabbah 1:5; B. Sanhedrin 104b).

Solomon, Odes of a pseudonymous collection of forty-two odes—short lyric poems or hymns—written in Syriac or Greek by a Christian author or authors, probably in Syria in the late first or the second century C.E. The Odes are sometimes called the earliest extant Christian hymnbook. In the modern period, they were known only by title and a few short excerpts until 1909, when a fifteenth-century Syriac manuscript of Odes 3–42 was discovered. Since then, another partial Syriac manuscript of the tenth century with Odes 17–42, a fourth-century Coptic manuscript containing Odes 1, 5, 6, 22, and 25, and a third-century Greek manuscript with Ode 11 have all come to light. Ode 2—and possibly portions of Odes 1 and 3—are still lost.

The Odes are generally similar in content and form to the biblical Psalms. The author (or authors) of the Odes typically expresses praise of and thanksgiving to "the Lord" for the spiritual benefits that the Lord has bestowed on the author. These benefits are expressed in terms of "joy," "rest," "salvation," "eternal life," "immortality," and "incorruption." The author feels that the Lord has manifested to the author a special love, sometimes expressed as the Lord's dwelling or growing within the author. Like the biblical Psalms, the Odes frequently cite God's power to vanquish the author's personal enemies.

The Odes often refer to the earthly career of the redeemer, Jesus. The author often puts the redeemer's words in the first person, and sometimes the "I" of the author slips almost indistinguishably into the "I" of the redeemer.

Although many scholars have asserted that the Odes contain various ideas and motifs that are characteristic of Gnosticism (see especially Odes 23, 24, 32, 33, 38, 39, and 41), they certainly do not evince a fully developed Gnosticism. However, they do seem to stem from an ideological milieu in which both "Gnostic" and more "mainstream" Christian concepts are expressed together as part of a coherent thought system. In this respect the Odes resemble the Gospel of John.

The main purpose of the Odes seems to be to exhort and inspire their audience. While it is sometimes theorized that the Odes originated in a prophetic milieu, others hold that they derive from a baptismal context. In all, the Odes attest to a profound sense of spirituality and theistic devotion in their author and in the communities in which the Odes were used.

Solomon, Psalms of a collection of eighteen psalms ascribed to King Solomon. Allusions to Pompey's invasion of Jerusalem in 63 B.C.E. date a significant part of the collection to the middle of the first century B.C.E. (Ps. Sol. 2:30–31, 8:16–28). A Greek translation of the Hebrew original is included in eleven medieval manuscripts of the wisdom books of the Greek Bible. A Syriac version, whose relationship to the Greek is uncertain, has been preserved in four manuscripts that also contain the Odes of Solomon or other prayers.

The Psalms of Solomon can be divided roughly into two types: those dealing with issues of concern to the nation (1, 2, 7, 8, 11, 17, 18); those focusing on individual and communal concerns of the pious (3, 4, 5, 6, 9, 10, 12, 13, 14, 15, 16). Parallels in vocabulary and themes indicate that both types stemmed from the same religious circles. The central theme is the righteous judgment of God, who chastises and purifies the covenant people and individuals among them and punishes the arrogant gentile oppressors. Related to this is the explicit contrast between the righteous and the sinners. The former are pious Jews who attend to their covenantal obligations, including the responsibility to atone for inadvertent sins. The latter include Jews who are careless about these obligations as well as Gentiles like Pompey. The difference between the two groups is explicated in Psalms of Solomon 3 (especially) and Psalms 13, 14, and 15. Psalm 4 criticizes hypocritical sinners, who sit in the council of the righteous.

The Psalms of Solomon have usually been attributed to the Pharisees. References to resurrection (3:11–12, 13:11, 14:9–10, 15:10–13) and free will (9:7) parallel similar teachings of the Pharisees, but our lack of detailed knowledge about the religious sociology of first-century Judaism cautions against a simple attribution to this group. References to "the communities of the pious" (Gr.: *synagogai hosiōn*) and the repeated contrast between righteous and sinners does indicate, however, a provenance in a community or group of communities who self-consciously identified themselves over

other Jews whom they considered to be less pious. This does not point to "the Hasidim" as a specific group, but the parallel references to (the community of) the pious ([*kehal*] *hasidim*) in canonical psalms like 132, 148, and 149 and in the noncanonical psalms in 11QPs^a 19–22 are suggestive of a general religious ambience. The repeated references to religious assemblies and acts of worship indicate an important element in the religious life of the authors. The intended function of the Psalms of Solomon is uncertain, although the didactic tone in many of them is more pronounced than in most of the compositions in the canonical Psalter.

The reason for the Solomonic ascription of the collection is unclear. The lengthy attention to the coming Davidic king in Psalms of Solomon 17–18 and the parallel between Psalm 2:31–35 and Wisdom of Solomon 5–6 fit the ascription, but there seems to be nothing specifically and uniquely Solomonic in the Psalms.

The uncertainty of their precise provenance notwithstanding, the Psalms of Solomon offer an important component for reconstructing the religious thought and practice of first-century Palestinian Judaism.

Solomon, Testament of a pseudepigraphic Christian writing of the first to third centuries C.E. in which Solomon describes how he used various demons and magical powers to build the Temple in Jerusalem. As Solomon builds the Temple, God grants him a magical ring with which Solomon can summon various demons and subdue them or enlist their aid.

The text, of twenty-six chapters, was probably composed in Greek, in either Egypt, Palestine, or Asia Minor. It is probable that the Testament is based on Jewish traditions about Solomon, and it is possible that the present text is a reworking of an earlier tale. The text survives in fifteen Greek manuscripts of the fifteenth and sixteenth centuries and in one fifth-century fragment. The Testament, rife with magic, demonology, angelology, and magical-medicinal lore, appears to be an early example of the many legends that grew up documenting Solomon's magical prowess (cf. 1 Kings 4:29–34).

Solomon, Wisdom of a pseudonymous Jewish religio-philosophical treatise that extols the wisdom and benefits of belief in the Jewish God and denounces idolatry and other pagan religious practices. The Wisdom of Solomon was written in Greek by an unknown Hellenistic Jew, almost certainly in Alexandria, Egypt, probably between 30 B.C.E. and 50 C.E. Couched in strongly philosophical language, it demonstrates to its diaspora audience not only that Judaism is respectable within a strongly Hellenized cultural context, but also that Jewish faith and practice, in fact, embody the highest expression of Hellenistic philosophy. Despite its philosophical orientation and espousal of various typically Graeco-Roman intellectual ideals (e.g., the immortality of the soul), the Wisdom of Solomon is strongly committed to traditional Judaism, and also displays a number of literary features that are typical of the Hebrew Bible. Although some commentators on the Wisdom of Solomon have questioned its literary integrity, modern scholarship is virtually unanimous in affirming its composition by a single author.

The Wisdom of Solomon is an example of the Hellenistic literary form of "protreptic" or "exhortatory" discourse. That is, it exhorts its audience, through a series of logical arguments, examples, and analogies, to accept its main theses and follow the course of action that it recommends. In addition, the work represents the genre of the encomium, a literary form that praises and persuades its audience to admire some person or ideal. In this case, the ideal is "Wisdom" (Gr.: *sophia*), a feminine hypostasis (personified form) of God, through which God created the world, and which serves as the main object of devotion by which humans can strive to reach God.

In content and structure, the Wisdom of Solomon can be divided into three main sections. The first, 1:1–6:21, exhorts the reader to strive for the goal of immortality, portrayed as a gift of Wisdom, and promises that those who are faithful to God and to the Mosaic covenant will achieve this goal.

In the second section (6:22–10:21), the main focus shifts to the figure of Wisdom herself, who is personified as God's partner in creation, whose nature, virtues and gifts are extolled, and who is portrayed as the object of the author's own quest for spiritual truth.

The third section, 11:1–19:22, constitutes a lengthy *synkrisis,* or "comparison," in which the author lays out a series of seven contrasting examples from the history of the Exodus to show that the evil Egyptians were punished by God through the same means by which the virtuous Israelites were saved. This section also contains two excurses, the first (11:15–12:22) dealing with the nature of God's mercy as demonstrated by God's gracious treatment of the Canaanites, and the second (chaps. 13–15) attacking the evils of idolatry.

Like other Jewish literature from the period between the Bible and the Mishnah, the Wisdom of Solomon effected little sustained influence in Jewish tradition, but was preserved instead in Christian circles. The work is today included among the Apocrypha, a body of early Jewish literature considered "deuterocanonical" (secondarily canonical) in Roman Catholic churches, but regarded as noncanonical by Protestants.

sōma (Gr., body) The term could be used generally for the human body or in the sense of something substantial, but it takes on a philosophical and theological significance in debates about the relationship of the person to body and soul (Gr.: *psyche*). Some saw the body in a negative light. *See also* PSYCHĒ.

Somn. *see* DE SOMNIIS

Song of Solomon, Targum to *see* SONG OF SONGS, TARGUM TO

Song of Songs, Targum to The Targum to the Song of Songs was composed after the completion of the Babylonian Talmud, perhaps in the seventh century C.E. Its language has elements in common with both Jewish Palestinian Aramaic and the dialect of Targum Onkelos. The author of this targum reinterprets the Song of Songs as an allegorical history of Israel's relationship with God. In doing so, he or she uses large amounts of aggadic material, swelling the targum to several times the size of the Hebrew text.

Song of Songs Rabbah commentary to the Song of Solomon, which reads the verses of the Song of Songs as a sequence of statements of urgent love between God and Israel, the holy people. This is expressed mainly through symbols. The exegetes set forth sequences of words that connote meanings, elicit emotions, stand for events, and form the verbal equivalent of pictures, music, dance, or poetry. They appeal to a highly restricted list of implicit meanings, calling upon some very few events or persons, repeatedly identifying these as the expressions of God's profound affection for Israel, and Israel's deep love for God. The message of the document comes not so much from stories of what happened or did not happened, assertions of truth or denials of error, but rather from the repetitious rehearsal of sets of symbols. In reading the love songs of the Song of Songs as the story of the love affair of God and Israel, sages identify implicit meanings, which are always few and invariably self-evident; no serious effort goes into demonstrating the fact that God speaks or that Israel speaks; the point of departure is the message and meaning the One or the other means to convey. To take one instance, time and again, a certain expression of love in the poetry of the Song of Songs is interpreted as God's speaking to Israel about the sea, Sinai, and the world to come, or about the first redemption (the one from Egypt), the second redemption (the one from Babylonia), and the third redemption (the one at the end of days). The repertoire of symbols covers Temple and schoolhouse, personal piety and public worship, and other matched pairs and sequences of coherent matters, all of them seen as embedded within the poetry. Here is scripture's poetry read as metaphor, and the task of the reader is know that for which each image of the poem stands. Thus Israel's holy life is expressed as metaphor through the poetry of love and beloved, Lover and Israel. This symbolic vocabulary conveys messages not through propositions but through images, whether visual or verbal. To take one example, the nut tree and Israel are compared with this result: First, Israel prospers when it gives scarce resources for the study of the Torah or for carrying out religious duties; second, Israel sins but atones, and Torah is the medium of atonement; third, Israel is identified through carrying out its religious duties, for example, circumcision; fourth, Israel's leaders had best watch their step; fifth, Israel may be nothing now but will be in glory in the coming age; sixth, Israel has plenty of room for outsiders but cannot afford to lose a single member. What we have is a repertoire of fundamentals, dealing with Torah and Torah-study, the moral life and atonement, Israel and its holy way of life, Israel and its coming salvation. The theological purpose therefore is to arrange and rearrange a few simple propositions, represented by a limited vocabulary of symbols. In such a structure the exegetes of the Song of Songs organize set-piece tableaus, rather than putting forth and demonstrating propositions.

Song of the Three Children a hymn of thanksgiving placed on the lips of the three youths in the fiery furnace. It is inserted into the Greek version of Daniel 3 between verses 23 and 24, where it is joined to the Prayer of Azariah by some brief prose. Together, the two pieces—confession of sin and thanksgiving for deliverance—add to the heroes' faith an appropriate expression of liturgical piety. The dating and original language of the hymn are uncertain.

The hymn begins with a doxology (vv. 29–34), and following the general order in Genesis 1, it makes a threefold appeal for the whole creation to join in the praise of God (vv. 35–51, 52–60, 61–65). The content of the hymn appears to paraphrase Psalm 148. Its structure recalls Psalm 136, and the wording of verses 67–68 reflects Psalm 136:1–3.

The hymn's liturgical character has led to its continued inclusion in Christian hymnals and liturgies, often under its Latin name, *Benedicite opera omnia. See also* AZARIAH, PRAYER OF.

son of God a metaphor based on the father–son relationship, used in a variety of ways to designate a close relationship to God. In the Hebrew Bible, "son" can literally refer to a male child sired by a father, or more broadly as a kinship term within a particular clan or tribe with the meaning "descendant" (like "the sons of Esau" in Deut. 2:4, 12, 22, 29 or "the son of Judah" in Joel 3:6). Inhabitants of a particular geographical location can also be characterized by the father–son metaphor, like "the sons of Jerusalem" (Isa. 51:18; Jer. 5:7), "the sons of Egypt" (Ezek. 16:26), or "the sons of the East" (Judg. 6:3; Isa. 11:14). The father–son relationship, extrapolated from the empirical observation that children physically resemble their parents, is also used to attribute certain characteristics to men, such as "sons of injustice" (wicked men; 2 Sam. 3:34; Hos. 10:9), "sons of Belial" (scoundrels; Deut. 13:13; Judg. 19:22), a "son of peace" (a peaceful man; Luke 10:6).

The father–son metaphor also stands behind the designation of Israel collectively as "my [i.e., god's] son" (Hos. 11:1), "my [i.e., god's] firstborn son" (Exod. 4:22; Sir. 36:17; 2 Esd. 6:58), and "child of God" (Wisd. of Sol. 18:13), or individually as "sons (and daughters) of God" (Deut. 14:1; Hos. 1:10; Wisd. of Sol. 9:7), and "children of God" (Wisd. of Sol. 12:7, 20–21, 16:10, 21, 26; Jdt. 9:4, 13; 3 Macc. 6:28, 7:6). This father–son and parent–child language serves to emphasize the special relationship that existed between YHWH and Israel involving both election and preservation. It also involves the discipline which parents must use to ensure the obedience of their children. Male descendants of the Davidic dynasty are also referred to as God's sons (2 Sam. 7:14; Ps. 2:7, 89:26f.; 1 Chron. 17:13, 22:10, 28:6), a royal title throughout the Near East. The phrase "son of God" is never actually used in this connection in the Old Testament. It is likely that the father–son language in royal coronation ritual is based on the metaphor of the adoption of the king by God. In Egyptian royal ideology, by contrast, the pharaoh was actually a god, whereas in ancient Assyrian royal ideology, as in Israel, the king was regarded as the adopted son of God. Angelic beings are frequently designated as sons of God (Gen. 6:2, 4; Job 1:6, 2:1, 38:7; Ps. 29:1, 89:6; Wisd. of Sol. 5:5; 1 Enoch 6:2, 13:8), or as sons of the Most High (Ps. 82:6), because while they are subordinate to God, they are members of his heavenly court. The phrase "son of the gods" (Dan. 3:25), means that someone appeared like a divine being. The Septuagint translates the Hebrew phrase underlying the English phrase sons of God as *aggeloi*, "angels," in Job 1:6, 2:1, 38:7. Finally, the righteous man is called the son or child of God because of the moral quality of his life (Wisd. of Sol. 2:13, 18; Sir. 4:10; Pss. Sol. 13:9; Jub. 19:29; Philo, *Spec. Leg.* 1.318 and *Quaest. Gen.* 1.92).

The title "son of God" is often considered a messianic title in late Second Temple Judaism, though the evidence in Jewish sources is relatively scanty. In the Qumran document 4QFlorilegium 10–14, 2 Samuel 7:12–14 is quoted and applied to the Messiah, providing evidence suggesting that son of God was probably a Messianic title in at least some strands of late Second Temple Judaism. Similarly, the Messiah is referred to in speeches attributed to God as my son (4 Ezra 7:28–29, 13:32, 37, 52, 14:9; 1 Enoch 105:2). Clear evidence for the messianic significance of the title Son of God, at least in Christian circles, is found in the New Testament (Matt. 16:16, 26:63; Mark 14:61–62; Luke 1:32–33, 4:41, 22:66–70; John 1:49, 11:27, 20:31; Acts 9:20–22).

The titles "Son" and "Son of God" are used frequently of Jesus in the New Testament and early Christian literature. While the application of the title "Son" to Jesus often implies an intimate relationship to God under the metaphor "Father" (Matt. 11:25–27; Luke 10:21–22; John 3:16, 5:19–24, 14:13, 167:1), the title "Son of God" is rarely used in this way. Jesus' reference to God as *abba* (construed by some as a nursery word for "father" equivalent to "daddy") presumes a unique filial relationship to God (Mark 14:26; see Rom. 8:15, Gal. 4:6). The "Son of God" title is one of the more important ways in which Jesus is identified in the Gospel of Mark. Jesus is initially identified as Jesus Christ, the Son of God (Mark 1:1), and a heavenly voice identifies him as "my [i.e., God's] son" at his baptism and transfiguration (1:11, 9:7). Demons address him as the Son of God (Mark 3:11, 5:7), as does the high priest at the trial of Jesus, in the form "son of the Blessed One" (14:61–62), and the Roman soldier at Jesus' crucifixion (15:39). The emphasis on the virginal conception pushes Jesus' unique sonship back to his birth (Matt. 1:18–25; Luke 1:35). The royal messianic connotations of the title in first-century Palestinian Judaism tended to be disregarded in the Graeco-Roman world where the title was more naturally understood as an affirmation of the uniqueness and divinity of Jesus. One pre-Pauline text that retains messianic significance is

Romans 1:3–4, where it is claimed that Jesus was designed Son of God at his resurrection. Here resurrection is understood as messianic enthronement (reflecting 2 Sam. 7:12–14). Paul (who uses the term "Father" of God nearly forty times) often uses the title to describe Jesus Christ as the unique and only Son of God, though he used the title "Lord" even more frequently. In both Pauline and Johannine literature, the title can be used of the preexistence of Jesus with specific reference to His being sent into the world (Rom. 8:3, 32; 1 Cor. 8:6; Gal. 4:4–5; John 3:17, 6:40–46, 8:42; 1 John 4:9, 10, 14; Bar. 5:11). The Son of God title is also used for the giving up of the Son to death (John 3:16; Rom. 8:32–34; Gal. 2:20). The divine sonship of the exalted Jesus is reflected (Rom. 1:3–4; 1 Thess. 1:9–10; Col. 1:13; Acts 13:33; Heb. 1:5, 5:5; Rev. 2:18). Paul also speaks of Christians as "sons of God" (Rom. 8:16, 17, 21, 9:7–8; Phil 2:15), based on God's adoption of them (Rom. 8:15, 23; Gal 4:5; see Eph. 1:5).

son of man (Heb.: *ben adam;* Aram.: *bar enash;* Gr.: *[ho] huios [tou] anthrōpou*). This generic Semitic expression for "human being" comes also to designate its opposite, a heavenly figure, and it becomes a significant New Testament designation for Jesus both as a human being and as a heavenly figure.

Is Psalm 8:4 "son of man" is used in parallelism with "man" as a designation for human being, who paradoxically functions as God's ruler over creation (Ps. 8:5–8). The vision in Daniel 7:13–14 presents a similar juxtaposition in reverse. In contrast to the beasts that represent four empires, Daniel sees a heavenly figure, who looks like a human being and is given dominion, glory, and kingship in heaven. This high angel, who is the patron of the suffering people of Israel, appears after the judgment of the last beast, and his heavenly enthronement is simultaneous with Israel's domination over all the kingdoms on earth. The precise sources of this vision are disputed, but it certainly depends on old mythic motifs and traditions from ancient Near Eastern religion.

In 1 Enoch 37–71 a major transformation in Daniel's tradition occurs. Although historians of religion have suggested many parallels from antiquity, Enoch's version is best explained as primarily a conflation of biblical traditions. The enthroned figure in Daniel (1 Enoch 46:1–2, 47) is designated as God's chosen one and is identified with Second Isaiah's exalted servant of YHWH (cf. 1 Enoch 48:1–7 and 49:4 with Isa. 49 and 42:1–2). He is also the Lord's "anointed one" and is described in language from Psalm 2 and Isaiah 11 (1 Enoch 48:8–10, 49:2, 52:4). This hybrid figure sits on God's throne and judges the persecutors of the righteous and chosen (cf. 1 Enoch 62–63 with the traditional reworking of Isa. 52–53 in Wisd. of Sol. 5). This conflation of enthronement traditions involves a threefold transformation. Texts about the earthly, Davidic king are now applied to a heavenly figure. The suffering and exalted servant of YHWH has become the heavenly champion of the suffering righteous. The one like a son of man, who is enthroned after the judgment in Daniel, is now the executor of that judgment.

Other forms of this conflated tradition appear in documents of the late first century C.E.: 2 Esdras 11–13, where the heavenly figure is the Davidic messiah; and the New Testament Book of Revelation, where he is the exalted Jesus. Some form of the conflated tradition has also influenced the gospel traditions about Jesus as son of man that are developing several decades earlier.

The designation of Jesus as son of man appears in the Gospels, always on Jesus' lips, in Acts 7:56, and in Hebrews 2:5–9. The gospel's son of man sayings fall into three groups relating to: the future exalted son of man; the activity and circumstances of the earthly son of man; his suffering, death, and resurrection. Scholarly literature on the subject is voluminous, and there is little consensus. Did the Jews even posit the existence of an exalted figure called son of man? Did the historical Jesus ever make reference to such a figure, and if so, was it himself or someone else? Do the traditions refer only to Daniel or also the figure as depicted in 1 Enoch?

Analysis of the texts suggests the following to the present writer. The judicial functions that many gospel texts ascribe to the son of man indicate contact with the tradition as modified in 1 Enoch. Texts about the son of man's death and resurrection reflect the pattern of the suffering and vindicated servant, as this appears in Wisdom of Solomon 2 and 5 in a tradition related to 1 Enoch 62–63. Paul's references to the Lord's glorious return and function as judge derive from son of man traditions also attested in the gospels (1 Thess. 4–5; 1 Cor. 4:1–5, 15:20–28).

sophia (Gr., wisdom) usually refers to wisdom of a more intellectual, philosophical, or theological sort, in contrast to practical wisdom (Gr.: *phrōnēsis*). The concept is personified or hypostatized as the figure of Wisdom known to us from Proverbs, the Wisdom of Solomon, and other Jewish writings.

Sophist term derived from the Greek word *sophos* (wise person). The Sophists were originally individuals in fifth-century B.C.E. Greece who taught for a fee, especially the subjects of rhetoric and debating. They were criticized and caricatured in the writings of Plato so that the term came often to be used pejoratively for those clever at speech and rhetorical tricks rather than possessing true wisdom or philosophy. Philo of Alexandria agrees with this opinion, viewing the sophist as one who leads the unwary astray by verbal tricks that counterfeit true understanding and knowledge.

sophos (Gr., wise person) The term could be used generally, but it also became a technical term in theological and philosophical discussion for the learned individual, the "sage," especially one knowledgeable in true philosophy. It overlapped with "philosopher," which was the more specific term.

Sophronius (560–638 C.E.) patriarch of Jerusalem. He wrote long biographies of Cyrus and John, two Alexandrian saints, and a number of poems that speak of the Persian invasion of Palestine in the sixth century C.E. He notes that the Jews joined the Persians in their siege of Jerusalem.

sōphrosynē (Gr., moderation) one of the four cardinal virtues. The idea of the "golden mean" (everything in balance, nothing in excess) was a concept widespread in ancient Greek thought. It also fit well into Jewish ethics and is found in the works of Jewish writers, such as Philo of Alexandria.

sorites a literary argument (also called *climax* or *gradatio*) that ascends step by step so that one conclusion or fact forms the basis for the next stage of the argument, often by repeating key words from the previous stage. It was popular in Graeco-Roman literature and is also found in rabbinic writings.

Sosius Roman governor of Syria (38–37 B.C.E.) who defeated Antigonus and conquered Jerusalem in 37 B.C.E. He installed into power Herod the Great, who had been appointed king of Judea by the Roman Senate in 40 B.C.E.

sotah *see* ACCUSED WIFE

Sotah Mishnah tractate on the ordeal inflicted upon the wife accused of adultery. The tractate discusses invoking the ordeal (chap. 1); narrates the ordeal (chaps. 1–3); sets forth the rules of imposing the ordeal, exemptions, and testimony (chaps. 4–6); describes rites conducted in Hebrew in addition to that involving the accused wife (chaps. 7–9); discusses the priest anointed for battle and draft exemptions (Deut. 20:1–9) (chap. 8); and describes the rite of breaking the heifer's neck in connection with the neglected corpse (Deut. 21:1–9) (chap. 9).

sōtēr (Gr., savior) a term with a strongly positive connotation, often taken as an epithet by kings. It was also a technical term in theological discussion for one who brings salvation, a messiah figure or deliverer.

soul the innermost, most vital, and intimate part of a human being—the part that is sentient, decision-making, morally responsible, subject to emotion and feeling, susceptible to religious experience, and liable to divine judgment. It is considered one's true self, what causes one to be alive.

In the Hebrew Bible, the terms "soul" and "spirit" are similar in meaning when they denote an aspect of the human personality. In general, there is also no clear-cut distinction in biblical literature between a person's "soul" or "spirit" and "body": the person is a unified whole. However, the concept of "soul" or "spirit" underwent a basic transformation during the period of biblical Judaism.

Although intertestamental Jewish literature for the most part continues the biblical uses of "soul" and "spirit," these terms also acquire new connotations in this period. Perhaps most important is the idea that the soul survives the death of the body. For example, both 4 Ezra (7:32–101) and 2 Baruch (chap. 30) describe the soul's fate as it awaits God's judgment after the body's death. A favorite theme in these and other books is that the souls of the dead live in "storehouses" or "treasures" until the day of judgment (4 Ezra 4:35, 42; 2 Bar. 21:23; Ps-Philo 32:13).

The idea of the immortality of the soul, or "eternal life," is particularly common in Greek-influenced Jewish writings of the first centuries B.C.E. and C.E.—especially the Wisdom of Solomon, Pseudo-Philo, 4 Maccabees, and the writings of Philo. In some cases, the soul is depicted as leaving the body and ascending to heaven after physical death (4 Ezra 7:78; Test. Abr. A20:12). Furthermore, this notion of the soul's survival after death implies that the soul is distinct and different from the body; this anthropological dualism was a highly important, Greek-influenced development in intertestamental Jewish literature. Rabbinic literature also manifests a clear-cut distinction between soul and body.

Characterization of the "soul" and "spirit" in early Christian literature is generally consistent with that found in contemporary Jewish writings. Jewish Hellenistic ideas of the soul's being distinct from the body, and surviving death, are common in early Christianity.

The logia of Jesus in Mark 14:38 and Matt. 10:28 manifest a clear dualism between "body" and "soul." Accounts of the martyrdoms of Jesus and Stephen both picture their "spirits" leaving their bodies at the time of death. The idea of an anthropological and metaphysical distinction between "flesh" and "spirit" is basic to Paul's soteriology. Finally, Revelation portrays "souls" or "spirits" surviving death and waiting in a heavenly storehouse for judgment (6:9, 20:4).

Like earlier Judaism and formative Christianity, rabbinic sources view the soul as the inner, animating element of human beings, in contrast to the physical body, which is the soul's vehicle. Like the Hebrew words generally translated as soul—*nefesh, neshamah,* and *ruah,* which refer to breath—in rabbinic texts the soul is associated primarily with respiration, narrowly signifying the life force. Unlike other ancient Near Eastern cultures, here the soul is not broadly associated with appearance, destiny, or power.

The talmudic literature envisions a close connection between body and soul. Rabbinic authorities do not conceive of the soul's immortality separate from that of the body. Nor do they imagine the transmigration of the soul from one body to another. Body and soul, rather, are seen as separate only in origin, with the body deriving from human parents and the soul originating with God. In practice, the soul, created and bestowed upon the body by God, is taken back to God at death. At the time of the resurrection, it will be restored to that same body (see Jerusalem Talmud Kilaim 8:4, 31c; and B. Berakhot 60a).

The notion that the soul originates with God is expressed in rabbinic texts that proclaim all human souls were brought into existence during creation, having been aspects of the wind or spirit (*ruah*) of God referred to at Genesis 1:2. The messiah will come either when all of the prepared souls have been used or, alternatively, when God has finished creating all of the souls that he intended to create from the beginning (see, e.g., B. Abodah Zarah 5a; B. Hagigah 12b).

The soul enters the womb at the time of conception, conscious of its origins and accompanied by divine messengers (B. Berakhot 60b). During life, the soul's divine origin remains significant. While the body sleeps, for instance, the soul is understood to ascend to heaven, returning renewed in the morning (Gen. Rabbah 14:9). The soul protests its birth into the world but also protests the body's death. It hovers near the body for three days, hoping that it will return to life (Tanḥuma; Miketz 4; Pekudei 3). After three days the soul returns to God to await the time of resurrection, when it and the body will be judged together (B. Sanhedrin 90b–91a).

sovereignty-verses (Heb.: Malkhuyot) selection of verses of scripture that refer to God as ruler of the world, recited in a section of the New Year Additional Service devoted to the themes of God's sovereignty, God's remembrance, and God's revelation through the sound of the ram's horn (shofar).

Spartans, Jewish kinship with According to 1 Maccabees 12:7–23, as well as Josephus, Judas Maccabeus and one of his brothers, Jonathan, exchanged letters with the Spartans, claiming that they shared a common ancester in Abraham because the Spartans were descended from him through Keturah. It is generally accepted that the Jews did write such a letter, though whether the Spartans replied in the affirmative as alleged is more controversial. It has been suggested that it was an old piece of Jewish propaganda, which Jonathan may have thought to be genuine. About the same time, the Romans and Spartans also claimed to have found a common ancestry.

Spec. Leg. *see* DE SPECIALIBUS LEGIBUS

spices the products of aromatic trees and plants that were native to such places as Africa, Arabia, Persia, India, and Ceylon. Because they were imported from great distances they were expensive and considered very precious. Spices could be used alone or compounded; often their powdered form was mixed with oil. They could be used as condiments, but more often were employed in perfumes, oil for anointing, incense for cultic purposes, embalming substances, and medicines. Perhaps the longest catalog of spices in a Jewish text appears in 1 Enoch 28–32, which purports to be an account of a journey from Jerusalem, along the spice routes, to paradise in the northwest. More down to earth accounts of spices and the trees and plants from which they come appear in writers such as Theophrastus (*History of Plants*) and Pliny the Elder (*Nat. Hist.*, books 12–13).

spirit (Heb.: *ruaḥ*; Gr.: *pneuma*) an incorporeal being. Jewish and Christian literature uses the term with a wide range of referents. On the divine side, it refers to God's creative power (Gen. 1:2) or prophetic inspiration. Wisdom of Solomon 1:7 identifies it with heavenly Wisdom, the force that created and sustains the world. More generically, it can denote one of a whole range of heavenly beings (often called angels), or indeed "evil spir-

its," clients of the archdemon. Spirit denotes the human being as a living creature, and some texts envision the human spirit as a separate entity, released from the body at the time of death, and difficult to distinguish from "soul" (Heb.: *nefesh*; Gr.: *psyche*; cf. 1 Enoch 102:4–103:8). *See also* ANGEL; SOUL.

spirit of error an evil spirit who leads people astray into idolatry, moral error, or wrong interpretation and practice of the Torah. The term is common in the Testaments of the Twelve Patriarchs (cf. also 1 Enoch 99:14 and 1 John 4:6). Implied is the counterpart, the spirit(s) of truth. *See also* SPIRIT OF TRUTH; SPIRITS, TWO.

spirit of truth a good spirit who leads people on the path of moral rectitude, defending them from the spirit(s) of error, who would cause them to stray. This construct of the two spirits is typical of the Testaments of the Twelve Patriarchs and the Qumran Community Rule 3–4. In Christian texts, the spirit of truth is also known as the "advocate" (Gr.: *paraklētos*). *See also* ADVOCATE; SPIRIT OF ERROR; SPIRITS, TWO.

spirits, two two major opposed figures of the spirit world. In Zechariah 3, "the accuser" (Heb.: *haSatan*) and the angel of YHWH engage in a legal dispute about Joshua's fitness for the high priesthood. The "Prince of Mastema" and the angels of the presence have a similar confrontation in Jubilees 17:15–18:12, but Mastema is also the chief demon. In the Qumran Community Rule 3:18–25, the Prince of Light and the Angel of Darkness lead people on the ways of truth and perversity respectively, and in Testament of Asher 6:4–5 they recompense this conduct at death. Revelation 12:7–12 depicts the battle between Satan and Michael in the imagery of Isaiah 14. *See also* WAYS, TWO.

spirits, unclean a frequent term in the Gospels for spirits who infest humans, causing sickness, especially mental disturbances. They challenge the exorcist (Jesus), opposing his divine power to dislodge them. Their uncleanness derives from participation in a spirit realm opposed to the true God. Compare Jubilees 11:4 and 22:16–17, where evil spirits participate in the cultic uncleanness of idolatry. *See also* DEMONS.

spiritual gifts special skills or endowments considered beyond natural human abilities and resources and therefore necessarily thought to have been bestowed by God. In the Hebrew Bible the Spirit of God is credited with the exceptional wisdom or skill of particular individuals (Exod. 31:3, 35:31), as well as with the extraordinary military successes and feats of strength of the Israelite judges (Judg. 3:10,

6:34, 11:29, 14:6, 19, 15:14). Similarly, the ability to prophesy is often attributed to the influence of the Spirit of God (1 Sam. 10:6, 10; 2 Chron. 20:14, 24:20; Ezek. 11:5; Mark 13:11; Acts 13:2, 4, 21:11; 1 Cor. 12:3). However, the term "spiritual gifts" is primarily associated with the New Testament. There the term *charisma*, formed from the verb *charidzomai* (to give freely and generously), refers to that which is freely and generously given, that is, a gift. The fuller expression "spiritual gift" (*charisma pneumatikon*) occurs in the New Testament only in Romans 1:11, where it refers generally to the blessings of God bestowed on the Roman Christians through Paul's presence. Elsewhere in the New Testament spiritual gifts are referred to as a *charisma*, gift (1 Pet. 4:10) or *charismata*, gifts (Rom. 12:6; 1 Cor. 12:4, 9, 28, 30, 31), as *pneumatika*, spiritual [gifts] (1 Cor. 12:1, 14:1), or *dorea*, "gift" (Eph. 4:7–8). Spiritual gifts appear to be a conception introduced by Paul, probably ground in the notion that the Holy Spirit is considered a gift of God (Luke 11:13; Acts 2:38, 10:45; 1 Thess. 4:8). There are five lists of spiritual gifts in the New Testament, none of which are precisely similar (Rom. 12:6–8; 1 Cor. 12:8–10, 12:28–30; Eph. 4:7–13; 1 Pet. 4:10–11). There appear to be two major categories of gifts, however, and the common thread linking them all is that they describe forms of corporate behavior that functions to promote and reinforce Christian beliefs and values: (1) miraculous and revelatory gifts (emphasized in 1 Cor. 12:8–10, 28–30), prophecy, discerning of spirits, wisdom, knowledge, speaking in tongues, interpretation of tongues, healing, and performing miracles; (2) gifts of ministry (emphasized in Rom. 12:6–8 and Eph. 4:7–13), apostleship, ministry (*diakonia*), teaching, and exhortation.

squatter's rights   *see* ḤAZAKAH

Standard Literary Aramaic   *see* ARAMAIC, STANDARD LITERARY

star, five-pointed, representation of   a minor motif in Jewish art of the Roman and Byzantine periods. This star gains magical properties in the Middle Ages as the Shield of Solomon, but in the biblical period it seems to have no special meaning. One of the earliest appearances of the five-pointed star is on the wall of a Hellenistic tomb from Marisa. Since this star is not repeated again in the cemetery, it is clearly not an important symbol. A five-pointed star in relief appears on a frieze at Capernaum next to flowers. A similar five-pointed star appears on a frieze at Chorazin with two other circlets containing repeated petals or peaks.

star, six-pointed, representation of   a minor motif in Jewish art of the Roman and Byzantine periods. This star gains magical properties in the Middle Ages as the Shield of David, but in the biblical period it seems to have no distinct meaning. One of the earliest appearances of the six-pointed star is on coins of Year Two of the Redemption of Israel, or coins of Bar Kokhba of 136 C.E. The star above the Temple facade has either four or six points. In synagogue art of the early Byzantine period the six-pointed star appears again. A six-pointed star in relief appears on a frieze at Capernaum at least twice. A similar six-pointed star appears on a frieze at Chorazin with two other circlets containing repeated petals.

stars   Biblical and Second Temple Jewish literature regularly associates or identifies the fixed stars and the planets with living divine beings. At times it is difficult to know whether the Hebrew *tzaba* ("host") refers to the heavenly army or simply to the aggregation of celestial bodies. In Judges 5:20 the stars (Heb.: *haKokhabim*) battle against Sisera. 1 Enoch 82:4–20 provides names for the leaders of "thousands," who are in charge of the stars. Whether one thinks of an identity or simply a close association between angels and stars, 1 Enoch 18:15 and 21:1–4 explicitly assign moral responsibility to these heavenly bodies. When the head of God's heavenly army visits Asenath (Joseph and Asenath 14), he appears in the heavens as a star and then materializes as "a man." Daniel 12:3 seems to assert that the righteous teachers of the community, exalted to heaven when they die, will partake of the immortality that belongs to the astral sphere. The oracle of Balaam employs the image of a star to depict the Davidic king (Num. 24:17), and 4QTestimonia seems to identify the star as the king, while Matthew 2:1–12 associates a special "star" with the birth of Jesus the Messiah, playing on common ideas about stars as signs.

stasis   (Gr., faction, or dissent) This became a term in political contexts, to be used to refer to everything from minor discord all the way to civil disorder and even revolt in the Hellenistic world. Discord in society was considered very bad, especially to the Romans after their civil war.

Statius   (45–96 C.E.) Roman poet, born in Naples. He lived in Rome and was a friend of the Roman emperor Domitian. His *Silvae* mentions the celebrated agricultural products of Judea. Another poem mentions M. Maecius Celer, the legate of a Syrian legion, who bridled the Palestinian cohorts and visited Idumea.

Statutus, Publius Aelius   official in Palestine under Diocletian. Two boundary stones found north of the sea of Galilee mention Aelius Statutus. He seems to have been the official who carried out the land survey in Palestine when Diocletian transformed the *annona* from an ad hoc requisition to a regular tax in kind.

Stephanus   civil governor of Palestine in the mid-sixth century C.E. In 556, the Jews and Samaritans rioted in Caesarea, plundering and burning many churches. Stephanus attempted to protect the Christians. The rioters attacked and destroyed his palace, and he perished in the conflagration.

steward   person entrusted with the management of households or estates (Gen. 43:16; 1 Kings 16:9); the financial aspect of businesses (Matt. 20:8; Luke 16:1–8); churches (Titus 1:5–9, the bishop as "God's steward"); and even revelation (1 Cor. 4:1–2, "of the mysteries of God") and spiritual gifts (1 Pet. 4:10)

stiffness of neck   a vivid expression for stubborn resistance to God's will. In the Hebrew Bible it is uniformly a designation for Israelites (Exod. 33:3, 5; 34:9; Deut. 9:6, 13), and in the wisdom literature it can describe the wicked person (Prov. 29:1; Ecclus. 16:11; Bar. 2:30). The power of the invective can be enhanced through combination with references to hardness, heaviness, or uncircumcision of the heart (Deut. 10:16; 1 Enoch 98:11; Acts 7:51). The latter three texts are noteworthy because the invective is directed against persons whose viewpoint and practice differ from the author's; one designates one's enemies as enemies of God. *See also* HEART, HARDNESS OF.

Stobi Synagogue   first- or second-century-C.E. house in the city of Stobi, Macedonia. Its lower floor was converted into a synagogue in the second century through the largess of its owner, Polycharmos. It was decorated with frescos of geometric designs. According to an inscription on a column, Polycharmos remained living on the second floor and violation of his donation was sanctioned by a large fine payable to the patriarch. A second synagogue, about 13 by 8 meters, was built over the house in the second or third century. It was decorated with frescos, a floor mosaic, and a Torah shrine on the east wall. In the fourth or fifth century a Christian basilica was built over the synagogue.

stoicheia   (Gr., elements, or elemental spirits) The term could be used in reference to the letters of the alphabet or to the physical elements of the universe, as Philo uses it. The *stoicheia tou kosmou* (the elements of the world) in Colossians 2:8 may have a Jewish background, though the precise meaning is disputed.

Stoicism   a Greek philosophy founded by Zeno in the fourth century B.C.E., named after the *stoa* (the porch) in Athens where Zeno taught. It was characterized by a view of the cosmos that saw everything as interrelated, with God (referred to as Logos, or "reason") coextensive with the universe. The key to human happiness was to accept everything that happened with equanimity as a part of the natural order, whether good fortune or misfortune. The only thing important was virtue; you were happy if you had that, but other goods (wealth, honor, and so on) were "indifferent" in that they did not affect the question. An extreme view was that only the truly wise could be virtuous and that anything less than perfect virtue was of no value, but later thinkers modified this perspective. Many Stoics were heavily deterministic, assuming that everything was predetermined. Many thought the universe was to go through a cycle that would finally culminate in the reduction of everything to its original elements in a final conflagration (Gr.: *ekpyrosis*). The philosophy was especially popular among the Romans but also influenced other philosophical systems. Philo of Alexandria shows considerable Stoic influence.

stone vessels   standing containers of soft, easily carved limestone characteristic of the first century C.E. Many examples are known from Jerusalem and environs and other sites. They were turned on a wheel much like a lathe wheel, powered by hand or by connection via gears to a water wheel. These stone containers are basically cylinders supported on a single leg and broad foot. The rims are formed into a profile resembling a molding. The surface is carefully smoothed and sometimes decorated with horizontal bands carved while the vessel was on the lathe. Each stone vessel stood 65–80 centimeters tall, though small vessels of such stone are also known. The latter comprise plates, bowls, and cups without handles. The smaller forms resemble popular pottery vessels of the period, but the large, standing vessels resemble goblets. A vessel that stood 75 centimeters in height on a foot of about 20 centimeters would hold around 70 liters. They may be the containers mentioned in M. Parah 3:3, "And at the door of the courtyard [of the Temple] was set up a vessel of purification." They may also be the vessels mentioned in John 2:6, "Now standing there were six stone vessels for the Jewish rites of purification, each holding two or three measures" (one measure = 36 liters). In recent excavations in Jerusalem, these stone vessels have been found in almost every pre–70 house investigated. This implies that they were not luxury items as assumed heretofore.

storm Symbolic of divine presence, testing, and judgment, a storm is a common theophanic occasion: Noah's flood and Jonah's wind are examples. Elijah's experience on Mount Horeb revealed God's presence in the silence after a great wind (1 Kings 19:11–12); in Job the theophany is the voice out of the whirlwind (chap. 38). Mark 4:36–41 (Matt. 8:23–27; Luke 8:22–24) depicts Jesus calming a storm and so both saving his disciples from drowning and demonstrating his divine power.

Strabo Greek writer of the first century B.C.E. (c. 65 B.C.E.–25 C.E.). His only extant work is the *The Geography,* but this was the most important treatment of the subject in antiquity. Included in it in Book 16 was the geography and some of the history of the Palestinian area. He also wrote an important *History* of the world. Although this has been lost, it was heavily used by Josephus in the *Antiquities of the Jews.* Much of Josephus's account of the Hasmonean dynasty and state depend on Strabo and Nicolaus of Damascus. In a number of cases, Josephus quotes Strabo directly; these fragments show how important the Greek historian was for the surving information we have about this period. His account of the origins of the Jews is quite interesting in that his picture of Moses and the original religion seems quite positive, with Moses introducing a superior form of pure worship of God without images. However, he thinks that with time, credulous individuals became priests and introduced superstitions, which corrupted the religion with food taboos and circumcision. He considers Moses to have been an Egyptian priest who gathered "thoughtful" men with his teachings and made Jerusalem their home.

stranger *see* SOJOURNER

strategos (Gr., general, or leader) The term is often used of military leaders generically, but could also be applied to certain leaders and officials whose military role was secondary to their other functions in administration.

stumbling block (Gr.: *skandalon*) something that causes someone to fall, used metaphorically of a temptation to sin. Although the noun and the related verb *skandalizō* occur infrequently in Jewish literature, they are used quite often in the New Testament with two major referents. Jesus is a stumbling block to those who do not believe in him, that is, do not accept him as God's agent, or accept the authority of his teaching (Matt. 11:6; 15:12; 26:31; cf. Luke 2:34; 1 Cor. 1:23; and Rom. 9:33 and 1 Pet. 2:8, quoting Isa. 8:14). According to Paul, eating meat or eating food sacrificed to idols, while not wrong in themselves, cause others to sin if they imitate such behavior in violation of their consciences or in the belief that idolatry is permissible (Rom. 14:13–21; 1 Cor. 8:7–13). This concern not to lead others into sin is reiterated in Mark 9:42. In a passage playing on Simon's nickname, Peter (from Gr., rock), Jesus identifies the disciple as a spokesman for Satan, and hence a temptation to sin, when he tries to prevent Jesus from going to Jerusalem to die (Matt. 16:23).

Suburanus Aemilianus *see* AEMILIANUS, SEXTUS ATTIUS SUBURANUS

Suetonius (69–140 C.E.) Roman biographer. He spent some time as a lawyer and held several secretarial posts at the Roman court. He reports about the Jews' mourning after the murder of Julius Caesar; Augustus's negative attitude toward Judaism; Tiberias's meeting a certain Diogenes on Rhodes, who used to lecture on the Sabbath; and the harsh measures employed by Domitian's agents in collecting taxes from the Jews. He further notes that Claudius expelled the Jews from Rome because of a riot caused by a certain Chrestus. He exhibits a negative attitude toward Christianity, but does not express a direct opinion about Judaism.

suffering The Bible and early Jewish literature is replete with stories about and references to the suffering of God's people: sickness, famine and hunger, defeat by one's enemies, persecution because of one's faithfulness to God, oppression by the mighty, and the like. Interpretations of such suffering varied greatly. The standard Deuteronomic explanation was that suffering was punishment for one's disobedience to the covenant. This notion is questioned in many of the Psalms and strongly disputed by the author of the Book of Job. The prose framework of Job attributes his suffering to the accuser's (Satan's) attempt to disprove his righteousness, an idea attached to the story of the Akedah in Jubilees 17:16–18:16. For the author of Tobit and the Psalms of Solomon, God afflicts the righteous in order to "chasten" or "discipline" them for sins committed. 2 Maccabees 6–7 expounds the paradox that the innocent who suffer for their loyalty to the Torah in some sense help to pay for the sins of an apostate nation. The idea is expounded in more detail in 4 Maccabees and seems to be related both to Greek notions and to an interpretation of Isaiah 52:13–53:12. Christian texts take over the whole range of Jewish interpretations, ascribing vicarious suffering and death uniquely to Jesus, but positing the inevitability of Jesus' followers' suffering like their master.

An issue of concern within all religious systems, the existence of suffering implies (1) that God is not so powerful as to be able to prevent suffering, or (2) is not all good, so as to desire that his creatures do not suffer. Rabbinic Judaism responds to these concerns with an explanation rooted in scripture, which holds that suffering is a punishment for sin. In this view, people are responsible for their lot in life, with evil actions bringing about an evil return. In line with this approach, B. Berakhot 5a states: "If a person sees that sufferings afflict him, let him examine his deeds."

The weakness of this approach is that it does not explain apparently unearned suffering, for instance, of righteous adults or of innocent children. To account for such suffering as well as for the fact that the wicked often prosper, the rabbis developed a conception of immortality and afterlife. Positing final retribution and reward in a world to come permitted explanation of apparent inequities in the present world. In this approach, the wicked receive in this world their reward for any slight good they might do. In the coming world, however, they will find severe punishment. The righteous by contrast suffer in the present world for any slight infractions they might commit. As a result, they can look forward in the coming world to a perfect and complete reward. In line with this approach, the talmudic literature sometimes sees suffering as part of a process of purification—referred to as afflictions of love—through which individuals become closer to God. In this view, only those who can bear the burden of suffering are asked to do so, leading B. Taanit 8a to state that "one who gladly accepts suffering brings salvation to the world."

Alongside these understandings of suffering as a purposeful element in the relationship between people and God, the talmudic literature admits of a very different view. This other view holds that suffering may not be deserved and that those subject to it have reason to reproach God. The problem of suffering, accordingly, is beyond full human comprehension. Illustrating this view, M. Abot 4:19 holds that one should not rejoice at the suffering of his enemy, there being no way to predict whether or not he will himself soon be subject to similar misfortune. Comparably, in an account that depicts Moses's being shown a vision of the torture and death of Akiba, he protests to God, "Master of the Universe, is this the Torah and this its reward?" God responds simply, "Be silent, for this is the way I have determined it" (B. Menahot 29b).

This view of suffering holds that God is not entirely able to stop suffering and that he suffers along with this righteous creatures. This point is made at B. Berakhot 59b and parallels, which state: "When the Holy One, blessed be he, reflects that his children are plunged in distress among the nations of the world, he drops two tears into the Great Sea, and the sound is heard from one end of the world to the other."

suffetes Latin term for the Carthaginian chief magistrates. The word appears to be derived from the Phoenician/Punic *shofet,* a cognate of the Hebrew word for "judge." It is now thought that the Hebrew word included the concept of a ruler, like some of the "judges" of the Book of Judges, and not just the judicial idea.

sugya a unit of discourse; a complete topical or logical pericope within a rabbinic compilation; applied particularly to talmudic materials

suicide the taking of one's own life. Suicide in extreme circumstances, especially to save personal honor, was widely accepted in the Graeco-Roman world. There are a number of examples of suicide in early Jewish history, especially to avoid capture or humiliation. One of the most famous was the mass suicide at Masada in 73–74 C.E. Other examples are mentioned in 2 Maccabees 14:42 and 4 Maccabees 17:1. Josephus also formed a suicide pact with his companions when threatened with capture by the Romans, though he and a companion did not carry out their part of the bargain.

Rabbinic Judaism considered suicide morally wrong, a rebellion against God who gave life and who alone may choose to take it (B. Abodah Zarah 18a). The rabbis, however, treated death as a suicide only if the individual made explicit his desire to kill himself and people saw him act on that intention (Tractate Semahot 2:2). In this circumstance, burial rites performed out of respect for the dead were set aside, such that mourners did not rend their clothes and no eulogy was offered (Tractate Semahot 2:1). The mourners themselves, however, were to be comforted, and the mourning prayers were recited out of respect to them. In contrast to the prevailing attitude, B. Gittin 57b accepts suicide for people forced into sexual impropriety. This attitude follows from the rabbinic dictum that one should accept death rather than commit murder, worship an idol, or engage in licentious sexual behavior.

Sukkah 1. booth erected in celebration of Sukkot

2. Mishnah tractate devoted to the festival of Tabernacles. The tractate discusses objects used in celebrating the festival, such as the Sukkah, the lulab, and the citron (chaps. 1–3), and describes the rites and offerings (chaps. 4–5).

Sukkot *see* TABERNACLES, FESTIVAL OF

Sulpicius Severus (360–420 C.E.) historian and hagiographer from Aquitaine and southern Gaul. He composed a chronicle of sacred history from creation to 400 C.E., using Christian and non-Christian works. He reports that Titus supported those who wished to burn the Jerusalem Temple during the war of 66–73 C.E.

superstition *see* DEISIDAIMONIA

Sura city in southern Babylonia; for several centuries a most important center of rabbinic study, rivaled in significance only by Nehardea. The academy at Sura was established by Ra_b_ in 219 C.E. and, after his death, retained its preeminence under Ra_b_'s student, Ḥuna. Sura's importance diminished in the final years of the third century with the rise in stature of Pumbedita. But its centrality was regained in 367–427 C.E., under the leadership of Ashi, later understood to be one of the editors of the Babylonian Talmud. During Ashi's incumbency, the academy was moved to Mata Maḥasia, near Sura. After Ashi's death, Sura's academy diminished in importance, although it remained a center of Sa_b_oraic and, later, gaonic learning.

Susanna a tale about a Jewish woman who is falsely accused of adultery by her would-be seducers and is rescued from the sentence of death by Daniel. The story is prefaced to the Book of Daniel in the Greek Bible as an explanation of how the young Daniel rose to prominence in the Babylonian court (v. 64). The date and place of composition are uncertain. Wordplays in the Greek text are usually seen as an indication that the story was composed in that language, but they could also reflect a translator's cleverness.

The plot line of Susanna indicates that the story imitates the genre of court tales preserved in the Joseph cycle in Genesis 37–45, the story of Mordecai in the Book of Esther, the Mesopotamian Story of Ahikar, Daniel 3 and 6, and Wisdom of Solomon 2 and 5. Certain villains conspire against the protagonist and bring accusations that result in a death sentence. The protagonist is rescued from death, vindicated, and exalted, and the enemies are punished. In the present example, the story is democratized; the protagonist is a woman rather than a man and an ordinary righteous person rather than a member of the court. It is Daniel her rescuer, rather than she, who is exalted at court. Details in the story parallel the story of Joseph and Potiphar's wife (Gen. 39) and the Egyptian Tale of the Two Brothers, with the male and female roles reversed.

Although the story is set in the diaspora, the action takes place within the Jewish community. The antagonists are Jewish elders and not gentile opponents of the Jews as, for example, in Daniel 3 and 6. Susanna exemplifies virtuous conduct in the face of temptations that can arise within the religious community. The portrayal of the male elders as hypocritical lechers, whose pressures are withstood by a virtuous woman, would have had some countercultural sting, and it has sometimes been argued that the story was intended as a warning against careless legal proceedings that employed bad rules of evidence.

The story of Susanna was popular among early Christian writers and has been the inspiration for much visual art and music. Carlisle Floyd's powerful twentieth-century opera "Susanna" captures the anti-establishment polemic but tragically inverts the story by having the heroine capitulate to the persistent coercion of a traveling revival preacher.

Susiya *see* KHIRBET SUSIYA SYNAGOGUE

swastika a minor motif in Jewish art of the Byzantine period borrowed from the wider Roman and Byzantine world. The swastika is not an isolated emblem in early Roman art, but is rather a border consisting of a repeated cross pattern that resembles the swastika, but the cross with bent arms is connected to the next cross, and so on, to form a border that resembles a maze. This form of border is called a meander. This type of border is well known in non-Jewish contexts as well as Jewish contexts. A free-standing swastika is known as a major motif in one synagogue mosaic. This one stems from the Phase I mosaic floor in the synagogue of En Gedi on the west shores of the Dead Sea. In the central rectangular panel of the prayer hall there were three large squares in a row. In the southernmost square was a swastika pattern. The bent arms of the cross appear to rotate counterclockwise. It is surrounded by repeated triangles. In the synagogue at Eshtemoa in Judea, the swastika pattern appears in the earlier mosaic. A swastika design is repeated three times in the mosaic of the Susiya synagogue to separate the panel with menorahs and the Torah shrine from the central geometric mosaic. The mosaic floor in the synagogue of Maoz Hayyim shows the same repeated swastika panels separating birds and menorahs as can be seen at Susiya.

sword a bladed weapon for close combat. The blade could be single- or double-edged, curved or straight, pointed or blunt. The curved blade was primarily for slashing; the straight sword, for stabbing. The Iron Age (c. 1200 B.C.E.) saw the arrival of the straight, long sword as a major weapon; it reached a length of 30 inches and was strong enough to thrust and slash. In the Graeco-Roman period, Roman soldiers used a lighter sword of about 24 inches. In the War Rule from Qumran, the sword is to be of pure iron, straight, double-edged, pointed, and 1½ cubits long (about 25 inches) and four fingers (about 3 inches) wide. The hilt of the sword was to be of pure horn, with patterned bands in gold and silver and precious stones (1QM 5:11–14).

Besides references to the actual weapon, the sword came to symbolize aggression (4 Ezra 16:3; 1QpHab 6:10; Matt. 26:52), oppression (Dan. 11:33; CD 1:21; Luke 21:24), civic disorder (Matt. 10:34), but also the power of proper authority (Rom. 13:4). Frequently the sword images God's vengeance on sinners and apostates (Sir. 39:31; CD 1:4.17, 16:1); a special sword is given to Judas Maccabeus by the prophet Jeremiah (2 Macc. 15:15) as well as to those fighting on God's behalf (1 Enoch 90:19.34, 91:11; Rev. 6:4). The angel of God has his sword ready to bring judgment (Sus. 1:59), and swords in the sky are ominous (2 Macc. 5:2; Sib. Or. 3:672; 4 Ezra 15:41). The Lord of Spirits has a sword (1 Enoch 62:12; 63:12) as does God Himself (Wis. of Sol. 5:20; 1 QM 12:11; 4 Ezra 15:22; 3 En. 32:1–2). The Sword of God is almost personified (Ezek. 21:3; Zech. 13:7; 1 QH 6:29; 1 QM 15:3, 19:4.11).

The sword is also connected with the spoken word (Ahikar 100; Ps. 52:2; Ps. 57:4; Wisd. of Sol. 18:16; Eph. 6:17; Heb. 4:12). A two-edged sword proceeds from Jesus' mouth (Rev. 1:16, 2:12, 19:15.21). One also finds the thought expressed that the wicked angels teach humans the art of making swords (1 Enoch 8:1, 69:6, 88:2): here war is the opposite of the cooperation that should reign among humans.

Sychar *see* SHECHEM

Symmachus a translator of the Hebrew Bible into Greek, to take the place of the Septuagint. Although some reports make him an Ebionite, this has been disputed. Others think he was Jewish. His translation is characterized by good Greek style and free, rather than literal, translation.

symposium (from Gr.: *symposion,* drinking party) As one might expect, many such occasions exhibited the usual concerns of drink and sex, but they also served for philosophical and literary discussion, some of which have been written up as symposium literature. *See also* SYMPOSIUM LITERATURE.

symposium literature several Greek and Latin writings have as their supposed origin a symposium discussion. One well-known example is the *Deipnosophista* (Supper Sophists) of Athenaeus; another is Plato's dialogue *The Symposium,* which forms an influential debate on the question of love.

These vary widely, sometimes being devoted simply to the delights of an extravagant host. For example, "Trimalchio's Feast" in Petronius focuses almost entirely on sensual pleasure and "ostentatious consumption." More standard, though, is a literary or philosophical discussion in which the participants attempt to show their learning or to exchange knowledge or debate. An example in Jewish literature is the Letter of Aristeas. According to it, Jewish sages from Jerusalem, brought to Egypt to translate the Bible, were entertained by the Ptolemaic ruler and demonstrated to him their wit, wisdom, and agility of mind in their table talk. They are presented as being perfectly at home in this common Hellenistic institution. Some think that the Passover Haggadah has been influenced by this literature; it certainly has some points in common with the symposium format.

synagogue (Heb.: *beit kennesset;* Aram.: *kenishtah;* Gr.: *proseuchē sabbation, synagōgē*) term used for the place of Jewish assembly and, at various time and locations, for scripture reading, sermons, or prayer. The term initially may have referred not to a building, per se, but to a meeting in private dwellings.

The synagogue is widely reputed to be the most distinctive institutional development of Judaism in antiquity. Its origin is uncertain. The conventional theory holds that the synagogue is the product of the Babylonian exile, but there is no evidence to prove that claim. Evidence for the synagogue comes from archaeological remains, the writings of Josephus, the New Testament, rabbinic literature, the church fathers, and pagan writers. All this evidence together does not yield a consistent picture of the synagogue and its functions in antiquity. There is a scholarly consensus that the synagogue probably fulfilled various functions, depending on its location, the nature of discrete Jewish communities, and surrounding culture.

The following dates and places display the range of the evidence for the synagogue. There is inscriptional evidence of a synagogue in Egypt in the third century B.C.E. A second century B.C.E. synagogue, probably founded by Samaritans, has been excavated on the island of Delos. There are only three excavated synagogues in the Land of Israel that archaeologists are prepared to date to Second Temple times: one in Gamla in the Golan Heights, one at Herodium, and one at Masada. A synagogue from the second or third century C.E. has been excavated at Sardis. A particularly interesting synagogue is the one discovered in Dura-Europos, in Syria, dated to the mid-second century C.E.

which has elaborate frescoes, murals of biblical events and figures, and different representations of the Temple.

In the New Testament, Jesus is frequently pictured as teaching in the synagogues of Galilee (Matt. 4:23, 9:35; Mark 1:21, 39, 6:2; Luke 4:15–16, 6:6; John 6:59, 18:20). Acts of the Apostles speaks of synagogues in Jerusalem (6:9) and in the diaspora: synagogues as places of prayer and teaching; synagogue leaders as public, community officials who often expel Paul and who struggle to maintain community discipline and boundaries. The descriptions of synagogue activities in the Gospels and Acts probably reflect the time of the authors, the late first century C.E. They verify the existence of the synagogues, especially in the diaspora, but do not attest to the places or kinds of buildings in which synagogues assembled. Besides the Gospels and Acts, only two other New Testament books mention synagogues. Revelation refers to Jewish opponents in Smyrna and Philadelphia as slanderers and liars who say they are Jews but are not, as a synagogue of Satan (2:9, 3:9). James mentions a synagogue of the Christian assembly (2:2).

Evidence for synagogues increases from the late second into the third and fourth centuries C.E., particularly in the Land of Israel, especially in Galilee. In this period, synagogue remains suggest large, well-decorated structures with fixed places (niches and *bimah*s) for Torah scrolls.

On the basis of the evidence, there is no clear picture of the functions the synagogue served. It may not have filled the same role in all places. Most scholars judge, however, that reading from the Torah and possibly from the prophets was a likely function of the synagogue. Literary evidence makes the same suggestion. Prayer may have been said in the synagogue, but that is not certain in all times and locations.

Until the fourth century and possibly later, particularly outside the Land of Israel, the synagogue appears not to have been under rabbinic control. There is no evidence that rabbinic liturgy was translated into Greek, so in Greek-speaking communities, the influence of rabbis was slight. The art of the Dura-Europos Synagogue could not have been predicted on the basis of rabbinic writings.

By the fourth century, the notion of the synagogue as a surrogate for the Temple is evident in both Jewish and pagan writings. In some cases, it appears that the house of study (*beit midrash*) was within or alongside the synagogue. Evidence found at Merot in Galilee reveals a study room, dated to the sixth century, attached to the southern wall of the synagogue. The largest number of Jewish inscriptions has been found in synagogues. Hundreds are evident on walls, lintels, amulets, pillars, and mosaic floors.

synagogue poetry (Heb.: *piyyut*) poems added to the fixed schedule of prayers in synagogue worship, written for special occasions, such as Sabbath, Passover, praying for rain, and the Days of Awe. These fall outside of the regularly defined prayers and ornament the service of worship.

synagogues, diaspora those synagogues known by archaeological or epigraphic remains from the Graeco-Roman diaspora. Before 70 C.E. and the destruction of the Second Temple, Jews traveled for social or commercial reasons to most major urban centers in the Hellenistic East. Some were moved as slaves, but others were mercenaries, entrepreneurs, or public figures. Groups of Jews therefore developed as ethnic enclaves in urban centers with more or less contact with the Land of Israel. Since they wanted to be able to worship in accord with their traditions, they gathered in homes, rented space, and built structures in various parts of the Roman Empire and under other political and economic hegemonies.

The best known examples of synagogues or prayer halls are from Sardis and Priene in Ionia, Delos in the Greek islands, Stobi in Macedonia, Dura-Europos on the Euphrates in Roman Syria, and Ostia in Roman Italy. The earliest evidence is from Delos, the birthplace of Apollo, whose Jewish community is mentioned in 1 Maccabees and in Josephus. The community there dated from the second or first century B.C.E. The prayer hall (Gr.: *proseuchē*) was a modified local house. It appears that the house was reconstructed in the late second century B.C.E. and in the mid-first century C.E. as a cultic or community center for the Jewish settlement. The reconstruction or renovation of the house consisted mainly of the division of one large room into two small rooms by the erection of a partition wall with three doors. Both rooms thus formed could be entered either from the attached, roofed porch or from the other room. In the northern or main room, low benches were built against the west and north walls and a stone chair was built into the west wall opposite the entrance from the porch. It is assumed that this marble chair was for a synagogue functionary. A few fragmentary inscriptions attest to the fact that the worshipers here served the "Highest God."

There is no distinctively Jewish art or decorative element in this building, so the scholarly opinion is that this building served the Jewish enclave before the destruction of Jerusalem and the Second Temple in 70 C.E. There would be no social need for identification of the users by art, decoration, or even by inscriptions before that date. In fact, the building faces directly toward the sea, which suggests the foreign (Jewish) origin of its users, as other structures built by foreigners in ancient port cities often face the sea rather than some local landmark.

A Samaritan community is also attested at Delos by inscriptional evidence, though as yet no worship edifice or synagogue has been identified. According to the inscriptions, however, they had their own prayer hall or proseuchē.

At Priene one can see more unambiguous remains. The building in question was a modified house of imposing dimensions (16 × 19.5 meters), perhaps of late Hellenistic origins. It was located in a block of homes sharing common walls, but each accessible to the others only via the street entrances. Renovation of the house for worship included razing shops and building new walls for the area for the congregation on the west end of the house. At the east end a niche was installed into the back wall of the house, and this niche actually intruded into the space of the next house to the east. Presumably the tenant of the east house was Jewish or was persuaded to allow use of this space. About half the renovated house was devoted to an assembly area, and the rest seemed to be reserved for an apartment or perhaps a set of rooms used for hospitality of visitors to the community.

At Ostia the synagogue was in use the longest of these diaspora synagogues, namely, from the first to the fourth centuries C.E. Recent scholarship has suggested that the building was not originally built as a prayer hall as formerly thought but was also a renovated house. It has been suggested that the original house underwent renovations first with the addition of a dining room, probably to enable use of the building for Jewish assemblies. In its second renovation, a second story was added to the assembly room, in effect doubling the volume of the room. This renovation required thickening the walls and adding two columns to support the roof. With this second renovation the congregation added an aedicula, or two-columned Torah Shrine, at the rear of the assembly hall and the use of menorahs as Jewish art and symbols. A *bimah*, or raised platform, graced the wall opposite the Torah Shrine. At least one of these renovations included a Greek inscription on the Torah Shrine honoring the donor.

The synagogue at Stobi in Macedonia is a rebuilt house that originally belonged to Claudius Tiberius Polycharmos, who is referred to in the dedicatory inscription for the synagogue as "father of the synagogue at Stobi." During the fourth century, this renovated house-synagogue was converted to larger space by the simple addition of as much space as the original prayer hall occupied. Furthermore, in the donor inscription of Polycharmos there is a stipulation that his heirs are to continue to live in the living quarters of the converted house. The demise of this synagogue occurred in the fifth century when a Christian basilica was built over the site of the original prayer hall.

The synagogue of Sardis in Asia Minor was a spectacular basilical building, originally built by the citizens of Sardis as a public building, actually probably dressing rooms (apodeuteria) of the public bath next door. Sometime in the late first or early second century C.E., the citizens of Sardis deeded the three dressing rooms to the Jewish community of Sardis for their own use. This building underwent many beautiful renovations and redecorations over four centuries of use. Synagogue assemblies in the building had use of two aediculae, or shrines, on either side of the central entryway at the east end of the building. Decoration includes two Lydian lions and "Roman" eagles in prominent places at the west end of the building. An inscription in the center of the long hall honors a local "priest and teacher of wisdom" who bears the local name of Samoe. A lectern stood on piers just east of the west end of the building, which contained an apse with concentric benches.

The synagogue at Dura-Europos on the Euphrates in Syria was a house renovated to allow for assemblies of the Jewish community about 150–200 C.E. In this renovation the exterior of the house remained untouched, but on the interior a Torah niche was added to the back, interior wall. A cross-wall divided the main part of the house into a colonnaded porch and a small assembly hall or prayer hall. In the second synagogue, the interior assembly was reduced in size, but benches were added on four walls. The Torah niche was still in use. There may be provision for a lectern in the center of the hall. A smaller assembly room with benches around all four walls stood at the opposite end of the house. In the final renovation of the house, the interior was completely remodeled to form a large, colonnaded courtyard and a large assembly hall or prayer hall still using the same Torah niche. Part of a house next door was added to the space in use for worship. This last synagogue or prayer hall was decorated with stunning wall frescoes depicting biblical scenes. Certain donors are also honored in Greek inscriptions, one of whom is the elder, priest, and archon Samuel bar Yedaya, perhaps the original owner of the house that was converted to synagogue worship.

synagogues, Palestinian those synagogues known by archaeological or epigraphic evidence from ancient Palestine. The source for the term synagogue is the Greek term, *synagōgē*, to gather. It is used in the New Testament, in Josephus, and rabbinic sources for a Jewish community or building, or possibly both. The origin of the synagogue as a Jewish place of assembly and prayer is unknown. Several theories have been advanced: it developed during the Babylonian exile; at the time of the Deuteronomic reformation; or in Hellenistic Egypt. What is known from the textual sources is that the synagogue was in existence in Palestine by the first century C.E. and became the main focus and center of Jewish life following the destruction of the Temple in 70 C.E. Archaeological evidence from Palestine is less secure. An inscription uncovered in Jerusalem and dated to the first century C.E. describes a synagogue built by one Theodotus for the reading of the law, studying the commandments, and for use as a hostel. No mention is made of prayer, perhaps because of the building's proximity to the Temple. Torah reading was of primary importance. Four buildings in Palestine have been identified as synagogues predating the Temple's destruction: Masada, Herodium, Gamla, and Migdal. Masada and Herodium have reconfigured rooms in fortress palaces built by Herod the Great and occupied by zealots during the first Jewish revolt. Gamla, a town in the Golan occupied by zealots, has a large, unadorned building with benches along its interior walls. Migdal, on the west shore of the Sea of Galilee, has a small building with benches, that later became a water reservoir. Except for Masada, where scrolls and ostraca were found within the building, the evidence to support the identification of the other sites as synagogues is inconclusive.

Synagogue excavations began in earnest in Palestine at the beginning of the twentieth century. Over one hundred synagogues have since been excavated. Their plans display great diversity, but all are variations on the Roman basilica, with a roofed hall, usually rectangular with inner columns, and entered from either its narrow or long side. Basilicas were used by the Romans for functions requiring a large interior space, an important consideration for synagogue builders who needed to design buildings with rooms large enough to house a congregation gathered together for prayer and study. Synagogue plans fall into three broad categories.

The Galilean-type, found primarily in Galilee, has three doors on the synagogue's south facade opening onto a hall divided by two longitudinal rows of columns and a north transverse colonnade forming a U-shape. The building's focus, then, becomes the entry wall facing south toward Jerusalem. A portable Torah shrine and *bimah* may have stood between the doors. Evidence for permanent shrines in Galilean-type synagogues remains inconclusive. The plan requires a worshiper to make a 180-degree turn upon entering the synagogue in order to face south toward Jerusalem to pray. Galilean-type synagogues were built from the third to the fifth centuries, for example, Capernaum, Chorazin, Meron, Kefar Baram.

The broadhouse is found in Galilee and Judaea and is so called because its focus is on a permanent Torah shrine and/or *bimah* located on the broad wall facing toward Jerusalem. These synagogues have been found with interior colonnades. The earliest known example, dated to the second century, was uncovered at Nabratein in Galilee. The building has two bemas flanking its Jerusalem wall, and there is possible evidence of a table in the center. Horvat Rimmon, Eshtemoa, and Khirbet Susiya located in Judaea share the same basic plan, with entrances on the narrow east wall and a Torah shrine and *bimah* on the Jerusalem wall. The plan requires the worshiper to make a 90-degree turn to face toward Jerusalem to pray. The synagogues are dated from the second to the sixth centuries. Examples are Khirbet Shema and Nabratein in Upper Galilee, Horvat Rimmon I, Eshtemoa, and Khirbet Susiya in Judaea.

Longitudinal or apsidal synagogues are scattered throughout the country. A longitudinal axis leads from a court and/or narthex through entrances into the synagogue. Its interior is divided by two rows of columns into a central nave and flanking aisles. The axis continues down the nave to the synagogue's focal point, often an apse projecting off a short wall facing Jerusalem and the Torah shrine and *bimah*, which may be fenced off by a chancel screen similar to ones found in churches. Worshipers, upon entering the synagogue complex, transversed a longitudinal route leading from the secular to the increasingly sacred that culminated at the Torah shrine, the focus for prayer. These buildings are dated from the fifth century onward. Examples are Beth Alpha, Beth Shean A, Gaza, Maoz Hayim and Maon.

All three categories demonstrate the importance of prayer being directed toward Jerusalem. The longitudinal or apsidal plan may be related to developments in church architecture and illustrates an increase in the sacrality of the synagogue and a concomitant emphasis on prayer that evolved in the years following the Temple's destruction.

Diversity is evident in the decoration of synagogues. Galilean synagogues were primarily decorated with sculptural motifs, whereas the broadhouse and apsidal synagogues often had mosaic pavements and possibly frescoed walls. Eagles, lions, peacocks, and zodiacs are the most popular secular motifs. Lions appear in mosaic pavements and as three-dimensional and relief sculpture. Eagles are usually in relief, and peacocks and the zodiac are only found in mosaic pavements. The menorah is by far the most popular Jewish motif. Several three-dimensional menorahs have been found, but the majority are either relief sculpture or depicted in mosaic pavements along with the shofar, lulab, and etrog. In mosaic pavements the menorah and ritual objects may be shown flanking a Torah shrine. Biblical scenes are sometimes depicted in mosaic pavements. Possibly the most famous is the binding of Isaac at Beth Alpha.

Regionalism also can contribute to the diversity found in Palestinian synagogues. Different regions were exposed to different cultural influences that impacted on the synagogue's appearance. Synagogues in remote rural areas were less likely to exhibit figurative art than those close to Greek cities or trade routes. Diversity can be documented in synagogues located within a single region, for example, the broadhouse synagogue at Khirbet Shema and its Galilean neighbor at Meron. As more excavations are conducted, more will be understood about Palestinian synagogue architecture.

Syncellus, George Byzantine writer in Greek who worked in Constantinople at the beginning of the ninth century C.E. (c. 784–806 C.E.). His main work was the *Chronographical Excerpts,* a world chronicle from Creation to Diocletian; it was evidently planned to extend to his own time, but he died first. The chonological benchmark is the birth of Christ in the year 5500 after creation. The work does not show any particular originality or critical acumen but is mainly a compilation. In fact, much may have been copied from just two earlier Christian chronographers. Nevertheless, whatever its immediate source(s), it is extremely valuable because of having at its base a variety of historical and other works from the Graeco-Roman period that have since been lost. This includes a number of early Jewish works that until recently were known only or primarily through him. Although more recent discoveries have superseded his evidence in some cases, he is still the main representative of the Greek text of some works; this includes the important Greek version of 1 Enoch, which he quotes extensively. He also uses Jubilees a good deal; however, he seldom quotes it directly but rather reworks it.

syncretism the union or mixture of different cultures and religions. It is a term used by modern scholars in religious discussions but too often indiscriminately. In reality, it is rare to find true syncretism, in which two religions are blended together into a single unit. More frequent is influence, which leads to the borrowing of various elements, which are then incorporated into the existing religion. Also, plurality may not be the end result of the process, as was once thought about ancient Israelite religion, but rather the beginning of it, as most scholars now believe.

synodos (Gr., assembly) The term could be used of any assembly or meeting, official or unofficial, though often it referred to official conferences called by the government or administration. It was often a synonym of *synedrion* (Sanhedrin).

Syria In light of the proximity of Syria to the Land of Israel and the large number of Jews who, by the rabbinic period, lived there, rabbinic law treats Israelite-owned land in Syria as exactly like property in the Land of Israel itself (M. Ḥallah 4:11). The case of leased property (M. Ḥallah 4:7) and other ambiguous situations, by contrast, show the law not to have been completely settled: some rabbis deemed Syria to be like the Land of Israel proper, while others took seriously the fact that it is not within the area assigned by God to the twelve tribes.

Syria, Jews in During the Roman period, the historian Josephus claims that Syria had the highest percentage of Jewish inhabitants in the empire. Antioch, the major city in Syria, had a large and well-established Jewish community that dated from the third century B.C.E. He also mentions several other major cities: Tyre, Sidon, and Apamea. Much of the other evidence for Jewish presence comes from the late Roman period. Inscriptions indicate that Jews lived in Byblos and Beirut on the coast and Palmyra in the eastern desert. Later Syriac sources suggest interaction between Jews and Christians in Edessa and eastern Syria as well as northern Mesopotamia. It is likely that Jews were broadly present in all parts of Syria.

Syria, Roman province of The name Syria was used by the Seleucid dynasty, the predecessors of the Romans, for the geographical area east of the Meditarranean Sea and west of the Euphrates River from the Taurus Mountains in Asia Minor all the way to Egypt. During the Roman period, however, the southern portion of that area, including Lebanon and Israel, was divided into various kingdoms and provinces and the northern portion became the province of Syria. Since this province was at the border of the Roman Empire, its governors were entrusted with military operations and defense against the Parthians and later the Sassanids in Mesopotamia. The emperor appointed as governor a legate of senatorial rank who was a former consul. The legate commanded a strong force of legions and auxiliary troops. The eastern boundary of Syria was not a clearly marked geographical line. It varied with the advances and withdrawal of the Roman army and the waxing and waning influence of political powers in the East. Syria included a large number of ethnic groups, but literary, inscriptional, and material remains testify to the pervasive presence of Greek culture and language. *See also* SYRIA PALAESTINA.

Syriac an Eastern dialect of Late Aramaic, the use of which was centered in Syria. Used by the Eastern Church, it is the best documented Aramaic dialect, with the Peshita translation of both the Old Testament and the New Testament, as well as extensive commentaries, sermons, and other religious literature. It is written in three different scripts—Estrangela, Nestorian, and Jacobite—all of which differ from the standard block script of most other Aramaic dialects.

Syria Palaestina more popularly, Palestine ("the land of the Philistines," a designation found in Herodotus); the official Roman name given to the province that included Israel after the Bar Kosiba War (132–35 C.E.). Previously it had been called Judaea, a term that continued to be used unofficially.

Syro-Palestinian Christian Aramaic *see* ARAMAIC, CHRISTIAN PALESTINIAN

Syrophoenicia the coastal area northwest of Galilee, also known simply as Phoenicia, after its ancient inhabitants, the Phoenicians. In the Gospel of Mark (7:26), a woman who is a Greek, a Syrophoenician, approaches Jesus of Nazareth to ask him to cure her daughter.

taanit (Heb.) fasting; *see also* ASCETICISM

Taanit a tractate on fast days in the Division of Appointed Times (Moed) in the Mishnah, Tosefta, and both Talmuds. In manuscripts and first printings of all but the Babylonian Talmud, as well as in gaonic and medieval citations, the tractate is called Taaniyot (fast days). The Mishnah tractate's first two chapters concern fasts decreed because of a drought. Topics concern individuals exempt from such fasts, the procedures followed in instituting a fast, including the length of the fast and the range of prohibited activities, the prayers recited on fast days, and occasions on which fasting is prohibited. Chapter 3 turns to fasts decreed for reasons other than drought, for instance, by towns suffering from pestilence, blight, or other communal problems, such as animals attacking children. The tractate concludes in chapter 4 with miscellaneous material, covering a range of topics, not all of which are directly related to the overall topic of the tractate: the recitation of the priestly benediction on fast days, the rules for the members of the priestly watch and the communal delegation to the Temple, the law of the wood offering, the reasons for and rules of the fast days of the ninth of Ab and seventeenth of Tammuz, and a description of a special ceremony held on the fifteenth of Ab and the Day of Atonement, in which young women danced in the fields to attract husbands.

Within the talmudic treatment of the tractate, chapter 3 of the Babylonian Talmud is of particular interest. Devoted almost entirely to aggadah, it contains many stories of the early Ḥasidim, pious men believed to have had a special relationship with God. These materials develop M. Taanit's presentation of the story of Ḥoni the Circle Maker.

Taanit Esther fast of Esther, celebrated on the thirteenth of Adar, the day prior to Purim

Tabari, Abu Jafar Muhammad ibn Jarir al- (839–923 C.E.) historian and theologian, born in Tabaristan, northern Iran. His commentary on the Quran and his universal history of the world from creation to his own time became standard reference works. His history provides important information about the Jews under the Persian Empire.

tabernacle the tent of meeting and the place in which YHWH dwells when He is with his people. It contains the Ark of the Covenant and other artifacts and vessels of cultic significance. Ben Sira calls it the "house of the curtain" because it included an inner room or secluded area, the Holy of Holies, into which the high priest alone could enter on the Day of Atonement. The covenanters of Qumran thought of themselves as either the Temple or the tabernacle itself, and they defined their priests as the Holy of Holies itself (Community Rule).

Although the portable tent of meeting became immovable in Solomon's Temple, it is not certain whether the Second Temple also contained a tabernacle. Eupolemus's stress on the consideration kings had given to the tabernacle and Temple does not help to resolve the issue. By the first century C.E., there was some confusion about the layout and structure of the tabernacle but not about its replication of a divine prototype. Although we do not know of any prior nonliterary representation, the tabernacle and its priests were represented in the art of the third-century-C.E. synagogue at Dura-Europos.

Tabernacles, Festival of (Heb.: Sukkot) week of rejoicing beginning on the fifteenth of Tishrei, the date of the first full moon after the autumnal equinox. The festival is "the season of our rejoicing," when Israelites eat their meals in a tabernacle, or fragile hut, covered with boughs but with the sky showing through, in remembrance of the wanderings in the wilderness. It is also a harvest festival; prayers for rain during the coming rainy season are recited.

Tabiomi b. Ashi *see* MAR B. ASHI

table fellowship Practiced by the Therapeutae, Essenes (*Vita. Cont.* 40–89; see 1QSa 2), and various other Jewish groups (see Josephus, *Ant.* 14.10.8, on Caesar's permission for Jews to engage in feasting according to their customs) and by early Christians (1 Cor. 11:17–34; Acts 2:46), table fellowship had both social and religious import. Religious banquets, Christian *agape* feasts, *Haburah* meals, and other group meals were, in general, formal occasions in which group members consumed food made sacred through strict tithing or symbolic representation, such as sacrificial associations. Participation, which served to reflect and maintain social boundaries, often required prior initiation (circumcision, immersion). Table fellowship and meal settings also served as literary conventions for situating philosophical discussions.

tablets, heavenly *see* BOOKS, HEAVENLY

Tacitus (c. 55–120 C.E.) Roman historian. He wrote two main works: the *Histories* originally covered the period from 69 C.E. to the reign of Domitian; the *Annals* was devoted to the reign of Tiberius through that of Nero. Significant portions of both works have been lost, though they were made use of by Dio Cassius. In addition to providing general information on the history of the first-century Roman Empire, Tacitus is one of the most important Roman writers on the Jews and provides a useful supplement and corrective to Josephus for this period. Although he is not particularly favorable toward Judaism, he can give an even-handed account of historical events involving it. He briefly presents several accounts of Jewish origins, though he focuses on the one that ascribes them to the expulsion of disease-disfigured individuals from Egypt. He also states that Antiochus IV's attack on Judaism was to rid it of its superstitions. But he is better on descriptions of Roman rule over Judea, and his account of the siege of Jerusalem during the 66–70 war provides important information. He also makes various references to the Jews and Judaism in passing.

Tafnith location corresponding to Tabnin; referred to at T. Shebiit 4:11 as demarcating a border area of the Land of Israel

Taḥanun penitential supplications said silently in the daily synagogue prayer service both morning (*shaḥarit*) and afternoon (*minḥah*), but omitted on special occasions. Taḥanun grew out of an ancient custom of a private daily confession, then private prayer of any variety, and became finally, in the Middle Ages, the Taḥanun. Influenced ultimately by Christian penitential piety, Taḥanun is a collection of prayers invoking God's mercy despite human sin. It is omitted in Reform and many other liberal congregations.

Taheb an eschatological figure among the Samaritans. Much of the information on him is taken from very late sources, some produced in the twentieth century. What is clear is that the Mosaic prophet concept of Deuteronomy forms the core. This much is early, whereas other features may be due to Jewish or Christian influence.

tahor, tamei (Heb., clean/unclean) the concept that a person or object can be in a status that precludes contact with the Temple or cult. Uncleanness, that is, ritual impurity, is transferred to other persons or objects in a variety of ways, including contact, supporting the weight of an unclean object, or being under the same roof with it. The state of uncleanness is unrelated to any tangible condition, such as being physically dirty, but it is corrected primarily through ablution, which renders the individual clean, that is, ritually pure.

The Pharisees, followed by the Mishnah's rabbis, extended the scriptural notion that purity matters primarily in the Temple. They held that all food should be eaten in cleanness, as though it were a sacrifice on the Temple altar. Numerous laws make clear the practical implications the rabbis understood these matters to have. Along with a general prohibition against imparting uncleanness to foods, the rabbis legislated against prayer and study of religious texts by individuals in a state of uncleanness. Since scripture holds that cleanness is comparable to holiness, the rabbinic perspective intended in a concrete manner to transform the entire people of Israel into a holy nation of priests. At the same time, the people never meticulously followed these laws. The rabbinic sources speak of a small group of individuals, designated "associates" (ḥa-

verim), who were distinguished by their consumption of common foods in a state of cleanness. Additionally, many rabbinic laws refused to segregate those who are unclean, or even to deny them the right to participate in the synagogue or academy.

takkanah (Heb., remedy) an official rabbinic legal decree often enacted to accommodate Jewish law with historical conditions after extraordinary social or economic upheavals. In one such instance, Hillel the Elder ordained the prosbul to circumvent the cancellation of debts in the sabbatical year. Simeon b. Shetaḥ enacted compulsory education. Yoḥanan b. Zakkai legislated *takkanot* (plural) concerning the calendar and Temple ritual. Through the Takkanot of Usha (2d c. C.E.), the Sanhedrin sought to repair the social fabric of family life after the disastrous Hadrianic persecutions. Thus, fathers were required to support minor children and not inflict harsh punishment on them. *Takkanot* became more commonplace in the Middle Ages, and they became a means to regulate business, taxes, charity, and the ritual affairs of a community. Rabbenu Gershom b. Judah of Mainz (d. 1028 C.E.) enacted a *takkanah* for Ashkenazic Jews of France and Germany that prohibited both polygamy by Jewish men and the divorce of a woman against her will.

talent a unit of weight in the ancient Near East. As generally with weights and measures, it was not standardized over the region. It is sometimes defined as 3,000 shekels. Archaeological findings indicate that in ancient Israel it was usually reckoned as approximately 70 pounds (30 kg).

talith (Heb.; pl., *talitoth*) the mantle of the Roman period, woven of one rectangular piece of linen and worn over the tunic. This garment was called the *pallium* in Latin and the *himation* in Greek. Many examples of mantles were found in the Judean desert caves, notably the Cave of Letters, though only one was found largely intact. They are also known from the paintings in the synagogue and church at Dura-Europos, from Egyptian coffin paintings of the Roman period, from statuary in Palmyra, and from the Ravenna mosaics in Italy. The intact example from the Judean Desert Caves was 2.7 meters long and 1.4 meters wide. This talith had four gamma-shaped patterns with notched ends woven near the four corners (see illustration). Each gamma pattern is about 4 centimeters wide and 10 centimeters long on each leg. These gamma patterns are dyed in contrasting colors, namely, blue or black. The selvedges of the mantle are also blue or black. The notched gammas mark the mantle for a woman. The excavator hypothesizes that

the mantles doubled as blankets, since the width is roughly the height of an average Roman woman. This mantle was dyed yellow with saffron. Other mantles with gammas were dyed in many different colors, though reddish-brown and blue-black predominate. Men's mantles typically have a notched band about 1.5 to 3 centimeters wide and 10 to 30 centimeters long near each of the four corners. The band is also dyed blue or black. Mainly white or light yellow, the men's mantles with notched bands occur in fewer colors than do the women's mantles. It has been noticed that in a late Jewish document, the Sifrei to Deuteronomy, men are enjoined not to wear color, while women are enjoined not to wear white.

talitha cumi (Aram., girl, arise) the words spoken by Jesus to the dead daughter of the synagogue leader, Jairus, exhorting her to come back to life (Mark 5:41). It parallels the similar usage of the Aramaic expression, *ephphata*, at Mark 7:34.

tallit *see* PRAYER SHAWL

talmid hakham *see* DISCIPLE OF A SAGE

Talmid Ḥaver (Heb., student-colleague) in the Babylonian Talmud, a title of distinction for a disciple who has achieved the status of being a colleague to his teacher (B. Baba Batra 158b). In the Jerusalem Talmud, the same concept is expressed by the phrase Talmid veḤaver, "student and colleague" (Y. Shekalim 3:1, 47b).

Talmud a sustained, analytical reading and interpretation of a Mishnah tractate, in which a systematic and critical program aims at explaining the meaning and concrete application of the Mishnah-rule, on the one hand, and harmonizing one Mishnah-rule with others with which it intersects, on the other. "A Talmud" accomplishes the work of Mishnah-commentary and explanation by forming a moving ("dialectical") argument, from point to point, in which all possibilities are systematically taken up and examined. What is talmudic about the two Talmuds is that mode of thought, which is a critical, systematic application of applied reason and practical logic, moving from a point starting with a proposition and (ordinarily) ending with a firm and articulated conclusion. The two talmuds, the Talmud of the Land of Israel (the Yerushalmi, or the Jerusalem Talmud, or the Palestinian Talmud), completed c. 400 C.E., and the Talmud of Babylonia (the Babli), completed c. 600 C.E., share many formal traits, though their character and most of their contents differ radically. As commentaries to the Mishnah, they are alike, but in their canonical context, they also are different from all other documents, hence forming a genus made up of two species. But that which speciates vastly overrides that which units the species into a genus—the form is common; the substance, unique to the respective species. *See also* BABLI; YERUSHALMI.

Talmud of Babylonia   *see* BABLI

Talmud of the Land of Israel   *see* YERUSHALMI

Talmud Torah   study of Torah; education; *see also* TORAH STUDY

Tamar   **1.** the widow of Er and Onan who, disguised as a prostitute, became pregnant by her father-in-law Judah (Gen. 38; Ruth 4:12, 18–22; 1 Chron. 2:4). Philo (*Virt.* 220–222; *Nob.* 6), Pseudo-Jonathan, and T. B. Sotah 10 view Tamar as a Jewish proselyte. Jubilees 41 and Testament of Judah 10:1 call her a "daughter of Aram" and so preserve the ethnic ambiguity of Genesis 38. Because Judah orders her burnt for adultery (Gen. 38:24; cf. Lev. 21:9), Genesis Rabbah 85:11 states she is the daughter of the high priest Shem. Matthew's genealogy (1:3) associates her with Ruth, Rahab, and "the wife of Uriah" (Bathsheba). Jubilees and the Testament of Judah decry Tamar's activities but blame Judah's Canaanite wife for refusing to allow her son Shelah to fulfill his levirate duties. Genesis Rabbah 85 and T. B. Horayot 10b (R. Ulla) compare her adultery positively to that of Zimri. T. B. Sotah 10a (cf. T. P. Sotah 5a, 16d) vindicates Judah by attributing sinful activity to Tamar.

2. the daughter of David and Maacah whose rape by her half-brother Amnon precipitates her brother Absalom's revolt (2 Sam. 1–22)

3. Absalom's beautiful daughter (2 Sam. 14:27).

tamei   unclean; especially, unsuitable to enter the holy part of the Temple; *see also* TAHOR, TAMEI.

tamid   (Heb.) the daily whole offering

Tamid   Mishnah tractate narrating how the daily whole offering is presented. The narrative describes how priests prepare the altar (chaps. 1–2); select the lamb (chap. 3); clear the ashes from the altar (chap. 3); slaughter the lamb (chap. 4); bless the congregation and place the limbs on the altar (chap. 5); and clear the ashes (chaps. 5–6).

Tammuz   tenth month of the Jewish calendar, corresponding to June/July

Tammuz, Seventeenth of   *see* SHEBA ASAR BETAMMUZ

Tanakh   (also Bible or Torah) terms used by Jews to designate the same body of books that Christians call the Old Testament. It is regarded by both groups as authoritative scripture. The word Tanakh is an acronym made up of the first letters of the Hebrew names for its three basic divisions: Torah (divine teaching and law), Nebiim (prophets), and Ketubim (writings). The Tanakh is divided into twenty-four books. In the Christian Old Testament

the same material is divided into thirty-nine books and arranged somewhat differently. The Tanakh does not include the Apocrypha, Jewish works contained in the Bibles of some Christian groups (e.g., Roman Catholics). In the attempt to avoid calling this collection by a term with confessional (Jewish or Christian) overtones, scholars often refer to the Tanakh as the Hebrew Bible or the Hebrew scriptures.

Tanhuma   *see* MIDRASH TANHUMA

Tanhuma b. Abba   Palestinian amora of the second half of the fourth century C.E.; a student of Huna. A prolific midrashic scholar, he is held to have produced the Tanhuma Midrash and is best known for his place in the proem form, which frequently is introduced: "R. Tanhuma opened his discourse with this verse. . . ." Tanhuma is reported to have outreasoned the emperor and, as a result, to have been thrown into an arena with wild beasts (B. Sanhedrin 39a).

Tanhum b. Hanilai   Palestinian amora of the second half of the third century C.E.; referred to in the Jerusalem Talmud as Ilai or Ben Hanila; a student of Joshua b. Levi. He is known primarily for his scriptural exegesis, which is marked by his method of connecting the end of one verse to the beginning of the next (see, e.g., Lev. Rabbah 3:4).

Tanhum b. Hiyya   Palestinian amora of the late third and early fourth centuries C.E.; referred to in Babylonian compilations as Tanhum of Kefar Akko. In Galilee he was active in the intercalation of the calendar (Y. Sanhedrin 1:2, 18c). He is primarily known for scriptural interpretation.

Tanhumei Abelim   (Heb., the comforting of mourners) a specific liturgical practice during Tannaitic times by which mourners were offered comfort. It is no longer extant.

Tanhum of Kefar Akko   *see* TANHUM B. HIYYA

Tannaite, Tannaitic   (from Heb.: *tanna*, professional repeater) assigning the status of Tannaite authority to a document or to a saying. Thus "Tannaitic literature" means literature produced by authorities of Tannaite status, including the Mishnah, Tosefta, and *baraitot*, or traditions preserved outside of finished compilations and assigned to Tannaite standing and authority.

Tarfon   Tannaitic authority active immediately following the destruction of the Jerusalem Temple in 70 C.E.; a priest; a leading authority in the academy at Yabneh. He is frequently cited in dispute with Akiba. He was the teacher of Judah b. Ilai.

targeman   *see* METURGEMAN

targum   Hebrew and Aramaic word with the general meaning of translation. In our period, the word is used primarily to designate the translation of the Hebrew Bible into Aramaic. We currently possess targum texts to all but three books of the Hebrew Bible, namely, Ezra, Nehemiah, and Daniel. Targums contain translations that vary from being extremely literal (as in the case of Targum Onkelos) to being not merely paraphrastic but even inclusive of large amounts of nontranslation material (for example, the Targum to the Song of Songs). Most of the targums we now possess were written by Jews in the rabbinic period of Judaism, although at least one targum has been discovered at Qumran (first century C.E.) and others stem from the early Middle Ages. They were probably used in both synagogue worship and education when Aramaic was more widely used than Hebrew among Jews.

targum, forbidden   *see* FORBIDDEN TARGUM

targum festival collections   assemblages of Torah readings for specific festivals, such as Shabuot, the seventh day of Passover, and Purim. These readings usually consist of additions from the Palestinian Targum tradition and occasionally include *haftarah* readings as well. Sometimes an alphabetic acrostic poem introduces the collection. Such collections appear as brief independent collections, in Maḥorim and in Fragmentary Targums—most notably the Paris Targum.

targumic poems   These poems were usually constructed through an alphabetic acrostic (the first line begins with *aleph,* the next with *bet,* and so on) and were usually located in a topically relevant spot in a targum manuscript. The poem "Etzel Moshe," for instance, concerns Moses and the Red Sea and appears after Exodus 14:29 in the Fragmentary Targum in Paris. Other poems occur as introductions in targum festival collections. The earliest of such poems may have been composed in fourth- or fifth-century Palestine.

Targumic Toseftot to the Prophets   *see* PALESTINIAN TARGUM TO THE PROPHETS

targumist   the writer of a targum; occasionally used to designate a scholar who studies targums; *see also* TARGUM

Targum Jonathan   *see* TARGUM TO THE PROPHETS

targums and rabbinic literature   The targums have an ambiguous relationship with rabbinic literature. On the one hand, they are closely linked. The Babylonian Talmud treats Targum Onkelos to the Pentateuch and Targum Jonathan to the Prophets as official targums, often quoting from them and using them as sources for halakhah. The targums and the rabbinic texts often share the same exegetical concerns, with similar interpreta-

tions of passages appearing both in targums and in rabbinic midrashim or talmudic literature. Sometimes the interpretations agree; at other times they take different sides of the same issue. There are also important differences between the targums and rabbinic literature. Only the targums are continuous, following the narrative lines of scripture without break (although some early medieval targums to the Writings interrupt the narrative with multiple translations of the same passages). Most rabbinic texts, by contrast, consist of series of short, discrete units. Furthermore, the targums generally attempt to insert their interpretations into the translations, interweaving the two so that the interpretation appears as part of the translation. Most rabbinic midrashim and legal texts are written in such a way that the interpretation is set apart from the biblical passage being interpreted.

targums and the New Testament   The rabbinic targums share a surprising number of features with the New Testament's books. This is most evident for the Gospels, but also holds true for its letters. Both Gospels and targums use wording that avoids speaking of God anthropomorphically or anthropopathically. They share many key theological concepts: Father in heaven, this world/the world to come, Son of Man, resurrection, the great Day of Judgment, Gehenna, and paradise. They also contain similar—and occasionally identical—interpretations of passages from the Hebrew Bible. These common features demonstrate that these two sets of texts can be used to interpret each other. The problem with comparing these texts lies in their dating. Most of the New Testament books have been dated to the first century C.E.; the earliest of the rabbinic targums (Targum Onkelos, Targum Jonathan, and some of the Palestinian Targums), stem from the second century or later. Of course, many targums contain earlier material, but identifying that material has proved to be difficult. With regard to language, the earliest targums from Palestine may prove useful in reconstructing the Aramaic dialect spoken by Jesus.

targums and the text of the Hebrew Bible   The translations of the Hebrew Bible into Aramaic, known as targums, have not proved useful witnesses to the Hebrew text. Two reasons explain this failure. First, many of the targums derive from the Masoretic text and thus provide no independent witness to it. Indeed, many of the targums—Targum Pseudo-Jonathan and the Targums to the Writings, for example—were clearly composed long after the Hebrew text was fixed. Second, many of the targums are highly interpretive—adding new material, shaping the translation to reflect their writers' beliefs—even when they are at their most literal. Thus, the targums generally provide little help in establishing the original biblical text.

targums at Qumran   The only unquestionable targum found at Qumran is that of Job (11QtgJob). Its fragments cover portions of the book extending from Job 17:14 to 42:11. Aramaic fragments of Leviticus 16:12–15 and 18–21 have also been found; it is unclear whether these evidence a targum, however, because they are short enough to have simply been a biblical quote within a text of another type. The Genesis Apocryphon, which relates stories about Noah and Abraham, should also be mentioned. Although written in Aramaic, the apocryphon belongs, strictly speaking, to the category of rewritten Bible. It retells several stories about Abraham and Sarah, adding a significant amount of aggadic material and making little attempt to present a literal translation of the Hebrew. Aramaic fragments of Tobit were also found in the Qumran caves. It is thought that these fragments stem from the original Aramaic text of Tobit and thus are not a targum.

Targum Sheni   the second (Heb.: *sheni*) targum to Esther; *see also* ESTHER, TARGUMS TO

Targums to the Five Megillot   Each of the Five Megillot (scrolls)—Kohelet, Ruth, Song of Songs, Lamentations, and Esther—have been translated into Aramaic. These are individual targums composed under widely differing circumstances and not a single targum, as for the Pentateuch and the Prophets. However, they all seem to be written in a mix of Eastern and Western Aramaic—probably indicating their composition in the early Middle Ages.

Targums to the Pentateuch   *see* ONKELOS, TARGUM; PALESTINIAN TARGUMS TO THE PENTATEUCH

Targums to the Writings   (Hagiographa) There is no single targum covering the Writings, as there are for the Pentateuch and the Prophets. Although most of the hagiographic books have targums (only Ezra, Nehemiah, and Daniel do not), they use different styles of translation—suggesting they were composed by different people. Despite these differences, many of these targums share several characteristics: most use material from the Babylonian Talmud, the Palestinian Targums, and other Palestinian rabbinic documents, and their language is usually a mixture of eastern and western elements of Aramaic. All this evidence suggests that the Targums to the Writings were composed in the early Middle Ages by eastern Mediterranean Jewry after Targum Onkelos became the dominant Pentateuchal targum.

Targum to the Prophets   a translation of the books of the Former and the Latter Prophets into Aramaic. This targum has traditionally been called Targum Jonathan (Yonatan) because the Babylonian Talmud (Meg. 3a) attributes it to Jonathan b. Uziel. However, this attribution is fanciful, and the exact circumstances of the targum's origins are unknown. The known features of the Targum to the Prophets are similar to those of Targum Onkelos: the Targum to the Prophets attained its current form between the third and fifth centuries in a non-Palestinian (eastern) form of Aramaic, although it is probably based on an earlier targum. The Prophets targum is also generally literal, although it contains more nonliteral material than Targum Onkelos. Among Babylonian Jewry, Targum Jonathan became the authoritative translation of the prophetic books—valid even for questions of halakah. In the early Middle Ages, this targum became dominant among western Jews as well, replacing a Palestinian Targum to the Prophets.

targum use in synagogue and school   The use of the targums in synagogues and schools during the rabbinic period remains unclear. Rabbinic literature reveals that translation—particularly into Aramaic—plays a role in both worship and education. But it is not obvious whether translation was performed extemporaneously or through the memorization and repetition of written translations. So although we can speculate that the targum texts may have been used in these institutions, we do not know if any written targums, let alone the ones we now possess, were in fact used there. Despite this caveat, the practice of translation reveals the social context against which the relationship between scripture and Aramaic should be seen: in the synagogue, Hebrew scripture was read out loud to the worshipers and then translated into Aramaic—orally, not read from a written targum. Other rabbinic texts (Sifrei Deuteronomy 161) indicate that while the first order of study in a *beit sefer* (elementary school) constituted study of the Torah in Hebrew, the second focused on the Torah's translation into Aramaic. Targums could have been used in these religious situations, but we do not know if they were. *See also* SCRIPTURE READING IN THE SYNAGOGUE.

Taricheae   *see* MAGDALA

Tarngola   a location north of Caesarea Philippi, referred to at Tosefta Shebit 4:11 as demarcating a border area of the Land of Israel

Tartarus   the place in which, according to Greek mythology, the Titans were imprisoned. The Titans were an older generation of gods defeated by Zeus and his fellow Olympians. Since the prison was located in the underworld, or Hades, the two came to be associated. In Judaism, Tartarus was the prison of the fallen angels. According to the tradition in 1 Enoch, the angels who rebelled against God were seized at his command, bound, and imprisoned in Tartarus until the final judgment. A similar tradition seems presupposed by Jude 6. As with Hades, the word came to designate a place of punishment.

tashlikh (Heb., you shall cast) a ceremony of posttalmudic origin in which, on the first day of Rosh Hashanah, Jews throw bread crumbs or empty their pockets into a sea, lake, or other body of running water, symbolically casting away their sins. The ceremony's name derives from Micah 7:19: "You shall cast all of our sins into the depths of the sea." The earliest reference to *tashlikh* occurs in the early fifteenth century C.E.

tax collectors a variety of officials, native and foreign, entrusted with collecting local and imperial taxes in Israel. For many periods of Israel's history, we lack specific and detailed knowledge of national and imperial taxes and methods of assessment and collection. The high priest was often in charge of collecting tithes for the Temple and taxes for paying tribute to the imperial authorities. In the Persian period, the Persian governor probably collected imperial tribute, and the Levites collected tithes for their support (Neh. 10:32–39). In the Hellenistic period, the high priests generally collected tribute for the Ptolemies and Seleucids. When increased revenue was needed, the taxing agent could be changed. In the third century B.C.E., the Tobiads won the right to collect Ptolemaic taxes, and in the second century B.C.E., Antiochus Epiphanes appointed new high priests, who promised increased revenues.

Under the Romans, collection of the land and head (poll) taxes was generally not farmed out to the highest bidders (publicans) but was carried out by direct employees of the Roman governor (e.g., the prefects of Judea) or the Jewish king (e.g., Herod the Great [r. 37–4 B.C.E] and his son Herod Antipas in Galilee [r. 4 B.C.E.–39 C.E.]). Taxes on goods in transit were collected by toll collectors (Gr.: *telonai*), who appear in the New Testament in major commercial centers, such as Capernaum and Jericho (Mark 2:14; Luke 19:2). During the Roman period, tithes for the priests, Levites, and Temple were probably collected by representatives of the Jerusalem priesthood or possibly by the Jewish ruler when there was one. For example, early in the Revolt against Rome, the two priests who accompanied Josephus to Galilee collected a large sum of money from tithes to bring back to Jerusalem (*Vita* 63). In the diaspora, the half-shekel tax was collected by local community leaders for the support of the Temple. Professional tax collectors were generally despised. In the New Testament, they were classed with sinners (Matt. 9:10–11), and in the Mishnah, they were classed with murderers and robbers (M. Nedarim 3:4). *See also* TAXES.

taxes a variety of levies imposed by local and imperial rulers. Taxation systems varied widely by locale and period. The most important tax was collected from owners of agricultural land, who in turn collected a percentage of the crop from tenants. The other most common tax was the poll, or head, tax, either a flat rate for each person in a social class or a percentage of one's wealth. Tolls were collected on goods in transit and in marketplaces by local publicans, who paid a flat rate for the right to collect these taxes. Other special taxes could be levied as needed. An especially burdensome exaction was the maintenance of an army in the vicinity.

Land and poll taxes were collected by the local or imperial authorities or publicans. In the Persian Empire, each of the twenty satrapies was responsible for paying a fixed amount of tax in precious metal yearly. The amounts were generally realistic and based on a thorough system of assessment. Under the Ptolemies in the third century B.C.E., taxes were first paid in a lump sum by the high priest, who collected them from the people. Later, the right to collect them was sold to publicans, notably the Tobiads. Papyri indicate that thorough records were kept on land and people. Under the Seleucids in the second century B.C.E., the high priests collected and paid the tribute. Jason and Menelaus received appointment as high priests because they promised Antiochus Epiphanes greater revenues. Simon the Hasmonean finally freed himself from paying tribute to the weakened Seleucids in 142 B.C.D, a sign that Judea was independent (1 Macc. 13). During the Roman period, independent cities and client kings, such as Herod the Great (r. 1st c. B.C.E.) and Herod Antipas in Galilee (r. 1st c. C.E.), collected taxes as they wished and paid a fixed tribute to Rome. For example, Herod the Great instituted a market tax in Jerusalem and was notable for heavy taxation to finance his military adventures, extensive building projects, and generous donations to his imperial patrons. In the first century C.E., the prefect of Judea and Samaria collected the land and poll taxes directly for Rome. All Jews, including those in the diaspora, paid a half-shekel tax to the Temple. After the destruction of the Temple, this tax became the fiscus Judaicus, a two-drachma tax paid for the Temple of Jupiter in Rome through community leaders.

The tithes and offering mandated by the Bible for the support of the Temple underwent development during this period as well and should be understood as a kind of tax as well as a form of offering to God. For example, during the Persian period, the people were obligated to support the Temple and its priests and Levites by contributing the firstfruits of the earth and trees, the firstborn of animals and humans (to be redeemed), a dough offering, wine, and oil (Neh. 10:35–39).

Reflecting the ancient system of support for the Levites as local cultic functionaries, the Book of Nehemiah says that the Levites collected their tithes locally as prescribed in the Pentateuch. But the ascendency of the priests and centralized Temple can be seen in the requirement that a priest be present and that both people and Levites offer a tithe to the priests in the Temple. In addition, sacrificial offerings of animals and produce continued to support the Temple and priests. In the Graeco-Roman period, Levites were securely subordinated to the priests as a subordinate order of functionaries entrusted with Temple music, order, and the like. These developments were systematized in the mishnaic system of tithing and offerings, which included an offering from all agricultural produce for the priests, called heave-offering (*terumah,* usually interpreted as one-fiftieth), a first tithe for the Levites, a tithe of that tithe given to the priests, a second tithe to be eaten in Jerusalem or redeemed with money taken to Jerusalem, a tithe for the local poor instead of the second tithe every third and sixth year of the Sabbatical cycle, and a dough offering (one twenty-fourth) for the priests. In addition, offerings of firstfruits and sacrifices continued as sources of support for the Temple.

tax-farmers *see* PUBLICANS

Taxo a mysterious figure from the tribe of Levi in the Testament of Moses 9. Taxo exhorts his seven sons to join him in dying innocently for the Torah, in order to trigger God's vengeance against Israel's gentile oppressors. The meaning of the name cannot be settled for certain. It has been seen as an allusion, by gematria, to the martyred scribe Eleazar in 2 Maccabees 6:18–31 and as a translation (Gr.: *taxōn,* orderer) of the Hebrew *meḥokek,* the staff, a leader and interpreter of the Torah mentioned in the Damascus Document 6:3–9. The story

of Taxo and his sons bears similarities to the story of Mattathias and his sons and the account of the martyrs in 1 Maccabees 2, as well as the martyr legends about Eleazar and the mother and her seven sons in 2 Maccabees 6–7. In common, also in the case of the *meḥokek,* is the notion of a religious leader acting through word and deed to remove God's wrath from apostate Israel.

Teacher of Righteousness (Heb.: *moreh ha Tzadik*) revered leader of the group of Jewish sectaries who lived at the settlement at Khirbet Qumran and stored their library in the caves nearby. There are fifteen references to the Teacher of Righteousness in the published Qumran scrolls; some are so fragmentary that they yield only his title (1 QpeshHab 1:13; 4QpPs^b frgs. 1 and 2), but the other references yield a certain amount of information about this shadowy figure.

Although attempts have been made to argue that Teacher of Righteousness was a title held by a succession of individuals, the consensus is that it was the title given to a specific individual whose career was closely bound up with the founding of the settlement at Qumran. The Damascus Document, followed by the Habakkuk Commentary and the Commentary on Psalm 37, yields the most information about the Teacher. When the allusions in the various documents are pieced together, the Teacher's career can be reconstructed as follows: sometime in the early second century B.C.E. he becomes the leader of a distinct group of Jews (probably the Essenes) already in existence; by them he is called the Unique Teacher, and fidelity to his inspired teaching is considered necessary for salvation. He was, however, opposed by the Man of Lies, who founded a breakaway congregation. In this context, certain of the Hodayot (1QH 1, 2, 7–11) that are thought to have come from the Teacher's pen may be relevant: these hymns portray a leader who possesses special knowledge given by God and who is persecuted by enemies who espouse rival teachings. Perhaps as a result of this conflict with the Man of Lies, the Teacher and his followers went into exile in the "land of Damascus," probably to be identified with the settlement at Qumran. Outside the sect, the Teacher had another opponent, the Wicked Priest (usually identified with Jonathan the Maccabee), who followed him to his exile and attempted to disrupt the observance of the Day of Atonement by the sect (1QpeshHab). All of the Teacher's conflicts are controversies about halakhic matters, matters of calendar, purity, and ritual observance. The occupation of the office of high priest by the Hasmoneans, originally thought to be the reason for the Teacher's self-exile from Jerusalem, does not now seem to be a cause of conflict. The death of the Teacher is mentioned in CD 20.

It it possible to identify the Teacher? The Commentary on Psalm 37 says that the Teacher is a priest, leading some scholars to claim that he was the high priest in Jerusalem during the seven years between the death of Alcimus and the appointment of Jonathan as high priest in 152 B.C.E. The evidence for this, however, is tenuous at best. It remains safest to say that, while the Teacher of Righteousness loomed large in the history and thought of the Qumran sect, he escaped the notice of sources outside the Qumran corpus (much like Jesus of Nazareth at a later time). His identity thus remains uncertain.

teaching   Instruction, which was probably given in schools, encompassed detailed religious training, business advice, etiquette, and scribal arts. The remains of such teaching are located particularly in wisdom literature such as Proverbs, the Letter of Aristeas, the Sentences of Pseudo-Phocylides, and Ahikar. Ben Sira 51:23 mentions a "house of study" (Heb.: *beit midrash*) where the instructions Ben Sira presents were taught. Training in artistry (pottery, metallurgy) occurred through guilds; in the passages 24:30–34, 33:16–18, and 34:9–12 of the book bearing his name, Ben Sira delineates his qualifications for teaching. Teaching was also carried out in the home by relatives (Tob. 1:8). Priests, prophets, and probably scribes taught theology, morality, history, and other subjects. (2 Chron. 17:7–9; Matt. 13:51). The founding figure of the Qumran community, the Teacher of Righteousness (*moreh haTzadik*), was probably a priest displaced by Hasmonean politics. His works include scriptural interpretation (1QpHab) and, likely, liturgical compositions (1QH). In contradistinction to Qumran, Hellenistic gymnasia were constructed both locally and in the diaspora to instruct Jews in Greek rhetoric, philosophy, and athletics (Wis. 7:17–22).

The Gospels render *rabbi* (Heb., my lord; a title of respect) as *didaskalos* (teacher; e.g., Matt. 8:19). Jesus, who is called "teacher" (Mark 5:35, 9:17; etc.), instructed through parables, *chreia*, and exemplary action. His followers institutionalized the office of teacher (1 Cor. 12:28–29; Eph. 4:11; 1 Tim. 4; cf. Matt. 28:20) but their actual instruction is not delineated in detail. The Epistle of James 3:1–2 warns of the difficulties of the profession.

From the destruction of the Jerusalem Temple in 70 C.E. and on, the preeminent teacher in Judaism

has been the rabbi or rav. The former term referred to sages ordained through the laying on of hands, which was performed only in the land of Israel; the latter word was employed in Babylonia. As sole spokesmen for the oral Torah, rabbis increasingly became the central religious and legal functionaries of the Jewish community. In addition to their preeminent religious activity, study, and teaching of Torah, in the Talmudic period, rabbis served as judges, fixed the calendar, administered the community's system of social welfare, and promoted religious observance. These rabbis functioned much like other contemporary holy men and magicians, understood to have a particularly close relationship to God and, therefore, to possess special powers, including the ability to curse or to bless.

Mesharshaya, a Babylonian amora, is known for this statement about rabbinic learning (B. Keritot 6a): "When you want to go to learn before your master, first of all review your studies in the Mishnah, and then go to your teacher. And when you are in session before your teacher, watch the mouth of your teacher. . . . When you study any teaching, do it by the side of water. Just as water goes on and on, so may your learning go on and on." *See also* SCHOOL.

tebah   *see* ARK

tebel   rabbinic term for foods at the stage of growth or processing at which levitical and priestly tithes may be separated but from which those agricultural gifts have not yet been removed. Before use in a regular meal, *tebel* must be fully tithed. Until then, it may be consumed only as a snack, through which use the owner does not treat the untithed food as though it were entirely his own, available for any use he desires.

Tebet   fourth month of the Jewish calendar, corresponding to December/January

Tebet, Tenth of   *see* ASARAH BETEBET

tebul yom   (Heb.) one who has immersed and is waiting for the sun to set to complete the process of purification

Tebul Yom   Mishnah tractate on the uncleanness assigned to one who has immersed and is waiting for sunset to complete the purification process. The tractate discusses connection between a thing and a person, for example, when liquids or solid food touch what he has touched (chap. 3), and the uncleanness affecting the Tebul Yom (chaps. 3–4).

tedakah   *see* PHILANTHROPY

tefah   *see* HANDBREADTH

Tefasno Synagogue   (also Tafas, Tipasa) a probable synagogue site in southern Syria about 51 kilometers east of Tiberias. A three-line Greek inscription carved on a lintel was found there in the late nineteenth century. It reads as follows: "Jacob and Samuel and their father Clematios have erected this synagogue." It is likely that this represents remains of a third- or fourth-century-C.E. Jewish community in ancient Batanaea, a territory between Gaulanitis (the Golan Heights) to the west and Trachonitis to the east. It is also possible that this community belonged to the city territory of Dium. It has not been excavated.

tefillah   *see* AMIDAH; PRAYER

tefillin   (Heb., phylacteries) small leather cases containing passages from Exodus 13:1, 11, and Deuteronomy 6:4–9, 11:13–21, written on parchment. They are worn on the left arm and forehead by adult males in the morning service.

Tefillin   the title of one of the so-called minor tractates of the Talmud. A collection of Tannaitic sources in one chapter, it contains rules for writing the parchments placed in phylacteries and for wearing them in accord with the biblical requirement.

tefillin, archaeology of   the archaeological analysis of the remains of *tefillin* or phylactery cases from caves at Qumran and from the Wadi Murraba at near En Gedi. Among the minor finds in Qumran Cave 1 (1Q) were two intact phylactery cases of leather and parts of five others. One type had four small compartments for holding four tiny scrolls. The entire case was two centimeters long. Each compartment measured about 4 by 6 millimeters. The excavators identified these with four compartments as the type worn on the head. The four compartments would contain Exodus 13:9 and 13:16 and Deuteronomy 6:8 and 11:18. This type is formed of two pieces of leather stitched together. One piece of leather was pressed out wet to form the compartments. A second type had one compartment only and was therefore of the type worn on the arm. This single compartment case is formed of a single piece of leather folded in half, one-half deeply pressed to form a compartment to contain a minute scroll containing all four biblical verses. A thin leather thong for attachment is inserted at the middle. The halves fold over and are stitched together. The compartment measures 9 by 7 millimeters. The excavators of cave 1 published fifty-nine fragments of *tefillin* or phylactery texts. One of these texts, 1Q0, was rolled tightly but is too big to fit in any of the compartments in the leather pieces found.

Tehillim   (Heb.) psalms, especially in the phrase Sefer Tehillim (the biblical Book of Psalms); *see also* PSALMS

teḥiyat haMetim   *see* RESURRECTION

tekiah   (Heb.) the sounding of the shofar on the New Year

tekufah   (Heb.) season

tekufat Nisan   (Heb.) the vernal equinox

tekufat Tammuz   (Heb.) the summer solstice

tekufat Tebet   (Heb.) the winter solstice

tekufat Tishrei   (Heb.) the autumnal equinox

Tell Anafa   town site in eastern Upper Galilee on the west slopes of the Golan Heights. This was a town of perhaps 44 acres occupied in the Canaanite periods and also in the Persian and Hellenistic periods. A large building dating to the end of the second century B.C.E. was excavated upon which a later, residential building had been erected. A second large building, also of the Hellenistic period, had walls preserved to a height of three meters. This building was about 38 by 38 meters in extent and included one of the earliest heated baths in all of ancient Palestine. Tremendous amounts of glass were found at Tell Anafa in a period when glass was not common. This suggests that either Tell Anafa itself was a glass-manufacturing town or that glass was manufactured nearby. Since so many Jewish families were associated with glass making it may follow that this was a Jewish glass-manufacturing and exporting center. Many floors were exceptional stone and glass mosaics. There were also enormous amounts of Hellenistic red-slipped or red-glazed pottery and plaster painted in vivid colors with gilt attached, a sign of great wealth. The primary occupation of Tell Anafa is dated between 150 and 84 B.C.E. The settlement was completely abandoned by 75 B.C.E.

Tell el-Hesi   site with one of the largest artificial mounds in Israel located about 25 kilometers northeast of Gaza on the Wadi Hesi. The large mound is about 11 acres in area while the associated lower town is about 23 acres. Tell el-Hesi has been identified with biblical Eglon, a city prominent in the narrative of Joshua's conquests in the south of Canaan (Josh. 10). The tell has a long history of occupation, but in our era, beginning in the Persian period, the tell was apparently overwhelmingly reserved for huge grain storage pits, as were many other biblical cities in the region. That is, it had lost the majority of its population of artisans, farmers, and traders and was now a storage city for the region of the coastal plain where it was located. Not many families were needed to supervise and work the fields and inventory grain storage. The lack of settled population evidently contributed to its decline and disappearance in the Hellenistic period.

Tell Jemmeh (also Tel Gama) ancient mount nearly 10 kilometers south of Gaza on the south bank of the Wadi Gaza. The city has been identified with the ancient Egyptian city of Yerza. Josephus knew the city as Iorda or Orda (*War* 3.3.5, p. 51) and counted it as the extremity of Judea. Just south of the mound are Roman and Byzantine period remains, evidently of the city of Orda. The cemetery was the first to be discovered, since it had been pillaged by locals for many years. Recently a Byzantine church has been uncovered, which is in accord with the Madaba mosaic map in Jordan that locates the city of Orda south of Gaza and shows it as a fortress with six towers. Byzantine Orda evidently belonged to the territory of Gerar (Salus Gerariticus) and was a bishop's see.

Tell Megadim ancient Persian-period village on the Mediterranean coast about 2 kilometers north of modern Athlit. This small fifth-century-B.C.E. village was laid out in a square plan, a method of city planning called Hippodamian in the Hellenistic and Roman periods. The village was rectangular in plan, about 133 by 170 meters in extent. The village seems to have been based on agriculture, with ample facilities for storing grain and other commodities in storage jars. The village was fortified with a casemate wall, or a defense wall constructed of two parallel walls with cross walls forming rooms or casemates.

The village was suddenly destroyed near the end of the fourth century B.C.E., perhaps in the invasions of the kings of the twenty-ninth Egyptian dynasties or in some other major military attack. The village was not occupied again until the Roman period, when a staging post (*mutatio*) was built for travelers. The building featured large, paved courts as one would expect for a horse-changing station. This was probably the station at the eighth Roman mile south of Shikmona. In a text of the fourth century C.E. this station is identified as Certho, which suggests that its ancient Phoenician name was Karta (city, or town).

Tell Mevorah small mound in the Sharon Plain and on the south bank of the Wadi Taninim. During the Persian period this mound was an agricultural estate. The remains on the tell are of a single building, perhaps a villa. Meager remains of the Hellenistic period show that occupation continued, but it was too disturbed to reveal the nature of the occupation. A third-century-C.E. mausoleum with several marble sarcophagi was discovered at Tell Mevorah, indicating that if there were no local population living there in the Roman period, others in the region did not hesitate to use the tell as a cemetery. Two of the sarcophagi are very elegant, with carved representations of the war between the Greeks and the Amazons.

Tell Mikhal (or Tel Michal) ancient mound about 5 kilometers north of Tel Aviv and 6.5 kilometers north of the Yarkon River. The entire occupational area is scattered over five hills. The site is not identified as a biblical city, although it was occupied during the biblical periods. During the Persian period, Tell Mikhal was a prosperous way station and command post on the coastal road from Egypt to Phoenicia. Tell Mikhal probably played an important role in grain and wine storage and trade of this period, namely, from the sixth to the fourth centuries B.C.E. Pottery kilns found at the site attest to the production of storage jars. A small temple, probably dedicated to the Phoenician god Baal Shamim, or Lord of Heaven, was found on a hill to the northeast of the site. In the Hellenistic period, the town underwent a major change and was built as a fortress about 25 by 25 meters, probably for Seleucid Greek rulers, the inheritors of the Persian hegemony. A second, Hasmonean fortress was built on top of the remains of the Seleucid fortress and probably served the military campaigns of King Alexander Jannaeus of Israel (103–76 B.C.E.). This fort was eventually abandoned and succeeded by a Roman fort of the first century C.E. It served the Roman military before and during the two revolts against Rome (66–73 C.E. and 135 C.E.) when the fort lay north of Jewish Jaffa, an independent port at the time.

Tell Sera (or Tel Shera) city mound in the southern Shephelah below the hills of Judea, about 23 kilometers inland from Gaza. Some identify the tell with the biblical city of Gerar. Tell Sera was clearly occupied during the resettlement of Judah under Persian rule, but not until the fourth century C.E. The main archaeological find from this period are large numbers of silos lined with mud bricks and used for storing grain. Some of the silos are 5 meters in diameter and contained such finds as Aramaic ostraca and Athenian red-figured pottery. The town declined during the Hellenistic period when it came under the control of Antiochus III (the Great), with all of Judea, after 219 B.C.E. Only a few families appear to have lived there in the Hellenistic period. In the Roman period the tell and its surrounding fields were part of a Roman farmstead within the territory of Idumea. The farmstead included a massive stone tower on the north side of the mound and a villa decorated in typical Roman painted plaster. Since the pottery wares of this villa were imported from the kingdom of Nabatea southwest of the Dead Sea, it is likely that these were Idumeans living after the Roman fashion.

Tell Sippor city mound near biblical Marisa in the territory of Idumea south of Judah. The city stood in the hills of central Judah/Idumea and was occupied in the Persian and Hellenistic periods. It probably served as an important agricultural center in those periods. Its ancient name is lost. The entire region reverted to the control of Antiochus III after 219 B.C.E.

telos (Gr., end, goal, or tax) The term came to be used in two separate senses: first, as a philosophical term with regard to the end or goal of philosophy, or as a theological term meaning the end of the age; second, as a general term for taxation and also for customs duties in particular.

temenos Greek term for a piece of land marked off for official purposes. It often had to do with property specifically dedicated to a god, such as a sacred precinct for worship, usually including an altar. The term is more general than "temple," which implied buildings and the like.

Temple the structure in Jerusalem that was the cultic center of Judaism. According to scripture, God had commanded the establishment of the Temple, sacrifices, and hereditary priesthood. The Temple was to be the link between God and humans, where God's presence would reside over the two cherubim at the Ark of the Covenant (Exod. 25:16–22). The Temple was the house of YHWH (Ezra 3:11)—not a place where anyone could enter—and only the high priest could enter its inner sanctum, the Holy of Holies, and he could do that only once a year, on the Day of Atonement.

The basic shape of the Temple was rectangular, 60 cubits long, 20 cubits wide, and 30 cubits high. (The royal cubit—20.9 inches—is probably intended.) Outside the Temple stood the altar of sacrifice and the bronze laver. One entered the Temple on one of the short sides by mounting steps to an open air forecourt. One entered the central room through a door of cypresswood carved with cherubim and palm trees and overlaid with gold. Lit by windows, the central room contained an incense altar, the altar of the Bread of the Presence and ten golden lampstands. Olivewood doors carved with cherubim, palm trees, and flowers and overlaid with gold led into the Holy of Holies. Inside this dark room was the ark of the covenant flanked by two cherubim.

The Temple in Jerusalem was built by Solomon as a focal point for national unity under the Davidic dynasty. Other cult centers persisted, but the Temple in Jerusalem came to symbolize national identity. At the Temple's destruction in 587/86 B.C.E., the Babylonians carried away its precious items and furnishings and then burned it (2 Kings 25:8–17), but probably the stone foundation and part of the superstructure survived. This would have been the basis for the Second Temple, built between 520 and 515 B.C.E. under Joshua, the high priest, and Zerubbabel, the governor appointed by the Persians, with the help of the prophets Haggai and Zechariah. Without a king, the Temple became the center of national life and the high priests more and more assumed civil-leadership functions within the community. The Temple at Jerusalem was plundered by Antiochus IV Epiphanes in 169 B.C.E. and then desecrated in 167 B.C.E. by the erection of an idolatrous structure on the altar of sacrifice. The daily sacrificial offering was suspended until the Temple was retaken by the Maccabees in 164 B.C.E. and purified and rededicated to YHWH. In 63 B.C.E. Pompey the Great besieged the Temple, where supporters of the rebellious Aristobulus had locked themselves in. He breached the walls, slaughtered some priests in the act of sacrifice, entered the Holy of Holies but took nothing, and said the cult could continue. Herod the Great (37 B.C.E.–4 C.E.) rebuilt the Temple complex on a vast scale, making the walled sacred area one of the largest in the Mediterranean world, with balustrades separating the Gentiles from the area where Israelites could enter (*War* 5:184–227; *Ant.* 15:410–420). The project was not entirely finished until just before the outbreak of the revolt against Rome, around 63 C.E. After fierce resistance by the Jewish rebels, the Temple was finally destroyed by the Romans in 70 C.E.

The magnificence of the Temple is praised by Sirach in his description of the activities of Simon, son of Onias (Sir. 50:1–21); it is there that Wisdom ministers before God (Sir. 24:10). The Temple and its furnishings are sumptuously described in Letter of Aristeas 84–104 and are the objects of Gentile admiration. 2 Macc 3:2 tells how kings embellished the Temple with the most splendid gifts. Philo of Alexandria states that Jews from all over the Roman Empire supported Temple worship (*On the Embassy to Gaius* 152). Jews generally paid the half-shekel Temple tax (Matt. 12:24), and Josephus (*Ant.* 18:312) describes how the Jews in Mesopotamia made dedicatory offerings in addition to this tax. Temple life was thus an extremely important facet of Jewish identity. God defends his Temple both in history (2 Macc. 3–15) and at the last days (Sib. Or. 3.701–731; cf. Tob. 13:9–18).

This does not mean that there were not some negative attitudes towards the Temple, or rather towards the way sacrifices were being offered. When the Second Temple was built, most rejoiced, but some wept when they remembered what the First Temple had been like (Ezra 3:12). The argument for continuity between the First and Second Temples found in 2 Maccabees 1:18–36, somewhat nullified by the following verses 2:1–8, is perhaps countering such opinions. For the author of 1 Enoch 89:73, all the bread on the altar was polluted and not pure. In 2 Baruch 68:5–6, the rebuilt Temple will be honored but not as fully as before. In the Martyrdom of Isaiah, Jerusalem is depicted as a center of apostasy, lawlessness, magic arts, and fornication (2:1–6). In this view, it is close to the critique of the Temple by the Qumran covenanters, who held that the Temple had been profaned by the priests who did not observe their stricter interpretation about menstrual flow (CD 5:6–11). The Wicked Priest indulged in abominable and unclean things that defiled the Temple (1 QpHab 12:3–8). The same critique is found in the Testament of Levi 14:5–8 and the Psalms of Solomon 2:1–3 and 8:8–21. The solar calendrical system used throughout 1 Enoch and Jubilees and by the Qumran community (CD 6:11–20; 1 QS 10:5; 1 QH 12:5–9) also evidences opposition to the existing Temple cult in Jerusalem that used a lunar-solar system, as does the notion of the Qumran community as a temple (1 QS 8:4–10; 1 QH 6:22–31; Eph. 2:19–22; 1 Pet. 2:4–10). In driving out the money changers from the Temple (Mark 11:15–18), Jesus too showed himself wishing to bring about a restoration in Israel.

After the destruction of the Temple in 70 C.E. the author of 2 Baruch finds consolation in the idea that the earthly sanctuary has a heavenly counterpart (4:2–6), an idea implicit in the Songs for the Holocaust of the Sabbath (4 Q 400–407). To the grieving author of 4 Ezra is shown a brilliant new Jerusalem (10:25–50), as in the document from Qumran describing the dimensions of the new Jerusalem that may have included a description of the eschatological Temple (5 Q 15). The author of the Letter to the Hebrews speaks of a new tent/temple (Heb. 9:1-24), while in Revelation there is no new temple, for its temple is the Lord God the Almighty and the Lamb (Rev. 21:22).

In rabbinic Judaism, obedience to the covenant expressed itself in fulfillment of the Torah, which promised sanctification in nature and salvation in history; piety also reached expression in individual prayer and synagogue study of Torah. Temple imagery and symbolism persisted in rabbinic writings.

Temple, Second sole cultic center for the worship of YHWH, located in Jerusalem; "Second Temple" usually refers to the Herodian Temple, constructed by Herod the Great beginning in 37 B.C.E. However, various forms of the Temple existed in Jerusalem after the destruction of the First Temple (586 B.C.E.), dating from approximately 538 B.C.E. until the destruction of the Herodian Temple in 70 C.E. After this destruction, the Temple was never rebuilt.

The First Temple, originally built under the direction of King Solomon, was destroyed in 586 B.C.E. by the Babylonians. At this time, the Babylonians deported all but the "poorest of the land" from Jerusalem (2 Kings 25:8-12). After about 50 years, the Persians gained control over Jerusalem and Palestine. About 538 B.C.E., the Persian monarch Cyrus issued a decree allowing the Jews to return and rebuild the Temple (cf. Ezra 1:2-3). Soon after, a group of Jews under the leadership of Sheshbazzar returned and erected a small altar where the Temple had stood. A further partial attempt to reconstruct the Temple was made by Zerubbabel in 521 B.C.E. During Nehemiah's rule (beginning c. 445 B.C.E.), Jerusalem increased in size and importance, but the Temple still was not rebuilt to its former splendor. During most of the third century B.C.E., Jerusalem was a part of the Ptolemaic kingdom of Egypt, and during the second century, it was ruled by the Seleucids. The overthrow of the Ptolemaic Empire was welcomed by the Jews, and the Seleucids allowed the Jews to live according to the traditions of their ancestors and even assisted in repairing the Temple.

The situation under the Seleucids swayed, however, from support of the Temple and the Temple activities to condemnation and plundering of the Temple resources when the Seleucid monarch Antiochus IV came under pressure from Egypt. As the second century continued, the Seleucids changed their policy of toleration of Jewish heritage and religion; they encouraged Hellenization of the Temple and even set up a graven image in the Temple. This infuriated the Jews, and eventually, in 164 B.C.E., the Hasmoneans under Judas Maccabeus conquered Jerusalem and cleansed the Temple. The Hasmoneans ruled in Jerusalem until 63 B.C.E., when the Roman ruler Pompey conquered the city. The Temple Mount area was also overthrown at this time.

After this, the Romans ruled Jerusalem under the

puppet tetrarch Herod. There was a brief three-year interlude, from 40 to 37 B.C.E., when the last Hasmonean king, Mattathias Antigonus, regained control of the city. Herod reconquered the city for the Romans in 37 B.C.E. and then, as king of the Jews, set about a series of ambitious building projects. The walls of the city were rebuilt and three massive towers were added to the fortifications. In addition to impressive public buildings, Herod also rebuilt entire sections of the city's residential areas. His greatest building accomplishment, however, was the rebuilding of the Temple.

Following Herod's death in 4 B.C.E., a total of 14 Roman procurators ruled Jerusalem until the Jewish revolt in 66 C.E. These rulers had ignored the sentiments of the Jewish inhabitants, and eventually a large scale revolt erupted among the Jewish population, led by the Zealots. The Zealots took over Jerusalem in 66 C.E., but they were overthrown by the Romans in 70 C.E. During this overthrow, Jerusalem was completely overrun. The Temple Mount area was one of the last areas conquered, but it too was completely destroyed.

The archaeological remains of the Second Temple retaining wall (the so-called Wailing Wall, or Western Wall) are some of the most impressive and well-known remains in Jerusalem today. Though the magnificent stones that make up this wall give the modern visitor some idea of the grandeur of the Second Temple, the archaeological remains that allow for a precise reconstruction of the Second Temple are rather small.

Due to the paucity of precise archaeological data, scholars rely on literary sources to supplement what can be determined archaeologically. One of the most important sources for the details about the construction of the Second Temple is found in the Mishnah in a section called the Tractate Middot. One of the oldest sections of the Mishnah, it is said to originate from Eliezer b. Jacob, who lived during the last days of the Second Temple. This information is supplemented by the writings of the historian Josephus. Though there are some discrepancies between the two sources, both agree on the major components of the Second Temple. Both hold that the core of the Second Temple consisted of the porch, the sanctuary, and the Holy of Holies. Both sources also describe an upper chamber, cells, and a stepped passageway.

The only artistic representations of the Second Temple porch that are preserved today are found on two different types of coins from the Bar Kokhba period. Both the coins and the literary sources suggest that the entrance to the porch comprised twelve steps. The representations on the coins differ, however, in several aspects from the literary tradition preserved in the Mishnah. The Mishnah describes the facade of the porch as plain, but the coins depict two and four columns flanking the entrance from the porch. This discrepancy may be solved by positing that the coins represent the entrance to the Temple from inside the porch: at the inside entrance stood a magnificent doorway, flanked by one or two columns on each side, while the facade of the porch was plain.

The sanctuary and the Holy of Holies were contained in the hallway through the entrance of the porch. Both had an identical width and height (20 cubits wide by 40 cubits high), but the sanctuary was twice as long as the Holy of Holies (40 cubits as compared to 20 cubits). The sanctuary and the Holy of Holies were separated by elaborately embroidered curtains decorated with figures of lions and eagles. The sanctuary was overlaid with gold; its furnishings included a menorah, the showbread table, and the incense altar. A graphic hint at the actual appearance of these items is found in an important archaeological find from the Jewish Quarter in Jerusalem. An incised piece of plaster, now displayed in the Israel Museum, contains a fragmentary pictorial depiction of the menorah, the showbread table and the incense altar. Since this pictorial representation dates from before the destruction of the Second Temple, it most likely contains a contemporary artist's representation of the vital cultic elements in the sanctuary.

In contrast to the sanctuary, the Holy of Holies did not contain furnishings. In fact, entrance into the Holy of Holies was prohibited. The only exception was the high priest, who was required to enter the Holy of Holies once a year on the Day of Atonement. On that day, he entered the Holy of Holies four times to carry out the procedure of atoning for the sins of the people.

As mentioned above, the archaeological remains of the foundation walls permit a glimpse at the likely plan of Herod's Temple Mount. Most of the information comes from the excavations of Charles Warren between 1867 and 1869. Warren studied the walls and the entrances to the Temple Mount by digging a series of shafts outside the walls of the Temple Mount. When he reached bedrock in one shaft, he would dig another shaft that was horizontal to the first. He connected these multiple shafts by horizontal tunnels that followed the plan of the foundation walls. His records, which were quite good for his day, provide much data for interpreting the outline of the Temple Mount and its entrances.

The Temple Mount in general was shaped like a rectangle, but it was not an even rectangle, as each side was a different length. Though different scholars have arrived at slightly different figures for the dimensions, the general dimensions are as follows: (1) the western wall was the longest, measuring about 484 meters; (2) the northern wall was about 315 meters long; (3) the eastern wall was about 470 meters long; and (4) the southern wall, the shortest, measured about 280 meters.

South of the Temple Mount are the remains of the entrances to the Second Temple. There are two gates that are walled up today, and these are likely two of the gates from Herod's period. The double gate is at the western side of the southern wall, while the triple gate is on the eastern side. Both led to tunnels that proceeded to the top of the Temple Mount.

Though the Second Temple was a spectacular building with incredibly large walls, the power of the Roman army was too much for the Jewish rebels: Jerusalem and the Second Temple fell for the last time in 70 C.E. Since that time, the Temple has never been rebuilt, though the remains of its foundation walls are an archaeological highlight of modern Jerusalem.

Temple Scroll scroll discovered in Cave 11, Qumran, in 1956 and purchased by Y. Yadin after the Six Day War in 1967 for the Shrine of the Book in Israel. Yadin published a Hebrew edition of the scroll in 1977 and a revised English edition in 1983; the scroll's title is abbreviated as 11QTemple.

The Temple Scroll is the longest complete scroll found at Qumran, being 7.94 meters long in its present condition. It consists of nineteen sheets of leather preserving sixty-seven columns of text; the scroll is written in Hebrew by two scribes, scribe A copying columns 1–5 and scribe B, the remaining columns. Yadin assigned a date of the Herodian period (late 1st c. B.C.E.) to the handwriting of the scroll. In addition to the large scroll from Cave 11, one or possibly two other copies were found in Cave 11 (11QTemple[b,c?]); further, fragments were found in Cave 4 that overlap with portions of the Temple Scroll, although they are not copies of the Cave 11 manuscript (4Q365[a]).

The Temple Scroll presents itself as a direct revelation from God (speaking in the first person) to Moses, who functions as a silent audience. That the recipient is Moses is clear from the reference in column XLIV to "thy brother Aaron." The text is a collection of *halakhot* (laws), which cover the following topics: col. II: the covenant relationship; cols. III–XII: the Temple building and altar; cols.

XIII–XXIX: feasts and sacrifices; cols. XXX–XLIV: the Temple courts; cols. XLV–XLVII: the sanctity of the holy city; cols. XLVIII–LI:10: purity laws; cols. LI:11–LVI:11: various laws on legal procedure, sacrifices, and idolatry; cols. LVI:12–59: the law of the king; cols. LX–LXVII: various legal prescriptions.

The material of the scroll is heavily dependent on Exodus, Leviticus, and especially Deuteronomy, of which it quotes whole sections. However, the Temple Scroll is a "rewritten Torah"; that is, it takes the biblical material relevant to the topic at hand and weaves it into a unified whole. Therefore, in many cases the Temple Scroll presents a thoroughgoing rewriting of large passages of the Pentateuch, often with additions of its own to make its halakhic position clear. That position is exceedingly strict, particularly in the laws regarding the purity of the Temple. So, for example, defecation is not allowed within the holy city, nor is sexual intercourse. These purity laws were meant to safeguard the sanctity of the Temple.

Many of the halakhic provisions of the Temple Scroll are interesting for their unusual nature. The architectural plan the scroll outlines for the Temple differs from the biblical accounts of either the First or the Second Temple, as well as differing from the descriptions of the Second Temple by Josephus or the Mishnah. The festival calendar includes a number of festivals not found in the Torah or rabbinic literature, for example the Festivals of New Wine and New Oil. The Law of the King contains several unique provisions, including the prohibition of royal polygamy and the subordination of the king to the high priest in matters of war. It should be recalled that all of this material is presented as a direct revelation from God.

The question of the sectarian nature of the Temple Scroll is a vexing one. As has often been remarked, the Temple Scroll contains no overtly sectarian concepts as is found in other Qumran documents, such as a community with a distinct hierarchical structure, predestination, dualism, or a new covenant. However, the scroll does have clear commonalities with some of the Qumran texts that have been identified as sectarian, for example, the Damascus Document and the Nahum Commentary. It espouses a solar calendar and a strict interpretation of the Torah. In addition, several smaller details of the Temple Scroll show affinity with other Qumran documents. The Festival of New Oil appears in 4QReworked Pentateuch (a text that, like 11QTemple, may not be Qumranic in origin), sexual intercourse is forbidden in the holy city in the Damascus Document 12:1–2, the purity laws for the holy city are similar to the camp rules of the War Scroll, and consanguinity between uncle and niece is forbidden in both the Temple Scroll and the Damascus Document. Therefore, it seems likely that the Temple Scroll, while not a strictly sectarian composition, is part of an older body of material (which would also include books such as Jubilees) inherited and used by the sectaries.

temple state A number of the small countries of the ancient Near East in the Persian and Graeco-Roman periods were not kingdoms or chiefdoms but temple states. This means that they had a temple as the central institution, and the government or administration fell to a high priest and/or a priestly hierarchy. Most temples in the various countries possessed land and had slaves or serfs to work it to produce income for the temple. The same was true with a temple state, except that the temple did not have to answer to a higher authority, such as a king or emperor. The actual citizens with civic rights (as opposed to slaves and free individuals without civic rights) might be a minority of the population, if the theory of a *Bürger-Tempel-Gemeinde* is accepted. Through much of the Second Temple period, Judah acted as a temple state, either independently or under the rule of one of the great powers. The chief executive was the high priest, though he had a council (*boulē, gerousia,* or Sanhedrin) to advise him and perhaps even to share power. During Hasmonean rule, the high priesthood became combined with kingship, so that the state was ruled by "priest-kings."

temptation attraction toward an action or object, usually negative in character. Moses, in his final address to the people (Deut.), warned them not to test or tempt the Lord again as they had done at Massah—a place that got its name from what they had done there (Deut. 6:16; see also Ex. 17:2–7). In Isaiah 7 King Ahaz appealed to the same principle when he refused God's invitation, delivered through the prophet, to ask for a sign that would confirm his reassuring words. He refused, he said, to test the Lord. The Book of Jubilees and the Testament of Joseph echo the biblical theme, found most clearly in Job, that the Lord Himself at times tempts or tries the righteous to test their strength (also in Gen. 22:1). In Jubilees, Abraham is subjected to ten trials, such as the forcible removal of his wife, Sarah (19:8), although the test involving the sacrifice of Isaac is attributed to the devil figure Mastema, not to God, as it is in Genesis 22 (see Jub. 18). In the Testament of Joseph, the hero recalls for his sons that he, too, endured ten trials from God (2:7). One meets the theme of tempta-

tion several times in the New Testament, with the most famous one being the story of Jesus' forty-day test in the wilderness. This episode, which is meant to remind the reader of Israel's forty-year trek in the wilderness, is recounted in Matthew, Mark, and Luke. Mark, the earliest writer, describes it very briefly and does not specify what Satan's temptations were (1:12–13). Matthew (4:1–11) and Luke (4:1–13), however, expand this base text greatly. They add the detail that Jesus also fasted during this period and put the three acts of temptation with accompanying dialogue at the end of the forty-day span. Matthew calls the devil "the tempter," and the three trials the devil fashions for Jesus are the invitations to make stones become food, to throw himself from the pinnacle of the Temple, and to possess all the world's kingdoms. To each, Jesus responds with a scriptural citation. Against the second test, he quotes Deuteronomy 6:16 (see above). Luke agrees with Matthew for the first temptation and biblical quotation, but he gives the second and third in reverse order. He concludes the section with the note that the devil ended his temptations and left to return at a fitting time. The Lord's Prayer, in Matthew 6 and Luke 11, contains the petition "Lead us not into temptation." Elsewhere in the New Testament, believers are encouraged to resist temptations and to withstand tests (see James 1:3; Luke 17:1), following as their model the Christ who was tempted as they were (Heb. 2 and 4). God Himself is not, however, the source of temptation (James 1). The Book of Revelation identifies the serpent in the story of the Garden of Eden as the great dragon and tempter or deceiver of the whole world (chap. 12), who is to be punished forever (chap. 20).

Rabbinic Judaism views temptation as a result from the *yetzer haRa* (see Gen. 8:21), the hypostatization of people's inclination to engage in wrong actions. While rabbinic authorities see this temptation as a force that must consistently be fought, they also recognize in it one of life's motivating powers. Without the *yetzer haRa,* people would not engage in business, marry, raise a family, or construct a house (Gen. Rabbah 9:7; B. Yoma 69b). Human productivity thus is a positive result of people's need constantly to avoid the temptation to sin. They succeed in this by recognizing the ever-present eyes and ears of God (M. Abot 2:1), and, especially, through study of Torah and practice of the law (B. Sotah 21a), viewed as the greatest antidote against temptation (B. Kiddushin 30b).

Temurah Mishnah tractate on the rules of substituting one animal for another, in line with Leviticus

27:14. The tractate discusses who may make a statement effecting the substitution of one beast that has been consecrated for another and how it is done (chaps. 1–2); the status of the offspring of substitutes (chaps. 3–4); and language used in effecting an act of substitution (chaps. 5–6).

Ten Commandments *see* DECALOGUE

tent temporary dwelling or shelter made of cloth or animal skin. Several symbolic uses of the word in the Hebrew Bible and later Jewish literature seem to derive from the tent's temporary nature as well as its ubiquity. The fortune or fate of a person or people is reflected in what happens to their tents (Job 8:22; Jer. 4:20; Hos. 9:6). The enlarging of one's tent indicates prosperity (Isa. 54:2). The tent symbolizes the frailty of human existence (Isa. 38:12; 2 Cor. 5:1). God's presence with Israel is indicated in the image of his wisdom dwelling in a tent (Sir. 24:8, 10). God's heavenly sanctuary can also be called a tent (Heb. 8:1–2).

ten thousand times ten thousand the number of God's attendants in the heavenly throne room according to 1 Enoch 14:22, 40:1, 60:1, 71:8; Daniel 7:10; Revelation 5:11. In all but the first text, the term is used in parallelism with "thousands of thousands" or "a multitude that could not be numbered," indicating that the number, one hundred million, is not to be taken literally. Rather, it denotes the vast and boundless resources at the disposal of the heavenly King and fits well with the rest of the larger than life trappings of the heavenly throne room described in these texts. *See also* ANGEL; HOLY ONES.

terefah (Heb.) torn, in line with Exodus 322:31: "You shall not eat any flesh that is torn by beasts in the field." This refers to a beast that has not yet died but that cannot survive, because of health problems. Beasts that are imperfect and may die on that account cannot be eaten by Israelites.

Tertullian (c. 160–c. 225 C.E.) Christian apologist and theologian. Tertullian was one of the most artful of early Christian anti-Judaists. Possessed of an acerbic wit, he made invidious comparisons of Judaism and Christianity, not only in his treatise *Against the Jews* but throughout his writings. He lambasted Jews for rejecting and killing Jesus and the prophets; persecuting, calumniating, envying, and otherwise offending Christians; sinning against God with idolatry, hardness of heart, ingratitude, blindness, and ignorance; outmodedness (*vetustas*); and hypocrisy. Tertullian was quick to invoke the Jews when he wanted to put a damning label on Marcionites, Gnostics, fellow Christians who offended, and, after his conversion to Montanism, Catholics.

terumah *see* HEAVE-OFFERING

Terumot Mishnah tractate devoted to the heave-offering, or priestly rations, separated by the farmers and handed over to the priesthood at the harvest. The tractate discusses how the heave-offering is separated (chaps. 1–4); the rule that a heave-offering that has been separated still is in the domain of the householder (chaps. 4–10); consumption of the heave-offering by a nonpriest and the penalties thereof (chaps. 6–8); seed grain having the status of heave-offering that has been planted (chap. 9); a heave-offering cooked or prepared with unconsecrated produce (chap. 10); and the disposition of the heave-offering in the hands of the priest and proper preparation of food having the status of heave-offering (chap. 11).

testament a literary genre that claims to preserve the last words of an ancient figure. Biblical examples include Jacob's blessing of his sons (Gen. 49) and Moses' blessing of the twelve tribes (Deut. 33). Both texts are predominantly predictions about the tribes of Israel.

The last chapters of Deuteronomy served as a model for two early Jewish testaments. 1 Enoch begins by paraphrasing Deuteronomy 33:1–2 (cf. 1 Enoch 1:1–9) and has Enoch address his sons (81:1–82:3, 91:1–3), providing ethical instruction (91:3–4, 18–19; 92–105) and a double prediction of the future (91:5–9, 11–17; 93:1–10; cf. Deut. 31–32). The Testament of Moses is a rewritten form of Deuteronomy 31–34 that provides a detailed prediction of Israel's history shaped with reference to their evil (mainly) or righteous conduct.

Later Jewish testaments have a predominately ethical function. The dying patriarch gathers his children and exhorts them to right behavior, basing his instructions on a retrospective narrative—usually about his own life—that exemplifies certain virtues or vices. The testament concludes with an eschatological section that may imply prophetic inspiration. Examples of such testaments include Tobit, Jubilees 20–22 (Abraham), 1 Macc. 2:49–70 (Mattathias), the Testament of Job, and the Testaments of the Twelve Patriarchs, which is Christian in its present form. New Testament examples include Mark 13, John 13–17, and Acts 20:17–38.

Testament of Abraham *see* ABRAHAM, TESTAMENT OF

Testament of Job *see* JOB, TESTAMENT OF

Testament of Moses *see* MOSES, TESTAMENT OF

Testament of Solomon *see* SOLOMON, TESTAMENT OF

Testaments of the Twelve Patriarchs *see* TWELVE PATRIARCHS, TESTAMENTS OF THE

Testimonium Hebrew sectarian composition, of which only one copy survives, found in Cave 4,

Qumran, in 1952 and published by J. M. Allegro in DJD V. The manuscript, whose title is abbreviated as 4QTest, dates from c. 100–75 B.C.E., pointing to a composition date not later than the late second century B.C.E.

The document was labeled "Testimonium" by analogy with early Christian documents that are collections of scriptural quotations. This text collects five biblical quotations and one sectarian text, presented in four groups, that pertain to the messianic teachings of the Qumran community.

Although the texts are presented without commentary, the subject matter of the quotes makes the referent clear. The first group, Deuteronomy 5:28–29 and 18:18–19, anticipates the coming of "a prophet like Moses." The second group, Numbers 24:15–17, with its mention of the "Star of Jacob" and the "Scepter of Israel," clearly refers to the Davidic, or royal, Messiah. The third group, Deuteronomy 33:8–11, presents a blessing of Levi, and, by extension, the priestly Messiah.

The last group begins with a quotation of Joshua 6:26, followed by an excerpt from the sectarian composition known as the Psalms of Joshua. The quotation concerns a man and his two sons, who are cursed for rebuilding the city of Jericho. The Psalms of Joshua excerpt goes on to state that the man (either the father or the elder son) has brought evil to Israel, and his reign (and that of his son or his brother) is characterized by violence and bloodshed. F. M. Cross has argued that the man and his two sons should be identified as Simon the Maccabee and his two sons, all three of whom were murdered at Jericho. Using this text as one of his proofs, he identifies Simon as the Wicked Priest, the great enemy of the sect found in other Qumran documents. J. T. Milik, however, identifies the three as Mattathias and his sons Jonathan and Simon, claiming that it is the sons who rule, not the father, and that this text is not necessarily a reference to the Wicked Priest. Neither argument is without flaws. Given the preceding material of the Testimonium, the quote must refer to an event of the last days before the coming of the Messiah; whether or not this was a past event when the Testimonium was written is unclear.

Testimonium Flavianum a passage in Josephus that mentions Jesus. Its authenticity is highly disputed since it states that "this was the Christ," a very unlikely statement for Josephus. Also, some versions do not have this or give a different wording. Most modern scholars think either that it was entirely an interpolation by Christian scribes or that Josephus did indeed mention Jesus but Christian

scribes added words and phrases to give a more favorable opinion. The latter explanation has tended to dominate. The title means "the Flavian testimony," since Josephus was adopted into the Flavian family.

testimony the statement of a witness given in a court of law. In rabbinic law, testimony of witnesses is not given under oath; a formal oath is deemed unnecessary in light of the Decalogue's admonition against bearing false witness (Exod. 20:16). An oath may, however, be imposed upon an individual to force him or her to indicate whether or not he or she knows testimony that will benefit a litigant. This is allowed because such a witness can refuse to speak without violating the Ninth Commandment. Outside of an oath, there is no means of compelling a person to testify in court.

Scripture refers to testimony "from the mouth of witnesses" (e.g., Deut. 17:16). Accordingly, rabbinic law insists on oral testimony, given in open court, before the judges, litigants, and other witnesses. Questioning is by the court, but the opposing litigant has the right to suggest to the judges points on which to cross-examine the witness. In criminal matters, testimony by deposition is excluded. In litigation over contracts, however, depositions may be allowed, for instance, if a witness is sick or in a different locale.

Rabbinic law follows scripture in requiring evidence from at least two witnesses for convicting the accused (Num. 35:10; Deut. 19:15; B. Sotah 2b; B. Sanhedrin 20a). In a case in which testimony of two witnesses would prove the claim, however, the evidence of one is deemed sufficient to require the accused to take an oath denying the claim. Testimony is not accepted from women, slaves, imbeciles, deaf-mutes or, in the view of some authorities, the deaf or mute, the blind, relatives, parties who are in any way involved in the matter, known criminals, sinners, or those who reject societal norms (who might perjure themselves).

Tetragrammaton (Gr., four letters) term used in reference to the divine name, which in Hebrew is written as the four consonants YHWH, the vowels not being directly preserved; see also GOD, NAMES OF; I AM

tetrarch (Gr., ruler over a fourth part) Originally the term referred to a ruler over a quarter of a kingdom; with time, however, it came to mean a ruler over a significant portion of a kingdom, not necessarily a quarter. For example, when Herod the Great died, his kingdom was broken up into three parts. Two of these parts were each somewhat smaller in size; they were called tetrachies and ruled by the tetrarchs Herod Antipas and Philip. Judah proper, which constituted the largest portion of Herod's old realm, was left intact to be ruled by an ethnarch, Archelaus.

Thallus a writer of a history of the world that apparently extended from the Trojan war to the first century B.C.E. or perhaps the first century C.E., since one of the fragments seems to include a date in the latter. The work and the author are difficult to characterize because the six fragments preserved often cite Thallus together with other historians, and it is not clear that more than one or two contain exact quotations. Thus, whether he was a Jew, Samaritan, or pagan cannot be said with any confidence. He apparently mentioned Moses and supposedly gave a euhemeristic interpretation to the god Saturn. He included chronographical data, as well.

thank-offering welfare sacrifice, an offering in gratitude to the Deity. It is a subdivision of the peace-offering that was divided between the altar, the priest, and the one who offered the sacrifice. The latter shared his portion, which had to be eaten on the same day, with family and friends. By the early rabbinic era, the thank-offering was treated as a meal consumed by those making the offering. Josephus and Philo consider some burnt offerings to be thanksgiving-offerings, although the biblical injunction is that burnt offerings were for atonement. The Mishnah classifies the thank-offering in the lower order of sacred offerings.

theater a popular form of entertainment and cultural expression in the Graeco-Roman world. Both comedy and tragedy arose out of religious celebrations. The plays themselves were written in poetry and, like those of Shakespeare, had value both as literature and as live performances, though the author might intend one more than the other. Little is known of theaters in a Jewish context, except that Herod the Great built one in Jerusalem. We also know that Philo of Alexandria had attended theater productions. Finally, the *Exagoge* of Ezekiel the Tragedian was in play format, though we cannot say whether it was ever performed.

theft *see* ROBBERY

theios anēr (Gr., divine man) term used of various charismatic teachers in the Graeco-Roman world who were alleged to have special powers from God. The figure in Greek literature who is generally put forward as the model is Apollonius of Tyana, though both ancients and moderns have seen an alternative in Socrates, whose "divine" attributes were intellectual, not miraculous. Some figures from Jewish history have also been compared. These include holy men noted for their piety and holiness but also with special powers. One example is Honi the Circler, who was alleged to have been able to bring rain, and Hanina ben Dosa. Also included are such ancient sages as Moses. Hence, the argument has been developed that the Jewish holy man had some characteristics in common with the Hellenistic *theios anēr* and that a comparable idea had developed in Hellenistic Judaism by the first century C.E. The concept has been used in New Testament scholarship to try to better understand Jesus. As a result, the term itself—or a related concept—has become widespread in modern scholarship in both the Jewish and Christian contexts, though the appropriateness of this has been debated.

theocracy (Gr., rule by God) term that seems to have been coined by Josephus, who states that Judea was a theocracy. He proceeds to explain that by this he means a state under priestly rule, presumably because the priests were in theory directed by God. The structure of the state was one with the high priest as the head and his fellow priests as his assistants and administrators. The high priest was advised by a council, which may have been composed largely of priests; at times the council may have shared power, as well. In short, a theocracy is essentially a temple state.

theodicy a defense of the justice of God. In a religion that asserted that God rewarded the righteous and punished the wicked, evident instances to the contrary caused consternation and required explanation. Explicit concern with the issue appears in many of the canonical Psalms (see, e.g., Ps. 73) and is dealt with in excruciating detail in the Book of Job. Writings composed in response to such events as the persecution by Antiochus IV, Pompey's invasion of Jerusalem, and the Roman destruction of Jerusalem in 70 C.E. are full of attempts to defend God's justice in the midst of great suffering. *See also* JUDGMENT, DIVINE.

Theodoret (393–466 C.E.) bishop of Cyrrhus, Syria, born in Antioch. He was a defender of Nestorius and an ardent critic of Cyril of Alexandria. He wrote a work against Judasim, now lost. His *Church History* contains many valuable documents, and his *Religious History* contains biographies of ascetics. He tells us that he debated Jews "in most cities of the east." He reports that upon the appointment of Peter as bishop of Alexandria, a mob of Jews and Greeks surrounded the church and threatened him with exile. He also records that the patriarchal family was descended from Herod.

Theodosius I (346–395 C.E.) Roman emperor born in Spain. In 379, Gratian appointed him Augustus of the East. Failing to expel the Visigoths, he signed a treaty with them in 382 which provided them with lands in Thrace. In 386 he and the Persians partitioned Armeania. He became baptized as a Christian early in his reign during a serious illness, and as emperor he supported the followers of the Nicean creed against the Arians. He deposed the Arian bishop of Constantinople, Demophilus, and attempted to replace him with Gregory of Nazianzus. At first he did not close the temples of the old Roman cults, but he did not punish fanatical Christians who destroyed them. Finally, in 391 he closed all their temples and banned their religious practices. Although Ambrose forced Theodosius to annul his order for the bishop of Callinicum to rebuild the synagogue he had destroyed, the emperor continued to speak out against fanatical Christians who destroyed synagogues. Theodosius forbade marriages between Jews and Christians, and in 393 he outlawed polygamy among the Jews. In 383 he annulled the law freeing the rabbis from participation in the curiae, but in 397 he excused the Jewish elders from taking part in non-Jewish communal religious services. He continued the previous policy of legislating against Jewish proselytism.

Theodosius II (401–450 C.E.) Roman emperor. He was not a strong emperor, and others in his court exercised real control of the empire. He had to engage in wars with Persia, the Vandals, and the Huns. In 438 the publication of the Theodosian Code succeeded in reforming the empire's legal system. He was an orthodox Christian, and during his reign Nestorius and Flavian, two bishops of Constantinople, were condemned for heretical beliefs by councils in Ephesus. To discourage conversion to Judaism, in 423 he decreed that the circumcision of a Christian was punishable by confiscation of property and exile, and in 429 any stipulation in a Jewish will that prohibited children who had converted to Christianity from inheriting from their parents was declared invalid. In 438 proselytism of any Christian to Judaism was punishable by death. Eventually, Jews were prohibited from acting as representatives of cities, serving in the army, becoming lawyers, or holding any public office. In 415 all cases between Christians and Jews had to be tried in ordinary civil courts. In 438 he decreed that new synagogues could not be built, and new ones could be repaired only if they were in danger of falling down. In 429 he apparently refused to appoint a patriarch as successor to Gamaliel VI, for a law mentions "the end of the patriarchs."

Theodosius of Rome a Roman Jew also known as Todos of Rome, of the late first century C.E., who instructed the Roman Jewish community to prepare "helmeted goats," roasted with the entrails and legs on the head, on Passover. In response, sages declared that were it not for Theodosius's personal status, they would have excommunicated him for having the people eat meat prepared as a sacrifice outside of the Temple.

Theodotion a translation of the Hebrew Bible into Greek. At its base seems to be the *kaige* recension, which was evidently a revision of the Septuagint. Theodotian was a Christian figure of the second century C.E. who apparently made further revisions to the *kaige* to improve the Greek style of the text.

Theodotus writer preserved in only a few fragments in Eusebius, forty-six lines in all. These focus on the city of Shechem and the incident recorded in Genesis 34: the rape of Jacob's daughter Dinah by Shechem, the son of Hamor, king of Shechem. Shechem then agreed to marry Dinah and even accept circumcision; subsequently, Simeon and Levi entered the city while the men were incapacitated by the recent circumcision and killed them all. It has been suggested that the work was called *On the Jews,* but this does not fit the exclusive focus on the one incident at Shechem. Also, it has been suggested that the author was Samaritan, again because of the concentration on Shechem. Although this remains a possibility, there are no specifically Samaritan features of the story; for example, nothing is said of a temple or worship. A Jewish writer could have been interested in the incident as a part of his heritage; the poem may even be seen as anti-Samaritan. The poem itself is in classical hexameters and shows knowledge of Homeric verse; the author clearly had a Greek education. Although the poem generally follows the biblical text, an oracle of God is given in justification for the slaughter.

theophany the visible manifestation of God. Although some biblical accounts of God's appearance to humans have little descriptive detail (Gen. 3:8, 15:1–21; Exod. 33:17–34:7), others recount cosmic quaking and storm-like phenomena (Exod. 19:16–19; Ps. 77:16–20; Hab. 3). While the Sinai theophany was unique, a number of biblical texts anticipate a similar theophany when God will descend to judge humanity (Isa. 24:17–23, 66:15–16; Jer. 25:31; Mic. 1:3–4). 1 Enoch 1:3–9 and the Testament of Moses 10:3–10 draw on these texts and Deuteronomy 33:2, to flesh out vivid descriptions of the final judgment. *See also* EPIPHANY.

Theophrastus (c. 370–285 B.C.E.) Greek writer from Lesbos. He was a disciple of Aristotle and succeeded him as head of the Lyceum (philosophical school). He became the most famous Peripatetic after Aristotle. He is probably best known for his *Characters,* a set of stereotyped personality sketches. Other works preserved include *On Plants,* but much of what he wrote has perished. He is possibly the first Greek writer to mention the Jews directly. He praises them as philosophers who discuss divine things and also make observations of the heavens. With regard to animal sacrifices he thinks they adopted these only reluctantly and are more enlightened about them than the Greeks. This is because they burn the victim straight away, only at night, and while they themselves are fasting (as will be clear, he has confused several things, such as assuming the Jews offer only holocausts). He is also quoted by Josephus as mentioning the oath of *korban* by name. Other references by him mainly concern the natural products of Syria-Palaestina: the date palm, basalm, and various other spices.

theosebes (Gr., fearer of God, or pious one) term sometimes found in Jewish writings and inscriptions in Greek in reference to pious Jews. However, there is also evidence that it could be used of proselytes and "God-fearers", that is, Gentile sympathizers who did not go all the way to conversion. *See also* GOD-FEARERS.

Therapeutai a Jewish monastic community described in the first century C.E. by Philo of Alexandria. His report, in the treatise *On the Contemplative Life,* provides the only information we have on this group. (The name is derived from a Greek verb meaning either "to heal" or "to worship.") Its members lived an ascetic life on a hill west of Alexandria, between Lake Mareotis and the Mediterranean Sea. They gave up their possessions upon entering the community, and devoted themselves to the study of scripture, prayer, and worship. They lived each in a consecrated room called a *monasterion,* devoting themselves six days a week to private spiritual exercises. On the seventh day, they gathered for communal worship, with men and women separated by a barrier constructed in their meeting hall, listening to a discourse by their leader and sharing a common meal. A special festival was observed for the fiftieth day (presumably meaning after Passover, i.e., Pentecost, or Weeks). This festival featured an evening supper and an all-night vigil devoted to antiphonal hymn singing and a choric dance. The vigil concluded at sunrise with special prayers. Philo contrasts the Therapeutai with the Essenes, the latter said to live a more "active" life in contrast to the "contemplative" Therapeutai. However, some scholars have suggested a link between the Palestinian Essenes and the Therapeutai of Egypt. The fourth-century Christian historian Eusebius interpreted Philo's account as a reference to the first Egyptian Christians, but no credence can be given to this.

theriolatry (Gr., worship of animals) term used in reference to cults in which images of the gods were represented in the form of animals. The Egyptians were the major example of this and were often caricatured as worshiping animals, not only by the Jews but also by the Greeks and Romans.

Theudas a first-century-C.E. Jewish prophet who led a group of Jews, with their possessions, to the Jordan River, in the expectation that it would part, so that they could journey on, presumably into the desert or exile, according to Josephus (*Ant.* 20.97–98). The Roman procurator Fadus (served 44–46 C.E.) attacked the group (numbering 400 according to Acts 5:36), killing, capturing, and scattering them. Theudas was beheaded. Acts anachronistically places Theudas much earlier than the time of Fadus. Theudas's movement was one of a number led by popular prophets protesting Roman rule.

Thirty-third Day of the Counting of the Sheaf of First Barley Grain (after the advent of the first full moon after the vernal equinox; Heb.: Lag baOmer) thirty-third day in the seven-week period of counting the omer, from the second day of Passover to Pentecost (Lev. 23:15); day of celebration for scholars

throne of God God's relationship to the world is often described in the Bible in terms of a king ruling over his domain, and like a king he is said to sit on a throne (Heb.: *kiseh;* Aram.: *kursa*): so, for example, Psalm 47:8–9, "God is king of all the earth. . . . God reigns over the nations. God sits upon his holy throne." Psalm 103:9 locates God's throne in heaven ("the Lord has established his throne in the heavens"), but Ezekiel 1:1–28 implies that it moves about, borne on a wheeled vehicle which in later tradition was known as the Chariot (*merkabah*) of God. Daniel 7:9 also speaks of the throne as having wheels. Since the throne symbolizes God's power, its mobility may express the extension of that power throughout the world. The throne, which is not described in detail (though Dan. 7:9 states that it is made of fire), is associated with judgment: it is the ultimate tribunal, and when God takes his seat upon it, surrounded by his retinue of angels, it is to judge the world (Ps. 9:5,8; 1 Kings 22:19; Dan. 7:9–10). Earlier and later visions of God's throne are recorded in 1 Enoch 14 and the Apocalypse of Abraham 17–19, respectively.

Royal imagery is further developed in the writings of the *merkabah* mystics. They locate God's throne, designated "the throne of glory" (*kiseh hakabod*), in the innermost of seven concentric palaces (*hekhalot*), which are in turn located in the seventh heaven. The adept is portrayed as a petitioner who desires to stand before the throne and see the king. Like the kings of Persia, God sits behind a veil and, although he is served by myriads of angels, only certain privileged archangels are allowed to see his face (cf. Esther 1:14). God alone is allowed to sit; everyone else must stand in his presence—a notion justified by the statement in Ezekiel 1:7 that the angels have "straight feet" or "straight legs," for example, they have no knee joints and so are physically incapable of sitting. This tradition is intended to stress God's uniqueness and to deny that there are "two powers in heaven." By way of contrast, in certain other early Jewish texts other beings beside God are depicted as sitting in heaven: see, for example, Mark 14:62 ("you will see the son of man seated at the right hand of power"), Revelation 4:4, and note the controversy in 3 Enoch 16 over the throne of Metatron. According to some texts, God only descends from hidden, upper heavens at certain times in the day to sit upon the throne and to preside over the sessions of the heavenly law court (*beit din shelemaalah*). The mystical literature describes in great detail the elaborate rituals of adoration, centered on the celestial *kedushah* (cf. Isa. 6:3), that accompany these levees. Many of these ideas were taken up and reinterpreted in the mediaeval Kabbalah, the throne of glory and the chariot being correlated in complex ways with the world of the Sefirot. The philosophers naturally insisted that the language was figurative. Saadia (882–942), for example, maintains that the throne was an entity specially created by God out of fire in order to reveal himself to the prophets (Book of Beliefs and Opinions I, 10).

thyrsus (Gr., reed) a cult object often used in Greek processions, especially those associated with the worship of Dionysus. Resemblances have been seen to the Sukkot procession, because this features palm leaves and other vegetation, and possible influence has been suggested.

Tiberianus governor of Palestine, 114 C.E. He is mentioned by John Malalas and John of Antioch in connection with an event that occurred when Trajan was in Antioch to begin his war with Parthia. Although John of Antioch probably depends on Malalas and the texts are problematic, there is no reason to reject their testimony.

Tiberias city named after the Roman emperor Tiberius. Tiberias was founded in the reign of Herod Antipas, the son of Herod the Great, in 20 C.E. Its location is on the western shore of the Sea of Galilee, north of the hot spring known as Hammat. The city's western boundary is marked by Mount Berenice, which rises to an altitude of 200 meters above the Sea of Galilee.

According to Josephus, the city was located "close to the finer parts of Galilee." In order to populate the city for its first inhabitants, the king built "houses at his expense, and granted them land" (Ant. XVIII, 36–38). In 61 C.E. Tiberias was annexed to the kingdom of Agrippa II, whose capital was Caesarea-Philippi (Banias). Berenice, Agrippa's sister and co-ruler, has no connection to the hill and the aqueduct of Tiberias, which bear her name. When the war against Rome began (67 C.E.), Tiberias was fortified, and these fortification walls remained standing even after the surrender of the city to the Roman legions. Tiberias remained part of Agrippa's kingdom until his death in 96 C.E. (Josephus, *Life*, 37–38).

When Tiberias came under Roman rule in 100 C.E., it shared the prosperity enjoyed by the entire empire. In Hadrian's reign, a temple was built in his honor. In the mid-second century, after the Bar Kokhba War, Tiberias was cleansed of the ritual impurity caused by graves within the city, thus clearing the way for Jewish religious scholars to settle there. At the end of the century, Rabbi Judah the Nasi (patriarch) moved his residence from Sepphoris to Tiberias. The institutions of the Jewish leadership were transferred from Sepphoris to Tiberias too: first the Sanhedrin, headed by Rabbi Johanan, and then the patriarchate held by Rabbi Judah (Nesiah). In Tiberias, Rabbi Johanan established the Great Beit Midrash (academy), possibly located at the foot of Mount Berenice. According to tradition, the greater part of the Jerusalem (socalled Palestinian) Talmud was codified in this academy, which is frequently mentioned in rabbinic literature.

When Tiberias had become the spiritual capital of the Jewish people, both in Eretz Israel and in the diaspora, it enjoyed a prolonged period of prosperity. Tiberias's fortunes improved after the Muslim conquest. The city became the capital of Jund Urdun (Jordan District) whose boundaries roughly corresponded to those of the Byzantine Palaestina Secunda, the capital of which had been Beth Shean. Under Muslim rule, Jews were still the majority among the inhabitants, side by side with a fairly large Christian community and a smaller Muslim one.

During the period of Muslim rule, Tiberias suffered several earthquakes. The most severe occurred in 749 C.E. The destruction it brought is evident in all the archaeological sites in the city and its environs. In 1033 another earthquake struck Tiberias, destroying many buildings. Despite the damage it had suffered, the city maintained its status as the capital of Galilee until its capture by the crusaders in 1099. Tancred, the commander of the crusader army, established Tiberias as the capital of the Galilee Principality, the area of which roughly corresponded to that of the Jordan District under Moslem rule. The city wall was restored, and a large fortress was built in the north of the Roman-Byzantine city. The inhabitants clustered around the fortress and abandoned the area of the city which had been settled before then. Thus, the nucleus of a new Tiberias came into being, which developed into the modern city.

In 1187, after the battle of Hattin, the city fell to Saladin and remained under Muslim-Ayyubid rule until 1240, when Tiberias and the entire Galilee once again came under crusader control for a brief period. In 1247 the city fell to the Mamluk forces and remained uninterrupted under Muslim rule until the British conquest in 1917–1918.

Exploration. The remains of ancient Tiberias's walls were first examined by V. Guérin in 1875. A more detailed survey of the walls at the top of Mount Berenice was carried out by G. Schumacher in 1887. A systematic excavation of the southern gate and its vicinity was carried out by G. Foerster in 1973–1974. In addition, a great number of salvage excavations has been carried out. The largest, in both scale and results, was conducted under the direction of B. Rabani (1954–1956). The excavators cleared a section of the city's central colonnaded street (cardo), as well as a bathhouse and vaulted market. To the east, not far from the lake shore, A. Druks (1964–1968) uncovered the remains of a basilical structure. In 1976, F. Vitto excavated a Roman tomb in Tiberias, and in 1989–1990, Y. Hirschfeld's salvage excavation at the foot of Mount Berenice exposed a Roman public building beneath the remains of Muslim dwellings. Later, in 1990–1994, Hirschfeld conducted the excavation on the summit of Mount Berenice.

City plan. Following the Roman urban tradition, Tiberias was a planned city from its inception. As in every Roman city in Eretz Israel, public buildings were constructed for governmental, administrative, and religious purposes, and as centers for culture and entertainment. The rabbinic literature mentions the city gate, the citadel, the council building, thirteen synagogues, academies of learning, marketplaces, a stadium, a bathhouse, a toilet, and monumental tombs. Other sources mention the harbor, the city wall, and a temple erected in honor of Hadrian. Churches and mosques were built in the city in the Byzantine and Early Arab periods.

Along with the public buildings, there were flourishing residential quarters and a workshop area with various industries, such as glass and pottery manufacturing. To the south of Tiberias, in the vicinity of the hot springs, Hammath Tiberias developed into a suburb of wide renown, which served the multitudes who came to bathe in the springs and benefit from their healing properties.

Tiberias developed along the narrow coastal strip between the Sea of Galilee and the eastern slopes of Mount Berenice. In the mid-sixth century, the city was enclosed by a massive wall about 2.8 kilometers long. The line of the wall formed a rough triangle, with its base along the shore and its apex at the summit of Mount Berenice (at about 200 m above the Sea of Galilee). This wall marks the maximal expansion of the city. Hammath Tiberias was also enclosed by a wall during this period. The overall area of Tiberias and Hammath Tiberias was about 230 acres, comparable to the area of the largest cities in the country. The population of the city during the Byzantine period is estimated at twenty to thirty thousand—almost that of present-day Tiberias.

Tiberias, Lake *see* GALILEE, SEA OF

Tiberius (42 B.C.E.–37 C.E.) in full, Tiberias Julias Caesar Augustus; son of Tiberius Claudius Nero and Livia; stepson of the emperor Augustus and his successor as Roman emperor (14 C.E.). Though he is maligned by the Roman historian Tacitus, Tiberius was generally a good administrator and modest leader. His personal qualities did not make him a popular leader, and his reclusiveness late in his life impeded efficient administration and resulted in some governors being left in office too long, such as Pontius Pilate in Judea (26–36 C.E.).

Tiberius Julius Alexander procurator of Judea (46–48 C.E.); born in Alexandria; the son of Alexander, a wealthy tax official, and the nephew of the Jewish philosopher Philo. Tiberius and his family were prominent in the imperial service for several generations. After some initial appointments, Alexander was named procurator of Judea. Though Alexander had ceased to live as a Jew, according to Josephus, he kept the peace by not interfering with internal Jewish affairs. During his procuratorship he executed James and Simon, two sons of Judas the Galilean, and he also had to deal with a famine. Little else is known of his tenure in Judea. He later fought in Armenia under Corbulo who was campaigning against the Parthians. He became prefect of Egypt, a very important post, in 66. Tiberius was the first provincial governor to support Vespasian's campaign to become emperor in 69. When Titus continued the war in Judea with the siege of Jerusalem in 70, Tiberius was one of his military advisors. Subsequently, he probably served as Vespasian's praetorian prefect in Rome.

Tigranes V Jewish ruler of Armenia (60–61 C.E.). Tigranes was Herod the Great's great-great-grandson. In 60 C.E., the Roman emperor Nero appointed him king of Greater Armenia as part of his plan to make use of loyal Herodians to govern Middle Eastern principalities. Armenia had a fairly substantial Jewish population at this time. It is likely that this population reflected the importance of the Jews in the east–west trade of commodities. None of the Herodian family had maintained any ties to Judaism, and Josephus did not consider any of them to be good Jews.

tikun olam (Heb., setting the world right) the concept of the role of humans in reestablishing the perfectly ordered world that existed at the time of the Creation. *Tikun olam* is accomplished through acts of charity and loving kindness, as well as through observance of the complete system of rabbinic laws.

times or seasons (Gr.: *chronoi ē kairoi*; Acts 1:7) a general term referring to the notion that God has predetermined the time of the end, which is preceded by a series of historical periods or ages. This understanding of history is reflected in a number of apocalypses that provide reviews of such historical periods (Dan. 7; 1 Enoch 85–90, 93:1–10, 91:11–17; 2 Bar. 53–72; cf. also 1QH 1:23–25; 4Q180). Such texts reflect the practice of trying to determine when the end would come. In Acts 1:7 Jesus counsels against such practice, claiming that God alone knows the times (cf. also Matt. 24:36). *See also* ESCHATOLOGY.

Timestheus, Gaius Furius procurator of Palestine, 232 C.E. He had a distinguished career, holding a number of procuratorships. He was probably procurator of Palestine when Severus Alexander began his Persian war. Timestheus was put in charge of collecting the *annona* to support the emperor's military campaign.

Tineius Rufus *see* RUFUS, QUINTUS TINEIUS

Tisha b'Ab *see* AB, NINTH OF

Tishrei first month of the Jewish calendar, corresponding to September/October beginning with Rosh Hashanah, New Year

tithe (Heb.: *maaser*) a tenth of the herd and crop, set aside for the Lord, to be used for the Temple, priesthood, and other scheduled castes

tithe of the tithe a tenth of the Levite's tithe, which is handed on to the priest

Titus (39–81 C.E.) Roman emperor; son of Vespasian. Titus Flavius Vespasianus led the Roman forces in the siege of Jerusalem (70 C.E.) and succeeded his father as Roman emperor (79–81). After early military service and a term as quaestor, Titus accompanied his father on his campaign against the Jews in Palestine (67 C.E.). He was intimately involved in the negotiations that led to his father's accession to the imperial throne in 69. He then led the Roman army in its conquest of Judea and siege of Jerusalem. After weeks of battle the walls fell in succession, then the Temple Mount, and finally the Upper City with its citadel, the palace of Herod. According to the historian Josephus, Titus tried numerous times to negotiate the surrender of Jerusalem and ordered that the Temple not be burned. Since Josephus was a client of Titus and his father Vespasian and sought to present a positive picture of the Flavians, the veracity of his account is uncertain. After the war Titus and his father were granted a triumph by the Roman Senate. Titus then served his father in high office, including that of praetorian prefect. Although he aroused some resentment because he suppressed dissent, when he succeeded his father as emperor in 79 he was known as an affable and generous ruler. He completed the Colosseum and the Baths of Titus, and he responded to the disasters caused by the eruption of Mt. Vesuvius (79 C.E.) and the plague and fire in Rome (80). He died of natural causes in 81.

Titus, Arch of arch located on the Via Sacra in Rome. Carved relief sculptures on either side of the passage show the triumph of Vespasian and Titus after the destruction of Jerusalem. The menorah, the Table of Showbread, trumpets, other items from the Temple, and the captives are featured prominently on one panel; Titus in his chariot crowned by victory is shown on the other.

TJ abbreviation for Targum of Jerusalem (Heb.: Targum Yerushalmi; Ger.: Targum Jeruschalmi), the earliest name for the Palestinian Targums to the Pentateuch

TJ1 (TJI) abbreviations (occasionally written as 1 JT, 1 TJ, TY I, or 1J) that designate Targum Pseudo-Jonathan, which is a component of the Palestinian Targums to the Pentateuch, whose earliest name was Targum of Jerusalem (TJ).

TJ2 (TJII) abbreviations (occasionally written as 2 JT, 2 TJ, TY II, or 2J) that designate the Fragmentary Targums, a component of the Palestinian Targums to the Pentateuch, whose earliest name was Targum of Jerusalem (TJ).

Tobiah an opponent of Nehemiah referred to in Nehemiah (2:10, 19; 4:3, 7; 6:1, 12, 14) as "Tobiah the servant, the Ammonite." He was the ally of Sanballat of Samaria and Geshem the Arab in opposing Nehemiah's policies in Judah, threatened military action against Nehemiah (Neh. 4:7), and hired prophets to discredit Nehemiah (Neh. 6:12–14). He had close ties with the Judean nobility (Neh. 6:17–19) and the Jerusalem priesthood (13:4–9). "Servant" (*ebed*) is probably an honorific title, and he seems to have been governor of the Ammonite region, east of the Jordan, under Persian rule. *See also* TOBIAH, HOUSE OF.

Tobiah, house of family founded by Tobiah, who was probably the opponent of Nehemiah described in the Book of Nehemiah, though one of the Lachish letters from the last days of Judah mentions a Tobiah who was a "servant of the king." By the third century B.C.E., the Tobiad family was established in the Ammonite region, east of the Jordan, in and around the fortress of Araq el-Emir, where the name Tobiah is engraved on the cliff at the entrance to the fortress (Qasr al-Abd). Something of the history of the family can be reconstructed from Josephus (*Ant.* 12:160–236), the Zeno papyri from the mid-third century B.C.E., 2 Maccabees 3:9–14, and the excavations at Araq el-Emir. Three generations of Tobiads (Tobiah, Joseph, Hyrcanus) supported the Ptolemies and opposed the high priestly family of the Oniads. Joseph became prosperous as a tax collector for the Ptolemies, and his son, Hyrcanus, had a large sum deposited in the Temple treasury (2 Macc. 3:11). Hyrcanus was later forced to retire to Transjordan, where he committed suicide on the accession of Antiochus IV Epiphanes (175 B.C.E.).

Tobit, Book of a fictional narrative about the suffering of two Israelite families in Assyria. The book was probably written in the third century B.C.E., but its folk motifs are doubtless much older. A translation of the originally Aramaic work was included in the Greek Bible, and Qumran Cave 4 yielded four fragmentary manuscripts of the Aramaic text and one of a Hebrew translation. Although Tobit was not accepted into the rabbinic canon, late manuscripts in Hebrew and Aramaic indicate its ongoing usage in other Jewish circles. Their place in the textual tradition must await publication of the Qumran texts.

A master storyteller, the author weaves two parallel plots into a common, but complicated resolution. Tobit, a pious Israelite from Galilee exiled to Nineveh, is regularly harassed and persecuted for his piety and righteous life. Blinded because of an act of kindness and the object of reproach, he prays for death to release him from his unfair situation. Certain that God will answer him, he sends his son Tobias across Mesopotamia to collect a large deposit of silver, first instructing him on his responsibilities to his mother and his obligation to marry a women of his tribe. Near Tobias's destination, Sarah, a distant relative, also prays for death because she is unjustly accused of the wedding-night deaths of her seven successive husbands, who in fact have been killed by a demon in love with her. The angel Raphael, sent in human form, guides Tobias on his journey, directs him to Sarah's house, dispatches the demon, fetches the money, and brings the couple back to Nineveh, where he cures Tobit's blindness, so that all live happily and prosperously ever after.

This complex and humorous plot mirrors the author's view of reality and makes a simple and serious point: a providential God orchestrates events toward a beneficent resolution for the pious even when they are totally oblivious of this fact. Tobit's and Sarah's story is paradigmatic for God's people in exile. Through suffering, God "scourges" righteous individuals and the nation for their sins, so that they may obtain "mercy"—release from their ills and return to a restored Jerusalem. Presumed throughout are the Israelites' covenantal obligations, epitomized in Tobit's observance of the Torah (regular visits to Jerusalem, the offering of tithes, and acts of kindness) and in divinely ordained familial obligations such as honoring one's parents and marrying an appropriate spouse.

The book is mainly prose narrative, and the portrayal of Tobit as a persecuted and restored courtier in Mesopotamia indicates the Story of Ahikar and Daniel 1–6 as parallels. However, the author's observations about human emotions and motivations give the story a novelistic color. Additionally, the narrative is embellished with genres such as prayers, testamentary wisdom instruction, an angelophany that includes a guided journey and a dual between two spirits, a hymn of praise, and a predictive summary of Israelite history related to 1 Enoch 93:1–10 and 91:11–17.

Although elements in Tobit recall the Book of Job, its mix of genres, sophisticated and clever narrative technique, use of subthemes, inclusion of magical and demonological elements, focus on Torah piety, emphasis on family, and concern about Israelite history combine to make a unique story.

The diaspora setting, repeated gentile antagonism to Tobit's piety, and emphasis on Israelite identity suggest that the story was composed in a predominantly gentile environment. *See also:* AHIKAR, STORY OF.

Tobit, Targum to a targum to the Greek Book of Tobit composed in the medieval period. The targum is fairly literal and follows the standard Greek texts closely. Fragments of an Aramaic version of Tobit were also discovered at Qumran and clearly represent a different text from that of the targum. It is presently thought that the Qumran fragments indicate that Tobit was originally composed in Aramaic.

Todos of Rome *see* THEODOSIUS OF ROME

Tohorot **1.** Mishnah tractate devoted to susceptibility to uncleanness of food, ordinarily at home. The tractate discusses susceptibility to uncleanness of Holy Things, heave-offerings, and unconsecrated food (chaps. 1–3); doubts in matters of uncleanness (chaps. 3–6); the relationship of observant and nonobservant Israelites in connection with preserving the ritual cleanness of food and drink (chaps. 7–8); and special liquids, olive oil, and wine (chaps. 9–10).

2. sixth division of the Mishnah, devoted to rules of ritual cleanness that govern in the Temple; and rules of ritual cleanness observed in the homes of those who wish to eat their everyday food at home in accordance with the laws governing the Temple priests' meals in the holy place

Tolidah one of the Samaritan Chronicles, also known as Chronicle 3. It consists mainly of a list of high priests with lengths of office, extending from Moses to the nineteenth century, but occasionally containing other data. Some have argued that this is the basis of all Samaritan priestly chronicles, but others disagree.

tomb *see* BURIAL; BURIAL SITES

toparchy (Gr., government of a district) Toparchies might be found in various places, but they seem to have been especially used as administrative units in Egypt, perhaps corresponding to the old *nomes.* The governor of a toparchy was referred to as a toparch.

Torah **1.** (Heb., instruction) referring especially to divine law, a fundamental concept in Jewish texts beginning with the Tanakh (Old Testament). The term is used in several senses, ranging from an individual commandment to the whole Tanakh. It often designates the first five books, Genesis through Deuteronomy, called the "Law of Moses" and regarded as the heart of the Tanakh. These books combine a number of originally independent law codes (e.g., the Ten Commandments in Exod. 20; the Holiness Code in Lev. 17–26; and Deuteronomy, or "the second law"), embedding them in the story of the foundational events of Israel's history (promises to the patriarchs, deliverance from Egypt, the formation of the covenant at Mount Sinai). The Torah stands in the context of the covenant between God and Israel; it is preceeded by divine grace and is itself an expression of grace. As the law, "Torah" is understood as the revealed will of God, which covers all aspects of life, religious and civil. Particular emphases of biblical law include the command to worship one God, the honoring of the Sabbath, circumcision, ritual purity, and dietary laws.

If the Torah is to regulate the life of all Jews, in various times and places, it requires interpretation. The tendency to expand and update the Torah is already evident in the different law codes that scholars have identified within the Tanakh. The texts of early Judaism (2d c. B.C.E.–2d c. C.E.) reflect various ways of expanding the Torah, as well as rival interpretations of it. Jubilees, a retelling of Genesis 1 through Exodus 14, underscores the authority of its peculiar interpretation of the Torah by presenting it as the contents of the "heavenly tablets" which were dictated by the "angel of presence" to Moses during his forty days on Mount Sinai (Exod. 24:18, Jub. 1:5, 2:27). Particular emphases include a solar calendar (which was also followed at Qumran but not in the Jerusalem Temple) and the correct observance of sabbath and festivals.

The authors of the Dead Sea Scrolls also believed that they had the exclusively true interpretation of the Torah, hidden from outsiders (CD 3:14), but revealed to the members of the sect (1QS 5:9). Entering the Qumran community is described as "entry into the Covenant of God" and being "converted to the Law of Moses" (1QS 5:7–11); the sect's interpretation of the law is presented as the only true and faithful one (cf. CD 6:2–11) The Scrolls polemicize against those who pervert the law (4QpNah 2:2, 8; 4QPs^a 1:18–19; 2:2–3), and specifically oppose the practices of the Jerusalem priesthood (CD 1:13–20, 5:6–7). A recently published fragmentary "Halakic letter"

(4Q394–99, also known as MMT) exhorts its addressee to forsake incorrect interpretations of certain laws (e.g., laws governing Temple offerings and other matters of purity). Similar polemics against rival interpretations of the Torah are found in the Epistle of Enoch (1 Enoch 92–105): "Woe to you who alter the true words and pervert the eternal covenant . . . (99:2). The Epistle makes exclusive claims for the instruction of "the wise" and claims that those who follow a different interpretation of the law ("falsehood") will be damned (99:9, 98:14).

Tension between the Torah and the ways of the Gentiles is evident in Tobit (1:4–20) and in 1 Maccabees, which describes the attacks on the Torah by the Seleucid king Antiochus IV and the courageous opposition of the Maccabean warriors and of the ḥasidim, ("pious ones") who "offered themselves willingly for the Law" (2:42). Willingness to die for the Torah is also exalted in the 2 Maccabees (6:18–31) and 4 Maccabees (9:1–2).

In Ecclesiasticus, the Torah is identified with the personified "Lady Wisdom," who was created by God before the ages, and whose counsel "is deeper than the great abyss" (Ecclus. 24, cf. 2 Bar. 48:24, 51:3). Philo of Alexandria identifies the Law of Moses with the law of nature (*Vita Mos.* 2.52; *Op. Mund.* 1–3) and devises an allegorical interpretation of specific commandments which gives them a philosophical meaning, without, however, denying that ordinary observance was obligatory. The Pharisees, who put particular stress on the laws of purity, teach a twofold Torah: the Written Torah revealed at Mount Sinai and the Oral Torah handed down in a chain of tradition which reaches from Moses to the Pharisaic rabbis (cf. M. Abot 1:1). Further development of the Pharisaic Oral Torah is recorded in the Mishnah (c. 200 C.E.) and the Talmud (5th–6th cs. C.E.), works which had formative influence on subsequent Jewish understanding of the Torah.

In the New Testament, Torah, translated by the Greek term *nomos,* has two main senses. In its first sense, "Scripture," the "Law" (the Old Testament) is universally affirmed as the Bible of the new Christian religion and a witness to Jesus Christ. In the sense of commandments that must be observed (the "Law of Moses"), there was no such unanimity (consider the controversies reported in Acts 15 and Gal. 1-3). Despite a number of stories which portray Jesus deliberately violating portions of the Torah, especially the Oral Torah (e.g., Mark 2), the general picture of Jesus that emerges from the Gospels is that of a Torah-observant Jew. After Jesus' death, some of those Jews who believed in him continued to observe the Torah (Acts 15:5, Gal. 2:11–14). The clearest enunciation of this position is found in the Gospel of Matthew, which presents Jesus as saying: "Until heaven and earth pass away not a letter or part of a letter will pass away from the law" (5:18). This summary statement is followed in 5:21–48 by a series of six commandments from the Law of Moses, which Jesus affirms and makes more stringent.

A very different position is reflected in the letters of Paul. While he regards the five books of Moses as authoritative Scripture (Rom. 3:21), Paul argues vehemently that observance of the commandments is not to be imposed on gentile Christians. For Paul, "Christ is the end (Gr.: *telos*) of the law" (Rom. 10:4). The word "end" means both "goal" and "termination." Paul, who describes his pre-Christian life as that of an especially zealous Pharisee (Phil. 3, Gal. 1), continues to affirm as a Christian that the Law of Moses is "holy" and that it reveals the will of God (Rom. 7:12). But he claims that the aim of the Torah, from the beginning, was to prepare for the saving message of Jesus' death and resurrection (Gal. 3:19). Having achieved its "goal" in these events, the law is now obsolete, or terminated.

Paul felt himself called to be an "apostle to the Gentiles" (Gal. 1:16), and his discussions of the Law of Moses take place in the context of an argument for the full equality of Jew and Gentile in the church. But his views on Torah observance were not merely a matter of expedience in the mission field. They reflect his apocalyptic theology, according to which the death of Christ brought the end of the old, evil age. As a Christian, Paul came to believe that the Torah, despite its divine origin, had become an instrument of the evil powers (sin and the flesh) which rule over the old age (Rom. 7).

Paul's views incited considerable controversy, beginning in his own day. This is especially evident in his letter to the Galatians, where he argues against rival Jewish Christian missionaries who say that gentile Christians must be circumcised and observe the commandments. In our own century, some scholars have claimed that Paul either misunderstood or deliberately distorted the Jewish understanding of Torah. While Paul's conception of the law was a minority position in the church of his own time, it quickly became the dominant Christian view as the church became increasingly gentile, though law-observant Jewish-Christian communities continued to exist for several centuries.

2. In rabbinic literature, the word "Torah" bears

seven meanings: (1) the written Torah; (2) the one whole Torah, oral and written, revealed by God to Moses at Sinai; (3) a particular thing, such as a scroll, containing divinely revealed words; (4) revelation in general; (5) a classification or rules, as in "the torah of . . . ," meaning "the rules that govern . . ."; (6) the act of studying the Torah; and (7) the status of a teaching, namely, deriving from the Torah, as against deriving from the scribes. "The Torah" speaks of the scriptures of ancient Israel (the Old Testament). Between the Mishnah, c. 200 C.E., and the Talmud of the Land of Israel, c. 400 C.E., "the Torah" lost its capital letter and definite article and ultimately became "torah." What for nearly a millennium had been a particular scroll or book thus came to serve as a symbol of an entire system. The word "Torah" reached the apologists for the Mishnah in its long-established meanings: Torah-scroll; contents of the Torah scroll. But even in the Mishnah itself, these meanings provoked a secondary development, the status of Torah as distinct from other (lower) statuses, hence, Torah-teaching in contradistinction to scribal teaching. With that small and simple step, the Torah ceased to denote only a concrete and material thing—a scroll and its contents. It now connoted an abstract matter of status. And once made abstract, the symbol entered a secondary history, beyond all limits imposed by the concrete object, including its specific teachings, the Torah-scroll. When a rabbi quoted in the Mishnah spoke of "torah," he no longer meant only a particular object, a scroll and its contents. Now he used the word to encompass a distinctive and well-defined worldview and way of life. Torah had come to stand for something one does. Knowledge of the Torah promised not merely information about what people were supposed to do, but ultimate salvation. The Torah as a book thus developed into an abstract and encompassing symbol, so that in the Judaism that took shape in the formative age, the first seven centuries C.E., everything was contained in that one thing.

When the rabbinical literature of late antiquity speaks of "torah," the term no longer denotes a particular book, on the one hand, or the contents of such a book, on the other. Instead, it connotes a broad range of clearly distinct categories of noun and verb, concrete fact and abstract relationship alike. "Torah" stands for a kind of human being. It connotes a social status and a sort of social group. It refers to a type of social relationship. It further denotes a legal status and differentiates among legal norms. As symbolic abstraction, the word encompasses things and persons, actions and sta-

tus, points of social differentiation and legal and normative standing, as well as "revealed truth." In all, the main points of insistence on the whole of Israel's life and history come to full symbolic expression in that single word. If people wanted to explain how they would be saved, they would use the word "Torah." If they wished to sort out their relationships with Gentiles, they would use the word "Torah" to explain what defined Israel as distinct from all other peoples. "Torah" stood for salvation and accounted for Israel's this-worldly condition and the hope, for both individual and nation alike, of life in the world to come. The Torah symbolized the whole, at once and entire. When "the Torah" refers to a particular thing, it is to a scroll containing divinely revealed words. The Torah may further refer to revelation, not as an object but as a corpus of doctrine. When one "does Torah" the disciple "studies" or "learns," and the master "teaches" Torah. Hence, while the word "Torah" never appears as a verb, it does refer to an act. The word also bears a quite separate sense, torah as category or classification or corpus of rules; for example, "the torah of driving a car" is a usage entirely acceptable to some documents. This generic usage of the word does occur. The word "Torah" very commonly refers to a status, distinct from and above another status, as "teachings of Torah" as against "teachings of scribes." For the two Talmuds that distinction is absolutely critical to the entire hermeneutic enterprise. But it is important even in the Mishnah.

Obviously, no account of the meaning of the word "Torah" can ignore the distinction between the two Torahs, Written and Oral. It is important only in the secondary stages of the formation of the literature. Finally, the word "Torah" refers to a source of salvation, often fully worked out in stories about how the individual and the nation will be saved through Torah. In general, the sense of the word "salvation" is not complicated. It is simply salvation in the way in which Deuteronomy and the Deuteronomic historians understand it: kings who do what God wants win battles; those who do not, lose. Thus people who study and do Torah are saved from sickness and death, and the way Israel can save itself from its condition of degradation also is through Torah. The expansion of the meaning of the word "Torah" to encompass not only the scriptures (Written Torah) but also the teachings and writings of rabbis of the first six centuries C.E. (Oral Torah) begins with the Mishnah. The framers of the Mishnah gave no hint of the nature of their book, so the Mishnah reached the political world of

Israel without a trace of self-conscious explanation or any theory of validation. They nowhere claim, implicitly or explicitly, that what they have written forms part of the Torah, enjoys the status of God's revelation to Moses at Sinai, or even systematically carries forward secondary exposition and application of what Moses wrote down in the wilderness. Later on, two hundred years beyond the closure of the Mishnah, the need to explain the standing and origin of the Mishnah led some to posit two things. First, God's revelation of the Torah at Sinai encompassed the Mishnah as much as scripture. Second, the Mishnah was handed on through oral formulation and oral transmission from Sinai to the framers of the document as we have it. These two convictions emerge from the references of both Talmuds to the dual Torah. One part is in writing. The other was oral and now is in the Mishnah. Thus the word "Torah" came to refer to not only the ancient Israelite scriptures but also much else and ultimately came to stand for the religion, Judaism.

The Mishnah places a high value upon studying the Torah and upon the status of the sage. A "*mamzer*-disciple of a sage takes priority over a high-priest *am-haAretz*" (M. Hor. 3:8). But if the Mishnah does not claim to constitute part of the Torah, then what makes a sage a sage is not mastery of the Mishnah in particular. The Torah is what comes from Sinai; all who stand in the chain of tradition from Sinai are bearers of the Torah. That is the turning point in the meaning of the word "Torah" as it evolved. The Torah, then, is what the sages of the Mishnah, Talmuds, and Midrash teach. In the tractate Abot, Torah is instrumental. The figure of the sage, his ideals and conduct, forms the goal, focus, and center. Abot regards study of Torah as what a sage does. The substance of Torah is what a sage says. That is so whether or not the saying relates to scriptural revelation. The content of the sayings attributed to sages endows those sayings with self-validating status. The sages usually do not quote verses of scripture and explain them, nor do they speak in God's name. But it is clear that sages "talk Torah." What follows is this: if a sage says something, what he says is Torah. More accurately, what he says falls into the classification of Torah. Accordingly, Abot treats Torah-learning as symptomatic, an indicator of the status of the sage. The beginning is to claim that a saying falls into the category of Torah if a sage says it as Torah. The end will be to view the sage himself as Torah incarnate. The Mishnah is held in the Talmud of the Land of Israel to be equivalent to scripture (Y. Hor. 3:5).

Once the Mishnah entered the status of scripture, it would take but a short step to a theory of the Mishnah as part of the revelation at Sinai—hence, oral Torah. The first Talmud claims that the Mishnah contains statements made by God to Moses. Just how these statements found their way into the Mishnah, and which passages of the Mishnah contain them, we do not know. This new usage of the word "Torah" found in the Talmud of the Land of Israel emerges from a group of stories that treat the word "Torah" (whether scroll, contents, or act of study) as source and guarantor of salvation. At this point the word "Torah" has ceased to constitute a specific thing or even a category or classification—stories about studying the Torah yield not a judgment as to status (i.e., praise for the learned man) but a promise of supernatural blessing now and salvation in time to come. To the rabbis, the principal salvational deed was to "study Torah," by which they meant memorization of Torah sayings by constant repetition and, as the Talmud itself amply testifies (for some sages), profound analytical inquiry into the meaning of those sayings. The innovation was that this act of "study of Torah" was held to impart supernatural power of a material character. For example, by repeating words of Torah, the sage could ward off the angel of death and accomplish other kinds of miracles as well. Thus Torah formulas served as incantations. Mastery of Torah transformed the man engaged in Torah learning into a supernatural figure, who could do things ordinary folk could not do. The category of "Torah" had already vastly expanded so that through transformation of the Torah from a concrete thing to a symbol, a Torah scroll could be compared to a man of Torah, namely, a rabbi. Now, once the principle had been established that salvation would come from keeping God's will in general, as Israelite holy men had insisted for so many centuries, it was a small step for rabbis to identify their particular corpus of learning, namely, the Mishnah and associated sayings, with God's will as expressed in scripture, the universally acknowledged medium of revelation. The key to the first Talmud's theory of the Torah lies in its conception of the sage, to which that theory is subordinate. Once the sage reaches his full apotheosis as Torah incarnate, then, but only then, the Torah becomes (also) a source of salvation in the present concrete formulation of the matter. Since the sage embodied the Torah and gave the Torah, the Torah naturally came to stand for the principal source of Israel's salvation, not merely a scroll, on the one hand, or a source of revelation, on the other. The history of the transformation of the word "Torah" from scroll to symbol proceeds from its removal from the framework of material objects, even from the limitations of its own contents, to its identification with a living person, the sage, and endowment with those particular traits that the sage claimed for himself. *See also* TORAH, ORAL; TORAH, WRITTEN.

Torah, Oral the orally revealed and transmitted part of the Torah. At Sinai, God gave the Torah to Moses in two media, oral and written; the oral part was formulated for memorization and handed on from master to disciple, in the model of God to Moses: "Moses received Torah at Sinai and handed it on to Joshua, Joshua to elders, and elders to prophets. And prophets handed it on to the men of the great assembly" (M. Abot 1:1). The Oral Torah was committed to writing, beginning with the Mishnah (completed c. 200 C.E.). Since the authorities of the Mishnah and related writings stood in the line of oral transmission of the Torah, what they said is accorded the status of Torah. Relating the Written Torah to the Oral Torah, which, people maintained, encompassed this law code, the Mishnah, presented a problem. The Mishnah presented one striking problem in particular: it rarely cited scriptural authority for its rules. Omitting scriptural proof-texts implied a claim to an authority independent of scripture; in that striking fact, the document set a new course for itself. From the formation of ancient Israelite scripture into a holy book in Judaism, in the aftermath of the return to Zion and the creation of the Torah-book in Ezra's time (c. 450 B.C.E.), new sacred writings had routinely cited the established canon of revelation (whatever its contents) to set their ideas into relationship with scripture. They did so by citing proof-texts alongside their own rules. Otherwise, in the setting of Israelite culture, the new writings would have found no ready hearing.

Over the six hundred years from the formation in writing of the Torah of Moses during the time of Ezra, from c. 450 B.C.E. to c. 200 C.E., four conventional ways to accommodate new writings—new "tradition"—to the established canon of received scripture had come to the fore. First and simplest, a writer would sign a famous name to his book, attributing his ideas to Enoch, Adam, Jacob's sons, Jeremiah, Baruch, and any number of others, down to Ezra. But the Mishnah bore no such attribution, for example, to Moses. Implicitly, to be sure, the statement of Abot 1:1 that "Moses received Torah from Sinai" carried the further notion that sayings of people on the list of authorities from Moses to

nearly their own day derived from God's revelation at Sinai. But no one made that premise explicit before the time of the Talmud of the Land of Israel. We note, in this connection, that the authors of the Gospels took the same view as did the authors of the Mishnah. They did not sign the names of Old Testament authorities either. They explained the origins of Jesus Christ by appeal to genealogy, just as in the tractate Abot, we find an explanation of the origins of the Oral Torah by appeal to genealogy: the genealogy represented by tradition. Second, an authorship might also imitate the style of biblical Hebrew and thus try to creep into the canon by adopting the cloak of scripture. But the Mishnah's authorship ignores biblical syntax and style. And the Gospel's authors, of course, did not even try. Third, an author would surely claim his work was inspired by God, a new revelation for an open canon. But, as we realize, that claim makes no explicit impact on the Mishnah. And it would be some time before the canonical Gospels were given the standing of revelation through the Holy Spirit; it is a claim they do not make on their own behalf. Fourth, at the very least, someone would link his opinions to biblical verses through the exegesis of the latter in line with the former so that scripture would validate his views. The authorship of the Mishnah did so only occasionally; far more commonly, it stated on its own authority whatever rules it proposed to lay down. In this regard, Matthew shows, for instance, in chapter 2, how this would have looked; much of Matthew's Gospel places into relationship prophetic teachings about the Messiah and the life, teachings, and actions of Jesus.

The Hebrew of the Mishnah and of the other writings of the Oral Torah complicates the problem, because it is totally different from the Hebrew of the Hebrew scriptures. Its verb, for instance, makes provision not only for completed or continuing action, for which the biblical Hebrew verb also allows, but also for past and future times, subjunctive and indicative voices, and much else. The syntax is Indo-European, just as Latin and Greek are Indo-European languages, in that we can translate the word order of the Mishnah into any Indo-European language and come up with perfect sense. None of that crabbed imitation of biblical Hebrew that makes the Dead Sea Scrolls an embarrassment to read characterizes the Hebrew of the Mishnah. Mishnaic style is elegant, subtle, exquisite in its sensitivity to word order and repetition, balance, and pattern.

The solution to the problem of the authority of the Mishnah, that is to say, its relationship to scripture, was worked out in the period after the closure of the Mishnah. Since no one then could credibly claim to sign the name of Ezra or Adam to a book of this kind, and since biblical Hebrew had provided no apologetic aesthetics whatever, the only options lay elsewhere. The two options were, first, to provide a story of the origin of the contents of the Oral Torah, beginning with the Mishnah, and, second, to link each allegation of the Oral Torah, again starting with the Mishnah, through processes of biblical (not Mishnaic) exegesis, to verses of the scriptures. These two procedures would establish for the Mishnah the standing that the uses to which the document was to be put demanded for it: a place in the canon of Israel, based on a legitimate relationship to the Torah of Moses. And with the notion that the Mishnah and later writings that amplified and explained its law formed a component of the Oral Torah, the writing down of the Oral Torah began. As people began to bring to the Written Torah, or Jewish scriptures, the questions of amplification and explanation that they brought to the Mishnah, they also wrote down the answers to their questions. These accumulated and were collected and organized in the Midrash-compilations concerning the biblical accounts of Creation, Adam, Noah, the Flood, Abraham, Isaac, Jacob, and the Ten Commandments. And that is how the Oral Torah came to be written down. The great sages, honored with the title of rabbi, transformed the Torah into a plan and design for the world, presenting the everyday as an instance of the eternal. They read scripture as God's picture of creation and humanity. They read the life of the streets and marketplaces, the home and the hearth, the nations and the world as an ongoing commentary on scripture and the potentialities of creation. *See also* TORAH, WRITTEN.

Torah, Written the written part of the Torah revealed by God to Moses at Sinai; generally equivalent to the books of the Hebrew scriptures (Pentateuch, Prophets, Writings). The piety of Israel in the Land of Israel encompassed not only prayer but also the public recitation and exposition of the scriptures. Scholars concur that by the first century, people observed the rite of the reading of the Torah, that is, the Pentateuch, as well as of prophetic lections in the synagogue. No one now can identify with certainty the lections in the prophets that accompanied various passages in the Pentateuch, nor do we know how long it took for the recitation of the whole Pentateuch—whether it took one year or three years. The interpretation of the contemporary meaning and requirements of

the Torah and of the prophets occupies a principal place in accounts of such special groups as the disciples of Jesus and the Essenes. Moreover, it formed the background of public life in a world that constantly and ubiquitously invoked the authority of the Torah as validation for the policies and practices of everyday life.

The contribution of the Torah to the common piety derived, in the end, from the conviction that "God revealed Torah to Moses at Sinai" (M. Abot 1:1f.). That meant that when people acted rightly and in conformity to the Torah, they carried out the requirements of the covenant that Israel had made with God. Life under the Torah was a life of sanctification in the here and now and salvation in the age to come, because all life found meaning under the aspect of the covenant. Clearly, the conception that the national life found definition in scripture rested on the premise that education, formal and informal, constituted a broad opportunity for the population at large. Certainly people learned scripture, which formed the center of synagogue worship and defined the nation's sense of itself in the world. We do not know whether a formal school system existed or what, beyond scripture and such aspects of piety as formal prayer, people might have learned in such schools. The absence of concrete information on schooling, however, should not obscure the fact that in every available account the population at large is represented as informed about the scripture and traditions of the nation. It must follow that these literary works found their way, through some institutional means, into the lives of the people. But beyond that simple surmise, nothing can presently be said. Certainly one mode of popular education lay in the translation of scripture into the vernacular, which was Aramaic in the countryside and Greek and Aramaic in the towns, such as Jerusalem. The scriptures, read in Aramaic, gained access to the people that public recitation in a language no one spoke would have denied them. We do not now have the Aramaic translations, or Targumim, exactly as these would have been read in the synagogue in the first century. *See also* TORAH, ORAL.

Torah scroll (Heb.: *sefer Torah*) the Hebrew scroll of the Pentateuch used in synagogue worship. The Hebrew Bible does not present Israel's scripture as sacred. In the Second Temple period, however, various texts refer to biblical writings as holy books. In this period, the rituals surrounding the production and reading of scripture are unclear, although special care in the production of biblical scrolls is evident at Qumran.

Rabbinic Judaism developed a distinctive theory and practice of scripture's sanctity, which is manifest in its treatment of the scroll of the Pentateuch (*sefer Torah*). Scripture had sacred status in rabbinic Judaism. Consequently, human dealings with scripture were circumscribed. Mishnah Yadayim 3:5 declares that "all the holy writings render the hands unclean" (also M. Kelim 15:6; Yadayim 3:2, 4:6). A scroll's sanctity extended to its blank margins (M. Yadayim 3:4; T. Yadayim 2:11) and its wrappings and containers (T. Yadayim 2:12). People were enjoined to violate Sabbath restrictions to save scripture and its wrappings from fire (M. Shabbat 16:1)—an exemption otherwise applied only to save a human life. A damaged, worn, or unfit scroll retained its sanctity and therefore was to be buried, by itself or in the coffin of a sage, but not burned or otherwise destroyed (B. Megillah 26b).

The category "holy writings" could include works in Hebrew and in translation (M. Shabbat 16:1), but the Torah scroll was the the scriptural paradigm and prototype. A Jewish community could do without a synagogue, an ark, or other books of scripture, but not a Torah scroll. The Talmud's elaborate rules for the scroll's production and treatment distinguish it from ordinary writing. The Torah scroll was used in worship and had to be written without vocalization. It had to be transcribed on specially prepared parchment marked with lines (B. Megillah 19a), in a particular script (B. Shabbat 104a), and with orthographic uniformity (B. Erubin 13a). In the scroll, seven Hebrew letters, each time they appeared, were to be drawn with three-stroke decorative crowns at the top of the letter (*tagin*) (B. Menahot 29b). A sheet of Torah parchment with four errors was to be buried, not corrected (B. Megillah 29b), but scrolls produced by heretics or sectarians were to be burned (B. Gittin 45b). Worshippers were to rise before the Torah scroll, and no other scroll could be put on top of it (Y. Megillah 4a; T. Megillah 3:20). It was unacceptable to touch the parchment of the Torah scroll with bare hands (B. Shabbat 14a).

Torah writing also could serve as an amulet. It was used in phylacteries and affixed to dwellings in *mezuzot*, both of which acquired sacred status because of the Torah writing they contained. Rabbinic culture judged that the sefer Torah distinguished Israel from the nations and generated God's loyalty to Israel (Sifra Behukotai, Perek 8:10). At the sight of a burned Torah scroll, rabbis were to perform the mourning ritual of *qeriah* (tearing one's clothes). For a torn Torah scroll, they were to do so twice, once for the parchment and once for the writing (B. Moed Katan 26a). These materials suggest that rabbis regarded the Torah writing itself as a sacred object.

Rabbinic teaching claimed that both the writing of the Torah scroll and the vocalization of the written consonants were the possession of rabbinic tradition, of Oral Torah. The Torah scroll was rabbinic Judaism's most revered and sacred artifact, the stable center for rabbinism's system of piety. Rabbis claimed that the Torah scroll was central to Israel's relationship to God and claimed mastery over it by making its reading and writing a part of their distinctive traditions.

Torah shebeal peh *see* TORAH, ORAL

Torah shebikhtab *see* TORAH, WRITTEN

Torah shrine *see* ARK

Torah study (Heb.: Talmud Torah) systematic memorization and recitation of teachings of Torah, whether the written or the oral Torah, and explanation of those teachings. Torah study is accorded the highest value in Judaism: "The Torah study outweighs all of the other [religious duties]."

Tosefta a corpus of complementary materials for the Mishnah, following the plan and order of the Mishnah, citing the same authorities, and cast in the same language and syntax. Since the Tosefta contains numerous verbatim citations of the Mishnah, the document as a whole certainly is later than the Mishnah, which was completed c. 200 C.E., and since its materials are cited in the Talmud of the Land of Israel, which was completed c. 400 C.E., the closure of the Tosefta should fall some time between those two estimated dates. A guess of c. 300 seems justified. The Tosefta is made up of three types of distinct statements. The first type cites and then glosses a sentence of the Mishnah. The second refers to a principle given in the Mishnah but does not cite it verbatim; this second type cannot be fully understood without reference to the Mishnah. The third sort stands completely separate from the Mishnah; it contributes a rule on a topic found in the Mishnah but in no way relates to, or intersects with, a rule on the same topic given by the Mishnah. The materials of the Tosefta tend to start with citation of the Mishnah's rule, then provide an amplification, and finally give those autonomous, free-standing statements that are essentially supplementary to the Mishnah's treatment of a given subject.

Tosefta targums Tosefta targums, or targumic *toseftot,* as they are sometimes called, are interpretive passages in Aramaic that add to or expand upon biblical verses. They appear either in different manuscripts of Targum Onkelos, sometimes inserted into the text, at other times placed in the margins or at the end of a book, or they are gathered into independent collections. In literary conception, they usually follow additional material found in the Palestinian Targums to the Pentateuch. In language, however, they contain many features of the Eastern Aramaic of Targum Onkelos. These two features suggest that the targumic *toseftot* are Palestinian traditions that were later revised by eastern Mediterranean Jewry to fit with the newly dominant Targum Onkelos.

tours of the cosmos Beginning in the Second Temple period and extending into the Middle Ages, there developed in Jewish and then in Christian literature a literary genre in which especially righteous individuals are given "tours of the cosmos" by heavenly, usually angelic, beings. The tour is normally construed as a reward for the individual's great piety. The seer is picked up from his everyday environment and whisked away into a supermundane, heavenly realm, where he is granted visions of supernatural phenomena. The tour often occurs at or near the end of the seer's life.

Normally, the tour's climax is a vision of God sitting on God's heavenly throne. The tours also typically involve journeys through heaven, multiple heavens, or parts of the earth usually inaccessible to humans. The heavenly being who conducts the tour often acts as "guide," pointing out unusual sights and answering questions. Because of their revelatory content, the tours, and the books that contain them, are often termed "apocalypses."

Although the Hebrew Bible itself describes no such extended tours, it does have a number of passages that influence or reflect the extrabiblical tours. Displacements of Enoch and Elijah into a realm of God or a heavenly realm are described in Genesis 5:24 and 2 Kings 2:11, respectively, while Ezekiel's intermittent spiritual journeys are related in the Book of Ezekiel. Exodus 24:9–11; 1 Kings 22:19–23; Isaiah 6:1–4; Ezekiel 1 and 10; and Daniel 7:9–14 all describe individual's visions of God and of other heavenly phenomena.

The first, and most influential, examples of full-fledged tours of the cosmos in Jewish literature occur in 1 Enoch, in the Book of the Watchers (chaps. 1–36) and the Book of the Heavenly Luminaries (chaps. 72–82). The Book of the Watchers contains three relevant sections—Enoch's ascent into heaven and vision of God's throne (chaps. 14–16), and two separate tours in which Enoch is conducted to the ends of the earth and shown various hidden natural and cosmic phenomena (chaps. 17–19, 20–36). The Book of the Heavenly Luminaries focuses on Enoch's visions of the courses of the sun and moon.

Later books describing tours of the cosmos generally feature similar types of revelatory experiences. There is an increasing tendency, however, for the tours to transcend the earthly plane and focus exclusively on heavenly realities. Sometimes "heaven" is a single plane, and the tour proceeds horizontally (e.g., the Parables of Enoch [1 Enoch 37–71]; Test. of Abr.; Apoc. Zeph.; Rev.). In other cases heaven is portrayed as being composed of various levels (usually three or seven), through which the seer sometimes proceeds in an ascent to God's throne in the highest heaven (e.g., 2 Enoch; Apoc. Abr.; Test. Levi 2–7; 3 Bar.; Asc. Isa.).

Many of the tours show a special interest in the fates of human souls after death (e.g., Test. Abr.). In general, however, the cosmic tours do not place a strong emphasis on eschatology. Various categories of later Jewish and Christian literature continue the tradition of the cosmic tour.

Trajan Roman emperor (r. 98–117 C.E.). His mother was Spanish and this may account for Nerva's adopting him. Nerva needed to quiet the criticism of the legions and the Praetorian Guards, and Trajan was respected as a general but was still considered to be a Roman "outsider." As emperor he distributed free corn to the needy, instituted a massive program of public works, probably financed by the booty he gained from the Second Dacian War, and took firm control of the Praetorian Guards. In 113 Trajan moved against Parthia who had removed Axidares as ruler of Armenia. In 114 he conquered Armenia, and by 115 Trajan captured Ctesiphon, Parthia's capital. However, in 116 there was a revolt in southern Mesopotamia, and Parthian troops attacked his forces in northern Mesopotamia, Armenia, and Adiabene. Apparently, the Jews joined the fighting against Trajan, and Lucius Quietus was appointed governor of Palestine after he quelled the rebellion. In 115 there were Jewish revolts in Egypt, Cyprus, and Cyrene and a short-lived uprising in Palestine. There is no evidence that the revolts in North Africa were related to the Jewish disturbances in either Mesopotamia or Palestine but seem to have been the result of continued tensions between the Greeks and the Jews of the region. *See also* TRAJAN, WAR OF.

Trajan, War of Jewish uprisings against Rome, 115–117 C.E.; called the War of Quietus in rabbinic literature. In 115 C.E., while Trajan was on a lengthy campaign in Mesopotamia fighting the Parthians on the borders of the Roman Empire, Jews in Egypt and Cyrene and later Cyprus and Mesopotamia attacked their non-Jewish compatriots and revolted against the Roman Empire. The cause of the uprising is unknown, but probably Trajan's absence in the east with substantial military forces left an opening for insurrection. Since the uprisings occurred only in a small number of Jewish diaspora communities and not in Palestine, the motives for the uprisings were probably local, deriving from intercommunal tensions, ongoing conflicts, previous persecutions, and present threats. In Egypt, a Jewish attack in 115 C.E. defeated the Greeks and the Roman governor, Marcus Rutilius Lupus, who were forced to withdraw to Alexandria, where they counterattacked successfully against the Alexandrian Jews, killing and imprisoning many. The next year (116 C.E.) battles between Jews and Greeks spread over the country and were put down only with the intervention of Roman legions. Many battles were fought in villages throughout the country, and extant papyri detail extensive damage and slaughter. Some areas of Egypt were devasted for years afterward. The conflict was so severe that even about eighty years later, a festival celebrating the defeat of the Jews was still celebrated in Oxyrhynchus. Though a Jewish community in Alexandria survived, it was moved outside the city and so weakened that it never exercised the influence and creativity of the first-century community.

In Cyrenaica to the west, the uprising became a war against Rome. According to a later Greek historian Dio, the Jews, led by Lucuas (or Andreas, in another source), tortured and massacred 220,000 inhabitants of the region and destroyed many public installations. Though Dio probably exaggerates the numbers and clearly wishes to sensationalize the atrocities of the war, his account shows the seriousness of the conflict. Archaeological excavations have revealed that many of the public buildings in the city of Cyrene were destroyed at this time and that other cities in Cyrenaica were damaged. Roads and temples were also destroyed by the Jews, as inscriptions concerning their rebuilding attest. The uprising was so widespread and violent that it became a revolt against Roman rule. The claim to kingship by the leader of the revolt may imply messianic hopes as one motive. Trajan sent one of his ablest generals, Marcius Turbo, to North Africa to put down the revolt in 116, a task that Marcius accomplished after a year-long, difficult campaign. Roman legions killed thousands of Jews in both Egypt and Cyrenaica. Peace was restored by the middle of 117. After the war, the number of Jewish names on tax lists and papyri decreased greatly, indicating that the community suffered substantial fatalities.

Inspired by the uprisings in Egypt and Cyrenaica, Jews revolted elsewhere in the Roman empire. Dio says that on Cyprus Jews, led by Artemion, killed 240,000 (probably another exaggeration) and destroyed Salamis, the capital city. When Roman legions restored control, they killed many Jews and banned all Jews from the island.

By 116, Trajan had conquered most of Mesopotamia and organized its regions into provinces. However, a Parthian counteroffensive from Media into northern Mesopotamia led to a general uprising against the Romans among the indigenous population, an uprising that included the Jewish communities throughout the east. Probably the Jews of Mesopotamia, along with other ethnic groups, hoped to throw off Roman rule with the help of the Parthians, under whom they had more intracommunal freedom. The Christian historian Eusebius speaks of a specifically Jewish revolt, but Jewish participation in a general uprising is more likely. Since this revolt threatened a sensitive border region of the Roman empire, Trajan ordered his general, Lucius Quietus, later governor of Judea, to put down the revolt. In the course of the campaign, thousands were massacred. After Trajan's death in 117, his successor, Hadrian, abandoned his eastern conquests as too costly to defend. Thus, eastern Jewish communities escaped Roman rule.

Though some fragments of evidence suggest unrest against the Romans in Palestine, no revolt of any consequence took place until almost twenty years later under Bar Kosiba (Bar Kokhba).

transgression going beyond the boundaries as a type of sin that connotes deliberate disobedience to God. This term is often used to translate the Hebrew root *pshʿ* (rebellion) and the Greek *parabasis* (transgression). Second Temple Jewish literature and the New Testament use these words especially to characterize the activities of those community members who are deliberately disloyal and do not lead proper lives according to God's law and commandments. Transgressors are conceived of as hardened sinners in deliberate and permanent defiance of God. *See also* SIN; TRESPASS.

Transjordan modern name for the area east of the Jordan that included at the end of the Israelite monarchies (from north to south) Karnaim east of the Sea of Galilee, Gilead and Ammon east of the

Jordan, and Moab east of the Dead Sea. Edom lay southeast and south of the Dead Sea. The Persian satrapy called "Beyond the River," that is, west of the Euphrates, consisted of the same place names during Persian hegemony, except the Jewish kingdom of the Tobiads which occupied the ancient Ammonite area south of the Jabbok and east of the Jordan, including the ancient cities of Abila, Tyrus (the capital), and Rabbath-bene-Ammon (The Height of the Sons of Ammon, later Philadelphia). The subsequent Hellenization of this entire area is made plain by the Greek names applied to the leading cities of Transjordan. From north to south these included Seleucia (biblical Abila), Berenice-Pella (biblical Pehel), and Philadelphia (biblical Rabbath-Ammon or Rabbath-bene-Ammon). About 144 B.C.E. Jonathan Maccabeus managed to win back roughly the area of the Tobiads from Demetrius, who represented the Seleucid Greeks. From this point onward the area would be known as Perea. It was apparently the policy of the Maccabees to replace Greek populations with Jewish populations wherever possible. In 128 B.C.E., the Jewish king John Hyrcanus I added the cities of Medeba and Esbus (biblical Heshbon) immediately south of Perea. His successor Alexander Jannaeus (104–76 B.C.E.) expanded the borders of his kingdom to include virtually every area his ancestor David had ruled. East of the Jordan rift from north to south, his rule included the Greek cities of Gaulanitis, such as Gamala and Hippos, similar cities of Galaaditis, such as Abila and Pella, the region immediately east of the Jordan with the cities of Ammathus, Gedor, and Macherus, and the region of Moabitis, which included Esbus and Medeba, but not Philadelphia. South of this territory lay the kingdom of the Nabateans.

With the coming of Rome in 63 B.C.E., the political divisions of the area east of the Jordan changed. The Roman general Pompey ceded Gaulanitis to the Itureans and Syria. The ten Greek cities in the north he joined into a league of ten cities—the Decapolis—including Scythopolis (biblical Beth Shean) west of the Jordan. Perea became a narrow strip of land about 100 kilometers by 26 kilometers, again not including Philadelphia or Gerasa. This state of affairs continued under Herod the Great, except that he expanded his territories eastward in the north to include Batanea, Trachonitis, and Auranitis. He also expanded Gaulanitis to the north to include Caesarea-Paneas. In the south he annexed Esbus by defeating the Nabateans in 32 B.C.E. At the death of Herod the Great, Perea passed to his son Herod Antipas, who ruled Perea until his exile in 39 C.E., when it passed under the control of Agrippa I (37–46 C.E.) and then to Roman procurators. Gradually, however, as Agrippa II (44–95 C.E.) proved an able administrator, many of the territories of his father were transferred to him. The central part of Transjordan, however, remained always under the control of the procurators. During the First Revolt of 66–73 C.E., the area east of the Jordan was under Jewish control until 68 C.E., when it returned to the Roman general Vespasian. In 97–98 C.E. the city of Capitolias was founded in the northern Transjordan area. Furthermore, in 106 C.E. the emperor Trajan annexed the kingdom of the Nabateans southeast of the Dead Sea and south of Perea as the province of Arabia. The cities of Dium and Philadelphia east of the Sea of Galilee were added to Arabia, so that Perea was now bordered by this new province on the south and east. During the Bar Kokhba Revolt (131–135 C.E.), Perea was administered from Jerusalem as a Jewish territory.

After the Bar Kokhba Revolt, Jerusalem was refounded as a Roman city under the name Aelia Capitolina, and Perea was ruled from Aelia as part of the province of Syria Palaestina. Sometime in this period the Decapolis broke up into independent cities. In 242 C.E., the emperor Philippus Arabus gave his native village in Syria municipal rights and the name Philippopolis. This state of affairs continued until about 400 C.E., when Perea was designated with Judea, Idumea, and Samaria as Palaestina Prima with its capital at Caesarea on the coast. Palaestina Secunda included Galilee, Gaulanitis, and the cities of the Decapolis, with its capital at Scythopolis. Early in the fifth century C.E., the emperor Theodosius could address an edict to the Jewish Sanhedrins of the "two Palestines."

With the royal patronage of Christianity given by Constantine the Great, ecclesiastical divisions became civil divisions. In Byzantine Palestine, Perea had shifted to Palaestina Prima. East of Perea were the city territories of Adraea, Gerasa, Philadelphia, Heshbon, and Medeba as part of the province of Arabia. On the other hand, Palaestina Secunda included the northern Transjordanian territories, including Clima Gaulanes (Gaulanitis), Hippus, Gadara, and Pella. In the former Auranitis new cities were founded, although their locations remain unknown: Constantia, Neapolis, and Hierapolis. A city of Maximianupolis was founded in Trachonitis.

Excavations in the cities of Transjordan in this period reveal a thriving population, sometimes mixed, sometimes wholly non-Jewish. Herod built temples at Esbus, for example, that rival anything west of the Jordan. A marvelous water system at Abila is rivaled only by the similar system at Sepphoris in Lower Galilee. Furthermore a Roman road system has been traced from southeast of the Dead Sea to Medeba, Heshbon, and Philadelphia. At Philadelphia a fork turned north and east to Bostra. The west fork lead to Pella, and from there to Hippos and eventually Damascus.

treasure (Gr.: *thēsauros, thēsaurizō*) metaphors for the heavenly accumulation of deeds that will affect one's fate in God's judgment. When Ezra worries about his fate, Uriel promises him that he has "a treasure of works laid up with the Most High" (2 Esdras 7:77; cf. 8:33, 36; 2 Bar. 14:12; Gen. Rabbah 9:9). The metaphor was especially at home in admonitions to the rich (Tob. 4:8–9, where retribution takes place in this world, and 2 Enoch 50:5). In two sayings ascribed to Jesus, the gathering of wealth on earth is contrasted to laying up treasures in heaven, through generosity and almsgiving (Mark 10:17–22; Matt. 6:19–21; Luke 12:33–34). The parables in Luke 12:16–21 and 16:1–9 and the story in Luke 19:1–10 make the same point. Thus good deeds, and especially the generous distribution of one's wealth, pay dividends when it counts. The idea that sin constitutes a debt may be the other side of this coin. The treasure image is extended to refer to the storing up of immortality and God's wrath in heaven (2 Esdras 8:54; Rom. 2:5; James 5:3). *See also* DEBT; JUDGMENT, DIVINE; REWARDS AND PUNISHMENT; WEALTH.

tree a multivalent symbol for people and groups that emphasizes vitality, strength, and, paradoxically, vulnerability. Its widespread usage reflects the agricultural environment in which it is used.

Psalm 1:1–3 depicts the righteous person as a tree that bears fruit as it draws life from the river of the Torah, and the Psalms of Solomon 14 extends the image to the community of the pious, who are "the Lord's paradise, the trees of life" (vv. 2–4), devoted to the Torah. Isaiah 61:3 also emphasizes this communal aspect, referring to the poor and afflicted of Israel as "oaks of righteousness" and the "plantation of YHWH." As texts like 1 Enoch 10:3, 16, 93:2, 5, 10 and the Damascus Document 1:7 indicate, the related image of the "plant of truth," begun with Noah or Abraham, becomes a regular way of speaking about Israel and the eschatological community of the righteous and chosen. New Testament sayings ascribed to John the Baptist and Jesus contrast the righteous and the wicked by describing them as good or evil trees that bear good or evil fruit, or no fruit at all (Matt.

3:8–10, 7:16–20, 12:33). Bearing fruit becomes a regular image for doing (good or evil) deeds—whatever plant envisioned in the metaphor (Mark 4:20; and Matt. 21:41 and John 15:1–8, probably reflecting Isa. 5:1–7). In a relatively rare use of agricultural imagery that may reflect his use of tradition, Paul contrasts Israel and the Gentiles, describing them as a cultivated and a wild olive trees (Rom. 11:16–24).

Ezekiel 31 and Daniel 4:4–26 employ the image of a great tree to depict the power of the kings of Egypt and Babylon. In each case, however, the mighty tree falls before the superior power of the axe wielded by God or God's agents. A similar notion occurs in Isaiah 10:33–34, which is followed immediately by reference to the shoot from the stump of Jesse, the Davidic king, an association that was not lost on the author of one of the Qumran commentaries on Isaiah (4QpIsaᵃ 8–10; cf. 2 Bar. 36–40). The saying ascribed to John the Baptist also describes God's judgment as the felling of trees (Matt. 3:10; cf. also Luke 13:6–9). Great strength and its vulnerability before God's judgment is the point of comparison in several texts that depict the prediluvian giants as fallen trees (CD 2:19; 4QEnGiantsᵇ 7–10; cf. 1 Enoch 83:4; 2 Bar. 36–37). *See also* TREE OF LIFE; TREE OF WISDOM.

tree of life one of two identified trees in the Garden of Eden, said to offer immortality to those who eat its fruit (Gen. 3:22–23). Although the idea appears to draw on ancient Near Eastern motifs, its precise origins are obscure. In eschatologically oriented Jewish and Christian texts, the righteous are promised that in the future they will receive the sustenance and eternal life that the tree provides (1 En. 25:3–6; Test. Levi 18:10–11; Rev. 2:7; 2 Esdras 8:52; 2 En. 8:3; perhaps Apoc. Moses 9:3–13:5 and Life of Adam and Eve 36:2). *See also* OIL OF LIFE; TREE OF WISDOM.

tree of wisdom primarily a metaphor for the source of divinely given wisdom, associated with the story of paradise. The association between wisdom and the first human being is explicit in the version of the Eden story preserved in Ezekiel 28:1–17. Different from Genesis 3, where "knowledge of good and evil" are wrongly sought after, here wisdom appropriate to the first human is corrupted (v. 17). Interpreting Genesis 2–3 and perhaps Ezekiel 28, 1 Enoch 32 describes Enoch's journey to "the paradise of righteousness," where he sees the tree of wisdom, whose fruit was wrongly eaten by the first parents but enables certain others (perhaps the angels) to understand great wisdom. Picking up the idea attested in

1 Enoch 32, the Life of Adam and Eve 29:2–11 ascribes to Adam apocalyptic knowledge of the future gained when he ate the tree of knowledge. 1 Enoch 82:1–3 implies the image of the tree of wisdom to describe the life-giving power of the apocalyptic wisdom that Enoch brought down from heaven. For Ben Sira, the Mosaic Torah is the tree of wisdom that grants life (Ecclus. 24:12–22), and allusions to the paradise story are close at hand (24:23–29). In various versions of the Gnostic myth, with their inverted exegesis of Genesis 2–3, the snake and the tree of wisdom provide the knowledge that allows Eve and Adam to overcome the ignorance imposed on them by the Creator, which impedes their salvation. *See also* PARADISE; TREE OF LIFE.

trespass   sin. The terms "trespass" and "transgression" are used to translate Hebrew words for sin derived from the root *psh*ᶜ (to rebel) and the Greek *paraptōma*. The latter is also translated as "debt." Trespasses generally are individual sins, which may be followed by repentance and improvement (Wisd. of Sol. 12:2; Rom. 5:15–20). *See also* SIN; TRANSGRESSION.

trials   *see* TEMPTATION

trials, legal   According to the Mishnah tractate Sanhedrin, the Great Sanhedrin was a court (as well as legislature) and conducted trials according to clearly articulated legal procedures. There is no evidence prior to the Mishnah, however, for either a standardized, formally constituted court or standardized regulated procedures. From the few cases for which we have accounts it appears rather that rulers governed and judged as the Roman overlords and the domestic balance of power allowed. Indeed, it was standard procedure for a ruler to convene a court (*synedrion*), but the ruler-convener could manipulate or circumvent the court. This is suggested by Josephus's accounts of Herod being summoned to trial for murder of the bandit-chieftain Hyrcanus in Galilee. In this case Herod manipulated the court under pressure from Sextus Caesar, the governor of Syria. Once established as king, Herod himself convened and manipulated both courts and wider assemblies at will—to frame the former high priest Hyrcanus II, to convict his own sons, or to condemn the scholars and their students who cut down the Roman eagle from over the Temple gate. The synoptic Gospel accounts of the trial of Jesus of Nazareth and Josephus's account of the trial of his brother James similarly portray the principal ruler, in these cases the high priest (Caiaphas and Ananus, respectively), convening

a court and virtually directing its verdict (Mark 14:53–64; *Ant.* 20.200). In Jesus' case the Roman governor ratified the verdict and carried out the execution by crucifixion, while in the latter case, the Roman authorities were displeased by Ananus's own execution of the condemned.

Rabbinic Judaism articulated clear and complete procedures for legal trials. A court of three judges had jurisdiction in civil matters, including divorce, conversion, and absolution from vows, and was empowered to penalize a defendant through fines, flogging, and even enslavement. Courts of twenty-three adjudicated criminal matters. Despite this fully defined system, in rabbinic times and thereafter, Jewish courts had only limited power. This was so particularly in capital cases, in matters involving a Jew and non-Jew, and in cases in which a Jew chose to resort to a non-Jewish court.

The trial depended upon oral testimony, given in open court before the judges, litigants, and other witnesses (see Deut. 17:16). The judges conducted the interrogation, but the opposing litigants had the right to suggest questions. In criminal matters, testimony by deposition was completely excluded; in litigation over contracts, it was allowed, for instance, if a witness was sick or in a different locale. Testimony was not given under oath, deemed unnecessary in light of the Decalogue's admonition against bearing false witness (Exod. 20:16). In criminal matters, testimony of at least two witnesses was required to convict the accused (Num. 35:10; Deut. 1915; B. Sotah 2b; B. Sanhedrin 20a). Testimony was not accepted from women, slaves, imbeciles, the deaf or mute, the blind, relatives, parties in any way involved in the matter, known criminals, sinners, and those who rejected societal norms (who might perjure themselves).

tribes, ten   ten of the twelve social units of Israel, all of which are presented as the direct descendants of Jacob's sons. The biblical tribal lists vary somewhat regarding the names for the ten. The ten sons of Jacob from whom the tribes come are Reuben, Simeon, Levi, Dan, Naphtali, Gad, Asher, Issachar, Zebulun, and Joseph (see Gen. 29–30). In the lists of tribes, Levi, the priestly clan that had no land, is often eliminated, but the number of tribes remains the same because Joseph is divided into two, which are named after his sons, Ephraim and Manasseh (see Num. 26). When Israel was split into two kingdoms after Solomon's reign, most of the tribes formed the Kingdom of Israel. In 1 Kings 11-12, the prophet Ahijah gives the new king, Jeroboam, ten of the twelve pieces into which he had torn a new garment; these symbolized the tribes (other than Judah and apparently Benjamin) over which he was to rule. This realm existed until 722–721 B.C.E., when the Assyrians killed or deported thousands (see 2 Kings 15–17). The fact that these tribes are not mentioned again in the Hebrew Bible has given rise to the idea of the ten lost tribes. They do, however, play a part in some extrabiblical texts. The Testament of Moses 3–4 predicts that the two other tribes, when exiled, will summon the ten to repent. They do so, but eventually they grow and spread out among the nations. In 2 Baruch (c. 100 C.E.), the remaining two tribes are said to have done more evil than the ten who were deported; 4 Ezra 13:39–50 looks to a return of the ten tribes in the last days. *See also* TRIBES, TWELVE.

tribes, twelve the basic constituent units of Israel, all descended from the twelve sons of Jacob. The sons' names are Reuben, Simeon, Levi, Judah, Dan, Naphtali, Gad, Asher, Issachar, Zebulun, Joseph, and Benjamin. For the tribal lists, Joseph is usually divided into two tribes, which are named after his sons, Ephraim and Manasseh, and Levi, the priestly tribe to which no land was given, is removed from the roster. These tribes are said to have grown in number in Egypt (Exod. 1) so that they became a great nation. After their Exodus and wilderness wanderings, they entered the land of Canaan, where nine and one-half tribes were allotted land, with the other two and one-half remaining on the east side of the Jordan River. They formed the united Kingdom of Israel in the time of Saul, David, and Solomon, but later split into two: ten tribes followed Jeroboam and established the new Kingdom of Israel; Judah and Benjamin remained under the rule of Davidic kings. The motif of the united twelve tribes did not die out with political rupture, however. Elijah referred to it when he took twelve stones for the altar that he rebuilt (1 Kings 18), and Ezekiel, in his vision of restored Israel, divides the land into twelve parts (chap. 47). After the return from exile and reconstruction of the temple by some Judeans, the number of sacrifices offered at the new sanctuary reflected the full number of the tribes (Ezra 6:17, 8:35).

Outside the Hebrew Bible, the clearest appeal to the number twelve is in the Testaments of the Twelve Patriarchs, which present what are supposed to be the final speeches of Jacob's twelve sons to their descendants. The Qumran community was governed by a council of twelve lay members representing the tribes (Manual of Discipline 8). The Temple Scroll, which describes a splendid, massive temple complex, has twelve gates in dif-

ferent courtyards, and they are named after the sons of Jacob. There are also areas for them in the complex (see cols. 39–41, 44), and sacrifices are connected with them (cols. 24–25). The War Scroll, which describes the final battles, mentions the presence of the twelve several times and says that their names were written on the great standard and on the shield of the prince of the congregation (cols. 2–3, 5). The Testament of Moses 3–4 predicts that the twelve tribes will have contact in their exile, while the Testament of Benjamin 9 pictures the twelve at the future temple. Testament of Abraham 19 speaks of their judgment, but Ben Sira prays that all may be gathered to their original inheritance (36:11). In the New Testament, Jesus' twelve disciples reflect the tribal number; in fact, they will judge the twelve tribes when the Son of Man sits on his throne (Matt. 19:28; Luke 22:30). The Epistle of James is addressed to the twelve tribes of the dispersion (1:1). In the Revelation of John, the twenty-four elders seated around the heavenly throne seem to represent the twelve patriarchs or tribes and the twelve apostles (chap. 4). The symbolic total of 144,000 redeemed people is reached by assigning 12,000 to each of the twelve tribes, all of which are listed (chaps. 7 and 14). The woman who represents God's people has twelve stars in her crown (chap. 12), and the holy Jerusalem that is lowered from heaven is surrounded by a wall with twelve gates named after the twelve tribes (chap. 21). *See also* TRIBES, TEN.

tribulation (Heb.: *tzarah;* Gr.: *thlipsis*) the great trouble expected to come upon God's people prior to their rescue as the end time, which is sometimes described as the "time of distress." This uniquely terrible time is first mentioned in Daniel 12:1, "There will be a time of distress such as has not been since the nation came into being until that time." The notion recurs in Testament of Moses 8:1, Mark 13:19, and Revelation 7:14, and many apocalyptic texts describe in detail the woes of this time of trouble. *See also* SIGNS, ESCHATOLOGICAL.

tribune Latin term for two sorts of official. First, there was the *tribunus plebis,* an official who served as an ombudsman for the people in Rome during the republic and empire. The office arose because of the old system in which the aristocracy governed. As a representative of the people, the tribune had a major say in legislation, including a veto against most judicial and legislative acts. A second sort of tribune, the *tribunus militum,* was a military officer above the centurion. Half a dozen were normally assigned to each legion, where they acted as magistrates, among other duties.

triennial cycle the practice in Israel in early rabbinic times of publicly reading in the synagogue the entire Torah, divided into weekly portions (each called a *parashah* or *sidra*) over a span of three years. The portions are probably based on the division of the Torah into 153, 155, or 167 *sedarim* (Heb., orders, or divisions). The Babylonian custom to complete the cycle in one year has been most widely practiced since the eighth century C.E., although some places used the triennial cycle during the Middle Ages. In the annual cycle, Genesis is divided into twelve portions, Exodus eleven, Leviticus ten, Numbers ten, and Deuteronomy eleven, for a total of fifty-four. That cycle begins after Sukkot in the fall. Special readings are added for festivals, the new moon, Purim, Hanukkah, fast days, and for four Sabbaths in Adar and Nisan. The sequence concludes on Simhat Torah with special recognition for those called to read the last section of Deuteronomy and the first of Genesis. Each portion was further subdivided among members of the congregation who each read several verses. Reading from the Torah in the synagogue was considered an honor. On the Sabbath seven men were called to come up to read (Heb.: *aliyot*). A priest was called to read the first segment, a Levite the second, and ordinary Israelites the remaining portions.

trumpet, eschatological God's signal for the return of the dispersion at the time of the end. The association between a trumpet blast and the beckoning voice of God appears already in the Sinai account in Exodus 19:13 and 16. In Isaiah 27:12–13, it sounds the signal for the gathering of the people of Israel lost in Assyria and driven to Egypt. 1 Enoch 102:1–3 refers to the mighty sound of God's voice as the theophany is imminent. Jesus' prediction of the end in Mark 13 alludes to Isaiah 27 in its description of the return of the diaspora (v. 27), but it is Matthew's revision of this passage that mentions the great trumpet (24:31). Both texts may be alluding to the resurrection of the dead, a traditional interpretation of the return of the dispersed; however, it is Paul who associates the trumpet explicitly with the resurrection (1 Thess. 4:16; 1 Cor. 15:51–52). This last passage is cited in Handel's oratorio, "Messiah," and in the "Tuba Mirum" of the Dies Irae in the Roman Requiem. *See also* SIGNS, ESCHATOLOGICAL.

trust *see* FAITH

truth and falsehood a construct that polarizes religion into two categories, what is right and receives God's favor, and what is wrong and leads to divine condemnation. The construct can include right and wrong conduct as well as right and wrong teaching. This teaching may involve the Torah and its interpretation or prophetic revelation. Three sets of texts promulgate this viewpoint: 1 Enoch, the Qumran scrolls, and the New Testament.

In 1 Enoch, truth and falsehood turn on the authors' claims to have received revealed wisdom and knowledge. Enoch received the contents of the astronomical book while guided through heaven by Uriel (chaps. 72–82). According to the Animal Vision (chaps. 85–90), Israel's history is marked by continual apostasy, depicted as blindness, which repeatedly falls under God's judgment. This blindness continues after the exile and includes a polluted Temple cult (89:73–74). In the Hellenistic period, a younger generation is enlightened, and the opening of their eyes leads to the struggles that culminate in the great judgment and the reversion of humanity to its pristine unity. Chapters 1–5 indict sinners for revisionism (that is, changing the Torah; 2:1–5:4), celebrate the eschatological gift of wisdom (5:8), and anticipate the great judgment and the reward and punishment respectively of the righteous chosen and the sinners (1:4–9, 5:5–9). Chapters 92–105 work these notions out in detail. Although the author is deeply concerned with social injustice, he also focuses on right and wrong religious teaching. Right and wrong conduct are described as walking on the paths of righteousness or truth and the paths of wickedness or perversity. Perversity and changing the commandments of the eternal covenant are at the heart of the evils that this author opposes (99:2, 104:9–11) and are tantamount to idolatry (99:1–2, 6–9). This error derives from false teachers who write lies and lead many astray with their errors (98:15–16). However, the author claims to possess revealed knowledge about God's Torah and about the rewards and punishments due the righteous and the sinners. All of this is given an eschatological cast in the Apocalypse of Weeks, which construes the postexilic generation as thoroughly perverse, but posits the receipt of "sevenfold wisdom and knowledge" and the revelation of righteous Torah, which will be available for "all the sons of the whole earth" (93:9–10, 91:11–14; cf. 104:12–105:2).

At Qumran, the Enochic scheme is enhanced by the imposition of a two-spirits theology with a cosmic dimension (1QS 3:15–4:26). These spirits—the Prince of Light, or Angel of Truth, and the Angel of Darkness—preside over humanity and influence human deeds. The repeated pairings of light and darkness, truth and falsehood, indicate that human virtue and wickedness are, to a considerable degree, the result of a right and wrong understanding of sin and righteousness. As in 1 Enoch, the Qumran texts describe a time when some in Israel come to understand the wrongness of their ways and turn to God, specifically through the tutelage of the Teacher of Righteousness (CD 1:3–18, 6:2–11; 1QS 8:1–10). Those responsible for writing these texts had strong halakhic differences of opinion with their opponents, whom they dubbed "interpreters of slippery things" and persons who "lead many astray through their false teaching, lying tongue, and deceitful lips" (4QpNah 2; cf. CD 1:18; 1QH 4:5–29). As in 1 Enoch, wrong halakhah includes error in the calendar (3:14–15) and also results in the pollution of the Temple (CD 5:6–7). This opposition between right and wrong Torah is exacerbated by conflict about right and wrong prophetic revelation (1QH 4:5–21). Thus, the Qumran sectarians orient their religious self-understanding and their place in history within a massive cosmic struggle between truth and falsehood. As the eschatological community of the chosen, they obey the true Torah as God has revealed it (1QS 5:8–11) and await vindication in the judgment that will also condemn the rest of humanity.

Many of the dualistic motifs in 1 Enoch and the Qumran literature recur in the New Testament and often govern the self-understanding of the New Testament authors. The crucial issue and principal eschatological factor is Jesus of Nazareth. In the Gospel according to Mark, Jesus, as the Son of God and presence of the Spirit, is pitted against a demonic realm, whose agents include the protagonists of the Torah itself: the scribes, Pharisees, and chief priests. Moreover, Jesus warns against false messiahs and false prophets who will lead many astray at the end time (Mark 13:5–6, 22). The Fourth Gospel epitomizes the viewpoint. Jesus, the heavenly Logos, descends to witness to the truth in the darkness of a world dominated by Satan. His revelation is accepted by a few, but rejected by most. Those who believe in him receive eternal life. The First Epistle of John sees human reactions to Jesus Christ as the criteria for truth and falsehood. *See also* DUALISM; ERROR; SPIRIT OF TRUTH; WAYS, TWO.

Tryphon, Diodotus general of the Seleucid emperor Alexandar Balas (r. 151–145 B.C.E.). After Alexander's death, Tryphon fought Demetrius II Nicator (r. 145–140/139 B.C.E.) for the throne in the name of Alexander's minor son, Antiochus VI (145–142 B.C.E.). He then killed Antiochus and sought the throne for himself, but was besieged in Apamea by Demetrius's brother Antiochus and committed suicide in 142 B.C.E.

tumtum   *see* HERMAPHRODITE

Turbo, Quintus Marcius Roman general under Trajan. He was born in Dalmatia. Trajan sent Turbo to quell the Jewish revolt in North Africa in 116 C.E., believing that the general was more important for that task than for continuing with Trajan's army against the Parthians. Most likely, Turbo's authority extended over the military leaders of both Cyrenaica and Egypt. Since he was given a joint naval and land force, he was probably charged with putting down the revolt in Cyprus as well. Eusebius tells us that Turbo faced a difficult situation and that it took many battles and a long time to stop the rebellion. It appears that Turbo succeeded in bringing peace to the area by the end of 117. The following year, Hadrian put him in charge of Pannonia and Dacia with a rank equal to that of prefect. Eventually, Hadrian became suspicious of Turbo and dismissed him from office.

turgeman   *see* METURGEMAN

Twelve Patriarchs, Testaments of the   a twelve-part collection of texts purporting to contain the deathbed instructions of Jacob's sons. The document is preserved in many Greek manuscripts and in Armenian and Slavonic translations of the Greek. Patent christological references indicate that *in its present form* the collection is a Christian product. Scholars have explained the origin of the document in three ways: (1) a Jewish collection of twelve testaments was Christianized through interpolation; (2) a nucleus of Jewish testaments was expanded by a Christian into a collection of twelve testaments; (3) a Christian author or authors composed the collection, making use of Jewish traditions. The discussion of these options has reached no consensus; however, it is generally recognized that interpretation should begin by accepting the collection as the Christian document that it presently is.

Each testament has the following formal components: (a) a deathbed setting in which the patriarch gathers his sons for instruction; (b) a narrative about the patriarch's life which illustrates his vices and/or virtues (excepting Test. Asher); (c) ethical exhortations that the sons should emulate or avoid the father's virtues or vices; (d) eschatological predictions that their descendants will not heed this advice; and (e) a description of the patriarch's death and burial.

The Testaments emphasize ethical issues, with the narrative, exhortations, and predictions supplementing one another to this end. Taken together the testaments provide instruction on a range of virtues and vices—both emotions and internal dispositions, and the behaviors they inspire. Two sets of opposing categories govern the Testaments' ethical viewpoint: love, compassion, and mercy, stand in opposition to hatred, anger, and envy; moderation, chastity, and continence are opposed to drunkenness, greed, and sexual promiscuity. Human actions and the emotions and dispositions behind them are functions of two opposing (groups of) spirits, who lead one along the right or the wrong path (see esp. Test. Asher). The list of vices and virtues that one can abstract from the Testaments has many parallels in Jewish wisdom literature, early Christian ethical exhortations, and pagan moral philosophy.

The narratives in the Testaments have been inspired by details in the Joseph cycle (Gen. 37–48) and elements in the testaments of Jacob and Moses (Gen. 49, Deut. 33). Joseph, especially, is presented as a model of virtues, and his brothers' actions against him as examples of vices. Parallels in Jubilees indicate that the Testaments draw on Jewish tradition, and some narrative details reappear in rabbinic literature and in the Targum Pseudo-Jonathan.

The Testaments' eschatology has four noteworthy features: the defeat of Beliar and his spirits, which will overcome the human disposition to sin; the salvation of the Gentiles and the condemnation of many in Israel; the appearance of a pair of anointed figures from Levi and Judah or a single figure descended from both tribes; a tendency to identify this figure, or one of the two, with Jesus.

The Jewish roots of the Testaments (however one hypothesizes the process of composition) are indicated by the following factors: the narrative parallels cited above; Qumran teachings about two anointed ones, with the priestly figure predominating; Jewish two-ways and two-spirits teachings. Manuscript evidence includes a Hebrew genealogy of Bilhah from Qumran that parallels Testament of Naphtali 1, several manuscripts of a Qumran Aramaic Levi document, and medieval copies of a Hebrew Naphtali testament and an Aramaic Levi document. Parallels to the Testaments' teachings are found in second- and third-century Christian writers such as Justin Martyr, Irenaeus, Hippolytus, and Origen, who quotes the Testaments. Thus, the Testaments provide a wealth of comparative material for the study of early Judaism and second- and third-century Christianity. *See also* SPIRITS, TWO; TESTAMENT; WAYS, TWO.

Twelve Prophets, Targums to *see* TARGUM TO THE PROPHETS

TY *see* TJ

tyche (Gr., fate, or destiny) The abstract concept is personified as a goddess, Tyche (Fortuna in Latin). The idea of fate was a strong one in the Graeco-Roman world, ranging from simple luck to a strong sense of one's future being laid out in advance according to a preconceived plan (e.g., in Stoicism). The concept is also well known in some Jewish literature. According to Josephus, the Essenes believed all was determined in advance. His own history exhibits an interest in destiny with regard to the nation, though here it was not impersonal but God fulfilling his plan.

tzaar baalei ḥayim *see* ANIMALS, CRUELTY TO

Tzaddok the Pharisee a founder of the "Fourth Philosophy," according to Josephus, and a leader of the revolt against the Roman census and Roman governor Quirinius (6–7 C.E.). Judas the Galilean enlisted Tzaddok to help arouse popular resistance to the census and the Romans. Josephus judges Tzaddok's teaching to be nontraditional and disastrous for Israel. *See also* FOURTH PHILOSOPHY.

tzaraat *see* LEPROSY

tzedakah *see* PHILANTHROPY

Tzidduk haDin (Heb., acceptance of the judgment) general term for the funeral rite. The phrase implies its theological purpose: accepting God's judgment of death.

tzitzit (Heb., fringe) the tassels referred to at Numbers 15:38–39, which Israelites are to place on the corners of their garments as a reminder of God's commandments. Rabbinic legislation defines the fringes (Sifre Num. 115), describes the garments that require them (B. Menaḥot 39b), and notes that the fringes must be removed before the garment is sold to a non-Jew (B. Menaḥot 43a). The rabbinic literature generally follows the scriptural view that the fringes remind people of their obligations and prevents them from engaging in inappropriate behavior (B. Menaḥot 44a).

Tzitzit the title of one of the so-called minor tractates of the Talmud. A collection of Tannaitic sources in one chapter, it contains rules for tying, dyeing, and wearing fringes on one's garments in accord with Numbers 15:38–40.

U

Uktzin Mishnah tractate on connections between different parts of food, for example, the twig and the apple, the husk and the nut. The tractate discusses susceptibility to uncleanness and joining together of distinct parts of the same piece of fruit (chaps. 1–2); connection in food (chap. 2); and susceptibility to uncleanness of food (chap. 3).

Ulam Rabata location corresponding to the town of Chula, referred to at T. Shebiit 4:11 as demarcating a border area of the Land of Israel

Ulla II Palestinian amora of the second half of the fourth century C.E.; cited infrequently in the Jerusalem Talmud and not at all in the Babylonian Talmud; a younger contemporary of Raba

Ulla b. Ishmael Palestinian amora of the second half of the third century C.E.; in the Babylonian Talmud called simply Ulla, without a patronymic; a student of Yoḥanan b. Nappaḥa, Simeon b. Lakish, and Eleazar b. Pedat. He frequently visited Babylonia, where he had contact with the exilarch (see, e.g., B. Shabbat 157b).

Ulpius Arabianus *see* ARABIANUS, MARCUS ULPIUS

Umm el-Amud *see* HORVAT AMUDIM

Umm el-Kanatir Synagogue synagogue site in the Golan Heights about 8 kilometers due east of the east shore of the Sea of Galilee. The village and its synagogue were located on a level plain on the east side of the Wadi esh-Shebib beneath a steep cliff. The building facade is oriented to the south. In antiquity a narrow porch or narthex, held up with two columns, stood at the facade. The nave was reached through a single entrance in the facade. A second means of entrance is a door that opened to the west aisle. The main hall measures nearly 19 by 14 meters, which is large for a village site. The building is a fine repository of ancient Jewish art, as the facade was decorated with an eagle in relief and the forequarters of a lion. A large stone slab in the shape of a triangle was probably a pediment of some kind; it is decorated with moldings. A vine scroll and grape clusters decorated a window frame. A second eagle with outstretched wings decorated yet another stone. The building is usually dated to the fifth century because a basket capital stood on one of the columns in the porch or narthex.

uncircumcised those who had not entered Israel's covenant by the initiatory ritual of circumcision. Uncircumcised males were classed with the unclean (Isa. 52:1; Ezek. 44:7.9; Rest of Esther 14:15) and metaphorically Jeremiah could condemn Israel for being uncircumcised in heart (Jer. 9:26). At the time of Antiochus IV Epiphanes, when Jason was high priest of Jerusalem, some Jews attempted to hide their circumcision (1 Macc. 1:14). As known from later Greek and Roman sources, there were two ways to do this: one could undergo minor surgery called epispasm or could attempt to hold some covering in place with a pin. The later Testament of Moses (8:3) suggests that epispasm was forced upon young Jews during persecution. In keeping with his sense of living at the end of time, Paul argues that a Gentile should not become circumcised, nor a circumcised man undergo epispasm (1 Cor. 7:18), and that what matters is not circumcision but a new creation (Gal. 6:16). In line with

Jeremiah, Paul maintains that real circumcision is a matter of the heart (Rom. 2:29). This idea of spiritual circumcision is continued in the Odes of Solomon 11:1–3. The apostolic council described in Acts of the Apostles 15 held that Jews were to stay circumcised, while Gentiles were not obliged to be circumcised, and Ephesians 2:11 holds that the division between the uncircumcised and the circumcised has been abolished. *See also* CIRCUMCISION.

unclean   *see* TAHOR, TAMEI

universalism   term used to describe a more open attitude toward the gentile world on the part of Jews. Although Ezra and Nehemiah show an exclusivistic attitude, others thought the community should be more outward looking and open to the surrounding culture. This reached a peak in the Hellenistic reform of Jason.

Urbanus   Christian governor of Palestine (304–307 C.E.). Eusebius mentions him as one of the governors during Diocletian's persecution of the Christians. He was in office at the time of Diocletian's fourth edict against the church in 304. He was executed in the fifth year of the persecutions, most likely in 307.

Urbinus, Codex   shortened name of the Codex Urbinates Ebr. 1, which was written (copied) in 1294. Now housed in the Vatican Library, the Codex Urbinus contains the texts of the entire Hebrew Bible, Rashi's commentary on the Pentateuch, Masorah Magna, Masorah Parva, as well as the Aramaic targums to the books of the Pentateuch, the Prophets, and some of the Writings.

Uriel   (Heb., light of God) one of seven holy ones (angels) who stand in God's immediate presence. In 1 Enoch 18 and 21, he oversees the prison for the watchers and the heavenly luminaries who have rebelled against God. In 1 Enoch 72–82, he guides Enoch through the heavens and explains the functions of the luminaries.

Ur of the Chaldeans   city in southern Mesopotamia, present day Tell el-Muqayyar; the home of Abram before he moved to Haran (Gen. 11:31). Tradition saw it as a center of idolatry and astrology and interpreted the name to refer to a fire (Heb.: *ur*) that destroyed the city's idols, from which God-fearing Abram was rescued. According to Jubilees 12, Abram burned the idol temple and then fled from Ur. In a revision of the Daniel 3 story in the Book of Biblical Antiquities 6, Abram refuses to help build the idolatrous Tower of Babel, and he is thrown into a fiery furnace, from which God rescues him.

Ursicinus   fourth-century-C.E. Roman general. In 351 Jews in Palestine under the leadership of Patricius revolted against Rome. The rebels first seized the armory in Sepphoris, and then, joined by Jews from Lydda and Tiberias, spread throughout the Galilee, capturing Lydda on the coast. The Roman forces, under Ursicinus, quickly defeated the Jews. In rabbinic sources Ursicinus ("the king") is described with respect. The Talmud indicates that during the time of Ursicinus the Jews of Sepphoris put on disguises to avoid capture, and a Torah scroll in the village of Sennabris, south of Tiberias, was burned. Some sages permitted the Jews to bake bread for Ursicinus's troops on the Sabbath.

Usha   town in Lower Galilee that was a site of Israelite habitation from biblical times. Usha was of particular importance following the Bar Kokhba Revolt, when it became the center of rabbinical study and the seat of the Sanhedrin. The establishment of this academy is described at Song of Songs Rabbah 2:5, 3, which notes the roles of Judah, Nehemiah, Meir, Yose, Simeon b. Yoḥai, Eliezer b. Yose the Galilean, and Eliezer b. Jacob, who called upon the sages of Galilee to gather in Usha.

Usha, archaeology of   Usha, a seat of the Sanhedrin after the destruction of the Second Temple, is identified with two possible sites: (1) Khirbet Hosha, a ruin 14 kilometers west-northwest of Sepphoris and lying within the city territory of Sepphoris; and (2) Horvat Amudim (the ruin of the columns), which stands 15 kilometers west-north-west of Sepphoris, but within the city territory of Tiberias. Khirbet Hosha has not been excavated, but surveys published as early as 1881 established that at the site one could see foundations of buildings, a mosaic floor, a well and plastered tank, and rock-cut tombs. Horvat Amudim, on the other hand, has been excavated and its synagogue was first reported in 1869. The synagogue is about 19 by 14 meters, one of the largest in Galilee. The facade faces south towards Jerusalem. The lintel on the central portal bore two lions with their forepaws resting on the head of a calf and a two-handled amphora above the calf. A lintel on the east was decorated with floral rosettes and a wreath. An Aramaic inscription in one of the walls reads: "Yoezer the hazan and Shimon his brother made this gate of the Lord of heaven." It is usually understood that "gate" refers to the synagogue itself, in which case Yoezer and Shimon were benefactors.

usury   *see* INTEREST

Uziel   *see* AZAEL

V

Vaballathus king of Palmyra (r. 267–271 C.E.). He was a vassal of Rome. He was a minor when his father was assassinated, so his mother, Zenobia, was the real ruler of Palmyra. Some Christian sources claim that Zenobia was Jewish and that she and her son were friendly to the Jews.

Valens, Flavius eastern Roman emperor (r. 364–378 C.E.). He was the brother of Valentinian, who gave him the traditional title Augustus and made him ruler of the East. He allowed Visigoths to cross the Danube and settle in Thrace (376), from where they plundered and threatened the East. Foolishly not waiting for Gratian's military support, Valens fought the barbarians at Adrianople, in Thrace, in 378. The Roman army was annihilated by the superior barbarian cavalry, and Valens lost his life—the last emperor killed by barbarians in battle until Nicephorus I in 811. Theodosius succeeded Valens in the East and made peace with the Visigoths; Arianism, together with religious toleration, which Valens had favored, fell with Valens.

Valentinianus governor of Palestine, 310/311 C.E. He is known from a dedication inscription to Galerius. His dates are mere conjecture, but this is the only year that is not covered by the governors mentioned by Eusebius in connection with Diocletian's persecution of the Christians.

Valerian Roman emperor (r. 253–260 C.E.). He was proclaimed emperor by his troops upon Gallus's death. During his reign, the empire was beset by internal revolts and external attacks. In 253 the Persians moved into Syria, captured Antioch, and probably raided Palestine. By 256 the Goths sacked Nicomedia, Nicaea, and other Bithynian cities in northwest Asia Minor. That same year, Dura fell to the Persians. In 260 Valerian gathered troops, including some from Judea, and marched against the Persians; however, at Edessa he was defeated and captured by the Persians. At this point, Palestine came under the control of Odenathus of Palmyra.

Valerianus, Lucius Valerius *see* VALERIUS VALERIANUS, LUCIUS

Valerius Gratus *see* GRATUS, VALERIUS

Valerius Maximus author about whom little is known, other than that he was a contemporary of the emperor Tiberius (r. 14–41 C.E.), to whom he dedicated his *Memorable Deeds and Sayings*. The nine books of *Sayings* are a didactic, preachy collection of limited value, consisting of tales, historical anecdotes, and judgments intended for rhetors and educators.

Valerius Valerianus, Lucius governor of Palestine. The dates of his tenure in Palestine are uncertain because of the questionable reading of a dedication to him set up in Caesarea. However, a date at the time of Caracalla seems preferable to a date at the time of Elagabalus. Between 214 and 240 he was prefect of Mesopotamia and Osroene at the same time.

valuation (Heb.: *arakin*) pledge of the value of a person, in line with Leviticus 27:1–8; *see also* ARAKIN

Varro (116–27 B.C.E.) Roman encyclopedist. Of his many works, only those on the Latin language and agriculture have survived. He had included a good deal on religion in his great work on the *Antiquities of Human and Divine Matters,* which has unfortunately perished except for quotations in such writers as the church father Augustine. In it he had dealt with temples, priests, festivals, sacred objects, and the gods. The preserved fragments give a quite positive view of the Jews. Varro opposed the use of images in worship and claimed that the Romans originally did not use them; instead, he held up the Jews as a good example for avoiding such inferior worship. He also identified the Jewish God with Jupiter, apparently because he thought the Jews worshiped the highest god and none was higher in the Roman pantheon. He was also aware that the Jewish God was called Iao in some contexts. He mentions the date palm, which bears fruit in Judea. In a historical reference, he makes mention of Pompey and his lavish expenses when he was campaigning in Judea, a fact also noted by Appian. Where he obtained his knowledge of Jewish beliefs is uncertain.

Varus, Publius Quinctilius Roman governor of Syria (7/6–4 B.C.E.). He put down the revolt and disturbances after the death of Herod the Great (4 B.C.E.) in two campaigns, during which he destroyed Sepphoris, relieved the besieged Roman soldiers in Jerusalem, and crucified two thousand rebels.

vaticinia ex eventu (Lat., prophecy after the event) Many prophecies of the Hebrew Bible and the Jewish Apocalypses give a review of history as if uttered by an ancient sage. A good example is Daniel 11. Much of these reviews will usually contain identifiable events of history, even with their somewhat disguised language. Rather than being genuine prophecies, though, the review of history would simply show the author's understanding of past history from his own perspective. When the author's own time is reached, however, the prophecy may become a genuine prediction of the future.

vegetarianism Genesis 9:3–4 suggests that only after the Flood was humanity granted permission to consume animal products. The Therapeutae were vegetarians, as were the Pythagoreans and the Jewish-Christian Ebionites but not—*pace* Jerome—the Essenes. Romans 14:2 labels those who eat only vegetables (perhaps those observing Jewish dietary laws) as "weak" but exhorts the carnivorous "strong" to refrain from judging them.

veil The veil was part of the outer garment (*himation*), as the Judae Capta coins illustrate. Several sources from diverse periods (Song of Sol. 4:1, 3; Isa. 47:2; 1 Cor. 11:2–16) note that women wore veils, but one cannot determine on the basis of these scattered references that all Jewish women throughout antiquity practiced this custom. Veils were worn by brides (Gen. 24:65–67) and Moses (Exod. 34:29–35; 2 Cor. 3:13), and a veil or curtain hung over the entrance to the inner sanctum of the Temple (2 Chron. 3:14; Mark 15:38; the heavenly counterpart of this veil is described in 3 Enoch 45). Paul argues that women must wear veils in worship (1 Cor. 11:2–16) "because of the angels," a statement variously interpreted as a reference to the watchers, who might be distracted by women, as a concern that Christian women not be regarded as prostitutes, and as a means by which gender distinctions could be enforced.

vengeance (Heb.: *nekamah*) punishment inflicted in retaliation for injury or offense. In the Hebrew Bible, revenge, that is, seeking recompense for wrongdoings, is usually given over to God. Thus God speaks in Deuteronomy 32:35, "Vengeance is mine, and recompense, for the time when their foot shall slip. . . ." Because of Israel's and, later, Judah's position of relative political powerlessness in the Ancient Near East, God is often portrayed as taking vengeance on a people or nation that has wronged the Israelites. A striking example of this portrayal occurs in Jeremiah 50, in which God declares revenge on the Babylonians for their treatment of Judah before and during the exile.

This concept of vengeance as God's peculiar right on behalf of his people continues into the Second Temple period, particularly in the Dead Sea Scrolls. In the sectarian writings among the Scrolls there is an expectation of a day in which God will vindicate the sect and punish its opponents. This is made explicit in the War Scroll, which calls the day of the final battle between the forces of good and evil the "day of vengeance." The War Scroll uses the word "vengeance" to denote the (military) action of God on behalf of the Community. In early Christianity, persecuted Christians also looked forward to a "day of vengeance," when they would be vindicated and their enemies brought low (cf. especially the Book of Revelation).

Like the Bible, the rabbis view vengeance as the primary tool used by God both to punish Israelites' wrongdoings and to bring to justice the nations that have oppressed Israel (Ruth Rabbah 45; Lev. Rabbah 34). While God's vengeance is generally understood to be a future act, the rabbis also depict as examples of God's vengeance the troubles that befall enemies of Israel (see, e.g., Lev. Rabbah 22, regarding God's vengeance against Titus). The importance of vengeance is indicated by Psalms

94:1, where the term appears between two references to the divine name ("God of vengeance, O Lord"). Vengeance is, however, solely God's tool. Israelites are forbidden from exacting vengeance (see Lev. 19:17–18), defined as any act of retaliation (Sifra Kedoshim 4).

Vespasian Roman emperor (69–79 C.E.), commander (67–69) of the Roman forces that fought in the war against the Jews in Palestine. Titus Flavius Vespasian had served as an army commander and in various offices when Nero appointed him to subdue the Jewish rebellion in 67 C.E. He conquered the northern part of the country, but when Nero died in 68, he became involved in the politics of succession. After the deaths of three emperors in a year, Vespasian was proclaimed emperor by the legions in the East. He ruled successfully for ten years and was succeeded by his two sons, Titus and Domitian. They are referred to as the Flavian dynasty.

vessels, hidden *see* HIDDEN FURNISHINGS AND VESSELS

Vetus Latina the Old Latin translation of the Bible that preceded the Vulgate. The Old Testament part of the Old Latin was usually translated from the Septuagint. Although the Vulgate became the standard Latin version, the Deutero-canonical books in it were taken over from the Vetus Latina.

vices *see* VIRTUES AND VICES

vidui *see* CONFESSION OF SIN

vindication (Heb.: *hitzdik;* Gr.: *dikaioō*) putting things right legally. Often used in a religious sense, the term denotes that someone is innocent of certain charges, has acted in a righteous or just manner, or has been upheld when treated unjustly. *See also* JUSTIFICATION.

vine and vineyard The grapevine was one of the most important crops in ancient Israel. The vine and vineyard, by virtue of their particular qualities, also assume figurative dimensions in the thought of biblical Judaism. For example, we find that while the vine is generally a symbol of prosperity and fruitfulness in the Bible, in the part of the Bible known as Prophets, the vine is typically used metaphorically, with Israel being the "vine" or "vineyard" of God (e.g., Jer. 2:21; Hos. 10:1). When the people of Israel disobey God, the vineyard will be destroyed (Jer. 5:10; Ezek. 19:12).

The vine and vineyard receive limited attention in intertestamental Jewish literature. In the Wisdom of Ben Sira 24:17–21, Wisdom compares herself to a fruitful vine and invites people to come and eat of her. In 4 Ezra 5:23, Israel is the "one vine" specially chosen by God from among all the trees of the earth.

There are two pseudepigrapha in which the "tree of knowledge" in Genesis 3 is represented as a vine. The first is the Apocalypse of Abraham, in which Abraham sees the tree of knowledge in the Garden of Eden as having fruit "like the appearance of a bunch of grapes of the vine," with Azazel as a serpent feeding the grapes to Adam and Eve (23:5–11). The second—3 Baruch—characterizes the "tree of knowledge" as a vine that was planted in Eden by Satan. God curses the vine and its seed and forbids Adam to touch it. Consequently, Satan becomes envious and tricks Adam and Eve into eating from the vine (3 Bar. 4).

The vine also figures prominently in 2 Baruch. According to that text, the earth will be so productive in the Messianic Age that one vine will have 1000 branches, each producing 1000 clusters, each yielding 1000 grapes, each giving 120 gallons of wine (29:5). In 2 Baruch 36–40, the seer has a vision in which a vine and a fountain, jointly representing the rule of God's messiah, overthrow a great forest, which stands for a major world kingdom that presumably is Rome.

Vines and vineyards provide important images in early Christian literature, notably in a number of striking parables and metaphors in the New Testament. In the eschatological parables in Matt. 20:1–16; Mark 12:1–12 and parallels; and Luke 13:6–9, Jesus uses a vineyard to represent the sphere of worldly activity. In Matt. 14:25 and parallels, he promises not to drink of the vine's fruit until the time of the eschatological kingdom. In John 15:1–11, Jesus identifies himself as the true vine, his "father" as the vinedresser, and his disciples as the vine's branches. Revelation 14:18–20 uses the harvesting of the vineyard as a metaphor for eschatological destruction.

According to Josephus, the image of a grapevine appeared around the top of the Jerusalem Temple, and the vine also appeared frequently on Palestinian synagogues, probably to demonstrate a link between the two institutions. As in the Bible, in the talmudic literature the vine and, in particular, the grape cluster symbolized what is desirable and good. The word for cluster (*ishkol*) was interpreted to refer to a perfect man, in which there is everything (*ish shekol bo;* B. Sotah 47b; B. Terumah 15b). Early rabbinic masters, held to have no blemishes (that is, faults), were symbolized as grape clusters (Mishnah Sotah 9:9; Tosefta Baba Kamma 8:13; Jerusalem Talmud Sotah 9:10). This interpretation may be related to Micah 7:1–2, which associates a scarcity of grape clusters with the perishing from the earth of godly and upright men. Aibu

(Gen. Rabbah 19:8) holds that grapes were the forbidden fruit eaten by Eve. Marrying one's daughter to a rabbinic scholar is equated with grafting one grapevine to another. This is contrasted with marrying the child of an unlettered man, which is deemed comparable to grafting a grapevine to the lesser berry bush (B. Pesahim 49a–b). *See also* GRAPES, GRAPEVINES; VITICULTURE.

vine scroll   a common motif in Jewish art as a variation on the vine trellis. The vine scroll is a repeated pattern of round openings formed by the vine itself, which may be a grape or ivy vine. An inhabited scroll contains animals, birds, or other figures in each round opening. Vine scrolls without inhabitations occur on tombs, synagogue floors, sarcophagi, and occasionally on architectural fragments.

vine trellis   a common motif in Jewish art formed of a geometric pattern shaped by vines, vine tendrils, and vine leaves. It is a motif borrowed from Graeco-Roman art, where it was exceedingly popular. Sometimes the vines represented are grape vines, but sometimes it is simply ivy. The vine trellis appears in mosaic floors as a repeating pattern of openings framed by the vines; then the openings are filled with figures. The inhabited scroll is an example of a vine trellis in which the tendrils form round medallions filled with the figure of an animal, bird, or other art motif. One of the most famous of these pavements is from the synagogue of Maon.

vipers, brood of   the insult hurled by John the Baptist at the Pharisees and Sadducees according to Matthew 3:7 (the parallel in Luke 3:7 addresses the crowds) and by Jesus at the Pharisees and scribes (Matt. 12:34). Matthew 23:33 implies that contact with these four groups of Jewish leaders is deadly (see Isa. 59:5; Job 20:16; and contrast Mark 16:18 and Acts 28:1-10).

virgin   The Hebrew word *betula* (separated) originally indicated an unmarried young woman, then a virgin. High priests could only marry virgins (Lev. 21:7–8, 13–15; also Philo and Josephus). Applied to cities and peoples, such as "virgin Israel" or Jerusalem (Jer. 18:13), the designation suggests virtuousness. Chastity and, hence, virginity received greater emphasis in the Graeco-Roman period: Philo's Therapeutrides; the stress on Asenath's virginity as well as on Joseph's in Joseph and Asenath; Abode of the Rechabites/Apocalypse of Zosimus 11:6–8; Pseudo-Phocylides 215–16 (on daughters). References to male and female virginity are found as well in early Christian material: Mary (Matt. 1:23, using the Greek *parthenos*, quotes from the LXX of Isa. 7:14; the Hebrew reads *alma* [young woman]); Philip's four unmarried daughters (Acts 21:9); and the 144,000 male virgins of Revelation 14:4. Paul exhorts virgin men and women in his congregations not to marry and acknowledges celibacy to be a spiritual gift (1 Cor. 7:7–9, 25–38).

Within rabbinic culture a virgin was the preferred bride, reflected in the value of her jointure, set at twice that of a widow (M. Ketubot 1:2). If the husband did not find her hymen intact, he could ask the court to annul the marriage, as a "purchase made in error" (M. Ketubot 1:6). In developing this idea, rabbis debated whether a woman whose hymen was broken but who never had intercourse should be deemed a virgin (Gen. Rabbah Parashah 60). While virginity was equated with sinlessness (Sifrei Deut. 321), the rabbinic obligation to procreate meant that celibacy was discouraged. The rabbis understood marriage and sexual relations within marriage to be a religious obligation.

Virt.   *see* DE VIRTUTIBUS

virtues and vices   The Greek word for virtue, *arete,* is used in reference to positive human characteristics in Greek philosophy as well as in Jewish and Christian religious literature. To define and list the qualities that should characterize humans at their best was a major concern among Greek philosophers from the time of Plato on, and especially in the thinking of Stoic philosophers. Jewish thought was influenced by this intellectual development, and in many writings from the second century B.C.E. and later, there is a shift of focus from the specifics of the moral laws in the tradition of Moses to the abstract principles and moral qualities that should characterize the people of God. Both the positive (virtues) and the negative (vices) features of the moral life are described.

In Plato's *Republic* (4.427–428), moral issues are focused on four principles: justice, wisdom, courage, and self-control. These moral qualities were affirmed by the Stoic philosophers as well. Aristo—a pupil of Zeno, who founded Stoicism—wrote, "Virtue, when it considers what should be done and what should not be done, is called prudence; when it controls desire and defines what is moderate . . . it is called self-control; when it is concerned with dealings and contracts with others, it is called justice." The Testaments of the Twelve Patriarchs identify the virtues as integrity, piety, uprightness, honesty, generosity, compassion, hard work, and self-control. The vices are sexual promiscuity, anger, envy, greed, envy, cruelty to fellow human beings, and debauchery.

Among the later historical books, 2 Maccabees describes Onias the high priest as one who is noble and good, modest in bearing and having a gentle manner, and trained from childhood in all that belongs to excellence. 4 Maccabees begins with the affirmation that devout reason is the absolute master of human passions, while the forces hindering temperance are gluttony, lust, malice, rage, fear, forgetfulness, and ignorance. Reason can lead to justice and courage (1:1–6). Pious reason produces a life in conformity with the law of God, while passion fosters pretentiousness, avarice, contentiousness, backbiting, and gluttony (2:1–15). Josephus observes that humans, created in God's image, should strive to participate in the perfection of virtue God possesses (*Ant.* 1.23).

Like Greek philosophers, rabbinic authors attempted to determine the essence of morality and proper behavior. The broadest and most complete statement of human virtues and vices was understood to be expressed by the system of rabbinic law itself. Within this law, the rabbis enumerated 613 commandments and 248 positive requirements believed to be parallel to the number of organs in the human body and 356 prohibitions corresponding to the number of days in the year.

A number of rabbinic passages attempt to ascertain the essence of this system of law and so to define the most basic virtues. B. Makkot 24a presents one of the most developed of these passages. Simlai cites biblical texts that he holds progressively condense the commandments into a smaller number of essential virtues. Psalm 15 lists eleven of these, ranging from not doing evil and honoring those who fear the Lord to not lending out money at interest. Isaiah 33:15 lists six virtues, including the refusal to listen to reports of bloodshed or even to look upon evil. Micah 6:8 comprehends the system of commandments as just three virtues: to do justice, love kindness, and walk humbly with God. Isaiah 61:1 expresses this in two concepts, observing justice and doing righteousness. Amos and Habakkuk finally present single ideals seen as capturing the essence of virtue as expressed by the rabbinic system: "Seek me and live" (Amos 5:4) or "The righteous man shall live by his faithfulness" (Hab. 2:4).

visions the sight of things not normally perceptible to human eyes, the most common mode of revelation in Jewish and Christian apocalypses. Visions in the Tanakh (Old Testament) include several which portray the throne of God (Exod. 24:9–11, Isa. 6:1–13, Ezek. 1:1–3:15, 1 Kings 22:19–23). In the prophets, the dominant mode of revelation is the oracle, but visions (e.g., Amos 7:1–9, Jer. 24) also occur. Visions are particularly prominent in the prophet Ezekiel (chaps. 1–3, 40–48), a book which is the forerunner of apocalyptic; compare, for example, Ezekiel's vision of heavenly throne of God (Ezek. 1:1–28, 10:9–17) with Daniel 7, 1 Enoch 14, and Revelation 4–5.

In the apocalypses, visions are associated with dreams and heavenly journeys, and their principal theme is revelation of the secrets of heaven and of God's plans for the end of history. The visions of Daniel 7–12, the only apocalypse in the Tanakh, depict the end of history in terms of battles, in which God and his angels defeat terrifying beasts (symbols of the human and superhuman powers of evil, including the Seleucid rulers of the author's own time). The apocalypse of 1 Enoch, a compilation of five originally independent books (3d c. B.C.E. to 1st c. C.E.), all ascribed to the shadowy biblical figure Enoch (Gen. 5:18–24), contains visions with quite varied content. Book 1, "the Book of the Watchers" (chaps. 1–36) portrays the fall of the angels (cf. Gen. 6:1–4) and also Enoch's journeys to heaven, where he learns heavenly secrets such as the sources of wind, water, and thunder. In Book 4 (chaps. 83–91), "the Dream Visions," Enoch tells his son Methuselah of two visions, one of the destruction of the cosmos and the second an extended allegory of the history of Israel, in which biblical figures are visualized as animals. Allegorical visions also play an important role in two apocalypses that reflect on the destruction of Jerusalem in 70 C.E., 2 Esdras and 2 Baruch.

In the New Testament, the two-volume work Luke-Acts reports Paul's vision on the road to Damascus (Acts 9:1–8) as well as several other visions (Luke 1:8–22; Acts 1:3–11; 7:55–56; 9:10–16; 10:1–6, 9–16; 11:5–10, 13–14; 16:9–10; cf. 12:7–11). In 2 Cor. 12:1–4, Paul, in a curious third person account, tells of being caught up to the "third heaven." The Revelation to John, the only New Testament apocalypse, consists almost entirely of visionary accounts, from an opening vision of Jesus as the exalted son of man (1:9–20) to the concluding visions of the last battle against Satan and the establishment of God's perfect reign (19:11–22:7). The central part of the book consists of a picture of the heavenly throne of God (chaps. 4–5), followed by three cycles of seven visions each, which repeat the story of God's eschatological judgment. These exhibit the general characteristics of apocalyptic visions: lavish use of symbols (animals, colors, numbers, etc.), many of which have become traditional, repetition (a series of visions that treat the same event or theme), the presence of heavenly intermediaries, and an emphasis on mystery and secrecy.

visitation (Heb.: *pekudah;* Gr.: *episkopē*) a common expression for God's judgment, whether to reward the righteous or punish the wicked. Some eschatological texts in the late Second Temple period envision God actually making a visit to the earth (1 Enoch 25:3), while in others the term is simply a synonym for judgment or retribution (1QS 4:6, 11). The Greek verb and noun mean "[to conduct] an inspection or investigation," although, like the Hebrew, they can mean simply "[to execute] judgment" (Luke 1:68). *See also* JUDGMENT, DIVINE.

Vita Con. *see* DE VITA CONTEMPLATIVA

Vita Mos. *see* DE VITA MOSIS

Vitellius, Lucius Roman legate in Syria (35–39 C.E.). He removed Pilate from office in 36 C.E. and sent him to Rome to answer for his attack on a Samaritan religious gathering. He also returned the care of the high priest's vestments to the Jerusalem Jews and abolished a market tax on fruit in Jerusalem. When campaigning against Aretas the Nabatean, he ordered Roman troops carrying images of the emperor on their standards to avoid Judea.

viticulture the branch of agriculture that deals with tending and exploitation of the vine, including the use of its fruit for making different products. In First Temple times, several different kinds of grapes were cultivated and the fruit was used for making wine, raisins, syrup and vinegar. Vine tenders were professionals known as *koremim* (Joel 1:11; 2 Chron. 26:10). After the destruction of the Solomonic Temple, the Babylonians exiled a certain segment of the population but retained on the land peasants and vine dressers (2 Kings 25:12; Jer. 52:16).

Very little pertaining to agriculture in general and viticulture in particular can be found in the later books of the Hebrew Bible. Nonetheless, the few references to viticulture suggest that this branch of agriculture flourished and was respected as seen in Proverbs 31:16, where planting a vineyard is mentioned as one of the activities of the diligent wife, or the several instances in Song of Songs where metaphorical references are made to vineyards (1:6, 8:11-12) or the grape vine (6:11, 7:9, 13).

Other written sources from late antiquity, such as the Zeno Papyri, suggest that during the Second Temple period, wine was exported from Palestine to Egypt. The Letter of Aristeas (dated to the Hellenistic period), in describing the richness of Palestine, mentions vineyards among other agricultural resources. Pliny in his *Natural History* (XIV, 103)

describes Syrian wine flavored with myrrh. Famous wines of that period were Sharon wine, Carmel wine, and Ammon wine. From the fourth to the seventh centuries C.E., Ascalon and Gaza were known for exporting excellent wine to Syria and Egypt. Wine exported from these cities reached as far as Gaul and Italy. Its production in the area surrounding Ascalon has been recently documented in survey work where kilns for amphora and wine presses were found.

During the Second Commonwealth most Jews were agrarians as reflected in descriptions contained in Tannaitic literature and in the writings of Josephus. According to Rabbi Tarphon, rich is one "who owns one hundred vineyards and one hundred fields" (Shab. 25b). Rabbi Johanan spoke of diversification as protection against agricultural loss, suggesting the division of land into three: cereals, olives, and vines (B.M. 107a). New vineyards were planted as one can see from R. Simeon b. Gamliel's involvement with the *orlah* law (B.Q. 69a). While during Mishnaic and Talmudic times most of the Palestinian economy continued to be agricultural, every region specialized in certain cultivars. The Galilee specialized in olives for oil, and grapes were cultivated in Judea and in the south. The fact that hardly any wine presses were found in the Golan suggests that its inhabitants imported wine from other regions.

Decrees made by the emperors Vespasian and Hadrian in the first and second centuries C.E. resulted in the decline of Jewish land ownership and Jews were reduced to the status of tenant farmers and sharecroppers. Although the two rebellions against the Romans caused agricultural destruction in many parts of the country, it continued to rely on agriculture. Only in the middle of the third century C.E., when bad economic times weakend most of the Roman Empire and Jews had to leave Palestine to find livelihoods elsewhere, the Jewish attitude toward agriculture changed and denigrated it as a means of earning a livelihood. This period sees the rise of large estates and the growing number of sharecroppers, tenant farmers, hired hands, and laborers.

Archaeological remains related to viticulture from the Persian and Hellenistic periods are scant. It can be safely assumed that during these periods viticulture practices developed in the Iron Age were maintained. Nevertheless, much archaeological information is available for wine making in the Roman-Byzantine period. Many wine presses were found in Judea, the southern Shephelah, and in the Negev, where wine presses were found in most of the so-called Nabatean cities. The large size of many of these wine presses suggests that they were operated not by small planters, but by either large land owners, groups of farmers, or by the government. Most wine presses have a treading floor, a tesselated collection tank with a sump, and plastered walls.

During late antiquity, viticulture continued to occupy a very important place in daily life and thus influenced many of its aspects, such as art. For example, mosaics as well as tombs and stone sarcophagi were decorated with motifs of the grape vine or bunch. Coins from different periods carried similar motifs. As early as the reign of Antiochus VIII (c. 126–125 B.C.E.), a coin struck in Jerusalem depicts on its reverse side a grape bunch. Herod the Great and Herod Archelaus used the motif of a grape leaf and cluster which became Jewish symbols. Coins of the first rebellion against the Romans bore on the reverse side a depiction of a grape leaf and cluster. The chalice or the amphora on the obverse side might have indicated a vessel used for wine libations. In the first half of the second century C.E., Bar Kosiba coins of different denominations also display a vine leaf or a grape bunch on the reverse side. Silver-plated Bar Kosiba coins displayed a grape bunch on the obverse side, as well. A suggestion was made that the grape leaf and cluster depict a golden decoration of Herod's temple. Being a Jewish motif is highlighted by the fact that other contemporary coins, as, for example, Nabatean coins, do not bear any viticultural motifs.

Vologases III Parthian ruler (r. 148–192 C.E.). His foreign policy was to foment rebellion against Rome in the frontier territories, and he probably encouraged Jewish anti-Roman activity in Palestine, Osrhoene, and Adiabene. Jews at this time did wage war against Rome, and those battles coincided with Parthian interests.

vow A promise either to forgo something not ordinarily forbidden, or a promise to perform some act in return for divine help or in thanksgiving for such help. Examples of the first category include the story of Paul's having his hair cut off (Acts 18:18) and the four Christians under vow who have to undergo some ritual of purification at the Temple of Jerusalem, which involves having their heads shaved (Acts 21:23–24). Examples of the second are attributed to Cyrus, king of Persia, who is said to have vowed to destroy Babylon and to restore the vessels taken from Jerusalem (1 Esdras 4:44), and Judas Maccabeus, who in the manner of Numbers 21:2–3, promised that the city of the

Baeanites would be devoted to the Lord in utter destruction if the battle was successful (1 Macc. 5:5). As for the thanksgiving vow, on coming to the throne, Darius and Artaxerxes, kings of Persia, are said to have vowed to rebuild Jerusalem (1 Esdras 4:43–45), and some of the Jewish leaders, after returning to Jerusalem, vowed to erect the Temple as best they could in thanks to God for bringing them back to Jerusalem (1 Esdras 5:44); Heliodorus, the Seleucid minister, made lavish vows to the Lord, who had spared him (2 Macc. 3:35). A person should think before making a vow, but if a vow is made, one is bound to perform it (Ecclus. 18:22–23; Letter of Jeremiah 6:35). The Temple Scroll at Qumran maintains the rules about vows found in Numbers 30 (11QTemple 53–54). Members of the Qumran covenant are required to vow to follow the Law, but they are not to vow to the altar articles acquired unlawfully, or the food of their own house, nor can they vow another to destruction by gentile law (CD 16:7–8, 13–15; 9:1).

Perhaps because of the ever present possibility that one who vows will not be able to fulfill his obligation, or perhaps because of the potentially devastating unforeseen consequence of vows (see Judg. 11:30–40, where a vow leads Jephthah to kill his daughter), rabbinic sages almost uniformly discourage vowing. Leviticus Rabbah 37:1 states that people who do not fulfill their vows in a timely fashion ultimately will worship an idol, commit fornication, and spill blood, claims proven from the experiences of the patriarch Jacob. Samuel (B. Nedarim 22a) and Dimi (B. Nedarim 77b) hold that a person who makes a vow, even if he fulfills it, is deemed wicked or sinful. B. Shabbat 32b argues that making vows results in the premature death of one's children.

In keeping with their negative attitude toward vows, the rabbis developed a sophisticated procedure through which vows can be annulled. This is quite different from biblical law, which recognizes only the absolution of the vow of an unmarried woman by her father, or of a married woman by her husband (Num. 30:3–15). By contrast, rabbinic law allows a court to annul vows brought before it by discovering an unforeseen circumstance, knowledge of which would have deterred the individual from making the vow in the first place. If, when made fully aware of the impact of the vow, the individual regrets having made it, the vow is deemed invalid *ab initio*.

Even while discouraging vows and allowing their annulment, rabbinic law is clear that an individual's statements are binding, so long as they were made voluntarily and he or she was aware of their scope and significance. Only vows made by mistake or under compulsion are not valid.

Vulgate the Latin translation of the Old Testament by the church father Jerome. He learned Hebrew while living in Bethlehem and translated directly from the Hebrew text, though he sometimes used Greek translations to help in understanding the Hebrew text, as well as being influenced by the Vetus Latina.

Wadi ed-Daliyeh site of a cave, Mugharet Abu-Shinjeh, in which Bedouin found papyri (the Wadi ed-Daliyeh or Samaria manuscripts) in 1962. The wadi arises out of the eastern edge of Palestine's central highlands west of Samaria and falls to the Jordan Valley about 15 kilometers north of Jericho. Several caves in the Wadi ed-Daliyeh were excavated in 1963 and 1964 to determine the findspot for the manuscripts and the circumstances of their deposit.

In 1962 the Bedouin middleman brought some papyrus fragments to the Palestine Museum. It was determined that the fragments belonged to the fourth century B.C.E., and they were purchased through a manuscript fund of the American Schools of Oriental Research. When the cave from which the papyri came was identified by the Bedouin, it was necessary that scientific excavation in the cave take place to confirm their findspot, determine an explanation for their presence in the cave, and recover any fragments or artifacts the Bedouin may have missed. Several other nearby caves in the wadi were also explored.

The manuscript area in the cave was evident from the digging and exploring of the Bedouin. It was thoroughly cleared and the dirt sifted. In addition a meter-wide trench was dug from the mouth of the cave back to the manuscript area and several recesses in order to determine the occupational history of the site. Fourth-century B.C.E. (Late Persian) occupation was confirmed, with an indication of a slight later Roman use.

Among the finds related to the fourth-century occupation were cloth, wood, bones, remains of food, a few small papyrus fragments, seals, a tiny silver coin, some jewelry, and much pottery.

In another cave slightly up the wadi, evidence of Second Revolt (132 C.E.) and Early Bronze Age (third millennium B.C.E.) occupation led to further excavation there. Twenty large ovoid storage jars and globular cooking pots found intact from the Early Bronze Age witnessed to cave habitation toward the end of the third millennium. Early Roman pottery and artifacts indicated that refugees had probably used the cave as a hideout in the early second century C.E.

From the story the Bedouin told and from the content of the papyri and the other finds from the cave clearance, an explanation for the deposition of the manuscripts can be given. According to the historians Josephus (*Ant.* xi. 297–345) and Q. Curtus Rufus (*Hist. Alex.,* iv. 8.9–10), the leaders of Samaria had rebelled against those Alexander the Great had left in charge. When the leaders who were implicated heard of Alexander's return from Egypt and march toward Samaria to take vengeance upon them, they fled down the Wadi Farah into the wilderness hoping for temporary refuge in the Wadi ed-Daliyeh cave. There were perhaps about a hundred of them, including members of their families. They brought with them large storage jars and cooking vessels, as well as various personal articles, and their seals and legal documents. Their origin and status is attested by these finds. They were discovered in their hiding place by Alexander's men, who may have built a fire in the entrance and suffocated them.

Wadi ed-Daliyeh Papyri fragments of documents found by Bedouin in the Wadi ed-Daliyeh. They were left by refugees from Samaria who fled from Alexander the Great in the third quarter of the fourth century B.C.E.

Many of the papyri are fragmentary. About twenty pieces are large enough to be numbered as papyri but none are complete. There were about two hundred small rolls in the first purchase and hundreds of small fragments. The original deposit may have consisted of more than a hundred documents. The main destructive element was worms, and their lacy patterns can be traced on the remaining fragments. A papyrologist was able to do some reconstruction by fiber analysis and a study of the destructive patterns.

The documents were sealed with bullae (clay seal impressions), and over a hundred of these seals have been recovered. The best preserved papyrus roll was sealed with seven bullae. Two other rolls had four seals. Two of the seals were inscribed in paleo-Hebrew, but they usually carried Attic motifs in the contemporary Greek style or Persian mythic and royal motifs.

The documents were all legal and administrative. Many are slave documents, while others are concerned with loans, sale of property, and marriage. The opening and closing formulas are preserved in some. They record that the contract was written in the province or city of Samaria and executed before the governor or prefect. In cases where the year in a governor's reign is given, it has been possible to date the document closely. The earliest is dated between the thirtieth and fortieth years of Artaxerxes II, between 375 and 365 B.C.E. Others are from early in the reign of Artaxerxes III (358–338 B.C.E.). The latest and best preserved papyrus was written on March 19, 335 B.C.E. The range is thus about 375 to 335 B.C.E.

The names that appear most often are Yahwistic, that is names combined with Yahweh. There are also foreign names reflecting the mixed Samaritan population. On one of the seals Sanballat is named as governor, perhaps Sanballat III, great-great-grandson of the Sanballat of Nehemiah's day. The name Nehemiah also appears as a slave for one of the nobles of Samaria.

The script of these papyri provide absolute dates for the fourth-century Aramaic cursive. When they are fully studied, the contents of the documents and the circumstances of their find will provide sig-

nificant historical and cultural information about this period.

wages *see* EMPLOYERS, EMPLOYEES

Wailing Wall *see* WESTERN WALL

walk (Heb.: *halakh;* Gr.: *peripateo*) to live one's life, righteously or wickedly. This major metaphor for the ethical dimension of human conduct implies the imagery of the two ways and is the source of the term *halakhah. See also* WAYS, TWO.

walled cities cities encompassed by walls. Such cities are subject to several special rules: (1) Hereditary property situated in walled cities may be redeemed from a purchaser for a year from the date of purchase (Lev. 25:29; M. Arakhin 9:3–8). But such property is exempt from the law of the Jubilee, which, every fifty years, has hereditary property returned to its original owners. (2) Following the practice recorded at Esther 9:18, in walled cities, the Scroll of Esther is read annually on the fifteenth of Adar, the day after it is read in cities without walls (M. Megillah 1:1–2). (3) Walled cities in the Land of Israel are held to have a higher level of sanctity than that of unwalled cities. Lepers may not remain in them, and corpses, once removed, may not be brought back into them (M. Kelim 1:8).

war armed conflict between nations using lethal force to compel one side to do the other's will or, in extreme cases, intending totally to obliterate the enemy. In the Hebrew Bible, war resulted in the annihilation of the defeated army and the capture of noncombatants, whose possessions were taken as spoils of war (see, e.g., Gen. 14:1–12, 34:25–29; Num. 31:21–30). Biblical law even makes provision for Israelite warriors to take wives from among captive women (Deut. 21:10–14). By contrast, in certain instances, especially when fighting an enemy understood to be hostile to Israelite theocracy, the defeated nation and all of its property were devoted to God and deemed forbidden for Israelite benefit. In such a circumstance, noncombatants as well as enemy warriors were killed and their possessions destroyed (see, e.g., Josh. 8). Failure completely to carry out such a ban of extermination had devastating consequences for the Israelites, whose act of sacrilege turned God against them (1 Sam. 15).

While war and the destruction of an enemy frequently were understood to be demanded by God, biblical law also required concerted attempts to avert bloodshed. Prior to the battle, terms of peace were to be offered. These demanded surrender and payment of tribute or providing of forced laborers (Deut. 20:10–11; see, e.g., Judg. 1:28, 30, 33, 35). If the enemy did not accept terms of surrender, a siege would ensue with the ultimate purpose of killing all of the enemy's males and taking the women, children, and property as booty. While sieges were brutal and affected noncombatants as well as soldiers, the level of permissible devastation was in some respects limited. Israelites were forbidden from cutting down fruit-bearing trees, since destroying the food supply would make the land desolate and permanently uninhabitable (Deut. 20:19–20).

Service in the Israelite army was by conscription, which may explain the Israelite census procedure that counted only those of military age and required payment of a ransom of atonement (see, e.g., Exod. 30:12–16) similar to that required of a person guilty of manslaughter (Exod. 21:29–31). When the army faced battle, those who might not fully dedicate themselves to the task were allowed to return home. These included the fearful, anyone who had just built a new house, planted a vineyard, or betrothed a wife. Such people were to enjoy their new possessions rather than risk death (Deut. 20:5–10). I Maccabees 3:56 speaks of the implementation of this practice.

The Pentateuch and historical writings view war positively, expressing the perspective of an Israelite nation pursuing the divine commandment to take control of the land of Israel. The prophetic literature, by contrast, considers war from the vantage point of a small and weak people beset by significantly more powerful adversaries. Within this context, Jeremiah advises submission to Babylon rather than entry into a war that the Israelites will certainly lose (Jer. 27:12–22). In general, the prophets depict war in all of its horror. They portray the messianic age as a time in which there will be no more war, when swords will be beaten into plowshares and spears into pruning hooks (Isa. 2:4; Mic. 4:3; Joel 3:10).

The rabbinic literature discusses the morality of going to war and the conditions under which war is permissible or even required. The rabbis broadly distinguished a discretionary war (*milḥemet reshut*) from one that was mandatory (*milḥemet ḥobah, milḥemet mitzvah*) (M. Sotah 8:7). A mandatory war was required to repel an attack on an Israelite city and could be declared by the king acting alone. This was in contrast to a discretionary war, which was initiated by the Israelites themselves in order to increase their territory. Such a war needed to be declared by the full Sanhedrin of seventy-one members (M. Sanhedrin 1:4). According to the rabbis, the Bible's exemption of certain people from fighting applies only in a discretionary war.

By contrast, in the case of an obligatory war, even a bride and bridegroom were required to join the battle (M. Sotah 8:7).

Rabbinic sources differ regarding the offer of terms of peace required by Deuteronomy 20:10–14. Sifre Deuteronomy 199 is explicit that terms of surrender are to be offered only in the case of a voluntary war; if Israel is attacked, no such negotiation is permitted. Leviticus Rabbah 17:6 and Deuteronomy Rabbah 5:13, by contrast, propose that Joshua offered the Canaanites terms of surrender, suggesting that Deuteronomy 20:10–14 applies even in the case of an obligatory war. Additional regulations control the actual conduct of the battle. For instance, while a siege should not be initiated within three days of the Sabbath, once started it is to be maintained even on the Sabbath until successful (Tosefta Erubin 4:7).

The Talmud holds that during the war for the conquest of the land of Israel, Israelite troops were permitted to eat meat found in Canaanite homes, even though such foodstuffs were normally forbidden under the dietary laws (B. Ḥullin 17a). In general, rabbinic texts propose that soldiers are released from ritual obligations that would impede their ability to find and prepare food in order to carry out their military objectives.

While the rabbis provide a system of laws indicating the circumstances under which wars may be fought and defining the conditions under which the enemy is to be engaged, their interest is largely theoretical. Though speaking of wars declared by king or Sanhedrin in defense of or to enlarge the territory of the land of Israel, the rabbis lived and worked in a period in which there was neither king nor Sanhedrin and in which Jews did not control the promised land. In practice, the rabbis' attitude toward war is illustrated by the actions attributed to Yoḥanan b. Zakkai, the founder of the rabbinic academy at Yabneh. In 70 c.e., unable to convince the Jews to give up their fight for freedom from Roman dominion, Yoḥanan reportedly escaped the besieged Jerusalem and went to the Roman camp, where he received permission from Vespasian to establish a center for study and religious observance (B. Gittin 56a–b). Rabbinic Judaism thus is founded on the precept that God demands that the people of Israel observe the terms of the covenant through the practice of its religious and social precepts and that war is not the best path to achieve God's messianic promise. *See also* WAR, HOLY.

war, holy Since "YHWH is a man of war" (Exod. 15:3), the idea that God fights for and with his covenant people, and sometimes against them (Amos 1–2), runs throughout biblical literature. Placing all the God-led wars of the Bible together led scholars to construct a "holy war" typology, with motifs of consultation of the deity, trumpet blasts to call an assembly and attack, consecration of the soldiers, YHWH's leadership, the need for total belief, the enemy's loss of courage as "divine terror" overtakes them, the carrying out of the ban, and dismissal of the army. More recent scholars have correctly pointed out that this scheme is only a construct and actual wars were not fought following this outline. Nevertheless, an early attempt to bring together disparate elements of a war code is found in Deuteronomy 20, and this summary was to be influential in later depictions of wars.

After the end of Judah's independence, which occurred with the destruction of the First Temple in 587 B.C.E., the language of holy war was used more and more to describe a final battle between YHWH and hostile nations (e.g., Zech. 14). One can note, however, how the Temple Scroll from Qumran carries on and develops the code of Deuteronomy 20, particularly emphasizing the need for sexual purity and consultation of the deity (11 QT 58:3–21), and how elements of holy-war language are found in the descriptions of battles fought by the Maccabees (e.g., 2 Macc. 8:12–29; 1 Macc. 3:17–24, 3:42–4:25. In 2 Maccabees one also has descriptions of divine helpers (10:29–30, 11:8), and here, besides the influence of Hellenistic historiography, one might also see the synergism between the heavenly and the earthly realms. Conflict between the Israelites and their enemies on earth is seen as but one aspect of a cosmic event. To the earthly war corresponds a war in heaven, alluded to in Daniel 10:20–11:1 but most fully sketched in the War of the Sons of Light against the Sons of Darkness (1QM). There one sees all the cultic requirements of the holy war fulfilled as the Israelites battle the Kittim, but this battle reflects the angel Michael's battle with Belial, and all are subsumed under the cosmic categories of light and darkness.

Finally, sometimes God acts with human agents (e.g., 1 Enoch 90:19), sometimes not (Dan. 7:26, 8:25, 11:45); and sometimes God acts through a Messiah (4 Ezra 11:36–12:3; 12:31–34; Test. Levi 18; Test. Judah 24; Test. Dan. 5:10–13; Ps. Sol. 17) or a transcendent agent (1 En. 37–71; 4 Ezra 13; 11 Q Melchizedek; Mark 13; Rev. 16).

Talmudic rabbis conceived of a future war fought to fulfill the divine promise that the Israelite nation would dwell sovereign and secure in the Promised Land. The concretization of such thinking is evident in the rabbinic reports that Akiba deemed Bar Kokhba to be the messiah, such that the Jewish Revolt against Rome in 133–135 C.E. was fought both in the name of God and in the person of the messiah under divine leadership. While familiar in its underlying idea to scripture's holy war, the rabbis did not describe the battle through which the nation will fulfill its destiny within the covenantal relationship in the terms operative in the biblical and later Hellenistic typologies of such wars. On the one hand, they conceived of God personally fighting on behalf of the Israelites against the other nations of the world (e.g., Mekhilta Shirata 1). On the other, they failed to delineate the character of this future war or to describe, for instance, the consecration of soldiers, the need for total belief, or the prospective enemy's terror. The rabbis' relatively minor concern for the eschatological battle reflects their insistence that the path to salvation is not war at all but the fulfillment of their nation's covenantal duty through observance of Torah.

War of Quietus   *see* TRAJAN, WAR OF

War of the Jews   *see* JEWISH WAR, THE

War of the Sons of Light and the Sons of Darkness   *see* WAR SCROLL

War Scroll   an eschatological text describing the battle between the armies of God and Belial, first discovered in 1947 in Cave 1, Qumran. This manuscript, 1QM (also known as Serekh haMilḥamah or War of the Sons of Light against the Sons of Darkness), the most complete of the manuscripts of the War Scroll, consists of nineteen badly mutilated columns of text, and was first published by E. L. Sukenik in 1954. Six other fragmentary manuscripts were found in Cave 4 in 1952 (4QM^{a-f}) and were published by M. Baillet in *DJD* VII. The manuscripts range in date from the first half of the first century B.C.E. to the mid-first century C.E. The date of composition is disputed, ranging from the Hasmonean to the late Herodian periods (an impossible date, given the date of the oldest manuscript).

The War Scroll is a description of the final eschatological battle that will take place between the Sons of Light, which includes an army of angels led by the archangel Michael in addition to the sect itself, and the Sons of Darkness, headed by Belial and including apostate Jews, the nations of the world as listed in Genesis 10, and the Kittim of Asshur, who should be identified in the later stages of the work as the Romans. The War Scroll is a composite document, with columns 1 and 15–19 describing the war against the Kittim, columns 2–9 describing a war forty years in length, and columns 10–14 containing miscellaneous hymns and prayers. Therefore, certain inconsistencies are noticeable. The war against the Kittim will take place in seven "lots": in three lots the Sons of Light will prevail; in three, the Sons of Darkness; and in the seventh God will intervene to defeat the forces of Belial. The war against the various nations, however, will last forty years, during which the army will rest every seventh year, in accordance with the sabbatical law.

The latter points to an important characteristic of the scroll: its concern with the correct conduct of the army and the purity of the camp (because of the presence of angels) leads to some definite impracticalities in the conduct of war. For example, the warriors are between forty and fifty years of age, while the baggage handlers are between twenty-five and thirty! Also, the war will be conducted by priests; the absence of any mention of a Davidic Messiah is remarkable. For reasons such as these, the war described in the War Scroll resembles a choreographed dance, where the enemies fall or flee on cue, rather than a practical manual for the conduct of battle.

washing of hands Scripture requires priests to wash their hands and feet prior to cultic service (Exod. 30:18–21). The rabbinic system of ritual purity focuses in particular upon hands, which, if unwashed, are held to suffer from second-degree uncleanness. In this state they convey uncleanness to food that is heave-offering, so that it may not be eaten by the priest. The Pharisees and later rabbis extended this concern for cultic cleanness to common Israelites, whom they wished to consume everyday food as though it were a sacrifice at the temple altar. Cleansing of the hands required a minimum of a quarter log of water, which was poured over the hands up to the wrists prior to the consumption of food (M. Yadaim 1:1, 2:3). The concern of this procedure was cultic not hygienic. For this reason almost any water could be used, no matter how dirty (M. Yadaim 1:3), and it could be poured out over the hands from any vessel, even one made of dung (M. Yadaim 1:2).

A "tradition of the elders" ignored by the disciples (Matt. 15:1–20; Mark 7:1–23), the practice of washing the hands is contrasted by Jesus with internal cleanliness. The negative resonance of the practice for early Christians is heightened in the Matthean passion narrative, when Pilate washes his hands to symbolize his innocence in Jesus' execution (Matt. 27:24).

watchers (Aram.: *irin*) a class of heavenly beings in 1 Enoch and Daniel, who serve primarily as messengers or envoys. The term is often combined with "holy ones" (*kaddishin;* see also Dan. 4: 13–23). Used alone in 1 Enoch 6–16, "watchers" designates the rebels who lost their holy state by mating with women. The term is usually derived from the Aramaic *ur* (to be awake, watchful), as indicated in 1 Enoch 39:12 (those who sleep not) and perhaps 1 Enoch 14:23, but the derivation is contested. Where the Aramaic fragments of 1 Enoch are extant, "watcher and holy one" is the counterpart to "holy angel" (*angelos hagios*) in the Greek translation. *See also* HOLY ONES; ANGELS.

water In biblical Jewish culture, water was, as it is now, an indispensable component and sustainer of life, and, by virtue of having these qualities, water also acquired a symbolic significance. Since it has always been a scarce commodity in the Land of Israel, water's very presence was seen in the biblical world as a blessing from God and a symbol of God's care for creation.

Water is also important in the Bible as a cleansing agent that can remove impurity and render an object "clean" or holy for ritual and other purposes. In the context of God's creation of the world, water represents both one of the primordial elements of creation (Gen. 1:1–10) and also the chaos that God overcame to create the world. In the flood story in Genesis 6–9, God uses water as an agent to both destroy and cleanse the earth.

In intertestamental Jewish literature, water retains many of the significations it had acquired in earlier times. On the one hand, it represents abundance, goodness, and grace. Ben Sira (15:3) and 4 Ezra (14:47) use water as a symbol of knowledge and wisdom. Several texts speak of the salvific qualities of "living water" or the "water of life" (1 Enoch 17:4; 1QH 8:7–16; CD 19:34). Ritual submersion of humans in water figures in several contexts—in Pharisaic proselyte baptism, in the Life of Adam and Eve 6–17, and, perhaps most notably, at Qumran, where purificatory ablutions before meals and on other occasions were mandated.

Water often figures in intertestamental literature in narratives of the process of creation (2 En. 27–28; 4 Ezra 6:41–52; Jdt. 9:12). It can designate the primeval chaos (Wisd. of Sol. 19:7) or the turbulence and raging of the sea (Wisd. of Sol. 5:22, 13:2). In Daniel 7, as in Revelation 13, evil beasts arise from the sea. Apocalyptic texts sometimes picture the drying up of the sea as a sign of the end of the world.

In early Christian usage, water generally carries a positive valence, due to an increasingly spiritualizing interpretation and to the importance of baptism. Perhaps the best-known reference is the story in John 4 of the Samaritan women at the well whom Jesus promises to provide with "living water," an unceasing source of spiritual refreshment. Salvific "living water" is also mentioned in the Odes of Solomon 6:8–18, 11:6–8, 30:1–7; John 7:38; Revelation 7:17; Ignatius' Letter to the Romans 7:2; and Didache 7:1-3.

The notion of "living water" also functions in an eschatological context, in, for example, Revelation 21–22. Here baptism in water combines the idea of purificatory cleansing or salvific power with the concept that the washing is an initial or preparatory eschatological cleansing.

In the rabbinic literature, water frequently symbolizes divine teachings, produced by the master and "drunk" by the disciple (e.g., B. Ḥagigah 3a; B. Baba Metzia 84b). Abtalion (M. Abot 1:11) worries that the result of sages' inappropriate talk will be exile to a place of "bad water," which later disciples will drink, causing them to die and to profane the name of heaven. Alongside this metaphorical usage, throughout the rabbinic literature, attention is placed on the role of water in the processes of cultic purification and to the procedure through which water is to be collected and used in the ritual bath (*mikveh*).

Wayiqra Rabbah   *see* LEVITICUS RABBAH

way of the land   (Heb.: *derekh eretz*) normal custom, correct conduct, good manners, courtesy, or etiquette; also, mode of earning a living, job, career, or profession. Disciples of sages are expected to master both Torah-learning and *derekh eretz*, that is, to study the Torah and also earn a living. They also are supposed to show *derekh eretz* to masters, that is, to treat teachers with dignity; and all Israelites are expected to display *derekh eretz*, that is, courtesy, to all persons they meet.

ways, two   a metaphor for the good and evil alternatives of human conduct. Depicting human actions as walking along a path was common in antiquity, and the imagery of the two ways is attested in texts as disparate as Xenophon's *Memorabilia* 2.21.21–34 and Jeremiah 21:8. Jewish and early Christian texts develop the metaphor in great detail.

The ways are described by word pairs that characterize the alternative types of behavior (righteousness and iniquity, truth and falsehood), the source of this activity (light and darkness), and its outcome (life and death). Good and evil spirits are companions along the way, battling for one's loyalty as they prompt one to right or wrong actions.

Sin involves straying or turning aside from the right path. The roads end at a pair of gates leading to eternal life or destruction. The continuity implied in travel along a road can characterize one's behavior as already participating in life or death (Wisd. of Sol. 1–6).

In early Jewish literature, the metaphor appears in a variety of genres with a wisdom flavor (see, e.g., Ecclus 15:11–12 [a collection of proverbs]; Tob. 4:5–6 [a narrative containing a testament]; 1 Enoch 91:3–4, 18–19; 94:1–4 [an apocalypse in testamentary form]). The Qumran Community Rule provides our first example of a special genre that structures ethical instruction around the imagery. There are two ways and two angels; the deeds appropriate to each are cataloged with reference to the vices and virtues that motivate them; then follow lists of the rewards and punishments for the two kinds of behavior (1QS 3:15–4:26). The Testament of Abraham literalizes the metaphor's eschatological aspect. Abraham watches souls being taken down two paths toward perdition and life (Test. Abr. 11 [a]; cf. Test. Asher).

The Sermon on the Mount ends with reference to the two ways and two gates appropriate to those who obey or disobey Jesus' teaching (Matt. 7:13–14). In Galatians 5:16–26, Paul organizes his ethical exhortation according to the alternatives of flesh and spirit, his counterparts to the two angelic principles that are at war with one another, catalogs the respective deeds in a manner similar to the Community Rule 3–4, admonishes his readers to "walk according to the spirit," and then mixing his metaphors, refers to the consequences of such behavior—the reaping of corruption and eternal life (Gal. 6:7–10). Later Christian texts building on the form found in the Community Rule include Didache 1–6; Barnabas 18–20; and the Mandates in the Shepherd of Hermas. *See also* DUALISM; ERROR; LIGHT AND DARKNESS.

ways of the Amorites   (Heb.: *darkhei haAmori*) practices deemed superstitious and forbidden, for example, use of charms or good luck omens

wealth   Attitudes about the possession and use of wealth varied in early Jewish writings and the Christian texts that were influenced by them. In the Deuteronomic view, the accumulation of wealth might be seen as a sign of divine favor for one's piety, and, in any case, splendid tombs and burials paraded the accomplishments of the rich. On the other hand, the poor and their protagonists could rail against the oppression of the rich (1 Enoch 94–105), and a text like 1 Enoch 103:5–8 pits the two points of view against one another. In general, writings in the wisdom tradition see wealth as ambiguous. The Book of Tobit encourages alms-giving and the responsible use of one's resources. For the sage, Ben Sira, generosity was a virtue, and the abuse of wealth was to be avoided (Ecclus. 13). His observation about undue dependence on one's wealth (11:18–19) stands in a long tradition that sometimes condemns the rich (1 Enoch 97:7–10; Luke 12:16–21; cf. also Mark 8:36–37). In the New Testament, the Gospel of Luke and the Epistle of James, in particular, encourage the responsible use of wealth and warn that God judges the oppressive rich. *See also* ALMS; MAMMON.

wedding   *see* ḤATTUNAH; MARRIAGE

weights and measures   those objects and vessels devised in Palestine to weigh and measure commodities, land, cloth, and other items. In the Persian period the old biblical weights and measures still pertained, though in certain areas, doubtless, the Persian system was imposed. In the Bible, the basic unit of dry measure was the *log*, usually calculated at 0.3 liters. There were twelve *log*s to the *hin*, seventy-two *log*s to the *bath*, and seven hundred and twenty *log*s to the *kor*. In dry measures, some of the measurements come from the Babylonian system and some from the Egyptian, so there are often curious relationships. For instance, the basic unit of dry measure is the *qav*. There are 1.8 *qav*s to the *omer-issaron*, six *qav*s to the *seah*, eighteen *qav*s to the *ephah*, ninety *qav*s to the *letekh,* and one hundred and eighty *qav*s to the *homer*. In terms of weight, the basic unit is the *shekel*, which is observed to average about 10 to 11.4 grams from archaeological finds of stone weights inscribed "shekel" in Hebrew. One-half *shekel* was a *beqa*, inscribed examples of which have been found, and one-twentieth of a *shekel* was the *gerah*. Inscribed stone weights in the form of round, polished limestone objects with flat bottoms, occur as five *gerah*, one *beqa*, one *netsef* (which is perhaps 5/6 of a *shekel*), one, two, four, eight, and forty *shekel*s. The *netsef* does not occur in the Bible and may not be part of the *shekel* system at all. Many weights inscribed "pim" have been found and average about 7.8 grams. This name occurs in 1 Samuel 13:21. On the other hand, weights have been found that are inscribed "beqa," but they do not weigh one-half *shekel*. The Phoenician system was also in use on the coast, in which fifty Phoenician *shekel*s (or *skater*s) make one *mine*. The Phoenician system also has one-half *shekel* and one-sixteenth *shekel*

weights. Phoenician weights resemble bronze blocks with flat tops. These and other finds suggest that there was more than one weight system available in the biblical period.

In the Hellenistic period, the papyri from the Jewish colony of Elephantine in Egypt mention the *seah* and the *qav*. In the Septuagint, or the Greek translation of the Bible, there appears an addition to Daniel called Bel. In Bel 3, two measures appear, the Persian *artaba* for flour and the Greek *metretes* (measure) for olive oil. At Qumran, a jar has been found inscribed "two seah and seven log."

By the time of the Talmud, the biblical system was correlated with the Roman system. Furthermore there is some literary evidence that weights and measures after 200 C.E. varied according to three systems: the measure of the wilderness, the measure of Jerusalem, and the measure of Sepphoris (B. Eruvim 83a). The basic measure of volume was the *log*. There were four *log*s to the *qav*, twelve *log*s to the *hin*, and seventy-two *log*s to the *ephah* or *bath*. There were also larger measures of volume: five *bath*s to the *letekh* and ten *bath*s to the *homer* or *kor*. Other units of dry measure include the Greek *sextarius*, which was considered the equivalent of one *log*. There was also the Roman *modius*, which was equivalent to 2/3 *seah*. The *modius* is depicted in ancient Greek or Roman art as a basket on the head of an Eastern goddess of fertility, such as Ceres.

Soft limestone vessels with two handles, often called "measuring cups" by their excavators, appear to be intended to hold one *log*. Most of these cups contain about 0.54 liter. Since the Talmud says that the ratio of the *seah*s of the wilderness, of Jerusalem, and of Sepphoris is 144:173:207 (the number of eggs that can be placed in each *seah* measure), and if the stone cup is the *log* of Jerusalem, then the *log* of the wilderness was about 0.45 liter and the *log* of Sepphoris was about 0.65 liter.

Units of length in the Talmudic period are the *etzba* (fingerbreadth), *tefach* (handbreadth or palm breadth), *zeret* (span from thumb to little finger), and *ammah* (cubit). According to literary sources there are six handbreadths to the cubit, or seven handbreadths to the royal cubit. The cubit is usually reckoned at about 45 centimeters (estimates range from 45 to 53.3 cm), which makes the royal cubit 52.5 centimeters. The ratio of fingerbreadth to palmbreadth to span to cubit is 24:6:3:1. Other measures include the Roman mile of 5,000 Roman feet, or 2,000 cubits. The Roman mile was also reckoned at 7.5 *stadia*. The Persian league (*parasang;* Heb.:

parsah) was reckoned at thirty *stadia*. During this period one could also measure according to the Roman cubit of about 1.6 Roman feet.

During the Talmudic period, it appears that the *shekel* was about half the weight of the Biblical *shekel*. There was a mixture of Roman and Jewish systems. There were 3,000 *shekels* to the *kikkar* (*talent*, 34.2 kg), eighty *shekels* to the *mina* or fifty *shekels* to the Italian *mina*, twenty-five *shekels* to the *tartimar*, four *shekels* to the Roman *uncia*, and two *shekels* to the *sela* or Greek *tetradrachm*, actually a silver coin. One *zuz* weighed one-half *shekel*. The Roman *litra* or *libra* (lb, 360 g) was also in use. The *libra* was divided into twelve *uncia* or forty-eight *sicilici*. Many examples of Roman pounds or other weights have been excavated. One square and flat lead weight recovered at Sepphoris was inscribed with the name of the market official, Simon, and was evidently his official weight.

In the Byzantine period, the *libra* or *litra* was still in use, as was the *uncia* (Gr.: *ouggia*). The *libra* was further divided into seventy-two *numisma* (Gr.: *exagios*) or ninety-six *drachma*, which was also a coin. The *gramma* (Lat.: *scripulum*) was one-third of a *drachma*, the *obol* was one-sixth of a *drachma*, and the *keratios* (Lat.: *siliqua*) was one-eighteenth of a *drachma*. Byzantine weights are flat round discs or flat squares with the weight clearly inscribed on the top.

Measures of area in the Bible were usually expressed in square cubits, but in the Mishnah they are expressed as so many cubits by so many cubits. A second system is to describe the area by the amount of seed required to sow it. A field that required one *seah* of seed to sow would be described as a *beth seah*, which equals 2,000 square cubits. Other such areas include the *beth rova* of about 10.5 by 10.5 cubits, and the *beth kor*, which is a plot of land that requires one *kor* of seed to sow.

Western Aramaic   *see* ARAMAIC, WESTERN

Western Wall   (Heb.: Kotel Maara<u>bi</u>) wall of the Second Temple in Jerusalem, which survived the destruction of 70 C.E. and still stands as a Judaic shrine today

wheel   a minor motif in Jewish art, particularly Roman and Byzantine synagogue art. The wheel is simple and unadorned with varying numbers of spokes. For example, a wheel with nine or ten spokes appears to the left of an eagle with outstretched wings in a stone relief fragment from the synagogue of Umm el-Kanatir in the Golan Heights. A wheel with eight spokes was found painted on a ceiling in one of the catacombs of Beth Shearim. A nine-spoked wheel appears in low relief on a lintel in the synagogue of Eshtomoa south of Jerusalem. A six-spoked wheel appeared in low relief on a stone from the synagogue of Khirbet Kanef. The motif also appears on the bottom of late Byzantine lamps, but it was not intended to be seen. No one knows what such a wheel might represent.

Wicked Priest   the label given to one of the enemies of the Teacher of Righteousness, the leader of a group of Jewish sectaries who eventually settled at Qumran. The sobriquet "Wicked Priest" appears in the Habakkuk Commentary and the Commentary on Psalm 37, where a portrait emerges of a ruling high priest who persecutes the Teacher of Righteousness and his followers, but who is eventually punished by God. The Habakkuk Commentary describes him as one "called by the name of truth when he first arose. But when he ruled over Israel his heart became proud, and he forsook God and betrayed the precepts for the sake of riches. . . . And he lived in the ways of abominations amidst every unclean defilement" (1QpeshHab 8:8–13). Further, the Habakkuk Commentary claims that the Wicked Priest pursued the Teacher to his settlement, disrupting the Day of Atonement; and 4QpeshPs 37 states that he tried to murder the Teacher. Finally, however, the Wicked Priest is murdered by his enemies (1QpeshHab).

Two candidates emerge for the identification of the Wicked Priest: Jonathan and Simon, the Maccabees. Both held the office of high priest in the mid- to late second century B.C.E., and both died a violent death. However, the sect seemed to favor the Wicked Priest at the beginning of his rule, and only condemned him for iniquity later. This would seem to fit Jonathan slightly better, since he began his rule as the hero of the Maccabean war, but later fell into the habits of an oriental despot. Moreover, Jonathan was killed by his enemies the Seleucids, while Simon was murdered by his son-in-law. Overall, then, Jonathan seems the best candidate for the Wicked Priest.

widow   in biblical and Hellenistic traditions, a woman whose husband has died. A widow without sons may have entered into a levirate marriage or, if released, sought a new husband. Some widows, especially the wealthy, did as they pleased (Judith), yet others returned to their childhood homes (Tamar to her father's house; Orpah to her mother's). For widows without means, public protection was mandated (Deut. 10:18, 24:17–22; Isa. 1:17; Jer. 49:11, etc.). The Apocalypse of Zephaniah 7:4 (visiting widows and sick men); 4 Ezra 2:20; several passages in the Testament of Job; and Sibylline Oracles 2:76 and 270–271 emphasize proper treatment of widows, while Sibylline Oracles 3:75–93 describes Cleopatra as a widow whose universal rule is accompanied by cosmic destruction.

According to Luke 7:11–17, Jesus restores life to a widow's son, hails the Temple contribution made by a poor widow (the "widow's mite," Mark 12:42–44; Luke 21:1–4), and condemns those who "eat up widows' houses" (Mark 12:40). Christian teaching includes exhortations to maintain widows at the community's expense (1 Tim. 5:4, 16; see also Acts 6:1–6). The overlooking of Hellenist widows in the daily food distribution prompted the appointing of deacons (Acts 6:1-6). First Timothy 5:3–16 establishes three sets of widows: real, to be supported by the church; enrolled, to provide congregational service; and young, to be remarried lest they become idle gossips (1 Tim. 5:3–16).

Under rabbinic law, a widow could continue to live in her deceased husband's house or return to her own father's home. In either case, she was supported from her dead husband's estate until she either remarried or accepted full payment of her dowry and jointure. These sums could be exacted from any of the estate's assets, even landed property, which the widow had the right to sell in order to collect her due. The widow's claim upon the estate generally was prior to that of other creditors. The rabbis contemplate the widow's remarriage, although her apparently reduced value as a bride was reflected in the monetary terms of her new marriage contract. The stipulated jointure of a widow who remarried was 100 *zuz,* half that of a virgin-bride (M. Ketubot 1:2). While Leviticus 21:14 prohibits a high priest from marrying a widow, rabbinic law holds that, should appointment as high priest occur after the marriage, he may retain her as his wife (B. Yebamot 77a).

wilderness of Judea the narrow strip of rugged arid land, about ten miles wide, descending from the mountains stretching from Jerusalem–Jericho in the north to the southern end of the Dead Sea. It was a place of escape or retreat. In the wake of the Maccabean Revolt and the Hasmonean assumption of the high priestly office, a group of priests and scribes established their new exodus and covenantal community in the wilderness of Judea at Qumran near the northeast corner of the Dead Sea, where the Dead Sea Scrolls were found in 1947. Much farther south, Herod built his nearly impregnable fortress at Masada, where the Sicarii held out

against the Roman siege for years prior to their mass suicide. The Gospel of Matthew locates the preaching of John the Baptist in "the wilderness of Judea" (Matt. 3:1).

will the last instructions of a dying person to his family regarding the disposal of his property and their future conduct and often expressing a blessing for them, as in the wills or testaments of the biblical figures Abraham, Jacob, and Moses. Property distribution often was not a primary issue since it was fixed by rabbinic law, which allocated a double portion for the firstborn and equal inheritance for the remaining sons. Deathbed bequests had special validity in the rabbinic system. Written wills were accepted as valid by rabbinic authorities in accord with the prevailing local customs.

wine the primary beverage of antiquity. The rabbinic use of the Hebrew word for wine, *yayin,* connotes the undiluted extract of grapes. It was mixed or diluted with water before the liquid was consumed. Rabbinic custom prescribed that grace recited over every meal be accompanied by a cup of wine (Ber. 50a). The individual blessing over wine was central to the table ritual for the inauguration and conclusion of Sabbaths and festivals (namely, the rituals of *kiddush* and *habdalah*). Four cups of wine were drunk at the Passover Seder and a fifth was set aside for Elijah (M. Pesah. 10). Mourners drank several cups of wine as consolation according to custom (Ketub. 8b). The Talmud encouraged moderation in drinking wine, citing its medicinal and health values (B. Bat. 58b). Alcohol abuse was not a dominant concern, although the Talmud prescribed some remedies for drunkenness (Shabb. 66b). Wine used in pagan ritual was deemed unclean and prohibited. Any ordinary wine prepared or handled by non-Jews also was prohibited either because it was suspected to have been a libation to a pagan god or because the rabbis wanted to restrict social interaction between Jews and Gentiles (Abod. Zar. 36b).

Wine, Festival of New *see* NEW WINE, FESTIVAL OF

Wisdom, figure of Wisdom was pictured as a woman as early as Proverbs 8 and 9, and the figure continued to develop in later Jewish writings, such as the Wisdom of Solomon. In writings such as those of Philo of Alexandria, it moves on further to become a hypostasis and interchangeable with the Logos. The origin of the figure of Wisdom is much debated. Wisdom in Proverbs 8 and 9 seems more than just a personification of an abstract quality. Many think that the description has been influenced by the language used of various godesses, such as Isis and Maat from Egypt.

wisdom literature a modern designation for two types of texts in the Bible: (1) aphoristic sayings or instructions, and (2) reflective analyses of existence, particularly divine justice and life's meaning. Besides Proverbs, Job, and Ecclesiastes, wisdom literature includes two books in the Apocrypha, Sirach and Wisdom of Solomon. This king's reputation for wisdom led later editors to attribute the majority of the wisdom corpus to him, although others questioned the accuracy of that tradition. A few psalms, especially 37, 49, and 73, resemble Job and Ecclesiastes in asking profound questions. Both types of wisdom texts were common in Egypt and Mesopotamia, and some familiarity with these writings by Jewish authors appears likely.

Egyptian wisdom consists of instructions from as early as the third millennium and "sentences" from as late as the second century B.C.E. The most significant of the former are the Instructions of Ptah-hotep, Ani, and Amenemope, while Papyrus Insinger and Ankhsheshanky make up the most notable texts from the latter. The philosophical reflections are represented in a brief section of The Admonitions of Ipuwer, as well as The Dialogue of a Man with his Soul. Scribal texts and The Teaching of Duauf praise the profession of scholars. Mesopotamian wisdom, largely magic and incantation, contains reflection on suffering (A Man and His God; I Will Praise the Lord of Wisdom; The Babylonian Theodicy; and A Dialogue between a Master and His Slave) and proverbial collections (The Instructions of Suruppak; Sumerian, Neo-Assyrian, and Babylonian sayings). An incomplete Aramaic wisdom text, the Sayings of Ahikar, has survived.

The social location of the sages in Egypt and Mesopotamia was the school, whether secular or within temple precincts, and the profession was at times connected with the royal court. In Israel the earliest proverbial sayings arose among the folk, then were transmitted by parents instructing their children on ways to attain success. Over the years these teachings were given literary form so as to function in the professional education of male scribes, perhaps for the royal court in Hezekiah's day. The world of the aphorisms is the small town, with family at the center and ordinary life as the fundamental concerns.

Wisdom themes naturally cover a swath as wide as life itself, but its perspective is that of a reasoned analysis based on experience. Observation of nature and human behavior led to conclusions about laws governing one's efforts to master daily experience. By drawing analogies from one realm and applying them to another, sages endeavored to withstand all threat and to attain wealth, honor, progeny, and long life. Philosophical probings about life's meaning, divine justice, and the possibility of pure virtue complemented "practical" wisdom.

At the center of wisdom literature was the idea that religious devotion, the fear of the Lord, preceded all knowledge, indeed was its final destination as well. Good people were called wise, wicked persons fools. Foreign women posed the chief threat to sages; this expression may have been a religious designation for strange types of worship, including sexual behavior. Her rival, personified Wisdom, was the agent of creation and the guide of sages in their quest for knowledge. Early optimism about the power of human reason eventually waned and sages looked to sacred traditions to supplement a flawed intellect. In this way the distinctive perspective of wisdom literature was compromised by revelation.

Wisdom of Jesus ben Sirach *see* SIRACH, WISDOM OF

Wisdom of Solomon *see* SOLOMON, WISDOM OF

witness *see* TESTIMONY

woe a literary form that laments the fate of the wicked. Attested frequently in the prophetic corpus of the Hebrew Bible, woes begin with a stereotyped formula, "Woe to you (*or* those) who . . . ," that is followed by a description of the conduct, quality, or situation that is the cause for the lament and a prediction of judgment. Derived from mourning cries in ancient Israel, the form was employed by the prophets to express their distress over the sins of the people and the nations, and to contrast present arrogance, especially sins of social oppression, with the disasters that awaited the sinners when judgment was exacted on the day of YHWH (Isa. 5:8–22; Jer. 22:13; Amos 5:18, 6:1). The woe is one of several prophetic forms employed by Ben Sira (Ecclus. 2:12–14, 41:8–9). Its most striking use, however, is in 1 Enoch 92–105, where thirty-six woes, most of them shorter than their biblical counterparts, punctuate the seer's message of imminent judgment on the rich and powerful who oppress the righteous and poor. Similar woes are juxtaposed with Luke's version of Jesus' beatitudes, thus contrasting the future fate of the righteous and the wicked (Luke 6:24–26). *See also* BEATITUDE.

woes of the Messiah an expression that has been somewhat literally translated from the "birthpangs [Heb.: ḥebalim; Gr.: ōdines] of the Messiah." An idea current as early as the late Second Temple period was that the days preceding the Messiah would be ones of social trouble and even cosmic upheaval.

woman, born of circumlocution for "human being" (Job 14:1, 15:14), used in the Community Rule 11:20–21 parallel to the term "son of man." Paul employs it to refer to Jesus' humanity (Gal. 4:4; cf. Rom. 8:3).

women, in Jewish inscriptions the appearance of women's names and titles in inscriptions on material such as stone, ceramic, metal, ivory, or even glass. Inscriptions may consist of only a few letters or contain entire texts of several hundred words. Jewish inscriptions appear on a diversity of objects, from marble memorial or dedicatory plaques on synagogue walls to ceramic oil lamps used for lighting. Many of these inscriptions were created by women, or mention the names of women. Most frequently, names of women are found on tombs as parts of epitaphs. Sometimes the woman's name may be accompanied by a title such as the Greek *kura* (lady), which was popular in tomb inscriptions of Jewish women. A symbol such as a menorah, olive branch, or shofar may also appear on the epitaph.

Hebrew, Aramaic, Greek, or Latin are the languages in which Jewish inscriptions are written, although often women's names (and men's) may be transliterated from one language to another. For instance, an inscription may be written in Hebrew, but the names may be transliterations of Greek names, or it may be written in Latin with Hebrew names. There are many examples of this type of difference between the language of the inscription and the language of origin of the name.

An inscription on a coffin lid (late 2d c. C.E. to the beginning of the 3d c. C.E.) from Beth Shearim in Palestine provides an example of a Hebrew inscription with the title "lady" and where the woman's name is Mega, a Hebrew transliteration of the Greek word *megas* (large): "This is the coffin of the lady Mega, the wife of Rabbi Joshua, son of Levi. Peace."

Inscriptions about women are not limited to tombs, however. A number of inscriptions have been found in synagogues commemorating women donors. The Tralles synagogue at Caria contains a good example of a donation inscription (3d c. C.E.). The woman's name is a Greek transliteration of a Latin name: "I, Capitolina, most worthy and God-fearing, having made the entire threshold, decorated this staircase with mosaic on behalf of a vow for myself and my children, and for my family. Blessings."

Many more examples of Judaic women's inscriptions exist in ancient Jewish catacombs and synagogues, and include names from a variety of languages: Sara, Marame, Rahel (Heb.); Theodora, Artemis, Irene (Gr.); Julia, Veriana, Caelia (Lat.); Zera (Aram.). As well as being found in Palestine, these inscriptions have appeared in locations scattered all over the ancient Mediterranean, including Greece, Rome, Syria, Egypt and Africa.

women, position of *In biblical times.* The Bible envisioned a society in which men were heads of household and women were subordinate to and dependent upon them. The basis of biblical Judaism was a covenant struck between God and the Jewish people: in exchange for worshiping Him and performing prescribed acts of piety, God promised security, prosperity, and continuity. Although all stood at Sinai, the covenant was made with the men, and through the men, with the women. Evidence of this can be found in the Ten Commandments, which say—to men— "Do not covet your neighbor's wife" (Exod. 20:17) and in the holiness code in Leviticus 18, which lists the various consanguineous women with whom a man may not have a sexual relationship. Even though much of biblical law bound women as well, it was men who transmitted it to them and who were responsible for its implementation. In fact, biblical society was defined in terms of its male members, as indicated by the census in Exodus 30, and in Numbers 1 and 26, which counted adult males but no women or children.

The principal legal institutions of biblical society favored men. It was a man who took himself a wife, paid her father a bride-price, bound her to him, and set her aside for his exclusive use. It was therefore only he, and not she, who could end the marriage, by giving her a bill of divorcement and dismissing her from his home (Deut. 24:1). She could not choose to leave of her own accord or remain against his will. Within marriage, however, he was required to provide for all her needs.

Since marriage was not viewed as an exclusive relationship between the two members of a couple but as ownership of a woman by a man, adultery was defined as sexual relations between a married woman and any man other than her husband, either married or unmarried. Since married men were not forbidden to have sexual relations with unmarried women, it follows that wives had no claims on husbands for marital fidelity; husbands, however, could not only demand it of their wives but even test for innocence or guilt. Numbers 5:5–31 sets forth in gruesome detail the ordeal to which a wife must submit if her husband merely suspects her of extramarital sexual activity.

The punishments the Bible prescribes for crimes against women yield an even sharper understanding of women's status, both before and during marriage. The Bible deems the rape of an already betrothed girl far more serious than that of an unbetrothed girl—the former being a capital crime and the latter punishable only by forced, indissoluble marriage of the rapist to the woman he raped (Deut. 22:25–29)—because from the future husband's perspective, what he had paid for and had not yet taken possession of had been appropriated for use by someone else.

According to the Bible, it was incumbent upon a wife to bear children for her husband. The special case of levirate marriage, still in effect today, shows that the course of a woman's marital life was determined by her ability to fulfill this male prerogative (Deut. 25:5–10). If a man died childless, his widow was not free to remarry but was considered to be already betrothed to his brother. The purpose of her marriage to her levir was to produce an heir, presumably a male, who would continue the name and line of his father's deceased brother and inherit his property. In this situation, a woman glided from one marriage to the next, suffering no period of financial distress, but having no choice of life options or partners. It was only the levir who could choose to release his sister-in-law from the marital bond, by undergoing a ceremony called *halitzah;* she could not refuse to live with him.

In economic matters women were totally dependent on men. Real estate, the most valued asset, was usually owned by men. According to the Bible, the Land of Israel was to be distributed to men only (Num. 26:53, 27:6–11). Upon death, a man's parcel of land was to pass to his agnatic kin—sons, brothers, or uncles. In the event that he left no sons but only daughters, they were to supersede all other relatives and inherit their father's land, sharing it among themselves. In cases like these, women were required to marry within the tribe so as not to reduce its land holdings.

The laws of vows (Num. 30:2–17) provide an important—but limited—exception to the general rule of women's subordinate status. It was standard behavior in the biblical period for people to take a vow in order to influence or implore God to grant a request. In return for engaging in some form of self-denial, the vowing individual hoped to gain healing for a sick family member or the safe return from war of a husband or son. The main point of this section of Torah is to distinguish between

men's and women's vows. If a man takes a vow, no matter what transpires, he must keep his word; if a woman takes a vow, her intentions may be subverted by either father or husband. However, Numbers 30:11 notes, the vows of widows and divorcees may not be canceled by anyone. Thus women as women are viewed as competent and able to maintain absolute control over their own affairs, religious and even financial. But when they are under the aegis of a father or husband, their vows need approval.

In ritual areas, men predominated: it was the males of the priestly class who served as religious functionaries in the Temple and lay Israelite men who were bidden to make a pilgrimage to the Temple three times a year. Women, however, did take some part in organized religious life. Their ability to enter the holy precincts of the Temple was impaired by their regular periods of ritual uncleanness due to menstrual flow (Lev. 15:19–30). But when ritually clean, women could bring voluntary offerings and were even required to bring a sin-offering after each birth. As for ritual restrictions, such as not working on the Sabbath, fasting on Yom Kippur, and avoiding leaven on Pesah, women were bound by these rules, just as men were.

The one area in a woman's life in which she achieved parity with men was her status as a parent. In the eyes of the Bible, the older generation, both males and females, had absolute authority over the younger. A child was to honor and fear both its father and its mother; a son or daughter who cursed or struck either parent was to be put to death (Exod. 21:15, 17). Both mother and father had to declare a son rebellious for him to be punished (Deut. 21:18–21). Upon death, the same rites of mourning obtained for a mother as for a father (Lev. 21:2).

It is thus evident that Judaism in the biblical period was, in general, both androcentric and patriarchal. Women were dependent upon men but also protected and supported by them. Although important life decisions were made for a woman by others, and she had no involvement in or control over financial matters, she seems to have occupied a secondary but not insignificant role in society. Inasmuch as the Bible envisioned a sacred society, women were included in that vision but were accountable to men, who in turn were accountable for them to God.

One of the unresolved issues regarding the position of women in Judaism in the biblical period is the relationship of law to life. Did the social realities conform to the legal prescriptions? The narrative portions of the Bible suggest that women's position in society, although not equal to that of men, was still not as subordinate and marginal as one might have expected. The matriarchs, as well as other female biblical characters, exhibited independence of thought and action and critically influenced the course of Jewish history, although differently from men. Rebecca behaved more like a patriarch than did her passive husband, Isaac, securing the patriarch's blessing for her favorite son, Jacob, to whom it was meant to go, and thwarting Isaac's plan to bestow it upon Esau, his favorite (Gen. 27). Tamar (Gen. 38) and Ruth, in different ways, each enticed a man to engage in marital or quasi-marital sexual relations so that he would maintain the family's line. In reward for and acknowledgment of the merit of their actions, each of them became an ancestress of King David. These heroines, and scores of others who appear throughout the Bible, show that women, despite sociolegal limitations, could act resolutely to shape the future according to their own vision.

Traditionalist perspective. In the Mishnah, where we find the postbiblical law of Judaism, the dominant interest is in two crucial stages in the transfer of women and of property from one domain to another: (1) the leaving of the father's house for the husband's through marriage; and (2) the leaving of the husband's house at the marriage's dissolution through divorce, the husband's death, or the wife's infidelity. There is yet a third point of interest, though it is much less important than these first two stages: (3) the duration of the marriage. Women have numerous rights in the law of the Mishnah. Even while married, women may become property owners of substance, as their fathers leave them land. True, the husband enjoys the usufruct so long as the marriage continues. But the woman is ultimate owner. That means the husband has every material reason to want to preserve those conditions that will secure and perpetuate the marriage. Moreover, the Mishnah makes provision for a husband's relinquishing his rights over his wife's property, even as a condition of marriage. The Mishnah, within its theoretical frame, accords the woman rights of property. It secures the marriage, through the marriage contract and its settlement upon the occasion of divorce or death of the husband, so that the wife is not completely dependent upon the husband. The woman does not enjoy a position in her realm equivalent to that of the man, in his. But a woman's status in this system is not that of utterly lacking a measure of autonomy, dignity, and control of her own affairs. It is the point at which a woman is perceived as requiring legislation—when she has the capacity to become a wife and a mother but is not yet in a position of realizing it, or when she ceases to be a wife—that her status requires the regulation, ordering, and protection of Mishnah's elaborate and reverent intellectual attention.

Women are treated as anomalous by the law of Judaism represented in the Mishnah and its commentaries, the two Talmuds. The anomaly of woman is addressed at its most anomalous, that is, disorderly and dangerous, moment, the point at which women move from one setting and status to another. The very essence of the anomaly, woman's sexuality, is scarcely mentioned. But it always is just beneath the surface. For what defines a woman's status—what is rarely made explicit in the Division of Women—is not whether she may have sexual relations, but with whom she may have them and with what consequence. It is assumed that long before the advent of puberty, a girl may be married and in any event is a candidate for sexuality. From puberty onward, she will be married. But what is selected for intense and continuing concern is with whom she may legitimately have sexual relations, and with what economic and social effect. There is no sexual deed without public consequence; and only rarely will a sexual deed not yield economic results, in the aspect of the transfer of property from one hand to another. What is anomalous is the woman's sexuality, which is treated in a way wholly different from a man's. And the goal and purpose of Mishnah's Division of Women are to bring under control and force into stasis all of the wild and unruly potentialities of sexuality, with their dreadful threat of uncontrolled shifts in personal status and material possession alike.

The Mishnah invokes heaven's interest in this critical moment for individual and society alike. Its conception is that what is rightly done on earth is confirmed in heaven. A married woman who has sexual relations with any man but her husband has not merely committed a crime on earth. She has sinned against heaven. It follows that when a married woman receives a writ of divorce and thus is free to enter into relationships with any man of her choosing, this, too, is confirmed in heaven. What was beforehand a crime and a sin afterward is holy, not subject to punishment at all. The woman may contract a new marriage on earth, which heaven, for its part, will oversee and sanctify. What is stated in these simple propositions is that those critical turnings at which a woman changes domains produce concern and response in heaven as much as on earth. And the reason is that heaven is invoked specifically at those times, and in those circumstances, in which the Mishnah confronts a situation of anomaly or disorder and proposes to effect suitable regulation and establish order.

It is to a situation that is so fraught with danger as to threaten the order and regularity of the stable, sacred society in its perfection and at its point of stasis that the Mishnah will devote its principal cognitive and legislative efforts. For such a situation, the Mishnah will invoke heaven and express its most vivid concern for sanctification. What breaks established routine is subject to the fully articulated and extensive reflections of a whole division of the Mishnah. The Mishnah provides its own most reliable exegesis in calling each one of its six principal divisions an order (Heb.: *seder*). The anomaly of woman is worked out, that is, held in stasis, by assigning her to man's domain. It follows that the stasis is disturbed at the point when she changes hands. Then Mishnah's instincts for regulating and thereby restoring the balance and order of the world are aroused. Thus from the recognition of the anomalous character of women, we find ourselves moving toward the most profound and fundamental affirmations of the Mishnah about the works of sanctification: the foci and the means. Women are sanctified through the deeds of men. So, too, are earth and time, the fruit of the herd and of the field, the bed, chair, table, and hearth—but in the nature of things, women most of all. *see also* GENDER ROLES, IN RABBINIC JUDAISM; MARRIAGE; VIRGIN; WIDOW.

Woodgathering, Feast of festival mentioned by Josephus at the time of the siege of Jerusalem during the 66–70 C.E. war. It was apparently given in celebration of bringing wood for the altar. Such a festival is now known from the Temple Scroll found at Qumran, as are the Feast of New Wine and Feast of New Oil.

word of God (Heb.: *daḇar elohim;* Gr.: *logos tou theou* or *hrēma theou;* more idiomatically translated, the message of God) Since the God of the Bible is perceived as a personal God who is vitally concerned with human destiny, He is depicted as revealing His will to humanity in the form of speech, so that the word of God is the primary way in which the biblical God disclosed Himself to human beings. In the Hebrew Bible the phrase word of God is occasionally used of the revelatory message communicated to prophets and priests by God in the formula "the word of God came to Nathan" (1 Kings 12:22; see 1 Chron. 17:3; Luke 3:2), and the resultant message proclaimed by the prophet can be designated as "the word of God" (1 Sam. 9:27). The formula preferred in the Hebrew Bible, however, is "the word of YHWH," or "the word of the Lord," in such expressions as "the word of the Lord came to Ezekiel" (Ezek. 1:1; see 1 Sam. 15:10; 1 Kings 6:11; Jon. 1:1; Hag. 1:1; Zech. 1:1). The message which prophets proclaim is therefore called "the word of the Lord" (1 Sam. 8:10; 1 Kings 12:25; Isa. 1:10; Jer. 36:11), which can be proclaimed with the formula "hear the word of the Lord" (Isa. 1:10; Hos. 4:1). The Torah or Law which was revealed to Israel at Mount Sinai by Moses, particularly the Ten Commandments, is also understood as divine revelation and is called "the word of God" (Exod. 24:4, 34:21–27; Ps. 119:10–11). The Hebrew phrase translated "the Ten Commandments" literally means "the Ten Words" (Exod. 34:28).

In the New Testament "the word of God" is used from the Hebrew Bible or Greek Septuagint (Mark 7:13; Matt 15:6). In the Gospels the phrase is used for the teachings of Jesus only in Luke (5:21, 8:11, 21, 11:28), though the other Gospels use analogous phrases such as "the word" or "my [i.e., Jesus'] word" (Mark 2:2, 33, 4:14; John 8:31), "the word of the Kingdom" (Matt. 13:19). In the New Testament generally, the phrase "the word of God" is frequently used of the gospel or good news, that is, the early Christian proclamation of the saving significance of the death and resurrection of Jesus (1 Cor. 14:26; Col. 1:25; Phil. 1:14; Rev. 1:2, 9, 6:9, 20:4). This is particularly the case in Acts where "the word of God" is virtually used as a technical term for the Christian gospel (e.g., Acts 4:31, 6:2, 7, 12:24, 13:5, 7).

A special development of the phrase "word of God" occurs in the New Testament and early Christian literature when it is applied to Jesus in a variety of ways. In Revelation 19:13, the rider on the white horse depicted as the warrior Messiah (see Pss. Sol. 17:24 and Wisd. of Sol. 18:15–16), is implicitly identified as the returning Christ, and called "the Word of God." In John 1:1–5, in what appears to be a midrashic interpretation of Genesis 1:1–5, the preincarnate Jesus is called "the Word" and identified with God. The claim that this Word is the means whereby the universe was created (John 1:3) appears to be a development of the notion that the heavens were created "by the word of God" (Heb. 11:3; 2 Pet. 3:5), that is, by the command of God. In 1 John 1:1 (probably an interpretation of John 1:1–3), the incarnate Jesus is designated "the Word of life." *See also* LOGOS.

Words of the Heavenly Lights Hebrew composition for which three fragmentary manuscripts were found in Cave 4, Qumran, in 1952, and subsequently published in DJD VII in 1982. Their editor, M. Baillet, assigns a paleographic date of the mid-second century B.C.E. to the earliest of the three manuscripts; thus the date of composition must be prior to that.

The Words of the Heavenly Lights, or Words of the Luminaries, takes its title from the unusual fact that a probable title is actually written on the reverse of one of the fragments (Heb., Dibrei haMeorot). The contents of the text were collective prayers for each of the days of the week; the mention of the fourth day (Wednesday) and the Sabbath are preserved on the fragments. Most of the preserved text seems to be the prayer for Friday.

The prayers are pleas for the forgiveness of sin; the sin is spoken of in general terms ("we were sold because of our iniquities, but despite our offenses thou didst call us"); the plea to God for forgiveness is made on the basis of the chosenness of Israel ("For thou hast named Israel 'my son, my first born'"), and the language of the whole is heavily dependent on biblical imagery ("Thou hast carried us marvelously [on the wings of] eagles"; cf. Exod. 19:4). In form, content, and language these prayers are similar to the ancient "supplication" prayer found in the daily Jewish liturgy.

There is nothing that can be identified as sectarian in the language of the prayers; and the composition of the text, based on the date of the oldest manuscript, must take place before the founding of the settlement at Qumran (c. 150–135 B.C.E.). The mention of Adam and the Garden of Eden (frg. 8) are unusual in a Qumran document and may again point to a non-Qumranic origin. However, its lack of sectarian characteristics does not allow for the claim that this was not considered a sectarian composition by the sectaries themselves; the text was certainly stored by the sectaries at Qumran and may have been used by them in a liturgical context.

works *see* DEEDS, WORKS

world in the Hebrew Bible, the whole sphere of God's creation; the part of creation inhabited by humans.

Intertestamental Jewish literature continues these meanings, supplementing them with the idea of the "world" as the sphere of human activity. A common expression here is "the whole world," denoting all human life. Another important concept, expressed mainly in apocalyptic literature, is that God will one day "judge" and destroy the world.

The letters of Paul in the New Testament are among the earliest Judaism-based sources in which "world" takes on a distinctly negative connotation. Here the term denotes the lower element of an ontological dualism between "the world" and the realm of God. Paul not only recommends being "crucified" to the world (Gal. 6:14), but also speaks of "the god of this world" as a negative force (2 Cor. 4:4). In the New Testament's Gospel of John and Johannine letters, this dualism is carried to an extreme: the "world" is completely evil. Although some Jewish writings of the late first and the second centuries (e.g., 4 Ezra) speak of "this world" as a place of sorrow, corruption, and unrighteousness, none of them evinces the radically negative valuation of the "world" attested in many early Christian writings.

In rabbinic Judaism the concept of world is intertwined with that of Torah. The first of God's creations, the Torah comprised the blueprint subsequently used by God to make the world (Sifre Deut. 37; Gen. Rabbah 1:1, M. Abot 3:14; see Prov. 8:22). Concomitantly, the world was created for the sake of Torah (Gen. Rabbah 12:2). In rabbinic thinking, the law and the world thus are unitary and, as creations of God, perfect. Observance of the laws of Torah accordingly entails acts that are neither random nor discretionary. Through Torah, rather, people conform to the character of the world as God meant it to exist. Only because people have failed consistently to do this and so have destroyed God's originally perfect creation, do the rabbis look forward to a coming world, separate from current life. Unlike Paul and the Gospel of John, however, they do not view the current world as intrinsically evil or corrupt.

world to come *see* AGE TO COME

world year the concept that the world went through a cycle of several thousand years, at which time it came to an end or the cycle began again. The idea is found in Stoicism which taught that an evental *ekpyrosis* (universal conflagration) would destroy everything and begin the cycle again. Zoroastrianism developed a cycle of twelve thousand years. The idea of an end of history and the world was widespread in Jewish writings of the Second Temple period. It was probably in the first century C.E. that the idea of a world week developed, in which humankind was given six thousand years, followed by a seventh thousand of God's rule.

worship *see* CULT

wrath of God God's anger at opposition to divine holiness, righteousness, or intentions. God's wrath has concrete effects, from sickness and misfortune to military defeat and death. Divine wrath is provoked by human iniquity or ignorance and manifests God's righteousness. Violation of God's rules risks wrath, as when Uzzah touches the ark (2 Sam. 6:7) or Aaron's sons offer unholy fire (Lev. 10:1-3). Nations that oppress Israel and do not acknowledge divine sovereignty experience wrath (Exod. 15:7–8; Jer. 50:25; Jdt. 9:9). God is angered by Israel's transgressions of the covenant, such as idolatry (Exod. 32:10; Deut. 13), social injustice (Exod. 22:21–24; Isa. 1:21–25), and rebellion against God's rule (Deut. 1:26–45). But God is slow to anger (Exod. 34:6; Ps. 86:15; Joel 2:13), and divine anger is tempered by love or mercy (Ps. 51:1; Isa. 60:10). Pseudo-Philo is particularly concerned with the tension between God's anger and mercy.

In apocalyptic eschatology, God's coming wrath will soon punish the wicked (1 Enoch 1–5; Apoc. Abr. 28:4). The Dead Sea Scrolls and Daniel 8:19 and 11:36 refer to the present as the Age of Wrath. Paul and Revelation have an apocalyptic view that God's wrath will be revealed at the eschaton (Rom. 2:5; 1 Thess. 1:10; Rev. 6:16–17, 11:18, 14:10). For Paul, God's wrath is also operative in the present (Rom. 1:18; 1 Thess. 2:16). In the Gospels, both John the Baptist (Matt. 3:7) and Jesus (Matt. 13:37–43) preach God's coming wrath.

wreath a motif in Jewish art borrowed from Graeco-Roman art. The wreath is usually depicted as a closed circle woven of vines or a circle with a gap at the front (top). The wreath as a motif in Jewish art represents one woven of vines or made of gold, but even a gold wreath (or diadem) was modeled after the vine wreath. Wreaths in Roman and Byzantine synagogue art appear many times as the center of interest in a stone relief on a lintel flanked by lions, genii, or other animals. Sometimes in the center of the wreath in synagogue art there appears a menorah or knot of Hercules, or else the bottom of the wreath is itself tied in a knot of Hercules. Wreaths decorate the friezes of the synagogues of Capernaum and Chorazin. A wreath realistically depicted in the Tiberias synagogue mosaic contains a Greek dedicatory inscription: "Proclus the son of Crispus made it." Wreaths also appear on chancel screens in Byzantine synagogues. These wreaths usually enclose a menorah. Coins of Jewish rulers often featured wreaths. For example, on coins of John Hyrcanus I (135 B.C.E.) wreaths appear surrounding a Hebrew inscription: "Yonatan the High Priest and Council of the Jews." The wreath on coins is sometimes understood to

be a royal diadem and indicates the authority under which the coin was minted.

writing materials items such as inkwells, papyrus, vellem, and ink used for writing. While an almost countless number of items were used for some sort of written communication from the Persian period until the end of the Byzantine period, the following items were among the most common media used: papyrus, animal skins, bullae, seals, mosaics, ostraca, metal, pottery, ossuaries, and stone.

Perhaps the most familiar mediums of ancient writing to modern individuals are papyri and animal skins, because these were used for the famous Dead Sea Scrolls. Papyrus was used extensively in Palestine due to its close proximity to Egypt where the plants were grown. Papyrus leaves were woven together and then pressed to make writing sheets. Dried animal skins that were later pressed were a similar medium, and ink was used for writing on both surfaces. The majority of the Dead Sea Scrolls were written on animal skins, but some were written on papyrus. Papyrus was also used for legal contracts and letters, which were often sealed with bullae.

Bullae are simply tiny pieces of clay or wax that have been impressed with a seal in order to officially close or seal a letter, contract, deed, or other document. These seals often contained the name of the owner along with the name of his or her father ("Joseph, the son of Saul"). Seals are known to have belonged both to women and to men, and at times iconography was used to identify the owner instead of the name. The seals were commonly made of semiprecious stones and were engraved by artisans.

Pottery was also a common medium for writing. Individual vessels were often inscribed before or after firing with various labels identifying either the owner of the vessel or the contents of the vessel. Stray pottery sherds were also used for writing practice and for composing letters. These sherds were at times inscribed with some sort of sharp instrument, and at other times ink was used. When ink was used on a pottery sherd, the resulting piece of writing is called an ostracon.

Metal was also used as a medium for writing and was commonly inscribed as an amulet. Breastplates often contained short prayers or blessings. These amulets were often used in burials. Burials in general seem to have brought out the need for writing from earliest times. Stone tombs and ossuaries were often inscribed with messages commemorating the deceased, with warnings to potential grave robbers and prayers to God. Finally, mosaics were often used following the Hellenistic period for various types of inscriptions. This is especially important in Palestine, because many synagogues and churches contain mosaics with various types of inscriptions.

The study of the letters found on these different types of writing is called paleography. This study is often used to date unknown objects and archaeological levels by comparing the shape and style of a particular set of letters with a set of letters from the preceding and following time periods. Though some general conclusions can be reached through paleographic dating, the resulting dates are necessarily not specific and sometimes are unreliable, because, like today, there is often much variation in the style of letters from the same time period as a result of scribal habits. *See also* INSCRIPTIONS; OSTRACON; SEALS AND BULLAE.

Writings the English translation of the Hebrew term *ketubim;* a Jewish division of the Hebrew Bible containing the books of Psalms, Proverbs, Job, Song of Songs, Ruth, Lamentations, Ecclesiastes (Kohelet), Esther, Daniel, Ezra, Nehemiah, and 1 and 2 Chronicles. The Ketubim's books were among the last written, and some of them did not receive canonical status until a century or so into the common era.

Written Torah *see* TORAH, WRITTEN

X-Y

Xanthikos the name of a Macedonian month; appears in a number of Jewish sources, such as the writings of Josephus. Unfortunately, there was not a uniform usage; sometimes it corresponded to the Hebrew month of Adar (February/March) and sometimes to the month Nisan (March/April).

Yabneh town near the Mediterranean on the southern coast of the Land of Israel, where, after the destruction of the Temple in 70 C.E., sages assembled and conducted schools and courts, also referred to as Jamnia

Yabneh, archaeology of the ancient site of Yabneh, also known as Jamniah or Jabneh. Yabneh was a minor biblical city (2 Chron. 26:6) on the Huldah River near the coast of the Mediterranean and south of Jaffa. Josephus knew that it had been the seat of the governor of Idumea during the Hellenistic period (*Ant.* 12.7.4, p. 308). Greek troops under Seleucid command had used Yabneh as a base for the resistance to the Hasmoneans (1 Macc. 5:58). Simon Maccabaeus, however, conquered Yabneh and it remained in Jewish hands until the Romans came in 63 B.C.E. In rabbinic literature it is known as the seat of Yohanan ben Zakkai and Raban Gamaliel. A Sanhedrin sat at Yabneh. In the Byzantine period it is known as the seat of a bishopric. The site is replete with foundations of buildings, with tombs, and with fragments of sculpture of the Roman and Byzantine periods. Pottery fragments on the ground include those of the Persian period and earlier. A Greek and Hebrew inscription from Khirbet Hebra near Yabneh, of uncertain date, mentions Abram the son of the blessed Robel

of Pharbaithos, which is a city in the eastern Delta in Egypt. The Hebrew says, "Peace upon Jeshrun forever."

Yadayim Mishnah tractate on washing hands to remove ritual uncleanness. The tractate discusses washing hands (chaps. 1–2); the status of uncleanness imputed to hands (chap. 3); and the status of uncleanness imputed to sacred scriptures (Chaps. 3–4).

Yahrzeit anniversary of a person's death. It is a medieval innovation, whereby the annual anniversary of an immediate relative's death is marked. Those observing it recite the *kaddish,* and receive the honor of being called to the Torah (*aliyah*).

Yahu (Aram.: *yhw*) an abbreviated form of the divine name YHWH (Yahweh) found in Jewish papyrus letters written in Aramaic at Elephantine, in Egypt, about 400 B.C.E.

Yahweh *see* YHWH

Yamim Noraim *see* DAYS OF AWE

Yannai Palestinian amora of the early third century C.E.; a student of Judah the Patriarch and Hiyya; teacher of Yohanan and Simeon b. Lakish; also known as Yannai Rabbah (the Great). He was active at Akbara, in the upper Galilee, where he founded an academy (Y. Erubin 8:4, 25a). The Talmud suggests that he was wealthy (B. Kiddushin 11a), an owner of orchards and vineyards (B. Moed Katan 12b, B. Baba Batra 14a). *See also* ALEXANDER JANNAEUS.

Yannai b. Ishmael an infrequently cited Palestinian amora of the late third century C.E.; found in the Babylonian Talmud in several legal and exegetical passages

Yaoel a high angel who bears God's name (Yahu; YHWH). Unique to the Apocalypse of Abraham 10–17, this angel mediates the vision of God precipitated by the sacrifice in Genesis 15 and teaches Abraham the song of God's heavenly attendants. *See also* ABRAHAM, APOCALYPSE OF.

Yattir a location northwest of Khura. The Cave of Yattir is referred to at T. Shebiit 4:11 as demarcating a border area of the Land of Israel.

Yazdagird I Sassanid ruler (r. 399–420 C.E.). Although he faced invasions by the Ostrogoths and Franks and revolts by Maximus and the city of Antioch, he did not focus on expanding his territory or fighting wars on his frontiers. He upheld his treaty with Byzantium, and he won the respect of the Roman emperor Arcadius. He ended the long and debilitating persecution of the Christians, and in 409 he permitted Christians to worship openly and rebuild their churches. However, strife between the magi and the Christians soon erupted, leading to a four-year persecution of the Christians, including destruction of churches and arrests of believers. However, Christian writers present a favorable picture of Yazdagird. The Jewish sources are also positive toward Yazdagird, some claiming that his wife was Jewish. But the stories of his Jewish wife are garbled and are unreliable. Perhaps women in Yazdagird's harem were sympathetic to the Jewish community. The rabbinic texts indicate that the exilarch enjoyed a good personal relationship with Yazdagird and his court. Amemar compared Yazdagird to Cyrus, and one source claims that the king knew scripture and the complicated requirements of the priestly garments, neither of which is likely.

Yazdagird II Sassanid ruler (r. 440–457 C.E.). After the death of of his father, Bahram V, he concluded a peace with Rome and ascended the throne. He engaged in successful campaigns against the Ephthalites of Transozania and forcibly converted Armenia to Zoroastrianism. At first he was tolerant toward Christianity, but he began to persecute Armenian Christianity, and in about 445–446 the persecutions spread to Iran. He subjected the Jews to the most severe persecutions they experienced in Persia. For more than fifty years, Judaism was considered an illicit religion, and the Jews were punished for practicing it. Jewish sources claim that he outlawed the Sabbath, and even commanded the Jews to violate the Sabbath. Other sources claim that he prohibited the recitation of the Shema and that he closed the Jewish schools. He also decreed that the Jews should live by Sassanid law and that their courts should be closed. The Jewish sources suggest that he virtually abolished Jewish self-rule in the Sassanid Empire and that he executed important rabbis and other Jewish leaders. It is possible that the king desperately needed the support of the Sassanid clergy and secured this support by persecuting both Christians and Jews.

Yazdagird III last Sassanid ruler (r. 632–651 C.E.). Crowned in the city of Istakhr, he inherited a weakened country, which was divided among generals and governors and exhausted after a long struggle with Rome. Bands of Arabs moved against the Sassanid territories after they defeated Syria. In 637, the Sassanid armies were defeated at al-Qadisiya and Jalula. Ctesiphon fell, and all of ancient Babylonia now was lost. In 641, the Moslems defeated the Sassanids at Nihavend, and in 643 Hamadan fell. Finally, in 651, Yazdagird III was murdered by his own forces.

Yazden Persian imperial finance minister (early 7th c.). Yazden's family possessed large estates in Karkha de Bet Slokh. He was a Nestorian Christian, whom Khusro II placed in office. He often accompanied the imperial armies to collect and protect the moneys seized in pillage or gained in ransom. He used his wealth to endow monasteries and support churches. After the Persian armies took Jerusalem, he sent a remnant of the "true cross" back to Ctesiphon and punished the Jewish population for their anti-Christian actions during the conquest. He also rebuilt Jerusalem's churches. Yazden fell from power during Khusro II's persecutions of the Christians.

Yebamot Mishnah tractate on levirate marriages. The first five chapters discuss establishing the levirate marital bond and severing the levirate bond through the rite of removing the shoe. Subsequent chapters discuss the special marital bond of marriage into the priesthood, covering when a woman may eat heave-offering (chap. 6); who may eat heave-offering (chaps. 7–8); severing the marital bond (chaps. 10–16), with these subdivisions: marital bonds subject to doubt (chaps. 10–11); severing the levirate bond through the rite of removing the shoe (chap. 12); severing the marital bond of a minor and the right of refusal (chap. 13); the infirm marital bond of a deaf-mute (chap. 14); and severing the marital bond through the death of the husband (chaps. 15–16).

Yehoshua *see* JOSHUA

Yehuda *see* JUDAH

Yehudiyeh, Tell el- the modern name of ancient Leontopolis, a Ptolemaic and Roman city about 56 kilometers north of modern Cairo. The modern Arabic name comes from the many Jewish tombstones found here, for there was apparently a considerable Jewish population under the Ptolemies and the Romans. King Ptolemy VI Philometor (180–145 B.C.E.) gave Onias permission to build a Jewish temple at Leontopolis. This temple was an active worship center for Jews of Egypt until the emperor Vespasian closed it in 74 C.E., presumably in response to the slaying of the last Jewish defenders of Judea at Masada at about the same time. So far, the exact location of the temple has not been determined. On the other hand, many Jewish tombs have been examined. They are of the loculus type, well known in ancient Palestine and in ancient Alexandria in the Jewish necropolis of Alexandria. The Jewish epitaphs and other inscriptions from Leontopolis are a gold mine of information about the people and the city. All are in Greek Over half of the names in the epitaphs are recognizably Jewish, with names such as Iesous (Joshua), Rachelis (Rachel), Abramos (Abram), Mikkos (Micah), and the like, but also Theodosius (Nathaniel), Sabbatios (one born on the Sabbath), Aristoboulos (common in Judea), and the like. The people mentioned in the epitaphs are from all walks of life, for they are soldiers, city magistrates, and women who died in childbirth. At least one inscription of the mid-second century B.C.E. mentions the place of prayer or *proseuche,* so there must have been a prayer hall.

Yemar Babylonian amora; successor of Ashi as head of the academy at Sura, 417–432 C.E.; also cited as Meremar. Seder Tannaim veAmoraim reports that upon his death, a pillar of fire appeared in the sky for thirty days.

Yermeyahu *see* JEREMIAH

Yerushalmi Talmud produced in the Land of Israel, c. 400 C.E., as a commentary to the Mishnah's first, second, third, and fourth divisions, primarily composed of amplification and extension of passages of the Mishnah. Approximately 90 percent of the document comprises Mishnah-commentary, which falls into four categories: (1) text criticism; (2) exegesis of the meaning of the Mishnah, including glosses and amplifications; (3) addition of scriptural proof-texts of the Mishnah's central propositions; and (4) harmonization of one Mishnah passage with another Mishnah passage or with a statement of Tosefta. The text criticism and exegesis remain wholly within the narrow frame of the Mishnah passage subject to discussion. The scriptural documentation and the reconciliations take an essentially independent stance vis-à-vis the Mishnah pericope at hand.

The Mishnah is read by the Yerushalmi as a composite of discrete and essentially autonomous rules, a set of atoms rather than an integrated molecule; the most striking formal traits of the Mishnah are obliterated. The Mishnah as a whole and complete statement of a viewpoint no longer exists. Its propositions are reduced to details. Then, on occasion, the details may be restated in generalizations encompassing a wide variety of other details across the gaps between one tractate and another. The Yerushalmi provides some indication of efforts to establish the correct text of various passages of the Mishnah. This nearly always is in the context of deciding the law. It is not a random search for a "perfect" text. It rather represents a deliberate and principled inquiry into the law as revealed by the phrasing of a passage. That is why, in the bulk of these passages, the legal consequences of one reading as opposed to another are carefully articulated, and sometimes even tied to a range of other points subject to dispute. The Mishnah rarely finds it necessary to cite a scriptural proof-text for a proposition. The Yerushalmi, by contrast, cites scriptural proof-texts for the propositions of the Mishnah whenever possible.

When the Yerushalmi proceeds beyond Mishnah-exegesis, it sets forth four types of discussions: (1) *Theoretical questions of law not associated with a particular passage of the Mishnah.* There is some tendency to move beyond the legal boundaries set by the Mishnah's rules. More general inquiries are taken up. These, of course, remain within the framework of the topic of one tractate or another, although there are some broader modes of thought, characteristic of more than a single tractate. (2) *Exegesis of scripture, separate from the Mishnah.* It is under this rubric that we find the most important instances in which the two Talmuds present materials essentially independent of the Mishnah. The repertoire produced is substantial and striking. While many items may be linked to a theme of the Mishnah, if not to a specific rule, virtually all of the items stand totally separate from the Mishnah. They pursue problems or themes through what is said about a biblical figure, expressing ideas and values simply unknown to the Mishnah. (3) *Historical statements.* The Yerushalmi contains a fair number of statements that something happened, or narratives about how something happened. While many of these are replete with biblical quotations, in general, they do not provide exegesis of scripture, which serves merely as illustration or reference point. (4) *Stories about, and rules for, sages and disciples, separate from discussion of a passage of the Mishnah.* The Mishnah contains a tiny number of tales about rabbis. These serve principally as precedents for, or illustrations of, rules. The Talmuds, by contrast, contain a sizable number of stories about sages and their relationships to other people. These, too, may be adduced as evidence of the values of the people who stand behind the two Talmuds—the things they thought important. These tales rarely serve to illustrate a rule or concept of the Mishnah. The main, though not the only, characteristic theme is the power of the rabbi, the honor due to the rabbi, and the tension between the rabbi and others, such as the patriarch, the heretic, or the Gentile.

To sum up, the Talmud of the Land of Israel forms a composite of three kinds of materials: exegeses of the Mishnah, exegeses of Scripture, and accounts of the men who provide both. The Yerushalmi might be viewed as a reworking of its two antecedent documents: the Mishnah, lacking much reference to scripture, and scripture itself. The Yerushalmi synthesizes the two, both by reading scripture into the Mishnah and by reading scripture alongside of, and separate from, the Mishnah.

Yerushalmi, Targum   *see* TARGUM TO THE PROPHETS

Yeshahu   *see* ISAIAH

yeshiba   (Heb.) session; talmudic academy

yetzer haRa, yetzer Tob   *see* INCLINATION, EVIL AND GOOD

YHWH   the Tetragrammaton, the four-lettered name of God; Yahweh; *see also* GOD; GOD, NAMES OF; I AM; TETRAGRAMMATON

Yiḥud   isolation of a woman and a man, for purposes of sexual relations, as part of the marriage rite

Yizkor   (Heb., may God remember . . .) the standard formula for the memorial prayer said in memory of immediate relatives and martyrs. It is of medieval provenance, but frequently it is assumed, incorrectly, to date from rabbinic times because of the general anachronistic dating of the practice of memorializing the dead. *See also* HAZKHARAT NESHAMOT.

Yobal   *see* JUBILEE YEAR

Yodfat   (or Jotapata) the city that took the brunt of Vespasian's siege in his first attack on Galilee in the Jewish Revolt. Yodfat stood about five miles north of Sepphoris, the capital of the area, in a range of high hills. In the Mishnah, Yodfat is listed as one of the cities that harken back to the time of Joshua (Arach. 9.6). The same document distinguishes Yodfat and Old Yodfat, which suggests that the devastation of the city by Vespasian resulted in a new construction, perhaps to the north. Josephus relates the story of the siege of Yodfat in which he, Josephus, was the defending general against Vespasian. This is also the site of Josephus's personal surrender to Vespasian and the place where Josephus prophesied that Vespasian would become emperor. After the destruction of the Second Temple the priestly course of Miyamin settled at Yodfat. Excavations at the site have revealed a city wall, houses with associated ritual baths, or *mikvaot,* and industrial installations. There are also signs of later occupation north of the hill of Yodfat perhaps as late as the Mameluke period (1250–1517).

Yofiel   According to Targum Pseudo-Jonathan (Deut. 34:6), Yofiel was the angel who laid Moses on his deathbed. He was considered a wise sage among the angels. In medieval times, the Zohar, a Kabbalist text, considered him a great angel chief and a prince of Torah.

Yoḥanan b. Berokah   Tannaitic authority at the beginning of the second century C.E., cited ten times in the Mishnah and ten times in the Tosefta. Tosefta Sotah 7:9 associates him with Eleazar Ḥisma and suggests that these two individuals may have been students of Joshua b. Ḥananiah. Tosefta Terumot 7:14, by contrast, describes a visit by Yoḥanan b. Berokah to Yoḥanan b. Nuri, who scholars accordingly suggest may also have been his teacher. Yoḥanan b. Berokah was father to the Tannaitic authority Ishmael b. Yoḥanan b. Berokah.

Yoḥanan b. Nappaḥa   an eminent Palestinian authority of the end of the second century C.E.; active in his native Sepphoris and later in Tiberias, where he started an academy; referred to either as Yoḥanan, without the patronymic, or simply as Bar Nappaḥa. He was an orphan, raised by his grandfather. His first teachers were of the final generation of Tannaitic authorities.

Yoḥanan b. Nuri   Tannaitic authority active in Beth Shearim in the first half of the second century C.E. He transmits sayings of and was active in deliberations in the presence of Eliezer b. Hyrcanus, who may, therefore, have been his teacher. He frequently appears in the Mishnah in disputes with Aqiba and was also an associate of Eleazar b. Ḥisma. Sifre Deuteronomy 16 reports that after Gamaliel promoted Yoḥanan b. Nuri and Eleazar b. Ḥisma to membership in the Sanhedrin, they continued to sit among the students. As a result both individuals lost their positions of authority. Yoḥanan b. Nuri lived through the Bar Kokhba Revolt, and following the war, Judah the Patriarch reportedly visited him in Beth Shearim (T. Sukkot 2:2).

Yoḥanan b. Torta   Tannaitic authority; a contemporary of Akiba in the second century C.E., known for his response to Akiba's acceptance of Bar Kokhba as the messiah: "Akiba, grass will grow out of your jaws, and the son of David will not yet have come!"

(Y. Taanit 8:8, 68d). Born a Gentile, Yoḥanan reportedly converted to Judaism upon seeing a cow that refused to work on the Sabbath (Pesikta Rabbati 14). In that story, he is referred to by his cognomen alone, Ben Torta, that is, "son of a cow."

Yoḥanan b. Zakkai principal rabbinic authority of the first century C.E.; head of the sages at Yabneh after the destruction of the Temple. He taught the leading sages of the late first and early second centuries; established the foundations of the Mishnah; and is noted for his teaching, "If you have learned much Torah, do not puff yourself up on that account, for it was for that purpose that you were created."

Yoḥanan the Sandal Maker Tannaitic authority in the first half of the second century C.E., a native of Alexandria (Y. Ḥagigah 3:1). He is listed as one of the rabbis who gathered in the valley of Bet Rimmon at the end of the persecutions that followed the Bar Kokhba Revolt in order to renew the study of Torah (Y. Ḥagigah 3:1). His name appears several times in the Mishnah, generally in association with students of Akiba.

yoke of the Torah a metaphor for submission to God's sovereignty through obedience to, and study of the Torah. The notion appears first in the Ecclesiasticus, with reference to the yoke of wisdom, which Ben Sira identifies with Torah (Ecclus. 6:23–31, 51:23–26). Both passages emphasize study, and Pirkei Abot 3:6 appears also to refer to such study, which releases one from other obligations (cf. Ecclus. 39:1 in contrast to chap. 38). The yoke imagery recurs in Matthew 11:28–30, where Jesus speaks as the voice of wisdom. Comparison with Ben Sira does not indicate that Jesus' invitation implies a contrast between his commands and the Torah construed as a burden.

Yokneam (or Jokneam) biblical city, important since the time of Joshua (Josh. 12:22) and one of the largest tells in ancient Palestine. Yokneam stood at a major pass through the Carmel range from the coast inland to the Jezreel Valley, today's Wadi Milh. In the Persian and Hellenistic periods there seems only to have been a large village here that exploited the rich agricultural area around the tell. The village prospered. In the fourth century Eusebius knew the town as Kammona or in Latin, Cimona (*Onomast.* 116.21). After the Jewish Revolt, Kammona belonged to the city territory of Legio, established first as the base for the Roman VI legion, but afterwards a major regional city.

Yoma Mishnah tractate dealing with Temple rites on the Day of Atonement, in line with Leviticus 16. The first seven chapters discuss conduct of the rites on the Day of Atonement. Chapter 8 discusses the laws of the Day of Atonement, for example, not eating or drinking; what the day atones for; and what repentance and reconciliation must accomplish.

Yom haBikkurim *see* SHABUOT

Yom Kippur (Day of Atonement) holy day falling on the tenth of Tishrei and observed by fasting, prayer, repentance, and confession. The Temple rites are described in Leviticus 16. After the destruction of the Temple, day-long synagogue prayer became the principal observance of the penitential day.

Yonah *see* JONAH

Yonatan *see* JONATHAN

Yose b. Abin Palestinian amora of the fourth century C.E.; one of the latest rabbis referred to in the Jerusalem Talmud. According to tradition, he had a significant role in the editing of the Jerusalem Talmud. For a time he was in Babylonia, so he also transmits Babylonian sayings and practices.

Yose b. Akabiah Tannaitic authority of the second century C.E., said to be equivalent to Joseph of Husal, Joseph the Babylonian, Issi b. Gur Arye, Issi b. Judah, Issi b. Gamaliel, Issi b. Mehallel, and Yose Kittunto (B. Pesaḥim 113b; Y. Baba Kamma 3:7, 3d). These identifications are not certain; in particular, the identification with Issi b. Judah appears to be incorrect.

Yose b. Assi *see* YOSE B. YASYAN

Yose b. Dormaskit Tannaitic authority of the late second century C.E.; born in Damascus; cited only once in the Mishnah, at M. Yadyim 4:3. Several of his statements are preserved in midrashic documents. He seems to prefer the plain meaning of scripture (see, e.g., Sifrei Deut. 1).

Yose b. Ḥalafta Tannaitic authority of the mid-second century C.E.; referred to in the Talmud simply as Yose. Born in Sepphoris, he was a late student of Akiba, ordained by Judah b. Baba (B. Sanhedrin 14a), and active following the Bar Kokhba Revolt.

Yose b. Ḥanina Palestinian amora of the second half of the third century C.E.; active at the academy at Tiberias. He was a student and colleague of Yoḥanan, was a teacher of Abbahu, and is known as a judge (B. Baba Kamma 39a). He seems to have been wealthy (B. Baba Batra 90b) and to have outlived his children (B. Taanit 13b).

Yose b. Judah Tannaitic authority of the mid-second century C.E.; a colleague of Judah the Patriarch, with whom he is frequently in dispute. The Talmud holds that in the Mishnah, statements of his are at times cited without attribution (see, e.g., B. Erubin 38b).

Yose b. Kipper Tannaitic authority of the late second century C.E. His name is absent from the Mishnah but appears in the Tosefta and both Talmuds. He reportedly was sent to Babylonia to collect funds to support rabbinic authorities in the Land of Israel (B. Gittin 14b; Y. Gittin 1:6, 43b).

Yose b. Kisma Tannaitic authority at the beginning of the second century C.E.; active in Tiberias. Several of his exegetical statements are extant.

Yose b. Meshullam Tannaitic authority at the end of the second century C.E.; a close colleague of Judah the Patriarch, though infrequently cited in the Mishnah. According to Y. Maaser Sheni 2:10, 53d, Yose b. Meshullam and Simeon b. Menasyah led "the holy congregation in Jerusalem" and ate ordinary food in a state of ritual purity.

Yose b. Saul student of Judah the Patriarch at the beginning of the Amoraic period in the third century C.E., known chiefly for transmitting his teacher's sayings

Yose b. Yasyan Tannaitic authority; a contemporary of Simeon b. Gamaliel II; sometimes called simply Ben Yasyan; probably also identical with Yose b. Assi

Yose b. Yoezer an early sage; along with Yose b. Yoḥanan, listed at M. Abot 1:4 as the first of the pairs; active at the beginning of the second century B.C.E. He is known for the statement: "Let your house be a gathering place for sages; and wallow in the dust of their feet; and drink in their words with gusto."

Yose b. Yoḥanan an early sage; along with Yose b. Yoezer, listed at M. Abot 1:4 as the first of the pairs; active at the beginning of the second century B.C.E. He is known for the statement: "Let your house be wide open; and seat the poor at your table; and don't talk too much with women."

Yose b. Zebida Palestinian amora active at the beginning of the fourth century C.E.; a student of Hela; referred to in the Jerusalem Talmud without the patronymic. In the Jerusalem Talmud, he frequently appears in debate and, in general, in close association with Jonah, who was also his business partner. He was a contemporary of Yose b. Abin, with whom his name sometimes is interchanged.

Yose b. Zimra Palestinian rabbi of the late second century C.E., at the nexus of the Tannaitic and Amoraic periods; known primarily for his interpretations of scripture, which appear in the Talmuds and Amoraic midrashic compilations

Yose Kittunto *see* YOSE B. AKABIAH

Yose the Galilean Tannaitic authority active in the late first and early second centuries C.E. He was a colleague of Eleazar b. Azariah, Tarfon, and Akiba, and he frequently abandoned his own views in favor of those of Yose (B. Ḥagigah 14a; B. Pesaḥim 36b). Yose is remembered for his mastery of law as well as his piety, on account of which later authorities recalled that his prayers for rain invariably were answered. Little is known of his youth. Genesis Rabbah 17 reports of his unhappy married life and eventual divorce.

Yose the Priest Tannaitic authority at the end of the second century C.E.; a student of Yoḥanan b. Zakkai, commended by his teacher for his piety (M. Abot 2:8). Little of his teaching is preserved. According to Y. Ḥagigah 2:1, 77a, he studied chariot mysticism.

Yosi *see under* YOSE

Yosippon *see* JOSIPPON

Yotapata *see* YODFAT

Yubka location referred to at T. Shebiit 4:11 as demarcating a border area of the Land of Israel

Yudan Palestinian amora of the fourth century C.E.; cited exclusively in the Jerusalem Talmud and midrashic compilations. He is known for exegetical statements aimed at comforting his Jewish contemporaries, who were subject to persecution by Christian Rome. This authority is distinguished from a later Palestinian amora, Judah b. Shalom, who, in the Jerusalem Talmud, also is referred to as Yudan.

Yudan b. Ishmael Palestinian amora of the third century C.E.; possibly a brother of Yannai B. Ishmael

yuḥasin (Heb., relations) refers to genealogical classes, relationships, or records. In the rabbinic literature, the term appears in the title Sefer Yuḥasin, "Book of Genealogy," a commentary to Chronicles that purportedly disappeared in Roman times (B. Pesaḥim 62b). M. Kiddushin 4:1 uses the term *yuḥasin* in speaking of ten castes who left the Babylonian captivity and returned to the land of Israel: (1) priests, (2) Levites, (3) Israelites, (4) impaired priests, (5) converts, (6) freed slaves, (7) mamzers, (8) Netins, (9) silenced ones (people whose fathers' identities are unknown), and (10) foundlings (people whose parents' identities are unknown). Within these castes, priests, Levites, and Israelites are permitted to marry one another; Levites, Israelites, impaired priests, converts, and freed slaves are permitted to marry one another; and converts, freed slaves, mamzers, netins, silenced ones, and foundlings are permitted to marry among one another.

Z

zab *see* FLUX

Zabdai b. Levi Palestinian amora active in the circle of Hoshayah in the mid-third century C.E. He is known in particular for his exegetical comments, in which he often appears in dispute with Rab and Joshua b. Levi.

Zabim Mishnah tractate on the flux-uncleanness described in Leviticus 15. The tractate discusses becoming a *zab* (chaps. 1–2) and transferring the uncleanness affecting the *zab* to other objects (chaps. 2–5), especially through pressure (chaps. 2–4).

Zadok a priest of David in Jerusalem. In 2 Samuel 15:24–37 he first appears with the Ark of the Covenant, in association with Abiathar, the other priest appointed by David. Zadok supported Solomon in the succession struggle at the time of David's death (1 Kings 1:22–39), and thus became the chief priest in the Jerusalem sanctuary during the reign of Solomon (1 Kings 2:35). The descendants of Zadok, the Zadokites, remained the dominant priestly family in Jerusalem until the exile (587 B.C.E.). In Ezekiel's program for Temple's the restoration, the Zadokites are the only legitimate priests (Ezek. 44:6–31). In reality, after the return from exile, the Zadokites regained control of the high priesthood and retained that office until the deposition and murder of Onias III in the early second century B.C.E. (2 Macc. 4:33–34).

In the postexilic literature, the name Zadok appears most prominently in the sectarian texts of the Dead Sea Scrolls. In the Damascus Document 4:1–4, the members of the sect, usually identified with the Essenes, are called the "sons of Zadok," indicating the priestly leanings of the sect. In the Community Rule, authority in the Community is given to "the priests, the Sons of Zadok" (e.g., 5:2b–3a). This emphasis on priestly authority and particularly the importance of the Zadokite priests led some scholars to posit that the reason for the foundation of the settlement at Qumran and for the sect's split from the rest of Judaism was the assumption of the high priesthood by the non-Zadokites Jonathan and Simon the Maccabees. In recent years, however, this theory has been discredited, and more emphasis has been placed on the sect's halakhic disagreements with the rest of Judaism as the reason for the schism.

Zadokite a presumed descendent of Zadok, the high priest under David. The high priest does not seem to have had an important function in the Hebrew Bible. This changed in the Second Temple period, when according to Ezekiel, the high priesthood was to be confined to the line of Zadok. Under the Hasmoneans, there was a dispute over the office of high priest, and in some cases the rivals would accuse each other of not being a true Zadokite. For example, the Qumran texts make an issue of the fact that their priests were Zadokites, accusing those in Jerusalem of being illegitimate or implying it.

Zagnazgael (also Seganzagel, Zagzagel, Zamzagiel) according to Targum Pseudo-Jonathan to Exodus 3:2, the angel who was the flame of fire that appeared to Moses in the burning bush. According to 3 Enoch, Zagnazgael is another name for Metatron.

Zaradusht middle Iranian form of Zarathustra, the founder of Zoroastrianism or Mazdaism, sixth century B.C.E. He believed in a dualistic monotheism, in which the universal lord fathered twin spirits, the good and the evil, an eventual transformation of life and existence, and inward religiosity.

Zarvai a location on the east bank of the Jordan River, referred to at T. Shebiit 4:11 as demarcating a border area of the Land of Israel

zeal, jealousy The same Hebrew root *kn'*, translated by the Greek *zēloun,* includes both the positive meaning "zeal"—an ardent interest in pursuit of something—and the negative "jealousy"—an intolerance of rivalry or unfaithfulness. A human's concern only for his/her own glory is to be avoided: "jealousy and anger shorten life" (Sir. 30:24), and envy is the opposite of love (Test. Simeon 3, 4:7; Test. Gad 7:6–7; 1 Cor. 13:4; 2 Cor. 12:20; James 3:14, 16; 4:2). The author of Acts says the Jews persecuted the early Church out of jealousy (Acts 5:17, 13:45, 17:5). Jealousy is thus usually found in lists of vices (1QS 4:10; Gal. 5:20). Remarkably, the Romans are praised for lack of jealousy in 1 Maccabees 8:16.

This singleminded devotion can be turned to something beyond oneself, and so one can be zealous for someone or something. One should be zealous for goodness (Sir. 51:18; Titus 2:14; 1 Pet. 3:13) and just laws (1QS 4:4). The Master at Qumran is to be a man zealous for the precept (statute, law), whose time is for the Day of Revenge (1QS 9:23). The zeal of Elijah (Sir. 48:2) and Phinehas for God is praised (Sir. 45:23) and imitated (1 Macc. 2:26). But zeal must be focused on the proper goal: the opponents of the Qumran covenanters can have zeal (1QH 2:31), the preconverted Paul zealously persecuted the Church (Phil. 3:6), and Paul recognizes that his opponents acted out of misdirected zeal (Rom. 10:2; Gal. 4:17–18). Paul hopes to stir up the zealousness of the Jews so that they will convert (Rom. 11:11, 14). The two spirits of truth and falsehood are in a zealous quarrel, according to the Rule at Qumran (1QS 4:17).

As in the Hebrew scriptures (Exod. 34:14), God in his zeal (1QS 2:15) is described as destroying backsliders from his covenant. God will wage war against his people's enemies, putting on the armor of his zeal (Wisd. of Sol. 5:17). Paul worries that Corinthians partaking of food offered to idols might provoke the Lord to jealousy (1 Cor. 10:22).

Rabbinic texts understand human jealousy as a result from competition between people of equal stature (B. Abodah Zarah 55a). Such jealousy can be productive, increasing, for instance, the wisdom of scholars (B. Baba Batra 21a, 22a), or negative, leading to conflict between people (B. Berakhot 28a). At least some rabbis do not see human jealousy as a particularly serious problem. They hold that simply by eating breakfast in the morning, one can supplant jealousy with love (B. Baba Metzia 107b).

The biblical cognate of jealousy—religious zeal—occurs infrequently in the rabbinic literature, for instance, in a description of Moses' determination to kill the Egyptian taskmaster (Exod. 2:11–12; Lev. Rabbah 32:4). The Hebrew term generally rendered in English as "zeal" derives from a different root entirely and refers to the speed and exactitude with which an individual carries out a religious obligation. The rabbis hold that a zealous person fulfills religious responsibilities as promptly as possible (Sifrei Tazria Perek 1).

Zealots term used by the historian Josephus to characterize groups of peasant bandits who had been forced off their land by the advance of the Roman army toward Jerusalem in 67 C.E. These Zealots took over the city, rejected the leadership of the chief priests and aristocracy, elected lowborn priests to serve as high priests, and allied themselves with John of Gischala who eventually gained control of the group. In a series of conflicts they killed many of the priests and nobility, including the high priest Ananius, and caused many to flee from Jerusalem. Their animosity toward the wealthy governing families probably reflects a history of conflict between the Jerusalem landowning class and the peasants in the villages. As the war progressed the Zealots split into two groups and then reunited. They fought each other and the forces of Simon bar Giora in a civil conflict which weakened Jerusalem and made Roman conquest of the city inevitable.

The term "zealots" is often used in modern historical accounts in a very broad sense to include all opponents of Roman rule from the first century B.C.E. to 70 C.E. Some connect Ezekias, a Galilean bandit, with Judas the Galilean (one of the founders of the so-called "Fourth Philosophy") and with various resisters to Roman rule in the first century C.E. and finally with the Zealots, the Sicarii, and followers of Simon bar Giora at the time of the war against Rome. This imprecise use of the term "zealots" should not imply that there was a long-term, organized resistance movement against Roman rule. Rather, various independent figures and groups rose up during the 130 years of Roman sovereignty preceding the war as a response to a variety of complaints and to national goals.

Zebaḥim Mishnah tractate devoted to rules of everyday animal sacrifice in the Temple. The tractate discusses improper intention on the part of the priest and how it invalidates the act of sacrifice (chaps. 1–4); rules for the sacrifice of animals and fowl (chaps. 5–7); and rules of the altar (chaps. 8–12). The chapters on altar rules address disposing of sacrificial portions or blood that has been confused with portions or blood from another offering (chap. 8); the altar's sanctification of what is appropriate but not of what is not (chap. 9); precedence in the use of the altar (chap. 10); blood of the sin-offering that spurts onto a garment (exposition of Lev. 6:27–28) (chap. 11); dividing hides of animals among eligible priests (chap. 12); and proper location of the altar (Jerusalem alone) and the act of sacrifice (Chaps. 13–14).

Zebid Babylonian amora active in the fourth century C.E.; head of the academy at Pumbedita, 377–385. A number of his talmudic dicta concern economic and social relations with Gentiles, in particular, prohibitions to ensure that Israelite products do not come to be used in the pagan cult (see, e.g., B. Abodah Zarah 83b). He is also called Zebid of Nehardea.

Zeboim, Mount mountain referred to at M. Ḥallah 4:10 and M. Bikkurim 1:3. It may be a mountain next to or in the valley of Zeboim, mentioned at 1 Samuel 13:18. Alternatively, the site may be related to the town of Zeboim of the postexilic period, listed at Nehemiah 11:34.

Zechariah, Targum to *see* TARGUM TO THE PROPHETS

Zechariah b. Berechiah (LXX: Barachiah) biblical prophet to whom the book of Zechariah is ascribed (1:1). Matthew 23:34–36 (cf. Luke 11:51) confuses the prophet with Zechariah the son of Jehoiada, who is slain in the Temple (2 Chron. 24:20–22). The apocryphal Protevangelium of James 23–24 further confuses the issue by ascribing a similar fate to Zechariah the father of John the Baptist (cf. Luke 1).

Zedekiah b. Chenaanah prophetic opponent of Micaiah ben Imlah (1 Kings 22). According to the Martyrdom of Isaiah 2:12, he was the uncle of the Samaritan false prophet Belchira, the opponent of Isaiah.

Zeira I Palestinian amora of the third century C.E.; a native of Babylonia, where he was a student of Ḥuna at Sura and of Judah b. Ezekiel at Pumbedita. His love of the Land of Israel is expressed in the stories of his crossing the Jordan in his clothing and of his expressing concern over his own worthiness to enter a place that even Moses could not go. In the Land of Israel, he studied under Yoḥanan in Tiberias and was in close relationship with Ammi, Assi, and Abbahu. Later in life, he apparently again spent time in Babylonia (B. Shabbat 14a–b). He is one of the most frequently cited rabbinic authorities, referred to sometimes as Zera.

A Zeira with the Babylonian honorific Rab is mentioned several times in the Talmud and may be a distinct figure, active at the beginning of the fourth century C.E. Alternatively, he may be the same individual as Zeira I, referred to by the Babylonian title prior to his emigration to the Land of Israel.

Zeira II Palestinian amora of the mid-fourth century C.E.; active in the circle of Mani II; a student of Jeremiah; also called Zera

Zeiri Babylonian amora of the third century C.E.; in the Jerusalem Talmud, called Zeiri b. Ḥinena. Born in Babylonia, he studied in the Land of Israel under Ḥanina b. Ḥama and Yoḥanan. Later, he returned to Babylonia where, at the academy at Nehardea, he was the teacher of Ḥiyya b. Ashi and others.

Zekarya *see* ZECHARIAH

zekhut in Judaic writings, term of art signifying both the protecting influence of good conduct (sometimes translated as "merit") and consequent advantage, privilege, or benefit. Only through using the word *zekhut* do authors of compositions and authorships of composites express the first sense. However, the two senses are not really separable, since the "protecting influence of good conduct" is always understood to yield "advantage, privilege, or benefit." The advantages or privileges conferred by *zekhut* may be inherited and also passed on; the notion stresses entitlement because advantages or privileges invariably result from receiving *zekhut* from ancestors or acquiring it on one's own; the word "virtue" is used to refer to those supererogatory acts that demand a reward because they form matters of choice, the gift of the individual and his or her act of free will, an act that is at the same time uncompelled by the obligations imposed by the Torah but also valued by the Torah. *Zekhut* bears the capacity to unite the generations in a heritage of entitlements; *zekhut* is fundamentally a historical category and concept, in that, like all historical systems of thought, it explains the present in terms of the past, and the future in terms of the present. Because *zekhut* is something one may receive as an inheritance, out of the distant past, *zekhut* imposes upon the definition of the social entity Israel, a genealogical meaning. It furthermore imparts a distinctive character to the definitions of way of life. Thus the task of the political component of a theory of the social order, which is to define the social entity by appeal to empowerment, and of the economic component, which is to identify scarce resources by specification of the rationality of right management, is accomplished in a single word, which stands for a conception, a symbol, and a myth. All three components of this religious theory of the social order turn out to present specific applications, in context, for the general conception of *zekhut*. The first source of *zekhut* derives from the definition of Israel as family, the entitlements of supernatural power deriving from virtue, and then care, inherited from Abraham, Isaac, and Jacob. The second source is personal: the power one can gain for one's own heirs by virtuous deeds. *Zekhut* deriving from either source is to be defined in context: what can one do if one possesses *zekhut* that one cannot do if one does not have *zekhut,* and to whom can one do it? The answer to that question addresses empowerment by *zekhut*.

The word *zekhut* has been given the confusing translation of "merit." But one may receive *zekhut* from one's ancestors, and that is not by reason of one's own merit—by definition. "Unearned grace" is more appropriate in that context. Scripture, for example, knows that God loves Israel because he loved the patriarchs (Deut. 4:37); the memory or deeds of the righteous patriarchs and matriarchs appear in a broad range of contexts, for example, "Remember your servants, Abraham, Isaac, and Jacob" (Exod. 32:13), for Moses, and "Remember the good deeds of David, your servant" (2 Chron. 6:42), for David. At stake throughout is giving people what they do not merit, to be sure. But in these contexts, "remembering" what X did as an argument on behalf of favor for Y does not invoke the word *zekhut,* and the context does not require use of the word either. Accordingly, our problem of definition requires limitation to precise usages of a given word. Were we to propose to work our way back from situations that seem to exhibit conceptual affinities to the concept represented by the word under consideration, cases, for instance, in which someone appeals to what is owing the fathers on behalf of the children, we shall not accomplish the goal at hand, which is one of definition of a word that bears a very particular meaning, and, more to the point, carries out a highly critical systemic role.

Zekhut stands for the empowerment, of a supernatural character, that derives from the virtue of one's ancestry or from one's own virtuous deeds of a very particular order. No single word in English

bears the same meaning, nor can one identify a synonym for *zekhut* in the canonical writings in the original. The difficulty of translating a word of systemic consequence with a single word in some other language (or in the language of the system's documents themselves) tells us that we deal with what is unique, beyond comparison and therefore beyond contrast and comprehension. An indication that we have found our way to the systemic center is that we cannot easily translate with a single English equivalent the word that identifies what we conceive to define the system's critical tension and generative concept. What is most particular to—distinctive of—the systemic structure and its functioning requires definition through circumlocution, such as, "the heritage of virtue and its consequent entitlements." A further mark of the systemic importance accorded to the notion of *zekhut* is that even though a man was degraded, one action sufficed to win for him that heavenly glory to which rabbis in lives of Torah-study aspired. The mark of the system's integration around *zekhut* lies in its insistence that all Israelites, not only sages, could gain *zekhut* for themselves (and their descendants). A single remarkable deed, exemplary for its deep humanity, sufficed to win for an ordinary person the *zekhut* that elicits the supernatural favor enjoyed by some rabbis on account of their Torah study. The centrality of *zekhut* in the systemic structure—the critical importance of the heritage of virtue together with its supernatural entitlements—therefore emerges in a striking claim. Even though a man or a woman was degraded, not a sage or rabbi at all, one action sufficed to win for him or her that heavenly glory to which rabbis in general aspired.

zekhut abot   (Heb., merit of the fathers) the theological doctrine of inherited merit. According to this concept, later generations, undeserving of God's grace, may expect it anyway on account of the abundant meritorious acts of the patriarchs.

Zeno   emperor of the Eastern Roman Empire (r. 474–491 C.E.). In 488, he ended the danger of a German invasion of Constantinople. The moderate party among the Monophysites made peace with him and the government in 482, and he expelled the Nestorians from Constantinople. In 484, he suppressed the Samaritan revolt and built a Christian church over the place where the Samaritan altar had stood. He was known for his anti-Jewish attitudes and was pleased when he heard the news that Jews had been burned in the riots at Antioch.

Zenobia   queen of Palmyra (r. 254–273 C.E.). Upon the death of her husband, Odenathus, in 266, she became the actual ruler of Palmyra because the new king, her son Vaballustus, was a minor. She had built a large empire by exploiting the weaknesses of both Rome and the Sassanid Empire, maintaining Palmyrene rule in Palestine and even extending it over Asia Minor and Egypt, assuming the title of Augusta in 271. Because Rome's suppression of Palmyra was her first step in reestablishing her position in Mesopotamia, it was in the Sassanids' interest to support Zenobia against the Romans. However, in 273 she was captured by Aurelian, who put an end to the Palmyran domination of Asia Minor and Egypt. Some Christian sources claim that she was Jewish. Even though she did rebuild a synagogue in Egypt, there is no sound evidence that she had converted to Judaism.

Zephaniah, Apocalypse of a pseudepigraphical Jewish writing of the first century B.C.E. or first century C.E. that describes the visionary experiences of Zephaniah as he leaves his earthly city, journeys to various parts of heaven and the underworld, and then ascends in glory through the heavens. The Apocalypse's text survives only in three fragments, which comprise some fourteen short chapters; these probably represent about one-quarter of the original text. The Apocalypse was composed in Greek, possibly in Egypt. It is written in an apocalypse's typical form, with the seer being guided by angelic figures who lead his ascent and describe the significance of what he sees.

The earliest source for the Apocalypse's text is a Greek quotation in Clement of Alexandria's *Stromateis*. The longest witness is an Akhmimic (Coptic) manuscript, containing eighteen pages, from the end of the fourth century. There is also a Sahidic (Coptic) manuscript of two pages from the early fifth century.

The longer, Akhmimic, text opens with Zephaniah, accompanied by an angel, looking down from a distance over his own city, apparently after dying. After seeing human souls being punished, Zephaniah learns from the angel that there are two groups of angels that record the good and evil deeds of humans; these records are then given to the "great angel" and the "accuser," respectively, who present them to God. Zephaniah visits Hades, where he has a vision of both the great angel and the accuser. Since his own good deeds have outweighed his bad, he ascends from Hades and "crosses over" into heaven, assuming an angelic garment. An angel trumpets three times, signaling progressive stages of Zephaniah's salvation. The prophet sees sinners being punished and saints praying for them, and then receives a forecast of the eschaton.

The Apocalypse's chief concern is the fates of good and evil humans in the afterlife. This concern is manifested in the literary form of the apocalypse, in which the human seer is shown all the facets of the afterlife and human judgment by an angelic interpreter. Although the Apocalypse's audience and occasion of writing are unknown, it must be assumed that its author's main purpose was parenetic—to exhort readers to eschew sin and to embrace righteousness. The author's other main concerns are the importance of repentance and of intercessory prayer.

Zephaniah, Targum to *see* TARGUM TO THE PROPHETS

Zera *see* ZEIRA I; ZEIRA II

Zeraim first division of the Mishnah, devoted to the rules governing agriculture in the Holy Land, with special reference to God's share in the crops, the Sabbatical year, and tithing and gifts to the priesthood

Zered, Brook of brook mentioned at Numbers 21:12 as an Israelite camping place and referred to at T. Shebiit 4:11, Sifrei Deuteronomy 51, and elsewhere, as marking a border of the Land of Israel. Scholars associate it with Wadi al-Ḥasa, which flows for 28 miles up to the Dead Sea.

Zerika Palestinian amora; a student of Eleazar b. Pedat and Ammi

Zeus the great sky-god of the Greeks who sends rain and whose weapon is the thunderbolt. Ruler of the gods at Olympus, Zeus was protector of the king and his rights, and protector of civic rights, law, and morals. During the Hellenistic period, his name was often given to the chief deity of any group or nation, as to the god Ammon of Thebes in Egypt. During the Maccabean revolt, the Temple in Jerusalem was renamed the temple of Zeus Olympios while that at Gerizim became the temple of Zeus Xenios (2 Macc. 6:2).

Zeuxis, letter to In *Antiquities of the Jews*, Josephus quotes a letter of Antiochus III to a governor of Phrygia named Zeuxis. Antiochus proposes to send two thousand Jewish families from Babylonia to Lydia and Phrygia, in Asia Minor. They are to be settled in fortresses in the area to help stop the revolts of the local people, because of their alleged piety toward God, which will presumably make them loyal to the king. They had been loyal to Antiochus's forefathers. Although many scholars accept the letter as genuine, some disagree and argue that it is only Jewish propaganda.

zikhronot *see* REMEMBRANCE-VERSES

Zimun (Heb., invitation) specifically, the invitation to join in the grace after meals; *see also* BIRKAT HAMAZON

Zion   in the Hebrew Bible, a designation variously for the Temple, the Temple Mount, the city of Jerusalem, the Land of Israel, and the people of Israel. This variation of usage is continued in the traditions of early Judaism and early Christianity. Here, in addition, the term Zion receives more spiritualized and apocalyptic applications: it can represent a place where eschatological visions are seen or a "spiritual" reality such as the heavenly Jerusalem.

One remarkable feature of the term Zion in early Jewish literature is the breadth of its semantic range and fluidity of its application. Indeed, the term is often used in poetic or metaphorical contexts in which a general, nonspecific meaning is intended. Thus Sirach 51:12 (Hebrew), "Give thanks to him who has chosen Zion, for his mercy endures forever," or 2 Baruch 6:2, "I was grieving over Zion and sighed because of the captivity which had come upon the people."

Elsewhere, the intended application of the term is more specific. In 2 Baruch 61:2, and 68:5, "Zion" clearly refers to the Temple itself. The more specific "Mount Zion" designates the Temple Mount; see Jubilees 1:29; 1 Maccabees 4:37, 5:54, 7:33. In 4 Ezra 14:31, "Zion" represents the land of Israel, whereas in Sirach 48:24, 2 Baruch 4:9, and 2 Baruch 61:7, it clearly stands for the city of Jerusalem.

An especially noteworthy aspect of the term "Zion" is its application in spiritualized or apocalyptic contexts. Jubilees 4:26 states that Mount Zion "will be sanctified in the new creation for the sanctification of the earth." In 2 Baruch 13:1 and the prologue to the Slavonic version of 3 Baruch, Zion is the site of eschatological revelations to Baruch. In 4 Ezra 10:44, the heavenly Jerusalem seen by Ezra is called "Zion," and in chapter 13, Mount Zion is the site of an eschatological battle (see also 2 Bar. 40:1, 44:7, 59:4).

The sparse use of the term "Zion" in early Christian literature reveals several interesting peculiarities. Most of the few references here appear in quotations of Jewish scriptures. Hebrews 12:18–22 contrasts the earthly Mount Sinai with "Mount Zion and . . . the city of the living God, the heavenly Jerusalem" (cf. Gal. 4:24–26; 5 Ezra 2:33–48). In apocalyptic contexts, John of Patmos in Revelation 14:1 and Ezra in 5 Ezra 2:42–47 see visions, respectively, of the "Lamb" and the "Son of God" standing on Mount Zion (cf. 4 Ezra 13).

zob   *see* FLUX

zodiac and the four seasons   a motif in ancient synagogue art, especially in mosaic pavements. The depiction of the zodiac is in the form of a circle with the twelve signs arranged radially around a circle containing Helios in the chariot of the sun. The four seasons are personified as busts of women in the four corners of a square frame around the zodiac. These are seen in synagogue floors of the fourth to sixth centuries C.E. None appear in Christian buildings.

At least seven zodiac pavements are preserved in Palestinian synagogues at Hammath Tiberias, Khirbet Susiya, Naaran, Husifa, Yafia, Beth Alpha, and Sepphoris. All repeat the same basic composition of the circle of the zodiac around Helios. The zodiac is inscribed in a square with the four seasons in the spandrels (corners). The zodiac panel is most often combined with a representation of a Torah shrine flanked by menorahs and other objects used in the Jewish liturgy.

Illustrated astronomical treatises may have played a role in the dissemination of zodiac compositions in ancient Jewish society. A miniature painting in the Vatican museum depicts Helios in the central circle driving the chariot of the sun drawn by four white horses through the blue sky. In the outer circle are the representations of the twelve signs of the zodiac.

The representations of the signs of the zodiac exhibit an increasing tendency toward stylization, but the iconography remains faithful to the classical prototypes: a ram for Aries; a bull for Taurus; the twins of Gemini; the crab for Cancer; a lion for Leo; a draped female for Virgo; scales for Libra; a scorpion for Scorpio; an archer for Sagittarius; a goat for Capricorn; a water bearer for Aquarius; and a fish for Pisces.

The representations of the four seasons constitute one of the strongest survivals of classical imagery. Such images were most widespread in the late antique period, with the same types repeated again and again with little variation. The seasons' representations that appear in the zodiac pavements are among the last monuments to preserve the Graeco-Roman type of the isolated female bust with an attribute.

Like the signs of the zodiac and the personifications of the seasons, the figure of Helios in the center of the zodiacal circle is based on earlier prototypes. Helios stands in the chariot of the sun in the center of the composition, a visual translation of Aratus's description: "In them, twelve in all, has the sun his course as he leads the whole year, and as he fares around this belt all the fruitful seasons have their growth."

The zodiac in itself is not new to synagogue decoration. The signs of the zodiac decorated some of the ceiling tiles of the synagogue of Dura Europos, and were carved in relief on the lintel of the synagogue at Er-Rafid. A long and unusual inscription in the pavement of the synagogue at En-Gedi lists the signs of the zodiac followed by the names of the Hebrew months. The figure of Helios is frequently found on Jewish magical amulets, often with inscriptions naming the deity and the names of the angels.

There seems to be abundant evidence for the practice of astrology among the Jews in late antiquity. In tractate Shabbat (156b) of the Babylonian Talmud there is a debate about the validity of astrology for Jews. Rabbi Hanina, a Babylonian who came to Palestine to study with Rabbi Judah Ha Nasi (d. before 230 A.D.), says: "The planetary influence gives wisdom, the planetary influence gives wealth and Israel stands under planetary influence." In contrast to this, Rabbi Yoḥanan, who lived in Tiberias c. 250, declares: "There are no constellations for Israel." The rest of this section of the Talmud is devoted to the arguments put forth in support of Rabbi Yoḥanan's position against planetary influence.

The Sefer haRazim (Book of Secrets), a text of the late third or early fourth century discovered among the texts in the Cairo Geniza, is particularly important because it was widely influential even among rabbinic Jews. Among the prayers is one to Helios. In Greek, but written in Hebrew letters, it reads "Holy Helios who rises in the east, good mariner, trustworthy leader of the sun's rays . . . who of old didst establish the mighty wheel of the heavens." The text names the angels who are in charge of the twelve months of the year. The apocryphal Book of Jubilees refers to the four seasons and names them the "angels of winter and of spring and of autumn and of summer."

The liturgical poems read during the service in the synagogue, the *piyyutim* of the late antique and early Byzantine period provide numerous references to the zodiac. Thus, in an acrostic poem to Exodus 12:2 found in the Cairo Geniza, we read, "There arose a dispute among the months, when the August One sent to the land of Egypt. Come let us cast lots on the zodiac, that we might know in which of us Israel is to be redeemed." In a lamentation of the Ninth of Ab—still recited on the eve of that day in the Ashkenazic ritual—the first eight signs of the zodiac bewail the fate of Jerusalem, while the last four are practically accused of betrayal. A parallel poem found in some Geniza manuscripts, which are thought to preserve remnants of ancient eastern prayerbooks, describes the joyous reaction of the constellations on the successful return of the high priest from the Holy of Holies on the Day of Atonement. To these we may add the better known poems of Eliezer ben Kallir, who was the outstanding representative of the classical *piyyut* and lived in Palestine in the late sixth century. In two of his most famous compositions, On Rain, read in the synagogue on Sukkoth, and On Dew, read at Passover, every other stanza contains a prayer for rain or dew in one of the Hebrew months and the following stanza mentions one of the signs of the zodiac.

The texts and the images indicate that there was an underlying theological basis that accounts for the frequency of the zodiac theme in synagogue decoration, and, at the same time, explains why this decoration was never used by Christians. The iconography of the synagogue pavement (the zodiac, the Torah shrine, and the liturgical objects) presents a coherent decorative scheme that expresses Jewish political and eschatological hopes.

zonah *see* PROSTITUTION

Zoroastrianism, influence on Judaism The Iranian religion founded by Zoroaster became the official religion of the Persian, Parthian, and Sassanian empires. Since many Jews lived in the areas controlled by these empires, Judaism was exposed to Persian religious influences from the sixth century B.C.E. on. That there was some influence is widely accepted, though the exact amount is disputed. The modified dualism of Qumran, with its constant war between "the sons of light" and "the sons of darkness," has certain points in common with Zoroastrianism, though it differs in not being an absolute dualism. Jewish eschatological views, which included the concepts of resurrection of the body, the judgment of the soul after death, and a final resurrection and judgment of all the dead looks very much like the Iranian model; however, this form of eschatology was not universal in Judaism, and there is debate as to how early it arose in Zoroastrianism. The development of an elaborate angelology and demonology in Judaism coincides to some extent with Persian rule, but the roots for this can also be found in Israelite tradition. Thus, it is easy to postulate influence, but the extent is more difficult to determine.

Zoroastrians followers of the religion taught by the Iranian prophet Zoroaster (properly Zarathustra), who reformed the indigeneous religion of his people sometime prior to the fifth century B.C.E., and reduced its complex polytheism to an ordered hierarchy of divine beings, ruled by a supreme creator god, Ahura Mazda (Wise Lord). Zoroaster taught an absolute moral and metaphysical dualism of good and evil, personified as a conflict pitting the god Ahura Mazda and his assisting spiritual powers against the antigod Angra Mainyu (Aggressive Spirit) and his pan-demonium. The history of the universe involves the ongoing battle between these two opposing forces.

The Zoroastrian social ethic promotes generosity, hospitality, moderation, prosperity, and the value of family. Every good deed that a human performs assists Ahura Mazda, while every evil act weakens the good and assists the cause of Angra Mainyu in the world. Everyone will be rewarded by admission to paradise or punished by exile in hell according to their conduct in life. In addition to judgment of the individual at death, the world will experience a general judgment at the end of time, at which the souls that have been punished in hell will be released into paradise.

All Zoroastrians wear a special white undershirt (*sudreh*), bound by a sacred thread (*kusti*); the ritual act of retying the *kusti,* accompanied by formulaic recitations, performed several times each day, constitutes a constant reminder of the Zoroastrian's dedication to Ahura Mazda. Zoroastrian religious life includes prayer at least five times a day, and an annual cycle of seven seasonal festivals. Sacred fires, symbolizing purity, are kept perpetually burning and guarded from pollution in Zoroastrian temples. The individual Zoroastrian combats the pollution of Angra Mainyu by performing lustrations (*padyab*) of the commonly exposed parts of the body (while recalling Ahura Mazda) upon rising in the morning, after calls of nature, before meals, and before prayers. More elaborate baths and purifying acts, assisted by priests and accompanied by lengthy prayers, are performed for extraordinary contamination, such as that incurred by contact with a dead body. Dead bodies are exposed to the sun in designated places, where they will be devoured by vultures and not pollute earth, water, or fire.

The Zoroastrians collected their sacred writings into the twenty-one books of the Abestag (Avesta) in the time of the Sassanid Empire (3d–early 7th c. C.E.). However, much of the Abestag has been lost through the traumas of the religion's history. *See also* ZOROASTRIANISM, INFLUENCE ON JUDAISM.

Zugot (Heb., pairs) the designation given pairs of sages understood to have transmitted Torah between the biblical prophets and the earliest Tannaitic authorities (M. Peah 2:6). M. Abot 1:4–12 lists five pairs: Yose b. Yoezer of Seredah and Yose b. Yohanan of Jerusalem, Joshua b. Perahiah and Nittai the Arbelite, Judah b. Tabbai and Simeon b. Shetah, Shemayah and Abtalyon, and Hillel and Shammai. The earliest of these, in the period of the Maccabean revolt, received Torah from Simeon the Righteous. The latest, in the time of Herod the Great, were followed by Gamaliel. According to M. Hagigah 2:2, the first listed individual in each pair was patriarch (*nasi*), while the second served as head of the court (*ab beit din*).

Zurvan the principle of time in the Pahlavi texts. Zurvanism was a new Iranian dualism, which developed during the Sassanid period. It reflects a tendency to reconcile the original Zoroastrian dualism with Babylonian astral religion and Mesopotamian demonology. Time, Zurvan, is at the center of Zurvanist speculation and a protagonist in the cult's mythology. Zurvanism modified the dialectic of Zarathusda, which held that Good and Evil were absolutely separate entities. According to Zurvanism, evil could be explained by attributing all power to Zurvan, the supreme god who sired both Ormazd and Ahriman.

Zutra *see* MAR ZUTRA

zuz a small coin; a penny

Notes

Notes